1000
BIBLE STUDY
OUTLINES

"Whoso is armed with the text, the same is a right worker, and my best advice and counsel is, that we draw water out of the True Fountain, that is, diligently to read in the Bible. He is learned that is well grounded in the Bible, for one text and sentence out of it is of far more esteem and value than many writings and glosses, which neither are strong, sound, nor armor of proof." —*Martin Luther*

1000
BIBLE STUDY
OUTLINES

F. E. Marsh

Foreword by
F. B. Meyer

kregel
PUBLICATIONS

Grand Rapids, MI 49501

1000 Bible Study Outlines, by F. F. Marsh. Foreword by F. B. Meyer. First published in 1970 by Kregel Publications, a division of Kregel, Inc., P. O. Box 2607, Grand Rapids, MI 49501. Formerly published under the title *1000 New Bible Readings*. All rights reserved.

Library of Congress Catalog Card No. 75-125115

ISBN 0-8254-3247-2 (pbk.)

9 10 11 12 Printing/Year 94

Printed in the United States of America

Preface

Through the goodness of our God and Father, the grace of the Lord Jesus, and the ministry of the Holy Spirit, my *500 Bible Readings* [now published by Kregel Publications as *500 Bible Study Outlines*] have gone through many editions in Great Britain and America. Now comes a volume of *1000 Bible Readings* [presently published as *1000 Bible Study Outlines*]. I place these readings at the feet of Him, who is the Author, the Illuminator, and the Applier of the Book, and pray that He may use them in helping many in the Lord's service. The themes are meant to be suggestive to busy workers, and not crutches to lazy shirkers.

I especially call attention to the wise and weighty words found in the helpful Foreword of beloved and esteemed Dr. F. B. Meyer. Those who know him, love him; and the more he is loved, the better he is known. I would also ask the student of God's Word to carefully ponder the introduction to these readings, and the article on the Bible.

My conviction is, the more the Bible is studied, the more there is found in it to be studied. Fresh light, assurance, power, joy, help, grace, and blessing, break out from it. It is like the dawn, ever new in its light; like the air, ever fresh in its vitality; like the food, ever nourishing in its feed; like the flowers, ever beautiful in their variety; like the body, ever unifying in its organism; like the blood, ever pulsating in its energy; and like the electric current, ever powerful in its movement.

F. E. MARSH

"I adore the plenitud of the Scriptures, in which every letter is a word, and every word is a verse, and every verse is a chapter, and every chapter is a book, and every book is a Bible; in which every twig is a branch, and every branch is a tree, and every tree a forest, in which every drop is a rivulet, and every rivulet is a river, and every river a bay, and every bay an ocean, and every ocean all waters."

—Tertullian

Foreword

It is a pleasure to write these lines of Foreword to the Bible readings prepared by my friend, Dr. F. E. Marsh, who has devoted his life to the study of the Bible, and the unfolding of its treasures to others.

We believe in the plenary inspiration of Scripture. The word *"inspiration"* is equivalent to *"inbreathed."* There is a quality there which is found to the same extent and in the same manner nowhere else, and it is self-evident.

One summer's day, as I was exploring the western coast of Scotland, I came on what seemed to be a large inland lake, but when I descended to its shores, and dipped my finger in the water, placing it to my lips, I knew by the saline taste that the Lough was an inlet from the Atlantic. The quality of the water was evidence of its origin. So
In the Bible There Is a Divine Quality,
which the spiritual mind recognizes as being its exclusive characteristic. "All Scripture is given *by inspiration of God*, and is profitable" (2 Tim. 3:16).

The heart of Scripture is "the Word of God." As our Lord became incarnate in human flesh, with the weakness and needs of human nature, though not its sins, so He is—so to speak—incarnate in Scripture. There is a sense, therefore, in which we may say that in the Holy Scripture, the Word has become flesh and tabernacles among us.

The late Hudson Taylor used to kindle his little lamp, and spend two hours at night reading his Bible, while the Chinese who shared the inn with him lay around asleep. He said that it was only by the written Word that he could feed on Him who is the Spirit and Life of Scripture. "The connection between the *written* Word and the *Incarnate* Word is so close and intimate that you can no more separate them than you can separate body and soul, or soul and spirit."

This involves the unity of Scripture. Its theme is one, and its Author is one. The unities of the Bible are specially remarkable, and confirm this thought of the unity of Scripture. Certain threads of suggestive symbolism may be traced from Genesis to Revelation—such as the garden, the serpent, the river, the Lamb, the blood-covenant, redemption, the advent, faith, love, the triune Being of God.

This thought justifies the whole scheme of these Bible readings. To follow them will resemble

The Discovery of New Paths Through the Woods,

or on the hills, and as we follow the track here marked out by an experienced guide, we shall catch rare glimpses of new and heavenly horizons. In majestic prose, in lyric poetry, in lovely imagery, in massive argument, there is the same *motif* and refrain. Now you sit at the feet of a prophet; again you hear the voice of a sweet singer; and yet again, as you read the love-epistles of St. John, or the massive reasonings of St. Paul, you say to yourself: "This is but another setting of the Old Melody with a delightful variation."

In all Bible study we must seek the teaching of the Holy Spirit. "The natural man receiveth not the things of the Spirit of God . . . because they are spiritually discerned" (1 Cor. 2:14).

A striking illustration of this was presented in the conversion of one of China's *literati*. He had complained to a missionary, who was at the moment preparing a cup of tea for him, that he did not find the Chinese Bible, of which he had possessed himself, especially interesting. At that moment the kettle was near boiling point. "See," said the missionary, "the fire is needed to cause the water to boil; so, tonight, if you take up the Christian Scriptures, you must ask the God of Heaven to give you the Holy Spirit to enable you to understand them aright, then the Book will become a new book to you, and it will soon mean more to you than any book in the world." That night he asked the Spirit of the Unknown God to turn a dull book into an interesting one. "O God," he said, "if Thou be a God, give me thy Holy Spirit, and help me to understand this Book." As the evening hours passed he became more and more engrossed with the Book, and as he turned over its pages a new spirit took possession of him. The Savior of whom he read became vividly real to his heart. The words spoken long ago were living and powerful, and brought him peace and healing.

We should never open our Bibles without first lifting our heart for that Spirit by whom holy men were led to write.

Beneath His Touch Rocks Will Yield Water,

blank pages will become illuminated, and fountains arise where the soil had seemed sterile. To that Spirit who has spoken His messages to the hearts of men, as into a dictaphone I commend this book of Bible study outlines to all students of the Sacred Word, praying that it may give back to them the holy truth in words that melt and thoughts that burn.

F. B. MEYER

Introduction

THE best way to prove the truth of the Bible is to study it. As the Living Word Himself proves His Deity, so the Written Word itself evidences its Divinity. Theories about Inspiration provoke controversy, but the fact of Inspiration commands attention. As life in its essence cannot be explained, so inspiration in its heart is beyond human ken. The living man proves the fact of life. The Living Book proclaims the Living Author. Men's books are bushes without the burning flame; the Word of God is a Bush flaming with the fire of God. "Inspired of God" is the Word's claim, and it contains the life of God. It is God-breathed and God-breathing. As the Creator breathed into man's body the breath of life, and thus united man's body with his created spirit, so God has taken the body of human language and united to it the Holy Spirit, and breathed the breath of the Living Christ in its sacred revelation. We do not worship the Book as a Book, but we worship Him who is revealed in it, and because of Him we prize the Book.

The adaptability of the Book to meet all people is one of the most cogent proofs of its source and its secret. J. H. RITSON, of the British and Foreign Bible Society, says:

"It is very wonderful that though the Bible deals with the deepest truths, yet it is the most translatable book there is. The Koran and other sacred books remain imprisoned in the languages in which they were written—the power of their appeal is largely inherent in their original tongue. The Bible is not only the most translatable book, but it is the Book which suffers least in translation. Further, when once it is translated it speaks to every human being in his mother tongue at any moment when he is free and willing to hear. When a man has the Bible he need not wait for the services of the house of God in order to hear the truth, he is not limited to the teaching of the Sabbath day; he continues to feed on the Word when he is remote from any human teacher, and when the missionary is broken in health and is compelled to go on furlough. The Bible is free from the limitations which beset the missionary. There is no prison for the Word of God."

There are many ways in which we can study God's Word, some of which I have indicated in my "Fully Furnished" or "Christian Worker's Equipment:" in which will be found, on pages 150-172, ten ways in which the Bible may be studied, namely:

GEOGRAPHICALLY	TOPICALLY	CONCENTRATINGLY
GEOLOGICALLY	COMPREHENSIVELY	CRITICALLY
GRAMMATICALLY	COMPARATIVELY	TEXTUALLY
	and PRACTICALLY	

Broadly speaking, if the following seven rules are followed the student will find himself so full of the truth of God's Word that he will never be wanting for a theme.

1. **Study the Text in the Light of its Setting.** Sometimes the division between two chapters will mar the beauty of association. We have such an instance in John's Gospel. Chapter three begins, "There was a man of the Pharisees named Nicodemus." The particle "now" which is supplied in the Revised Version leads the reader to see what has gone before. In the latter part of the second chapter we are told Christ did not commit Himself to certain disciples who professed to believe on Him, but He did commit Himself to Nicodemus, hence, in the conversation with him, as Sir Stevenson Blackwood once pointed out, Christ practically revealed to him every truth of the Gospel.

One other instance of the importance of context is the first word of John iii. 16. Illuminated texts generally begin with "God so loved the world," etc., leaving out the conjunction "for." Reading the "For," we find that Christ showed the necessity of His death, in that the Son of Man "must be lifted up," before He revealed the cause of that death, is the love of God, who gave His only begotten Son. The setting of a Scripture is as important as the diamond in a ring. When the diamond is lacking the diamond ring is wanting. The ring is essential to the diamond's setting, and the diamond is necessary to give the ring importance and value.

2. **Study Words and Phrases.** A phrase of frequent occurrence in the Epistles is "In Christ." It will be found in at least three associations. It is an *Inclusive* term, for we are blessed by God the Father with all spiritual blessings "in

Christ" (Eph. i. 3). "In Christ" is an *Exclusive* term. When Paul would designate himself, he speaks of himself as "a man in Christ" (2 Cor. xii. 2). Being "in Christ" believers are no longer in sin, in the world, in condemnation, and in the flesh. Then "In Christ" is a *Conclusive* word, hence Peter speaks of "your good manner of life in Christ" (1 Peter iii. 16). At once we see the importance of the association of a phrase.

The importance of distinguishing words is necessary. There are two words rendered "Son" in the New Testament, namely *"Teknon,"* and *"Whyos,"* *"Teknon* denotes one who is born, from *"Tikto"* to bear. Like the Scots, "Bairn" from *"Beran"* to bear, a child, a descendant. *"Teknon"* is never used of Christ for He was not a descendant of God nor of man, hence, this word is never used of Him as The Son of God nor as the Son of Man. Yet the word to bear is used of His birth, because as man He was actually born—Luke ii. 7. How accurate was the prophecy about Him, "Unto us a child is born, a Son is given" (Isa. ix. 6). As the Son He was not born, but given. As the child He was born and given. *"Teknon"* is applied to believers, because we have a spiritual origin—John i. 12, 13, R.V., hence heirship is based on sonship—Rom. viii. 16, 17.

"Whyos" is used in an adoptive sense, and is always applied to Christ as The Son of God and The Son of Man. It is written of Him, "Jesus Christ the Son of David, the Son of Abraham" (Matt. i. 1), and "Jesus Christ the Son of God" (Mark i. 1). It is written, "She brought forth her First-born Son" (Matt. i. 25) on the human side, but on the Divine side, "God gave His only Begotten Son." The "Son" Mary brought forth was actually born, but He was not a descendant of man. He was "the Only Begotten Son in an official sense for us, and is for us "called the Son of God" (Luke i. 35). Therefore as to humanity He was not the Son of man, but the Son of God; and as to His Deity, He was not a descendant of God, but God the Son. "Adoption of sons" (*Whyothesia*) is applied because of our identification with the Son of God, and the glory we are to have with Him. While we are not waiting for our relationship as children of God, we are waiting for our place as adopted sons—Rom. viii. 15, 23; Eph. i. 15; Gal. iv. 5.

3. **Find Out About Eastern Customs**. When a corn chandler in this country measures corn, he puts the corn as

lightly as possible in the measure, and then uses a "strike" to level the corn with the rim; but in the East it is the man who buys the corn who measures it.   It is to this Christ refers when He says, "Give and it shall be given you, good measure, pressed down, and shaken together, and running over" (Luke vi. 38). GEIKIE describes the process:

"When grain is bought after harvest, for winter use, it is delivered in sacks, and the quantity in these is always tested by a professional measurer.   Sitting on the ground, this functionary shovels the wheat or barley into the measure, which is called a *tinmeh*, using his hands to do so.   When it is quite full, he shakes the *tinmeh* smartly, that the grain may settle; then fills it to the brim again, and twists it half round with a swift jerk as it lies on the ground, repeating both processes till it is once more filled to the top.   This done, he presses the contents with his hands to fill up any vacant space, till at last, when it will hold no more, he raises a cone on the top, stopping when it begins to run over at the sides, and this only is thought to be good measure. "

What an illuminating explanation is given in the Eastern custom above, illustrating as it does the abundant giving of God in return for our giving to Him.   Many more illustrations might be given evidencing the importance of knowing the customs of the East.

4. Be Sure of Facts.   Many a skit has been made about Jonah being swallowed by a whale!   We are sometimes told "a whale has not a gullet big enough to swallow a man." That may be true of a Greenland whale, but not so with the Mediterranean whale.

FRANK BULLEN, in his book on "The Cruise of 'The Cachalot,'" refers to the blunder which a popular M.P. made some time ago, when he referred to a whale in the following words: "Science will not hear of a whale with a gullet capable of admitting anything larger than a man's fist. "   Bullen relates the fact that a sperm whale, on one occasion in its death agony, vomited a piece of cuttle fish as big as their hatch house.   He says: "For the first time it was possible to understand, that, contrary to the usual notion of a whale being unable to swallow a herring, here was a kind of whale that could swallow—well, a block four or five feet square. " On another occasion Bullen relates: "The ejected masses of food were of enormous size, one piece of cuttle fish being eight feet by six feet. "

Another mistake about Jonah is made, namely, that he was alive in the sea-monster. His body was in the fish, but he cried "from the belly of Hell" (Jonah ii. 2), which proves he was in the place of disembodied spirits, for "Hell" is the Hebrew "*Sheol,*" which corresponds to the "Hades" of the New Testament. To be a perfect type of Christ, Jonah must have died and been raised from the dead—Matt. xii. 40, for this was the "sign" or miracle to the people of Nineveh—Matt. xii. 39, 41.

5. Scripture will Explain Scripture. As the light in the lampstand gave "light over against it" (Exod. xxv. 37), so Scripture illuminates and explains Scripture. In Genesis xxxvii. 25-29; xxxix. 1, there seems to be two parties to whom Joseph was "sold"—"Ishmaelites" and "Midianites. " Higher Criticism immediately comes to the conclusion there are two narratives which contradict each other. "According to J, " he was sold (so we are told) to the "Ishmaelites, " and "according to E. , " "The Midianites sold Joseph into Egypt to Potiphar. " Then the critics further say, "If (mark the "if") the text were a unity the Midianites would have been the Ishmaelites. " That is just what they were. How do we know? In Judges viii. 24, we are told that the Midianites whom Gideon defeated were Ishmaelites. All Midianites were not Ishmaelites, but all Ishmaelites were Midianites; just as all Englishmen are Britishers, but all Britishers are not Englishmen, as our Scots friends are quick to remind the English when an Englishman talks about England and he means Great Britain.

Another case where Scripture explains Scripture is in the use of the word "these" in John xxi. 15. Some have thought that "these" refers to the fish, but the remote context shows Christ refers to Peter's fellow-disciples. In Matthew xxvi. 33, Peter says, "Though all" ("men" is in italics; see Mark xiv 29), that is "all" the rest of the disciples, "shall be offended because of Thee, yet will not I. " So Christ seems to say, "Lovest Thou Me more than these? You professed to do so, Peter, but you were no better than the rest, although you professed more. My Word was true, all of you were offended and proved unfaithful. "

This goes to prove the desirability of comparing Scripture with Scripture, and of patient reading and study.

6. **Benefit of a Correct Translation**. Even one who does not know Hebrew and Greek, with a good concordance and lexicons can get a correct text. Take a simple illustration. There is the primary particle *ei.*, which Strong in his concordance called "a particle of conditionality," but of which Bullinger in his lexicon says, "But if in the indicative mood, assumes the hypothesis as an actual fact." Take a few passages where the particle is rendered "if," and instead of "if," read "since."

Luke iv. 3: "If Thou art the Son of God."—"*Since* Thou art the Son of God."

Romans viii. 31: "If God be for us."—"*Since* God is for us."

1 Thessalonians iv. 14: "If we believe."—"*Since* we believe."

Colossians iii. 1: "If ye then be risen with Christ."—"*Since* ye then are risen with Christ."

1 John iv. 11: "If God so loved us."—"*Since* God so loved us."

See the importance of reading "Since" instead of "If" in the case of the temptation of Christ.

GODET says: "If Thou art, expresses something very different from a doubt, this 'if' has almost the force of 'since'." This must be, as the context proves. Satan had just heard Christ was the Son of God, and immediately he says, "Since Thou art the Son of God, command these stones be made bread."

7. **Essentials to Remember**. In the Revelation which God has given of Himself in Christ and in the Book, we have all the essentials for salvation and godliness, but we need eyes to see. The Spirit's inward illumination is essential to understand the Divine Revelation. There are seven things to remember.

(1) The Bible is a SPIRITUAL BOOK. Christ declares, "The words that I speak unto you, they are spirit, and they are life" (John vi. 63); and further, we are reminded the Word of God is living—Heb. iv. 12. The Words of Christ and the Word not only contain life, or a medium of life, but they are life, even as a tree alive is a living tree.

(2) A SPIRITUAL MIND is essential to understand the spiritual Book. We are told, "The natural man receiveth not the things of the Spirit of God, for they are foolishness unto him, neither can he know them, because they are spiritually discerned" (1 Cor. ii. 14). An artist who invited a friend to come and see a picture,

first shut his friend up in a dark room and left him there. The friend wondered why he was so treated, and afterwards, in answer to the question, said, "I knew if you came into the studio with the glare of the sun in your eyes, you could not appreciate the fine colouring of the picture, so I left you in the dark room till the glare had worn out of your eyes." When earth lights are glaring in our eyes we cannot see the deep and hidden meaning of the things of God.

(3) THE SPIRITUAL TEACHER is requisite for the spiritually minded to understand the Spiritual Book. "Eye hath not seen, nor ear heard, neither have entered into the heart of man, the things which God hath prepared for them that love Him. But God hath revealed them unto us by His Spirit: for the Spirit searcheth all things, yea, the deep things of God" (1 Cor. ii. 9, 10). A minute form of life, called a Rotifer, in a drop of water cannot be seen by the naked eye, but by means of a powerful microscope it can not only be seen, it is revealed in all the inness of its being, and its heart is manifest in its beating. Through the light of the Spirit's microscopic power we can know the minute working of His grace and the spirituality of His teaching.

(4) THE SPIRITUAL SAINT. Constant reference is directed to spirituality as a quality of being to be effective in Christian life, service, and inward condition. The one who is "spiritual" is the one who is qualified to "restore" an erring brother—Gal. vi. 1, and no other. The one block in the Spirit's work in the Church at Corinth was because the many were "carnal" instead of being spiritual. When the spiritual food—1 Peter ii. 2, R.V., is nourishing the inner life, then the unspiritual things of the old man will be thrown off, even as the rising sap in the tree will throw off any of the old leaves which may be clinging to it. A spiritual saint is one who is dominated by the Holy Spirit. Dominated in the Spirit of his self-consciousness in fellowship with the Lord; concentrating the soul of his life-consciousness by being attracted to the Lord; and swayed in the body of his sense-consciousness; and by recognising the body is the temple of the Holy Spirit.

(5) SPIRITUAL BLESSINGS, or the blessings of the Spirit, are "all" found "in Christ" (Eph. i. 3). Who can estimate these in their worth, or comprehend them in their totality? Among

those blessings of the Spirit, if the books of the Bible are pondered in relation to the Holy Spirit, it will be found He is unveiled in a specific way, giving qualification to meet a special emergency. Thus in Genesis He is seen as the Spirit of Power, in Exodus as the Spirit of Wisdom, and in Judges as the Spirit of Victory. Everything is wanting if He is not acting, but all is met when He is in absolute possession. All blessing is found in Christ alone, but the Spirit Himself must make them known.

(6) SPIRITUAL THINGS—1 Cor. ii. 13. At first glance there may seem to be no difference between "spiritual blessings" and "spiritual things, ' but the setting of the latter illuminates its importance. We are exhorted to compare "spiritual things with spiritual, " or, as Darby translates, "Communicating spiritual things by spiritual means;" or, as Godet, "Appropriating spiritual things to spiritual men;" by those "spiritual things" are what "the Spirit teacheth, " therefore the obvious sense, the Spirit is the One who communicates those things. He gives the spiritual things, and He alone can communicate to those who are spiritually minded. What those "spiritual things" are, or some of them, is brought out in chapters i. and ii., where we have enumerated the things of God and of Christ, such as "the will of God, " "the Church of God, " "the Grace of God, " "the Testimony of Christ, " "the Coming of our Lord, " "the Day of our Lord Jesus Christ, " "Fellowship in His Son, " "the Name of our Lord, " "the Cross of Christ, " "the Power of God, " "the Wisdom of God, " "the Foolishness of God, " "the Weakness of God, " "the testimony of God, " "Deep Things of God, " "the mind of Christ. "

(7) "SPIRITUAL SACRIFICES" (1 Peter ii. 5). These we are to offer up to God, which by means of Christ will ascend to Him, like the burnt offering, as a sweet-smelling savour. The odour of love's affection, the fragrance of faith's reliance, the perfume of life's consecration, the incense of prayers' intercession, the savour of praise's worship, the frankincense of fidelity's faithfulness, and the myrrh of help's ministry, are ever the delight of the Lord's appreciation.

After all, the written needs to be incarnated in the experience of a devoted life. Bengel's two rules must ever apply: "Apply thyself wholly to the Word, and apply the Word wholly to thyself. "

The Bible

The word "Bible" is not found in the Bible. The word simply means "The Book," so "there was a time," as Trench says, "when bible might be applied to any book," but in our present use of the word we use it in a restricted sense of the one Book. The *Imperial Dictionary* says: "The Bible is the Sacred Scriptures of the Old and New Testaments, as received by the Christian Church as a Divine Revelation."

There are seven things about these Holy Writings.

1. **What is It?** They claim to be "inspired of God" (2 Tim. iii. 16, 17). The word "inspired of God" is *Theopneustos*. *Theos* is the word for God, and the other part is a presumed derivation of *pneo*, which means to breathe or blow hard. It is rendered "bloweth" in John iii. 8, and "wind" in Acts xxvii. 40. Thus the word means to divinely breathe in. Some would render the sentence, "The Scriptures are the Divine breathing." Our English word "inspired" only occurs in one other place, and that is Job xxxii. 8—"There is a spirit in man, and the inspiration of the Almighty giveth them understanding." As God breathed into man the breath of life, and he became a living soul, so God has breathed this Book, and it breathes out what He has breathed in. It breathes life into the spirit, love into the soul, understanding into the mind, determination into the will, grace into the heart, beauty into the life, and harmony into the being.

2. **Who Inspired It?** "Holy men of God spake as they were moved by the Holy Spirit" (2 Peter i. 21). The Holy Spirit is the Author and the Interpreter of the Book. The "men" who were "moved" were men, human beings; but they were not the common herd of men, they were "men of God," and not only so, they were "holy men of God." These men were in fellowship with God. "Holy men" and "the Holy Spirit" needed to be in touch with each other to produce holy results. The word "moved" means to be "borne along," and is used of a ship being *"driven"* by the wind—Acts xxvii. 17, of a man being *"brought"* on a bed—Luke v. 18, and of one who is carrying another—

xvii

John xxi. 18. This at once makes the Bible different from all other books.

3. Who Were the Instruments Used? "The prophets" (1 Peter i. 10). We naturally think of a prophet as one through whom events are forecast; but the primary meaning is a seer, that is, one who sees. "A prophet, " as one has said, is—

"One who speaks forth openly before anyone, a proclaimer of a Divine message; among the heathen, the interpreter of the oracles. In the Septuagint, it is the translation of the earlier 'seer,' showing what really constituted the prophet, was immediate intercourse with God. The usage of the word is clear, it signifies one on whom the Spirit of God rested— Num. xi. 17, 25, 26, 29; one to whom and through whom God speaks—Num. vii. 2; one to whom God makes known His mysteries—Amos iii. 7, 8; hence it means one to whom God reveals His truth, and through whom He speaks. . . . In the Old Testament prophets, their preaching was a prophesying of a salvation and purposes of grace and glory yet to be accomplished; while in the New Testament prophets, their prophesying was a preaching of those purposes of grace already accomplished, and also a foretelling of the purposes of glory which were still future. "

4. What was the Purpose of the Bible's Revelation? Christ Himself answers the question, for He says of the Scriptures: "They are they which testify of Me" (John v. 39). He is *light* in the lantern, to show the way; He is the *life* in the tree, to make it grow; He is the *kernel* in the nut, to make it worth; He is the *glory* in the temple, to make it beautiful; He is the *heart* in the body, to cause it to live; He is the *spring* in the watch, to make it to go; and He is the *power* in the wire, to electrify the machine.

The Old Testament characters in the Bible are types of Him. He is the Last Adam, to quicken; the offering Able, to sacrifice; the faithful Abram, to separate; the peaceful Isaac, to substitute; the working Jacob, to secure; the providing Joseph, to store; the leading Moses, to guide; the priestly Aaron, to represent; the valiant Joshua, to subdue; the strong David, to conquer; the wise Solomon, to teach; and the Kinsman-Redeemer, to redeem.

The offerings were all foregleams. He is the Passover, to

protect; the Burnt-offering, to please; the Sin-offering, to be judged; the Trespass-offering, to release; the Peace-offering, to reconcile; the Drink-offering to rejoice; and the Red Heifer-offering, to cleanse.

All Scripture contains in Him, and He is the contain of all Scripture.

5. **What are the Two Fundamental Themes of the Bible?** Christ Himself answered the question to the two disciples as He journeyed with them to Emmaus, and to the eleven gathered in the upper room—Luke xxiv. 27, 36.

The sufferings and glory of Christ are the couplings of God, which couple up everything. Calvary and Olivet are His viewpoints. The Cross and the Crown are the Alpha and Omega of Revelation. The Lamb and the Throne are the fulcrum and lever of God's purpose. The Passover and the Lamb are His starting point and goal; and the Altar and the Skekinah are the Genesis and Revelation of everything.

6. **What the Bible Imparts?** Among the many things to which it is compared is seed—1 Peter i. 23. There are two things which are characteristic of seed. It contains life, and produces like to its kind. Faith in the Living Word comes by means of the Written Word; and when the Living Word, by means of the Written, operates in a living soul, the character of the Word is reproduced. It is a Holy Word, to sanctify; a Righteous Word, to rectify; a Living Word, to fructify; a Wise Word, to edify; a Peace Word, to pacify; a Powerful Word, to electrify; and a Loving Word, to intensify.

7. **What the Bible Does?** This raises another question: "What does it not do?" One has tersely said of the Bible in a general way: "Every hour I read you, it kills a sin, or lets a virtue in to fight against it."

Many are the things the Bible does; the following will illustrate a few of the things:

Acquaints us with the theme of the Gospel—1 Cor. xv. 3, 4.

Blesses us as we obey its precepts—Psa. cxix. 2.

Consecrates us as we follow its injunctions—Num. vi. 1-7.

Defeats the enemy as we use it against him—Matt. iv. 4, 7, 10.

Edifies the life as we heed it—Acts xx. 32.

Fires the heart to a faithful testimony—Jer. i. 1; xxiii. 29.

Guides those who follow its light—Psa. cxix. 105.

Heals the spirit as it is applied—Psa. cvii. 20.
It forms the mind as to its secrets—1 Cor. ii. 9; Isa. lxiv. 4.
Judges the conduct and maketh wise—Psa. xix. 9-11
Keeps us abiding in Christ's love—John xv. 10.
Leads to the true and beautiful—Prov. vi. 20-24.
Moulds us like to itself—Rom. vi. 17.
Nourishes the spiritual life—1 Peter i. 2.
Orders the steps of our life—Psa. cxix. 133.
Purifies the mind—2 Cor. vii. 1.
Quietens the heart—Isa. xxx. 15.
Rewards those who keep it—Psa. xix. 11.
Sanctifies those who live in it—John xvii. 17.
Teaches those who are led by it—Psa. xxv. 4, 5.
Unites us to the Lord—Psa. lxxxvi. 11; John xvii. 8.
Verifies the experience—2 Peter i. 19, 20.
Warns the observant—Psa. xix. 11.
'Xamines the heart—Psa. xxvi. 1-3.
Yokes us with Christ—John xvii. 8.
Zeals the soul—Psa. lxix. 9; John ii. 17.

A Prayer

OUR GOD AND FATHER IN CHRIST, I THANK THEE
THAT THOU HAST GIVEN THY HOLY WORD FOR MY
INSTRUCTION. ENABLE ME IN THE GRACE OF THE
HOLY SPIRIT TO LOVE THY WORD SUPREMELY, TO
BELIEVE IT WHOLLY, TO LIVE IT OUT TRULY, TO
FOLLOW   IT   EARNESTLY,   TO   REST   ON   IT
CONTENTEDLY, TO FOLLOW IT CONTINUALLY, TO
PRACTISE   IT   CONSISTENTLY,   TO   OBEY   IT
UNHESITATINGLY, TO WITNESS TO IT FAITHFULLY,
TO PROVE ITS PROMISES FULLY, TO HEAR ITS VOICE
ATTENTIVELY, TO SEE ITS PROPHECIES MINUTELY,
TO ANSWER TO IT LOVINGLY, TO HANDLE IT
REVERENTLY, AND TO ENTER INTO ITS SPIRIT
DEVOTEDLY:—IN HIS NAME, WHO ALONE IS
WORTHY, I PRAY. AMEN.

1000 BIBLE STUDY OUTLINES

1. "ABOUT" OF GRACE

1. Protection of Grace. "Hast Thou not made an hedge *about* him?" (Job i. 10).

2. Pathway of Grace. "God led the people *about*, through the way of the wilderness of the Red Sea" (Exod. xiii. 18).

3. Discipline of Grace. "He led him *about* and instructed him" (Deut. xxxii. 10).

4. Diligence of Grace. "I must be *about* My Father's business" (Luke ii. 49).

5. Direction of Grace. "Let your loins be girded *about*." "Girt *about*" (Luke xii. 35; Eph. vi. 14).

6. Life of Grace. "Always bearing *about* in the body," etc. (2 Cor. iv. 10).

7. Aim of Grace. "Went *about* doing good" (Acts x. 38).

2. "ABOVE"

"Born from above" (John iii. 3).

1. Christ, who came "from above" did a work for us which was outside in its merit and worth—John iii. 31.

2. Life. The life which qualifies us for the Kingdom of God is "from above"—John iii. 3, 5. The word "again" should be "above," and is so given in John iii. 31.

3. Love. The "perfect gift" of God's love and grace is "from above," as well as every good gift of His providence—Jas. i. 17.

4. Wisdom. The wisdom which makes us wise is "from above"—Jas. iii. 17.

5. Affection. To set our affection on "things above" is to evidence we need resources above and beyond us—Col. iii. 1, 2.

6. Protection. We need "above all" the Shield of Faith (Christ) to shield us from the enemies' attacks—Eph. vi. 16.

7. Satisfaction. Covering all and in all the Lord Himself, who is above, is the One who can take out of danger and bring us into untold blessing—Psa. xviii. 16-19.

1

3. ABRAM'S JOURNEY OF FAITH

Gen. xii. 4-9; xiii. 1-4, 14, 18

THERE is a path to be found, and God alone can find it; so if we would find the path we must find God by being found by Him.

1. **The Departure of Faith**—xii. 4. Abram "departed out of Haran," the half-way place of compromise, and this was "as the Lord had spoken to Him." Faith's authority and action is always based upon what God says—Rom. x. 17. Obedience is the act of faith. When we will what God wills, we show our faith.

2. **The Destination of Faith**—xii. 5; "This land" (ver. 7). "They went forth" to "Canaan," and "into the land of Canaan they came," and there "Jehovah appeared unto Abram, and said, Unto thy seed will I give this land." The land was God's gift of earthly possession to Abram and his seed. God has given to faith "all spiritual blessing in Christ" (Eph. i. 3). See how many blessings are mentioned in Ephesians i., and "name them one by one."

3. **The Worship of Faith.** Three times we read of Abram in connection with an altar, and in three different relations. First, when Jehovah gave Abram the land—xii. 7; second, when he was restored after his backsliding into Egypt—xiv. 4; and third, as he progressed on his journey—xiv. 18. The altar, in its typical meaning, is worship founded on sacrifice. The Cross of Christ's sacrifice is the basis of God's giving—Rom. viii. 32, the plea for restoration—Heb. ix. 13, 14, and the spur to progress in Christian life and service—2 Cor. v. 14-16. The only place where we can worship God is in and at the Cross of Christ's atoning sacrifice. We cannot worship Him if we are in the Egypt of the world and lack heart separation to Him. The altar and tent are not mentioned as long as Abram is in Egypt—see Gen. xii. 9—xiii. 4.

4. **The Declension of Faith.** Abram "went down into Egypt," and when he had "come into Egypt" he compromised with Sarah, caused Pharaoh pain, told a lie about Sarah, and was sent away by the Egyptians—xii. 10, 14, 17, 19, 20. When a child of God gets out of communion with the Lord, he will often do what a man of the world would scorn to do. Our faith will wane if we are not watchful, even as a plant will languish for want of attention. A musty room means the exclusion of light, sun, and air, and a declining faith will cause the whole spiritual life to be lacking in the warmth of love, the light of knowledge, and the air of the Spirit's life-imparting grace.

5. **The Vision of Faith**—xiii. 14-16. The Lord told Abram to "look," after he was separated from Lot. Lot was the man

who looked on the plains of Jordan—xiii. 10, and soon was in Sodom. He followed the eyes of his inclination, but Abram followed the direction of the Lord. When we see things at the Lord's bidding we always find a blessing; but when we look with the eyes of self-will we are courting a bane. To see the Lord is to see things in their true light.—Heb. xi. 27. To see things truly there is a needs be for the heart to be clean, the hands right, the spirit possessed by Christ, and the soul dominated by the Spirit.

6. **The Journey of Faith.** There are seven stages in the journeyings of Abram.

From the Ur of idolatry to the Haran of compromise—xi. 31.

From the Haran of compromise to the Canaan of blessing—xii. 4, 5.

From the Canaan of blessing and the "Moreh" of conflict to the Bethel of prayer—xii. 6-8.

From the Bethel of prayer to the "going and journeying" (margin) to "the south" of bordering on the Egypt of the world, and to the Egypt of straitening—xii. 9-20.

From the Egypt of backsliding to the Bethel of restoration—xiii. 1-4.

From the Bethel of restoration to the Hebron of fellowship—xiii. 18.

7. **The Advance of Faith.** When the Haran of compromise is left, the Egypt of the world is abandoned, and Lot is cut off; then Abram is able to "look" with God into His purpose for him, and to "walk" through the land, and dwell with the Lord in the Hebron of fellowship—xiii. 14-18. Hindrances gone, faith advances. When faith advances in the ways of God, it enjoys His word and keeps on in fellowship with Him.

4. ABRAHAM'S INTERCESSION

Genesis xviii. 18-33

Dr. Joseph Parker, in referring to Sodom, and Abraham's prayer for it, and God's knowledge of its sin, said: "There are four great facts to consider. 1, That God holds inquest upon the moral condition of cities. 2, That God is accessible to earnest human appeal. 3, That the few can serve the many. 4, That human prayer falls below Divine resources."

There are several traits in Abraham's intercession.

1. He was **confident in spirit**, for he stood before the Lord—22.

2. He was **definite in his plea**, for he prayed that Sodom might be spared for the sake of the righteous in it—23-25.

3. He **pleaded what the Lord was**, and His righteousness, as arguments for his prayer to be answered, for he confessed the Judge of all the earth would do right—25, 26.

4. His intercession was **humble in tone**, for he confessed he was but dust and ashes—27.

5. And his **petition was persistent in spirit**—28. And yet it failed in its continuance, for he left off in his intercession before the Lord left off in His giving—32, 33.

5. ABRAHAM'S VISION
Genesis xviii. 1, 2

FELLOWSHIP is the soul of friendship, or the common interest that the one has with the other.

The Lord appeared to him—1, 2. If the different occasions when God appeared to Abraham are looked up, it will be found they were crisis points in his history. On this occasion God promised a son to him. Every true Christian experience begins with a vision of Christ, and we fail to see anything that is worth seeing till we have seen Him. Recall how this fact is illustrated in the lives of—

1. **Moses, the Leader**—Exod. iii. 2.
2. **Isaiah, the Prophet**—Isa. vi. 1.
3. **Paul, the Apostle**—Acts ix. 3-5.
4. **Peter, the Fisherman**—Luke v. 8.
5. **John, the Disciple**—Rev. i. 17.
6. **Gideon, the Warrior**—Judges vi. 12.
7. **Jacob, the Prince**—Gen. xxxii. 24-30.

6. "AGREE"

THE Greek word for "agree" in Matthew xviii. 19, means to symphonise and suggests a musical harmony, where chords are tuned to the same key, and struck by a master hand.

1. There is a symphonising which we should **avoid**, that is, a concert for the furtherance of evil, like Ananias and Sapphira, when they "agreed together" to tempt the Holy Spirit—Acts v. 9.

2. There is a symphonisation which we should **recognise**, namely, when the working of God's providence agrees with the fulfilment of God's Word (see the word "agree" in Acts xv. 15).

3. But the symphony which is **specially pleasing to the Lord** is when His people agree in a concert of prayer, as Judah did—2 Chron. xx. 4, as the disciples did in the upper room—Acts i. 14, as the Church did for Peter—Acts xii. 12, and as Nehemiah and his workers did—Neh. iv. 9.

7. ABUNDANT SUPPLY

"ABLE to do exceeding abundantly above all we ask or think" (Eph. iii. 20).

"The principal and most valuable characteristic of the cod is its amazing fecundity. It has been calculated that a single fish will deposit nine millions of eggs, a number which in its vastness simply bewilders us, for we cannot at all realise what such a mighty host means. " What is true in this realm of Nature is true in every other, and especially in the realm of grace, for the Lord provides—

1. **Abundant Grace** to save us—Rom. v. 20.
2. **Abundant Pardon** to forgive us—Isa. lv. 7.
3. **Abundant Satisfaction** to fill us—Psa. xxxvi. 8.
4. **Abundant Peace** to quieten us—Phil. iv. 7.
5. **Abundant Life** to equip us—John x. 10.
6. **Abundant Joy** to gladden us—Phil. i. 26.
7. **Abundant Power** to energise us—Col. i. 11.

8. "ACCORDING TO"

In EPHESIANS I

1. **Predestination.** "According to the good pleasure of His will, " He hath predestinated us to the place of children (5).

2. **Benediction.** "According to the riches of His grace, " He has blessed us in Christ (7).

3. **Revelation.** "According to His good pleasure, " He hath made known to us the secret of His will (9, 10).

4. **Inheritance.** "According to the purpose" of His counsel, He hath given us an inheritance in Christ (11).

5. **Power.** "According to the working of His mighty power, " He energises us for life and labour (19).

9. A GROUP OF GLAD ONES

THE words "Glad," "Rejoice," etc., are one and the same in the Greek.

1. A Glad **Saviour**—Luke xv. 5.
2. A Glad **Sinner**—Luke xix. 6; Acts viii. 39.
3. A Glad **Servant**—Acts xi. 23.
4. A Glad **Sufferer**—Col. i. 24.
5. A Glad **Saint**—2 John 4.
6. A Glad **Surveyor**—Col. ii. 5.
7. A Glad **Scoffer**—Luke xxiii. 8.

10. ACTIVITIES OF GOD

AMONG the activities of God on behalf of His people, we have—

1. **Hurrying Feet** in Grace for our blessing—Luke xv. 20.

2. **Holding Hands** in Power for our security—John x. 29.

3. **A Loving Heart** in Sympathy for our encouragement—John xvi. 27.

4. **Listening Ears** in Attention for our prayers—Psa. xxxiv. 15.

5. **Watching Eyes** in Outlook for our enablement—2 Chron. xvi. 9.

6. **Gracious Lips** in Promise for our faith—S. of S. v. 13.

7. **Everlasting Arms** in Upholding for our sustainment—Deut. xxxiii. 27.

11. "AFAR OFF"

THERE are many characters who are said to be "afar off."

1. **A Demon-Possessed Man**, when he "saw Jesus afar off," ran and worshipped Him (Mark v. 6).

2. **The Women at the Cross** were "beholding" Him "afar off" (Matt. xxvii. 55).

3. **Peter** followed his Lord "afar off" when he ought to have been near (Luke xxii. 54).

4. **The Lepers**, conscious of their disease, "stood afar off" (Luke xvii. 12).

5. **The Publican**, knowing his sin and unworthiness, stood "afar off" (Luke xviii. 13).

6. **The Gentile Sinners** are "afar off" from Jewish blessings and promises (Acts ii. 39; Eph. ii. 13, 17).

7. **Old Testament Saints** did not enjoy to the full the blessings of the Gospel, but they saw them "afar of" (Heb. xi. 13).

12. ACTIVITIES OF JESUS

IN JOHN XI

THE Man of men, the greatest Person who ever lived.

1. **The Listening Friend.** "Jesus heard" (4).

2. **The Loving Lord.** "Jesus loved" (5).

3. **The Gracious Teacher.** "Jesus answered" (9).

4. **The Wondrous Speaker.** "Jesus saith" and "spake" (13, 23).

5. **The Timely Visitor.** "Jesus came" (17).

6. **The Located Saviour.** "Jesus was" (32).

7. **The Seeing Helper.** "Jesus saw" (33).

8. **The Troubled Groaner.** "He groaned and was troubled" (33, 38).

9. **The Weeping Compassionator.** "Jesus wept" (35).

10. **The Believing Son.** "Jesus lifted up His eyes and said, Father" (41).

11. **The Commanding Life-Giver.** "He cried" (43).

12. **The Constant Worker.** "Jesus did...done" (45, 46).

13. **The Undisputed Witness.** "This Man doeth many miracles" (47).

14. **The Delivering Substitute.** "Jesus should die" (51, 53).

13. ACTIVITIES OF THE CHRISTIAN LIFE

1. **Shining.** Arising to shine—Eph. v. 14.
2. **Running.** Running to win—1 Cor. ix. 24-27.
3. **Helping.** Helping to succour—Phil. iv. 3.
4. **Sowing.** Sowing to reap—Gal. vi. 7-9.
5. **Fighting.** Fighting to subdue—1 Tim. vi. 12.
6. **Praying.** Praying to bless—1 Tim. ii. 1, 2.
7. **Fishing.** Fishing to catch—Matt. iv. 19.

14. ACTIVITIES OF THE CHRISTIAN LIFE

1. **Following** to prove—John x. 27.
2. **Growing** to attain—Eph. iv. 15.
3. **Walking** to accomplish—Eph. v. 1, 2.
4. **Working** to benefit—Rom. xii. 6-16.
5. **Wrestling** to conquer—2 Tim. ii. 5.
6. **Washing** to cleanse—John xiii. 14.
7. **Reaching** to gain—Phil. iii. 13, 14.

15. "ALL" IN ROMANS

1. **Sin.** "All have sinned" (Rom. iii. 23).
2. **Subjection.** "All under sin" (Rom. iii. 9).
3. **Sacrifice.** "Gave Him up for us all" (Rom. viii. 32).
4. **Supply.** "Freely give us all things" (Rom. viii. 32).
5. **Supplication.** "All who call upon Him" (Rom. x. 12).
6. **Superintendence.** "Lord over all" (Rom. x. 12).
7. **Support.** "The God of Peace be with you all" (Rom. xv. 33).

16. "AGAIN"

THE importance, intensity, and repetition of a given act, or the statement of a truth, is seen in the word *palin*, rendered "again." The importance of distinguishing words given "again" is seen if we contrast two other words. "Again" should be "above" in the sentence, "Born from above" (John iii. is given "above" in verse 31). Another word, "again," is the word associated with Christ rising "again" from the dead. It means to stand up. Strictly speaking, "again" can only be applied to a second act. Christ did rise the second time. He was standing in life before He died, and He stood up again in resurrection; but in the instances where *palin* is used of Christ, it means a repetition.

1. **Life Given and Taken**. "I lay down My life, that I may take it again" (John x. 17, 18). Here is the double purpose of deliberate action. His death and resurrection were no accident.

2. **"Written" and "Written Again."** To Satan's partial quotation of Scripture, Christ gave him an utterance of full statement. "Jesus said to him, It is written again" (Matt. iv. 7).

3. **Hands Upon Eyes and Again**. There was a double touch with Christ in His healing of the blind man—Mark viii. 23-25.

4. **Christ's Repeated Statement**. The disciples were astonished at Christ's teaching about riches, but He emphasised His statement by repeating it—Mark x. 23, 24.

5. **Peace and Peace**. "Jesus saith to them again" (John xx. 21). He gives a double peace. The peace of the Cross and the peace of Himself—John xiv. 27.

6. **Prayer and Prayer**. "He went away again" (Matt. xxvi. 42, 44). To pray again is to get into the heart of things.

7. **Coming and Coming**. "I will come again" (John xiv. 3). His future coming is associated with His first.

17. "AFTER THAT"

1. **Trusting** after hearing—Eph. i. 13.
2. **Communion** after cleansing—Lev. xiv. 8.
3. **Revelation** after separation—Gen. xiii. 14.
4. **Service** after consecration—Num. viii. 15, 22.
5. **Power** after the Spirit's coming—Acts i. 8.
6. **Thanksgiving** after blessing—Deut. xvi. 13-17.
7. **Glory** after suffering—1 Peter v. 10.

18. ACTS OF CHRIST

THE acts of Christ are frequently referred to in connection with the word "FORTH. "

1. **His Power to Heal.** "Put forth His Hand" (Matt. viii. 3).

2. **His Power to Send.** "Jesus sent forth" (Matt. x. 5).

3. **His Power to Sow.** "Sower went forth to sow" (Matt. xiii. 3).

4. **His Power to Manifest.** "Manifested forth His glory" (John ii. 11).

5. **His Power to Direct.** "Putteth forth His own sheep" (John x. 4).

6. **His Power to Evidence.** "Jesus Christ might shew forth" (1 Tim. i. 16).

7. **His Power to Return and Reward.** "Will come forth and serve" (Luke xii. 37).

19. "ALL THINGS"

"ALL things" occurs 221 times in the Bible.

1. They are of God as to their **Source.** "All things are of God" (2 Cor. v. 18).

2. Are for the sake of the believer as to their **Object.** "All things" are yours—1 Cor. iii. 21.

3. Work together for good as to their **Purpose.** "All things work together for good to them that love God" (Rom. viii. 28).

4. Christ Head over the Church as to their **Arrangement.** "Head over all things to the Church" (Eph. i. 22).

5. The believer may know, hence his **Privilege.** "Teacheth you of all things" (1 John ii. 27).

6. The believer can do, hence his **Power.** "Do all things through Christ which strengtheneth" (Phil. iv. 13).

7. Granted in answer to **Prayer,** hence his dependence. "All things, whatsoever ye shall ask in prayer" (Matt. xxi. 22).

8. Only possible to **Faith,** hence his responsibility. "All things are possible to him that believeth" (Mark ix. 23).

9. Are to be **Proved,** hence his diligence. "Prove all things" (1 Thess. v. 21).

10. **Thanks** to be given for, hence his gratitude. "Giving thanks for all things" (Eph. v. 20).

11. Their **End** at hand, hence his watchfulness. "The end of all things is at hand" (1 Peter iv. 7).

12. To be **Inherited** by the believer, hence his hope. "Inherit all things" (Rev. xxi. 7).

20. ALL-NESS OF THE CHRISTIAN LIFE.

How many of God's saints know the fullness of blessing found in connection with the little word "all" in the following Scriptures.

1. God has blessed us with "**all** spiritual **blessings** in Christ" (Eph. i. 3).

2. He has "given **all things** that pertain to life and holiness" (2 Peter i. 3).

3. He is able to make "**all grace** abound toward you" (2 Cor. ix. 8).

4. "**All** the **promises** of God are yea and amen in Christ" (2 Cor. i. 20).

5. He desires we should be filled into "**all**" His **fullness** —Eph. iii. 19.

6. He can supply "**all**" our **need**, according to His riches in Christ Jesus—Phil. iv. 19.

7. He assures us "**all things**" are ours—1 Cor. iii. 21, 22.

21. THE "ALL" PSALM

Psa. xxxiv., R. V.

1. **A Joyful Chorister**. "I will bless Jehovah at *all* times" (v. 1).

2. **A Delivered Suppliant**. "Jehovah...delivered me from *all* my fears" (v. 4).

3. **A Saved Saint**. "Jehovah...saved him out of *all* his troubles" (v. 6).

4. **A Confident Witness**—v. 17. "Jehovah heard, and delivered out of *all* troubles."

5. **Escaped Believer**—v. 19. "Afflictions...Jehovah delivereth him out of them *all*."

6. **A Preserved Servant**—v. 20. "He keepeth *all* his bones."

22. "ALTOGETHER"

1. What **man is**. "Every man at his best is altogether vanity" (Psa. xxxix. 5).

2. What man **has become**. "Altogether become filthy" (Psa. liii. 3).

3. What **God's Word is**. "The judgments of Jehovah are true and righteous altogether" (Psa. xix. 9).

4. What **God thinks** about man's thinking about Himself. "Thou thoughtest that I was altogether such a one as thyself" (Psa. l. 21).

5. **What the convicted saint knows** God knows. "There is not a word in my tongue, but, lo, O Jehovah, Thou knowest it altogether" (Psa. cxxxix. 4).

6. God's **other blessing** of His people. "Thou hast altogether blessed them these three times...what the Lord saith, that will I speak" (Num. xxiii. 11, 26; xxiv. 1, 10, 13).

7. The **secret of blessing.** "That which is altogether just shalt thou follow, that thou mayest live and inherit the land" (Deut. xvi. 20).

23. "ALL THAT HE," OR "SHE HAD"

1. **A Clean Separation.** "Abram went up out of Egypt... and all that he had" (Gen. xiii. 1).

2. **A Beautiful Type.** "Abraham gave all that he had unto Isaac" (Gen. xxv. 5; John iii. 35).

3. **A Worthy Ruler.** "All that he had he put into his hand" (Gen. xxxix. 4, 6).

4. **A Prosperous Man.** "The blessing of the Lord was upon all that he had" (Gen. xxxix. 5).

5. **A Bankrupt Servant.** "Commanded him to be sold... and all that he had" (Matt. xviii. 25).

6. **A Weary Quest.** "Spent all that she had, nothing bettered" (Mark v. 26).

7. **A Magnificent Gift.** "Cast in all that she had" (Mark xii. 44).

24. ANGEL'S RESURRECTION MESSAGE
Matt. xxviii. 1-10: 18-20

THE angel's message is full of the grace and glow of the Gospel. Weigh his sevenfold message.

1. The **"Fear not"** (5) **of Love.** The earthquake caused the keepers to shake and quake; we are therefore not surprised that the lightning countenance of the angel should fill the women with consternation.

2. The **"I know" of Appreciation.** The angel knew the loving quest of the women. He knew they wanted to see the loved form that they had last seen on the cruel Cross. Faith's memory always centres in the Cross.

3. The **"He is not here" of Reminder.** He had said He would not remain in the grave. We do not always find what we expect, but we discover the unexpected to our joy and comfort.

4. The **"He is risen" of Joy.** He travelled through the realm of Hades, and preached the Gospel to the spirits in prison—1 Peter iii. 18; iv. 6; and now He is risen triumphant over death, Hell, the grave, and the Devil—Heb. ii. 14; Rev. i. 18.

5. The "**See the place**" of Observation. The place of expiation was Calvary—Luke xxiii. 33; the place of glory will be in the Father's mansions—John xiv. 2, 3; and the place of resurrection was an empty tomb.

6. The "**Go quickly**" of Commission. To go and "tell" others that "He was risen from the dead" when they expected still to find Him lifeless, gave wings to their feet and a glow in their hearts.

7. The "**Ye shall see Him**" of Expectation. To hear He was risen was good, but to have the assurance of seeing Him was better.

25. ANXIETY AND COMMITTAL

"Be not anxious" Matt. vi. 25, R. V.

"GLASS, with anxiety!" Strange expression this! What does it mean? These words accompanied a parcel sent from Norway to England, and they were intended to indicate that the sender feared, from the fragile nature of the contents, that some mishap might befall it.

Is there not a lesson here for Christians? Might not some of us be rightly labelled, "Christians with anxiety?" In many instances there is no need for a label, as anxiety is only too plainly stamped upon the countenance, although the apostolic injunction is, "In nothing be anxious" (Phil. iv. 6. R. V.). Some obey this command in certain circumstances only, while others reverse the reading, and live as though they were to be anxious for everything. The Lord wishes His children to carry their worries and anxieties to Him; and to leave them with Him. Here are seven things which He bids us cast upon Him, or commit unto Him.

1. **Commit Yourself unto Him.** "He is able to keep that which I have committed unto Him against that day" (2 Tim. i. 12). Paul deposited himself in the hands of the Heavenly Banker; and, as the money in the Bank of England is kept safe in the strong-rooms within and by the guard without, so was the apostle, for he was kept by the Holy Spirit within, and by the Lord who encamped round about him.

2. **Commit Your Soul unto Him.** "Wherefore let them that suffer according to the will of God commit the keeping of their souls to Him in well-doing, as unto a faithful Creator" (1 Peter iv. 19). Suffering we shall have, but if we commit the keeping of our souls unto the Lord in well-doing, as the three Hebrew young men did, we shall, like them, cut loose our bonds, and gain the company of Jesus.

3. **Commit Your Spirit unto Him.** "Into Thine hand I commit my spirit" (Psa. xxxi. 5). If the Lord has the control of our spirit, He will control us altogether.

4. **Commit Your Way unto Him.** "Commit thy way unto the Lord; trust also in Him; and He shall bring it to pass" (Psa. xxxvii. 5). If we commit our way unto Him, we shall never stray from Him.

5. **Commit Your Works unto Him.** "Commit thy works unto the Lord" (Prov. xvi. 3). If the Lord controls the works and the workers, there will be no clashing in the working.

6. **Commit Your Burden unto Him.** "Cast thy burden upon the Lord" (Psa. lv. 22). If the Lord is our Burden-bearer, we shall be free to bear one another's burdens.

7. **Commit Your Care unto Him.** "Casting all your care upon Him, for He careth for you" (1 Peter v. 7). One, John Careless, a martyr, in writing to a friend, said: "Now my soul is turned to her old rest again, and has taken a sweet nap in Christ's lap. I have cast my care upon the Lord, who careth for me, and will be careless, according to my name." If we cast all our cares upon Him, He will take all care of us.

26. APPRECIATION

MANY appreciations were given of the Right Hon. JOHN MORLEY. Mr. A. G. Gardiner, writing in the *Nation*, says of him: "In an active life that covered nearly half a century of history, he played a part as disinterested, as elevated, and as free from blemish as that of any man in our public annals. Neither as journalist, author, nor statesman, did he fall on any great issue below the high standards which he professed, and by which he lived. He never trimmed his sails to the popular breeze, never deserted a cause which he believed to be just, never put truth in the balance against any private end. To his essay 'On Compromise' he affixed this motto: 'It makes all the difference in the world whether we put truth in the first place or in the second place.' It may, I think, be said with confidence that no man in our public life ever lived more steadily and unfalteringly by the lamp of truth than John Morley."

Thus says one of the great statesmen, as viewed from the outside. Sometimes we lack in appreciating each other as believers in Christ. We need to follow Paul's example, and record what we see in others.

1. Of the **Nameless Brother**, he said his praises were in all the churches—2 Cor. viii. 18.

2. Of **Epaphras**, he said, "He laboured fervently in prayer" (Col. iv. 12).

3. Of **Epaphroditus**, he said, "He ministered to my wants" (Phil. ii. 25).

4. Of **Onesimus**, the slave, he said, He is "a faithful and beloved brother" (Col. iv. 9).

5. Of the **Women in Philippi**, he said, "They laboured with me" (Phil. iv. 3).

6. Of the **Thessalonian Saints** he said, "From you sounded out the Word of the Lord" (1 Thess. i. 8).

7. Of **Onesiphorus**, he said, "He oft refreshed me, and was not ashamed of my chain" (2 Tim. i. 16).

27. "ARM OF THE LORD"
Isa. liii. 1

1. **Redeeming Arm** to Deliver—Exod. vi. 6.
2. **Great Arm** to Achieve—Exod. xv. 16; Psa. xcviii. 1.
3. **Persistent Arm** to Accomplish—Deut. iv. 34.
4. **Promising Arm** to Overthrow—Deut. vii. 18, 19.
5. **Powerful Arm** to Overawe—Deut. xxvi. 8.
6. **Strong Arm** to Scatter—Psa. lxxxix. 10, 13.
7. **Strengthening Arm** to Empower—Psa. lxxxix. 21.

28. A SERVANT OF JESUS CHRIST

THE Greek word for "servant," in the Book of Revelation, means a slave, and is rendered "bondman" and "bond"—vi. 15; xiii. 16; xix. 18. It occurs fourteen times, and in eleven instances indicates a servant of God, or of Christ.

1. **Revelation.** "Shew unto His servants" (i. 1; xxii. 6). God reveals to His servants what He does not make known to the world.

2. **Possession.** "His servant John" (i. 1). We are the Lord's by creation, calling, purchase, and possession.

3. **Opposition.** "Seduce My servants" (ii. 20). Satan and his emissaries do not trouble those who are his, but he and they are always at work to beguile and blast the Lord's.

4. **Preservation.** "Sealed the servants of our God" (vii. 3). Things are sealed for security and secrecy, so the Lord hides and preserves His own.

5. **Completion.** "As He hath declared to His servants" (x. 7). God will fill to the full all He has declared shall be.

6. **Compensation** "Shouldest give reward unto thy

servants" (xi. 18). The Lord has eyes to see, a heart to appreciate any service done to Him, and a reward is in His hands for those who have served.

7. **Recognition.** "Moses, the servant of God" (xv. 3). The Lord knows each of His servants by name.

8. **Retribution.** "Avenge the blood of His servants" (xix. 2). The saints who are saintly do not vindicate themselves, but the Lord does.

9. **Ascription.** "Praise our God, all ye His servants" (xix. 5). Worship is the out-going of the heart in praise, gratitude, and adoration to the Lord.

10. **Consecration.** "His servants shall serve Him" (xxii. 3). "Serve Him." To serve *Him* means loyalty, affection, thoroughness, and disinterestedness.

29. A SEVENFOLD EXHORTATION
Hebrews xii

1. **Stripped Bodies.** *"Lay aside* every weight," etc. (v. 1). The simile used is the putting off of a garment, as the athlete who lays aside every encumbrance before he runs in the race.

2. **Looking Eyes.** *"Looking unto* Jesus" (v. 2). The figure indicates the looking away from one object to another. Christ is the Leader and Completer of faith. We have a Perfect Example of faith to follow, and a Perfect Indweller to impart the faith He requires.

3. **Lifting Hands.** *"Lift up* the hands," etc. (v. 12). A loving heart to Christ in remembering how He lifted us up from sin to Himself, will prompt us to have hands for Christ in helping others in need.

4. **Straight Paths.** "Make *straight* paths," etc. (v. 13). The best way to restore others is to be perfectly sure we are right with God ourselves. We need to be straight ourselves if we would straighten others.

5. **Pursuing Feet.** *"Follow* peace," etc. (v. 14). Peace is the terminus which is reached by travelling in the way of holiness.

6. **Alert Attention.** *"Looking* diligently," etc. (v. 15). Not to take in supplies is to be devoid of provender. To fail the grace of God is to fail to take God in His grace, who never fails.

7. **Good Service.** *"Serve* God acceptably," etc. (v. 28). To be well-pleasing to God is the highest form of service. Acceptable service has love for its motive, truth for its guide, the Spirit for its power, and God's glory for its end.

30. "AS HE HATH PROMISED"

THE Lord binds Himself to His Word of Promise, and we command His fulfilment when we obey the conditions attached thereto. Ponder the words, "as He hath promised," in the following Scriptures.

1. **Bestowment.** After Jehovah had brought Israel into the land of Canaan, "as He" had promised (see seven "I wills" in Exod. vi. 6-8), they were to call to mind God's giving in redemption by keeping the feast of the Passover. A lively memory causes the heart to sing in loving praise. To forget His redeeming love, His saving grace, His liberating, His supplying gifts, His gracious presence, His guiding Word, and His willing service, is to express the deepest ingratitude.

2. **Enlargement.** "When the Lord thy God shall enlarge thy border, as He hath promised, thou mayest eat flesh" (Deut. xii. 20). Previously to this command, the children of Israel were prohibited from eating only such animal food as had been offered in sacrifice, but now they could have as much as they desired; and the reason given is, because they were enlarged, that is, having greater facilities for production, there was greater provision for supply. An enlargement of soul always means an enlargement of capacity to appreciate what the Lord gives.

3. **Avouchment.** "The Lord hath avouched thee this day to be His peculiar people" ("a people for His own possession," R.V.), "as He hath promised thee" (Deut. xxvi. 18). Israel had avouched the Lord to be their God—v. 17, and He responds by taking what they gave. Nothing gives the Lord greater pleasure than to possess us when we want to be possessed; when we love Him well we are willing to let Him take all. Adam's sleeping—Gen. ii. 21; Abram's giving—Gen. xxii. 16; Rebekah's going—Gen. xxiv. 58; Moses' forsaking—Heb. xi. 24-27; Ruth's clinging—Ruth i. 16; Jonathan's surrendering—1 Sam. xviii. 4; David's growing—1 Chron. xii; mighty men's risking—1 Chron. xi. 17-19; widow's casting—Luke xii. 59; Mary's anointing—John xii. 3, are a few illustrations of what results when the Lord possesses.

4. **Accomplishment.** "For the Lord your God fighteth for you, as He hath promised you" (Joshua xxiii. 10). Israel was an instrument of judgment to repel the inhabitants of Canaan because of their sins. We who believe in Christ have foes of a different character to contend with, namely, principalities and powers in heavenly places. When we walk with the Conqueror we shall surely conquer. Mark what the "Lord your God" is

said to have done all down Joshua xxiii., and don't forget the whole reason is in the "FOR" of verse 10. When the Lord drives out we can chase out our enemies.

5. **Fulfilment.** "The Gospel of God, which He had promised afore by His prophets in the Holy Scriptures, concerning His Son, Jesus Christ our Lord" (Rom. i. 1-3). The Scriptures are meaningless unless we see Christ in them, but they are meanful if we see Him. Adam, the man; Abel, the shepherd; Noah, the saviour; Enoch, the godly; Abraham, the giver; Isaac, the offered; Jacob, the toiler; and Joseph, the provider, foregleam His glory. The offerings are types of the many-sidedness of His atoning sacrifice; and the messages of the Psalms and the prophets proclaim His worth and work.

6. **Advent.** "Now He hath promised...Yet once more I shake not the earth only, but also Heaven" (Heb. xii. 26). If the passage is pondered from which the writer to the Hebrew Christians quotes—Haggai ii. 5-9, it will be seen it has to do with the Lord's Coming in power to set up His Kingdom on the earth. The nations will then recognise the Lord in Jerusalem, for when He shakes the earth and the Heavens, and the nations, then the nations will acknowledge the Lord, for "the precious things of all the nations shall come" (ii. 7, R. V.), that is, shall be brought as offerings—see Zeph. iii. 10; Zech. xiv. 16.

7. **Enrichment.** "Blessed is the man that endureth temptation, for when he is tried he shall receive the crown of life, which the Lord hath promised to them that love Him" (Jas. i. 12; ii. 5). Crown-wearers are first of all cross-bearers. Those who stand the test of trial take their place among those who have triumphed.

31. "AT ALL TIMES"

1. **Trust.** "Trust in Him at all times" (Psa. lxii. 8).

2. **Praise.** "I will bless the Lord at all times" (Psa. xxxiv. 1).

3. **Love.** "A friend loveth at all times" (Prov. xvii. 17).

4. **Righteousness.** "Blessed...is he that doeth righteousness at all times" (Psa. cvi. 3).

5. **Desire.** "My soul breaketh for the longing that it hath unto Thy judgments at all times" (Psa. cxix. 20).

6. **Faithfulness.** "It is good to be zealously affected at all times" (Gal. iv. 18, R. V.).

7. **Concern.** "He maintain the cause...of His people at all times" (1 Kings viii. 59). "The Lord...give you peace at all times" (2 Thess. iii. 16, R. V.).

32. "AS MANY"

1. "As many as were **baptised** into Jesus Christ" (Rom. vi. 3).
2. "As many as are **led** by the Spirit of God, they are the sons of God" (Rom. viii. 14).
3. "As many as **walk** according to this rule" (Gal. vi. 16).
4. "As many as be **perfect**" (Phil. iii. 15).
5. "As many as I **love**, I rebuke" (Rev. iii. 19).
6. "As many as **received** Him, " etc. (John i. 12).
7. "As many as were **ordained** to eternal life" (Acts xiii. 48).

33. AT—IN TIME TO COME

THE objective of Christ's Coming is often found associated with the Greek preposition "*en*," which denotes a fixed position, as being in a place, state, or time.

1. "**At His Coming**," those who are "Christ's" will be claimed by Him—1 Cor. xv. 23.
2. "**At the Last Trump**, " those who are the Lord's will be "changed in the twinkling of an eye" (1 Cor. xv. 52).
3. "**At His Appearing**, " Christ will reward those who have endured trial with "praise, honour, and glory" (1 Peter i. 7).
4. "**At His Coming**, " we may be "ashamed before Him" if we are not found abiding in Christ—1 John ii. 28.
5. "**At the Revelation**" (1 Peter i. 13) of Christ we shall have a fresh revelation of God's grace.
6. "**At that Day**" of His appearing, Christ will give those who have loved His approach a crown of righteousness— 2 Tim. iv. 8.
7. "**At Hand**" is the time when the predictions of the Revelation will be fulfilled—Rev. i. 3; xxii. 10.

34. AT CERTAIN PLACES

PLACES in which people were found.

1. "**At the Beautiful Gate**" a poor cripple was found —Acts iii. 10.   Like many Christians, he had life, but not liberty.
2. "**At the Door**" Peter knocked for admittance—Acts xii. 13.   The saints often need to be knocked up to have fellowship with them.

3. "At the Sepulchre" Mary Magdalene was found—John xx. 11. Where she had last seen Him dead, she met Him alive.

4. "At His Feet" Mary fell, to find comfort about the death of her brother—John xi. 32.

5. "At the Fire" Peter "warmed himself," when he ought to have been near his Lord—Mark xiv. 54.

6. "At Home" is the place to show piety at first—1 Tim. v. 4.

7. "At the Door" the Lord is found when a church is wrong, instead of being inside—Rev. iii. 20.

35. "AT HAND"

THE italicised words in the Scriptures are the same in the Greek.

1. An Hour of Woe. "The hour is *at hand*" (Matt. xxvi. 45).

2. A Means to an End. "By the which we *draw nigh* unto God" (Heb. vii. 19).

3. A Reciprocal Action. "*Draw nigh* unto God, and He will *draw nigh* unto you" (James iv. 8).

4. A Cheering Lord. "Jesus Himself *drew near*, and went with them" (Luke xxiv. 15).

5. A Returning Saviour. "The Coming of the Lord *draweth* nigh" (James v. 8).

6. A Near Redemption. "Your redemption *draweth* nigh" (Luke xxi. 28).

7. An Approaching Day. "The Day is *at hand*" (Rom. xiii. 12; Heb. x. 25).

36. A THREEFOLD TAKING

THREE times the compound word "*paralambano*" occurs in John's Gospel. The word means to take near to one's self, hence to have with one the object thus taken. "*Lambano*" occurs many times in the aforesaid Gospel, at least forty-five times, and is generally given "*receive*" and "*took*;" but where the prefix "*para*" is added to "*lambano*" it means to take near to one's self.

1. Rejection. The Spirit's lament about Christ's own is, "His own *received* Him not" (John i. 11). Being His kinsmen and possessions, they should not only "receive" (*lambano*) Him, but receive Him near with glad hearts, surrendered wills, and communing spirits. What an added touch of meaning is given when the Spirit goes on to say, "As many as received (*lambano*) Him, to them gave He the right to become the children of God" (i. 12). Those who were not His kinsmen who receive Him, become His kinsmen. Those who had not the

relationship of life, by the life of relationship enter into a closer bond.

2. **Crucifixion**. "And they took (*paralambano*) Jesus and led Him away." This was after Pilate had weakly and against his conviction delivered Him to be crucified. Wicked hands took Him near to themselves and led Him to the "place of a skull." Their ill-intent of wickedness carried out the God-intent of purpose—Acts ii. 23. The manner of His death was prophesied —John xix. 37; its cause was sin—Rom. iv. 25; its power was love—Gal. ii. 20; its basis was grace—Heb. ii. 9; its unfolding is wisdom—1 Cor. i. 23; its practicality is separation from self, sin, and the world—Rom. vi. 6; Gal. v. 24; vi. 14; and its end is identification with Christ—Matt. xxvii. 44; Gal. ii. 20. The word "crucified with" in these passages signifies co-crucifixion.

3. **Expectation**. "I will come again and receive you to Myself," or, as it might be given, "I am coming to take you to be near to Myself" (John xiv. 3). When Christ returns for His own, He comes as the Saviour to redeem—Rom. viii. 23; as the Uniter to gather—1 Thess. iv. 13-18; as the Blessed Hope to gladden—Titus ii. 13; as the Transformer to glorify—Phil. iii. 20, 21; as the Lover to present—Eph. v. 27; as the Lord to reward—1 Cor. iii. 14; iv. 5; and as the Friend to receive to Himself.

37. ATONEMENT

THE atonement of Christ's death is—

1. The **Sin-cleanser** of the sinner's conscience—1 John i. 7.
2. The **Self-annuller** of the old life—Gal. ii. 20.
3. The **Soul-sanctifier** of the saint's life—Heb. xiii. 12.
4. The **Service-inspirer** of the believer's work—2 Cor. v. 14.
5. The **Victory-giver** in the warrior's conflict—Rev. xii. 11.
6. The **Magnet-drawer** to the Church's communion— 1 Cor. x. 16.
7. The **Song-incentive** of Heaven's praise—Rev. v. 9.

38. ATTITUDES OF THE BELIEVER
IN RELATION TO CHRIST

THERE are some terms which relate to the Christian life which are of pressing importance, because of the issues which are involved in relation to them. The following seven words indicate a few aspects of the Christian's life, namely, "Believe," "Pray," "Abide," "Walk," "Take," "Stand," "Watch."

1. To **Believe on Christ** is the **secret** of the Christian life— Gal. ii. 20,

2. To **Pray to Christ** is the **stay** of the Christian life—Phil. iv. 6.

3. To **Abide in Christ** is the **strength** of the Christian life—John xv. 4.

4. To **Walk as Christ** is the **shining out** of the Christian life—1 John ii. 6-9; 1 Peter ii. 21.

5. To **Take from Christ** is the **supply** of the Christian life—Isaiah xxvii. 5.

6. To **Stand with Christ** is the **staple** of the Christian life—Eph. vi. 14.

7. To **Watch for Christ** is the **standing order** of the Christian life—Mark xiii. 33. The term watchfulness is a comprehensive one. It signifies far more than merely holding the truth of the Lord's Coming. It covers the whole trend of the spiritual life in the variety of its traits.

39. ATTENTION OF GRACE

"FEAR not! Ye are of more value than many sparrows" (Luke xii. 7).

The careful attention of the Lord to details is aptly expressed when we remember He—

1. **Names** His sheep—John x. 3.
2. **Numbers** our hairs—Matt. x. 30.
3. **Counts** our steps—Job. xxxi. 4.
4. **Books** our thoughts—Mal. iii. 16.
5. **Bottles** our tears—Psa. lvi. 8.
6. **Takes** our hands—Isa. xli. 13.
7. **Supplies** our need—Phil. iv. 19.

40. AUTHORITY

WHEN we are under the authority of Christ, we have all His authority behind us. The usage of the word for authority (*exousia**) is instructive and inspiring.

1. **Authority to Heal** "Power (*exousia*) to heal sicknesses" (Mark iii. 15).

2. **Authority over Demons.** "Power (*exousia*) over unclean spirits" (Mark vi. 7).

3. **Authority to Preach.** "Go...all power (*exousia*) is given unto Me" (Matt. xxviii. 18).

4. **Authority to Become.** "Power (*exousia*) to become the children of God" (John i. 12).

* "*Exousia*" is translated "authority" in John v. 27, "right" in Rev. xxii. 14, "jurisdiction" in Luke xxiii. 7, "liberty" in 1 Cor. viii. 9, and "power" in John x. 18.

41. BANDS OF LOVE

Hosea xi. 4

1. Christ's Life Illustrates His Love. See how often He is said to be "moved with compassion" (Matt. ix. 36; xiv. 14; xv. 32; xx. 34; Mark i. 41; v. 19; Luke vii. 13). His life, like the sun in its shining, was beneficent in its ministry.

2. Christ's Cross Displays His Love. "He gave Himself up" (Gal. ii. 20, R.V.; Eph. v. 2, 25, R.V.). Think of what He *gave up*, to what and for whom He gave Himself, and the *outcome* of His giving.

3. Christ's Grace Confirms His Love. Believers are loved, loosed, and lifted—Rev. i. 5, R.V., and nothing can separate from His love. See the seven things that ordinarily can separate in Romans viii. 35; and the ten things that would divide in Romans viii. 38, 39.

4. Christ's Truth Affirms His Love. The words of truth assure us of the continuity of His love—John xiii. 1, as well as the measure and manner of it—John xv. 9, 12.

5. Christ's Friends Testify to His Love. His love is particular in its affection—John xi. 5, sympathetic in its service —John xi. 35, and confiding in its fellowship—John xiii. 23.

6. Christ's Spirit Imparts His Love—Rom. v. 5; 1 John iv. 16. He leads to the love that saves, imparts the love that sanctifies, and is the secret of the sacrificing love that serves.

7. Christ's Operation through us Demonstrates His Love—2 Cor. v. 14. The constraining power of His love is the moving force to impel in holy service and lowly sacrifice.

42. "BE"

THE commands of the Lord are always imperative. They leave no choice with us, but to choose His choice.

1. "Be Holy." "Be ye holy in all manner of conversation" (1 Pet. i. 15, 16), and the reasons are, "Because" God is "Holy," and because He calls us to this devoted life in separation to Him.

2. "Be Perfect." (2 Cor. xiii. 11). "Perfect" means to be in joint, to be adjusted, and is used of nets being mended—Matt. iv. 21, of being "joined together" (1 Cor. i. 10), and of one being restored to what he was before—Gal. vi. 1.

3. "Be Still" (Psa. xlvi. 10). The secret of knowing God is to be still in humbleness before Him, and let every voice **but** His be hushed.

4. "Be Sober." "Be sober," that is, hold oneself in hand, so that others shall not take us unawares—1 Pet. v. 8.

5. **"Be Faithful"** (Rev. ii. 10). When faith and love burn within the temple of our being, faithfulness will characterise the life.

6. **"Be Clean."** "Be ye clean that bear the vessels of the Lord" (Isa. lii. 11). If the heart of the inner life is clean the hand of outward service will correspond.

7. **"Be Filled"** in the Spirit—Eph. v. 18. This is the most essential, for when the Spirit pervades the being, the atmosphere of His presence will be known.

43. BAGS

1. **Weights** in a bag—Deut. xxv. 13.
2. **Stones** in a bag—1 Sam. xvii. 40, 49.
3. **Transgressions** in a bag—Job xiv. 17.
4. **Holes** in a bag—Haggai i. 6.
5. **Gold** in a bag—Isa. xlvi. 6.
6. **Covetousness** in a bag—John xii. 6; xiii. 29.
7. **A Hand** in a bag—1 Sam. xvii. 49.

44. BARNABAS—FULL OF THE SPIRIT
Acts xi. 22-24

EVIDENCES of being full of the Spirit.

1. **A Seeing Eye.** "Had seen the grace of God."
2. **A Glad Heart.** "Was glad."
3. **A Ready Foot.** "He came."
4. **A Helpful Tongue.** "Exhorted them all."
5. **A True Character.** "He was a good man."
6. **A Consecrated Man.** "Full of Holy Spirit" (see iv. 36. 37).
7. **A Believing Soul.** "Full of faith."

45. "BEAR"

CHRIST bore our sins on the Cross, and bears the iniquity of our holy things.

1. **Personally,** when anyone sinned he was liable to bear the consequence of his act, whether he knew his sin or not. "If a soul sin...though he wist it not, yet is he guilty, and shall *bear* his iniquity" (Lev. v. 17).

2. **Substitutionary,** atonement for sin was only made by the shedding of blood. The blood of the bullock and the goat on the great day of atonement was specifically to "make an

atonement. " No less than sixteen times does the verb occur in Leviticus xvi. After the blood of the goat had been shed, by a priestly act of transference, he is said to place the sins of the children of Israel "upon the head of the live goat, " and he shall *"bear* upon him all their iniquities" (Lev. xvi. 21, 22).

3. **Representatively,** Aaron being the representative of Israel, he appeared before the Lord to act for them, and wore the priestly garments that he might *"bear* the iniquity" of their holy things (Exod. xxviii. 12, 29, 30, 38).

4. **Typically,** the sin-offering was essentially "to *bear* the iniquity of the congregation, to make atonement for them before the Lord" (Lev. x. 17). This was its counterpart in John's message about the Lamb of God, who "taketh" (*beareth*) away the sin of the world.

5. **Prophetically,** in the unfolding of the Spirit's utterance, Christ is said to have *"borne* our grief, " and to *"bear* the sin of many" (Isa. liii. 4, 12).

6. **Dogmatically,** the Holy Spirit declares that Christ was "manifested to take away our sins" (1 John iii. 5). The meaning of "take away" is to *bear* by taking up the load upon one's self, and thus to take away the load of guilt resting upon others.

7. **Practically,** the sins and their consequence are removed for the believer, for it was for "our sins" He was manifested; and now we are dead to the sins that put out Lord to death— 1 Peter ii. 24.

46. BELIEVER'S ATTITUDE

TO THE DOCTRINE (TEACHING) OF THE HOLY SPIRIT

1. Continue in it **stedfastly** as whole-hearted believers in Christ—Acts ii. 42.

2. Be shaped by it **continually** as pliable saints—Rom. vi. 17.

3. Feed upon it **personally** as dependant disciples— 1 Tim. iv. 16.

4. Attend to it **regularly** as diligent scholars—1. Tim. iv. 13.

5. Take heed to it **thoroughly** as earnest stewards— 1 Tim. iv. 16.

6. Teach it **faithfully** as consistent doers—1 Tim. vi. 3; Titus ii. 7, 10.

7. Preach it **tenaciously** as zealous workers—2 Tim. iv. 2; Titus ii. 1.

8. Hold it **firmly** as convinced witnesses—Titus i. 9; 2 John 10.

9. Abide in it as **satisfied** servants—2 John 9.

47. BECAUSE

1. **The Exciter of Wrath.** Sin. "Because of these things (sins) cometh the wrath of God" (Eph. v. 6).

2. **The Reason of Love.** God's love. "We love Him because He first loved us" (1 John iv. 19).

3. **The Cause of Failure.** Want of faith. "Because of unbelief" (Heb. iii. 19).

4. **The Evidence of Life.** Love to others. "Because we love the brethren" (1 John iii. 14).

5. **The Secret of Preservation.** Christ's livingness. "Because I live, ye shall live also" (John xiv. 19).

6. **The Power of Quickening.** The Holy Spirit. "The Spirit is life because of righteousness" (Rom. viii. 10).

7. **The Prompter of Kindness.** Christ's ownership. "Because ye belong to Christ" (Mark ix. 41).

48. BECOMINGNESS

THE word in italics in the texts is one and the same in the Greek.

1. **A Subjective Saviour.** "Thus it *becometh* us to fulfil all righteousness" (Matt. iii. 15).

2. **A Suffering Kinsman.** "It *became* Him," etc. (Heb. ii. 10).

3. **A Holy Priest.** "Such an high priest *became us*" (Heb. vii. 26).

4. **A Woman's Attitude.** "Is it *comely* (becoming) that a woman?" (1 Cor. xi. 13).

5. **A Saintly Walk.** "As *becometh* saints" (Eph. v. 3).

6. **A Corresponding Act.** "Which *become* sound doctrine" (Titus ii. 1).

7. **An Answering Life.** "Which *becometh* women professing godliness" (1 Tim. ii. 10).

49. "BEFORE GOD"

IN THE BOOK OF REVELATION

1. "**Stood** before God" (viii. 2).

2. "**Ascended** up before God" (viii. 4).

3. "**Voice**...before God" (ix. 13).

4. "**Witnesses**...before the God of the earth" (xi. 3, 4).

5. "**Elders**...sat before God" (xi. 16).

6. "**Accused** before God" (xii. 10).

7. "**Remembrance** before God" (xvi. 19).

8. "**Stand** before God" (xx. 12).

50. "BEGAN TO BE——"

1. **A Mighty Hunter.** "Began to be a mighty hunter" (Gen. x. 8).

2. **An Amazed Saviour.** "Began to be sore amazed" (Mark xiv. 33).

3. **A Perplexed Band.** "Began to be sorrowful, and to say... Is it I?" (Mark xiv. 19).

4. **A Wilful Bankrupt.** "Began to be in want" (Luke xv. 14)

5. **A Mutual Joy.** "They began to be merry" (Luke xv. 24).

6. **A Glorious Theme.** "Great salvation; which began to be spoken by the Lord" (Heb. ii. 3).

51. "BEFORE GOD"

1. **"Righteous** before God" (Luke i. 6).

2. **"Favour** before God" (Acts vii. 46).

3. **"Memorial** before God" (Acts x. 4).

4. **"Present** before God" (Acts x. 33).

5. **Truth** "before God" (Gal. i. 20).

6. **"Acceptable** before God" (1 Tim. v. 4).

7. **Charged** "before God" (1 Tim. v. 21).

52. BELIEVER'S CALLING

GOD called Abram from the land of idolatry to go with Himself to a land of promise—Heb. xi. 8. See from Deuteronomy viii. what kind of land it was.

Those who believe in Christ are called—

1. **From the darkness of sin and ignorance,** to the knowledge and light of God—1 Peter ii. 9.

2. **From the bondage of legalism** (doing things because we ought) to the liberty of the Gospel—Gal. v. 13.

3. **From the turmoil of unrest** and disquietude, to the peace and quietness of reconciliation with God—Col. iii. 15.

4. **From the death of spiritual death** of trespasses and sins, unto eternal life—John v. 24.

5. **From the unholiness of the self life** to the holiness of fellowship with God—1 Peter i. 15.

6. **From the wrangling of self-interest,** to partnership with Christ's sufferings—1 Peter ii. 21; iii. 9.

7. **From the uncertainty of the future,** to the "eternal glory" in Christ—1 Peter v. 10.

Let us walk worthy of our calling—Eph. iv. 1; and make it "sure" by our obedience—2 Peter i. 10.

53. BEHOLD THE CHRIST

1. "**Behold My Servant**" (Matt. xii. 18). See Him in His life, labour, and love.
2. "**Behold the Lamb**" (John i. 29, 36). See Him in His sinlessness and sacrifice.
3. "**Behold the Man**" (John xix. 5). See Him in His beauty and sympathy.
4. "**Behold the Sower**" (Matt. xiii. 3). See Him in words, works, and faithfulness.
5. "**Behold your King**" (John xix. 14). See Him in His might, majesty, and authority.
6. "**Behold the Greater**" (Matt. xii. 41, 42). See Him in supremacy, pre-eminence, and glory.
7. "**Behold your God**" (Isa. xl. 9). See Him in His Deity, dignity, and giving.

54. BELIEVERS ARE

1. **Saved** from condemnation—Rom. viii. 1.
2. **Accepted** in the Beloved—Eph. i. 6.
3. **Made meet** for the inheritance—Col. i. 12.
4. **Sanctified** in Christ—1 Cor. i. 2.
5. **Sealed** with the Holy Spirit—Eph. i. 13, R.V.
6. **Possessors** of eternal life—1 John v. 12.
7. **Blessed** in Christ with all spiritual blessings—Eph. i. 3.
Here are riches indeed!

55. BELIEVERS ARE CALLED

1. "**Children**" for kinship—1 John iii. 1, 2, R.V.
2. "**Saints**" for holiness—1 Cor. i. 2.
3. "**Christians**" for identification—Acts xi. 26.
4. "**Brethren**" for fellowship—Heb. ii. 11.
5. "**Sheep**" for character—John x. 3.
6. "**Servants**" for employment—Matt. xxv 14
7. "**Friends**" for companionship—John xv. 15.
When we are called anything, we are supposed to be true to what we are called.

56. BELIEVER'S OUTLOOK

BRIEFLY summarised, we may say there is a sevenfold outlook of blessing before the believer.
1. We shall "**meet**" Christ—1 Thess. iv. 17, and that means, as the word "meet" suggests, we shall be caught up to meet Him in the air, and come back with Him to the earth.

2. We shall "**see** Him as He is" (1 John iii. 2), not as He was in humiliation and death, but as He is in glory and incorruptibility.

3. We shall be **received** by Him—John xiv. 3, as He promised, "I will receive you to Myself," which means He will take us to His heart.

4. We shall **stand before** Him that our life and service may be tested, and our conduct towards our fellow-believers scrutinised—Rom. xiv. 10; 1 Cor. iii. 12-15; ix. 5; 2 Cor. v. 10.

5. We shall be **rewarded** by Him, for when we stand before the judgment seat of Christ it is that each may have his praise from God—1 Coi. iv. 5.

6. We shall be "**like**" Him in all the beauty of His manhood, and body of glory—1 John iii. 2; Phil. iii. 20, 21.

7. We shall be **with** Him, and have the joy of His companionship for ever—1 Thess. iv. 17.

57. "BE SOBER"

FREQUENTLY we are exhorted to "be sober," to "think soberly" (Rom. xii. 3), and to "live soberly" (Titus ii. 12).

1. "**Be...Sober**" in all the spheres of life, that the office filled may be commended—1 Tim. iii. 2.

2. "**Be Sober**" in wakefulness, and not allow the sleep of slothfulness to mar us—1 Thess. v. 6.

3. "**Be Sober**," and put on the armour of faith, love, and hope, and thus be prepared for the assaults of the enemy—1 Thess. v. 8.

4. "**Be Sober**," and thus be vigilant to qualify against the assaults of the Devil, and overcome his devices—1 Peter v. 8.

5. "**Be Sober**," and "watch unto prayer," for the end of all things is at hand—1 Peter iv. 7.

6. "**Be Sober**," is the command to young and old—Titus ii. 2, 4, 6, for unless we watch we shall be worried.

7. "**Be Sober**," and "hope to the end"—1 Peter i. 13, for the Coming of the Lord draweth nigh.

58. "BE NOT AFRAID"

1. "Be not afraid" when Christ says, "**It is I**" (Matt. xiv. 27).

2. "Be not afraid" when He says, "**Arise**" (Matt. xvii. 7).

3. "Be not afraid" when told to "**go**" and "**tell**" (Matt. xxviii. 10).

4. "Be not afraid" when Christ says, "**Believe**" (Mark v. 36).

5. "Be not afraid" of what may happen, provided **God is feared**—Luke xii. 4-7.

6. "Be not afraid" when God commands us to **"speak"** (Acts xviii. 9).

7. "Be not afraid" when ungodly men are a **"terror"** (1 Peter iii. 14).

59. "BE STRONG"

GOD's commands are His promises, which enable us to carry out His precepts.

1. "Be strong" to **possess God's possessions**, as He urged upon Joshua—Joshua i. 6.

2. "Be strong" to **obey Jehovah's commands**, by unfaltering response to them—Joshua i. 7.

3. "Be strong" in the **face of difficulties**, because the Lord is with us to see us through them—Joshua i. 9.

4. "Be strong" in the **face of the declension** of others, for the Lord bids us to be of "good courage"—Joshua i. 18.

5. **Pass on His Word**, "Be strong," to others, as Joshua did to the children of Israel, and overcome all your enemies—Joshua x. 25.

6. "Be strong," **for the Lord bids thee** "fear not" those who oppose us, for He pledges Himself not to fail us—Deut. xxxi. 6.

7. "Be strong," for **the Lord hath sworn** to give what He has promised—Deut. xxxi. 7.

60. "BEWARE"

GOD's commands remind us of our responsibilities. Beware of—

1. **The Bane of Covetousness.** "Beware of covetousness" (Luke xii. 15).

2. **The Dogs of Evil.** "Beware of evil workers" (Phil. iii. 2).

3. **The Traditions of Men.** "Beware lest any man spoil you through philosophy and vain deceit, after the traditions of men" (Col. ii. 8).

4. **The Leaven of Self-righteousness.** "Beware of the leaven of the Pharisees" (Luke xii. 1).

5. **The Blight of Forgetfulness.** "Beware lest thou forget the Lord" (Deut. vi. 12).

6. **The Concision of Judaism.** "Beware of the concision" (Phil. iii. 2).

7. **The Error of the Wicked.** "Beware lest ye also be led by the error of the wicked" (2 Peter iii. 17).

61. BIBLE

B BEAUTIFUL in its language—Psa. xxiii.

I INCORRUPTIBLE in its nature—1 Peter i. 23.

B BLESSED in its bestowments—Psa. xxxii.

L LOVING in its message—John iii. 16.

E ENLIGHTENING in its guidance—Psa. cxix. 105.

62. BIBLE STUDY

ON HEBREWS XIII. 20, 21

THIS is one of the green pastures, and the provendor is thick, sweet, and nourishing.   Every word is weighted with intrinsic worth and holy wealth.

1. **Personal Title of God.**   "The God of Peace."   The God of Peace proclaims the calm of His holiness, the quiet of His love, the stillness of His rest, the power of His Word, the resources of His grace, the steadiness of His purpose, the harbour of His care, the beauty of His character, and the glory of His nature.

2. **Powerful Act of God.**   "That brought again from the dead our Lord Jesus."   Without disturbing swathing bands, weight of spices, heavy stone, God brought Christ through them all.   Hades could not hold Him, nor the grave detain Him, nor Hell hinder Him.   The resurrection of Christ proclaims the greatness of God's power, and also its might.

3. **Pastoral Character of Christ.**   "That great Shepherd of the sheep."   His sheep are blood-bought, hand-kept, spirit-led, grace-guarded, word-sanctified, divinely-marked, and promise-fed.   He is great to do all these things, and loves to serve them. He lives to bless them, as He died to purchase them.

4. **Propitiating Blood of the Covenant.**   "Through the blood of the everlasting covenant."   By means of (as "through" signifies) Christ's Blood, Heaven is satisfied, justice is magnified, law is gratified, Hell is stultified, saints are sanctified, sinners are vivified, Christian workers are intensified, and believers will be glorified.   The covenant was made between Father and Son, and we get the benefit, and that benefit is eternal in its blessing.

5. **Perfecting of the Saints.**   "Make you perfect in every good work to do His will."   To answer to God's will by being thoroughly adjusted to His Word, is to be perfect.   For this perfection we need the Perfect One.   The will of God, nothing less, nothing more, nothing else.   When God has His way with us we get our way with Him, because we only want what He gives.   To be God-made is to be God-stayed.

6. **Performance of the Lord.** "Working (margin, "doing")
in you. " Mark the present tense, "working. " Not "did work"
nor "will work, " but is "working. " When the Lord puts His
hand to the plough He never looks back. There is no looking
back with Jehovah. When He takes up, He never gives up.
When He begins He completes.

7. **Pleasing to the Lord.** "That which is well-pleasing
in His sight. " The consciousness of the Lord's presence is the
soul of consecration. To please the Lord always produces a
pleasure to the one who does it. Here again the Lord is the
end, as well as the beginning and centre. The Leviticus of His
pleasure is reached by the Exodus of His redemptive leading;
and the Genesis of His grace.

8. **Preposition of Grace.** "Through Jesus Christ. " The
preposition "through" means, by means of the active agency
of our Lord. His activities did not cease at the Cross; they
began there with a new purpose and power. He is still the
active agent by means of whom all blessing flows to us. We
never can get beyond the sphere of His grace. Any and everything we need as saints and servants, as well as sinners, is
"through Jesus Christ" our Lord.

9. **Praise to the Lord.** "To whom be glory for ever and ever,
Amen. " We may well bless Him with our praises, since He has
blessed us with His mercies. A thankless man is a disgrace and
a dishonour, but a thankful man is a delight and an honour.

63. BLUNDERS

THE blunders of God's saints, as recorded in His Word, are
meant to be beacons to tell us to keep off the rocks upon which
they went.

1. **David's laziness,** and his consequent fall—2 Sam. xi. 1-4.

2. **Solomon's lustfulness,** and the consequent backsliding—
1 Kings xi. 1-6.

3. **Hezekiah's pride,** and its resultant captivity—Isa.
xxxix. 1-8.

4. **Miriam's jealousy,** and the leprosy which came to her
as punishment—Num. xii. 1-10.

5. **Lot's selfishness,** and his humiliating rebuke from the
Sodomites—Gen. xiii. 11; xix. 9.

6. **Peter's self-confidence,** and his consequent downward
course—Luke xxii. 33.

7. The **self-exultation** of the Church at Corinth, and the
resultant chastisement—1 Cor. xi. 30, are all recorded that
we may avoid their mistakes and escape their punishments.

64. BLESSINGS OF THE UPRIGHT

ONE said of a devoted Christian man in his business, "He commands my custom, for all his goods are Christian;" and of another, "He sells a Christian shovel." When we are "upright in heart and life and business, we need no recommendation."

The upright man, and not the leaner, is ever the blessed one. If the Book of Proverbs is carefully studied, it will be found there are many blessings which come to the upright.

1. The upright "**dwell in the land**" of promised blessing— ii. 21.

2. The upright have **Jehovah as their strength**—x. 29.

3. The integrity and righteousness of the upright bring **guidance and deliverance**—xi. 3, 6, 11.

4. The upright are **a joy to the Lord**, and He delights to answer their prayer—xi. 20; xv. 8.

5. The upright find that **the Lord keeps them**, causes them to flourish, and obtain definite direction—xiii. 6; xiv. 11; xxi. 29.

6. They find "**good things in possession**" (xxviii. 10).

"No good will Jehovah withhold from them who walk uprightly" (Psa. lxxxiv. 11).

65. BLESSED ONES

THE word "blessed" in the following passages means "happy." The soul of happiness may be summarised as contentment, peace, and joy.

The blessed or happy ones are those:

1. "Whose **robes** are washed in the Blood of the Lamb" (Rev. xxii. 14, R.V.).

2. Whose **iniquities** are forgiven through God's grace— Rom. iv. 7, 8.

3. Who **obey** Christ's Word to minister to others—John xiii. 17.

4. Who **endure** temptation by getting the victory—James i. 12.

5. Who **give** of their substance rather than receive—Acts xx. 35.

6. Who **have not seen Christ**, and yet believe in Him— John xx. 29.

7. Who **fulfil** the conditions embodied in the twelve Blesseds of Christ found in Matthew's Gospel—Matt. v. 3-11; xi. 6; xiii. 16; xxiv. 46.

66. BLESSINGS WHICH COME TO THE MEEK

1. **Satisfaction.** "The meek shall eat and be satisfied" (Psa. xxii. 26).
2. **Discretion.** "The meek will He guide in judgment" (Psa. xxv. 9).
3. **Instruction.** "The meek will He teach His way" (Psa. xxv. 9).
4. **Salvation.** "Save all the meek of the earth" (Psa. lxxvi. 9).
5. **Exaltation.** "The Lord lifteth up the meek" (Psa. cxlvii. 6).
6. **Beautification.** "He will beautify the meek" (Psa. cxlix. 4).
7. **Valuation.** "A meek and quiet Spirit" (1 Peter iii. 4).

67. BLIND MAN'S CONFESSION
John ix.

To truly confess Christ is to stand with Him, and tell what one knows experimentally. Mark the use of the personal pronoun "I."

1. The "I am" of **personality**—9.
2. The "I went" of **obedience**—11.
3. The "I received" of **blessing**—11.
4. The "I know not" of **ignorance**—12.
5. The "I washed" of **cleansing**—15.
6. The "I know" of **experience**—25.
7. The "I see" of **sight**—25.
8. The "I have told you" of **emphasis**—27.
9. The "I might" of **desire**—36.
10. The "I believe" of **faith**—38.

68. BLINDNESS OF SINNERS

NATURALLY we are—

1. Blind to our **condition** before God—Rom. iii. 11.
2. Blind to the **beauty** of Christ—Isa. liii. 1.
3. Blind to the **grace** of God—Rom. xi. 8.
4. Blind to the **things** of the Lord—1 Cor. ii. 9-14.
5. Blind to the **presence** of Christ—Rev. iii. 18, 19.
6. Blind to the **need** of the new birth—John iii. 3-7.
7. Blind to the **evil** around—Eph. ii. 2, 3.

69. BODY

1. **A Sacrificing Priest**—Rom. vi. 13; xii. 1. The words "yield" and "present" are the same.

2. **A Sacred Temple**—1 Cor. vi. 19; iii. 16. Faith recognises what we have in Christ, and makes it true in the experience by the Holy Spirit.

3. **A Possessed House**—1 Cor. vi. 13, 15. The Lordship of Christ is an essential truth which is sadly neglected.

4. **A Preserved Saint**—1 Thess. v. 23. The Lord expects us to be blameless, and He can keep us so if we trust Him.

5. **A Diligent Keeper**—1 Cor. ix. 27. If the body has the uppermost place, it will retard and injure the spiritual life.

6. **An Obedient Slave**—1 Cor. vi. 20. The believer, as a slave, is responsible to recognise the Lord's claim, and to allow Him to have absolute control of the entire being.

7. **A Saved Believer**—Rom. viii. 23; Phil. iii. 20, 21. Believers are waiting for their glorified bodies. When they have them their salvation will be complete.

70. BODY OF FAITH

1. **Eyes** of faith, to see—Heb. xi. 1.
2. **Ears** of faith, to listen—John v. 24.
3. **Hands** of faith, to grip—John i. 12.
4. **Feet** of faith, to walk—John x. 27.
5. **Mind** of faith, to think—Phil. ii. 5.
6. **Heart** of faith, to love—Rom. x. 9.
7. **Taste** of faith, to appreciate—1 Peter ii. 3.

71. "BROUGHT"

1. **Brought Out.** "The Lord hath brought him out of prison" (Acts xii. 17).

2. **Brought Forth.** "He brought Jesus forth" (John xix. 13).

3. **Brought To.** "He brought him to Jesus" (John i. 42).

4. **Brought Up.** "Brought again from the dead" (Heb. xiii. 20).

5. **Brought Low.** "Brought low for their iniquity" (Psa. cvi. 43).

6. **Brought Near.** "Brought thee near to Him" (Num. xvi. 10).

7. **Brought Home.** "The Lord hath brought me home" (Ruth i. 21).

72. "BORN AGAIN ALL OVER"

"WHEN I was born again, I was born again *all over.*" I am afraid there are some, who, while they are born again—that is, have life in Christ—are not born again *"all over;"* but they are like one who, when he was asked if he was religious, said, "Yes, in parts." To be wanting in any department of the Christian life is like the children of Israel, of whom it is said, they "came short" (Heb. iv. 1). Of Mephibosheth we read, he was "lame on both his feet." The Lord does not want any of His children—

1. To be **lame** in their experience—Heb. xii. 13.
2. To be **puffed up** with the big head of pride—1 Cor. iv. 6, 18, 19.
3. To have the **twist** of sectarianism—1 Cor. i. 10-12.
4. The **swelling** of conceit—Rom. xi. 25.
5. The **listless hand** of sloth—Prov. xx. 4.
6. The **feeble knees** of a decrepit experience—Heb. xii. 12.
7. The **hard heart** of unbelief—Heb. iii. 12.
8. The **coming short** of His purpose—2 Peter i. 4-11.

73. BOW OF PROMISE

Genesis ix. 13.

THERE is a sevenfold bow of promise. He promises—

1. **Help** in need—Heb. xiii. 5, 6.
2. **Strength** in weakness—Isa. xli. 10.
3. **Cheer** in despondency—Matt. xiv. 27.
4. **Guidance** in perplexity—Psa. xxxii. 8.
5. **Peace** in trouble—Isa. lxvi. 12.
6. **Joy** in sorrow—Isa. lxi. 3.
7. **Power** in service—Acts i. 4-8.

74. "BROTHERLAND"

"ALL one in Christ." If we are in Christ, we share a common brotherhood in Him. One relates how, in the days of the war, "I was at the front in the early days, and after a bad bit of an engagement I came upon a German officer in a shell-hole. He was in a terrible state, poor fellow, and we couldn't take him in, so I decided to stay with him. His mind was perfectly clear, and he said, 'Colonel, don't you think this is strange?' 'What's strange?' I asked. 'Well,' said he, 'if you and I had met in the trenches, I suppose you would have tried to kill me for the sake of the Motherland, and I should have tried to kill

you for the sake of Fatherland; yet here you are trying to save
me for the sake of—Brotherland.' More of the same kind he
said in those last hours, and when the end came he was in my
arms and his head was on my breast, and I don't mind telling
you I—I kissed him. "

The Brotherhood of Believers in Christ—

1. Christ Himself is the **Centre** of brotherhood—John xvii. 6.

2. Faith in Christ is the **Beginning** of Brotherhood—
John i. 12.

3. The Holy Spirit is the **Power** of Brotherhood—1 Cor.
xii. 13.

4. The Word of God is the **Guide** of Brotherhood—Col. iii. 11.

5. Love is the **Evidence** of Brotherhood—John xiii. 34, 35.

6. The recognition of Christ is the **Responsibility** of
Brotherhood—1 Cor. xii. 1-27.

7. The witness of Christ to the World is the **Business** of
Brotherhood—John xvii. 21.

75. "BROUGHT OUT "

THE word *Exago* is rendered "led out, " "brought out, " and
"fetch out. "

1. **Separation.**   "Led him out of the town" (Mark viii. 23).

2. **Crucifixion.**   "Led Him out to crucify Him" (Mark
xv. 20).

3. **Benediction.**   "Led them out as far as Bethany" (Luke
xxiv. 50).

4. **Destination.**   "Leadeth them out" (John x. 3).

5. **Liberation.**   "The Lord brought him out" (Acts xii. 17).

6. **Redemption.**   "Brought out"... "lead out" (Acts vii. 36;
xiii. 17; Heb. viii. 9).

7. **Expulsion.**   "Brought them out, and desired them to
depart" (Acts xvi. 37, 39).

76. BUILDED, FOUNDED, AND GROUNDED

To build a true and lasting character.

1. We need to **rest on** the ground work of Christ's atonement
for safety—Gal. ii. 20.

2. To be **united to** the living rock of Christ's personality
for life —Matt. xvi. 18.

3. To be **empowered by** the power of Christ's Spirit for
ability—Acts i. 8.

4 To be **fused** and **fired by** the love of Christ's nature for practical love—2 Cor. v. 14.

5. To be **dominated by** the truth of Christ's Word for sanctity—John xvii. 17.

6. To be **held in** the grip of Christ's keeping for security—John x. 28.

7. To be **swayed by** Christ's aim to please God in the life—Rom. xv. 3.

8. To **have Christ Himself** dwelling in the heart of the will—Eph. iii. 17.

77. BUNDLE OF BLESSINGS
IN 2 THESSALONIANS II. 13-17

1. "**Loved**" by the Lord and "beloved."
2. "**Chosen**" by the Lord and saved.
3. **Sanctified** by the Spirit and The Truth.
4. **Called** by the Gospel to the glory.
5. **Given** by Christ and The Father "everlasting consolation and good hope through grace."
6. **Comforted** hearts, stablished feet, and holding hands "in every good word and work," and to "hold fast" the things taught.
7. **Specification.** Mark the centre flowers. "Loved," "salvation," "sanctification," "truth," "gospel," "glory," "consolation," "hope," "grace," "comfort," and "good."

78. BUNDLES

1. A **Bundle of Money** which brought trouble—Gen. xlii. 35.
2. A **Bundle of Life** which brings blessing—1 Sam. xxv. 29.
3. A **Bundle of Myrrh** which speaks of love—Cant. i. 13.
4. A **Bundle of Sticks** which contained a viper—Acts xxviii. 3.
5. A **Bundle of Tares** which foretells judgment—Matt xiii. 30.

79. BUSINESS
"Not slothful in business" (Rom. xii. 11)

THERE is a story related of a great English nobleman of the last century (Lord PALMERSTON), who witnessed an accident in London, when a little girl fell down and smashed a pitcher with a quart of milk in it. Lord Palmerston said to her: "My dear, don't cry, don't cry! I have not any change with me now, but I will meet you here to-morrow at twelve o'clock on this bridge, and I will give you a shilling to buy another pitcher and some more milk. " The next day Lord Palmerston was in a business meeting with a large company of gentlemen, and when the hour came to meet the little girl he said, "Gentlemen, I have an engagement. " "Oh!" was the reply, "but there is important business going on, sir. " "I cannot help it. I have a previous engagement made yesterday. I must keep the word of my promise to meet the individual. "

In all our business it is well that we mind the Lord's business. His injunction to us as His servants is : "Do business till I come, " for when He returns He will want to know "what business" we have "done" (Rotherham's Translation of Luke xix. 13, 15).

The word for "business" in Romans xii. 11, is rendered "haste, " "diligence, " "carefulness, " "forwardness, " and "earnest care. " Our business for the Lord should be done—

1. With a **set purpose**, as Mary when she went with "haste" into the hill country—Luke i. 39.

2. With **"diligence, "** as he who "ruleth" is exhorted to do—Rom. xii. 8.

3. With **"care, "** as in the sight of God—2 Cor. vii. 12.

4. With **attention** to detail, as Paul recognised, when he spoke of the "carefulness" of the saints' repentance in Corinth— 2 Cor. vii. 11.

5. With **earnestness**, as in the case of Titus, when the apostle recognised the "earnest care" in him—2 Cor. viii. 16.

6. With **specific aim**, as the Spirit enjoins believers to give "diligence" to add to their faith—2 Peter i. 5.

7. With the **main object** in all "business" to be serving the Lord—Rom. xii. 11.

80. CALLED OUT OF EGYPT

Exodus ix. 1

THE call has a double application. It was a call to Pharaoh: "Let My people go that they may serve Me, " and it was a call to the Israelites to get out of Egypt.

1. It was a call **based upon God's covenant** with Abraham, to give to him and his seed the promised land—Exod. vi. 2-4.

2. It was a call **of deliverance**, for Jehovah had determined to deliver Israel from the burden and bondage of Egypt— Exod. vi. 5, 6.

3. It was a call **based on sacrifice**, as the whole of Exodus xii. depicts in the Passover ordinance.

4. It was a call **based on promise**, for Jehovah had said,

"I will take you to Me for a people, and I will be to you a God" (Exod. vi. 7).

5. It was a call **associated with** what Jehovah calls "a difference" which He put "between the Egyptians and Israel" (Exod. xi. 7).

6. It was a call **illustrating power**, for the night of Israel's deliverance was an exhibition of the right hand of God's delivering grace for Israel, and His outstretched arm of judgment against the Egyptians—Exod. xii. 42.

7. It was a call **associated with a memorial feast** to remind Israel of what Jehovah had done in bringing them out of Egyptian bondage—Exod. xii. 43-51.

81. CALLING—CONDUCT

REMEMBER what you are called, and *be* what you *are*—

1. As a **Saint**. Be holy—Rom. i. 7; 1 Cor. i. 2.
2. As a **Christian**. Be Christlike—Acts xi. 26.
3. As **Salt**. Be pungent—Matt. v. 13.
4. As a **Light**. Be true—Matt. v. 14.
5. As an **Epistle**. Be legible—2 Cor. iii. 2.
6. As a **Soldier**. Be valiant—2 Tim. ii. 3.
7. As a **Child**. Be obedient—1 Peter i. 14, 15.

82. "CANDLES" AND "LAMPS"

THE word for "candle" is rendered "lamp" (Exod. xxvii. 20) and "light" (2 Sam. xxi. 17).

1. A **Lighted Candle**. "Thou wilt light my candle" (Psa. xviii. 28).

2. A **Supplied Lamp**. "Oil to cause the lamp to burn" (Exod. xxvii. 20).

3. An **Ordained Lamp**. "I have ordained a lamp for mine anointed" (Psa. cxxxii. 17).

4. A **Constant Lamp**. "Her lamp goeth not out" (Prov. xxxi. 18).

5. A **Protected Lamp**. "That thou quench not the light of Israel" (2 Sam. xxi. 17).

6. A **Used Lamp**. "Search Jerusalem with candles" (Zeph. i. 12).

7. An **Extinguished Lamp**. "The lamp of the wicked shall be put out" (Prov. xiii. 9).

83. "CANDLES"

1. **A Lighted Candle.** "Light a *candle*" (Matt. v. 15).
2. **An Essential Candle.** "The *light** of the body is the eye" (Matt. vi. 22).
3. **A Useful Candle.** "Light a *candle*, and sweep," etc. (Luke xv. 8).
4. **A Shining Candle.** "He was a burning and a shining *light"** (John v. 35).
5. **A Burning Candle.** "Your *lights** burning" (Luke xii. 35).
6. **A Necessary Candle.** "sure Word...a *light** that shineth," etc. (2 Peter i. 19).
7. **A Glorious Candle.** "The Lamb is the *Light** thereof" (Rev. xxi. 23).

84. "CANNOT"

THINGS the sinner cannot do.

1. Cannot **reverse what God does.** "I cannot go beyond the Word of the Lord" (Num. xxii. 18).
2. Cannot **find God by Himself.** "I cannot perceive Him" (Job xxiii. 8, 9).
3. Cannot **supply what is lacking.** "What is crooked cannot be made straight" (Eccles. i. 15).
4. Cannot **please God**—Rom. viii. 8.
5. Cannot **see** or **enter the Kingdom** of God—John iii. 3, 5.
6. Cannot **be where Christ is.** "Whither I go ye cannot come" (John viii. 21, 22, 43).
7. Cannot **pass the gulf** which divides the saved from the unsaved in the next life—Luke xvi. 26.

85. "CANNOTS" IN JOHN'S GOSPEL

1. The natural man **"cannot see"** or "enter the Kingdom of God" (iii. 3, 5).
2. The sinner **"cannot come"** or "go" where Christ is, as long as he is unsaved—vii. 34, 36; viii. 21, 22.
3. The unregenerate **"cannot hear"** Christ's Word (viii. 43).
4. The "Scripture **cannot be broken"** (x. 35).
5. The world **"cannot receive"** the Holy Spirit (xiv. 17).
6. The believer **"cannot bear fruit"** of himself (xv. 4).
7. Conditions often limit Christ's revelation to us, so He has said, **"Ye cannot bear** them now" (xvi. 12).

*The Greek word "*luknos*" is rendered "candle" and "light" in the above verses.

86. "CANNOT"—SOME THINGS GOD CANNOT DO

1. He cannot **break His Word.** "Scripture cannot be broken" (John x. 35).
2. "God cannot **lie**" (Titus i. 2).
3. "God cannot **deny Himself**" (2 Tim. ii. 13).
4. "God cannot **be tempted of evil**" (Jas. i. 13).

87. "CHRISTIAN ENDEAVOUR"
"We endeavoured" Acts xvi. 10

A GOOD Christian endeavourer is—

1. **Christ Encircled.** "In Christ" (2 Cor. xii. 2).
2. **Christ Enthroned.** "Christ sanctified as Lord in the heart" (1 Peter iii. 15, R.V.).
3. **Christ Empowered.** "Can do all things in Christ" (Phil. iv. 13).
4. **Christ Enlightened.** "Christ shall give thee light" (Eph. v. 14).
5. **Christ Enjoyed.** "I rejoice in the Lord greatly" (Phil. iv. 10).
6. **Christ Experienced.** "Christ liveth in me" (Gal. ii. 20).
7. **Christ Expanded.** "Grow up into Him in all things" (Eph. iv. 15).

88. CHANGES

1. **Repentance** is a change of purpose—Luke xv. 18; 1 Thess. i. 9.
2. **Salvation** is a change of position—Eph. ii. 6-8.
3. **Justification** is a change of state—Rom. v. 1.
4. **Adoption** is a change of family—Eph. i. 5.
5. **Redemption** is a change of masters—Eph. i. 7.
6. **Sanctification** is a change of life—1 Thess. v. 23, 24.
7. **Consecration** is a change of will—Rom. xii. 1, 2.

89. CHAIN OF GOLDEN LINKS
2 CORINTHIANS V. 17-21

1. **Divine Origin.** "If any man be in Christ Jesus he is a new creation" (margin). The Christian life is an implantation of the Divine, a translation into the Divine, and a reproduction of the Divine.
2. **Divine Operation.** "All things are of God, who hath reconciled us to Himself by Jesus Christ." Three things are

stated here—the worker, the means, and the blessing. The
Worker is God. We are God-called, saved, justified, kept,
used, filled, and sanctified. The means of our blessing is "by,"
or more correctly, "by means of Jesus Christ;" and the blessing
mentioned is, "we are reconciled to Himself."

3. Divine Ordination. "Given to us the ministry of reconciliation...committed unto us the word of reconciliation."
All believers have this ministry and word committed and given
to them. The word is that "God was in Christ, reconciling the
world unto Himself," and the end and aim of all ministry, to
get men reconciled to God and each other.

4. Divine Office. "Now then we are ambassadors for
Christ." The counterpart of Christ for us is, we are for Christ.
As lights to shine for Him, as witnesses to testify for Him, and
as an embassage to be on service for Him.

5. Divine Opportunity. "We pray you in Christ's stead,
be ye reconciled to God." As the priests of old acted for God
and the people, so believers act for God and others. We pray to
men for God, and we pray to God for men.

6. Divine Offering. "For He hath made Him to be sin for
us." He is a Message that has in it the melody of Heaven's
music, and yet how deep its meaning and mystery! "Made
sin!" Made what I was and did! Yes, and that's the reason
He can make us other than what we are.

7. Divine Obtainment. "That we might be made," or
become, "the righteousness of God in Him!" Being "in Him,"
who is the Righteousness of God, we must be what He is, even
as the ingrafted shoot is part of the tree.

90. CHARACTERS AROUND THE CROSS
Luke xxiii

In the scene of scenes many characters are seen. Heaven's
greatest giving, and man's greatest sin. If the chapter is read
through it will be observed how many people are seen in their
different relations to Christ—

1. The Accusing Multitude
2. Weak Pilate
3. Smiling Herod
4. Murderous Barabbas
5. The Cruel Rabble
6. Bearing Simon
7. Weeping Women
8. Sinful Malefactors
9. The Loving Father
10. The Deriding Rulers
11. The Mocking Soldiers
12. The Praying Thief
13. The Believing Centurion
14. The Beholding Relatives
15. The Mourning People
16. The Religious Authorities
17. Thoughtful Joseph

91. CHARACTERISTICS OF A BELIEVER IN CHRIST

AS REVEALED IN JOHN XV

EVERY metaphor and simile of the Christian life elucidates some trait of the character of a Christian.

1. **A Branch for Fruitfulness**—5. A branch in a vine is the outcome of the productive quality of the root and stem, and is dependent for its fruitfulness from them. Through the branch the vine manifests itself in fruit. It needs to be cleansed, and pruned to bring its fruit to perfection. Being united to Christ, we bring forth fruit, and as we allow the Vine-dresser to develop us, we bring forth the "more fruit," yea, "much fruit," and the fruit that remains—2, 8, 16. The fruit is "love" (Gal. v. 22).

2. **A Disciple for Faithfulness**—8-10. Discipleship is evidenced by fruitfulness. Being a disciple, we "learn" of Christ, we follow Him, and we are obedient to Him—Matt. xi. 29; Luke ix. 23; John xiii. 34.

3. **A Friend for Communion**—15. Three things evidence friendship, namely, confidence, sympathy, and fellowship. We might call these love in exercise, like the love of Jonathan for David.

4. **A Chosen One for Holiness**—16. When anyone or anything is set apart for a given purpose, and that purpose is achieved, the election is seen. We prove our election by selecting the things that faith adds to itself—2 Peter i. 10.

5. **An Ordained One for Benefit**—16. Fruit is produced for another's benefit, is lasting in its blessing, and is a forerunner of answered prayer. See the "that" in verse 16.

6. **A Servant for Employment**—20. To serve such a Master is a privilege, even though we may have to suffer because of our association with Him. He has saved us to serve, and we save ourselves from many things in serving.

7. **A Witness for Testimony**—27. A witness is one who knows, and is able to tell out what he has seen and heard. The thing that gave power and brought conviction in the early days was what was evidenced in the disciples—Acts i. 8; ii. 37; iv. 13.

92. CHARACTERISTICS OF GOD'S WORD

THE following characteristics of the Word will indicate in some measure what it means to preach it.

1. "The Word of **God**" to reveal (Heb. iv. 12).
2. "The Word of the **Lord**" to command (1 Thess. i. 8).
3. "The Word of **Christ**" to inspire (Col. iii. 16).
4. "The Word of the **Gospel**" to gladden (Acts xv. 7).

5. "The Word of **Salvation**" to deliver (Acts xiii. 26).
6. "The Word of **Reconciliation**" to preach (2 Cor. v. 19).
7. "The Word of **Grace**" to build up (Acts xx. 32).
8. "The Word of **Faith**" to assure (Rom. x. 8).
9. "The Word of **Truth**" to arm (2 Cor. vi. 7).
10. "The Word of **Righteousness**" to feed (Heb. v. 13).
11. "The Word of **Life**" to attract (Phil. ii. 16).
12. "**The** Word" in its exclusiveness (Matt. xiii. 19, 20, 21, 22, 23).
13. "The **Faithful** Word" to instruct (Titus i. 9).
14. "The **Engrafted** Word" to save (Jas. i. 21).
15. "The **Sincere** Milk" to feed (1 Peter ii. 2).
16. "The **Sure Word** of Prophecy" to enlighten (2 Peter i. 19).

93. CHRIST

JESUS as the Christ was the Messiah, the Sent One of God to do a work for us (see the 43 times in John's Gospel He is spoken of as the One who was "sent," and the purpose why He was sent—John xx. 31).

As the Christ He has—

1. "**Died** for us"—Rom. v. 8.
2. He was **raised** for us—Rom. vi. 9.
3. He **lives** in us—Gal. ii. 20.
4. He has **redeemed** us—Gal. iii. 13.
4. He **brings** us near to God—Eph. ii. 13.
6. He **strengthens** us—Phil. iv. 13.
7. He is the **Object** for our concentration in life—Phil. i. 21.

94. CHRIST AND EVIL SPIRITS

THERE are many who are possessed by evil spirits still.

1. The evil spirits of the **greed of covetousness**—1 Tim. vi. 10.
2. The **love of the world**—2 Tim. iv. 10.
3. The **inflation of pride**—1 Tim. iii. 6.
4. The **exaltation of self**—3 John 9.
5. The **blight of error**—1 Tim. i. 19, 20.
6. The **division of sectarianism**—1 Cor. i. 11-13.
7. The **demon of envy**—Acts vii. 9. These are some of the evil spirits around. Christ can expel these, and cure from the ill effects, as He did of old—Luke viii. 2.

95. CHRIST ABOUT HIS FATHER'S BUSINESS

WHAT was His Father's business?

1. To do the Father's **work**—John x. 37.
2. To proclaim the Father's **words**—John xvii. 8.
3. To reveal the Father's **character**—John i. 14, 18.
4. To glorify the Father's **Name**—John xii. 28.
5. To carry out the Father's **will**—Luke xxii. 42.
6. To unfold the Father's **love**—John xvi. 27.
7. To bring to the Father's **house**—John xiv. 2.

96. CHRIST AND HIS FINISHED WORK

CHRIST and His finished work is—

1. The **Panacea** for the ill of sin—1 John i. 7.
2. The **Peace-maker** for our reconciliation with God—Col. i. 20.
3. The **Price** for our redemption from sin's slavery—Titus ii. 14.
4. The **Power** which enables us to overcome Satan's malice—Rev. xii. 11.
5. The **Potentiality** which constrains us to live for God—2 Cor. v. 15.
6. The **Pattern** for our imitation in dying to self—John xii. 24, 25.
7. The **Propeller** in Christian service—2 Cor. v. 14.

97. CHRIST AND PROPHECY *re* HIS CRUCIFIXION

A WHOLE host of prophecies gather round the Cross of Christ. No candid reader of the Scriptures can doubt for one moment that such passages of Holy Writ as Psalm xxii. and Isaiah liii. had a literal fulfilment in the death of Christ. There are several particulars in relation to the crucifixion of Christ which are specified as fulfilments of prophecy.

1. The **casting of lots** about His clothes—John xix. 24; Psa. xxii. 18.
2. His **thirst**—John xix. 28; Psa. lxix. 21.
3. His **bones** not being broken—John xix. 36; Exod. xii. 46; Psa. xxxiv. 20.
4. His **body** being pierced—John xix. 37; Zech. xii. 10.
5. His being **crucified** according to the Roman law, and not being stoned to death according to Jewish custom—John xviii. 31, 32; Matt. xx. 19.

6. His being **numbered** among the malefactors—Mark xv. 28; Isa. liii. 12.

The above are a few of the many fulfilments of prophecy in the crucifixion of the Saviour.

The fulfilment of prophecy is a *comfort* to God's saints, for it demonstrates His carefulness to keep His Word, and a *warning* to the unsaved, for since He keeps to the minutiæ of His promise to His people, He will surely fulfil His threats to the ungodly.

98. CHRIST AND "MANY"

1. Many **healed** by touching Him—Matt. xiv. 36.

2. He gave His life a **"Ransom** for many" (Matt. xx. 28).

3. He **"shed"** His Blood for "many" "for the remission of sins" (Matt. xxvi. 28).

4. Christ **"cast out** many devils," and delivered them who were possessed—Mark i. 34; Luke iv. 41.

5. "Many hearing Him were **astonished**" at His teaching (Mark vi. 2).

6. "As many as **received**" Him are "born of God" (John i. 12, 13).

7. Gives **"eternal life** to as many as Thou hast given Him" (John xvii. 2).

99. CHRIST AND THE HOLY SPIRIT
IN LUKE IV

EVIDENCES of being "full" of the Holy Spirit are seen in Christ's experience.

1. **Led.** "Led by the Spirit."
2. **Tested.** "Tempted of the Devil."
3. **Word Used.** "It is written."
4. **World Refused.** "Get thee behind Me Satan."
5. **God only Recognised.** "Him only shalt thou serve."
6. **Victory.** "Satan departed."
7. **Testimony Borne.** "The Spirit of the Lord is upon me."

100. CHRIST AS THE BOY OF NAZARETH
Luke ii. 40-52

How many stars shine in the sky of Christ's early days as the Boy of the humble home of Nazareth.

1. **The Growing Child.** The Child grew. He was supernatural in His being as "The Son," but He was perfectly natural in His childhood.

2. **The Strong Spirit.** "Waxed strong in spirit." The spirit nature in man is evidenced in his individuality and in his intelligence—1 Cor. ii. 11.

3. **The Wise Mind.** "Filled with wisdom." To be wise is good, but to be filled with wisdom is better. Wisdom is the right application of knowledge.

4. **The Graced Boy.** "The grace of God was upon Him."

5. **The True Israelite.** He went with His parents to Jerusalem to keep the Passover—41, 42.

6. **The Tarrying Lad**—43. The reason why He tarried is given by Himself. He felt He must be about His Father's business—49. The consciousness He had come into the world to do a definite work was pressing upon Him.

7. **The Missed Son**—43-45. The parents of Jesus lost Him in one day, and it took three days to find Him. They supposed He was with them, but suppositions do not make realities. It takes a longer time to recover our blessings than it does to lose them.

8. **The Central Figure**—47. He was found "in the midst" of the doctors, "hearing them, and asking them questions."

9. **The Higher Relationship**—49. How startled Mary must have been when she heard the words: "Wist ye not I must be about My Father's business?" especially following her statement: "Thy father and I have sought Thee sorrowing."

101. CHRIST CRUCIFIED

THERE are several ways in which the crucifixion of Christ is spoken of.

1. The **fact** of it. The manner of His death. The fulfilment of Scripture—John xix. 18-24.

2. The **place** where He was crucified: "Where our Lord was crucified"—Rev. xi. 8; Luke xxiii. 33.

3. The **sinful act** of crucifixion. The word, "to crucify" in Acts ii. 23, means to fix with ill intent and act.

4. The **associates** of His crucifixion were two thieves—Luke xxiii. 32, 33.

5. The **crucifixion** of Christ is the theme of the Gospel—1 Cor. i. 23, 24; ii. 2; Gal. iii. 1.

6. The **subjective power** of the Cross is death to self, sin, the flesh, and the world—Rom. vi. 6; Gal. ii. 20; v. 24; vi. 14.

7. The **grave consequence** of apostasy from Christ is to make Him bleed again—Heb. vi. 6.

102. CHRIST AND THE INNESS OF THINGS

CHRIST ever taught the inness of things.

1. To Nicodemus it was **inward life**—John iii. 7.
2. To the woman of Samaria, **inward supply**—John iv. 14.
3. To Saul of Tarsus, **inward light**—Acts xxvi. 13-19.
4. To the demoniac, **inward liberty**—Mark v. 15.
5. To the palsied man, **inward blessing**—Mark ii. 5, 9.
6. To Simon the Pharisee, **inward love**—Luke vii. 47.
7. To the Pharisees, **inward cleansing**—Matt. xxiii. 25, 26.

Whitewash is good for cellars, but it is no good for sinners. Sinners need to be washed white in the Blood of the Lamb.

103. CHRIST CAUSES THE LAME TO WALK
Matt. xv. 31

How many people are walking by the aid of spiritual crutches. The crutches of self-help, the crutches of dependence upon others, the crutches of worldly means, and the crutches of carnal reason. The Lord can make us—

1. **"Walk in newness of life"** (Rom. vi. 4).
2. To **walk "by faith"** (2 Cor. v. 7).
3. To **walk "in the Spirit"** (Gal. v. 16).
4. To **walk "in love"** (Eph. v. 2).
5. To **walk "in wisdom"** (Col. iv. 5).
6. To **walk "in the truth"** (3 John 4).
7. To **walk "after His commandments"** (2 John 6).

104. CHRISTIANITY—WHAT IS IT?

"CHRISTIANISE your modern Christianity," so said Joseph Cook, of Boston, on one occasion. Or, as it has been put in another quarter, "There is a tremendous lot of Ianity, but very little Christianity." That leads one to ask the question, "What is Christianity?"

There is only one answer—"Christ."

1. Christ in the **glory of His Deity**—Matt. xvi. 16.
2. Christ in the **glow of His Love**—2 Cor. v. 14; Gal. ii. 20.
3. Christ in the **reality of His Humanity**—1 Tim. ii. 5.
4. Christ in the **sufficiency of His Death**—Heb. ix. 14, 28.
5. Christ in the **indwelling of His Spirit**—Eph. iii. 17.
6. Christ in the **beauty of His Character**—Heb. vii. 26.
7. Christ in the **hope of His Glory**—Col. i. 27.

105. CHRIST DECLARED GOD

"He hath declared Him" John i. 18

"SIX-YEARS-OLD tip-toed softly up to the little low crib where one. of the world's very latest hopes was lying throned and swathed in the coverlets that love had sewn for its coming," writes *Collier's Weekly*. "Big brother's face was gravely intent, his eyes bright and shining. He stooped far over and gazed down at that wrinkled, peevish bit of a face.

"'Now, baby brother,' he whispered into one tiny red ear half hid by the clustering black hair, 'tell me about God before you forget.'

"Before the world closes in on the new life you have brought to our greying days. Before work and money and clothes, and what people say, can matter to you. Before these earthly things have their way, and you lose touch with that eternal mystery and glory of which you were a part only such a little while ago.

"'Quickly, brother, before you forget!' If only we grown-ups could remember. There was One once who did."

"There was One who did" tell us about God, and who did not "forget," and that One was Christ. He did not forget—

1. **God's Will**, but delighted to do it—Heb. x. 7; Psa. xl. 8.

2. **God's Word**, but made it known—John xvii. 8.

3. **God's Ways**, but walked in them—Acts ii. 22; x. 38.

4. **God's Work**, but fulfilled it—John xvii. 4; xix. 30.

5. **God's Worth**, but revealed it—John iii. 16.

106. "CHRIST" IN EPHESIANS V

1. CHRIST—in the **sacrifice of His atonement**. "*Christ...* hath given Himself for us" (2).

2. CHRIST—in the **wealth of His Kingdom**. "Kingdom of *Christ*" (5).

3. CHRIST—in the **light of His grace**. "*Christ* shall give thee light" (14).

4. CHRIST—in the **authority of His headship**. "*Christ* is the Head" (23).

5. CHRIST—in the **dominion of His claims**. "Church is subject unto *Christ*" (24).

6. CHRIST—in the **purpose of His love**. "*Christ* also loved the Church" (25).

7. CHRIST—in the **care of His attention**. "As *Christ* also the Church" (29, R.V.).

107. CHRIST IN CONTRAST TO PHARISEES.

CHRIST plainly indicates the outward observances of ceremonies will not suffice, but the inward life of consecration to God. He says, we must have a righteousness which exceeds that of a religious Pharisee—Matt. v. 20. If we contrast the conduct of a Pharisee with the character of Christ's holy principles, we shall see how much the latter goes beyond the former.

1. The Pharisee thought that **the whitewash of religiosity** would do—Matt. xxiii. 26, but Christ emphasises the purity of a clean heart—Matt. v. 8.

2. The Pharisee was satisfied with **the inflation of self-righteousness**—Luke xviii. 11, but Christ calls for the denial of self itself—Luke ix. 23.

3. The Pharisee measured himself with **the rule of self-importance**—Matt. xxiii. 6, 7, but Christ gauges everything by the holiness of God—Matt. vii. 24.

4. The Pharisee was **pugnacious in his hold upon little things** of minor importance, but loose in his obedience to the weighty claims of Jehovah—Matt. xxiii. 23, but Christ points to the path of loving obedience—John xiii. 34.

5. The Pharisee was an **expert in laying burdens upon others**—Matt. xxiii. 4, but Christ was the Example of lifting burdens from the oppressed—Matt. xi. 28.

6. The Pharisee **boasted of his earthly relationship** to Abraham—Matt. iii. 9, but Christ declares likeness to God in action is of more importance—Matt. v. 44, 45.

7. The Pharisee **would not go near the sinners** to help them —Matt. ix. 11, but Christ sought to benefit them by His teaching and grace—Luke xv. 1.

8. The Pharisee believed in **the form of fasting**—Matt. vi. 16, but Christ emphasised the needs be of being right with God—Matt. vi. 33.

108. CHRIST CRUCIFIED
"The power of God" 1 Cor. i. 24

1. Power to **reconcile** to God—Eph. ii. 16.
2. Power to **separate** from the world—Gal. vi. 14.
3. Power to **exalt** to the highest place—Phil. ii. 9.
4. Power to **extinguish** the flesh—Gal. v. 24.
5. Power to **remove** the handwriting of ordinances—Col. ii. 14.
6. Power to **put off** the old man with his deeds—Rom. vi. 6.
7. Power to **ignore sinful self**—Gal. ii. 20.
8. Power to **set forth** Christ before others—Gal. iii. 1.

109. CHRIST IN HEBREWS

1. He **saves** to the uttermost—vii. 25.
2. He **lives** eternally—vii. 25.
3. He **obtains** redemptively—ix. 12.
4. He **appears** continually—ix. 24.
5. He **sits** permanently—x. 12.
6. He **pleads** incessantly—vii. 25.
7. He **succours** effectively—ii. 18.

110. CHRIST IN HIS HUMANITY

HE was—

1. **Divine** in His origin—Mark xv. 39.
2. **Faultless** in His character—Luke xxiii. 4.
3. **Powerful** in His actions—Matt. viii. 27.
4. **Loving** in His grace—Luke xv. 2.
5. **Wonderful** in His teaching—John vii. 46.
6. **Perfect** in His offering—Heb. x. 12.
7. **Unchanging** in His priesthood—Heb. vii. 24.

111. CHRIST IN 1 PETER

1. **Resurrection** of Christ our Hope—i. 3.
2. **Appearing** of Christ our Reward—i. 7.
3. **Suffering** of Christ our Glory—i. 11.
4. **Blood** of Christ our Redemption—i. 19.
5. **Sacrifice** of Christ our Acceptance—ii. 5.
6. **Footsteps** of Christ our Example—ii. 21.
7. **Death** and **Resurrection** of Christ our Pledge—iii. 18, 22.
8. **Suffering** of Christ our Joy—iv. 12, 13.
9. **Eternal Glory** of Christ our Call—v. 10.

112. CHRIST IS ALL

EVERYTHING comes easy when we know Christ
He is—

1. **Oil** to the wheels of life—1 John ii. 20.
2. **Light** in the lamp of the heart—John viii. 12.
3. **Salt** in the character of being—Col. iv. 6.
4. **Power** in the machinery of service—Phil. ii. 13.
5. **Love** in the dwelling of home—John xi. 5.
6. **Food** on the table of need—John vi. 35.
7. **Sweetness** in the cup of trial—1 Peter i. 7, 8.

113. "CHRIST IS ALL"
Col. iii. 11

He is—
1. **Life** to the body of truth—Col. iii. 16.
2. **Light** to the realm of thought—Eph. iv. 20, 21.
3. **Energy** to the machinery of work—1 Cor. i. 24.
4. **Music** to the notes of life—Heb. ii. 12.
5. **Soul** to the sphere of conduct—Gal. ii. 20.
6. **Love** to the heart of affection—2 Cor. v. 14.
7. **Grace** to the beautifying of character—Eph. iii. 8.

"I never was anything till I knew you," said Tom Hood to his wife; and we are never anything until we know Christ and the Holy Spirit.

114. CHRIST, OUR EXAMPLE IN HUMILITY
"Let this mind be in you" Phil. ii. 5

THERE are many illustrations of Christ's humility.
1. In the **manger** of His birth—Luke ii. 7.
2. In the **bedlessness** of His life—Luke ix. 58.
3. In the **dependence** upon others—Luke viii. 3.
4. In the **service** to His disciples—John xiii. 14.
5. In the **borrowing** of an ass—Matt. xxi. 2.
6. In the **asking** for a drink—John iv. 7.
7. In the **burial** in another's grave—Luke xxiii. 53.

He who takes the lowest place on earth will find himself exalted to the highest place in Heaven.

115. CHRIST, OUR EXAMPLE IN OBEDIENCE
"Obedient unto death" Phil. ii. 8

HIS obedience was not to death as a master, but His path of obedience, in the things He did and suffered, led Him to obedience unto death as a goal—Heb. v. 8; Psa. xl. 8. Obedience is the—
1. **Proof** of Love—John xiv. 15, 21.
2. **Badge** of Loyalty—Rom. xvi. 19.
3. **Soul** of Liberty—Rom. vi. 16.
4. **Securer** of Blessing—Isa. i. 19.
5. **Spirit** of Service—Joshua xxiv. 24.
6. **Meaning** of Worship—Heb. xi. 8.
7. **Livery** of Holiness—1 Peter i. 14.

116. CHRIST "HIGHER THAN THE HEAVENS "

THE Holy Spirit rings the changes on the word *"made"* in the Epistle to the Hebrews, in calling attention to what Christ has been "made."

1. As **Man**, He is *"made* a little lower than the angels" (Heb. ii. 7).

2. As **Kinsman**, He is *"made* like His brethren" (Heb. ii. 17).

3. As **Sufferer**, He is *"made* perfect" through His sufferings (Heb. v. 9).

4. As **High Priest**, He is *"made* an high priest after the order of Melchisedec" (Heb. vi. 20).

5. As **Surety**, He is *"made* surety of a better covenant" (Heb. vii. 22).

6. As **Inheritor**, He is *"made* so much better than the angels" (Heb. i. 4).

7. As **Exalted**, He is *"made* higher than the Heavens" (Heb. vii. 26).

He took the lowest place when He was made "a little lower than the angels" in His incarnation (Heb. ii. 7); but He has obtained the highest place by His ascension, for He is made higher than the angels.

The expression, "made higher than the Heavens," at once puts Christ in contrast to others.

117. CHRIST RISEN

"He is risen" Matt. xxviii. 6

THE fact Christ had been in the tomb proclaimed three things: sin's climax, love's giving, and Christ's accomplishment.

1. **Sin's Climax.** "He was buried" is the Spirit's affirmation, and is a part of the Gospel's message (1 Cor. xv. 1-4). One of the answers to the question, "Why did Christ die?" is, He died to give a satisfaction for man's sin. If we.eliminate the fact of sin's presence and penalty, His death has no meaning. Professor Orr declared: "The whole of Christianity is but a Divine counsel and provision for repairing the ruin of man's sin." At the Cross sin abounded to its wicked climax, for there it superabounded beyond anything it had done before, and yet there, grace did much more abound. One has well said: "The Cross is God's final treatment of sin, the one compendium work of grace, and the hinge of human destiny. Apart from sin, the Cross has no meaning. It was the exhibition of the worst in the heart of man, and the best in the heart of God."

2. **Love's Giving.** God delivered Christ up for our offences, and raised Him on account of our justification—Rom. iv. 25.

Our beloved Lord deliberately gave up His life for us. Love alone gave Him to die for our sin. Love alone enabled Him to give Himself out in death, and love could not be satisfied with anything else.

> "Love saw the need, and all the need has met;
> Love gave its best when life so rich He gave;
> Love spent its all when for our sins He died;
> Love comes in grace, and with His blood doth save."

3. **Work Accomplished.** Christ not only died, but accomplished what no other could do in dying. Death did not come to Him in the fulfilment of His mission; it was the fulfilment of His mission. His death was no accident (Luke xxiii. 46, R.V.). His star of destiny was His death on Calvary. Dr. Denny says of Christ's death: "It is in this the atonement lies. Christ finished it. He finished it alone. No one can do it after Him. No one needs to do it." Happy are we if we know our individual interest in Christ's death, and can say with the old Scottish woman, who was asked about her soul's salvation, "The Father and the Lord Jesus settled the matter of my salvation between them, and I got the benefit."

118. CHRIST, OUR POWER

1. The power of His **resurrection** to raise us above an earthly and selfish life—Phil. iii. 10.

2. The power of His **grace** to strengthen in trial—2 Cor. xii. 9.

3. The power of His **Spirit** to make Himself a reality to us—Eph. iii. 16, 17.

4. The power of His **preservation** to keep to His heavenly inheritance—1 Peter i. 4.

5. The power of His **love** to bestow all things which pertain to life and godliness—2 Peter i. 3.

6. The power of His **ministry** to operate through us—Acts i. 8; iii. 12; iv. 3.

7. The power of His **strength** to enable us to be faithful—2 Tim. i. 12, R.V., margin.

119. CHRIST, OUR RANSOM

"Who gave Himself a Ransom for all" 1 Tim. ii. 6

THE word *antilutron*, in the above passage of Scripture, means a procuring price paid instead of others.

Frequently we are reminded Christ gave Himself to meet our liabilities. His ransom was a—

1. **Sin-answering Ransom.** "Gave Himself for our sins" (Gal. i. 4).

2. **God-man Ransom.** "Who gave Himself a Ransom for all" (1 Tim. ii. 6).

3. **Sinner-answering Ransom.** "Gave Himself for us, that He might redeem us from all iniquity" (Titus ii. 14).

4. **Love-provided Ransom.** "He gave His only begotten Son" (John iii. 16).

5. **Life-substituted Ransom.** "Give His life a ransom for many" (Matt. xx. 28).

6. **Grace-given Ransom.** "Bread that I will give is My flesh" (John vi. 51).

7. **Grateful-remembered Ransom.** "This is My Body given for you: this do in remembrance of Me" (Luke xxii. 19).

120. CHRIST, OUR SUBSTITUTE
IN ISAIAH LIII

1. He was a **Bearing** Substitute, for "He hath borne our griefs" (4).

2. He was a **Crushed** Substitute, for He was "wounded," "bruised," and chastised (5).

3. He was a **God-punished** Substitute, for Jehovah "laid on Him the iniquity of us all" (6).

4. He was a **Silent** Substitute, for "He opened not His mouth" (7).

5. He was a **Sinner's** Substitute, for "He was numbered with transgressors" (12).

6. He was a **Sin-made** Substitute, for He was made "an offering for sin" (10).

7. He will be a **Rewarded** Substitute, for "He shall see of the travail of His soul and be satisfied" (11).

121. CHRIST'S AGONY IN GETHSEMANE

1. **"Began to be sorrowful"** (Matt. xxvi. 37). Like an on-coming storm which causes the barometer to fall, so the conflict through which Christ was about to pass caused Him to be weighted with sorrow.

2. **"Began to be sore amazed"** (Mark xiv. 33). "Sore amazed" is rendered "greatly amazed" (Mark ix. 15) and "affrighted" (Mark xvi. 5, 6). As an apparition will cause the observer to be frightened, so as Christ looked into the cup He was about to drink it startled Him with the awfulness of its ingredients.

3. **"To be very heavy"** (Mark xiv. 33). The word is given in Phil. ii. 26, "full of heaviness." As the liquid cement hardening

in a vase filled with it will cause it to be weighted beyond intention, so Christ was made heavy with the weight of sin, as He contemplated the punishment it deserved.

4. **"My soul is exceeding sorrowful unto death"** (Mark xiv. 34). He was not only "sorrowful," but "exceedingly" so; that is, He was completely surrounded with grief, even as a tropical plant might be by a blasting frost, and His sorrow was "unto death." Some would tell us Christ was afraid He would die before He reached the Cross, but He said He would die and rise again—see Matt. xx. 17-20; John x. 17, 18. "Unto" means "until," and, as Bullinger points out, means "marking the continuance of an action up to the time of another action."

5. **"Being in an agony"** (Luke xxii. 44). The word "agony" is rendered "conflict" in Colossians ii. 1. How His holy soul was torn as He entered into "the hour" of the nearing Cross —Mark xiv. 35, 41, as he looked into the cup He was about to drink, as He felt the powers of darkness by which He was surrounded, and as He beheld the death for sin He was about to die; no wonder He "sweat great drops of blood."

The practical lesson for us is, like Christ, to glory in the will of God, for His will is our highest good.

122. "CHRIST'S"

1. **Christ's Possession.** "Ye are Christ's" (1 Cor. iii. 23).

2. **Christ's Gospel.** "Preach Christ's Gospel" (2 Cor. ii. 12).

3. **Christ's Property.** "If any man trust to himself that he is Christ's...as he is Christ's, even so we are Christ's" (2 Cor. x. 7).

4. **Christ's Bestowment.** "If ye be Christ's, then are ye Abraham's seed, and heirs according to the promise" (Gal. iii. 29).

5. **Christ's Claim.** "They that are Christ's have crucified the flesh with the affections and lusts" (Gal. v. 24).

6. **Christ's Liberty.** "He that is called, being free, is Christ's servant" (1 Cor. vii. 22).

7. **Christ's Coming.** "They that are Christ's at His Coming" (1 Cor. xv. 23).

123. CHRIST'S ABILITY
"He is able" Eph. iii. 20

RESPONSIBILITY is man's response to God's ability.

1. He is able **to save** to the uttermost, for He lives to do it, therefore rest in Him and be glad—Heb. vii. 25.

2. He is able **to make all grace** to abound towards us, therefore be satisfied with Him, and be thankful—2 Cor. ix. 8-11.

3. He is able **to give us the victory** when tempted, therefore take Him as Victor, and be an overcomer—1 Cor. x. 13.

4. He is **able to keep us** from falling, therefore lean upon Him and be upheld—Jude 24.

5. He is able **to shield us from harm**, therefore abide in Him, and be at rest—Psa. cxxi. 3-8.

6. He is able **to make us active**, therefore let Him work effectively through us, and be useful—2 Tim. i. 12, R.V., margin.

7. He is able **to keep us always**, therefore let Him tend us, and be fresh and sweet—Isa. xxvii. 2, 3.

124. CHRIST'S ATONEMENT AND ADVENT

THIS double truth of atonement and advent might be multiplied. The following brief outline will emphasise:

1. Christ's sufferings and glory is **the theme of the Scriptures** "The prophets...prophesied...of the sufferings of Christ, and the glory that should follow" (1 Peter i. 10, 11).

2. Christ's suffering and glory was **the topic of Christ's conversation** with the two disciples, as He journeyed with them to Emmaus—Luke xxiv. 26.

3. "Till He come," we **observe the memorial feast** which proclaims His death—1 Cor. xi. 26.

4. The **assurance of the resurrection** of our loved ones who have fallen asleep, and the quickening of the living ones, is based on "Christ died"—1 Thess. iv. 14.

5. "Who died for us," are the Spirit's words as He declares **the ground** why we are appointed (placed in) to the salvation of the future—1 Thess. v. 9, 10.

6. The Church will be set before the Lord without a spot or wrinkle, or any such thing, because **He loved** her and gave Himself for her—Eph. v. 25.

7. We are exhorted to be **looking for that Blessed Hope**, and the appearing of the glory of the great God and Saviour, who gave Himself for us—Titus ii. 13.

The cords of God's love bind us to the altar of Christ's sacrifice, and its flame fuses us into God's nature; and the glory of Christ's Coming attracts us to the Heaven of His holiness. Since the Lord has such a claim upon us, and we have been called to such a glory, what manner of persons ought we to be? With such a past of His passion, and with such a prospect of His glory, we cannot, if we know Him, be anything else than wholly devoted to Him.

125. CHRIST'S ATTRACTABILITY

ALL sorts of people were attracted to Christ by the magnetism of His fascinating personality.

1. **Mothers** brought their children to Him—Mark x. 13, 14.
2. **Children** were attracted to Him—Matt. xix. 13, 14.
3. **Sinners** came to Him—Luke xv. 1.
4. **Men** followed Him—Luke v. 11, 28.
5. **Mary** loved Him—John xii. 3.
6. The **soldiers** were charmed by Him—John vii. 46.
7. The **centurion** confessed Him—Luke xxiii. 47.
8. The **people** wondered at Him—Matt. xv. 31.
9. **Pilate** was astonished at Him—John xviii. 33-38.
10. The **Samaritan** praised Him—Luke xvii. 15, 16.
11. The **shepherds** worshipped Him—Matt. ii. 11.
12. **Martha** served Him—Luke x. 38.
13. The **released demoniac** wanted to be with Him—Mark v. 18.
14. The **people** gathered unto Him—Mark v. 21.

126. CHRIST'S AUTHORITY

THE Greek word *exousia* is rendered "power," "authority," "liberty," "right," and "jurisdiction."

1. Authority to **lay down His life**—John x. 18, 19.
2. Authority to **forgive sins**—Matt. ix. 6. 8.
3. Authority over **demons**—Mark i. 27.
4. Authority over **sickness**—Mark iii. 15.
5. Authority to **judge**—John v. 27.
6. Authority **over all men**—John xvii. 2.
7. Authority **in Heaven** and earth—Matt. xxviii. 18.

127. CHRIST'S BLOOD

WE may know more perfectly what the precious Blood of Christ has done for us when we call to mind the following seven things—

1. It **averts** the judgment of God against sin, as the blood of the paschal lamb did on the night of the Passover—Exod. xii. 13; 1 Cor. v. 7.

2. It **converts** the one who believes in the Substitute, even as the blood of cleansing changed the position and condition of the cleansed leper—Lev. xiv. 14; Rev. i. 5.

3. It **inverts** the position we once occupied to the world, for instead of being in it, we are now separated from it, even

as God said to Pharaoh of Israel: "I will put a redemption (margin) between thy people and My people" (Exod viii. 23).

4. The Blood of Christ **inserts** us in a new place, even as the blood of the covenant enabled Moses and the seventy elders to draw nigh and see the God of Israel—Exod. xxiv. 5-10.

5. It **asserts** that the blessing of pardon—Eph. i. 7; peace—Col. i. 20; power—Rev. xii. 11; purity—1 John i. 7; and paradise are secured in Him—Rev. vii. 14.

6. The Blood of Christ **exerts** a powerful influence in its practical bearing, for it kills sin—Rom. vi. 1-15; slays self—2 Cor. v. 15; and overcomes pride—Phil. ii. 5-8.

7. And the Blood of Christ **subverts** the powers of Hell, which have been conquered by His death; even as when the sacrificial lamb was offered by Samuel, and the Lord discomfited the Philistines in consequence—1 Sam. vii. 9, 10; Heb. ii. 14; Col. i. 14.

128. CHRIST "SAW"

How frequent we read of Christ seeing and appreciating. Take what we find in Luke's Gospel—

1. "He saw" the **faith** of the four men and healed their friend—v. 20.

2. He saw **Matthew**, and called him to higher service—v. 27.

3. He saw the **bound woman** and released her—xiii. 12.

4. He saw the **lepers** and cleansed them—xvii. 14.

5. He saw **Zacchaeus** and saved him—xix. 5.

6. He saw the **widow** casting in her two mites and commended her—xxi. 2.

7. He also revealed the fact the Father saw **the prodigal** in his need and met it—xv. 20.

129. CHRIST'S CHARACTER
Hebrews vii. 26

1. "**Holy**" in His nature—Luke i. 35.
2. "**Harmless**" in His actions—Acts x. 38.
3. "**Undefiled**" in His life—1 John iii. 5.
4. "**Separate**" in His service—John xvii. 19.
5. "**Meek**" in Spirit—Matt. xi. 29.
6. "**Humble**" in heart —Phil. ii. 5.
7. "**Devout**" in purpose—Heb. v. 7-9, R.V.

130. CHRIST'S BODY OF GLORY

"We shall be like Him" 1 John iii. 2

ONE of the things which He will give to His own, when He comes as the Saviour, is a body of glory. He will fashion anew the body which has been humiliated by sin, and make it like to His body of glory—-Phil. iii. 20, 21. What is His body of glory like? We have a description given to us in Revelation i. We recognise Christ is alone in the absoluteness of His Deity; but His glory as revealed to John is that of the Son of Man, and therefore there will be a similarity between Him and us, when it is said we shall be "like Him."

1. **"Like Him" in the Glory of His Immortality.** "I am He that liveth, and am alive for evermore." He could not die again, for He lives in the power of an indissoluble life— Heb. vii. 16, R.V. Immortality is more than deathlessness, it is a state of holiness and bliss in a glorified body from which we can never fall.

2. **"Like Him" in the Purity of His Spotlessness.** His head and His hair are said to be as white as snow. Being as white as snow is always a symbolical expression of purity— Psa. li. 7. As the sunlight which shines into a muddy pool cannot be contaminated by its contact with it, so, being like Him in the holiness of His nature, we shall be incapable of contamination.

3. **"Like Him" in the Eyes of His Penetration.** His eyes are as a flame of fire. What we shall see we cannot tell, but we shall have the capacity to see into the heart of things, which we do not now possess.

4. **"Like Him" in the Feet of His Capacity for Endurance.** His feet are said to be like unto "fine brass, as if they burned in a furnace." Brass is an enduring metal, and is therefore typical of that which endures; and the burning in a furnace suggests intensity of purpose. "He maketh His angels as a flame of fire." Being like Him, we shall have the capacity to endure in His service without tiredness, and to glow with intense love as we are on His business.

5. **"Like Him" in His Voice of Power.** His voice is said to be as "the sound of many waters." Some conception of what is meant may be gathered from the flow of many waters that tumble over Niagara, and the generating force of its onrush. The thought is the inherent quality which is able to produce effects.

6. **"Like Him" in the Right Hand of His Administrative Ability.** The seven stars are seen in His right hand, which

represent the messengers of the seven Churches. Christ Himself hints that some of His glorified ones will have rule over His hemisphere—Luke xix. 17, 19; Matt. xxv. 21.

7. "Like Him" **in the Effectiveness of His Ministry.** "Out of His mouth went a sharp two-edged sword." The two-edged sword is identified with the power of His Word—Heb iv. 12, and with His ability to smite the nations—Rev. xix. 15. Here again it indicates an inherent quality which breaks down all opposition in carrying out the will of God.

8. "Like Him" **in the Glory of His Personality.** His countenance is said to be as the sun shineth in his strength. There are many things suggested by the sun shining as described, such as light, heat, colour, and healing; but perhaps the main thing is that of luminosity. The Lord is said to clothe Himself as with light, and it may suggest that which our first parents lost by sin—namely, that they were clothed with light as with a garment, and their transgression robbed them of this, and, therefore our glorified body will have a luminosity which will be dazzling in its appearance and wonderful in its glory. Human language cannot describe what the glorified body of the believer will be like, and, therefore, we must summarise it as the Spirit of God does, "His Name shall be in their foreheads," for name stands for nature. He will look upon us and see Himself.

131. CHRIST'S COMING

THE words "therefore" and "wherefore" in connection with Christ's Coming, give us reasons for our attitude in relation to His return.

1. The "therefore" of "**watch.**" Because of those who are "perverse," and that the Lord may reward us, be on the alert against the evil, and alive to the future "inheritance"—Acts xx. 31, 32.

2. The "wherefore" of **acceptability.** "Wherefore" we labour, or "make it our aim," that we may be "well-pleasing" to the Lord when we stand before His judgment seat—2 Cor. v. 9, 10, R.V.

3. The "wherefore" of "**comfort**" and edification. Because we are going to "live with" Christ, we are to be mutually interested in each other's welfare—1 Thess. v. 11.

4. The "wherefore" of "**grace.**" Because of the grace that we are to experience at the revelation of our Lord, we are to gird up the loins of our mind, set the hope perfectly, and be sober (1 Peter i. 13).

5. The "wherefore" of **calling.** If we make our calling sure

by adding to our faith what the Lord enjoins, He will add to us an abundant entrance into the everlasting Kingdom at His return—2 Peter i. 10, 11.

6. The "wherefore" of **remembrance**. We are apt to forget "these things" which relate to our present duty, and future glory of His Kingdom—2 Peter i. 12-19.

7. The "wherefore" of **blamelessness**. The righteous character of the new Heavens and the new earth should exercise such an influence upon us, that we should be like them in character—2 Peter iii. 14.

132. CHRIST'S COMING
BLESSEDNESS FOR THOSE WHO ARE FOUND WATCHING

IN the parable of the lord returning from the wedding, Christ enforces and emphasises the Coming of Himself—Luke xii. 35-48. The distinctiveness of our Lord's return is declared no less than nine times in connection with the words: "He cometh," "will come," "come," "The Son of Man cometh," and "He shall come." In relation to the last, our Lord declares that when "He shall come" and find His servants waiting and watching, those servants are "blessed." They shall be "blessed" in many ways—

1. They shall be "blessed" **with His approval**, because they will be ready to "open unto Him immediately," when "He cometh and knocketh" (36).

2. They shall be "blessed" **with His service**, for, finding them watching, "He will come forth and serve them" (37).

3. They shall be "blessed" **in not suffering loss**, for Christ implies in the parabolical language used, the man who does not watch against "the thief" finds his house "broken through"—39, 40.

4. They shall be "blessed" **for faithful and wise stewardship** in being appointed rulers over the Lord's household, and in ministering to others—42-44.

The fact that those who are found watching shall be "blessed" implies that those who are not so found, will suffer loss and disapproval; yea, more, those servants will be "beaten with many stripes," who knew their Lord's will and did not "prepare" themselves; and also those who did not know their Lord's will, receive few stripes; and yet again, those who professed to be His servants, and presumed upon their position, will be "cut" off—45-48.

133. CHRIST'S COMING

A PRESBYTERIAN minister said to the writer: "I was never taught anything about the Coming of the Lord when I was in the theological college." Then he asked me about the best book on the theme, and I immediately replied, "The New Testament." No one can read through that Book without being convinced of the following—

1. That Christ is personally Coming back again, **as He promised**—John xiv. 1-3.

2. That His Coming is **pre-Millennial**, that is, before the Kingdom of righteousness can be ushered in, the King must return—Luke xix. 12.

3. That He has committed to His servants the pound of the Gospel, with which they are **to trade** until His return—Luke xix. 13, 14, R.V.

4. That the Lord's purpose in this dispensation is not to convert the world, but **to gather out** a people for His Name—Acts xv. 13-18.

5. That **evil will abound** and increase under the rule of man, and the god of this world—2 Tim. iii. 1-9.

6. That Christ will Come for His people and **remove them** from the world, and raise the blessed dead, before He comes with them in judgment—1 Thess. iv. 13-18.

7. That Christ will **destroy the Man of Sin** by His personal appearing, and overthrow all the forces of evil—2 Thess. ii. **8.**

134. CHRIST'S COMING AND OUR RESPONSIBILITY
Luke xii. 35-48

1. **Announcement** of His Coming. "When He cometh" (36).

2. **Watching** for His Coming. "Shall find watching" (37).

3. **Reward** of His Coming. "Will come forth and serve them" (37).

4. **Blessedness** of His Coming. "Blessed are those servants" (38).

5. **Loss**, if not ready for His Coming—39.

6. **Command** about His Coming. "Be ye therefore ready" (40).

7. **Faithfulness** and reward *re* His Coming—42-44.

8. **Effect** of not expecting His Coming—45.

9. **Judgment** upon those who are not ready for His Coming —46-48.

135. CHRIST'S "COMING FORTHS"

1. **Prediction.** "There shall come forth a rod out of Jesse" (Isa. xi. 1).

2. **Incarnation.** "I came forth from the Father" (John xvi. 28).

3. **Humiliation.** "Came Jesus forth wearing the crown of thorns" (John xix. 5).

4. **Crucifixion.** "Bearing His Cross went forth" to "Golgotha, where they crucified Him" (John xix. 17, 18).

5. **Revelation.** "Come forth" (Lev. xvi. 24; cf. Heb. ix. 28).

6. **Compensation.** "Will come forth and serve them" (Luke xii. 37).

7. **Opposition.** "Jehovah shall go forth as a mighty man... He shall prevail against His enemies" (Isa. xlii. 13).

136. CHRIST'S CONQUESTS IN THE BOOK OF THE REVELATION

THE one predominating thought in the Book of the Revelation is, the Lamb, in all the livingness of His death, puts down His foes, and reigns over His enemies. The wounded One of Calvary is the Warrior conquering His enemies. The Book of the unveiling is the revelation that—

1. God's Little Lamb shall conquer **the red dragon** of Hell—xii. 9-13.

2. He will put down **the seven-headed and ten-horned beast** of a revived Roman Empire—xvii. 12-14.

3. He will blast **the false prophet of Antichrist**, by the brightness of His Coming—xix. 20.

4. He will cause **the corrupt woman** of Christendom to be slaughtered by the confederates—xvii. 15-18.

5. He will wipe out the sin-riddled and **demon-possessed City** of Babylon—xviii. 16-24.

6. He will break **the nations** who oppose Him with the rod of His power—xix. 11-15.

7. He will **remove all who stand in the way** of His sway as He merges the kingdoms of the world to crown Him King of kings and Lord of lords.

The Lamb that was slain is the Conqueror. He was once trodden in the winepress because of man's sin, and because of this He shall conquer His enemies as He treads them down in the fierceness of God's wrath—xix. 16-18.

137. CHRIST'S COMING INTRODUCES THE MILLENNIUM

THERE are many portions of Scripture which foretell what will take place when Christ returns, but we concentrate upon what the Lord will do in connection with two phrases which occur several times in the prophecy of Isaiah, namely, "the Lord shall Come" or "will Come." The expression is connected with two thoughts, the overthrow of His enemies, and the inauguration of the Millennium. As the Lord of Hosts, He will come to fight for Mount Zion and to defend His people—Isa. xxxi. 4, 5. He will not only defend Jerusalem, but He will pass all over it, as a mother bird hides her young under her wings to protect them.

1. As the **Bringer of Blessings**, He says He will come and save, and there are many blessings which shall ensue as a result of His Coming. See the twenty "shalls" in Isaiah xxxv. 4-10, R. V.

2. As the **Mighty One**, He will come to rule His flock like a shepherd—Isa. xl. 10, 11. The eastern sheik was the one that not only tended his flock, but ruled his own household. When our Lord comes His arm shall rule, and He shall feed His flock like a shepherd.

3. As the **Redeemer**, He will come to Zion to turn away ungodliness from Jacob—Isa. lix. 20. Birks renders "come to Zion," "for the sake of Zion," or "out of Zion," as in Romans xi. 26. The Hebrew is "for" in the sense "on behalf of." The thought undoubtedly is, He comes to give deliverance from transgression and ungodliness.

4. As the **Avenger**, the Lord will come with fire to overthrow the enemies of His people and to plead with all flesh; and following this, He brings in the new Heavens and the new earth, and He shall cause the children of Israel to be brought by the nations as an offering unto the Lord, and all flesh shall worship Him—Isa. lxvi. 15-23.

138. CHRIST'S CURE

IT is said of the impotent man he was "cured," "made whole," "healed," "took up his bed and walked" (John v. 9, 10, 13, 14).

1. When we are "cured" from the **disease of sin**—Psa. ciii. 3.

2. "Made whole" from the **effects of sin**—1 Cor. vi. 11.

3. Healed to **health in the Lord**—1 Peter ii. 24.

4. Master that which once **mastered us**—Phil. iii. 7, 8.

5. **Walk in the ways** of the Lord—Mal. ii. 6, then we evidence Christ has blest us indeed.

139. CHRIST'S COMMENDATIONS

HE commended—

1. The **unjust steward** for providing for the future—Luke xvi. 8.

2. The **widow**, for bountifulness in giving—Luke xxi. 3.

3. The **woman**, for her importunate pleading—Luke xviii. 3-7.

4. The **Syrophenician woman**, for her largeness of faith—Matt. xv. 28.

5. The **Samaritan** leper, for his grateful thanks—Luke xvii. 18.

6. The **Apostle Peter**, for his confession of faith—Matt. xvi. 17.

7. **Mary of Bethany**, for sitting at His feet—Luke x. 42.

8. The **Good Samaritan**, for his unselfish kindness—Luke x. 36.

9. He also **reminds us** that ministry to His brethren—Matt. xxv. 40, down even to a cup of cold water, will not miss its reward—Mark ix. 41.

140. CHRIST'S DEATH—EIGHT QUESTIONS

1. **For whom did Christ die?** Christ is said to have died for "sinners" and for the "ungodly," and that God's "enemies" are reconciled to Him by the death of His Son—Rom. v. 6, 8, 10.

2. **For what did He die?** "Our sins." "He died for our sins according to the Scriptures" (1 Cor. xv. 3).

3. **Why did Christ come into the world?** To "put away sin by the sacrifice of Himself" (Heb. ix. 26). "He was manifested to take away our sins" (1 John iii. 5).

4. **Did God have anything to do with that death for sin?** He made "His soul an offering for sin" (Isa. liii. 10). "He made Him to be sin for us" (2 Cor. v. 21). "God sending His Son... by a sacrifice for sin, condemned sin in the flesh" (Rom. viii. 3, margin).

5. **Did Christ die willingly?** "He gave Himself for our sins" (Gal. i. 4).

6. **What did He do with our sins?** "Bare the sins of many" (Isa. liii. 12). "Offered to bear the sins of many" (Heb. ix. 28).

7. **Where did He bear our sins?** "In His own body on the tree" (1 Peter ii. 24).

8. **Is it necessary for Him to repeat the act?** "Christ died (R.V., margin) for sins once" (1 Peter iii. 18). Offering of the body of Jesus Christ once for all—Heb. x. 12.

141. CHRIST'S COMPASSION
Luke vii. 13

COMPASSION reveals the tenderness of the heart of Christ and the power human grief has over Him. "Compassion" means to be intensely moved. The word is often rendered "moved with compassion." There are seven instances where we find He was "moved with compassion"—

1. When He saw the **scattered multitude**—Matt. ix. 36.
2. When He saw the **multitude of sick**—Matt. xiv. 14.
3. When He beheld the **hungry crowd**—Matt. xv. 32.
4. When He met **the blind men**—Matt. xx. 34.
5. When He was appealed to by **the leper**—Mark i. 41.
6. When He pictured His life's ministry in the act of the **Good Samaritan** and in the parable of **the Prodigal Son**—Luke x. 33; xv. 20.
7. When He saw **the widow's grief.**—Luke vii. 13.

He is still the same.

142. CHRIST'S DEATH

WE do well to remember Him who died on our account, for that death is—

1. The **basis** of faith's confidence—Rom. iv. 25.
2. The **spring** of love's service—2 Cor. v. 14.
3. The **window** of hope's expectation—1 Thess. iv. 14.
4. The **joy** of reconciliation's blessing—Rom. v. 11.
5. The **motive** of affection's regard—1 John iii. 16.
6. The **soul** of the believer's praise—Rev. i. 5.
7. The **theme** of the Gospel's witness—1 Cor. xv. 3, 4.

143. CHRIST'S DEATH FORETOLD AND EXPLAINED

1. Predicted He would **die**—Isa. liii. 5.
2. The **manner** of His death was foretold—Psa. xxii. 16.
3. He **said** He would die—John x. 18.
4. He **showed** the love of God in dying—Rom. v. 8.
5. He died for our **sins**—Gal. i. 4.
6. He died to **destroy** the Devil's works—1 John iii. 8.
7. He died that we might **live** to Him—2 Cor. v. 14, 15.

The determination of His will is seen in His "flint" face of purpose—Isa. l. 7, and in that He set His face to go to Jerusalem—Luke ix. 51, 53, and He was not satisfied till He could say "accomplished." The word rendered in John xix. 30, "It is finished," would be better given "accomplished."

144. CHRIST'S DEATH

1. His **star of destiny** was His death on Calvary—Heb. ix. 26.

2. His death was no accident, but **a deliberate purpose**—John x. 18.

3. His death was a **goal**, a terminus—Phil. ii. 8.

4. His death was an **accomplishment**, a work done for us—Rom. vi. 10.

5. His death was essential, **a necessity** to meet a need—John iii. 14, 15.

6. His death was **a smiting** of the Rock, that the living waters might flow—John vii. 37-39.

7. His death is the **gate of life**, which leads to the plains of glory—1 Thess. v. 9, 10.

8. His death is a **mould** to shape and make us—Rom. vi. 17, margin.

145. CHRIST'S DEATH

THE death of Christ is the fact of the Gospel, and in that fact is the factor of all blessing. His death was—

1. **Unjustified in Cause.** "Wicked hands crucified" (Acts ii. 23).

2. **Unique in Fulfilment.** "Saying of Jesus might be fulfilled, which He spake, signifying what death He should die" (John xviii. 32).

3. **Unparalleled in Experience.** "He, by the grace of God should taste death for every man" (Heb. ii. 9).

4. **Substitutionary in Fact.** "He suffered the Just for the unjust" (1 Peter iii. 18).

5. **Reconciling in Effect.** "Reconciled to God through the death of His Son" (Rom. v. 10).

6. **Separating in Influence.** "Baptised into His death... Dead unto sin" (Rom. vi. 3, 11).

7. **Conforming in Power.** "Being conformed to His death" (Phil. iii. 10).

146. CHRIST'S DEATH IN ITS DEPTHS

WHO can sound the depths of Christ's death?

1. Think of the **sufferings** of His death. "He endured the Cross"—Heb. xii. 2.

2. Muse upon the **reality** of His death. He tasted death—Heb. ii. 9.

3. Ponder the **necessity** of His death. He was made sin for us—2 Cor. v. 21.

4. Meditate upon the **love** of His death. He willingly gave Himself for us—Gal. ii. 20.

5. Call to mind the **character** of His death. He was made a curse for us—Gal. iii. 13.

6. Remember the **benefits** of His death. He emptied out His life in atonement, that He might empty into our lap the very fullness of God—2 Cor. viii. 9.

7. And then don't forget the grand purpose of His death. It was that He might **bring us to God**—1 Peter iii. 18.

147. CHRIST'S DEATH—SEVEN FACTS

1. **Effective in Blessing.** "By means of* death...they which are called might receive the promise of eternal inheritance (Heb. ix. 15).

2. **Victorious in Outcome.** "By means of "death He might annul him that had authority over death" (Heb. ii. 14).

3. **Acknowledged in Resurrection.** "Save Him from ("ἐκ, " out of) death" (Heb. v. 7).

4. **Honoured in Place.** "Because of (dia, with accusative means "because of") the suffering of death, crowned with glory and honour" (Heb. ii. 9).

5. **Glorious in Purpose.** "Through* death to present you holy and unblameable and unreproveable before Him" (Col. i. 22).

6. **Exemplary in Pattern.** "Let this mind be in you... obedient unto death" (Phil. ii. 5, 8).

7. **Remembered in Love.** "Ye do shew the Lord's death until He come" (1 Cor. xi. 26).

148. CHRIST'S FACE

1. A **Glorious Face** in Transfiguration—Matt. xvii. 2.

2. An **Agonised Face** in Supplication—Matt. xxvi. 39.

3. An **Insulted Face** in Persecution—Matt. xxvi. 67; Isa. l. 6.

4. A **Covered Face** in Derision—Mark xiv. 65.

5. A **Steadfast Face** in Determination—Luke ix. 51.

6. A **Set Face** in Destination—Luke ix. 53; Isa. l. 7.

7. A **Struck Face** in Opposition—Luke xxii. 64.

8. A **Marred Face** in Substitution—Isa. lii. 14.

9. An **Illuminating Face** in Ministration—2 Cor. iv. 6.

10. A **Revealed Face** in Reproduction—Rev. xxii. 4.

*Dia with the genitive signifies "by means of," as an active agent procuring a result.

149. CHRIST'S DEATH IN JOHN XII. 21-33.

1. Christ's death in the "hour" of its occasion—23, 27. There was no accident in connection with Christ's death.

2. Christ's death in the principle of its act. He lost His life as the corn of wheat loses its first root—24, 25.

3. Christ's death in the intensity of its reality. His soul was troubled. He knew what was before Him—27, R.V., margin.

4. Christ's death in the Father's appreciation. The Father had glorified Christ at His baptism and transfiguration, and promises to do it again—28.

5. Christ's death in the conquest of His victory. The Cross proclaims the judgment of the world, and its conquest over Satan—31.

6. Christ's death, and the life into which it leads—25, 26.

150. CHRIST'S DEATH, BLOOD, AND SUFFERING
In 1 Peter

1. "Sanctification...unto obedience and the sprinkling of the Blood of Jesus Christ" (i. 2).

2. Revelation in the Scriptures of Christ's sufferings and glory—i. 10-12.

3. Redemption from an empty manner of life by "the precious Blood of Christ" (i. 18, 19, R.v).

4. Identification with Christ in suffering, although we are right and thus following in His steps—ii. 20-23.

5. Substitution for us, for He "bore our sins in His own body on the tree" (ii. 24; iii. 18).

6. Separation from sin, for He died for our sins, that we should be "dead" to them—ii. 24; iv. 1, 2.

7. Partnership with Christ in His sufferings, in enduring trial and persecution—iv. 12-16.

151. CHRIST'S FIVE "MYS"
In John x

1. "My Life" (15, 17), laid down and taken again.

2. "My Voice" (16), heard by the sheep and heeded.

3. "My Sheep" (27), loved, kept, known, purchased, led; and the sheep hearing and following.

4. "My Hand" (28), holding and held.

5. "My Father" (17), loving (17), directing (18), witnessing (25), giving (29), holding (29), revealing (32), and proving (37).

152. CHRIST'S FASCINATION

WHAT Christ was to the Apostle Paul is seen in Philippians iii, in the relative expressions that are found in connection with the names of our Lord Jesus Christ.

1. The **Sphere of Joy.** "Rejoice in the Lord" (1).
2. The **Object of Glory.** "Glory in Christ Jesus" (3, R. V.).
3. The **Supreme Attraction.** "Counted loss for Christ" (7).
4. The **Super-Knowledge.** "The knowledge of Christ Jesus my Lord" (8).
5. The **Greatest Gain.** "That I may win Christ" (8).
6. The **Perfect Righteousness.** "Righteousness...through the faith of Christ" (9).
7. The **Desired Attainment.** "That I may apprehend that which also I am apprehended of Christ Jesus" (12).
8. The **Highest Prize.** "The prize of the high calling of God in Christ Jesus" (14).
9. The **Wonderful Outlook.** "We look for the Saviour, the Lord Jesus Christ" (20).

153. CHRIST'S FAULTLESSNESS

PILATE and the believing thief both confessed there was "no fault" in Him, and that He had done "nothing amiss" (Luke xxiii. 14, 41). The word "amiss" is rendered "harm" (Acts xxviii. 6), and "unreasonable" (2 Thess. iii. 2), in the two other places where "*atopon*" occurs. There was nothing un-reasonable in Christ's teaching, there was no harm in His actions, and not anything amiss in His character.

1. **He did no sin**—1 Peter ii. 22.
2. **In Him was no sin**—1 John iii. 5.
3. **He knew no sin**—2 Cor. v. 21.
4. **He was holy,** harmless, and undefiled, and separate from every vile association—Heb. vii. 26.

The greatest character that ever lived died the most shameful and undeserved death that was ever experienced.

154. CHRIST'S FIVEFOLD GLORY
ISAIAH IX. 6

ONE of the names of Christ is: "Wonderful—Counsellor—The Mighty God—The Everlasting Father—The Prince of Peace." "His *Name*," not His names, is thus expressed. Christ exemplified every one of the five sections of "His Name" in His life.

1. He was the **"Wonderful"** in the perfection of His holy life—Heb. vii. 26.

2. He was the "**Counsellor**" in the life-giving and light-imparting words of His love—John vi. 63.

3. He was "**The Mighty God**" in the wonder-working of His miracles—Acts x. 38.

4. He was "**The Everlasting Father**" in the Revelation He made and was of the Father—John xiv. 7.

5. He was "**The Prince of Peace**" in the peace He made by the Blood of His Cross, in what He is; and He will be the Prince of Peace when He comes to set up His Kingdom, for then, and not till then, "Of the increase of His government and peace there shall be no end" (Isa. ix. 7).

155. CHRIST'S GOAL

CHRIST unfolds that the purpose of His first advent was His atoning death at Calvary. This may be fully apprehended if we connect, what Luke alone brings out, the references to Jerusalem.

1. "**His Decease**, which He should accomplish at Jerusalem" (ix. 31).

2. "**Stedfastly** set His face to go to Jerusalem" (ix. 51).

3. "His face was as though **He would go to Jerusalem**" (ix. 53).

4. "**Teaching** and journeying toward Jerusalem" (xiii. 22).

5. "It cannot be that **a prophet perish** out of Jerusalem" (xiii. 33).

6. "It came to pass **as He went** to Jerusalem" (xvii. 11).

7. "**Behold**, we go up to Jerusalem" (xviii. 31).

8. "He was **nigh** to Jerusalem" (xix. 11).

9. "He **went before**, ascending up to Jerusalem" (xix. 28).

There are no less than thirty-two references to Jerusalem in Luke's Gospel, and nearly all of those mentioned, from the transfiguration scene to the accomplishment of His sacrificial atonement on Calvary, have their focus-point in His death.

156. CHRIST'S HEADSHIP

1. "Head of **The Corner**" of God's Building—Acts iv. 11.

2. "Head of **every man** is Christ." Head of humanity—1 Cor. xi. 3.

3. "Head of the **Church**" (Eph. v. 23).

4. "Head of all **Principality and Power**" (Col. ii. 10).

5. "Head of **Administration**"—Eph. iv. 15.

6. "Head of Christ is **God**" (1 Cor. xi. 3).

7. "Head over **all things**" (Eph. i. 22).

157. CHRIST'S HOUR

AGAIN and again we have a specified time stated in the hour of His destiny to die.

1. **Destined Hour** in the time of God's eternal purpose; hence, He was the Lamb slain from before the foundation of the world—1 Peter. i. 19, 20.

2. **Determined Hour** of Scripture's prediction, as prophesied through Daniel—Dan. ix. 25, 26.

3. **Divine Hour** of God's atonement as typified in the day of atonement—Lev. xvi. 29-34.

4. **Defined Hour** of sin's climax, for it was in the end of the ages, He appeared to put away sin by the sacrifice of Himself —Heb. ix. 26.

5. **Demonstrated Hour** of God's love, for it was in "due time" (the appointed time) God commended His love towards us—Rom. v. 8, 9.

6. **Distinct Hour** of the appearance of God's grace in bringing salvation—Titus ii. 11.

7. **Distinguished Hour** of time and eternity, of which Christ declared, "The hour is come"—John xii. 23.

158. CHRIST'S "I GIVE'S" IN JOHN

THE Greek word *didōmi*, coupled with the personal pronoun "I" in the following passages in John's Gospel, is rendered "will give," "have given," and "shall give." The word means to give freely, ungrudgingly, and unforced.

1. **The Living Water.** "The water that I shall give" (iv. 14). Living, leaping, loving, lifting, lasting, fructifying, and satisfying is this water.

2. **The Satisfying Bread.** "Bread that I will give" (vi. 51). Bruised in death, beneficent in feeding, real in substance, and holy in character is this bread.

3. **The Eternal Life.** "I give unto them eternal life" (x. 28). The life is the nature of Him who is Love, and must be eternal in duration.

4. **The Worthy Example.** "I have given you an example" (xiii. 15). He is the Pattern for our imitation and the Power to imitate the Pattern.

5. **The New Commandment.** "A new commandment I give" (xiii. 34). Grace lifts to higher ground than law, and enjoins greater responsibility.

6. **The "My Peace."** "My peace I give unto you" (xiv. 27).

The peace He leaves is the legacy of the dying man, the peace He gives is the gift of the Living Lord.

7. **The "Given Words."** "I have given unto them the words...Thy Word" (xvii. 14). The words give in detail what is found in the Word. The Word is love's revelation, faith's foundation, hope's life, the servant's authority, the saint's sanctifier, the pilgrim's cordial, the Lord's promise, and the believer's rule.

8. **The Bestowed Glory.** "The glory which Thou gavest Me I have given them" (xvii. 22). The Son's givings are the passings on from the Father.

159. CHRISTSHIP OF JESUS

THERE is a progressiveness of Revelation regarding Jesus as The Christ.

1. **Personally,** as the Anointed of God, He does work for us which we could not do for ourselves—John xx. 31.

2. **Positionally,** as the Anointer with the Holy Spirit, He is made Lord and Christ—Acts ii. 36.

3. **Mystically.** "Christ" as the Head and Members make up the mystical body of Christ—1 Cor. xii. 12.

4. **Representatively.** Christ is the One "in" whom believers are found—2 Cor. xii. 2.

5. **Provisionally.** Christ is the Reservoir where all blessing is treasured—Eph. i. 3.

6. **Potentially.** Christ is the Indweller to reproduce His life in ours.—Gal. ii. 20.

7. **Prospectively.** The Church will be "with Christ" whether at death—Phil. i. 23, or His return—Col. iii. 4.

160. CHRIST'S I "HAVE'S" IN JOHN XVII

1. "I have **glorified** Thee" (4).
2. "I have **finished** the work" (4).
3. "I have **manifested** Thy Name" (6).
4. "I have **kept**" (12).
5. "I have **given** them Thy Word" and "Words" (8, 14).
6. "I have **declared** Thy Name" (26).
7. "I have **known** Thee" (25).
8. "I have **sent**" (18).
9. "I have **given** them Thy glory" (22).

161. CHRIST'S INCARNATION

As the Incarnate One, Christ—

1. Bears the **Sweetest Name** ever given—"Jesus"—Luke ii. 21.

2. Embodies the **Greatest Power** ever known—"Emmanuel, God with us" (Matt. i. 23).

3. Stooped to the **Lowest Place** ever taken. "For our sakes became poor, " or a beggar (2 Cor. viii. 9).

4. Came on the **Mightiest Mission** ever undertaken. "He took...destroy" (Heb. ii. 14-16).

5. Is the **Greatest Unfolding** ever seen. "God manifest in the flesh" (1 Tim. iii. 16).

6. Bearer of the **Grandest Blessing** ever bestowed. "Life" (John x. 10).

7. Is the **Most Potent Force** ever communicated. "Rise and fall of many" (Luke ii. 34).

162. CHRIST'S IDENTIFICATION WITH US

"I sat where they sat" (Ezek. iii. 15.)

1. **Place of Condescension** in being born in a stable—Luke ii. 7.

2. **Place of Agony,** in being in the "place called Gethsemane" (Matt. xxvi. 36).

3. **Place of Suffering,** in being in the "place called The Pavement, " or Gabbatha (John xix. 13).

4. **Place of Substitution,** when He was found in "the place called Calvary" (Luke xxiii. 33).

5. **Place of Identification,** in two others being crucified with Him—John xix. 18.

6. **Place of Need.** The place where He was crucified was "nigh to the city" (John xix. 20).

7. **Place of Death.** "The place where they laid Him" (Mark xvi. 6).

163. CHRIST'S "I SPEAK" IN JOHN'S GOSPEL

1. **The Claim of Deity.** "I that speak unto thee AM" (iv. 26; "*He*" is in italics). He is the Jehovah, the great "I AM. " He speaks.

2. **The Claim of Inspiration.** "The words that I speak ...are spirit and life" (vi. 63).

3. **The Promise of Knowledge.** "If any man will do His will, he shall know...I speak" (vii. 17).

4. **The Revelation of Truth.** "I speak to the world," etc. (viii. 26).

5. **The Obedient Son.** "My Father hath taught Me, I speak" (viii. 28, 38; xii. 49, 50).

6. **The Discriminating Lord.** "I speak not of you all" (xiii. 18).

7. **The Absolute Authority.** "Words which I speak unto you," etc. (xiv. 10).

164. CHRIST SITTING

1. **A Weary Saviour.** "He *sat* on the well, being wearied" (John iv. 6).

2. **A Powerful Teacher.** "I *sat* daily with you teaching" (Matt. xxvi. 55; Luke iv. 20; v. 3; John viii. 2).

3. **An Approachable Man.** "As Jesus *sat* at meat...many publicans and sinners came and *sat* down with Him" (Matt. ix. 10).

4. **A Scripture Fulfiller.** "*Set* Jesus thereon" (Luke xix. 35). "Jesus *sat* upon him" (Mark xi. 7, R.V.).

5. **An Accomplishing Worker.** "When He had made purification of sins, *sat* down," etc. (Heb. i. 3, R.V.).

6. **A Glorious Priest.** "We have such a high priest, who *sat* down," etc. (Heb. viii. 1, R.V.).

7. **An Unsurpassed Example.** "Looking unto Jesus... is set down," etc. (Heb. xii. 1-3).

165. CHRIST SITTING

1. **Upon an Ass**, in fulfilment of Scripture—John xii. 15.

2. **In the House**, at a meal receiving sinners—Matt. ix. 10.

3. **Upon the Mount** of Olives, revealing the future to His disciples—Matt. xxiv. 3.

4. **In the Temple**, teaching—Matt. xxvi. 55.

5. **On the Well**, and blessing the woman of Samaria—John iv. 6.

6. **On the Right Hand of God**, in resurrection power—Col. iii. 1.

7. **On the Right Hand of the Majesty on High**, as the Great High Priest—Heb. i. 3; x. 12.

8. **On the Throne**, in judgment—Matt. xix. 28; xxv. 31.

166. CHRIST'S KINGDOM

WHAT will be the character of His Kingdom? We need to ponder the whole country of the Old Testament prophecies to answer the question. But if we confine ourselves to the prophecies in Daniel ii. and vii. we shall find a simple and unmistakable answer.

1. **Received Kingdom.** "There was given Him dominion, and glory, and a kingdom" (vii. 14).

2. **Powerful Kingdom.** "A stone...smote the image. and brake it in pieces" (ii. 34).

3. **Victorious Kingdom.** "Take away his dominion, to consume and to destroy it unto the end" (vii. 26; viii. 25).

4. **Recognised Kingdom.** "Shall serve and obey Him" (vii. 27).

5. **Universal Kingdom.** "Filled the whole earth" (ii. 35). "All people, nations, and languages shall serve Him" (vii. 14).

6. **Lasting Kingdom.** "His dominion is an everlasting dominion, which shall not pass away" (vii. 14). "An everlasting Kingdom" (vii. 27).

7. **Set Kingdom.** Set as to time as well as to being. "In the days of these kings" (ii. 44).

167. CHRIST'S KINGDOM PREDICTED
IN PSALM LXXII

PSALM lxxii. has a reference to Solomon, but he cannot fulfil all its statements, and therefore has a wider application to great David's greater Son. Its truth has a present application to every believer in Christ, for when our Lord reigns in the heart there will be purity in the mind, righteousness in our transactions, holiness in the life, truth in the lips, help in our hands, love in the walk, and beauty in the character.

The wider application of the Psalm points on to the time when Christ shall have received the Kingdom from the Father and returned to the earth—Luke xix. 11-15. The many-sidedness of the characteristics of that Kingdom is brought out in the frequent statements prefaced by what "HE SHALL" do. Note the many "shalls" in the Psalm, and seven "He shalls." His Kingdom will be—

1. **Righteous in its rule.** "He shall judge the people with righteousness" (2). He will do the right thing because it is the right thing to do. A straight ruler makes a straight line.

2. **Saving in its strength.** "He shall save" (4). As the bread saves the needy from starving, and the strong man helps

the weak, so He will vindicate all who are oppressed and in
need.

3. Blessing in its bestowment. "He shall come down
like rain" (6, 7). As the rain softens the earth, germinates the
seed, and causes the fruit to come forth, so Christ will bless all.

4. Universal in its sway. "He shall have dominion" (8).
All will own Him as King or be made to do so.

5. Succouring in its help. "He shall deliver the needy"
(12). His heart of love will prompt Him to exercise His hand
of help, even as it does the mother with her child.

6. Redemptive in its exercise. "He shall redeem their
soul" (14). Freedom from sin and all its attendant evils
will be the boon of His reign.

7. Lasting in its endurance. "He shall live... His Name
shall endure for ever" (15, 17).

The ills of earth call for the Coming of the Lord.

168. CHRIST'S KNOWLEDGE

NOTHING can be hid from the all-searching eyes of the Lord.

1. **David's** experience—Psa. cxxxix. 1-12.

2. Christ's messages to the **seven churches**—Rev. ii. and iii.
Note His frequent "I know."

3. His perception of **the Jews**—John ii. 24.

4. His knowledge of **the Pharisees'** thoughts—Matt. xii. 25.

5. His insight into the grumbling of **His disciples**—
John vi. 60, 61.

6. His foresight of the evil intent of **Judas**—John xiii. 11.

7. His knowledge of the **impotent man**—John v. 6.

8. His knowledge of the **disciples' wish** about His sayings—
John xvi. 19, all go to prove He knows all about all men.

169. CHRIST'S LORDSHIP

THERE are three things embodied in the title of Lord—

1. His Ownership, hence "the earth is the Lord's"
(Psa. xxiv. 1).

2. His Authority, hence the Lord delivered to the servants
the talents which they were responsible to use for Him—
Matt. xxv. 20-23.

3. His Power, hence when the Lord sent forth His servants
"the Lord" was "working with them" (Mark xvi. 19, 20).

170. CHRIST'S LOVE
AS REVEALED IN JOHN XIII

1. **Persistency of Love.** "Loved to the end" (1).
2. **Portion of Love.** "Jesus knowing that the Father had given all things into His hands" (3).
3. **Promise of Love.** "What I do thou knowest not now, but thou shalt know hereafter" (7).
4. **Pattern of Love.** "I have given you an example" (15).
5. **Place of Love.** "Jesus' bosom" (23).
6. **Precept of Love.** "Love one another" (34).
7. **Power of Love.** "By this shall all men know" (35).

171. CHRIST'S MESSAGE ON BEING SAVED

THE pages of the New Testament ring with the word "saved."

1. Christ's **message** was, "That ye might be saved" (John v. 34).

2. He said those who **entered** into the shepherd fold of His grace should "be saved" (John x. 9).

3. His **commission** to His disciples was that those who believed should "be saved" (Mark xvi. 16).

4. He **assured** a woman who came in penitence to Him, "Thy faith hath saved thee" (Luke vii. 50).

5. He **declared** that Satan's machinations were to keep men from receiving His Word, lest they should "believe and be saved" (Luke viii. 12).

6. He **revealed** that God sent Him into the world that it might "be saved" (John iii. 17).

172. CHRIST'S NAMES AS THE INCARNATE ONE
IN MATTHEW II

1. "**Jesus**" of Bethlehem, a Saviour for us—1.
2. "**King** of the Jews," a King over us—2.
3. "**Christ**," the Anointed One sent to us—4
4. The "**Governor**," to rule over Israel—6.
5. "The **Young Child**" (mentioned nine times). His actual humanity—8.
6. "**Son**," as One with God, and One given to us—15.
7. The "**Nazarene**," as the Separated to God and His service—23.

173. CHRIST'S NEED

"THE Lord hath need of him" (Luke xix. 31), was the reply given for the loan of the ass's colt. Christ's care that Scripture might be fulfilled—Zech. ix. 9, was the reason of His request. The Lord can do without any of us, but He is pleased to do with us.

1. He has need of our **faith**, that we may please Him as Enoch did—Heb. xi. 5.

2. He has need of our **love**, that we may minister to Him as Mary did—John xii. 3.

3. He has need of our **service**, that He may work in us as He did with the apostle—Eph. iii. 7.

4. He has need of our **heart**, that He may live in us as He did in Paul—Gal. ii. 20.

5. He has need of our **house**, that He may be received into it as Martha received Him—Luke x. 38.

6. He has need of our **minds**, that He may think in them as He did in men of old—2 Peter i. 21.

7. He has need of our **possessions**, that He may use them as He did the man's colt—John xii. 14.

174. CHRIST'S OUTLOOK

WHEN Christ first came he had two things before Him, namely, His sufferings and the glory that should follow—Luke xxiv. 26. The bitterness of the Cross lies behind, and the brightness of the crown lies before Him. When Daniel saw the world-powers depicted in the image and four wild beasts—see Dan. ii. and vii., he saw also the powers of their "dominion taken away," and further, the Ancient of Days gave to the Son of Man "dominion and glory," and all nations are made to serve Him (Dan. vii. 12-14). What that glory will be in its manifold splendour we cannot fully comprehend, but at least it will be sevenfold in its manifestation.

1. He will have the glory of **peculiar honour**, in having the Name which is above every name—Phil. ii. 9.

2. He will have position above every **position**, for He will be King of kings and Lord of lords—Rev. xix. 16.

3. He will have the outshining of **majestic power**, which will crush the opposition of the Man of Sin—2 Thess. ii. 8.

4. He will have the glory of **unsurpassed victory**, for He will overthrow the great usurper and consign him into the Lake of Fire—Rev. xx. 2, 10.

5. He will have the glory of a **majestic reign** as given in detail in Psalm lxxii.

6. He will have the glory of being **glorified** in His saints— 2 Thess. i. 10.

7. He will have the glory of the **glorified Lamb** lighting up the New Heavens and the New Earth—Rev. xxi. 23. What an outlook for Him, when He shall see the travail of His soul and be satisfied.

175. CHRIST'S PASSION

THE passion of His atoning death is ever the secret and soul of the Gospel. It speaks of—

1. Sin's **hindrance** removed—Heb. ix. 26.
2. Sin's **guilt** answered for—Heb. ii. 17.
3. Sin's **author** overthrown—Heb. ii. 14.
4. Sin's **gulf** spanned—Heb. x. 19, 20.
5. Sin's **pollution** removed—Heb. x. 10.
6. Sin's **power** broken—Heb. x. 16-18.
7. Sin's **victory** destroyed—1 John iii. 8.

176. CHRIST'S PRAYER IN GETHSEMANE

THE prayer of Christ was the greatest that was ever uttered.

1. It was a **lonely** prayer. He withdrew Himself from the disciples in the garden—Luke xxii. 41; and we are told He "went forward," and again "He went away"—Mark xiv. 35, 39. His very action of withdrawing is suggestive of the fact there are some places to which He alone could go.

2. It was a **humble** prayer. "He fell on the ground and prayed" (Mark xiv. 35). The posture of His body indicated the attitude of His spirit. Matthew tells us He fell on His face —xxvi. 39, and Luke says that He "kneeled down"—xxii. 41.

3. It was a **filial** prayer—Mark xiv. 36. He said, "Abba, Father." The intimacy of His relation to the Father is at once suggested. His heart of obedience beats in unison with the heart of the Father's love.

4. It was an **earnest** prayer—Luke xxii. 42; Heb. v. 7. The pressure upon Him caused the blood to ooze from His body, but instead of discouraging Him, "He prayed the more earnestly," yea, with "strong crying and tears."

5. It was a **persevering** prayer, for He not only went away and prayed the same words, but He did it three times—Mark xiv. 39. Is there not a suggested association with Christ's own

teaching about prayer in the words, "Ask, seek, knock" (Matt. vii. 7), and there certainly is a suggested connection with Paul when he asked thrice for the thorn to be removed—2 Cor. xii. 8.

6. It was a **resigned** prayer. At first Christ asked for the cup to be removed, but puts in the proviso, "Nevertheless not what I will, but what Thou wilt" (Mark xiv. 36). Matthew gives an added touch in Christ's second praying when Christ says, "O My Father, if this cup may not pass away except I drink it, Thy will be done" (Matt. xxvi. 42). In the first prayer we see the two wills, "My will" and "Thy will," but in the second prayer the Father's will alone is mentioned; but afterwards He evidently got beyond this, and said, "The cup which My Father giveth Me, shall I not drink it?" (John xviii. 11).

7. It was an **answered** prayer—Luke xxii. 43.

> "The Father heard, and angels there
> Sustained the Son of God in prayer,
>   In sad Gethsemane;
> He drank the dreadful cup of pain,
> Then rose to life and joy again.

> "When storms of sorrow round us sweep,
> And scenes of anguish make us weep,
>   To sad Gethsemane
> We'll look, and see the Saviour there,
> And humbly bow, like Him, in prayer."

177. CHRIST'S PERFECTNESS

1. His perfect **Work**. "Nothing can be put to it" (Eccles. iii. 14).

2. His perfect **Forgiveness**. "Nothing to pay" (Luke vii. 42).

3. His perfect **Care**. "Lacked nothing" (Deut. ii. 7; Neh. ix. 21).

4. His perfect **Victory**. "Nothing in His hand" (Judges xiv. 6).

5. His perfect **Supply**. "They lacked nothing" (1 Kings iv. 27).

6. His perfect **Grace**. "That ye may be perfect, and entire, wanting nothing" (Jas. i. 4).

7. His perfect **Operation**. "If this Man were not of God, He could do nothing" (John ix. 33).

Our emptiness and inefficiency are the opportunity for the display of God's sufficiency and fulness.

178. CHRIST'S REBUKES

1. **A Delivering Lord.** "Jesus *rebuked* him, saying...Come out of him" (Luke iv. 35).
2. **A Soothing Saviour.** "He stood over her, and *rebuked* the fever; and it left her" (Luke iv. 39).
3. **A Silencing Christ.** "He, *rebuking* them, suffered them not to speak" (Luke iv. 41).
4. **An Authoritative** Subduer. "*Rebuked* the wind...and there was a calm" (Luke viii. 24).
5. **A Cleansing Jesus.** "Jesus *rebuked* the unclean spirit" (Luke ix. 42).
6. **A Gracious Man.** "He turned, and *rebuked* them, and said, Ye know not what manner of spirit ye are of" (Luke ix. 55).
7. **The Answering Redeemer.** "Peter took Him, and began to *rebuke* Him...He *rebuked* Peter" (Mark viii. 32, 33).

179. CHRIST'S REPLY TO LAODICEA

PONDER the personal pronoun "I" to the Church in Laodicea—Rev. iii. 15, 18-21.
1. The "**I know**" of Discernment.
2. The "**I would**" of Desire.
3. The "**I will**" of Disgust.
4. The "**I counsel**" of Direction.
5. The "**I love**" of Devotion.
6. The "**I rebuke**" of Discipline.
7. The "**I stand**" of Demeanour.
8. The "**I will**" of Communion.
9. The "**I will**" of Promise.
10. The "**I also**" of Victory.

180. CHRIST'S RESURRECTION

THE whole fabric of Christianity rests upon Christ's Resurrection. It is—
1. The **keystone** to the arch of truth—2 Tim. ii. 8.
2. The **warrant** to faith—Rom. x. 9, 10.
3. The **pith** of the Gospel—1 Cor. xv. 3, 4.
4. The **ground** of hope—1 Thess. iv. 13, 14.
5. The **harbinger** of glory—1 Peter i. 3.
6. The **evidence** of the supernatural—Eph. i. 19, 20.
7. The **incentive** to holiness—Rom. vi. 4.
8. The **basis** of assurance—Rom. viii. 33-39.

181. CHRIST'S RESURRECTION
"Him that Liveth" margin, Luke xxiv. 5

1. **He Lives in Spite of Death.** Peter, on the Day of Pentecost, declared three things of Christ as the One who had been in the grip of death—Acts ii. 24. (1) God raised Him up, and His act in causing Him to stand out from among the dead is the exhibition of "the exceeding greatness of God's power" (Eph. i. 19, 20). (2) God has "loosed Him from the pains of death." "Loosed" means to unloose what is fast bound, as the unloosing of a colt—Mark xi. 5, the unloosing of dumb tongue—Mark vii. 35, etc. (3) Then we are told the reason: "Because it was not possible that He should be holden of it." "Holden" means to "hold fast," and is so given in Revelation ii. 25, hence to have rule or authority over anything, but it was "not possible" for Christ to be held by the power of death. The life within Him and the power of God around Him were factors which burst the powers that held Him, even as a living seed, dropping between the crevices of a tombstone, will lift and part it asunder.

2. **He Lives, as He Said He Would**—Luke xxiv. 8. There was no accident in the death of Christ. His star of destiny was His death on Calvary. He had a purpose in dying—Heb. ix. 26, namely, "To put away sin," the sin which kept us from God and kept God from us. He said He would die and rise again, and He kept His word. Well would it have been if the women and others had only remembered what Christ had said. "I have got a good forgettory," said a little girl who had forgotten what she ought to have remembered.

3. **He Lives: the Empty Tomb is the Evidence of It.** The "young man" in the tomb invited the women to come and "see the place where they had laid Him" (Mark xvi. 6), and when they entered the tomb they saw not the body of the Lord Jesus—3. He had been there in death, He was not there, for He was raised, and He will never be there again. A crucifix is not an emblem of Christianity, but an empty tomb is. How much that empty tomb proclaims! Scripture fulfilled—1 Cor. xv. 3, 4; Sin answered for—Rom. iv. 24, 25; Satan vanquished—Rev. i. 18; Col. ii. 12-15; Salvation proclaimed—Rom. x. 9, 10; Sanctification assured—Heb. xiii. 20, 21; Sorrow assuaged— 1 Thess. iv. 13, 14; Strength communicated—Acts ii. 32, 33.

4. **He lives: the linen clothes attest it**—Luke xxiv. 12. Peter entered into the sepulchre and "Beheld the linen clothes," and went away "wondering;" but when John entered in, he "saw and believed" (John xx. 8). What was it that impressed the disciples? The empty tomb; but there must have been something peculiar about the clothes. The grave clothes were not

a shroud, but a swathe; that is, a band wrapped round the body as one swathes an infant. Christ had passed through the swathing, and the one hundred pounds of spices, without disturbing them. Just as the chrysalis of the butterfly, after the butterfly has emerged from the case, the case retains the form of the chrysalis, although the butterfly is gone, so Christ had gone through the clothes, and they were left in all their convolutions as if they were still wrapped round the body. So there was a miracle in a miracle. The resurrection was a miracle, and there was a miracle in the miracle in that Christ had gone through the clothes without disturbing them. The same double miracle is seen in the raising of Lazarus. He that was raised came forth from the grave "bound hand and foot" (John xi. 44). He could not "come forth" naturally, because he was "bound hand and foot," hence all the old pictures represent him as gliding forth.

Do we know Christ is alive in our lives? A gentleman once saw a boy holding a piece of string, but could not see to what object it was attached; and he asked the boy what he was doing, and the boy replied, "Flying my kite." "But I cannot see any kite," said the short-sighted gentleman; so the boy said, "Ah! sir, I know it's there, because I can feel it pull." So those who know Christ risen from the dead, know the pull of His risen life.

182. CHRIST'S RESURRECTION ("PROOFS")

Acts i. 3

THERE are many "infallible proofs" of Christ's resurrection. Among the proofs may be noted—

1. **God-ward**, it was the display of God's power—Eph. i. 19, 20.

2. **Christ-ward**, it was the declaration of His Deity— Rom. i. 4.

3. **Spirit-ward**, it is the demonstration of His life— Rom. viii. 11.

4. **Believer-ward**, it is the denomination of God's grace— Eph. ii. 1-4.

5. **Hell-ward**, it was the defeat of Satan's realm—Rev. i. 18.

6. **Death-ward**, it is the destroyer of sin's sting—1 Cor. xv. 54-57.

7. **Glory-ward**, it is the day-star of hope's assurance— 1 Thess. iv. 13-18.

Other proofs might be enumerated, such as the undisturbed clothes in the sepulchre—John xx. 4-9; the many witnesses who saw Him alive—Acts x. 40, 41; and the difference Christ made in the lives of those who received Him—1 Cor. vi. 9-11.

183. CHRIST'S RESURRECTION

"Now is Christ risen" (1 Cor. xv. 20)

As we behold the fact of the starry Heavens in their order and movement, and see their relative importance; so as we ponder the star fact of Christ's resurrection we find there are several stars of truth that are relative to it and depend upon it. These may be classified in the following words—prediction, crucifixion, resurrection, vivification, consecration, indissolubility, and revelation.

1. **Prediction.** Christ predicted His death and resurrection, as His enemies testified when they urged Pilate to make the tomb secure, for they said, "Sir, we remember that this Deceiver said, while He was yet alive, After three days I will rise again" (Matt. xxvii. 63).

2. **Crucifixion.** "Christ being raised from the dead, dieth no more: death hath no more dominion over Him, for in that He died, He died unto sin once, but, in that He liveth, He liveth unto God" (Rom. vi. 9, 10). The emphasis here, is, the Risen One has "died," that He died "once," that He died in dealing with "sin," that He will "no more" die. Death can never have dominion over Him again, and that in a new way for us "He liveth unto God."

3. **Resurrection.** The resurrection of Christ not only meant to be roused and then to rise up, but He is always said to be "raised from the dead." This is always the emphatic word in the epistles—Rom. iv. 24; viii. 11; x. 9; Gal. i. 1; Eph. i. 20; Col. ii. 12; 1 Thess. i. 10; 1 Peter i. 21, the apex of the apostles' message—Acts iii. 15; iv. 10; xiii. 30, and the essential thing as a moving and magnetic power in the life of the believer— 2 Cor. i. 9; iv. 10; Phil. iii. 10. His out-resurrection was peculiar in that He would never come under the power of death again, like Lazarus. That out-resurrection secures the out-resurrection of all His own.

4. **Vivification.** Livingness is the one thing which characterises Christ. "He shewed Himself alive" (Acts i. 3) is the Spirit's word; and the ringing testimony of the "certain women" was, "He is alive" (Luke xxiv. 23). The message of the apostle was the same, he "affirmed He was alive" (Acts xxv. 19); and Christ's message to John at Patmos was the same, "I am alive" (Rev. i. 18; ii. 8). Since He is alive, what need we fear? Whether it be the condemning past, the anxious present, or the ominous future, He bids us not to fear.

5. **Consecration.** The Spirit, referring to Christ's non-succession priesthood, says He is "consecrated for evermore," or as it should be rendered, "to the age" (Heb. vii. 28), or

"unto the ever," for His priesthood is, like Himself, "for ever" (Heb. xiii. 8). The priests of the past were compassed by sin, infirmity, death, and change, but not so Christ, for as the Living One in His new office of unchanging priesthood He lives to succour, save, and sustain completely.

6. **Indissolubility.** Christ is "made" as our High Priest "after the power of an endless life" (Heb. vii. 16). "Endless" does not express the character of the "life." "Indissoluble" is the meaning of "*akatalutos*," which signifies the life is incapable of being loosed down by any power, death or otherwise; so He could not die again if He wanted to. What is there wrapped up in this for us? The assurance that every one who shares His life will share His indissolubility.

7. **Revelation.** Christ's affirming word, as He looks out of the cycles of eternity, is, "I am alive for evermore" (Rev. i. 18). "Evermore" would be better rendered "unto the ages of the ages." What other language can express infinitude, durability, perpetuity, reliability, continuity, and eternity? And, as the Living One, Christ assures, "I have the keys of Hades and of death." Therefore, whatever the future holds, and whatever fastnesses are ahead, He has the keys to open and shut. What a revelation is this! How fully Christ has brought life and immortality to light. How all this confirms our faith, inspires our love, stimulates our zeal, moves our services, calls forth our worship, and brightens our hope.

184. CHRIST'S RESURRECTION
Matt. xxviii. 6

How many voices are heard in that silent tomb! We listen to three, as found in the following sentences: "As He said," "He is risen," "He goeth before you" (Matt. xxviii. 6, 7).

1. **Proclamation.** "He said" He would rise. He looked beyond the shame of the Cross and the gloom of the tomb. His prevision enabled Him to see beyond the shades of the unseen, and caused Him to proclaim in anticipation, "Thou wilt not leave My soul in Hades, nor suffer Thine Holy One to see corruption." The disciples, too, recognised this, for after "He was risen from the dead" they remembered He had said "this to them;" and the consequence was, "They believed the Scriptures," and the word He had said (John ii. 22).

2. **Power.** There have been men in the past justly renowned for their prowess and power. We think of such a man as Cæsar, who tramped on his way with unparalleled success; of Alexander the Great, who in his onward march of conquest was like the

incoming tide, sweeping all before Him; we call to mind a man like Napoleon the First, whose raised hand made thrones and dynasties tremble; we think of the iron Bismarck, who made France bite the dust in the seventies; and in our own time we have seen the self-inflated William of Germany making the nations bleed and suffer. But these, with one exception, have had to bow before the King of Terrors, and to-day they are but a memory.

Who can dispute with death? Only One, and that One, our Lord Jesus Christ. In His uprising from among the dead we behold the display of the "exceeding greatness of God's power." Not merely His "power," but the "greatness," yea, the "exceeding greatness of His power." Creation reveals God's power, but Christ's resurrection manifests the "exceeding greatness" of it.

3. **Presence.** Mark, the Spirit emphasises through angelic message "He is risen," and "He goeth before you," and ye "shall see Him;" and as the women went on their directed way "Jesus met them," and greeted them with the salutation, "All hail!" And they "held Him," and "worshipped Him," and He assured them they should see "Him" after they had told the disciples He was risen.

As the Philistines knew the reality and power of Samson's presence when he took away the doors, the gate, and the posts of the city of Gaza, and laughed at his enemies to their discomfort, so Christ, after He had carried away the gates of Hades by His death and resurrection, spoiled principalities and powers, and made a show of them openly. Now He stands before us in the glow and glory of His victorious presence, and says, "I am He that liveth, and was dead; and, behold, I am alive for evermore. Amen; and have the keys of Hades and of death."

185. CHRIST'S SCARS

WE shall recognise Christ by the scars of Calvary. How much those scars proclaim! They at least reveal a sevenfold colour of grace and love. They proclaim—

1. The **satisfaction** of atonement for sin—Rom. iii. 25.
2. The **price** of emancipating redemption—Eph. i. 7.
3. The **ground** of Divine forgiveness—Col. i. 14.
4. The **assurance** of eternal peace—Col. i. 20.
5. The **overthrow** of Hell's authority—Heb. ii. 14.
6. The **basis** of all blessing for spirit, soul, and body—Heb. xiii. 12, 20.
7. The **harbinger** of coming glory—1 Thess. iv. 14.

186. CHRIST'S RESURRECTION IN ROMANS

1. **Power Proclaimed.** "Declared to be the Son of God with power...by the resurrection from the dead" (i. 4).

2. **Righteousness Reckoned.** "Was raised again on account of our justification" (iv. 24, 25).

3. **Partnership Proved.** "Like as Christ was raised up from the dead, even so, " etc. (vi. 4, 9).

4. **Claim Cancelled.** "Dead to the law by the body of Christ, married to another, to Him who is raised from the dead" (vii. 4).

5. **Death Defeated.** "He that raised up Christ from the dead shall quicken your mortal bodies" (viii. 11).

6. **Accuser Answered.** "Who is He that condemneth? Christ that died, yea rather, that is risen?" (viii. 34, margin).

7. **Confession Confirmed.** "If thou shalt confess... believe...God raised Him from the dead...saved" (x. 9).

8. **Ownership Owned.** "Christ rose...that He might be Lord both of the dead and living" (xiv. 9).

187. CHRIST'S SEVENFOLD CHARACTER

In LUKE i. 5-17, 26-33; ii. 25, 26, 36, 37, 38.

1. **"The Lord"** (i. 17). John's mission was to "make ready a people prepared for the Lord, " or, as the Revised Version, "To make ready for the Lord a people prepared." A Lord for the people to meet their need, and the people for the Lord to be His joy.

2. **"Jesus"** (i. 31; ii. 21). A common name among the Jews, and yet how uncommon because of Him who bears it.

3. **"Son of the Most High"** (i. 32, R.V.). The first time God is called "The Most High God" is in Genesis xiv. 18, 19, 20, and as such He is "The Possessor of Heaven and earth." Coupled with the statement of the angel regarding Christ as "the Son of the Most High, " we see how He illustrates the original title, for as such He will be "great, " have the throne of His father David, reign over the House of Jacob, and have an unending Kingdom. Ponder the seven "shalts" and "shalls" of verses 31-33.

4. **"The Son of God"** (i. 35). Christ was God the Son before He became the Son of God; that is, in the essence of His being He was eternally the Son of God, but when the Father would express Himself in human form He became a Son.

5. **"The Consolation of Israel"** (ii. 25). "Consolation" means something or someone near who encourages, enables, and helps us along, hence to console or comfort. The words

"comfort" and "consolation" occur ten times in 2 Corinthians i. 3-7.

6. **"The Lord's Christ"** (ii. 26). When the aged Simeon took up the infant Christ in his arms he not only saw "the Lord's Christ" in the infant, but also the "Salvation," and "the Light to lighten the Gentiles" and "the glory of Israel" (ii. 30, 32).

7. **"Redemption"** (ii. 38). Christ has paid the price by His precious Blood, that He might set us at liberty—Eph. i. 7. He frees us from sin's penalty and power, and will ultimately free us from sin's presence.

188. CHRIST'S RESURRECTION PROCLAIMED

No one can read through the Book of the Acts without being convinced that Christ's resurrection is the predominating theme of its witness.

1. Luke opens his treatise by **affirming** it—i. 3.

2. Matthias is added to the apostleship that he may **bear witness** to it—i. 23.

3. Peter, on the Day of Pentecost, unfolds certain Old Testament Scriptures as **embodying the fact**—iii. 31, 32; and affirms the same fact in connection with the healing of the lame man—iii. 15.

4. The first persecution was caused by the **declaration** of Christ's resurrection—iv. 2, 10, 33.

5. Peter **preached** the resurrection of Christ again and again—v. 29-32; x. 39-41.

6. Paul is constant in his **testimony** to the resurrection of Christ—Acts xiii. 30-38; xvii. 31; xxiii. 6-10; xxiv. 15, 21; xxvi. 23.

189. CHRIST'S WORDS

OUR Lord emphasises the importance and influence of "words." His words are:

1. **God-given** in their origin—John xvii. 8.

2. **Life-giving** in their nature—John vi. 63, 69.

3. **Faith-producing** in their influence—John viii. 30.

4. **Prayer-inspiring** in their working—John xv. 7.

5. **Peace-assuring** in their benediction—Luke xxiv. 36-44.

6. **Soul-sustaining** in their intercession—John xviii. 1.

7. **Wonder-begetting** in their ministry—Luke iv. 22; xxiv. 8.

190. CHRIST'S RETURN

A MINISTER who was talking with a Christian worker said: "Christ came again twenty years ago, when He came into my heart." Whereupon the Christian worker replied: "I read in my Bible that certain things are to happen when Christ returns, and among them, the dead in Christ shall be raised and the living believers in Him will be changed. Have either of these taken place?" The question non-plussed the minister! No honest reader of the discourse of Christ as recorded in Matthew xxiv. and xxv. can deny His word about His Coming again.

His return is—

1. **Promised** by Christ—John xiv. 3.

2. **Declared** by the two men who stood by the disciples when He went away—Acts i. 11.

3. **Announced** by Peter—Acts iii. 20.

4. **Described** by Paul—1 Thess. iv. 13-18.

5. **Urged** by James—Jas. v. 7.

6. **Affirmed** by John—1 John iii. 2.

7. **Quoted** by Jude—14.

191. CHRIST'S UNCHANGINGNESS

"I change not" Mal. iii. 6

A RECENT author says: "The universe seems like a clock running down with no mechanism for winding it up again. All the uranium in the world is breaking down, and we know of no source from which new uranium can come. Under these circumstances it seems strange that there should be any uranium. But if, like some insects, we lived only for a single spring day, we should think it strange that there should be any ice in the world, since we should find it always melting and never being formed. Perhaps the universe has long cycles of alternate winding up and running down."

If men would only turn to the Sacred Page of God's Word, they would find that it has a good deal to say about God's world. To take but one passage, namely, Colossians i. 16, 17, we find creation in relation to Christ—

1. "By ("in"—"*en*") Him were all things **created**." "In Him" as to source and substance.

2. "All things were **created** by Him" as to means, for the meaning of "by," *dia* with the genitive, is an active agent producing things.

3. "All things were **created**...for Him," that is, "unto

Him, " for the "for" is *eis*, and signifies the things were for Him as the objective.

4. "He is before all things, " for He is said to be "the First-born of every creature, " or, more correctly, "born before all **creation**" (Col. i. 15).

5. "By ("in, " *en*) Him all things **consist**, " subsist, or are held together. He is the cohesive power which prevents things from being dissipated, or scattered.

Since everything depends upon the unchanging Christ, we may be sure that everything will serve its purpose. Things cannot "run down, " since all depends upon Him who upholds "all things by the Word of His power" (Heb. i. 3).

192. CHRIST'S SEVENFOLD SUFFERING

How intense were the sufferings of Christ! He suffered in a sevenfold manner.

1. At the **hands of Satan**, being tempted—Luke iv. 2.

2. He suffered at the **hands of God**, as the surety for us. "Christ hath suffered for us" (1 Peter iv. 1)

3. He suffered by **way of anticipation**. The Cross was ever before Him. "The Son of Man must suffer many things" (Luke ix. 22).

4. He suffered at the **hands of friends**. Judas betrayed Him, Peter denied Him, and all His disciples forsook Him—Luke xxii. 21, 60; Mark xiv. 50.

5. He suffered **as His holy soul came in contact with sin**—John xii. 27.

6. He suffers **in His members**—Acts ix. 4.

7. He suffered at the **hands of His enemies**—Luke ix. 22.

193. CHRIST'S SUFFERING IN HIS BODY

THINK of what they did to His body.

1. His face was **marred**—Isa. lii. 14.

2. His back was **lacerated**—Isa. l. 6.

3. His brow was **scarred**—Matt. xxvii. 29.

4. His side was **pierced**—John xix. 34.

5. His hands were **nailed** to the Cross—Luke xxiv. 39.

6. His feet were **torn**—Psa. xxii. 16.

7. His body was **exposed** to the unholy gaze of a mob—Matt. xxvii. 36-42.

194. CHRIST'S SUFFERINGS AT THE HANDS OF MEN

THINK of who His enemies were, and what they did to Him.

1. He was **reproached** by the scribes and elders—Mark xv. 1.
2. He was **despised** by the people—Matt. xxvii. 25.
3. He was **laughed** at by the crowd—Matt. xxvii. 39, 40.
4. He was **railed** at by the thieves—Luke xxiii. 39.
5. He was **falsely accused** by the priests—Mark xv. 3.
6. He was **derided** by the rulers—Luke xxiii. 35.
7. He was **questioned** by the Sadducees—Matt. xxii. 23.
8. He was **grumbled** at by the Pharisees—Mark ii. 16.
9. He was **hunted** by Satan—Luke iv. 2.
10. He was **hated** by the world—John xv. 18.
11. He was **betrayed** by Judas—Luke xxii. 47.
12. He was **played with** by Pilate—John xix. 1-10.
13. He was **mocked** by Herod—Luke xxiii. 11.
14. He was **crucified** by the soldiers—John xix. 23.

195. CHRIST STANDS ALONE

"Never Man...like this Man" John vii. 46

1. In the **Deity of His Personality**, for He is the Son of God, and God the Son—Gal. ii. 20.
2. In the **sufficiency of His atoning death**, for in the eternal value of Himself He gave Himself for us—Heb. ix. 26-28.
3. In the **vitality of His life** making men alive unto God—John x. 10.
4. In the **sublimity of the Revelation** He brings as the Word—John i. 1-14.
5. In the **suitability of His invitation** to give and find rest in Him—Matt. xi. 28, 29.
6. In the **sinlessness** and beauty of His character—Heb. vii. 26; Song of Songs v. 9-16.
7. In the **promise** of the future—John xiv. 1-6.

196. CHRIST'S STEADFASTNESS

THERE were many things which might have daunted Christ. Think of—

1. The **denial** of Peter—Luke xxii. 61.
2. The **Betrayal** of Judas—Mark xiv. 43-46.
3. The **forsaking** of His friends—Mark xiv. 50.

4. The **agony** of Gethsemane—Luke xxii. 44.
5. The **suffering** of Gabbatha—John xix. 1-6.
6. The **forsaking** by God—Matt. xxvii. 45, 46.
7. The **piercing** of the Cross—John xix. 16-18.
8. The **sin** He was to be made—2 Cor. v. 21.
9. The **curse** of a broken law He would endure—Gal. iii. 13.
10. The **judgment** He would bear—Rom. viii. 3.
11. The **wrath** through which He would pass—Rom. viii. 32-34.
12. The **life** He would lose—John xii. 24-33.
13. The **shame** He would suffer—Heb. xii. 2.
14. The **death** He would die—1 Peter iii. 18.

197. CHRIST TAKING HOLD

1. **The Omitting Redeemer.** "Not of angels, doth He *take hold*" (Heb. ii. 16, R.V.).
2. **The Incarnate Saviour.** "He *taketh hold* of the seed of Abraham" (Heb. ii. 16, R.V.).
3. **The Living Deliverer.** "*Took hold* of him" (Matt. xiv. 31, R.V.).
4. **The Children's Friend.** "He *took* a little child" (Luke ix. 47, R.V.).
5. **The Gracious Healer.** "He *took* him and healed him" (Luke xiv. 4).
6. **The Loving Leader.** "When I *took* them by the hand" (Heb. viii. 9).
7. **The Sight Giver.** "He *took hold* of the blind man by the hand" (Mark viii. 23, R.V.).

The Greek word *Epilambanomai* occurs in each of the above Scriptures, and signifies "to catch hold," "to lay hold," and "to take." It is rendered *"caught"* in Acts xvi. 19; *"lay hold"* in 1 Timothy vi. 12; and *"take hold"* in Luke xx. 20.

198. CHRIST, THE BELIEVING ONE

"He trusted in God" (Matt. xxvii. 43).
"I live by the faith of the Son of God" (Gal. ii. 20).

CHRIST is the Author and Finisher of faith—Heb. xii. 2. His life was a life of constant and unswerving faith in God. We need Christ Himself to live His life of faith, that we may have a faith which corresponds to Him. What kind of faith was Christ's?

1. **Grounded on the Scriptures.** "That the Scriptures

might be fulfilled" is not only said of Him (Matt. 12. 17;
Luke xxiv. 44), but He was ever careful to fulfil them—John
xix. 24, 36. There is no faith in God nor likeness to Christ's
faith that is not founded and grounded on the Word of God.

2. **Guarded by Prayer.** The attitude of Christ's faith is
demonstrated in His constant act of looking up to His Father—
Mark vi. 41; vii. 34. Faith is defenceless in itself, so it ever
appeals to the Lord that He may hedge the heart and life by
His protecting Presence—Job i. 10.

3. **Graced by Love.** Christ's faith was ever looking to His
Father to supply the need of others—Matt. xiv. 19. The
"work of faith" is ever wedded to the "labour of love"—
1 Thess. i. 8.

4. **Guided by the Spirit.** Christ was always dependent
upon the Spirit's guidance. He did not move in service till
He was empowered by the Spirit—see Luke iv., how this is
emphasised, verses 1, 14, 18. "Faith" for and in service is
one of the Spirit's gifts—1 Cor. xii. 9.

5. **Growth of Faith.** Of Christ in His faith, and personal
grace, it is said, "He increased in wisdom and stature" (Luke
ii. 52). Well for us if it can be said of us because of Him
"Your faith groweth exceedingly" (2 Thess. i. 3).

6. **Goal of Faith.** The object of faith is God Himself. The
enemies of Christ taunted Him that His trust in God brought
Him no relief. They looked on with the eyes of reason. Christ
trusted to reach the goal of purpose. "Have faith in God"
(Mark xi. 22) is Christ's direction, and the Spirit's commendation—1 Thess. i. 8.

7. **Glory of Faith.** Faith is a God-honouring grace, for it
brings everything to God in prayer and truth, and brings God
into everything to guide and govern. How fully Christ
illustrates, and how evidentially it is illustrated in the lives
of those mentioned in Hebrews xi.

199. CHRIST, THE CENTRE

IF we find our centre in Christ we shall find ourselves in the
circumference of life.

1. Christ is the **Central Revelation** of the Godhead. "Express
Image" (Heb. i. 3).

2. He is the **Central Cause** in creation. "All things were
created by Him" (Col. i. 16).

3. He is the **Central Figure** in History. "No man hath seen
God at any time, the Only Begotten Son...hath declared Him"
(John i. 18).

4. He is the **Central Attraction** in the Church.   "They saw the Lord" (John xx. 19-26).

5. He is the **Central Sufferer** on the Cross.   "Jesus in the midst" (John xix. 18).

6. He is the **Central Power** in the life.   "Christ liveth in me" (Gal. ii. 20).

7. He is the **Central Object** in worship.   "In the midst of the lampstands" (Rev. i. 13-20).

8. He is the **Central Glory** of the New Jerusalem.   "The Lamb is the Light thereof" (Rev. xxi. 23).

200. CHRIST, THE FOUNDATION

CHRIST is the Foundation, and if we build deep into Him, we shall become like Him.   He is a—

FIRM Foundation for stability—1 Peter ii. 6.

ORDAINED Foundation for sacrifice—1 Peter i. 20.

UNITING Foundation for security—1 Peter ii. 5.

NAMED Foundation for selection: "elect"—1 Peter ii. 6.

DURABLE Foundation for sureness—Isaiah xxviii. 16.

APPOINTED Foundation for supremacy: "chief"—1 Peter ii. 6.

TRIED Foundation for testing—1 Peter ii. 8.

INVALUABLE Foundation for preciousness: "precious"—1 Peter ii. 6.

ONLY Foundation for salvation—1 Cor. iii. 11.

NOTABLE Foundation for choice: "chosen"—1 Peter ii. 4.

201. CHRIST, THE LIVING ONE

1. **Foundation.** As "the Son of the Living God," He is the Basis of the Church—Matt. xvi. 16.

2. **Supply.** As "the Living Water," He supplies and satisfies—John iv. 10, 11.

3. **Food.** "As the Living Bread," He feeds and nourishes—John vi. 51.

4. **Power.** As the Fountain of Life, "floods of living water" flow from Christ—John vii. 38.

5. **Access.** We have access to the Lord through Him who is "the New and Living Way"—Heb. x. 20.

6. **Union.** As the "Living Stone," He makes us living stones in His life—1 Peter ii. 4.

7. **Glory.** As "the Living Hope," He gives to His own a living and lasting inheritance—1 Peter i. 3.

202. CHRIST, THE GREAT ONE
"He shall be great" Luke i. 32

THIS is one of the positive statements Gabriel gave to Mary regarding the Infant Christ. There are seven "shalt's" and "shall's." The "shalt" of incarnation: "Thou shalt conceive;" the "shalt" of designation: "shalt call His Name Jesus;" the "shall" of exaltation: "He shall be great;" the "shall" of determination: "shall be called the Son of the Highest;" the "shall" of identification: "The Lord God shall give unto Him the throne of His Father David;" the "shall" of dominion: "He shall reign over the house of Jacob for ever;" and the "shall" of continuation: "Of His Kingdom there shall be no end." Christ is great in many ways.

1. **"Great God" in Being**. "Our Great God and Saviour" (Titus ii. 13, R.V., margin). He is great in many ways. Great in *Nature*, for He is "Love;" great in *Character*, for He is holy; great in *Name*, for He is Jehovah; great in *Creation*, for His works declare His skill; great in *Revelation*, for He expresses the Father; great in *Promise*, for He is "yea and amen;" and He is great in *Purpose*, for He is the Sum of all things.

2. **"Great Love" in Action**. "Great love wherewith He loved us" (Eph. ii. 4), To take only the setting of this statement, we see seven things love does among the many, namely, *quickens* in His life, *saves* by His grace, *raises* by His power, *fashions* us by His skill, *makes* us *nigh* by His Blood, *reconciles* by His Cross, and *gives* us *access* by His Spirit—ii. 4-18.

3. **"Great Salvation" in Blessing**—Heb. ii. 3. Salvation is at least a sevenfold blessing. God is its Author, *Christ* is its Embodiment, *man* is its object, the *Holy Spirit* is its Power, *deliverance* is its meaning, *holiness* is its fruit, and *glory* is its consummation.

4. **"Great Mercy" in Grace**. "Great is His mercy towards them that fear Him" (Psa. ciii. 11). Mercy is lovingkindness in action. Joseph's lovingkindness to his brethren, David's to Mephibosheth, Ahasuerus' to Esther, Boaz's to Ruth, the Good Samaritan to the robbed, and Christ in His many acts of mercy.

5. **"Great Power" in Operation**. "Great is our Lord and of great power" (Psa. cxlvii. 5). See how His power is stated in Psalm cxlvii. Ponder the setting of the words, "healeth," "bindeth," "telleth," "lifteth," "casteth," "covereth," "prepareth," "giveth," "maketh," "filleth," "sendeth," "sheweth," etc.

6. **"Great Light" in Revelation**. "People that sat in darkness saw great light" (Isa. ix. 2). In all the religions of the

world they only lead man in on himself to fruitless effort to be good, and into the bogs of despair and the darkness of uncertainty; but not so with Christ, in Him is light to illuminate, life to quicken, love to inspire, liberty to free, bread to satisfy, joy to gladden, and power to be.

7. **"Great Rock" in Protection**. "Shadow of a great rock in a weary land" (Isa. xxxii. 2). Weariness and woe in all around us. Sorrow and pain oft distress us. Trials and temptations often haunt and harass us. Things often seem to go wrong, and we know not what to do. Then the Saviour is found to be all we need as we shelter beneath His protecting presence; and as we nestle under Him we realise the warmth of His heart, the power of His hand, and the sufficiency of His grace.

8. **"Great Shepherd" in Power**. "Great Shepherd of the sheep" (Heb. xiii. 20). Sin, Hell, death, disease, and the grave all stood in His way when He was on earth, but He banished disease, put away sin by the sacrifice of Himself, conquered the powers of Hell, vanquished death, and was victorious over the grave. Now He can overcome our enemies, keep us by His power, and lovingly tend us by His sufficient grace.

9. **"Great King" in Splendour**. "The city of the Great King" (Psa. xlviii. 2). None so great as He. He is glorious in holiness, munificent in grace, beautiful in character, unsurpassed in love, exceptional in giving, constant in care, faithful in promise, almighty in power, victorious in battle, altogether lovely in appearance, and righteous in rule.

203. CHRIST, THE OBJECT OF WONDER

THERE were many things in Christ which excited admiration and wonder.

1. His **words of grace**. "Wondered at His gracious words" (Luke iv. 22).

2. His **works of power**. "The multitude wondered when they saw," etc. (Matt. xv. 31).

3. His **way of silence**. "The governor marvelled" (Matt. xxvii. 14).

4. His **will of might**. The disciples "marvelled" when they saw Him still the tempest—Matt. viii. 27.

5. His **word of pardon**. "The multitude" "marvelled" when they "saw" what He did for the palsied man—Matt. ix. 8.

6. His **word of authority**. "Amazed at the mighty power of God and wondered" (Luke ix. 43).

7. His **wondrous Person**. The disciples "wondered" when the saw Christ—Luke xxiv. 41.

204. CHRIST, THE LADDER

Genesis xxviii. 12

"BEHOLD a ladder" (12). From John i. 51 we know that this ladder was a type of Christ as the means of communication between God and man, and man and God—John xiv. 6.

1. Christ is **a safe ladder**. He is the only means of escape from the wrath to come, from the grasp of Satan, from the dominion of sin, and the whirlpool of iniquity. A company of shipwrecked sailors, cast on the coast of Scotland at the bottom of a great precipice, where the incoming tide would have broken up their vessel and drowned them, found a ladder hanging down the precipice, which they reached from the ship's mast, and thus escaped. In like manner Christ is the way of escape from the waves of eternal death, and the righteous wrath of God.

2. Christ is **a strong ladder**. A friend of mine in going down into the hold of a vessel of which he was captain, did not know that one of the rungs of the ladder was loose or weak, and when he put his foot upon it, it gave way, and down he fell into the hold. There is no fear of Christ's giving way beneath a soul that rests on Him, for He is the Eternal Rock of ages—Isaiah xxvi. 4, margin, the sure foundation—Isa. xxviii. 16, and the strong arms of omnipotence—Deut. xxxiii. 27.

3. Christ is **a spansive ladder**. The top of the ladder that Jacob saw reached to Heaven. It did not go part of the way. The men of Babel built a tower to reach to Heaven—Gen. xi. 4. but it ended in confusion, as all man's efforts do. Not so with Christ: He goes all the way, and brings us into communication and connection with God; even as the Tay Bridge spans the Tay and connects Fifeshire with Forfarshire.

205. CHRIST, THE LIGHT

CHRIST reveals Himself as the great "I AM," as "the light of the World." Think of the beautiful metaphor of Light as applied to Christ; as the Light

1. **Christ scatters** the darkness—Exod. x. 23
2. **Christ eradiates**—Job xxxvi. 30.
3. **Christ illuminates**—Exod. xxv. 37.
4. **Christ stimulates**—Psalm cxii. 4.
5. **Christ emancipates**—Isaiah lviii. 8-10.
6. **Christ dominates**—Isaiah lx. 1-3.
7. **Christ compensates**—Psalm xcvii. 11.

206. CHRIST, THE OBJECTIVE OF LIFE

"For me to live—Christ" Phil. i. 21

IF Christ lives out His life in ours, we shall find ourselves in the objective of the life He lived, and we shall live—

1. In the **manger** of His humility—Luke ii. 7.
2. In the **workshop** of His business—Matt. xiii. 55.
3. In the **Jordan** of His submission—Matt. iii. 15, 16.
4. In the **wilderness** of His temptation—Matt. iv. 1.
5. In the **synagogue** of His Church—Luke iv. 16.
6. In the **home** of His love—Luke ii. 51.
7. In the **mountain** of His prayer—Luke vi. 12.
8. In the **world** of His compassion—Matt ix. 36.
9. In the **friendship** of His help—John xv. 14.
10. In the **boat** of His testimony—Luke v. 3.
11. In the **sphere** of His work—John ix. 4.
12. In the **will** of His Father—Luke xxii. 42.
13. In the **place** of His triumph—Col. ii. 15.
14. In the **purpose** of His determination—Heb. x. 7.
15. In the **Gethsemane** of His sorrow—Mark xiv. 32-34.
16. In the **Gabbatha** of His persecution—Mark xv. 16-20.
17. In the **power** of His Spirit—Acts i. 8; x. 38.
18. In the **Cross** of His death—John xix. 18.
19. In the **might** of His resurrection—Rom. viii. 11.
20. In the **glory** of His ascension—Col. iii. 1, 2.
21. On the **Mount** of His Transfiguration—Luke ix. 28-36.

207. CHRIST, THE REFUGE

1. Christ is a **Great Refuge**, like the city of refuge. "The Eternal God is thy refuge" (Deut. xxxiii. 27).

2. Christ is a **Goodly Refuge**, like a harbour. "Jehovah will be the Harbour of His people" (Joel iii. 16, margin).

3. Christ is a **Guarding Refuge**, like a fortress. "God is our Refuge" (Psa. xlvi. 1).

4. Christ is a **Glorious Refuge**, like a palace. "He shall hide me in His pavilion" (Psa. xxvii. 5).

5. Christ is a **Good Refuge**, like the ark. "An ark to the saving of his soul" (Heb. xi. 7).

6. Christ is a **Gracious Refuge**, like the home. "Be Thou my strong habitation" (Psa. lxxi. 3).

7. Christ is a **Gentle Refuge**, like the mother bird with her young. "He shall cover thee with His feathers" (Psa. xci. 4).

208. CHRIST, THE OVERCOMER

"The Lamb shall overcome" Rev. xvii. 14

BEFORE the days of rapid communication as we have it to-day, there was a way of transferring news by flare. When Wellington was leading our forces against France, the issue of the battle of Waterloo was to be communicated by the above means from a tower at Winchester. The message seemed to read: "Wellington defeated." The message cast gloom all over England. But it turned out that the fog and mists had obscured the message, and when it was repeated and more clearly seen, it read: "Wellington defeated the enemy." What an illustration of Christ overcoming the enemy of our lives. Christ has gotten a sevenfold victory.

1. He has been **victorious over the strong enemy**, and taken away his goods—Luke xi. 22.
2. He has "**overcome the world**" (John xvi. 33).
3. He has **destroyed the works of the Devil**—1 John iii. 8.
4. He has **spoiled principalities and powers**—Col. ii. 15.
5. He has **taken away the power of death**—Heb. ii. 14.
6. He has **bruised the serpent's head**—Gen. iii. 15.
7. He holds the **keys of Hades and of death**—Rev. i. 18.

209. CHRIST, THE SECRET OF SPIRITUAL LIFE

1. Life **from** Christ—John v. 25.
2. Life **in** Christ—Rom. viii. 2.
3. Life **with** Christ—1 Cor. i. 9.
4. Life **by** Christ—John vi. 57.
5. Life **to** Christ—2 Cor. v. 15.
6. Life **for** Christ—Phil. ii. 16.
7. Christ living **in** the believer is the secret of all—Gal. ii. 20.

210. CHRIST, THE SIGHT GIVER

THE opening of the eyes of the blind is typical of the opening of the eyes of our understanding—Acts xxvi. 18.

The Lord causes us—

1. To **see the evil** in ourselves—Rom. vii. 23.
2. To **see His worth** and work—Heb. ii. 9.
3. To **see the need** of preparing for the future—Heb. xi. 7.
4. To **see the meaning** of spiritual things—1 Cor. ii. 9
5. To **see the fulfilment** of God's promises—Heb. xi. 13.
6. To **see the end** of the Lord in discipline—James v. 11.
7. To **see the beauty** of Christ—1 Peter i. 8.

211. CHRIST, THE SON OF GOD

1. He **commended** Peter for confessing that He was more than the Son of Man—Matt. xvi. 13-17.

2. He **taught** that only God could forgive sins, and as He forgave them, therefore He must be God—Mark ii. 6-10.

3. He **affirmed** He was God when He was put upon His oath by Caiaphas to declare if He were such—Matt. xxvi. 63. 64.

4. He was **crucified** as a felon because He said He was God— Matt. xxvi. 64-66.

5. He **demonstrated** He was Deity by His resurrection from the dead—Rom. i. 4.

212. CHRIST, THE STONE

In Acts iv. 11

1. **Peculiar in Substance.** "*This* Stone" (Matt. xxi. 44). "Chief...elect, precious" (1 Peter ii. 6).

2. **Laid in Place.** "Behold, *I lay* in Zion a chief corner stone" (1 Peter ii. 6).

3. **Living in Bestowment.** "*Living* Stone...ye also, " etc. (1 Peter ii. 4, 5).

4. **Rejected in Work.** "Builders *disallowed*" (1 Peter ii. 7).

5. **Exalted in Position.** "Is *become* the *Head* of the corner" (Acts iv. 11).

6. **Mighty in Conquest.** "The Stone *smote* the image... *filled* the whole earth" (Daniel ii. 35).

7. **Stumbling in Opposition.** "Stone of *stumbling*" (1 Peter ii. 8; Rom. ix. 33).

213. CHRIST, THE TEACHER

As the gardener trains the rose tree to climb in the direction, so Christ teaches the mind to think the things of God. Some of the great things that Christ taught were—

1. The **evil of sin**—John iii. 19.

2. The **necessity of the new birth**—John iii. 3.

3. The **requirement of His death** to answer for sin— John iii. 14.

4. The **love of God** in the gift of Himself—John iii. 16.

5. The **possession of eternal life** through faith in Himself— John iii. 36.

6. The **proof of discipleship**—John viii. 31.

7. The **secret of fruit-bearing**—John xv. 5.

214. CHRIST, SON OF GOD AND GOD THE SON.

THE first chapter of Hebrews gives a fourfold Sonship of Christ.

1. His **Eternal** Sonship—1, 2, as Creator and Heir.

2. His **Expressed Sonship**—2-4, as the "Express Image" of the Godhead.

3. His **Exalted** Sonship—5, as raised from the dead.

4. His **Exhibited** Sonship—6-9, as the One who will come again.

215. CHRIST, THE SUBSTITUTE

Luke xxiii. 25

BARABBAS was released because Christ took his place, and that by the wicked choice of the people, although behind the act of man we see the hand of God's purpose. We all by our sin were parties to Christ's crucifixion. His death was no accident, it was an accomplishment of Divine intent; therefore we find in the Holy Writ that He was the—

1. **God-provided** Substitute—Rom. v. 8.

2. **Sin-made** Substitute—2 Cor. v. 21.

3. **Curse-bearing** Substitute—Gal. iii. 13.

4. **Life-sacrificed** Substitute—1 Cor. v. 7.

5. **Grace-imparting** Substitute—Rom. viii. 31-34.

6. **Holy-inspiring** Substitute—Titus ii. 14; 1 John iii. 16.

7. **Glory-securing** Substitute—1 Thess. iv. 14.

216. CHRIST, THE SUPERIOR ONE

As REVEALED IN COLOSSIANS I

1. He is **superior to all**, for He is "the Image of the invisible God" (15).

2. He is **superior in order**, for "He is before all things" (17).

3. He is **superior in creation**, for "By Him were all things created" (16).

4. He is **superior in power**, for "By Him all things consist" (17).

5. He is **superior in position**, for "He is the Head of the Body, the Church" (18).

6. He is **superior in resurrection**, for "He is the First-born from the dead" (18).

7. He is **superior in content**, for "all fulness" dwells in Him (19).

217. CHRIST, THE WORTHY ONE

1. **As Lord**, He is worthy of all homage and praise—Rev. iv. 11.

2. **As Overcomer**, He is worthy to open the Book of Earth's Government—Rev. v. 1-9.

3. **As the Lamb**, He is worthy to be exalted by, and above, angelic hosts—Rev. v. 12.

4. **As the "Good" Shepherd**, He is worthy of our faith and love, because He gave His life for us—John x. 11.

5. **As the One who bears the "worthy" Name**, He is greatest of all—James ii. 7.

6. Christ is counted worthy of **more honour than Moses**—Heb. iii. 3.

The adjective "good" in No. 4 is the same as rendered "worthy" in James 2. 7.

218. CHRIST WAS "MADE"

THINK of the *seven things* He was made.

1. As to His **humanity**, he was "made of a woman" (Gal. iv. 4).

2. As to His **genealogy**, He was "made of the seed of David" (Rom. i. 3).

3. As to His **identity**, He was "made like unto His brethren" (Heb. ii. 17).

4 As to His **humility**, He "made Himself of no reputation" (Phil. ii. 7).

5. As to His **ignominy**, He was "made a curse" (Gal. iii. 13).

6. As to His **responsibility**, He was "made under the law" (Gal. iv. 4).

7. As to His **substitutionary work**, He was "made...sin for us" (2 Cor. v. 21).

219. COMMANDS OF THE LORD

FOR WARFARE IN EPHESIANS VI

1. The **"Be Strong"** of enduement—10.
2. The **"Put On"** of equipment—11.
3. The **"Take"** of achievement—13.
4. The **"Stand"** of environment—14-17.
5. The **"Sword"** of armament—17.
6. The **"Praying"** of endowment—18.
7. The **"Watching"** of endurement—18.

220. "COATS" OF THE BIBLE

1. A **Son's Coat**. "Joseph's coat"—Gen. xxxvii. 3-33.
2. A **Priest's Coat**. "A broidered coat"—Exod. xxviii. 4, 39.
3. A **Child's Coat**. "His mother made him a little coat" (1 Sam. ii. 19).
4. A **Giant's Coat**. "Armed with a coat of mail" (1 Sam. xvii. 5).
5. A **Rent Coat**. "Came to meet him with a rent coat" (2 Sam. xv. 32).
6. A **Backslider's Coat**. "I have put off my coat" (Cant. v. 3).
7. The **Redeemer's Coat**. "His coat" (John xix. 23).
8. A **Fisherman's Coat**. "His fisher's coat" (John xxi. 7).

221. "COLD" AND ITS EFFECTS

1. A **Faithful God**. "Cold and heat, and summer and winter shall not cease" (Gen. viii. 22). The seasons are a faithful witness to His unceasing attention.
2. A **Faithless Sluggard**. "Who will not plow by reason of the cold" (Prov. xx. 4). Conditions are meant to harden us and not to be excuses for laziness.
3. A **Faithful Saying**. "As cold water is to a thirsty soul, so is good news from a far country" (Prov. xxv. 25). The good news that comes to us from the far country of God's grace is, that Christ Jesus came into the world to save sinners.
4. A **Fearful Disciple**. Peter warmed himself at the world's fire, because "it was cold" (John xviii. 18).
5. A **Fearless Apostle**. Among the many things that Paul enumerates were "fastings often and in cold" (2 Cor. xi. 27).
6. A **Faulty Condition**. "The love of many shall wax cold" (Matt. xxiv. 12).
7. A **Timely Gift**. "A cup of cold water" (Matt. x. 42).

222. COLD THINGS

1. A **Cold Day**. "Camp in the hedges in a cold day" (Nahum iii. 17).
2. A **Cold Disciple**. "It was cold" (John xviii. 18).
3. A **Cold Heart**. "Love of many shall wax cold" (Matt. xxiv. 12).

4. A Cold Drink. "Cup of cold water" (Matt. x. 42).

5. A Cold Worker. "Will not plow because of the cold" (Prov. xx. 4).

6. A Cold Apostle. "In fastings often and in cold" (2 Cor. xi. 27).

7. A Cold Harvest. "As the cold of snow in the time of harvest," etc. (Prov. xxv. 13).

223. COMFORT

THE Hebrew word *"Nacham"* means to sigh with another, and thus to have fellow-feeling. There are seven strands in this cord of love.

1. Sympathy. The sons and daughters of Jacob "rose up to comfort him," when it was thought Joseph was slain—Gen. xxxvii. 35.

2. Help. Ruth said to Boaz: "Thou hast comforted me" (Ruth ii. 13).

3. Rest. Job said, "My bed shall comfort me" (Job. vii. 13).

4. Assurance. "The Lord hath comforted His people" (Isa. xlix. 13).

5. Affection. "As one whom his mother comforteth" (Isa. lxvi. 13).

6. Supply. "Thou shalt comfort me on every side" (Psa. lxxi. 21).

7. Courage. "I, even I, am He that comforteth you" (Isa. li. 12).

224. COMFORTERS

1. The Divine Comforter. "Comfort ye,   .nfort ye My people, saith your God" (Isa. xl. 1).

2. The Tender Comforter. "As one whom his mother comforteth" (Isa. lxvi. 13).

3. The Merciful Comforter. "Thy merciful kindness to comfort me" (Psa. cxix. 76, margin).

4. The Timely Comforter. "The Lord shall comfort Zion : He will comfort all her waste places" (Isa. li. 3).

5. The Saving Comforter. "Thine anger is turned away, and Thou comforteth me: behold God is my Salvation" (Isa. xii. 1, 2).

6. The Pastoral Comforter. "Thy rod and staff they comfort me" (Psa. xxiii. 4).

7. The Loving Comforter. "The Lord...to comfort all that mourn" (Isa. lxi. 1, 2).

225. COMFORTS

1. "The **God of all Comfort**" comforts us by His Word—2 Cor. i. 3-7, R.V.

2. The **Lord Jesus comforts** us by His work. The word "Advocate" in 1 John ii. 1, is the same as used of the Holy Spirit as the "Comforter."

3. The **Holy Spirit comforts** us by His presence—John xv. 26.

4. The **Word comforts** us by its assurance—Matt. ix. 2, 22; xiv. 27; Mark x. 49; John xvi. 33; Acts xxiii. 11. The words "cheer" and "comfort" are the same.

5. **Brethren comfort** us by their fellowship—Rom. i. 12.

6. The **ministry of the Word** is meant to **comfort** or help those who listen to it—Eph. vi. 22; Col. iv. 8, 11.

7. **Christ's Coming again** is meant to **comfort** those who sorrow for their loved ones who have fallen asleep—1 Thess. iv. 13-18.

226. COMING OF CHRIST
IN 2 THESSALONIANS II

PAUL supplements and expands the truth of Christ's Coming in his second letter.

1. **Vindicator of the Tried**—i. 4-7. Mark the words "persecutions," "tribulations," "troubled," "suffer." He will trouble the troublers, and tribulate the tribulationists.

2. **Punisher of the Godless**—i. 7-9. Those who know not God, and the disobedient, will be banished from His glory and presence, into "everlasting destruction."

3. **Glorifier of His Saints**—i. 10-12. Clothed with His beauty, like Him in glory, and with Him in power, the saints will be admired by those who once afflicted them.

5. **Gatherer of His Own**—ii. 1. As a mother bird gathers her young under her wings and feathers, so the Lord will assemble His own to Himself.

5. **Destroyer of the Man of Sin**—ii. 8. In the "brightness of His Coming" the wicked one will be made to see his sin, and will be crushed to his undoing.

6. **Completer of Salvation**—ii. 13. That salvation is described as "the obtaining of the glory of our Lord Jesus Christ" (ii. 14), which means being "like" Him.

7. **Patient One Satisfied**—iii. 5, R.V. He is waiting to be with us and then the Patient One will be satisfied.

227. COMING OF CHRIST
EFFECTS OF BELIEVING IN HIS RETURN

IF we believe in the Coming of our Lord we shall be—

1. **Pure in Heart**. For every one that hath this Hope purifieth himself, even as He is pure—1 John iii. 3. Purity within is essential to rightly see without.

2. **Resolute in Purpose**. We are exhorted to "gird up the loins of our minds, be sober, and hope to the end, for the grace that is to be brought at the revelation of Jesus Christ" (1 Peter i. 13). As the girdle braces up the body, so the truth of the Lord's Coming will hold together in a resolute purpose the mind of our determination.

3. **Sanctified in Life**. The reason why the Lord sanctifies and cleanses His Church now, is that He might "present it to Himself a glorious Church" (Eph. v. 26, 27). The spotless garments of a sanctified life have a qualifying recognition in the glory of the future—Rev. xix. 7; xxi. 2.

4. **Ardent in Love**. The reason why Paul served the Lord so faithfully was because he loved the Lord so devotedly— 2 Tim. iv. 6-8.

5. **Patient in Trial**. When James exhorted patience under persecution, and a steady persistence amid ridicule, he said: "Be patient, therefore, brethren, unto the Coming of the Lord," and repeats his exhortation by saying: "For the Coming of the Lord draweth nigh" (James v. 7, 8).

6. **Expectant in Attitude**. Of the early Christians, it is said they were waiting for the Son of God from Heaven, and the outcome of knowing the grace of God is, we shall be looking for that Blessed Hope and the glorious appearing of our great God and Saviour Jesus Christ—Titus ii. 11-14; 1 Thess. i. 10.

7. **Faithful in Service**. Our Lord has bid us to occupy till He come, and as we are faithful to Him in trading with the pound of the Gospel, which He has committed to our trust, we shall be rewarded accordingly—Luke xix. 12-26.

228. COMING SUPERMAN

IN many ways the coming superman is spoken of, and in many portions of God's Word. Suppose we take one—namely, Daniel xi. 36-45. If the passage is carefully pondered, it will be found this man is—

1. **Royal in Place**, for he is called "the king."
2. **Wilful in Spirit**, for he will do "according to his will."
3. **Proud in Soul**, for "he shall exalt himself."

4. **Self-inflated in Importance**, for he will "magnify himself."

5. **Bombastic in Speech**, for "he shall speak marvellous things against the God of gods."

6. **Prosperous in Wickedness**, for "he shall prosper."

7. **Infidel in Worship**, for "he shall not regard the God of his fathers," etc. (37, 38).

8. **Despotic in Rule**, for "he shall cause them to rule."

9. **Covetous in Heart**, he "shall divide the land for gain."

10. **Victorious in War.** Mark what is said in verses 40-43.

11. **Cruel in Action**, he "shall go forth to destroy and make away many."

12. **Humiliated in Overthrow.** "He shall come to his end, and none shall help him."

229. COMMANDS OF THE LORD
JAMES IV. 7-10

WITH every command of the Lord there is a promise of help.

1. **Submission.** "Submit yourselves unto God." To give unto the Lord is to find He gives Himself to us.

2. **Opposition.** "Resist the Devil and he will flee from you." The sword of the Spirit is the sure weapon to defeat the adversary.

3. **Communion.** "Draw nigh to God, and He will draw nigh unto you." If we draw near to Him in faith and faithfulness, He will draw near to us in power and grace.

4. **Purification.** "Cleanse your hands." Dirty hands are a disgrace to a Christian and a defilement to others.

5. **Concentration.** "Purify your minds ye double-minded." Singleness of heart is the concentration of consecration.

6. **Affliction.** "Be afflicted and mourn." A contrite spirit, a weeping heart, and tears in the eyes are appreciated by God.

7. **Humiliation.** "Humble yourselves in the sight of the Lord." Humility is the queen of graces and Heaven's livery.

230. COMMANDS TO SAFEGUARD

1. "**Lay not** up for yourselves treasures upon the earth" (Matt. vi. 19).

2. "**Lean not** unto thine own understanding" (Prov. iii. 5).

3. "**Let not** your heart be troubled" (John xiv. 1).

4. "**Look not** at the things which are seen" (2 Cor. iv. 18).

5. "**Lose not** those things which we have wrought" (2 John 8).

6. "**Love not** the world" (1 John ii. 15).

7. "**Lie not** one to another" (Col. iii. 9).

231. COMPANIONS OF THE DEVIL

"WALKETH *about*, seeking whom he may devour" (1 Peter v. 8), is the description of the occupation of the adversary. There are others, like him, up to mischievous practices, who are, therefore, allied with him.

1. **A Meddlesome Talebearer.** "He that *goeth about* as a talebearer revealeth secrets" (Prov. xx. 19).

2. **A Spark Maker.** "Compass yourselves *about* with sparks," etc. (Isa. l. 11).

3. **A Gadding People.** "Why gaddest thou *about* so much to change thy way?" (Jer. ii. 36).

4. **A Backsliding Daughter.** "How long wilt thou go *about*, O thou backsliding daughter?" (Jer. xxxi. 22).

5. **A Beset Company.** "Their own doings have beset them *about*" (Hosea vii. 2).

6. **A Self-righteous Nation.** "Going *about* to establish their own righteousness" (Romans x. 3).

7. **An Idle Gossip.** "Wandering *about* from house to house" (1 Timothy v. 13).

232. COMPLAINTS

FROM WHICH THE CHURCH IN CORINTH WERE SUFFERING.

1. **Fits of Sectarianism.** "There are contentions among you" (1 Cor. i. 11-13). Self-elation is the mother of a party spirit.

2. **Fever of Discontent.** "There is utterly a fault among you, because ye go to law with one another" (1 Cor. vi. 1-8). We have rights that we may give them up.

3. **Carnality of Unspirituality.** "Ye are yet carnal" (1 Cor. iii. 1-3). A saint in a carnal state is worse than a sinner in a dead state!

4. **Swelled Head of Pride.** "Ye are puffed up" (1 Cor. v. 2). Pride always causes the head to swell with conceit, and blurs the vision. Puffed eyes indicate a bad heart.

5. **Palsy of Sloth.** The Church at Corinth allowed a brother in sin to remain in their midst, and gloried in it, hence the command to "purge out" the leaven—1 Cor. v. 1-8.

6. **Ague of Disorder.** There was a babble of tongues, and a confusion in the assembly, hence the exhortation of 1 Corinthians xiv.

7. **Hardness of Unbelief.** Unbelief is the mother of many ills. Find out those mentioned in 1 Corinthians ix. and x.

233. CONDITION OF MAN AS A SINNER
IN ROMANS V
1. **Helpless.** "Without strength" (6).
2. **Godless.** "Ungodly" (6).
3. **Sinful.** "Sinners" (8).
4. **Rebels.** "Enemies" (10).
5. **Dead.** "Death passed upon all" (12).
6. **Deficient.** "All have sinned," namely, missed the mark (12).
7. **Condemned.** "Judgment came upon all men unto condemnation" (18).

234. CONDITIONS
EVERY promise and blessing is based on conditions. When we fulfil God's conditions He fills to the full His promises.
1. **Rest of heart** comes to those who are yoked with Christ in God's will—Matt. xi. 29.
2. **Manifestations of Christ's glory** come to those who keep His commandments—John xiv. 21.
3. **Confidence towards God** is born from an uncondemning heart—1 John iii. 21.
4. **Abiding in Christ** is the secret of fruitfulness—John xv. 4.
5. **Laying aside** every weight is the precursor to winning the race—Heb. xii. 1.
6. **Spiritual-mindedness** is the essential to see God's secrets—Eph. i. 18.
7. **Prayer** is the attitude of soul to which the Spirit of God ever comes with His grace and power—Acts i. 14; ii. 1; iv. 31; xiii. 2.

235. CONFESSION
*Con*fession means more than *pro*fession. Confession means to stand with, to be in agreement with, the thing or person to whom reference is made.
1. **Confession of Sins.** "If we *confess* our sins" (1 John i. 9).
2. **Confession of Christ.** "Whosoever shall *confess* that Jesus is the Christ is born of God" (1 John iv. 15).
3. **Confession of Salvation.** "With the mouth *confession* is made unto salvation" (Rom. x. 10).
4. **Confession of Jesus as Lord.** "If thou shalt *confess* Jesus as Lord" (Rom. x. 9, R.V.).
5. **Confession to the Name.** "The fruit of our lips which make *confession* to His Name" (Heb. xiii. 15).

6. **Confession of Separation.** *"Confessed* they were strangers and pilgrims" (Heb. xi. 13).

7. **Christ's Own Confession.** "Witnessed the good *confession"* (1 Tim. vi. 13, R.V.).

Ponder Timothy's example—1 Tim. vi. 12; the Spirit's exhortation—Heb. iv. 14, R.V.; and Christ's promise—Luke xii. 8.

236. CONFESSION (DANIEL'S)
Daniel ix. 5, 6

1. **"We have sinned."** Missed the mark of God's law.
2. **"Committed iniquity."** Perverting the right.
3. **"Done wickedly."** Wrought violation and brought disturbance.
4. **"Rebelled."** Clenching the fist and defying God to His face.
5. **"Departing from Thy precepts."** Turning aside from the right way.
6. **"Departing from Thy judgments."** Ignoring the right.
7. **"Not hearkened."** Not responding to His call.

In all this there had been what Daniel calls "trespass," that is, unfaithfulness to the Lord—ix. 7.

237. CONSECRATION
AND ITS CONNECTIONS

1. **Contrition** before the Lord—Isa. lvii. 15.
2. **Concentration** on the Lord—Phil. iii. 13, 14.
3. **Conformity** to the Lord—Rom. xii. 2.
4. **Controlled** by the Lord—Phil. ii. 13.
5. **Confidence** in the Lord—Heb. x. 35; xi. 6.
6. **Contentment** with the Lord—Phil. iii. 12, 13, R.V.
7. **Confession** of the Lord—Rom. x. 9, R.V.

238. CONSECRATION

1. **Surrender** is the act of consecration—1 Chron. xii. 18.
2. **Thoroughness** is the meaning of consecration—Lev. i. 9.
3. **Obedience** is the life of consecration—Rom. vi. 17, margin.
4. **The Holy Spirit** is the Power of consecration—Acts i. 8.
5. **Joy** is the outcome of consecration—Acts v. 41.
6. **The Glory of God** is the end of consecration—2 Thess. i. 12.
7. **Christ** is the secret of consecration—Gal. ii. 20.
8. **Cleansing** is the prelude to consecration—2 Cor. vii. 1.

239. CONSECRATION

CONSECRATION may be summarised under three divisions.

1. Consecration **to God**, which means yielding all to Him—Rom. vi. 13; xii. 1.

2. Consecration **by God**. As He filled the Tabernacle—Exod. xl. 34; consumed the sacrifice on mount Carmel—1 Kings xviii. 38; and kept anything "devoted" to Him—Lev. xxvii. 28.

3. Consecration **in God**, that is, finding all in the Lord Himself, and experiencing the blessings of the 91st Psalm.

240. CONSIDER

"Consider what I say" 2 Tim. ii. 7

1. The **Sinner's Stock-taking.** "Consider your ways" (Haggai i. 5-7).

2. The **Wise Man's Pertinent Advice**. "Consider the work of God" (Eccles. vii. 13).

3. The **Student's Lesson-book**. "I will consider Thy testimonies" (Psa. cxix. 95).

4. The **Believer's Constant Outlook**. "Consider the Apostle and High Priest," etc. (Heb. iii. 1; xii. 3).

5. The **Saved One's Call to Separation**. "Hearken, O daughter, and consider" (Psa. xlv. 10).

6. The **Brethren's Provocative Action**. "Let us consider one another to provoke unto love and to good works" (Heb. x. 24).

7. The **Christian's Lessons** in botany and natural history. "Consider the lilies," "Consider the ravens" (Matt. vi. 28; Luke xii. 24).

241. "CONSIDER" AND CONCLUDE

THE word "consider" in the following Scriptures means to perceive and to see clearly, and thus come to a right conclusion.

1. "Consider **the ravens**," and "lilies," and trust in the Lord—Luke xii. 24, 27.

2. Let us consider **the "beam"** of fault in ourselves, lest we receive the rebuke of Christ, because we "consider not"—Matt. vii. 3.

3. Consider **what God does**, as Moses did the burning bush, when he "drew near to behold (consider) it"—Acts vii. 31, 32.

4. Consider **what the Lord brings** before us, like Peter when he "considered" the vision—Acts xi. 6.

5. Consider **not the natural** when a Divine promise is given, like Abraham when he "considered not his own body"—Rom. iv. 19.

6. Consider **fellow believers**, for we are charged to "consider one another"—Heb. x. 24.

7. Consider **the Lord Jesus** in His Priesthood and Apostleship—Heb. iii. 1.

242. CONTEMPT

CONTEMPT is the act of derision against another, to the depreciation of that one, and self-inflation at the expense of the contemptuous one.

1. **Sneer** of contempt.   Satan's word to Eve: "Yea, hath God said?" (Gen. iii. 1).

2. **Pride** of contempt.   Goliath's taunt to David—1 Sam. xvii. 42, 43.

3. **Self-righteousness** of contempt.   The Pharisee's reflection on the publican—Luke xviii. 11.

4. **Ridicule** of contempt.   Young men's mockery of Elisha— 2 Kings ii. 23, R. V.

5. **Aloofness** of contempt.   Pharisees and Scribes objecting to Christ receiving sinners—-Luke xv. 2; xix. 7.

6. **Mistake** of contempt.   Corinthians' reference to Paul's infirmities—2 Cor. x. 10; xi. 12.

7. **Unbelief** of contempt.   The passers-by at the Cross— Matt. xxvii. 40.

243. CONTENTMENT

"Godliness with contentment is great gain" (1 Tim. vi. 6).

CONTENTION and contentment are the same in the contents of their first two syllables, but what a difference in their contents as a whole.   The Greek words *arkeo* and *arketos* give a chain of Scriptures which tell of the soul and secret of contentment. The words are rendered "enough," "sufficient," "suffice," and "content."

1. **A Dark Past**.   "The time past of our life may suffice us" (1 Peter iv. 3).

2. **A Divine Saviour**.   "Shew us the Father and it sufficeth us," etc. (John xiv. 8).

3. **A Glorious Assurance**.   "My grace is sufficient for thee" (2 Cor. xii. 9).

4. **A Happy Companionship.** "It is enough that the disciple be as His Lord" (Matt. x. 25).

5. **An Imperative Command.** "Be content with such things as ye have" (Heb. xiii. 5).

6. **A Needful Reminder.** "Sufficient unto the day is the evil thereof" (Matt. vi. 34).

7. **A Contented Conclusion.** "Having food and raiment, let us therewith be content" (1 Tim. vi. 8).

244. "CONTINUE"

1. "Continue **following the Lord** your God" (1 Sam. xii. 14).
2. "Continue **in My Word**" (John viii. 31).
3. "Continue ye **in My Love**" (John xv. 9).
4. "Continue **in the Grace of God**" (Acts xiii. 43).
5. "Continue **in the Faith**" (Acts xiv. 22).
6. "Continue **in Prayer**" (Col. iv. 2).
7. "Continue **in Faith and Charity**" (1 Tim. ii. 15).

245. "CONTINUED"

1. Continued **Prayer**—Acts i. 14.
2. Continued **Practice**—Acts ii. 42, 46.
3. Continued **Knocking**—Acts xii. 16.
4. Continued **Ministry**—Acts xviii. 11.
5. Continued **Speech** —Acts xx. 7.
6. Continued **Fasting**—Acts xxvii. 33.
7. Continued **Testimony**—Acts xxvi. 22.

246. "CONTRARY TO JESUS"

PAUL acknowledged he was wrong when he acted as Saul, although he thought he was right—1 Tim. i. 13. He was acting "contrary to the Name of Jesus" (Acts xxvi. 9). We are always wrong when we act "contrary" to Him.

To go contrary to Him is when we are—

1. **Blinded** by prejudice—2 Kings v. 11.
2. **Surfeited** by worldliness—Luke xxi. 34.
3. **Obsessed** by error—1 Tim. i. 10.
4. **Swayed** by Satan—Luke xxii. 31-34.
5. **Inflated** with pride—1 Tim. iii. 6.
6. **Dominated** by self—3 John 9.
7. **Moved** by envy—Acts xiii. 45.

247. CONTRARINESS

1. Contrary **Walk**—Lev. xxvi. 21, 23, 27, 40.
2. Contrary **Wind**—Matt. xiv. 24.
3. Contrary **Worship**—Acts xviii. 13.
4. Contrary **Ways**—Acts xxvi. 9.
5. Contrary **to God's Word**—Rom. xvi. 17; 1 Tim. i. 10.
6. Contrary **to each other**—flesh and Spirit—Gal. v. 17.
7. Contrary **things removed** by the Cross—Col. ii. 14.

248. CONVERSION OF PAUL

AS GIVEN IN ACTS XXVI. 13-15, 19

PAUL was arrested by Christ, convicted of his sin—13, 14, and then acknowledged Christ as "Lord" (15), and then bears his testimony to his obedience to the "Heavenly Vision" (19). That "vision"—

1. Gave him a **sight of himself**—1 Tim. i. 13.
2. Caused him **to appreciate Calvary**—Gal. ii. 20.
3. Made him **to see the Risen Christ**—1 Cor. xv. 8.
4. Brought him **forgiveness of sins**—Acts xiii. 38.
5. **Fired him** with a holy passion—2 Cor. v. 14.
6. **Moved him** to sacrifice himself—Phil. ii. 17, R.V.
7. Opened his eyes **to a different outlook**—Titus ii. 12.

249. CONVERTING POWER OF THE CROSS

"Christ crucified, the power of God" (1 Cor. i. 23, 24).

WHAT do the Scriptures say the Cross is? It is—

1. The **burden and symbol** of His sufferings for sin—John xix. 17-19.
2. The **lowest rung** in the ladder of His obedience—Phil. ii. 8.
3. The **means** by which **reconciliation** is made—Col. i. 20-22.
4. The **remover** of the claim and curse of the law—Col. ii. 14.
5. The **effective power** to bless—1 Cor. i. 17.
6. The **cause of condemnation** to those who despise it—1 Cor. i. 18.
7. An **example for the believer** to follow Him—Heb. xii. 2; Matt. xvi. 24.

250. "COULD NOT"

1. **An Impossible Task.** To be justified by law. "Could not be justified" (Acts xiii. 39).

2. **An Incompetent Ritual.** The sacrifices under law "could not make...perfect" (Heb. ix. 9).

3. **An Inadequate Medium.** "What the law could not do, in that it was weak through the flesh" (Rom. viii. 3).

4. **An Incomparable Saviour.** "He could not be hid" (Mark. vii. 24).

5. **An Impassionate Cry.** "They could not cure him" (Matt. xvii. 16).

6. **An Immovable House.** "Could not shake it" (Luke vi. 48).

7. **An Indifferent State.** "Could not believe" (John xii. 39; Heb. iii. 19).

251. COURAGE

Joshua i

COURAGE is the grace of fearlessness. It is born of truth; it is dominated by righteousness, and its highest form is begotten by the fear of God.

1. **Feet of Courage**—2, 11. "Go over this Jordan" is the Lord's distinct and definite command. There were many things in the way of their going; the Jordan in its flow, Jericho with its walls, and the Canaanites in their opposition; but when the Lord says "Go," it is not for us to reason, but to respond. The one thought that dominated the minds of our soldiers and thinking men in the Great War was that they were contending for the right against the arrogance of might, hence they had winged feet in their cause. When we know we are right, difficulties will not daunt us, but, like Paul, we shall press forward –Phil. iii. 14; 2 Tim. iv. 7, 8.

2. **Ground of Courage**—6, 9, 18. The ground of courage is the Lord's command and His promise. When the Lord commands us and we obey, courage will come to us; His presence will sustain us; His promises will cheer us; and what He pledges will attract us. Ruskin says of the Book of Joshua, "It is a book which tells us, straight from the lips of God, all we ought to do, and need to know; a book to be trusted as a Captain's order, to be heard and obeyed at our peril."

There are many commands which may be found in Joshua i. The following nine are some of them: "Go over," "Be strong,"

"Be of a good courage, " "Observe to do, " "Not depart, " "Meditate, " "Be not afraid, " "Be not dismayed, " and "Remember. "

3. **Action of Courage**—7, 8. "Observe to do" is the clarion note which is sounded right through the chapter. "The law" was what they were to "observe to do. " They were to observe "*all,*" not some of it. They were not to deviate from it either "to the right hand or to the left. " The law was not to depart out of their mouth, and it was to be always with them; hence they were to "meditate therein day and night;" and then the Lord promised them good success and prosperity.

4. **Face of Courage**—9. If we can with confidence look into the face of God, we shall be able to look into the faces of men, for the Lord bids us "not to be afraid" nor "dismayed. " One of the greatest things that was said of John Knox was, he never feared the face of man; and when he heard one of Queen Mary's attendants say of him, "He is not afraid, " as the attendant referred to the anger of the Queen against Knox, he replied, "Why should the pleasing face of a gentlewoman afray me, when I have looked into the faces of many angry men, and yet have not been afraid?" When our heart is in the will of God, and we are following in the steps of Him who set His face like a flint—Isa. 1. 7, we can go steadfastly on, though, as with Him, a cross of Calvary lies in front of us—Luke ix. 51.

5. **Mind of Courage**—8, 13. The twofold injunction which relates to the mind is: "Meditate" and "Remember. " When the mind muses on the Word of the Lord with an intense regard, it will cause the fire of devotion to burn with an ardent flame, which will show itself in a ready response to what the Lord enjoins; and when we "remember" what the Lord has promised, it will cause us to enjoy what He has given. If the mind of memory is keen to do the Lord's biddings, the music of the life will harmonise with it.

6. **Strength of Courage**. The Lord said, "I will be with thee" (5), and He followed it up by saying, "The Lord thy God is with thee, whithersoever thou goest" (9). The presence of the Lord is the secret of everything. It is the Giver of rest, as Moses found; it is the Soul of prosperity, as Joseph experienced; it is the Cause of victory, as David knew; it is the Sustainer in trial, as Paul enjoyed; and it is the Companionship in solitude, as John in Patmos discovered.

Someone once wanted to frighten Billy Bray as he journeyed home on a dark night along a country lane, by shouting to him out of the hedge, "Billie, the Devil is in the hedge, " to which he replied, "Bless the Lord, I did not think he was so far off as that, " and went on his way singing.

252. "COVERED"

1. **Worship**, or a covered face. "He covered his face" (Isa. vi. 2).

2. **Work**, or the covered Heavens. "His glory covered the Heavens" (Hab. iii. 3).

3. **Grace**, or the covered sinner. "I covered thy nakedness... I covered thee with silk" (Ezek. xvi. 8, 10).

4. **Blessedness**, or sin covered. "Blessed is the man whose sin is covered" (Psa. xxxii. 1; lxxxv. 2; Rom. iv. 7).

5. **Goodness**, or God's provision. "The pastures are clothed with flocks, the valleys are covered with corn" (Psa. lxv. 13).

6. **Beautified**, or grace's adornment. "Though ye have lien among the pots, yet shall ye be as the wings of a dove covered with silver, and her feathers with yellow gold" (Psa. lxviii. 13).

7. **Protection**, or covered servant. "I have covered thee in the shadow of Mine hand" (Isa. li. 16).

253. CRAFTINESS

THE word "craftiness" is rendered "subtilty" in 2 Corinthians xi. 3; and "cunning craftiness" in Ephesians iv. 14.

1. Craftiness **looks out for number one**, like Judas—John xii. 6.

2. Believes in **securing the best**, like Jacob—Gen. xxvii. 36.

3. **Sacrifices principle** to gain its own end, like Balaam—2 Peter ii. 15; Jude 11.

4. **Juggles with its conscience**, like Ananias—Acts v. 2.

5. **Passes itself off for what it is not**, like the spies employed by the priests—Luke xx. 23.

6. And **baits the hook of disobedience** with the bait of plausibility, like Satan did for Eve—2 Cor. xi. 3.

254. CREATION PROVES A CREATOR

THERE is one of two things to do: either to accept what the Scriptures affirm, that there was a "beginning" to creation, and hence a Creator; or accept the hypothesis there was no Creator, and everything produced itself!

What do the Scriptures affirm?

1. God is the **Originator of all things**, for in "the beginning God created the Heaven and the earth" (Gen. i. 1).

2. God is the **Creator of man**, and that man owes his being to Him, who caused him to be—Gen. i. 27; v. 1, 2; vi. 7; Isa. xlv. 12.

3. The **seen things** of creation **proclaim** Him, who made them what they are—Rom. i. 20.

4. That creation is referred to as **an illustration of God's grace**, for He who caused the light to shine out of darkness hath shined in our hearts—2 Cor. iv. 6.

5. The creature is **dependent upon the Creator** for his existence, for in Him we live and move and have our being—Acts xvii. 24-28.

6. The man of God **recognises he needs the help** of the Creator to help him in time of need—Psa. cxxi. 2; Acts iv. 24.

7. That **everything** was made by, sustained in, **created for Christ**—John i. 3; Col. i. 16-19.

Thus we see Christ, God, and the Scriptures centre in and are held together by God the Creator. Accept the extreme position of evolutionists, and we have nothing but the nebulous gas of pantheism; but receive the Scriptures as they reveal God, and in Christ we find One who cares, and loves, and blesses.

255. CRIES IN PLACES

1. A cry in the **wilderness**. John the Baptist—Matt. iii. 3.

2. A cry in a **cemetery**. The demoniac—Mark v. 5.

3. A cry by the **roadside**. The blind man—Matt. ix. 27.

4. A cry in the **temple**. "Children crying in the temple" (Matt. xxi. 15).

5. A cry in the **night**. "At midnight there was a cry" (Matt. xxv. 6).

6. A cry in a **garden**. The Saviour in Gethsemane—Heb. v. 7.

7. A cry in the **heart**. Spirit in the believer—Gal. iv. 6.

256. CRITICS AND GOD'S WORD

THESE critics often remind us of those who—

1. **Handle** the Word of God deceitfully—2 Cor. iv. 2.

2. **Corrupt** it wickedly—2 Cor. ii. 17.

3. **Wrest** it wrongfully—3 Peter iii. 16.

4. **Make** shipwreck of the faith disastrously—1 Tim. i. 19.

5. **Deny** the faith vigorously—1 Tim. v. 8.

6. **Err** from the faith woefully—1 Tim. vi. 10.

7. **Who** have itching ears continually—2 Tim. iv. 3.

257. CROSS ASSURES THE MILLENNIUM

THE Cross of Christ's atoning sacrifice is the basis by which sin will be taken away, for this is essential before there can be any Millennium. John's message, "Behold the Lamb of God which taketh away the sin of the world" (John i. 29) is far-reaching in its effects.

1. **Provisionally,** Christ's death declares sin is "put away" as a hindrance between God and man—Heb. ix. 26.

2. **Substitutionally,** Christ has borne our sins in His own body on the tree—1 Peter ii. 24.

3. **Practically,** sin is put away from the life of the believer in Christ, for he has died to it in Him, and it is no longer his master—Rom. vi. 17, 18.

4. **Prophetically,** sin will ultimately be rid out of the world; although not completely so in the Millennium, it will be in the golden age of the Lamb, when in the new Heavens and in the new earth righteousness will dwell, and that because the Lamb will be the light. All things will be reconciled "unto Himself," by means of Him who shed His precious blood on the Cross; yea, the Spirit says, "By" (By means of Him), "whether they be things in (upon) earth, or things in Heaven" (Col. i. 20).

258. CRUELTY TO PAUL

PONDER the many expressive words which embody the acts of cruelty as stated in Acts xxi., xxii., and xxiii.

1. The **"stirred"** of unholy agitation.

2. The **"laid hands** on them" of arresting hate—xxi. 27.

3. The **"moved"** of troublesome opposition.

4. The **"took"** of violent arrest—xxi. 30.

5. The **"went to kill"** of diabolical intent—xxi., 31; xxiii. 12.

6. The **"beating"** of wanton malice—xxi. 32.

7. The **"bound"** of curtailed liberty—xxi. 33.

8. The **"violence"** of turbulent rage—xxi. 35.

9. The **"away with him"** of unjust persecution—xxi. 36; xxii. 22.

10. The **"scourging"** of unkind treatment—xxii. 24.

11. The **"pulled in pieces"** of malicious handling—xxiii. 10.

12. The **"kept"** of solitary confinement—xxiii. 35.

If we suffer for Christ rightly we shall get the suffering from the world rigorously. Suffering is better than sinning; as Mr. Spurgeon says, "There is more evil in a drop of sin than in an ocean of affliction. Better burn for Christ than turn from Christ."

259. "CRUCIFIED TO THE WORLD"
Galatians vi. 14
1. Crucified to its "**sin**" (Rom. vi. 6).
2. Crucified to its "**wisdom**" (1 Cor. i. 20).
3. Crucified to its "**friendship**" (Jas. iv. 4).
4. Crucified to its "**things**" (1 John ii. 15-17).
5. Crucified to the "**pollutions**" of the world (2 Peter ii. 20).
6. Crucified to the "**elements**" of the world (Gal. iv. 3, 9; Col. ii. 8).
7. Crucified to the "**course**" of the world (Eph. ii. 2).
8. Crucified to the **contaminations** of the world (Jas. i. 27).
9. Crucified to the "**corruption**" of the world (2 Peter i. 4).
10. Crucified to the "**care**" of the world (1 Cor. vii. 32-34).
11. Crucified to the "**filth**" of the world (1 Cor. iv. 13).
12. Crucified to the "**spirit**" of the world (1 Cor. ii. 12).

260. CUT
A GOSPEL address may be compiled from the relative use of the word "cut."

1. **Obstacles Removed**. "Cut down their groves" (Deut. vii. 5; 2 Chron. xiv. 3; xxxi. 1; xxxiv. 7). The groves were identified with idol worship and sin.

2. **Oblation Made**. "Cut off out of the land of the living" (Isa. liii. 8; Daniel ix. 26). Christ's death was no accident. It was God's giving, and of God's laying down, but sin was its cause.

3. **Obstinacy Rebuked**. "Cut to the heart" (Acts v. 33; vii. 54), or, more correctly, "sawn through," so they were completely confounded.

4. **Offering Parted**. "Cut the ram in pieces" (Exod. xxix. 17; Lev. viii. 20). The ram was offered, and the blood of it was applied to Aaron and his sons at their consecration to the priesthood. The several parts of the ram were for Jehovah and the priests (Exod xxix. 17-28).

5. **Obstruction Uprooted**. "Cut it down" (Luke xiii. 7) means to cut out (*ek kopto*). There is only one thing to do with that which cumbers, and that is, remove the encumbrance— Rev. ii. 5.

6. **Omnipotence Displayed**. "Cut out of the mountain" (Dan. ii. 34, 45), which expresses Christ in His might overthrowing the world powers.

7. **Offensive Tongue**. "The froward tongue shall He cut out" (Prov. x. 31). The best way to deal with that which is dangerous is to remove it.

261. DANIEL

AN ACROSTIC STUDY IN CHARACTER

CHARACTER is what we are in the value of our being, as the gold coin rings out its worth as it is flung on the counter. Think of the character Daniel was. We might make an acrostic on his name.

Devout character, for the "Spirit of the holy" (Dan. v. 11) was seen in him, even as the prism reveals the colours of the rainbow.

Attractive character, for there was found in him "light," "understanding," and "wisdom," even as the light, heat, and colour are seen in the gaslight—Dan. v. 11.

Noble character, for even the king, who was condemned, appreciated his worth by clothing him in royal apparel and making him a ruler in his kingdom—Dan. v. 29.

Incisive character, for as the chisel cuts the wood, so Daniel by his insight into God's ways made known the handwriting on the wall—Dan. v. 25-27.

Excellent character. As the diamond flashes out its worth through the light, so the excellency of the prophet was acknowledged—Dan. v. 12.

Living character. No character is living in the truest sense which does not find its source and stream in God Himself. It is the living flower which emits perfume—Ezek. xiv. 14.

262. DANIEL'S PROTECTOR

AS SEEN IN DANIEL VI. 19-23

DANIEL's testimony regarding God's protection is explicit. There are seven things about the protection. It was—

1. **Divine in its help**, for it was "God" who shielded him.

2. **Personal in its benefit**, for Daniel said, *"My God."*

3. **Angelic in its medium**, for the "angel" shut the lions' mouths.

4. **Responsive in its blessing.** There are three reasons given why Daniel was delivered: "innocency was found" in him; he had "done no hurt" to the king; and he "believed in his God."

5. **Gladdening in its outcome**, for the king was "exceeding glad" when he found Daniel safe.

6. **Delivering in its end**, for Daniel was "taken out of the den."

7. **Perfect in its service**, for "no manner of hurt was found upon him"

263. DANIEL PRAYING

OR FAITH ILLUSTRATED—Dan. vi. 10, 11

1. The **Courage of Faith.** "When Daniel knew the writing was signed," etc.
2. The **Outlook of Faith.** "His windows being opened towards Jerusalem."
3. The **Humility of Faith.** "He kneeled upon his knees."
4. The **Method of Faith.** "Three times a day."
5. The **Worship of Faith.** "Prayed and gave thanks," etc.
6. The **Consistency of Faith.** "As he did aforetime."
7. The **Place of Faith.** "Before his God."

264. DAY BY DAY

1. **A Daily Burnt Offering.** CONSECRATION. "Daily burnt offering" (Num. xxix. 6). Attitude of the saint maintained as a result of the act of consecration in surrender.
2. **A Daily Worship.** THANKSGIVING. "Daily shall He be praised" (Psa. lxxii. 15). The essence of worship is praise to the Lord for what He is and does.
3. **A Daily Supplication.** NEED EXPRESSED. "I cry unto Thee daily" (Psa. lxxxvi. 3). "Give us this day our daily bread" (Matt. vi. 11). Prayer is the channel which keeps us in touch with God's supplies.
4. **A Daily Vigilance.** ALERTNESS. "Watching daily at My gates" (Prov. viii. 34). Watching for His leading and watching against our enemies.
5. **A Daily Cross.** DENIAL OF SELF. "Take up his Cross daily and follow Me" (Luke ix. 23). Following Christ in the denial of self, and in doing God's will.
6. **A Daily Searching.** TRACKING. "Searched the Scriptures daily" (Acts xvii. 11). Following on the trail of God's game till we catch the things of the Spirit and make them our own.
7. **A Daily Dying.** CO-CRUCIFIXION. "I die daily" (1 Cor. xv. 31). Reckoning we are dead with Christ, we are prepared to die for Him, and to die in Him.
8. **A Daily Care.** DUTY. "That which cometh upon me daily: the care of all the churches" (2 Cor. xi. 28). Duty fulfilled is blessing secured.
9. **A Daily Exhortation.** HELPFULNESS. "Exhort one another daily" (Heb. iii. 13). Love is concerned about the welfare of others.

265. DARKNESS AND ITS TREASURES

C. H. SPURGEON, on one occasion, was in Richmond Park with a friend, who was reading to him, and in the course of reading he read: "And it was now dark, and Jesus was not come to them." "Stay!" said C.H.S. "That is ugly! Dark! and Jesus was not come to them," and he relapsed into silence. Here are some sparklets of thought to pass on—

1. Don't be surprised when seeking the light if **you come into the dark.** Job long ago declared, "When I waited for light there came darkness" (Job. xxx. 26).

2. **When we are in the dark,** and have no light, we have the opportunity to trust in the Lord and stay upon Him—Isa. l. 10.

3. The **darkness is the opportunity** for the Lord's succour, for He maketh light to arise in the darkness—Psa. cxii. 4.

4. There are **"treasures of darkness,"** so don't be in a hurry to get out of it, lest you should miss them—Isa. xlv. 3.

5. There is **never a darkness** through which we may pass but what it is light in comparison to that which the Lord passed through for us on the Cross—Mark xv. 33.

6. If we seek **Christ in the dark,** like Mary Magdalene, who came to the sepulchre while "it was yet dark," we shall find Him—John xx. 1.

7. Christ will **not leave us in the dark,** so let us keep on rowing, as the disciples did, and it will not be long before we shall "see Jesus," and hear His, "It is I, be not afraid" (John vi. 17-21).

266. "DAY OF THE LORD"

IN Zechariah xiv. 4-21, we have seven times over what shall take place "in that day"—that is, the day of Millennial glory, when the Lord shall tabernacle amongst us again.

1. **Arrival of the Lord with His saints,** at the commencement of His tabernacling. "His feet shall stand in that day upon the Mount of Olives" (4).

2. **Darkness leading to light** will be the phenomenon "at that day." The American Revised Version of verses 6 and 7 reads: "In that day there shall not be light, the bright ones shall withdraw themselves (the stars)...but at evening time it shall be light"—that is, as Von Orelli says: "The light of salvation will break its way through the night of judgment"—see Isa. xxx. 26.

3. **Living waters blessing the earth.** "It shall be in that day living waters will go out of Jerusalem" (8). The river

described in Ezekiel xlvii. will bring blessing in its onward and deepening flow.

4. Christ's Universal Reign. "The Lord shall be King over all the earth in that day" (9). All the nations will know the right and might of His reign.

5. Christ's might Victorious over His enemies. The peoples that have warred against the Lord shall be brought under His judgment "in that day" (12-15, A.R.V.).

6. "Holiness unto the Lord" shall characterise everything "in that day" (20). Everything shall be sacred to Him.

7. Exclusion of the enemy. "In that day there shall no more be the Canaanite in the house of the Lord of Hosts" (21). The trafficker for self and sin will be excluded.

All this is preceded by Judah looking upon Him whom they have pierced, and in knowing Him who was smitten by the sword of Jehovah on their behalf—Zech. xii. 10; xiii. 7.

267. DEATH OF CHRIST

THERE are several ways in which the death of Christ is stated, each of which has its own touch of meaning.

1. A Sinful Act. "Being put to death in the flesh" (1 Peter iii. 18).

2. A Saving Atonement. "Through His Blood" (Eph. i. 7).

3. A Suffering Attachment. "The Cross of Christ...the marks of Jesus" (Gal. vi. 14-17).

4. A Slain Servant. "He came to give His life a ransom" (Matt. xx. 28).

5. A Soul Travailed. "The travail of His soul" (Isa. liii. 11).

6. A Sacrifice Given. "Christ our Passover is sacrificed for us" (1 Cor. v. 7).

7. A Submerged Saviour. "I have a baptism to be baptised with" (Luke xii. 50).

268. DEATH OF CHRIST
Continued

1. Proclamation of His Death. "Spake of His decease" (Luke ix. 31).

2. Place of His Death. "Where (Calvary) sin abounded, grace did much more abound" (Rom. v. 20).

3. Pleasure of His Death. "Gave Himself an offering and sacrifice to God for a sweet-smelling savour" (Eph. v. 2).

4. **Partakers** of His Death. "Died the Just for the unjust to bring us to God" (1 Peter iii. 18).

5. **Passion** of Christ's Death. "After His passion" (Acts i. 3).

6. **Provision** of His Death. "The Good Shepherd giveth His life for the sheep" (John x. 11).

7. **Planting** of Christ's Death. "Except a corn of wheat fall into the ground," etc. (John xii. 24, 25, 33).

269. DEBORAH THE PATRIOT
Judges iv. 1-16

THERE are three outstanding features we find in the Book of Judges. First, the repeated sin of the children of Israel and the consequent loss and bondage which came to them. Second, the Lord's gracious intervention in raising up deliverers when the children of Israel cried unto Him. Third, the power of the Holy Spirit which came upon the deliverers, qualifying them for their work.

1. **A Sad Repetition**—1, 2. The children of Israel did evil again, and it seems as if it was done with unblushing effrontery, for it was "in the sight of the Lord," and the result was the Lord sold them into the hand of Jabin, the king of Canaan. The repetition of sin will harden the heart, sear the conscience, darken the understanding, blur the vision, lower morality, divert the feet, and separate from God.

2. **A Supplicating Request**—3. The children of Israel "cried unto the Lord," and two reasons are given; because Jabin "mightily oppressed" them, and that for the long period of twenty years; and he seems to have done them unparalleled injury, for when he came against them he had many chariots of iron, and to these chariots of iron were fastened long scythes to the orbs of the wheels, which would cut those who were invaded in a terrible way. The only hope for them was the Lord, so they supplicated for His help. Prayer to the Lord will bring help from Him when everything else has failed. Prayer brought a nation out of Egypt—Exod ii. 23; victory to Hezekiah—2 Kings xix. 15-19; success to Nehemiah—Neh. iv. 9; salvation to Jonah—Jonah ii. 1-10; cleansing to the leper—Matt. viii. 2-4; help to Peter—Matt. xiv. 31; and power to the disciples at Pentecost—Acts i. 14; iv. 31.

3. **A Second Resource**—4-9. Deborah sent to Barak and advised him what to do in order that deliverance might come to Israel, but Barak would not go against the enemy unless Deborah went with him. She responded to the request, but she reminded Barak that a twofold loss would ensue, for it would

not be to his honour, and that Sisera, the leader of the foe,
would be delivered into the hand of a woman. We often find
that when man fails God uses a woman to accomplish His
purpose. The great lesson is that when the Lord calls us to do a
thing we should promptly obey His voice, for if we do not it
means loss to us.

4. A Sound Rout—10-16. With the encouragement of
Deborah, and the advice of Heber, Barak went up against
Sisera and completely routed all the invading host, so that every
one fell by the edge of the sword except Sisera, for the marginal
reading implies there was one left ("All fell...unto one").
Besides, we read that Sisera fled away to the tent of Jael, and, as
Deborah had predicted, he was slain by a woman—18-23.
God is recognised as the One who gave the victory over Israel's
enemies.   Reference should be made to the song of Deborah
and Barak as recorded in Judges v., for it is a tribute of praise
to the Lord's delivering grace. The Lord who gave victory
over the enemies of Israel is the One who will give us victory
over our enemies. Mr. Spencer Walton used to tell a story about
two boys who were fighting, and the boy who got the worst of
the fray said to the other one, "You wait here while I go and fetch
my big brother, and he will give you such a licking!" We
should never fight our own battles, but always call in the Lord
Jesus, who will crucify the flesh, conquer the world, and defeat
the Devil. When the hand of our faith grips the hand of our
Saviour, His hand of power will grip our hand and give us the
victory, so let us sing in faith:

> I'm gripped by Thine all-conquering hand;
> Thy hand shall hold me fast;
> Thy love and grace shall keep me safe
> And bring me home at last.

270. DEFINITE DETAILS OF PROPHECY

In 2 Thessalonians ii. 1-12 r.v.

1. The Definite Hope of the Believer. "The Coming of the
Lord Jesus and our gathering together unto Him." This is the
one event for which the Church is waiting.

2. The Definite Period of the Lord's Rule. "The Day
of the Lord." That is the 1000 years of Christ's reign on
the earth.

3. The Definite Apostasy Foretold. "*The* falling away."
Not *a* falling away, but "*the*" falling away, that is, the open
denial of the Father and the Son.

4. The Definite Character of the Anti-Christ. "The man
of sin," Not a system, but a "man."

5. **The Definite Title given to Anti-Christ.** "The Son of Perdition." Not one who goes into perdition, but who comes out of it.

6. **The Definite Place in which he will Sit.** "The Temple of God." Not a spiritual edifice, but a temple in Jerusalem.

7. **The Definite Mystery now at Work.** "The mystery of lawlessness." The spirit of self-will opposing God's will.

8. **The Definite Hinderer Removed.** "Until it be taken out of the midst." When the hindering power is taken away, the system of lawlessness will develop into the lawless one.

9. **The Definite Revelation of the Anti-Christ.** "Then shall *that* wicked one be revealed" ("the lawless one," R.V.). The word *"revealed"* means to uncover, so that which had been concealed shall be seen.

10. **The Definite Presence of Christ.** "Whom *the* Lord shall consume." The nailed hand of Calvary will effectually deal with the mailed might of satanic opposition.

11. **The Definite Means of Anti-Christ's Overthrow.** *"The* Spirit of His mouth." This, like Revelation xix. 15, and Hebrews iv. 12, is a symbolic expression to denote the authority and power of His commanding utterance.

12. **The Definite Manifestation of Christ's Coming.** "Shall destroy with the brightness of His Coming." The flashing out of Christ's inherent glory will blind and blast the Anti-Christ.

13. **The Definite Worker behind the Anti-Christ.** "Whose coming is after the working of Satan." The moving and moulding power behind the man of sin is the god of this world.

14. **The Definite Cause of the People Being Deceived.** "Because they received not the love of the truth." The truth is that which makes true, and to love it means to be made like it. Not to love the truth is to become a lie and lying.

15. **The Definite Lie Believed.** "That they should believe *the* lie," that is, the lie avowed that he is Christ.

16. **The Definite Unbelief Specified.** "Believed not *the* truth." Unbelief deforms the heart and life and makes them decrepit and dead.

271. DEGREES OF FAITH

1. **"Full faith"** of satisfaction (Acts vi. 5).
2. **"Great faith"** of confidence (Matt. xv. 28).
3. **"Continue in"** faith of progress (Acts xiv. 22).
4. **"Established in"** faith of steadfastness (Acts xvi. 5).
5. **"Joy of faith"** of exultation (Phil. i. 25).

6. **"Work of faith"** of effectuality (2 Thess. i. 11).
7. **"Unfeigned faith"** of sincerity (2 Tim. i. 5).
8. **"Full assurance of faith"** of consecration (Heb. x. 22).
9. **"Prayer of faith"** of intercession (James v. 15).
10. **"So great faith"** of excellence (Matt. viii. 10).

272. DEMONIAC
Before and After he Met with Christ
Before—Possessed by Demons
1. "Had devils" (Luke viii. 27).
2. "Among the tombs" (Mark v. 3).
3. "Bound with fetters" (Mark v. 4).
4. "No man could tame him" (Mark v. 4).
5. "Crying" (Mark v. 5).
6. "Cutting himself" (Mark v. 5).
7. "No clothes" (Luke viii. 27).
After—Liberated by Christ
1. "Devils were departed" (Luke viii. 35).
2. "At the feet of Jesus" (Luke viii. 35).
3. "Sitting" (Mark v. 15).
4. "In his right mind" (Luke viii. 35).
5. "Prayed Him" (Mark v. 18).
6. "Go home to thy friends" (Mark v. 19).
7. "Clothed" (Luke viii. 35).

273. DEVOTION OF THE VIRTUOUS WOMAN
The devotion of the "virtuous woman" described in Proverbs xxxi., is seen in her saintliness, service, and sacrifice. Mark seven traits of her character, and find the rest.

1. Her **Trustworthiness**. "Safely trust her" (11).
2. Her **Diligence**. "Worketh willingly" (13-15, 19, 22).
3. Her **Thoughtfulness**. "Considereth" (16).
4. Her **Helpfulness**. "She reacheth forth" (20).
5. Her **Influence**. "Her children call her blessed, and her husband praiseth her" (28, 29).
6. Her **Wisdom**. "She openeth her mouth with wisdom" (26).
7. Her **Prospect**. "She shall rejoice in time to come" (25).

Those who devote themselves for others' good, show their devotion to the Lord.

274. DEPRESSION

IT is said Mr. Spurgeon on one occasion was greatly depressed, and that one of the officers asked "those who had been converted or blessed under his ministry to rise," and 1200 rose to their feet. "Now," said the Deacon, "I charge you all to pray for your pastor."

Many of God's servants have got into the mire of depression, and we have the record of some of their experiences, that we may avoid their depressions.

1. **David:** "I shall one day perish by the hand of Saul" (1 Sam. xxvii. 1).

2. **Job:** "Why died I not from the womb?" (Job iii. 11).

3. **Elijah:** "O Lord, take away my life" (1 Kings xix. 4).

4. **Moses:** "I am not able to bear all this people" (Num. xi. 14).

5. **Psalmist:** "I watch, and am as a sparrow alone upon the housetop" (Psa. cii. 7).

6. **Jeremiah:** "Behold, O Lord, for I am in distress" (Lam. i. 20).

7. **Jonah:** "It is better for me to die than to live" (Jonah iv. 8).

Discontent and disappointment often lead to discouragement, and discouragement leads to depression, and these together will breed despair.

275. DISOBEDIENCE

DAMAGE and distress are sure to follow in the steps of disobedience.

1. **Abram** found it so when he left the Bethel of communion for the Egypt of compromise—Gen. xii. 7-13.

2. **Moses** lost the land of promise through using the rod of self-will—Num. xx. 10-12.

3. **Jonah** got an uncomfortable bed through not going to the Nineveh of ministry—Jonah i. 17.

4. **Peter** found his "net" broken through not letting down the "nets" of full obedience—Luke v. 4-6.

5. The **man of God** out of Judah lost his life through listening to the lying prophet of Bethel—1 Kings xiii. 20-26.

6. The **children of Israel** dug graves for themselves in the wilderness by means of their evil heart of unbelief—Heb. iii. 17.

7. **Solomon** got his soul hurt by getting into the trap of fleshly desire—1 Kings xi. 4.

276. DESIRABLE THINGS
IN 2 THESSALONIANS I
1. A **Growing** Faith—3.
2. An **Abounding** Love—3.
3. An **Enduring** Patience—4.
4. A **Righteous** Suffering—5-7.
5. An **Admired** Glory—10.
6. A **Worthy** Commendation—11.
7. A **Powerful** Work—11.

277. DIFFERENT KINDS OF CONSCIENCES
1. An **evil** conscience by sin—Heb. x. 22.
2. A **defiled** conscience by unbelief—Titus i. 15.
3. A **seared** conscience by hypocrisy—1 Tim. iv. 2.
4. A **convicted** conscience by Christ—John viii. 9.
5. A **weak** conscience by ignorance—1 Cor. viii. 10.
6. A **cleansed** conscience by Christ's blood—Heb. ix. 14.
7. A **perfect** conscience by Christ's perfect sacrifice—Heb. ix. 9; x. 2.
8. A **faithful** conscience by obedience—1 Peter ii. 19.
9. An **offenceless** conscience by carefulness—Acts xxiv. 16.
10. A **good** conscience by godliness—Acts xxiii. 1.
11. A **pure** conscience by fidelity—2 Tim. i. 3.
12. A **testifying** conscience by consecration—2 Cor. i. 12.

278. DIVINE QUALITIES AND POSSESSIONS
IN PSALM CXLIII   Faith's attitude to them
1. **Rest of Faith.** "Thy faithfulness. "
2. **Righteousness of Faith.** "Thy righteousness. "
3. **Responsibility of Faith.** "Thy servant. "
4. **Regard of Faith.** "In Thy sight. "
5. **Remembrance of Faith.** "Thy works. "
6. **Response of Faith.** "I muse on the works of Thy hands. "
7. **Request of Faith.** "Hide not Thy face. "
8. **Reciprocity of Faith.** "Cause me to hear Thy loving-kindness. "
9. **Reflection of Faith.** "Thy will. "
10. **Recognition of Faith.** "Thy Spirit is good. "
11. **Reliance of Faith.** "For Thy Name's sake. "
12. **Reiteration of Faith.** "Thy righteousness. "
13. **Refuge of Faith.** "Thy mercy. "

279. DIFFICULTIES

1. The **red sea** of difficulty—Exod. xiv. 13-22.
2. The **Saul** of persecution—1 Sam. xxvii. 1.
3. The **fret** of some thorn in the flesh—2 Cor. xii. 9.
4. The **loneliness** of some Isle of Patmos—Rev. i. 9.
5. The **prison** of man's hate—Acts xii. 3, 4.
6. The **fierce fire** of trial—1 Peter i. 7.
7. The **temptations** of the Devil—Matt. iv. 11.

280. "DIVERS," OR MANIFOLD

THE word rendered "divers" means *"manifold,"* and is so translated in 1 Peter i. 6; iv. 10.

1. **"Divers diseases"** (Matt. iv. 24). How many diseases afflict humanity! The cancer of lust, the palsy of doubt, the blindness of unbelief, the tumor of pride, the deafness of indifference, the lunacy of rationalism, the leprosy of worldliness, the gangrene of evil influence, the anaemia of lifelessness, and the waste of consumption.

2. **"Divers lusts"** (2 Tim. iii. 6). "Silly women laden with sins, led away with divers lusts." Two expressive similes are used to describe these: the life heaped up with sins as coals on a fire—see same word as "laden" rendered "heap" in Rom. xii. 20; and they are "led away" as a person "carried" by an outside power—see same word "led away" rendered "carried" in Acts xxi. 34. "Lusts" is the dominating force which burdens and leads away, and these are "manifold." "Lusts" means the inward desire of the soul, and is rendered "concupiscence" and "desire"—see Rom. vii. 8; 1 Thess. ii. 17.

3. **"Divers...pleasures"** (Titus iii. 3). "Pleasures" means that which gratifies self and the evil nature. The same word is translated "lusts" in James iv. 1, 3. "The pleasures of sin," while they are multiplied in form, last only for a season, while the pleasures in God's right hand last "for evermore" (Psa. xvi. 11, R.V.).

4. **"Divers and strange doctrines"** (Heb. xiii. 9). While there may be, to the carnal mind, doctrines which are various, they are "strange" to the mind of God, for they are contrary to what is revealed in His Word. The reason of their strangeness is found in the word "carried about," which means to be "carried about" as a vessel not under control is carried here and there by the wind—see Eph. iv. 14, Jude 12, or as a sick person is carried on a bed by others—see Mark vi. 55.

5. **"Divers miracles and gifts"** (Heb. ii. 4). The Revised Version reads, "manifold powers and gifts of the Holy Spirit." The manifestations and operations in the early days of Christianity were all the outcome of the Spirit's working. "Manifold" they were indeed in kind, and powerful in their effectiveness.

6. **"Manifold temptations"** (1 Peter i. 6). "Divers temptations" (James i. 2). Trials manifold and heavy come to the child of God, but we need to remember that trials make and prove us, even as the fire hardens the china clay, and burns in with lastingness the artist's colours.

7. **"Manifold grace of God"** (1 Peter iv. 10). The word "manifold" means "many coloured" and changing; but do not let us forget that the yellow of trial, when mixed with the blue of Heaven's grace, turns into the green of the pastures of profit; and that the red of temptation, when mixed with the blue of God's love, turns them into the purple of royal experience.

281. DIVINENESS OF THE GOSPEL

1. Divine **gift** bestowed—John iii. 16.
2. Divine **love** manifested—Rom. v. 8.
3. Divine **grace** revealed—Titus ii. 11.
4. Divine **righteousness** displayed—Rom. iii. 25.
5. Divine **power** exhibited—Eph. i. 19.
6. Divine **life** imparted—John i. 13.
7. Divine **promises** assured—2 Cor. i. 20.

282. DOCTRINE OF THE BIBLE
BIBLIOLOGY

THE doctrines of the Bible may be summarised under ten sections. The Bible, God, Christ, the Holy Spirit, Man, Sin, Salvation, the Church, Angels, and the Last Things.

1. **What is it?** The Word of God—2 Tim. iii. 16, 17.

2. **Who inspired it?** The Holy Spirit—2 Peter i. 20, 21.

3. **Who were the instruments** used to write it? "The prophets," "Holy men"—1 Peter i. 10, 11.

4. **What was the purpose** of its revelation? To reveal Christ—John v. 39.

5. **What are the two themes** of its unfolding? His sufferings and glory—Luke xxiv. 26, 27.

6. **What does it do?** "Discern (criticise) the thoughts and intents of the heart" (Heb. iv. 12).

7. **What does it impart?** Life—1 Peter i. 23.

283. DOCTRINE OF GOD
THEOLOGY
1. God in **creative skill**—Gen. i.
2. God in **righteous claim**—Exod. xx. 2-17.
3. God in **infinite love**—John iii. 16.
4. God in **active grace**—Luke xv.
5. God in **fatherly relationship**—John xiv.
6. God in **majestic power**—Eph. i. 19, 20.
7. God in **tender care**—Psalm xxiii.

284. DOCTRINE OF CHRIST
CHRISTOLOGY
1. His **Deity**—Heb. i. 3.
2. His **Humanity**—Heb. ii.
3. His **Ministry**—Acts x. 38.
4. His **Sufferings**—Isa. liii.
5. His **Message**—John iii. 1-21.
6. His **Priesthood**—Heb. vii.-ix.
7. His **Return**—1 Thess. iv. 13-18; 2 Thess. i. 7-10.

285. DOCTRINE OF THE HOLY SPIRIT
PNEUMATOLOGY
1. In **Creation**—Gen. i. 2.
2. In **Providence**—Psa. civ. 30.
3. And **Christ**—Luke iii. and iv.
4. And **Saints**—John xiv.-xvi.
5. And **Church**—1 Cor. xii.
6. And **Israel**—Ezek. xxxvii.
7. And **World**—John xvi. 8-11.

286. DOCTRINE OF MAN
ANTHROPOLOGY
1. Man **Created**—Gen. i. 27.
2. Man **Fallen**—Rom. iii.
3. Man **Cursed**—Gal. iii. 10.
4. Man **Loved**—Rom. v. 8.
5. Man **Saved**—Eph. ii. 1-10.
6 Man **Kept**—John xvii.
7. Man **Glorified**—Phil. iii. 20, 21.

287. DOCTRINE OF SIN
HAMARTIALOGY
1. The **Author** of Sin—1 John iii. 8.
2. The **Course** of Sin—James i. 15.
3. The **Nature** of Sin—1 John iii. 4, R.V.
4. The **Wages** of Sin—Rom. vi. 23.
5. The **Sin** of Sins—John xvi. 9.
6. The **Judgment** of Sin—John v. 27-29.
7. The **Sacrifice** for Sin—2 Cor. v. 21.

288. DOCTRINE OF SALVATION
SOTERIOLOGY
1. **Grace**, the source of salvation—Titus ii. 11, 12.
2. **Redemption**, the meaning of salvation—Heb. ix. 14.
3. **Faith**, the life of salvation—Heb. xii.
4. **Love**, the soul of salvation—1 Cor. xiii.
5. **Holiness**, the blessing of salvation—1 Thess. v. 23.
6. **Prayer** in the Spirit, the language of salvation—Jude 20.
7. **Hope**, the outlook of salvation—Rom. viii. 18-25.

289. DOCTRINE OF THE CHURCH
ECCLESIOLOGY
1. **Place** of the Church—Acts xv. 14-18.
2. The **Name** of the Church. "His Body"—Eph. i. 23.
3. The **Head** of the Church. Christ—Col. i. 18.
4. The **Administrator** of the Church. The Holy Spirit—1 Cor. xii.
5. The **Calling** of the Church—Heb. iii. 1.
6. The **Gifts** in the Church—Eph. iv. 8-13.
7. The **Glory** of the Church—Eph. v. 25-32.

290. DOCTRINE OF ANGELS
ANGELOLOGY
1. The **Archangel**—Jude 9; 1 Thess. iv. 16.
2. The **Cherubim**. Living creatures—Ezek. i. ; Rev. vi. R.V.
3. The **Seraphim**—Isaiah vi.
4. The **Principalities**—Eph. i. 21; iii. 10; vi. 12.
5. The **Powers**—Eph. i. 21; iii. 10; vi. 12.
6. **Named Angels**. Gabriel, etc.—Luke i. 26, etc.
7. **Angels generally**—See Angels in the Book of the Revelation.

291. DOCTRINE OF THE LAST THINGS
ESCHATOLOGY

1. **Intermediate** State—2 Cor. v. 1-10.
2. **Resurrection** of the Body—1 Cor. xv.
3. **Israel's** Future—Rom. xi.
4. **Judgment** Seat of Christ and **Rewards**—Rom. xiv. 10; 1 Cor. iii.-iv. 15; 2 Cor. v. 9, 10, R. V.
5. **Great** White Throne—Rev. xx. 11-15.
6. **Heaven**—Rev. xxi. ; xxii. 6.
7. **Hell**—Mark ix. 42, 49; Luke xvi. 19-31.

292. DOUBLE BLESSINGS

1. **Rest.** Salvation and holiness. "I will give you rest." "Ye shall find rest" (Matt. xi. 28, 29).
2. **Meetness.** Grace makes us meet for the inheritance—Col. i. 12; and the Holy Spirit makes us meet for service—2 Tim. ii. 21.
3. **Supply.** "Grace and peace be multiplied unto you through the knowledge of God and of Jesus our Lord" (2 Peter i. 2).
4. **Peace.** "Peace I leave with you, my peace I give unto you" (John xiv. 27).
5. **Keeping.** "Preserved," or kept "in" ("for", R.V.) "Jesus Christ." "Keep yourselves in the love of God" (Jude 21).
6. **Indwelling.** "He that keepeth His commandments dwelleth in Him, and He in him" (1 John iii. 24).
7. **Life and Joy.** "These things we write...that your joy may be full." "These things have I written...that ye may know ye have eternal life" (1 John i. 4; v. 13).

293. DYING WELL

THE reason why a child of God can die well is—

1. Because **he knows** Christ has died for his sins—1 Cor. xv. 3.
2. Given him **eternal life**—John 3. 36.
3. God has **made him beautiful** in the Beloved—Eph. i. 6.
4. Made **meet for the inheritance** of the saints in light—Col. i. 12.
5. **Begotten** unto an incorruptible inheritance—1 Peter i. 4.
6. **Kept by the power** of God for it—1 Peter i. 5.
7. **Christ has willed** in His last will and testament that he shall enjoy the glory of it—John xvii. 24.

294. DOUBLES

CHRIST'S blessings are always double.

1. The **double rest** of Matthew xi. 28, 29.
2. The **double character** of priesthood in 1 Peter ii. 5, 9.
3. The **double place** "in" and "out" of John x. 9.
4. The **double abiding** in John xv. 7.
5. The **double peace** of John xiv. 27.
6. The **double presence** of the Holy Spirit in John xiv. 17.
7. The **double association** with Christ in Galatians ii. 20.

295. DOUBLES OF THE CHRISTIAN

1. **Position.** "The Church...which is in God the Father and in the Lord Jesus Christ" (1 Thess. i. 1).

2. **Life.** "Your life is hid with Christ in God" (Col. iii. 3).

3. **Union.** "That they all may be one; as Thou, Father, art in Me, and I in Thee, that they also may be one in us" (John xvii. 21).

4. **Keeping.** "Neither shall any pluck them out of My hand...and no man is able to pluck them out of My Father's hand" (John x. 28, 29).

5. **Sendings.** Sent to redeem. "Sent forth His Son...to redeem." "Sent forth the Spirit of His Son in your hearts" (Gal. iv. 4-6).

6. **Power.** "In whom...ye were sealed with the Holy Spirit of promise." "Be filled with the Spirit" (Eph. i. 13; v. 18).

7. **Calling.** "The hope of our calling," which is to be with Him; and "The hope of His calling," which is for Him to be with us (Eph. i. 18; iv. 4).

296. "DRY" THINGS

1. A **Lifeless State.** Israel's state of death described as "dry bones" and "very dry"—Ezek. xxxvii. 2, 4.

2. A **Living Saviour.** "Root out of a dry ground" (Isa. liii. 2).

3. A **Manifested Miracle.** "Israelites passed over on dry ground" (Josh. iii. 17; Exod. xiv. 16-29).

4. A **Needy Saint.** "My flesh longeth for thee in a dry and thirsty land" (Psa. lxiii. 1).

5. An **Encouraging Sign.** "Let it now be dry only upon the fleece" (Judges vi. 37-40).

6. A **Constant Supply.** "Rivers of water in a dry place" (Isa. xxxii. 2).

7. A **Glorious Promise.** "I will pour floods upon the dry ground" (Isa. xliv. 3).

297. "DUST" IN THE BIBLE

SOMETIMES dust is used metaphorically, such as, "The clouds are the dust of His feet" (Nahum i. 3); sometimes "dust" expresses an act of humility—Josh. vii. 6; and often it denotes the actual dust of the ground.

1. **Creation.** "The Lord God formed man of the dust of the ground" (Gen. ii. 7). Man's lowly origin and frailty.

2. **Confession.** "Lord, what am I but dust and ashes?" (Gen. xviii. 27). To take a low place before God is to find a high place in Him.

3. **Conversion.** "He raiseth up out of the dust" (1 Sam. ii. 8). From the dust of sin, and shame, and self, the Lord raises to the realm of His salvation, love, and grace.

4. **Compassion.** "He remembereth we are dust" (Psa. ciii. 14). In His love He remembers we are of lowly origin, and helps us in our weakness.

5. **Consecration.** "Shake thyself from the dust" (Isa. lii. 2). Dusty garments are a disgrace, but the beautiful clothing of His grace beautifies us.

6. **Consideration.** "I exalted thee out of the dust" (1 Kings xvi. 2). What the Lord has done for us is worthy of our grateful consideration.

7. **Conquest.** "His enemies shall lick the dust" (Psa. lxxii. 9). When Christ reigns all shall submit to Him.

298. EARS—VARIOUS KINDS

1. The **uncircumcised ears** of rebellion—Acts vii. 51.
2. The **itching ears** of instability—2 Tim. iv. 3.
3. The **useless ears** of unbelief—Mark viii. 18.
4. The **willing ears** of the sacrificing Christ—Psa. xl. 6.
5. The **opened ears** by Love—Mark vii. 33.
6. The **attentive ears** of faith—Neh. viii. 3.
7. The **interested ears** of the Church—Acts xi. 22.

299. "EARS" IN ACTION

THE ear is often identified with expressive meaning and holy association.

1. **Bored Ear.** "His master shall bore his ear" (Exod. xxi. 6). The willing slave would rather serve his master than have his liberty.

2. **Consecrated Ear.** "Upon the tip of Aaron's right ear"

(Lev. viii. 23, 24). The blood and oil consecrates the ear to God's attention.

3. **Inclined Ear.** "Consider and incline thine ear" (Psa. xlv. 10). When we incline to a given direction we are practically gone to that way.

4. **Awakened Ear.** "He wakeneth mine ear" (Isa. l. 4). Listening to the Lord, we shall have something to say for the Lord.

5. **Hearing Ear.** "Let him hear" (Rev. ii. 7, 11, 17, 29; iii. 6, 13, 22; xiii. 9). The Spirit's voice calls for prompt, constant, and practical heeding.

6. **Uncircumcised Ear.** "Their ear is uncircumcised" (Jer. vi. 10). Circumcision means the cutting off of inattention, and not to have it signifies we are in rebellion.

7. **Dull Ears.** "Ears dull of hearing" (Matt. xiii. 15). To be deaf to the Lord is to shut our ears to our own interest.

300. EIGHT COMMANDS
IN PHIL. iv. 1-6

1. The **"Stand Fast"** of Fidelity (1).
2. The **"Same Mind"** of Unity (2).
3. The **"Help"** of Ability (3).
4. The **"Rejoice"** of Vivacity (4).
5. The **"Moderation"** (R.V., "Forbearance") of Consideration (5).
6. The **"Be Careful for Nothing"** of Non-anxiety (6).
7. The **"Prayer"** of Comprehension (6).
8. The **"Thanksgiving"** of Doxology (6).

301. EIGHT TOUCHES BY CHRIST

1. Touch of **Cleansing**—Matt. viii. 3.
2. Touch of **Cooling**—Matt. viii. 15.
3. Touch of **Opening**—Matt. ix. 29, 30.
4. Touch of **Assuring**—Matt. xvii. 7.
5. Touch of **Loosing**—Mark vii. 33.
6. Touch of **Blessing**—Mark x. 13.
7. Touch of **Quickening**—Luke vii. 14.
8. Touch of **Healing**—Luke xxii. 51.

302. EFFECTUAL THINGS

THE Greek word in the following passages signifies *to work effectually*, that is, to accomplish the desired end.

1. **Sin's Effectual Work.** "Sins which... did work in our members" (Rom. vii. 5).

2. **God's Effectual Work** for us. *"Working* of His mighty power, which He *wrought* in Christ, " etc. (Eph. i. 19, 20).

3. **The Spirit's Work** in us. "The power that *worketh* in us" (Eph. iii. 20; Phil. ii. 13; Col. i. 29).

4. **The Word's Effectual Work** upon us. "Which also *effectually worketh"* (1 Thess. ii. 13).

5. **The Righteous Man's Effectual Prayer.** "The *effectual fervent* prayer, " etc. (James v. 16).

6. **Christ's Effectual Ministry.** "Works *do shew forth* themselves in Him" (Matt. xiv. 2).

7. **The Believer's Power to Effectually Work** out his Salvation. "God which *worketh* in you both to will and *to do* of His good pleasure" (Phil. ii. 13).

303. "ELOHIM"

PSALM lxii

"GOD" is mentioned seven times in the above Psalm, and as it occurs in the plural, in the Christian sense as read in the reflected light of the Scriptures, it denotes the Father, Son, and the Holy Spirit, in their united action of power.

1. **Salvation.** "God, from Him cometh my salvation" (1).

2. **Expectation.** "God, for my expectation is from Him" (5).

3. **Protection.** "In God is my salvation and glory" (7).

4. **Power.** "The rock of my strength and refuge is in God" (7).

5. **Safety.** "God is a refuge for us" (8).

6. **Revelation.** "God hath spoken" (11).

7. **Possession.** "Power belongeth unto God" (11).

304. ENCOURAGEMENT TO FAITH

GOD's promises are the cause of our encouragement. Jehovah gave Abram four "I will's" of promise—Gen. xii. 1-3.

1. The "I will" of **Revelation.** "I will show thee. "

2. The "I will" of **Re-creation.** "I will make thee a great nation. "

3. The "I will" of **Renown**. "I will bless thee and make thy name great. "

4. The "I will" of **Reciprocation**. "I will bless them that bless thee. "

Faith not only honours God, but God honours faith. Jehovah's benedictions come to faith, and faith is always a benediction to others. Recall some men of God, who have been blessed by God, and who in turn have become a blessing to others. General Gordon, the faithful soldier; Moffat, the ardent missionary; Livingstone, the persevering explorer; Gladstone, the eloquent statesman; Muller, the devoted believer; Wilberforce, the slave emancipator; and Elizabeth Fry, the friend of prisoners.

305. "END"

THE word *telos*, rendered "end, " signifies the completion; not merely to end, but to perfect.

1. **End of Sin**. "The end of those things is death" (Rom. vi. 21).

2. **End of Holiness**. "Fruit unto holiness, and the end everlasting life" (Rom. vi. 22).

3. **End of the Law**. Christ answers to law. "Christ is the end of the law for righteousness to every one that believeth" (Rom. x. 4).

4. **End of the Commandment**. "The end of the commandment is love out of a pure heart" (1 Tim. i. 5).

5. **End of Faith**. "Receiving the end of your faith, even the salvation of your souls" (1 Peter i. 9).

6. **"End of the Lord"** is, to bring the saint to the end of himself, as in the case of Job—Jas. v. 11.

7. **End of the Sinner**. "Whose end is destruction" (Phil. iii. 19).

306. ENOCH

THERE are six things revealed about Enoch in his relationship to God.

1. He was **right before God**, for only those who are right before Him can walk with Him —Gen. v. 22.

2. He was **pleasing to God**—Heb. xi. 5.

3. He had **faith in God**—Heb. xi. 5.

4. He **walked with God**—Gen. v. 22.

5. He **witnessed for God**—Jude 14.

6. He was **translated by God**—Heb. xi. 5.

307. ENDUED WITH POWER

THE word for power is variously rendered, and means to be made strong by a power outside of us. We give the word in black type in each case.

1. "Saul **increased in strength**" to confound and convince unbelievers (Acts ix. 22).

2. "Abraham **was strong** in faith, giving glory to God" (Rom. iv. 20).

3. We need to be "**strong** in the Lord" to put on the whole armour (Eph. vi. 10).

4. "Christ **which strengtheneth** me," says Paul, is the power by which I am able to do all things (Phil. iv. 13).

5. The secret of the apostle's service was "Christ Jesus our Lord," as he said, "**who hath enabled me**" (1 Tim. i. 12).

6. The secret of enablement is to "**be strong** in the grace that is in Christ Jesus" (2 Tim. ii. 1).

7. To be "**strengthened**" by the Lord's presence is the secret of endurance under suffering (2 Tim. iv. 17)

8. "Out of weakness **were made strong**" is the Spirit's epitaph on the saints of old (Heb. xi. 34).

308. "ESCAPED"

THE SHIPWRECK STORY OF ACTS XXVIII

THE escape of Paul and those who were with him from death by drowning is an apt illustration of that greater escape which those who believe in Christ have experienced. The word translated "escaped" is rendered "saved" in 1 Peter iii. 20, "safe" in Acts xxiii. 24, "save" in Acts xxvii. 43, "heal" in Luke vii. 3, and "made perfectly whole" in Matthew xiv. 36.

The above Scriptures may be taken as illustrations of what the believer escapes from as he comes in contact with Christ.

1. In the ark of Christ's all-sufficient atonement we escape from **the deluge of condemnation**—John v. 24.

2. In the protection of Christ's presence we escape from **defeat in the hour of temptation**—1 Cor. x. 13.

3. In the keeping of Christ's power we escape being **taken by the enemy of our souls**—John x. 28.

4. In the healing touch of Christ's living grace we escape from the **disease of iniquity**—Psa. ciii. 3.

5. Through the grasp of faith we escape from **partial health of soul** by being "made perfectly whole"—Titus ii. 14.

309. EUNUCH AND PHILIP

As Mentioned in Acts viii

THERE are seven things we might briefly note in relation to the eunuch—

1. The **Book in his Hand**—28. The Word of God was his study. When the Scripture forms the theme of our meditation, we are sure to become acquainted with its Author, if our search is backed up by the teaching of the Holy Spirit—1 Cor. ii. 12.

2. The **Desire of his Heart**. The eunuch wanted to understand what he was reading—31-35. Philip told him of Jesus. Christ is the Key of Knowledge. If we understand *Him*, all is well—1 John v. 20.

3. The **Object in his Eye**—37. His attention is fixed on Christ, and he is captivated by Him to his conversion—Isa. xlv. 22.

4. The **Confession on his Lips**—37. There is no hesitation when he is asked for a confession as to his faith. When we know Christ in the heart, there will be no trouble to confess Him with the lips—Rom. x. 9, 10.

5. The **Companion in his Chariot**—31. To companion with those who know the Lord is to catch the aroma of His presence—Acts iv. 13.

6. The **Identification with Christ by Baptism**, which shows forth our oneness with Christ in His death, burial, and resurrection—Col. ii. 12.

7. The **Joy in his Soul**—39. When we know the joy of the Lord in saving us, the Lord's joy makes us joyful—John xv. 11.

310. ESSENTIALS FOR THE LORD'S WORK

As the four friends of the palsied man were the human instruments to bring him into contact with our Lord, so there are four essentials for the Lord's work on the human side.

1. **Prevailing Prayer**—James v. 16. The effectual fervent prayer of a righteous man availeth much. Fervency of supplication, like the greased slip beneath the vessel to be launched, causes our petitions to go easy to the throne of grace, and places us in the river of God's purpose. Prayer is the hand of our need grasping the hand of God's power, whilst He grasps our hand to accomplish His Divine salvation. Pray, brethren, pray, a ministry that is soaked with the oil of prayer must have in it an unction of power.

2. **Powerful Faith**. No ordinary faith will suffice if it is to accomplish effective work. One of the nine gifts of the Spirit

is faith—1 Cor. xii. 8-11; not the personal faith for our own salvation, but that which brings blessings to others. When Christ saw the faith of the four bearers, He said to the palsied man, "Thy sins be forgiven." Faith that can command blessing from God always achieves conquests for Him.

3. **Personal Love.** Love, like God, is a trinity. The heart of love is sympathy, the hand of love is help, and the act of love is sacrifice. He who died for our sins will impart His Spirit which led Him thus to die. We need to be conformed to His death, denying ourselves self-ease and pleasure that we may know the power of His resurrection. The tenderness of Jesus must operate through us. We may organise much, but we need to agonise too. Organisation alone is like a factory of cold machinery. Let the machinery work with power. Love much, do much. It is love's doing which makes duty performed a benediction—2 Cor. v. 14.

4. **Persistent Effort.** Continuance in well doing means doing a thing well. Individual effort is one of the secrets of success in Christian work. Going after some *one* person and gaining that one for Christ. The Divine order is ever when Christ finds Andrew and Philip and they each in turn find Peter and Nathaniel. Concentration of effort is the secret of success. Above all, follow Christ. His promise to make us "fishers of men" is preceded by His command to "Follow Me" (Matt. iv. 19).

311. "EVEN AS"

THE word *kathos* is sometimes rendered "as" (John xvii. 23), "according to" (Acts xi. 29), "according as" (1 Cor. i. 31), "How" (Acts xv. 14), and "even as." Its significance is one thing corresponding to another—like as, according as. Let us focus our thoughts upon the words "even as" or "as," as we find them used in John's Gospel in relation to Christ.

1. **Atonement.** "And *as* (even as) Moses lifted up the serpent in the wilderness, even so must the Son of Man be lifted up" (iii. 14). We find two things suggested by these words, namely, the necessity and the nature of Christ's death. Its necessity is embodied in the "must," and its nature is confirmed by Christ's after references to His lifting up—see John viii. 28; xii. 32, 34, and the "manner of His death" was because of our sins, for in that death He has given to God what we could never give ourselves, satisfaction on account of our sins.

2. **Adjustment.** "*As* I hear I judge," "*As* the Father hath taught Me," "*Even as* the Father hath said unto Me," "*As* the Father gave Me commandment," "*Even as* I have kept My Father's commandments" (v. 30; viii. 28; xii. 50; xiv. 31;

xv. 10). All Christ did and said was according to what His Father commanded and taught Him. Everything was adjusted to what His Father directed. He set the compass of His life and testimony to the sun of His Father's will.

3. **Alignment**. *"As* the living Father hath sent Me" (vi. 57; xvii. 18; xx. 21). Alignment is a bringing one object in line with another. Whether the reference is to Christ's sending His disciples as His witnesses into the world, or as living because of the "Living Father," there is the one thought of correspondence to law and order. As the train will reach the goal of its terminus if it keeps along the rails of the permanent way, so as we keep along the plan of truth, and are actuated by the law of love, we shall reach the goal of God's approval.

4. **Attunement**. *"As* I have done to you" (xiii. 15). As the musician attunes the musical instrument to the right pitch, so Christ has left us an example of loving and lowly service, to which our attitude and actions are to correspond. When love prompts the heart to serve, the hands are active in willing ministry.

5. **Affection**. *"Even as* I have loved you" (xiii. 34; xv. 12). The measure of love to each other is to be gauged and measured by the love which Christ has to us. Grace always places us on a higher plane than law, and in consequence expects more from us. Law demanded love to one's neighbour, even as one loved oneself; but grace commands us to love each other as Christ has and loves us.

6. **Affiliation**. Christ prayed for His disciples, and still prays "that they may be one, *as* we are" (xvii. 11, 22). What that affiliation or oneness is, in all its consecrated comprehensiveness may be gathered if we ponder the whole prayer. One in the "life eternal" (3), one in the knowledge of God's secrets through the words given—8; one in mutual possession—10; one in holy joy—13; one in consecrated separation—14; one in the sanctity of the truth—17; one in vital service—18; one in resplendent glory—22; one in glorious place—24; and one in undying affection—26.

7. **Acquaintance**. "I know Mine own, and Mine own know Me, *even as* the Father knoweth Me, and I know the Father" (x. 14, 15, R.V.). There are two words for knowing, one meaning the knowledge of perception, as seeing an orange tree is such; but the other word is the knowledge of personal acquaintance, that is the word which Christ uses. Seeing a peach growing on the wall, one has the knowledge of perception; but to eat the peach and enjoy its lusciousness is to have the knowledge of experience.

312. "EVEN SO"

THE "even so" in the following passages indicated a consequence of a certain action or a correspondence of one thing in answering to another.

1. **Provision.** "Even so must the Son of Man be lifted up" (John iii. 14). As the brazen serpent was the medium whereby life was brought to the bitten Israelites, so Christ by the means of His vicarious death brings eternal life to those who believe in Him.

2. **Corruption.** As a beautiful tomb may cover a corrupting body, "even so" an hypocrite "outwardly appears righteous unto men" (Matt. xxiii. 27, 28). The whitewashed exterior is no evidence that the inside is washed white. The outward profession is no guarantee of pureness of heart and holiness of life.

3. **Identification.** The practical outcome of being identified with the risen Christ is walking in the power of His risen life, for "as Christ was raised up from the dead by the glory of the Father, even so we also should walk in newness of life" (Rom. vi. 4). Oneness with Christ is proven by correspondence to Him.

4. **Presentation.** "As ye have yielded your members servants to uncleanness and to iniquity, unto iniquity; even so now yield your members servants to righteousness, unto holiness" (Rom. vi. 19). This yielding is definite in its crisis, and progressive in its process.

5. **Correspondence.** "As the Father gave Me commandment, even so I do" (John xiv. 31). He is the Model for our making, and the Magnet for our moving.

6. **Consequence.** "Ye shall know them by their fruits... even so every good tree bringeth forth good fruit" (Matt. vii. 16, 17). Correspondence to Christ is proof we are indwelt by the Spirit.

7. **Acquiescence.** "Even so, Father" (Matt. xi. 26). Christ's acquiescence is the example for our response, so we do well to say "even so" to all He says—Rev. xvi. 7; xxii. 20.

313. EVE'S THREE SINS

EVE did three things in connection with the Word of God. She added to it, took from it, and she altered it.

1. **She Took from the Word of God.** The Lord's command was as follows: "And the Lord God commanded the man, saying, Of every tree of the garden thou mayest freely eat" (Gen. ii. 16). Eve's answer to the serpent's tempting question was: "We may

eat of the fruit of the trees of the garden" (Gen. iii. 2). It will be seen that the woman left out of God's direction the word "freely," and by doing so she not only took from His Word, but cast a reflection upon His character.

2. **She Added to the Word of God.** God made one exception to the trees from which our first parents were to eat, and that was the tree of knowledge of good and evil. His command was: "But of the tree of knowledge of good and evil, thou shalt not eat of it: for in the day that thou eatest thereof thou shalt surely die" (Gen. ii. 17).

Eve's reply to the tempter is as follows: "But of the fruit of the tree which is in the midst of the garden, God hath said, Ye shall not eat of it, neither shall ye touch it, lest ye die" (Gen. iii. 3).

The woman added to the words of God, by saying, "Neither shall ye touch it." The Lord did not say anything about touching the tree. His command was that they were not to eat of the fruit of it.

3. **She Altered the Word of God.** The consequence of disobedience was stated very clearly and emphatically. The Lord said: "Thou shalt surely die" (Gen. ii. 17). But the woman altered the words to "Lest ye die" (Gen. iii. 3). Thus minimising the sharp and pungent words, "Thou shalt surely die."

Men are doing the same things to-day in connection with God's Word, and it becomes all of us to see to it that we do not do the same.

314. EVIDENCES

1. The **evidence of faith** is works, even as the fruit proves the tree—James ii. 14-26.

2. The **evidence of love** is sacrifice, even as the act evidences the heart—1 John iii. 16.

3. The **evidence of discipleship** is continuance, even as the walk demonstrates the life which moves—John viii. 31.

4. The **evidence of union** is fruitfulness, even as the child proves the parent—John xv. 5.

5. The **evidence of grace** is godliness, even as the sunlight proclaims the sun—Titus ii. 11, 12.

6. The **evidence of friendship** is consistency, even as the pulse speaks of the heart—John xv. 14.

7. The **evidence of the new birth** is love, righteousness, and victory—1 John v. 1, even as the living person proves life,

315. EVIDENCES
VISIBLE

1. **Judah's** staff and signet were evidences of his sin with Tamar—Gen. xxxviii. 25.

2. **Joseph's** bloody coat seems to speak of his death—Gen. xxxvii. 33.

3. **Joseph's** garment in the hands of Potiphar's wife was seeming proof of her false statement—Gen. xxxix. 12-18.

4. The unseen, but **bleating sheep**, bore evidence to Saul's disobedience—1 Sam. xv. 14.

5. The **clothes and boots** of the children of Israel proclaimed God's preserving care—Neh. ix. 21.

6. The **left garment** of Bartimaeus testified of his haste to reach Christ—Mark x. 50.

7. The **cloak** of Paul at Troas told of his presence there—2 Tim. iv. 13.

316. EVIDENCES OF ABIDING IN CHRIST

1. **Not Practicing Sin.** "Whosoever abideth in Him sinneth not" (1 John iii. 6).

2. **Keeping God's Commandments.** "He that keepeth His commandments abideth in Him" (1 John iii. 24, R.V.).

3. **Bearing Fruit.** "He that abideth in Me, and I in him, the same beareth much fruit" (John xv. 5, R.V.).

4. **Loving Each Other.** "He that loveth his brother abideth in the light." "Hereby we know we abide in Him" (1 John ii. 10; iv. 13, R.V.).

5. **Walking as Christ Walked.** "He that saith he abideth in Him ought himself also so to walk, even as He walked" (1 John ii. 6).

6. **Continuing in Christ's Word.** "If ye abide in My Word, then are ye truly My disciples" (John viii. 31, R.V.).

7. **Faithfulness to God's Truth.** "If that which ye heard from the beginning abide, ye also shall abide in the Son, and in the Father" (1 John ii. 24, R.V.). "Whosoever goeth onward (margin, "taketh the lead") and abideth not in the teaching of Christ, hath not God: he that abideth in the teaching the same hath both the Father and the Son" (2 John 9, R.V.).

317. EVIDENCES OF LIFE
Or, The Christian's Wardrobe

At one of the railway stations in the North of England, a man, whose clothes were covered with lime, got into one of the carriages of a train.   He was evidently employed in a neighbouring lime-kiln.   His fellow-passengers made room for him, and inly wished him in another compartment, by himself, as, brushing against them, he left his mark upon one and another.   Far from scorning the travelling toiler, who had an equal right with ourselves to the use of the carriage, we are indebted to him for a practical lesson.   As the Lord's children, let us be so clad that, wherever we go we shall leave a lasting impression behind us.   A man is often known by the clothes he wears; here is an inventory of a Christian's wardrobe:

1   "The **armour of light**" (Rom. xiii. 12).
2   "The **Lord Jesus Christ**" (Rom. xiii. 14).
3.   "The **whole armour of God**" (Eph. vi. 11).
4.   "The **breastplate of righteousness**" (Eph. vi. 14).
5.   "The **breastplate of faith**" (1 Thess. v. 8).
6.   "The **heart of compassion**" (r.v.), "kindness, humility, meekness, longsuffering" (Col. iii. 12).
7.   "**Love**" (Col. iii. 14).

If these were worn by Christians, under all circumstances, we should be able to make a deeper impression than we do at present upon those with whom we come in contact.

318. EVIDENCES THAT "WE KNOW"

The following "Hereby we know's" are tests as to our knowledge of spiritual things:

1. Obedience the Proof of Knowledge.   *"Hereby we do know* that we know Him, if we keep His commandments" (1 John ii. 3).

2. Faithfulness the Proof of Allegiance.   "Whoso keepeth His Word, in Him verily is the love of God perfected; *hereby know we* that we are in Him" (1 John ii. 5).

3. Love the Proof of Faith.   *"Hereby know we* love, because He laid down His life for us, and we ought to lay down our lives for the brethren" (1 John iii. 16, r.v.).

4. Christly Action the Ground of Assurance.   *"Hereby shall we know*...and shall assure our hearts" (1 John iii. 19; v. 2).

5. Commandments Kept, the Proof of Abiding in Him.   "He that keepeth His commandments abideth in Him...*hereby we know,"* etc. (1 John iii. 24, r.v.; iv. 13).

319. EXCEPT

LAW is the recognised authority or principle of any given thing. Thus the law of the mind is conscience; the law of sin is death; the law of the universe is attraction; the law of Sinai is righteousness; the law of grace is love; the law of the Gospel is faith; and the law of the Spirit is holiness. To each one of these laws there are subordinate principles. In thinking of the principles which operate in the Kingdom of grace, there are certain conditions to be fulfilled on our part, that we may know the power of them. Some of them are enunciated in Christ's use of the word "except" in John's Gospel.

1. **The Door of the Realm of Grace.** "Except a man be born from above (margin), he cannot see the Kingdom of God" (John iii. 3). As birth admits us into the natural kingdom, so the new life ushers into the spiritual realm of grace. This life is not the product of man, nor the bestowment of the creature, nor the result of will power, but is the result of a personal faith in Him whose death brings life to all who believe in Him— John i. 12, 13; iii. 14-16, 36.

2. **The Gain of Loss.** "Except a corn of wheat fall into the ground and die, it abideth alone: but if it die it bringeth forth much fruit" (John xii. 24). Christ illustrated His own precept by losing His life in death for us, and He has gained a ransomed host in consequence. Self-extinction is the way to gain distinction. To lose one's comfort in helping another in discomfort is to get the comfort of the Comforter; to lose one's ease in doing the task of a feeble brother, is to gain the thanks of appreciation; to lose one's good name in spreading Christ's fame, is to find it embrazoned in Heaven's fane, and to lose oneself for the sake of Christ Himself, is to find in Himself what self can never give—heart-satisfaction.

3. **The Source of Blessing.** "A man can receive nothing except it be given him from Heaven" (John iii. 27). "No man can come to Me except the Father...draw him" (John vi. 44, 65). There is no reluctance on God's part in giving, but He alone is the One who can give. We cannot will that He should give, any more than we can make the sun to shine; but He wills to give to all who will to receive, even as He willed in saying, "Let there be light," and light was. The right to give is His, the right to receive is ours. The might to draw is His, the weak to be drawn are ourselves. A man might wish to lift himself to the housetops by his shoe-strings, but his will would not

land him there; but a power outside of himself, like an elevator, would place him there quickly.

4. The Secret of Fruit-bearing. "As a branch cannot bear fruit of itself, except it abide in the vine; no more can ye except ye abide in Me" (John xv. 4). Fruit-bearing is the outcome of union with Christ. The vine branch is useless in itself—John xv. 5, but it is useful to the vine when the sap flows unhindered through it. What the sap is to the branch, so the Spirit is to the believer in Christ. We cannot have the fruit of the Spirit without the Spirit of the fruit. The fruit is His production, and where He is fruit is always found—Hosea xiv. 8. There are no fruitless branches in the True Vine. There are some who profess to be there, who are like fruitless branches.

5. The Means of Sustenance. "Except ye eat the flesh of the Son of Man, and drink His Blood, ye have no life in you" (John vi. 53). Spiritual participation of Christ by means of the Word through the Spirit is what is here meant, as Christ Himself says, "The words I speak unto you, they are spirit and life" (John vi. 63). As in nature insects become like the things upon which they feed, so those who feed on Christ become like Him. The way to get the truth of the Word is to feed upon the Word of truth.

320. EXHORTATIONS RELATIVE TO THE CHRISTIAN LIFE

In Colossians iii. 1-16

1. The first thing to "**seek.**" "Seek first those things which are above."

2. The essential thing to "**set.**" "Set your affection on things above."

3. The absolute thing to "**mortify.**" "Mortify therefore your members," etc.

4. The obnoxious thing to "**put off.**" "The old man and his deeds."

5. The necessary thing to "**put on.**" "Bowels of mercy," etc.

6. The gracious things to "**let.**" "The peace of God" to "rule," and "the Word of Christ" to "dwell."

7. The worshipful thing in "**singing.**" "Singing with grace in your hearts unto the Lord."

321. EXHORTATIONS IN HEBREWS
SELECTION I

1. **"Give Heed"** of earnest attention (ii. 1).

2. **"Consider"** (iii. 1). To consider Christ in the offices He holds for us is to find what He is to us.

3. **"Hold Fast"** (iii. 6; iv. 14). To grip God's things confidently is to find they grip consecratingly.

4. **"Hear"** (iii. 7, 15; iv. 7). To hear His voice is to obey His Word.

5. **"Take Heed"** (iii. 12). Watch the heart, or it will harden; cultivate it and it will be pliable.

6. **"Exhort"** (iii. 13). To stir one another by exhortation will prevent the life from defeat.

7. **"Fear"** (iv. 1). A godly fear is a stimulus to faith, an incentive to love, and a prevention of failure.

322. EXHORTATIONS IN HEBREWS
SELECTION II

1. **"Labour"** (iv. 11). Labour means to be diligent (R.V.). Leanness comes from laziness—see Josh. xviii. 3.

2. **"Come Boldly** (iv. 16). "Grace" and "mercy" come to those who come to the throne of grace.

3. **"Go on"** (vi. 1). To stop when the command is to "go on" is to miss God's end and intended goal.

4. **"Be not slothful"** (vi. 11, 12). Slothfulness is born of a weak faith, a dull heart, an unwatchful spirit, a morbid soul, a loose life, a neglected Bible, and a prayerless closet.

5. **"Draw near"** (x. 22). The conditions to "draw near" are a "true heart," a full assurance, a clear conscience, and a pure life.

6. **"Hold fast without wavering"** (x. 23). The Revised Version bids us "hold fast the confession of our hope." He will not waver in His promise, so we should not waver in our confession.

7. **"Provoke"** (x. 24). To "provoke" to "love," and labour is to enjoy His favour.

323. EXHORTATIONS IN HEBREWS
SELECTION III

1. **"Not forsaking"** (x. 25). To neglect the means of grace is to miss the grace which ministers.

2. **"Call to remembrance"** (x. 32). A short memory is a long loss.

3. **"Cast not away"** (x. 35). To throw away our confidence is to lose the anchor which keeps from drifting.

4. **"Believe"** (x. 39). To believe well is to be well, and to keep on believing is to reach the goal of salvation.

5. **"Lay aside"** (xii. 1). Weights and "the sin" are besetments which must be dropped, so strip them off.

6. **"Let us run"** (xii. 1). To run with patience is to be rewarded for endurance.

7. **"Looking unto Jesus"** (xii. 2). See Him as the "Author" of faith for imitation, and behold Him as the "Finisher" of faith for inspiration.

324. EXHORTATIONS IN HEBREWS
SELECTION IV

1. **"Consider Him"** (xii. 3). See how He acted, and you will know what to do.

2. **"Lift up"** (xii. 12). Hanging hands and feeble knees come from neglected prayer, and want of work.

3. **"Make straight"** (xii. 13). How can we walk straight if our path is not straight? Besides, we cause others to be crooked if we do not make a straight path.

4. **"Follow peace"** (xii. 14). Holiness and peace are the directors of our way, and the powers that stay.

5. **"Looking diligently"** (xii. 15). To fail the grace which will never fail us is the height of folly and the robber of supply.

6. **"See that ye refuse not Him that speaketh"** (xii. 25). To refuse Him is to deprive ourselves of blessing, to distress ourselves in life, and disqualify ourselves for the future.

7. **"Serve God"** (xii. 28). To serve Him is to serve our own interests. We can serve Him in everything, and He saves us to serve.

325. EXHORTATIONS IN HEBREWS
SELECTION V

1. **"Be not forgetful"** (xiii. 2). To entertain a stranger is beneficial to the entertainer, for an angel from Heaven may be found in the visitor.

2. **"Remember"** (xiii. 3). To remember those in "adversity" is to find ourselves in the Lord's university.

3. **"Be content"** (xiii. 5). Contentment finds a feast in a crust, and Heaven's wine in a cruse of water.

4. **"Whose faith follow"** (xiii. 7). To follow in the steps of those who have honoured God is to remember them in permanent appreciation.

5. **"Be not carried about"** (xiii. 9). If we drift with the tide of man's teaching we shall find ourselves in the ditch of error.

6. **"Go forth"** (xiii. 13). To go forth with Christ and find Him outside is to find many inside blessings.

7. **"Offer," "Do good," "Obey,"** and **"Pray"** (xiii. 15, 16, 17, 18) is the final quartette of exhortations. "Offer" to God His portion, "do good" to men, "obey" the Elders, and "pray" for the Lord's servants, and finally, don't forget to "salute" those who are in the places of responsibility—24.

326. "EYES LIFTED UP"

1. **Lifted Eyes of Backsliding.** "Lot lifted up his eyes and beheld all the plain of Jordan" (Gen. xiii. 10).

2. **Lifted Eyes of Faith.** "Lift up now thine eyes and look from the place where thou art" (Gen. xiii. 14).

3. **Lifted Eyes of Worship.** "He lift up his eyes...and bowed himself" (Gen. xviii. 2).

4. **Lifted Eyes of Appreciation.** "Balaam lifted up his eyes, and he saw Israel" (Num. xxiv. 2).

5. **Lifted Eyes of Submission.** "Joshua...lifted up his eyes and looked, and, behold...captain of the host of the Lord" (Josh. v. 13, 14).

6. **Lifted Eyes of Benediction.** "He lifted up His eyes on His disciples, and said, Blessed, " etc. (Luke vi. 20).

7. **Lifted Eyes of Despair.** "And in Hell he lift up his eyes, being in torments" (Luke xvi. 23).

327. FAITH IN JOHN'S GOSPEL

FAITH honours God by its trust, and God honours faith with His blessings. The following are a few of the blessings found in the mine of John's Gospel in response to believing in Christ.

1. **Sonship**—i. 12.
2. **Salvation**—iii. 15, 16.
3. **Eternal Life**—iii. 36.
4. **Satisfaction**—vi. 35.
5. **Blessing** to others—vii. 38.
6. **Preservation**—xi. 25, 26.
7. **Service**—xiv. 12.
8. **Assurance**—xx. 31.

328. FACES COVERED

1. A Shamed Face. "Shame hath covered my face" (Psa. lxix. 7).

2. A Sinner's Face. "Tamar had her face covered" (Gen. xxxviii. 15).

3. A Sorrowful Face. "David covered his face" (2 Sam. xix. 4).

4. A Schemer's Face. "They covered Haman's face" (Esther vii. 8).

5. A Servant's Face. "With twain he covered his face" (Isaiah vi. 2).

329. FAITH

1. Faith is **sure-footed,** for it stands on The Rock—Psa. xl. 2.

2. Faith is **eagle-eyed,** for it looks to Christ—Heb. xii. 2.

3. Faith is **quick-eared,** for it hears Christ's voice—John x. 27.

4. Faith is **firm-holding,** for it clings to Christ—Acts xi. 23.

5. Faith is **heart-loyal,** for it loves Christ—1 Thess. i. 8.

6. Faith is **resolute-willed,** for it says "I will" (Isa. xii. 2).

7. Faith is **keen-sensed,** for it responds to Christ—Heb. v. 14.

330. FAITH

FAITH is not concerned with itself, it is centred in Christ.

1. Christ is its **object**—Acts xx. 21.

2. The Spirit is its **power**—1 Cor. xii. 9; Gal. v. 22.

3. The Word of God is its **channel**—Rom. x. 17.

4. God is its **Originator**—Mark xi. 22, margin.

331. FAITH AND THE FAITH

FAITH's basis is the Word of God—Rom. x. 17. There is an intimate relationship between faith and *the* faith. Faith is the act of believing—John i. 12, and *the* faith is the truth believed.

1. The faith is the **food** which makes faith strong—Acts xiv. 22.

2. The faith is the **weapon** which faith wields—1 Tim. vi. 12, R.V.

3. The faith is the **rule** by which faith squares—Acts xxvi 18.

4. The faith is the **anchor** which faith fastens to its cable—Acts xvi. 5.

5. The faith is the **cheque-book** which faith signs—Rom. v. 1.

Faith goes up the stairs which Love has built, and looks out of the window which Hope has opened.

> "Faith is the subtle chain
> That binds us to the Infinite: the voice
> Of a deep life within. "

Faith says,

"I stand in God's will" like Stephen—Acts vi. 5.

"I rest in God's bosom" like Timothy—2 Tim. 1. 5.

"I am glad in His joy" as Paul says—Rom. v. 1.

"I am inspired by His love" like the Ephesians—Eph. i. 15.

"I am moulded by His truth" like Abraham—Rom. iv. 20.

"I am strengthened by His grace" as the Apostle enjoins—1 Cor. ii. 5.

"I glory in His Christ" as Paul illustrates—Phil. iii. 9.

"I am satisfied with Himself" as Christ dwells in the heart—Eph. iii. 17.

332. FAITH, LOVE, AND HOPE
1 Thess. i. 3

THE earliest of the Epistles is that written to the Church in Thessalonica, and in it we find all the truths of the Gospel, and how those truths affected the lives of the members of the Christian fraternity.

1. **An Active Believer.** "Your work of faith" (3). Faith is the Spirit's act and attitude towards the Lord. The act puts us in touch and relation to Him—John i. 12, and the attitude is the continuance of trust and obedience—Col. ii. 6. A workless faith is a worthless one. Faith in Christ is more than believing what He says is true, it is the grace that brings us into vital union with Him, and through the life He communicates we are able to do what He wishes and bids.

2. **An Inspired Worker.** "Labour of love" (3). The labour here signifies hard work, toil. The word is rendered "weariness" in 2 Corinthians xi. 27, and a relative word is given "toiled," in referring to the disciples who "toiled all the night" in fishing (Luke v. 5). How many of us have ween "wearied" (same word as "toiled," John iv. 6) in working for the Lord?

But what a toil toil is, if we only toil! Hence the importance of having love coupled with labour. Some of us will never have "LL.D." to our name; but we may have "L.L."—that is, "Loving Labourer." When love moves and moulds us, we move to purpose, and although we may be tired in toil, we will never be tired of toil. Carlyle says: "Blessed is he who has found his work; let him ask no other blessedness. He has a work, a life-purpose; he has found it, and will follow it."

3. **An Enduring Looker.** "Patience of hope" (3). Endurance is the meaning of patience. The word and its cognates are rendered "endurance" (see the six references in the Epistle to the Hebrews, x. 32, 36; xii. 1, 2, 3, 7), and mean not merely passiveness, but actively keeping on and not giving in, like Christ, who "endured the Cross" and "contradiction," and also, like the runner in the race, who keeps on till he reaches the goal. The drawing power which enables the believer to continue is the "hope" of the Lord's return. When "hope" is in the objective it always refers to the Lord's Coming for His people.

All these graces find their centre and circumference in the "Lord Jesus Christ," and live "in the sight," or presence, "of God and our Father."

333. FAITH'S ANSWER—"YES"

"Upon God's will I lay me down,
   As child upon its mother's breast;
No silken couch or softest bed
   Could ever give me such deep rest.
Thy wonderful, grand will, my God,
   With triumph now I make it mine,
And faith shall cry a joyous 'Yes,'
   To every dear command of Thine."

FAITH may be defined as saying "Yes" to the Saviour. There are several people who said "Yes" to the Lord, and they got what they wanted.

1. The **Blind Man** gave the "Yes"* of faith to Christ's ability (Matt. ix. 28).

2. The **Disciples** said "Yes, Lord,"* to Christ's question of teaching (Matt. xiii. 51).

3. The **Syrophenician Woman** replied "Yes, Lord," to His designation of "dog" (Matt. xv. 27).

4. **Martha** said "Yes, Lord,"* to His word (John xi. 27).

5. **Peter** said "Yes, Lord,"* to His question about love (John xxi. 15, 16).

6. **John** said, "Yes, Lord Jesus, come,"* to His announcement of His return (Rev. xxii. 20).

7. **Christ** is the Great Example, for He said "Yes, Father,"* to His will (Matt. xi. 26).

Obedience is the "Yes" of faith to God's Word. When we say "Yes" in fulfilling the conditions of the Lord's promises, He says "Yes" to the prayer of our requests.

* The word in each of the passages may be rendered "Yes," and is so given in Matthew xvii. 25, and other places. "Truth" (Matt. xv. 27), "Even so" (Luke x. 21). and "Surely" (Rev. xxii. 20).

334. FAITH'S ACT AND ATTITUDE

FAITH is the assent of the mind to the truth, that is, it is fully persuaded of its validity and reliability.

Faith is the *consent* of the will, hence it responds to the call of God by obedience to His Word.

Faith's *accent* is trust, for it shows itself in reliance on the Lord.

The first is to be persuaded *by* the Lord, the second is to have confidence *in* the Lord, and the third is to rest *upon* the Lord.

The three prepositions, *en*, *eis*, and *epi*, illustrate three steps of faith.

1. **Faith in** (*en*) **Christ** indicates the soul's rest in Him. *En* occurs in Galatians ii. 20; iii. 26; Ephesians i. 12.

2. **Faith into** (*eis*) **Christ** gives the thought of the individual going out of itself into another. *Eis* is used in John i. 12; iii. 15, 16, 36.

3. **Faith upon** (*epi*) **Christ** speaks of the believer's attitude in relying on Him. *Epi* with the dative occurs in Romans ix. 33; x. 11; xv. 12.

335. FAITH'S OBEDIENCE

"So Abram departed as the Lord had spoken" (Gen. xii. 4). He "got out" (Heb. xi. 8), and "removed into the land" (Acts vii. 4), and thus "obeyed." We, too, obey the Lord when we "come out" of evil associations (2 Cor. vi. 17), and dwell in the fulness of the grace and love of God—Eph. iii. 19.

Obedience to the Lord is proof of faith in Him. See what is said of those who "obeyed" the Lord.

1. Obedience is the **Secret of Blessing**—Gen. xxii. 17, 18.

2. Obedience is the **Soul of Success**—Gen. xxvi. 5.

3. Obedience is the **Sway of Power**—1 Chron. xxix. 23-25.

4. Obedience is the **Slayer of Self**—2 Chron. xi. 1-4.

5. Obedience is the **Submission of Faith**—Haggai i. 12.

6. Obedience is the **Sanctifier of Character**—Rom. vi. 17, R.V.

7. Obedience is the **Stamp of Approval**—Phil. ii. 12.

336. FAITH'S OCCUPATION

1. What the Lord **is**, is faith's delight. "The Author and Finisher of faith." (Heb. xii. 2).

2. What the Lord **does**, is faith's confidence. Abraham was "strong in faith, giving glory to God" (Rom. iv. 20).

3. What the Lord **has**, is faith's supply.   "Receiving the
end of your faith" (1 Peter i. 9).

4. What the Lord **promises**, is faith's stay.   "By faith
Isaac blessed Jacob and Esau concerning things to come"
(Heb. xi. 20-22).

5. What the Lord **commands**, is faith's obedience.   "By
faith Noah being warned of God, prepared an ark" (Heb. xi. 7).

6. What the Lord **desires**, is faith's will.   "By faith
Abraham, when he was tried, offered up Isaac" (Heb. xi. 17).

7. What the Lord **predicts**, is faith's expectation.   "By
faith" Abraham "sojourned...for he looked for a city" (Heb.
xi. 9, 10).

337. FAITH: ITS POWER, HEROES, AND PHASES
In Hebrews xi. 32; xii. 1, 2

1. **"By Means of Faith."**   The sentence "through faith,"
or "by faith," occurs many times in Hebrews xi.   It would be
better rendered "by means of faith."   In thus translating we
are reminded that faith is not a mere assent of the mind, but a
working force in the life.

2. **Heroes of Faith**—32.   There are seven heroes of faith,
namely, Gideon the brave—Judges vii. 20; Barak the victorious
—Judges iv. 16; Samson the strong — Judges xv. 14-20;
Jephthah the devoted—Judges xi. 40; David the psalmist—
2 Sam. xxii. 18; Samuel the consecrated—1 Sam. vii. 9; and
God's messengers, the prophets.

3. **Victories of Faith**—33, 34.   Faith is always a victorious
grace, for it brings everything to God by prayer, and thus
brings God into everything.

4. **Endurance of Faith**—35-37, 39.   Faith grips the hand of
the living Saviour, and is thus enabled to do things which are
impossible otherwise.

5. **Commendation of Faith**—38.   God takes note of faith's
reliance, and records His appreciation of its confidence.

6. **Anticipation of Faith**—39.   Faith looks beyond the
present, and knows that the faithful God will keep to the
promises of the future.

7. **Community of Faith**—40; xii. 1.   The "great cloud of
witnesses" mentioned in chapter eleven were but the precursors
of the whole host of the redeemed.

8. **Example of Faith**—xii. 2.   Christ is the "Author and
Finisher of faith," that is, He is the Pattern and Producer of
faith; hence we need to keep our eyes upon Him if we would have
faith like to His.

338. FEAR

1. A **Sorry Condition.** "No fear of God" (Psa. xxxvi. 1).

2. A **Saving Blessing.** "The fear of God came upon them" (1 Sam. xi. 7; 2 Chron. xiv. 14; xvii. 10; xix. 7).

3. A **Preventing Grace.** "I will trust, and not be afraid" (Isa. xii. 2).

4. A **Loving Word.** "Fear not" (Isa. xli. 10; xliv. 8).

5. A **Happy State.** "Happy the man that feareth alway" (Prov. xxviii. 14).

6. A **Commanding Power.** "The dread of thee, and the fear of thee" (Deut. ii. 25; xi. 25).

If we fear to disobey God we need not fear Him. Fear haunts us all the time if we do not fear God. Abiding in the secret place of the Lord's presence, no "terror" (fear) shall disturb us.

339. "FEAR"

1. A **Command.** "Fear God" (1 Peter ii. 17).

2. A **Caution.** "Be not high-minded" (Rom. xi. 20).

3. A **Consecration.** "Singleness of heart, fearing God" (Col. iii. 22).

4. A **Cause.** "Fear not, I am the First and the Last" (Rev. i. 17).

5. A **Company.** "Walking in the fear of the Lord" (Acts ix. 31).

6. A **Condition.** "Work out your own salvation with fear and trembling" (Phil. ii. 12).

7. A **Consequence.** "Perfect love casteth out fear" (1 John iv. 18).

340. "FEAR NOT"

THE beautiful flowers of God's "Fear Nots" are abundant in the country of the Scriptures. Let us call to mind a few of the New Testament ones.

1. The "Fear Not" of God's **Provision**—Matt. x. 31.

2. The "Fear Not" of **Prayer**—Luke i. 13.

3. The "Fear Not" of **Favour**—Luke i. 30.

4. The "Fear Not" of **Salvation**—Luke ii. 10.

5. The "Fear Not" of **Assurance**—Luke v. 10.

6. The "Fear Not" of **Promise**—Luke viii. 50; xii. 32.

7. The "Fear Not" of **Presence**—Acts xxvii. 24.

8. The "Fear Not" of **Victory**—Rev. i. 17.

341. "FEAR NOT"

PERSONS told not to fear:

1. **Zacharias**, the prayerful. "Fear not, Zacharias" (Luke i. 13).

2. **Mary**, the devoted. "Fear not, Mary" (Luke i. 30).

3. **Jairus**, the sorrowful. "Fear not, only believe" (Luke viii. 50).

4. **Simon**, the fisher. "Jesus said unto Simon, Fear not" (Luke v. 10).

5. Trembling **Disciples**. "It is I, be not afraid" (Matt. xiv. 27).

6. Seeking **Women**. "Fear not ye" (Matt. xxviii. 5, 10).

7. Valiant **Paul**. "Fear not, Paul" (Acts xxvii. 24).

342. "FEET"

1. **Kept** Feet. "He will keep the feet of His saints" (1 Sam. ii. 9).

2. **Lame** Feet. "Lame on his feet" (2 Sam. ix. 3, 13).

3. **Diseased** Feet. "Diseased in his feet" (1 Kings xv. 23).

4. **Speaking** Feet. "He speaketh with his feet" (Prov. vi. 13).

5. **Covered** Feet. "He covered his feet" (Isa. vi. 2).

6. **Beautiful** feet. "How beautiful are the feet of Him that bringeth good tidings" (Isa. lii. 7).

7. **Straight** Feet. "Their feet were straight feet" (Ezek. i. 7).

343. FELLOWSHIP WITH CHRIST IN SACRIFICE AND SUFFERING

WHAT does it mean to sacrifice and suffer with Christ?

1. The crucifixion of self—Gal. ii. 20.

2. The being spent and spending for Him and others—2 Cor. xii. 15.

3. The recognition of Christ suffering in us—Col. i. 24.

4. The being obedient unto death—Phil. ii. 8.

5. The sharing of the trials of others—2 Cor. i. 6.

6. Taking the sufferings, which come from the world, uncomplainingly—1 Peter ii. 20, 21.

7. The being sweet and kind amid the suffering—1 Cor. xiii. 4.

344. FEASTS OF JEHOVAH

THERE are seven feasts mentioned in Leviticus xxiii., each of which has a counterpart of significance in the New Testament.

1. The Feast of the **Passover** is typical of Christ our Passover sacrificed for us, in the benefit of His death for us—1 Cor. v. 7.

2. The Feast of the **Unleavened Bread** is representative of the outcome of faith in Him who died for us—namely, the purging out of the leaven of wickedness from the life—1 Cor. v. 6-8; Titus ii. 14.

3. The Feast of the **Firstfruits** proclaims the resurrection of Christ in His triumph over death—1 Cor. xv. 23; 1 Thess. iv. 13-18.

4. The Feast of **Pentecost** points to the coming of the Holy Spirit and His formation of the Church—Acts ii. 1-4; 1 Cor. xii. 12, 13.

5. The Feast of **Trumpets** denotes the Coming of Christ, when His redeemed will be gathered to Himself—1 Thess. iv. 16; 1 Cor. xv. 51, 52.

6. The Feast of the **Day of Atonement** embodies the outcome of Christ's atonement for the nation of Israel, and the consequent blessing to all—Lev. xvi.; Zech. xii. 10-13.

7. The Feast of the **Tabernacles** leads our thoughts on to the time when Christ shall tabernacle with men in His Millennial glory—Zech. xiv. 16-21.

345. FINDINGS OF CHRIST

1. **The Good Shepherd** finding the lost sheep. Sought until He found it—Luke xv. 4-6.

2. **The Treasure Seeker** finding the treasure and pearl. "When a man hath found." "Found one pearl" (Matt. xiii. 44, 46.

3. **The Disappointed Lord** finding only the leaves of profession. "He found nothing but leaves" (Mark xi. 13).

4. **The Agonising Saviour** finding sleeping disciples. "Found them asleep" (Matt. xxvi. 40, 43).

5. **The Appreciative Christ** finding a whole-hearted trust. "I have not found so great faith," etc. (Matt. viii. 10).

6. **The Counselling Master** finding those whom He had blessed. "When He had found him, He said" (John v. 14; ix. 35).

7. **The Searching Expeller** finding a desecrated temple. "Found in the temple those that sold...and drove them out" (John ii. 14, 15).

346. FIRST AND THE LAST WORD

"First of all...Christ died for our sins" (1 Cor. xv. 3). "The Lamb is the Light thereof" (Rev. xxi. 23).

Dr. Stuart Holden, in closing a meeting held in the Kingsway Hall, said: "My last word is this, that the basis of all sacrificial conflict, the basis of every life, and the inspiration of every career in fellowship with Jesus Christ, is the sacrificial life that He lived, is the unspeakable death that He died for our salvation. The last and ultimate thing to be said by any missionary, prospective or actual, in regard to his work, is this: 'He loved me, and gave Himself for me.'"

1. **Salvation.** The first and the last word for salvation is, "He gave Himself for me." Salvation is not Christ *and* me, but Christ *for* me—Gal. ii. 20.

2. **Sanctification.** "I am crucified with Christ...He liveth in me" (Gal. ii. 20). Holiness is not Christ *and* me, but Christ *in* me.

3. **Service.** "The love of Christ constraineth us...He died...we should live unto Him" (2 Cor. v. 14, 15). All true service is born of His service for us.

4. **Example.** "Suffered for us, leaving us an Example" (1 Peter ii. 21). We can do anything, or follow anywhere, where the magnetic influence of His Cross attracts us.

347. FIRST THINGS

1. The first thing to **seek**. "The Kingdom of God and His righteousness" (Matt. vi. 33).

2. The first thing to **preach**. "Delivered unto you first of all," etc. "The Gospel" (1 Cor. xv. 1-4).

3. The first thing to **do**. "First be a partaker" (2 Tim. ii. 6).

4. The first thing in **worship**. "First be reconciled to thy brother" (Matt. v. 24).

5. The first thing in life. "Cleanse first that which is within" (Matt. xxiii. 26).

6. The first thing in **holiness**. "Cast out first the beam out of thine own eye" (Luke vi. 42).

7. The first thing to **give**. "First gave their own selves to the Lord" (2 Cor. viii. 5).

8. The first thing in **prayer**. "First of all supplications, prayers, and intercessions" (1 Tim. ii. 1).

9. The first thing to **know**. "Knowing this first" (2 Peter i. 20).

348. FIVE LOOKS
ROMANS VI. 17, R.V

1. The **upward** look of thanksgiving. "But thanks be to God."
2. The **backward** look of remembrance. "Ye were the slaves of sin."
3. The **inward** look of decision. "Obeyed from the heart."
4. The **outward** look of appreciation. "Ye were delivered."
5. The **all-round** look of recognition. The Scripture in its entirety.

349. FLEE, FOLLOW, FIGHT
1 Timothy vi. 4-12

PAUL gave three "F's" to Timothy when he would set him on his guard. Look at them:

I. **"Flee these things"** (4-11).
  1. Swelling of pride (R.V.). "Puffed up."
  2. Folly of ignorance.
  3. Dotage of questionings (margin, "sick").
  4. "Strifes of words" (R.V., "disputes").
  5. Envy of jealousy.
  6. Strife of temper.
  7. Railings of incrimination.
  8. Surmisings of evil.
  9. Love of money.

II. **"Follow after"** (6, 11).
  1. "Righteousness" of life.
  2. "Godliness" of character.
  3. "Faith" of devotion.
  4. "Love" of faithfulness.
  5. "Patience" of endurance.
  6. "Meekness" of manner.
  7. "Contentment" of thankfulness.

III. **"Fight the good fight of faith"** (R.V., "The faith").
  1. By "a good profession" (12).
  2. By keeping "this commandment" (14).
  3. By charging the rich not to be "high-minded" (17).
  4. By being "rich in good works" (18).
  5. By laying "hold of eternal life" (19).
  6. By keeping "the faith" of the Gospel (20, 21).
  7. By being "ready to sympathise" (margin, R.V., 18).

350. "FOLLOW ME"

CHRIST's command is "Follow Me." Think of the places in which Christ was found, and see how we are called to follow to spiritual spheres.

1. He bids us follow Him to the **manger** of humility—Phil. ii. 5-8.
2. To the **Nazareth** of ministry—Luke iv. 18; Rom. xiii. 4-11.
3. To the **Jordan** of surrender—Matt. iii. 15; Rom. xii. 1.
4. To the **wilderness** of temptation—Luke iv. 1; 1 Cor x. 13.
5. To the **mount** of instruction—Matt. v. 1; 1 Cor. ii. 9-11.
6. To the **place** of transfiguration—Matt. xvii. 2; 2 Cor. iii. 18.
7. To the **field** of service—Acts x. 38; xx. 19.
8. To the **Garden** of Gethsemane—Luke xxii. 39-42.
9. To the **Cross** of Calvary—Heb. xiii. 12, 13.
10. To the **tomb** of resurrection—Rom. viii. 11.
11. To the **throne** of ascension—Col. iii. 1, 2.
12. To the **hope** of glory—1 John iii. 2, 3.

351. "FOLLOW ME"
John x. 27

THERE are at least eight distinct instances where Christ gives command, "Follow Me," and in these instances we have an eightfold call of Christ.

1. The call to **salvation**—John i. 43.
2. The call to **concentration**—John xxi. 19-22.
3. The call to **separation**—Matt. viii. 22.
4. The call to **self-denial**—Matt. xvi. 24.
5. The call to **consecration**—Matt. xix. 21.
6. The call to **imitation**—John xii. 26.
7. The call to **service**—Matt. iv. 19.
8. The call to **Himself**—Matt. ix. 9.

352. FOREHEADS

1. The **leprous** forehead of sin—2 Chron. xxvi. 19.
2. The **bold** forehead of the flesh—Jer. iii. 3.
3. The **holy** forehead of the priest—Exod. xxviii. 38.
4. The **marked** forehead of approbation—Ezek. ix. 4.
5. The **strong** forehead of service—Ezek. iii. 8, 9.
6. The **beautiful** forehead of glory—Rev. xxii. 4.
7. The **dented** forehead of judgment—1 Sam. xvii. 49.

353. "FORGET NOT"

A SHORT memory is a bad forgettory. To forget the Lord's things is base ingratitude.

1. "Forget not **the Lord**" (Deut. vi. 12; viii. 11, 14, 19). Ponder why He is not to be forgotten, as stated in the above Scriptures.

2. "Forget not how thou **provokest** the Lord thy God" (Deut. ix. 7). Remember past sins, and let them not be repeated.

3. "Forget not the **works of God**" (Psa. lxxviii. 7). Think upon His works if thou wouldest be large-minded, and provoked to praise.

4. "Forget not all **His benefits**" (Psa. ciii. 2). His benefits are beneficial and manifold.

5. "Forgot not **My Law**" (Prov. iii. 1). To forget God's Word is to ignore our responsibilities, and shut ourselves out of blessing.

6. "Forget not" "**to do good** and communicate" (Heb. xiii. 16). To be a blessing to others is to bless ourselves.

7. "Forgot not the **humble**" (Psa. x. 12). Jehovah will not forget the "crushed" and "humbled" (so Rotherham), therefore we should help them too.

354. "FORGIVEN"

THE several instances where Christ said to individuals "Thy sins are forgiven," are full of meaning, and illustrate how He forgives all sorts of sinners.

1. **The Palsied Sinner.** "Thy sins be forgiven thee" (Matt. ix. 2. 5).

2. **The Diseased Sinner.** "If he hath committed sins, they shall be forgiven him" (James. v. 15).

3. **The Weeping Sinner.** "He saith unto her, thy sins be forgiven thee" (Luke vii. 47, 48).

4. **The Trespassing Sinner.** "Having forgiven you all trespasses" (Col. ii. 13).

5. **The Iniquitous Sinner.** "Whose iniquities are forgiven" (Rom. iv. 7).

6. **The Transgressing Sinner.** "Blessed is the man whose transgression is forgiven" (Psa. xxxii. 1).

7. **The Atoned-for Sinner** is forgiven, and He above "Makes an atonement for him, for his sin...and it shall be forgiven" (Lev. iv. 20, 26, 31, 35; v. 10, 13, 16, 18; vi. 7).

355. "FORGIVEN "

THIS word is like a sweet songster warbling out its praise amid a scene of devastation.

This forgiveness is

1. **Specific** in its blessing. "Having forgiven you all trespasses" (Col. ii. 13). Sinners are the recipients. Mark the "trespasses" and "you."

2. **Sovereign** in its bestowment. "Thou hast forgiven the iniquity of thy people" (Psa. lxxxv. 2). If the Lord had not done it, it would never have been done.

3. **Sufficient** in its atonement. "It shall be forgiven," because "atonement has been made concerning his sin" (Lev. iv. 20. 26, 31, 35; v. 10, 13, 16). The blood of expiation is the ground of remission.

4. **Soul-stirring** in its enjoyment. "Blessed (or, "Oh! the blessedness") is he whose transgression is forgiven" (Psa. xxxii. 1).

5. **Certain** in its assurance. "Your sins are forgiven" (1 John ii. 12). Note the past tense, "are," and also the reason, "For His Name's sake."

6. **Exemplary** for our imitation. "Forgive and ye shall be forgiven" (Luke vi. 37), even "as God for Christ's sake" has "forgiven" you (Eph. iv. 32).

7. **Happy** in its enjoyment. "Blessed are they whose iniquities are forgiven" (Rom. iv. 7). When the load of sin is gone, then the man is joyful in his going.

356. "FORM" OF NEW TESTAMENT FACTS

1. **Christ's Eternal Character.** "Being in the form of God" (Phil. ii. 6).

2. **Christ's Humble State.** "Took upon Him the form of a servant"—slave (Phil. ii. 7).

3. **Christ's Risen Glory.** "He appeared in another form" (Mark xvi. 12).

4. **Christ's Indwelling Power.** "Christ be formed in you" (Gal. iv. 19).

5. **The Spirit's Teaching.** "That form of doctrine" (R.V., "teaching") (Rom. vi. 17).

6. **The Word's Healthfulness**. "Hold fast the form (pattern) of sound (healthful) words" (2 Tim. i. 13).

7. **The Sinner's Lack.** "Having a form of godliness, but denying the power thereof" (2 Tim. iii. 5).

357. "FORGIVENESS OF SINS"

1. **Medium** of forgiveness. "Through His Blood" (Col. i. 14).
2. **Measure** of forgiveness. "According to the riches of His grace" (Eph. i. 7).
3. **Giver** of forgiveness. "To give...forgiveness of sins" (Acts. v. 31).
4. **Receiver** of forgiveness. "By faith that is in Me" (Acts xxvi. 18).
5. **Proclamation** of forgiveness. "Preached unto you the forgiveness of sins" (Acts xiii. 38).

358. FORSAKEN

1. **A Forsaken God.** "Who have forsaken Me" (Jer. i. 16; ii. 13; 2 Chron. xxviii. 6; xxxiv. 25).
2. **A Forsaken Saviour.** "My God, My God, why hast Thou forsaken Me?" (Psa. xxii. 1).
3. **A Forsaken Law.** "He forsook the law of the Lord" (2 Chron. xii. 1).
4. **A Forsaken Man.** "God left* him to try him" (2 Chron. xxxii. 31).
5. **A Forsaken Heart.** "Therefore my heart faileth* me" (Psa. xl. 12).
6. **A Forsaken Servant.** "My master left* me" (1 Sam. xxx. 13).
7. **A Forsaken Sinfulness.** "He that covereth his sins shall not prosper, but whoso confesseth and forsaketh them shall have mercy" (Prov. xxviii. 13).

359. FOUR PROSPEROUS THINGS

1. **Prosperous Position.** "God hath prospered him" (1 Cor. xvi. 2). Prosperity in this life is due to the good hand of the Lord. Let us remember He expects a proportionate first fruit.
2. **Prosperous Journey.** "I might have a prosperous journey" (Rom. i. 10). The Lord goes before us to clear the road of difficulties, or He is with us to sustain us in them. If He goes with us all is well.
3. **Prosperous Health.** "Thou mayest prosper and be in health" (3 John 2). The Lord is the Healer of the body as well as the Health of the soul.
4. **Prosperous Soul.** "The soul prospereth" (3 John 2). Soul prosperity is the soul of all prosperity.

* Same word in Hebrew.

360. FORTRESS

INIQUITY shall never be our ruin if we do but cleave to Christ, for He is the—

1. **Strong Fortress** for safety in the time of peril—2 Sam. xxii. 2.

2. **Sheltering Fortress** for preservation from our enemies—Psa. xviii. 2.

3. **Sure Fortress** to keep from perplexity and doubt—Psa. xxxi. 3.

4. **Settled Fortress** for habitation—Psa. lxxi. 3.

5. **Supreme Fortress** for excellence, for none can do, or be, like Him—Psa. xci. 2.

6. **Suitable Fortress**, for He can meet the need of each and all—Psa. cxliv. 2.

7. **Succouring Fortress** in the time of affliction—Jer. xvi. 19.

361. "FOUND IN HIM"
Phil. iii. 9

1. As the man-slayer **in the City of Refuge**—safely—Num. xxxv. 6-32.

2. As the stone **in the building**—securely—1 Peter ii. 5.

3. As the jewels **in the breastplate** of the High Priest—acceptedly—Exod. xxviii. 29.

4. As the child **in the family**—affectionately—Eph. iii. 15.

5. As the partner **in the firm**—unitedly—Luke v. 7, 10.

6. As the branch **in the tree**—livingly—John xv. 5.

7. As the member **in the body**—submissively—1 Cor. xii. 13.

8. As the servant **in the household**—obediently—Eph. ii. 19.

9. As the plant **in the garden**—flourishingly—Matt. xv. 13.

10. As the arrow **in the quiver**—waitingly—Isa. xlix. 2.

11. As the vessel **in the hand**—usefully—2 Tim. ii. 21.

12. As the sheep **in the flock**—attentively—John x. 16, R.V.

13. As the scholar **in the school**—diligently—Matt. xi. 29.

14. As the steward **in the estate**—faithfully—1 Cor. iv. 1, 2.

362. FOURFOLD PEACE

REMEMBER these things—

1. Christ has **made** our peace—Col. i. 20.

2. Christ **is** our peace—Eph. ii. 14.

3. Christ **preaches** peace—Eph. ii. 17.

4. Christ **gives** peace—John xiv. 27.

363. "FOR YOU"

"ONE MAN SHOULD DIE"

WE must, in passing, note this "Divine mystery," and "the most monstrous act." Three times does the preposition *huper*, rendered "for," fall from the lips of Caiaphas—"Die for the people...Jesus should die for that nation...not for that nation only." The preposition with the genative case, means one acting on behalf of another. As applied to Christ's death, the main thought is, the provision God has made in His death for the salvation of men. There are other places where *huper* occurs. Six times Christ uses this word in relation to His death on our behalf—

1. **His Body.** "This is My body which is given for you" (Luke xxii. 19).

2. **His Blood.** "My Blood which is shed for you" (Luke xxii. 20).

3. **His Intention.** "My flesh which I give for the life of the world" (John vi. 51).

4. **His Gift.** "The Good Shepherd giveth His life for the sheep" (John x. 11).

5. **His Act.** "I lay down My life for the sheep" (John x. 15).

6. **His Consecration.** "For their sakes I sanctify Myself" (John xvii. 19).

364. FOUR ESSENTIAL THINGS FOR CHRISTIAN WORKERS

"A BED, and a table, and a stool, and a candlestick" (2 Kings iv. 10). Some years ago, a sister in Christ said to me: "Have you noticed that the four things which the Shunammite woman provided for the prophet Elisha are illustrative of the four things which the worker for Christ needs?" "No," I replied, "I have not." She said, "The four things are a bed, a table, a stool, and a candlestick" (2 Kings iv. 10).

1. The **bed** is the **symbol of rest** which is found in Christ, by coming to Him, and in being yoked in God's will with Him—Matt. xi. 28, 29.

2. The **table** is the **symbol of fellowship** with Him, for He spreads a table before us in the presence of our enemies—Psa. xxiii. 5, and bids us "come and dine" (John xxi. 12).

3. The **stool** is the **symbol of instruction** from Christ, for we must sit at His feet, and learn of Him, if we would be initiated in the secrets of His will—Deut. xxxiii. 3; Luke x. 39.

4. The **candlestick** is the **symbol of testimony** for Christ,

for He says we are the "light of the world," and His witnesses to testify of Himself—Matt. v. 14; Acts i. 8.

These things are not only illustrative of what the Christian worker needs, but the order in which they are given is suggestive too. Rest in Christ, by being yoked with Him in the will of God, is essential, in order to have fellowship with Him, and fellowship with Him is the qualification for instruction from Him, and instruction from Him is the precursor of effective testimony for Him.

365. FOUR REMARKABLE PRAYERS

THERE are four prayers mentioned in Mark v.

1. The prayer of the **demon-possessed** not to be tormented —6, 7.

2. The prayer of the **demons** to enter the swine—12.

3. The prayer of the **Gadarenes** that Christ would depart out of their coasts—17.

4. The prayer of the **emancipated one** to be with Christ—18.

All the prayers were answered except the last. God often denies His people what He grants to others. Christ gave the demons what they desired, and the swine were the means of landing them into the sea. When men and demons give themselves up to sin He leaves them alone in their sins, and thus gives them up to judgment—Rom. i. 23, 24, 26, 28.

366. FOURTEEN THINGS DONE TO CHRIST

1. **Spat** in His Face—Matt. xxvii. 30.
2. **Buffeted** His Cheeks—Matt. xxvi. 67.
3. **Bound** His Hands—Matt. xxvii. 2.
4. **Scourged** His Back—Matt. xxvii. 26.
5. **Stripped** His Body—Matt. xxvii. 28.
6. **Lacerated** His Head—Matt. xxvii. 29.
7. **Plucked** Off His Hair—Isa. l. 6.
8. **Took Away** His Garments—Mark xv. 24.
9. **Mocked** His Person—Matt. xxvii. 29, 39-47.
10. **Condemned** Unjustly—Luke xxiii. 41.
11. **Libelled** His Mission—Mark xv. 29, 30.
12. **Taunted** His Works—Mark xv. 31.
13. **Spiked** His Feet—Psa. xxii. 16.
14. **Speared** His Side—John xix. 34.

"They called Him 'Fool' and 'Traitor,' as through the land He went;
They cried out 'Agitator' and 'Brand of Discontent.'
From altar and from steeple, upon this man forlorn,
The priests and goodly people hurled wrath and bitter scorn.

They called Him 'Cheat' and 'Fakir,' and drove Him from the door;
They shouted, 'Mischief Maker, begone, and come no more!'
From border unto border they hounded Him, lest He
'Upset a stablished order and bring on anarchy.'
At length they seized and tried Him, that they might have their will,
And so they crucified Him upon a lonely hill.
The outcast agitator, driven by scourge and rod,
They called 'Fool' and 'Traitor,' and now we call Him 'God.'"

367. FULLY SAVED

1. Are you saved **from all doubt,** and do you enjoy full assurance of faith? This is the privilege of all believers as the sons of God—John v. 24; Rom. viii. 16; Gal. iii. 13; Col. ii. 13, 14; 1 John v. 10-13.

2. Are you saved **from the dominion of sin** and enabled to overcome the evil impulses of your natural heart? This is fully provided in Christ's great redemption. He is made unto us Sanctification—Rom. vi. 11-22; 2 Peter i. 2-4.

3. Are you saved **from the world,** its spirit, love, and aim? Christ's people are a separated people. The true believer overcomes the world—Gal. v. 24; Titus ii. 12-14; 1 John ii. 15, 16.

4. Are you saved **from Satan's power** and temptations, and do you triumph in His strength over all the power of the enemy? —Rom. viii. 37; 2 Cor. ii. 14; Col. i. 13.

5. Are you **filled with the Holy Spirit** as the light, life, joy, and power of your being? This is the very substance of Christ's salvation—John xiv. 23; xv. 11; Acts v. 32; Eph. v. 18.

6. Are you **consecrated to the service of God,** and working together with God for the Kingdom of Jesus and the souls of men?—John xv. 14; Rom. xii. 1, 2; Dan. xii. 3; Matt. xxviii. 18-20.

7. Are you saved **from sickness** and all Satan's power over your body?—Exod xv. 26; Psa. ciii. 3; cvii. 20, R.V.; Matt. xvi. 19, with margin of R.V. of Isa. liii. 4; James v. 14, 15.

368. "FURTHER"

"FURTHER" suggests something beyond that we have reached; and "no further" speaks of a limitation, or an arrestment.

1. **Control.** God controls the sea in all its movements, for He says to it, "Hitherto shalt thou come, but no further; and here shall thy proud waves be stayed" (Job. xxxviii. 11).

2. **Confession.** When the Lord revealed Himself to Job as the Almighty, he confessed, "Behold I am vile," and although

he felt inclined to say more, he pulled himself up by saying, "But I will proceed no further" (Job. xl. 1-5).

3. **Constrained**. When Christ would have "gone further," as He journeyed with the two disciples, "they constrained Him" by saying, "Abide with us" (Luke xxiv. 28, 29). We may by our prayers arrest Christ to our blessing.

4. **Carefulness**. "When they had gone a little further, they sounded again" (Acts xxvii. 28). The mariners did not recklessly go forward, but sought by their carefulness to see if they were warranted to do so. Carelessness is born of laziness, but carefulness is the companion of diligence.

5. **Corruption**. Paul speaks of "men" who have "corrupt minds, reprobate concerning the faith," but he says, "they shall proceed no further" (2 Tim. iii. 8, 9). God allows men to go a long way, but they find in the end they are pulled up to their confusion.

6. **Completion**. The Levitical priesthood did not make things complete, but Christ in His priesthood brings things to perfection, as the apostle implies when he says, "What further need was there that another priest should rise," but in Christ we have "an unchanging priesthood" (Heb. vii. 11, 24).

369. GARDENS

1. A garden **spoiled** by sin. Eden—Gen. iii. 1-24.

2. A garden **sanctified** by prayer.—Gethsemane—John xviii. 26.

3. A garden **hallowed** by Christ. Joseph's—John xix. 41.

4. A garden **prepared** for the Beloved—S. of S. iv. 12, 16.

5. A garden **watered** to its betterment—Isa. lviii. 11.

6. A garden **bringing forth** for others—Isa. lxi. 11.

7. A garden **destroyed** by judgment because of sin—Isa. i. 28-31.

370. GARMENTS

1. **White** garments for attraction—Eccles. ix. 8.

2. **Touched** garment for healing—Matt. ix. 20.

3. **Kept** garment for sacredness—Rev. xvi. 15.

4. **Left** garment for blessing—Mark x. 50.

5. **Wedding** garment for fitness—Matt. xxii. 11.

6. **Hated** garment of sin—Jude 23.

7. **Taken** garment for comfort—Acts xii. 8.

371. GARMENTS

"Put on thy beautiful garments" Isa. lii. 1

"THAT's me hanging up there." So said a vivacious lassie, as she pointed to some new clothes which had been purchased for her. There are garments which the Lord has provided for us.

1. **Salvation** garments for the needy sinner—Isa. lxi. 10.
2. **Substituted** garments for filthy ones—Zech. iii. 3-5.
3. **Beautiful** garments for adornment—Isa. lii. 1.
4. **Perfumed** garments for appreciated witness—Psa. xlv. 8.
5. **Holy** garments for priestly service—Exod. xxviii. 2-4.
6. **Anointed** garments for consecrated work—Lev. viii. 30.
7. **Fringed** garments calling for obedience—Num. xv. 38-41.

372. GARMENTS

1. **Washed** garments from the leprosy of sin—Lev. xiv. 8, 9.
2. **Parted** garments in atonement for sin—Psa. xxii. 18.
3. **Filthy** garments, descriptive of sin's pollution—Zech. iii. 3; Isa. lxiv. 6.
4. An **accusing** garment in the falsehood of sin—Gen. xxxix. 12-18.
5. **Rent** garments in humiliation for sin—1 Kings xxi. 25-29.
6. **Changed** garments from the prison of sin—2 Kings xxv. 29.
7. **Stained** garments in relation to the judgment of sin—Isa. lxiii. 1-3.

The words "garment," "clothes," in the above Scriptures are the same in the original.

373. GATES

"Go through, go through the Gates" (Isa. lxii. 10).

GATES are the means of entrance, and as we enter we find what is inside, to our benefit and enjoyment.

1. **Gate of the Tabernacle**—Exod. xxvii. 16. Type of Christ as the entrance into blessing—John x. 9, 10.
2. **"Gate of Heaven"** (Gen. xxviii. 17). Type of the experience of those who find Christ in their life's journey.
3. **"Gate of the Guard to the King's House"** (2 Kings xi. 19). When we are guarded by the King's guard of holiness and peace, we find it leads us to the place of the King's house.
4. **"Gates of Righteousness"** (Psa. cxviii. 19, 20). Nothing that is wrong can enter this gate. Being right and doing right, we square with the right.

5. Gates of Beauty—Isa. liv. 12. "I will make thy gates of carbuncles." When the Lord adorns us with His beauty, others are attracted by His grace.

6. "Gates of Praise" (Isa. lx. 18). Praise is the grace of gratitude opening its heart and life with thanksgiving and adoration to the Giver of all good.

7. "Gate of Jehovah" (Jer. vii. 2). To recognise Jehovah as the unchanging One, and the One who will cause things to be, is to find ourselves in the realm of His love.

374. GATES
IN THE NEW TESTAMENT

1. The **"strait gate"** of salvation—Matt. vii. 13.
2. The **"wide"** gate of sin—Matt. vii. 13, 14.
3. The **city** gate of sorrow—Luke vii. 12.
4. The **luxuriant** gate of sadness—Luke xvi. 20.
5. The **beautiful** gate of need—Acts iii. 2, 10.
6. The **closed** gate of opportunity—Acts x. 17.
7. The **iron** gate of deliverance—Acts xii. 10.
8. The **knocked** gate of gladness—Acts xii. 13, 14.

375. "GATHERED TOGETHER"

1. The Centre of Attraction. "Gathered together in My Name, there am I" (Matt. xviii. 20).

2. The Object of Calvary. "Gather together in one" (John xi. 52).

3. The Power of Prayer. "When they had prayed, the place was shaken where they were assembled together" (Acts iv. 31).

4. The Privilege of Service. "Assembled themselves with the Church" (Acts xi. 26).

5. The Joy of Believers. "Gathered the Church together... rehearsed all that God had done" (Acts xiv. 27).

6. The Purpose of Gathering. "Disciples came together to break bread" (Acts xx. 7).

7. The Church in Discipline. "When ye are gathered together...deliver such a one unto Satan" (1 Cor. v. 4, 5).

The word *sunago* in each of the above Scriptures might be rendered "gathered together."

376. "GAVE UP"

1. **Sinners given up to Sin given up by God.** "Wherefore God also gave them up," etc. (Rom. i. 24, 26, 28).
2. **The Saviour given up for our Sins.** "Who was delivered for our offences" (Rom. iv. 25).
3. **God's Love in Christ's Death.** "Delivered* Him up for us all," etc. (Rom. viii. 32).
4. **The Saviour's Voluntary Act in His Substitutionary Death.** "Gave Himself up for me" (Gal. ii. 20, R.V.; Eph. v. 2, 25).
5. **The Lord's Committal of Himself into the Hands of His Father.** "Committed* Himself to Him" (1 Peter ii. 23).
6. **The Devotion of the Lord's Servants to His Work.** "Men that hazarded* their lives" (Acts xv. 26).
7. **The Truth of the Gospel Given to the Saints.** "Faith once delivered* to the saints" (Jude 3).

377. "GIVETH"

THERE are many things which the Lord giveth. The following seven in the Old Testament are among the many:

1. **Wealth.** "It is He that giveth thee power to get wealth" (Deut. viii. 18).
2. **Songs.** "Who giveth songs" (Job. xxxv. 10).
3. **Power.** "He giveth power to the faint" (Isa. xl. 29).
4. **Food.** "Who giveth food" (Psa. cxxxvi. 25).
5. **Grace.** "He giveth grace unto the lowly" (Prov. iii. 34).
6. **Victory.** "God giveth avengement to me," etc. (2 Samuel xxii. 48, margin).
7. **Sleep.** "He giveth His beloved sleep" (Psa. cxxvii. 2).

378. GLORIOUS THINGS OF THE GLORIOUS GOSPEL

1. A Glorious **Work**—Psa. cxi. 3.
2. A Glorious **Past**—Isa. xi. 10.
3. A Glorious **Liberty**—Rom. viii. 21.
4. A Glorious **Power**—Col. i. 11.
5. A Glorious **Gospel**—2 Cor. iv. 4.
6. A Glorious **Body**—Phil. iii. 21.
7. A Glorious **Appearing**—Titus ii. 13.

* Same word in Greek.

379. "GIVETH"

MARK the present tense of the above word, as illustrating the constancy of God's grace:

1. **Life.** "He giveth to all life" (Acts xvii. 25).

2. **Increase.** "God giveth the increase" (1 Cor. iii. 7).

3. **Victory.** "Thanks be to God which giveth us the victory" (1 Cor. xv. 57).

4. **Wisdom.** "Giveth to all men liberally" (James i. 5).

5. **Abundance.** "Giveth more grace," etc. (James iv. 6).

6. **Service.** "The ability which God giveth" (1 Peter iv. 11).

7. **All Things.** "Who giveth us richly all things" (1 Tim. vi. 17).

380. "GLORY"

THE Bible says a great deal about "glory." Glory is the excellence of anything in display. The Heavens declare the glory of God's creative skill. The miracles of Christ displayed the glory of what He could do—John ii. 11. The following things "of glory" will further illustrate:

1. **"Hope of Glory"** (Col. i. 27). Christ within is the pledge of glory without.

2. **"Body of Glory"** (Phil. iii. 21, R.V.). When Christ comes He will make His own like to Himself.

3. **Partners of Glory**—Luke ix. 32; Col. iii. 4; Eph. i. 18. The scene on the Mount of Transfiguration is a pattern of things yet to be. We shall be with Him.

4. **"Liberty of the Glory"** (Rom. viii. 21, R.V.). Creation is to be brought into the liberty of the children of God. Creation is bathed in tears and blood, but it will be blessed and free.

5. **"Presence of Glory"** (Jude 24). Christ will "present" ("set") His own "faultless before the presence of His glory."

6. **"Throne of Glory"** (Matt. xxv. 31). The glory of His throne will extinguish all the lights of every earthly throne.

7. **"Appearing of Glory"** (Titus ii. 13, R.V.; 2. Thess. ii. 8). We are looking for the shining forth of our great God and Saviour as the coming of Him who is "the Blessed Hope."

381. "GO"

1. **"Go, and sin no more"** (John viii. 11) is the Saviour's word of direction to the sinner whom He frees from condemnation. For the world's doom is the precursor to departure from sin's domination, as Israel found when they were commanded to leave Egypt's association, having escaped its judgment.

2. **"Go in peace"** (Luke vii. 50) is the benediction which falls upon the pardoned one's ears. No more is sin to ruffle, Satan to tear, the world to traffic, the flesh to mar; but Christ's own peace is to reign supreme within the heart, however many temptations may rage without.

3. **"Go in this thy might"** (Judges vi. 14). The Lord's promised presence was to be Gideon's guarantee that he should save Israel. The foe was strong and numerous, but the Lord, the Mighty Man of valour, was with His servant, hence his victory was certain.

4. **"Go...and preach the Gospel"** (Mark xvi. 15). Here is the Lord's definite command to the Church as to her mission in the world. Her mission is not to amuse the world, nor herself, but to proclaim the glad tidings of the faithful saying, that Christ Jesus came into the world to save sinners.

5. **"Go, shut thyself within thine house"** (Ezek. iii. 24). The prophet was prohibited from speaking further to rebellious Israel. He was to find comfort in seclusion, and to pour out his heart in supplication. The secret place of the Lord's presence is the cure for every ill.

382. GOD
"We trust in the living God" (1 Tim. iv. 10).

1. God in the **holiness** of His nature—1 John i. 5, 6.
2. God in the **heart** of His love—John iii. 16.
3. God in the **revelation** of His Son—Heb. i. 1, 2.
4. God in the **might** of His Spirit—Acts i. 8.
5. God in the **sufficiency** of His grace—2 Cor. ix. 8.
6. God in the **purpose** of His will—Heb. xiii. 20, 21.
7. God in the **promise** of His Word—2 Peter i. 4.

383. "GOD HATH"
IN 1 CORINTHIANS.

1. **Revelation.** "God hath revealed" (ii. 10).
2. **Selection.** "God hath chosen" (i. 27).
3. **Preparation.** "God hath prepared" (ii. 9).
4. **Ordination.** "God hath set forth" (iv. 9).
5. **Resurrection.** "God hath raised up" (vi. 14).
6. **Vocation.** "God hath called" (vii. 15).
7. **Distribution.** "God hath distributed" (vii. 17).
8. **Combination.** "God hath tempered the body" (xii. 24).
9. **Situation.** "God hath set" (xii. 28).

384. "GOD"

1. **"Uncorruptible** God" in glory—Rom. i. 23.
2. **"Everlasting** God" in revelation—Rom. xvi. 26.
3. **"Invisible** God" in Christ—Col. i. 15.
4. **"Living** God" in power—1 Thess. i. 9.
5. **"True** God" in manifestation—1 Thess. i. 9.
6. **"Blessed** God" in grace—1 Tim. i. 11.
7. **"Great** God" in splendour—Titus ii. 13.

385. GOD AND INIQUITY

1. He **finds** it out—Gen. xliv. 16.
2. He **sets** them before Him—Psa. xc. 8.
3. He **marks** it, for He says, "Thine iniquity is marked before Me" (Jer. ii. 22)
4. He **dealt** with Christ on the Cross in relation to it—Isa. liii. 5, 6, 11.
5. He **takes** it away—Isa. vi. 7.
6. He **purges** it—Jer. xxxiii. 8.
7. He **forgives** it—Psa. lxxxv. 2.
8. He **subdues** it—Micah vii. 19.
9. He **redeems** from it—Psa. cxxx. 8.
10. He **punishes** for it—Amos iii. 2.

386. "GOD OF PEACE"

"THE God of Peace" is always associated with holiness.

1. Holiness of **His Presence.** "The God of Peace be with you" (Rom. xv. 33).
2. Holiness of **His Victory.** "The God of Peace shall bruise, " etc. (Rom. xvi. 20).
3. Holiness of **His Work.** "Be perfect...and the God of Peace be with you" (2 Cor. xiii. 11).
4. Holiness of **His Will.** "These things do, and the God of Peace be with you" (Phil. iv. 9).
5. Holiness of **His Power.** "God of Peace brought from the dead" (Heb. xiii. 20).
6. Holiness of **His Calm.** "The Lord of Peace be with you" (2 Thess. iii. 16).
7. Holiness of **His Call.** "God of Peace sanctify you wholly" (1 Thess. v. 23).

387. "GOD IS"

1. The **Essence** of God's being. "God is a Spirit" (John iv. 24).
2. The **Sublimity** of His nature. "God is love" (1 John iv. 8).
3. The **Splendour** of His perfection. "God is light" (1 John i. 5).
4. The **Reason** of His grace. "The Lord is good" (Nahum. i. 7).
5. The **Perfection** of His holiness. "God is holy" (1 Peter i. 15).
6. The **Height** of His personality. "The Lord is great" (Psa. xcvi. 4).
7. The **Refuge** of His protection. "God is a refuge and strength" (Psa. xlvi. 1).

388. GOD'S BRINGINGS

1. **A Saviour Heralded.** "Bring you good tidings...a Saviour" (Luke ii. 10).
2. **An End Accomplished.** "Might bring us to God" (1 Peter iii. 18).
3. **A Robe Investure.** "Bring forth the best robe" (Luke xv. 22).
4. **A Feast Provided.** "Bring hither the fatted calf" (Luke xv. 23).
5. **A Fruitful Branch.** "Bring forth more fruit" (John xv. 2).
6. **A Gracious Remembrancer.** "Bring all things to your remembrance" (John xiv. 26).
7. **A King's Retinue.** "Will God bring with Him" (1 Thess. iv. 14).
8. **A Divine Searcher.** "Bring to light" (1 Cor. iv. 5).

389. GOD'S CONSTANT MINISTRY

As Described in Job xxxvi. 27 to xxxvii. 13

Note the pronoun "He" as illustrating His service, goodness, and wisdom.

1. "He maketh" (xxxvi. 27). His skill.
2. "He spreadeth" (xxxvi. 30). His wisdom.
3. "He covereth" (xxxvi. 32). His power.
4. "He judgeth" (xxxvi. 31). His dealing.
5. "He giveth" (xxxvi. 31). His supply.

6. "He directeth" (xxxvii. 3). His guidance.
7. "He thundereth" (xxxvii. 5). His voice.
8. "He sealeth" (xxxvii. 7). His pleasure.
9. "He wearieth" (xxxvii. 11). His endurance.
10. "He scattereth" (xxxvii. 11). His strength.
11. "He commandeth" (xxxvii. 12). His word.
12. "He causeth" (xxxvii. 13). His purpose.

Notice that all these are in the present tense, as bringing out God's continued and continual oversight of all things.

390. GOD'S GIVINGS

1. He gives us **His love** to charm us—1 John iv. 9.
2. **His peace** to calm us—John xiv. 27.
3. **His word** to arm us—Eph. vi. 17.
4. **His promises** to cheer us—2 Peter i. 4.
5. **His joy** to strengthen us—Neh. viii. 10.
6. **His riches** to endow us—Eph. iii. 8.
7. **His grace** to empower us—2 Cor. xii. 9.
8. **His spirit** to guide us—John xvi. 13.
9. **His beauty** to beautify us—Psa. xc. 17.
10. **His glory** to satisfy us—Rom. viii. 17, 18.

391. GOD'S DELIGHTS

THERE are certain things in which God finds pleasure and satisfaction.

1. **Christ.** "In whom My soul delighteth" (Isa. xlii. 1). He delighted in what He is—the Holy One; He delighted in the death He died, for it was well-pleasing to Him; He delighted in the work He performed; He delighted in the obedience He gave; He delighted in the testimony He bore; He delighted in the words He uttered; and He delighted in His delight to do His will—Psa. xl. 8.

2. **Cross.** "He delighted in Him" (Psa. xxii. 8). The enemies of God said this of Him sneeringly, because He did not relieve Christ from the Cross. They knew not the loving purpose of God, nor the necessity of that atoning death, hence the contempt in their utterance.

3. **Men.** "My delights were with the sons of men" (Prov. viii. 31). It seems as the Lord desired the companionship of men, so He became a Man among men, that men might become the sons of God.

4. **"A Good Man."** "He delighteth in His way" (Psa. xxxvii. 23). When a man has his steps ordered by the Lord, he is a pleasure to the Lord. Seneca says, "He who would make his travels delightful must first make himself delightful."

5. **Prayer.** "The prayer of the upright is His delight" (Prov. xv. 8). It is the upright man's prayers which are a joy to Him. What a motive to be upright, and what an inspiration for the upright to pray.

6. **Mercy.** "He delighteth in mercy" (Micah vii. 18). Mercy is love's benediction blessing the undeserving. His mercy is not a dole thrown out, but the grace of God bestowed upon us with joy.

7. **Justness.** "A just weight is His delight" (Prov. xi. 1). God takes note of the actions of men. He puts a bad mark against frauds, cheats, hypocrites, and profiteers; and a good mark against those who give sixteen ounces to the pound.

392. GOD'S DELIVERANCE OF ISRAEL BY THE HAND OF MOSES

1. **Vindication.** It was a vindication of His servant, for the Lord had spoken through Moses to Pharaoh again and again, and had made him smart because of his disobedience— Exod. xi. 1. When God's servants act in obedience to His commands, He will vindicate their cause.

2. **Opposition.** Pharaoh again and again hardened his heart against the Lord, till at last the Lord left him in his hardened state, and in this sense we understand the sentence, "The Lord hardened Pharaoh's heart" (Exod. xi. 10). A self-elected choice against God always brings its own judgment.

3. **Help.** When God's people are in dire straits, He will often cause those who are not His people to help them, for that is the meaning of the words "borrowed" and "lent" (Exod. xii. 35, 36). The children of Israel asked for the things that the Egyptians gave them, as we read in the Revised Version, "So they let them have what they asked."

4. **Redemption.** The great consequence was that Israel knew God's delivering grace through their responsive obedience, for right through we find illustrated, if not stated, the children of Israel went and did so, as Jehovah commanded Moses— Exod. xii. 28. When we walk with the Lord in the path of obedience, He will always side with us in the might of His power. This is illustrated again and again in what Jehovah did for Israel as stated in Exodus xi. and xii.

393. GOD'S GRACE TO ISRAEL
HOSEA xi. 1-4

EIGHT things are stated in Hosea xi. 1-4, which demonstrate God's grace to Israel, and which are illustrations of His love to His children.

1. **Loved.** "When Israel was a child I loved him." Three things ever demonstrate love: affection, sacrifice, and service. Love loves because it is love, and not because of the worthiness of its object—1 John iv. 9, 10; sacrifices, because it loves—John iii. 16; and serves, because it delights to do so—John xiii. 1.

2. **Called.** "Called My son out of Egypt." Love does not suffer the object of its affection to remain in the Egypt of bondage and the thraldom of sin, but brings it "out of" it. Salvation and liberty are the inception blessings of the Gospel.

3. **Instructed.** "I taught Ephraim to go" (R.V., "to walk"). The beautiful picture of a mother teaching her child to walk is suggested by these words. It teaches us to walk consistently by the truth—3 John 4, consecratingly by His example—1 John ii. 6, and circumspectly by the Spirit—Eph. v. 15.

4. **Sustained.** "I took them on my arms" (R.V.). When the child gets tired, the mother carries it; so the Lord sustained and helped His people. Who can sink through the everlasting arms?

5. **Healed.** "I healed them." Three things are essential to a physician. He must know the disease, possess the remedy, and know how to deal with the patient. The Lord has all the qualifications.

6. **Attracted.** "I drew them with cords of a man, with bands of love." The metaphor seems to be of a plough being drawn by oxen, with the touch of a human, and that with bands (wreathen work) so strong that nothing could break them. The attractive power of a holy affection is magnetic, and far-reaching in its influence.

7. **Liberated.** "I was to them as they that take off the yoke on their jaws." Whatever the actual reference, there is the underlying sense of lifting something that galled, fretted, and oppressed. The yoke of sin is hard and heavy, while the Lord's yoke is easy and light.

8. **Provided.** "I laid meat unto them," or as Rotherham has it, "Holding out to him, I let him eat." The Lord not only turns us into green pastures, but He holds dainty bits to us, even as Boaz did to Ruth—Ruth ii. 14.

394. GOD'S "I HAVE'S"

1. **Pardoned.** "I have blotted out" (Isa. xliv. 22).
2. **Redeemed.** "I have redeemed" (Isa. xliii. 1; xliv. 22).
3. **Protected.** "I have covered" (Isa. li. 16).
4. **Chosen.** "I have chosen" (Isa. xliv. 1).
5. **Endowed.** "I have put my Spirit upon" (Isa. xlii. 1).
6. **Regarded.** "I have seen...I have heard" (Isa. xxxviii. 5).
7. **Loved.** "I have loved" (Isa. xliii. 4).

395. GOD'S PEOPLE ARE

1. **Harboured** in His grace for safety—Joel iii. 16, margin; Amos ix. 11, margin; Nahum i. 7.

2. **Holy** in His holiness for sanctification—Deut vii. 6; xiv. 2, 21; 1 Peter i. 15, 16.

3. **Helped** in His strength for suffering—2 Cor. xii. 9; Acts xxvi. 22; Heb. iv. 16.

4. **Honoured** in His fellowship for service—John xii. 26; 2 Tim. ii. 21.

5. **Hidden** in His presence for communion—Col iii. 3; Psa. xxvii. 5; cxxxii. 7; Isaiah xlix. 2.

6. **Happy** in His love for joy—Deut xxxiii. 29; Psa cxliv. 15; cxlvi. 5; Prov. xvi. 20.

7. **Heavened** in His glory for satisfaction—Psa. xvii. 15; 1 Cor. xv. 53; Phil. iii. 21; 1 John iii. 2.

396. GOD'S SUCCOUR

"She is sinking very fast," was whispered by an attendant in the dying chamber of a godly woman. "No, I am not sinking; I am in the arms of my Saviour," she said. To have the arm of Jehovah as our protection, and His arms beneath us for our comfort, means many things. Among the many, it means—

1. **The deliverances** of His grace—Deut. iv. 34; v. 15; vii. 19; ix. 29; xi. 2; xxvi. 8.
2. **The joy** of His victories—Psa. xcviii. 1.
3. **The comfort** of His love—Deut. xxxiii. 27.
4. **The attention** of His care—Isa. xl. 11.
5. **The upholding** of His power—Isa. li. 5.
6. **The succour** of His salvation—Isa. xxxiii. 2.
7. **The assurance** of His blessing—Mark x. 16.

397. GOD'S THOUGHT AND TESTIMONY ABOUT CHRIST

1. God **sent** Him for us—John iii. 17.
2. God **saves** us through Him—John iii. 17.
3. God **supplies** us in Him—Eph. i. 3.
4. God **speaks** to us of Him—Luke ix. 35.
5. God **sustains** us by Him—2 Cor. i. 4.
6. God **sanctifies** us in Him—1 Cor. i. 2.
7. God **strengthens** from Him—2 Cor. xii. 9.

398. GOD'S WILL

His will is for believers—

1. To be **sanctified** in Christ's work—Heb. x. 10.
2. To be **chosen** in His grace—Eph. i. 5.
3. To be **separated** from the world—Gal. i. 4.
4. To be **holy** in life—1 Thess. iv. 3.
5. To **suffer** in silence—1 Peter ii. 15.
6. To be **thankful** in everything—1 Thess. v. 18.
7. To **recognise** Him in all things—1 John v. 14.

399. GOD'S WORD

The Psalmist says: "Thou hast magnified Thy Word above all Thy Name" (Psa. cxxxviii. 2), therefore we do well to glorify it above everything else. It is—

1. **Divine in its Source.** To take but one book, the Acts, we find the Word is referred to thirty-five times. As "the Word of God" (iv. 31; vi. 2, 7; viii. 14; xi. 1; xii. 24; xiii. 5, 7, 44, 46; xvii. 13; xviii. 11; xix. 20) thirteen times; as "the Word of the Lord," eight times (viii. 25; xi. 16; xiii. 48, 49; xv. 35, 36; xvi. 32; xix. 10); as "the Word," thirteen times (iv. 4; vi. 4; viii. 4; x. 36, 44; xi. 19; xiii. 26; xiv. 3, 25; xv. 7; xvi. 6; xvii. 11; xx. 32); and as "Thy Word," once (iv. 29).

2. **Dynamic in its Operation.** Notice what it says about His Word in the Epistle to the Hebrews—i. 3; ii. 2; iv. 12; vi. 5; xi. 3; xiii. 7. There lieth in the dynamite of God's Word all the latent possibilities of the life of the Almighty.

3. **Definite in its Claim.** The Epistles to the Thessalonians illustrate the claims of the Word. It is "the Word" in its authority (i. 6), "The Word of the Lord" in its message (i. 8; iv. 15; 2. iii. 1), and "the Word of God" in its power (ii. 13). The Word claims the faith of our obedience, the loyalty of our love, and desire of our Hope.

4. Distinct in its Prophecy. The Book of the Revelation may illustrate what is found in many places. Christ is the Key— xix. 13, to keep it is our responsibility—i. 9; iii. 8, 10; vi. 10; xii. 11; xx. 4; and to bear record of it is our privilege—i. 2.

5. Distinguishing in its Message. The many qualifying words of the Word indicate its manifold message. It is a Word of Life to quicken—Phil. ii. 16; the Word of Faith to beget faith—Rom. x. 8; the Word of Reconciliation to assure—2 Cor. v. 19; the Word of God to slay—Eph. vi. 17; the Word of Christ to indwell—Col. iii. 16; the Word of the Lord to reveal— 1 Thess. iv. 15; the Word of Faithfulness to keep—Titus i. 9; the Word of Righteousness to adjust—Heb. v. 13; the Word of Incorruption to endure—1 Peter i. 23, 25; and the Engrafted Word to fructify—James i. 21.

6. Devoted in its Promises. The Word, as such, is coupled with what the Spirit calls "The word of all His good promise." Solomon confessed that not "one word" of God's good promise "failed" (1 Kings viii. 56). His promises and the performance of them is continually referred to—Psa. cv. 42; Acts xiii. 23, 32; xxvi. 6, 7; Rom. iv. 20; Gal. iii. 14-29; Heb. vi. 13-17; 2 Peter iii. 4, 9, 13.

Another interesting Bible study might be worked out in connection with the words "He," or "The Lord," "hath promised"—Exod. xii. 25; Deut. xii. 20; xxvi. 18; Josh. xxiii. 10; 2 Chron. vi. 15; Rom. i. 2; Heb. xii. 26; James i. 12; ii. 5; 1 John ii. 25.

7. Dedicating in its Influence. When we call to mind what the Lord says He will do by means of His Word, we can see how beneficent and practical it is in its in-working and out-working. Let us confine our thought to Christ and His teaching. He taught the Word was a fruit-producer—Matt. xiii. 23; a victory-gainer—Matt. iv. 4; a disciple-witnesser—John viii. 31; a sanctifying-obtainer—John xvii. 17; a love-prover—John xiv. 23; a prayer-answerer—John xv. 7; and a heart-assurer— John v. 24.

400. GOD THE ALL-WISE
As seen in Job xxxvi. 13-xxxvii. 13

No one who believes in God can doubt His wisdom. It is stamped—like the water-marks upon a Bank of England note— upon everything around us. The birds with their song speak forth the praise of wisdom; the cattle with their lowing and the sheep with their bleating tell out the fact; the flowers with their variegated beauty and sweet scent re-echo the same; the earth with its treasures, the sea with its supply, and the Heavens with their glory point out the wisdom of God.

There are many things that Elihu speaks of that point as so many sign-posts to the wisdom of God.

1. The **dew**, like pearls hanging upon the blades of grass—27.

2. The **rain**, like Rebecca supplying Eliezer, ministering to the thirsty earth—27.

3. The **clouds**, like a huge filter, purifying the vapour—28.

4. The **light**, like a messenger of good news, bringing joy and gladness, and like a great artist giving beauty and colour—30.

5. The **sea**, with its teeming life and its abundant supply for man like a huge larder, where he can go and be supplied —29, 30.

6. The **darkness**, like an extinguisher to put out the light, so that man is like a blind man without the help of God—32.

7. The **lightning**, with its vivid glare, like the gleam of a glittering sword uplifted to strike—xxxvii. 3.

8. The **thunder**, with its boom, as if the floor of Heaven was cracking—4.

9. The **snow**, like a mantle to keep the young shoots warm—6.

10. The **wind**, like affliction, takes away the rotten branches and strengthens the roots of the trees—9.

11. The **cold**, like trial, purifies and preserves—9.

401. "GOOD"

1. The **source** of "good works" is to be found by being in the creative hands of the Lord Jesus—Eph. ii. 10.

2. The **spring** of a "good conscience" is the outcome of whole-hearted allegiance to Christ—1 Tim. i. 5.

3. The **soul** of a "good conversation" (manner of life) is the result of following in the steps of Christ—1 Peter iii. 16.

4. The **inspiration** which shall enable us to war a "good warfare" is obtained by fellowship with Christ—1 Tim. i. 18.

5. The **motive** which shall prompt us to show all "good fidelity" to Christ has its rise in our desire to please Him—Titus ii. 10.

6. **Submission** to Christ is the secret of bringing forth "good fruit," for as the branch receives the sap which is in the tree, so we receive the life which is in Christ by our obedience to Him—Matt. vii. 17.

7. And the one thing which shall move us to be "good stewards" of the manifold grace of God, is to know in our own hearts **the grace** which has saved us—1 Peter iv. 10.

402. GOOD CHEER FOR BELIEVERS

SEVEN times the Lord gives the cheering salutation, "Be of good cheer." Once indirectly, and six times directly.

1. **Sins Forgiven.** "Son, be of good cheer; thy sins are forgiven" (Matt. ix. 2). The past annihilated by the Christ of Calvary.

2. **Faith Honoured.** "Daughter, be of good cheer; thy faith hath made thee whole" (Matt. ix. 22, R.V.). Life and health come by contact with the living Christ.

3. **Fears Banished.** "Be of good cheer; it is I; be not afraid" (Matt. xiv. 27).

"The word of His grace all fears doth efface;
Not one can live in the light of His face."

4. **Feebleness Met.** "Be of good cheer; rise, He calleth thee" (Mark x. 49, R.V.). The word of Christ put new life into him, for he "sprang up, and came to Jesus;" and thenceforth Bartimaeus was no longer the beggar sitting, but the disciple following.

5. **Foes Overcome.** "In the world ye shall have tribulation: but be of good cheer; I have overcome the world" (John xvi. 33). The world witn its god and Godless course need not daunt us, for Christ can give us deliverance.

6. **Further Service Indicated.** "The Lord stood by him and said, Be of good cheer...thou must bear witness also in Rome" (Acts xxiii. 11).

7. **Faith's Testimony and Blessing.** "Be of good cheer... wherefore be of good cheer...Then were they all of good cheer" (Acts xxvii. 22, 25, 36).

403. "GOOD WORK"

1. **Abounding.** "Abound to every good work" (2 Cor. ix. 8).

2. **Fruit.** "Fruitful in every good work" (Col. i. 10).

3. **Stablished.** "Stablish you in every good...work" (2 Thess. ii. 17).

4. **Diligence.** "Diligently followed every good work" (1 Tim. v. 10).

5. **Preparation.** "Prepared unto every good work" (2 Tim. ii. 21).

6. **Readiness.** "Ready to every good work" (Titus iii. 1).

7. **Perfection.** "Make you perfect in every good work" (Heb. xiii. 21).

8. **Completion.** "He which hath begun a good work in you, will perform it" (Phil. i. 6).

404. "GOOD" THINGS IN MATTHEW

1. "Good **Fruit**" (iii. 10).
2. "Good **Works**" (v. 16).
3. "Good **Gifts**" (vii. 11).
4. "Good **Tree**" (vii. 17).
5. "Good **Cheer**" (ix. 2; xiv. 27).
6. "Good **Comfort**" (ix. 22).
7. "Good **Ground**" (xiii. 8).
8. "Good **Seed**" (xiii. 27).
9. "Good **Work**" (xxvi. 10).

405. "GOING"

A GOSPEL MESSAGE

1. "**Going astray**" in the ways and wilfulness of sin (1 Peter ii. 25).
2. "**Going up**" to Jerusalem to accomplish a work (Matt. xx. 17).
3. "**Going through**" all opposition in Almighty Power (John viii. 59).
4. "**Going down** to the pit," and God's reason for not continuing in the course (Job. xxxiii. 24).
5. "**Going about**" to establish a righteousness which is not right (Rom. x. 3).
6. "**Going before**" to claim sin's judgment (1 Tim. v. 24).
7. "**Going out**" in God's keeping (Psa. cxxi. 8).

406. GOSPEL

THE Gospel we are called to preach is like the flowers, many-coloured, beautiful, and fragrant.

1. It is **Divine** in its source, for it is "of God" (Rom. i. 1).
2. It is **gracious** in its bestowment, for it springs from grace—Acts xx. 24.
3. It is **personal** in its message—Mark i. 1.
4. It is **life-giving** in its begetting—1 Cor. iv. 15.
5. It is **saving** in its work—Eph. i. 13.
6. It is **full** in its blessing—Rom. xv. 29.
7. It is **powerful** in its might—Rom. i. 16.
8. It is **practical** in its out-working—Phil. i. 27, R.V.
9. It is **glorious** in its consummation—2 Cor. iv. 4.

There is power in the Gospel we preach, but we need the power of God to preach it.

407. GOSPEL

THE Gospel is the good news of God's love in providing a Saviour—Rom. v. 8.

1. Proclaims that Christ died **for our sins**—1 Cor. xv. 3.
2. That He rose for our **justification**—Rom. iv. 25.
3. That His grace can **save**—Titus ii. 11.
4. That His Blood can **cleanse**—1 John i. 7.
5. That His power can **keep**—1 Peter i. 4.
6. That His Spirit can **qualify**—Acts i. 8.
7. That His joy can **gladden**—John xv. 11.
8. That His peace can **quieten**—John xiv. 27.
9. That He Himself can **satisfy**—Phil. iii. 7-9.

408. GOSPEL
"The Gospel of Christ" Rom. i. 16

"A NATIVE cook in Nigeria," said Mrs. F. W. Dodds, a missionary, at the Primitive Methodist Conference at Liverpool recently, "placed the text 'God is Love' on the kitchen door, and wrote underneath, 'No admittance.' "

The cook did not mean what the notice seemed to say, for the Gospel proclaims blessing for all.

1. God **loves** all, and calls all to believe in Christ and be saved—John iii. 16.

2. Christ died as a propitiation on **account** of all, for the sins of the world—1 John ii. 2.

3. The Spirit says, "**Whosoever** calleth on the Name of the Lord shall be saved" (Acts ii. 21).

4. Christ says, "Him that cometh unto Me, I will **in no wise** cast out" (John vi. 37).

5. The righteousness of God is **unto all**, and upon all who believe—Rom. iii. 22.

6. God makes no difference in **blessing all** who will be blest—Acts xv. 9.

7. Forgiveness of sin is proclaimed **to all** who believe in Christ—Acts xiii. 39.

8. **As many** as receive Christ are made the children of God—John i. 12.

409. GOSPEL'S THREEFOLD MESSAGE

THE Gospel is a three-fold message.

1. It is "the Gospel of the **grace of God**" (Acts xx. 24), proclaiming His favour to the undeserving.

2. It is the **Gospel of power**, telling out the good news that God never asks us to do a thing without giving us the power to do it—Rom. i. 16.

3. It is a **Gospel of glory**, declaring a better state of things in the future—2 Cor. iv. 4.

410. GRACE

"The grace of God" Titus ii. 11

PASCAL sings of grace. "To make a man a saint, grace is absolutely necessary, and whoever doubts it, does not know what a saint is or what a man is."

The following blessings, mentioned in Ephesians, which grace bestows will speak for themselves.

1. We are **accepted** in the Beloved to the "praise of the glory of His grace" (i. 6).

2. We are **forgiven** "according to the riches of His grace" (i. 7).

3. We are "**saved** by grace," that is, through His loving act, irrespective of what we are (ii. 5, 8).

4. We are **made trophies** of His love through "the exceeding riches of His grace" (ii. 7).

5. We are privileged to be **witnesses** of the Lord through the "grace given" (iii. 7, 8).

6. We are exhorted to **be channels** of blessings to others by a consistent life, that we may "minister grace" to them (iv. 29).

7. The benediction of love is, "**Grace** be with all who love our Lord Jesus Christ" (vi. 24).

411. GRACE AND GLORY

1. **Transferred** from death to life by grace—John v. 24.

2. **Transfigured** by the Spirit by looking at Christ—2 Cor. iii. 18, R.V.

3. **Translated** by the power of God at Christ's return—Heb. xi. 5.

4. **Transformed** by the Saviour, and made like to Him—Phil. iii. 20, 21.

412. "GREAT THINGS"

"Who has done great things, O God" Psa. lxxi. 19

C. H. SPURGEON, that prince of preachers, once said: "God's mercy is so great that it forgives great sins to great sinners after great lengths of time, and then gives great favours and great privileges, and raises us up to great enjoyments in the great Heaven of the great God. As John Bunyan well said, 'It must be great mercy or no mercy, for little mercy will never serve my turn.'"

Many are the great things the great God has done. The following are a few of the great things He shows us:

1. **Loved with a "Great Love"** (Eph. ii. 4). His love is a fathomless ocean, a mine of wealth, a lasting spring, a glorious provision, a sun of warmth, a lifting power, and an unceasing inspiration.

2. **Saved with a "Great Salvation"** (Heb. ii. 3). God is its source, man is its object, Christ is its embodiment, deliverance is its meaning, the Spirit is its power, faith is its receiver, holiness is its outcome, and glory is its consummation.

3. **Thrilled with a "Great Joy"** (Luke ii. 10; Acts viii. 8; xv. 3). The Saviour is its secret, substance, supply, and source. His joy makes our joy full and lasting.

4. **Strengthened with "Great Power"** (Acts iv. 33). The Spirit's enduement is the power to keep us right, and to work in and through us with effective might.

5. **Communing with "Great Delight"** (Song of Songs ii. 3). Sitting under the shadow of His Cross, and listening to the voice of His Word, and feeding on the promises of His grace, we have "great delight" in His presence.

6. **Enjoying the "Great Peace" of His Word** (Psa. cxix. 165). To love God's Word is to find the joy of His grace, the tenderness of His love, the holiness of His sanctity, and the peace of His promises.

7. **Expecting the "Great Glory"** (Luke xxi. 27). When Christ comes to the world His saints will come with Him. He will not have the glory apart from His saints, and it would be no glory if He were not with it.

413. "GROW UP," "GO OUT," "GET UP"

1. If we would "**grow up**" into Christ in all things—Eph. iv. 15.
2. We must "**go out**" from the world of sin—Gen. xii. 1.
3. And "**get up**" to the Bethel of prayer—Gen. xiii. 3, 4.

414. "GRIEVED" PEOPLE

1. A grieved **Saviour**—Mark iii. 5.
2. A grieved **disciple**—John xxi. 17.
3. A grieved **apostle**—Acts xvi. 18.
4. A grieved **brother**—Rom. xiv. 15.
5. A grieved **prophet**—Dan. vii. 15.
6. A grieved **sinner**—Mark x. 22.
7. A grieved **God**—Heb. iii. 17.

415. GRUBS

HERE are some grubs which the Lord's people are after.

1. The voracious grub of **covetousness**—Gen. xiii. 10, 11.
2. The slimy grub of **jealousy**—Luke ix. 46.
3. The black grub of **pride**—2 Chron. xxvi. 16.
4. The changing grub of **compromise**—2 Kings v. 18.
5. The stinging grub of **temper**—Phil. iv. 2.
6. The contaminating grub of **worldly companionship**—2 Chron. xviii. 1.
7. The poisonous grub of **disobedience**—1 Kings xiii. 21, 22.

416. HAND OF GOD

IN EZRA VII.-viii. 15-32

1. **A Ready Leader**—vii. 6. "Ready" means "skilful" or quick. The word comes from a root which means to flow easily, to be liquid, hence to be prompt, to answer, to do. There was no hesitation or trepidation. To be ready in the things of God shows we are in touch with the God of the things.

2. **Supplied Leader**—vii. 6. Behind the king's granting him "all his request" is "according to the hand of his God." Earthly stores come from the Lord's cupboard.

3. **Prepared Leader**—vii. 10. Before Ezra taught others he "prepared" himself, and he "prepared" himself by the best possible means, namely, "prepared his heart to seek the law of the Lord."

4. **Recognised Leader**. The King of Persia recognised that Ezra was a man who was instructed in the commandments and law of God—see the frequent references to the fact in vii. 11, 12, 21, 23, 25, 26. When we recognise God by our obedience to His Word He will cause others to recognise us to our honour.

5. **Thankful Leader**—vii. 27, 28. Ezra praised "the Lord God of our fathers," and acknowledged all that came to him through the king was from "the hand of the Lord my God."

6. **Associated Leader**—viii. 15-20, 24-30. A leader must have someone to lead, and each and all go to make the sum total of success. "The priests" and "the people," the "men of understanding" and the "man of understanding," the sons of Levi, and "all who were expressed by name" were required in the Lord's work and worship.

7. **Prayerful Leader**—viii. 21-23. Mark the expressive words: "To seek of Him a right way," "The hand of our God is upon all them for good that seek Him," "Besought our God for this, and He was entreated of us."

8. **Conquering Leader**—viii. 31, 32. Ezra not only started on his journey to Jerusalem, but he got there, and he was able because of the "hand of God" to lead his host, to keep from being ensnared, and conquered by the way.

417. HAND OF THE LORD IN THE ACTS

THE hand of God denotes His power to accomplish things. The Acts of the Apostles illustrate His hand as—

1. An **exalted** hand—ii. 33.
2. A **purposing** hand—iv. 28.
3. A **healing** hand—iv. 30.
4. An **honouring** hand—v. 31.
5. A **delivering** hand—vii. 25, 35.
6. A **converting** hand—xi. 21.
7. A **judging** hand—xiii. 11.

418. HAPPINESS

MANY a trite thing is heard in an omnibus. Riding along Whitechapel Road in a motor bus, an east-ender greeted the conductor in a sarcastic way, as he looked at his beaming face, by saying, "Whatever makes you look so happy?"

With a lightning retort the conductor replied, "It's what I'm looking at that makes me look so happy."

The writer complimented the official upon his reply, and the man said, "Yes, when a fool greets you that way the only way to down him is to give him biting sarcasm back."

Although the reply of the conductor was witty sarcasm, we may use it to a profitable end, for when our outlook is right, our inward condition will answer to it. The following instances which describe happy conditions are to the point.

1. **Source** of Happiness. "Happy is he that hath the God of Jacob for his help" (Psa. cxlvi. 5). When we are helped by God we are in a happy condition.

2. **Receivers** of Happiness. "Happy is that people whose God is the Lord" (Psa. cxliv. 15). When Jehovah the Unchanging One is our God, every case is met by Him.

3. **Soul** of Happiness. "Happy art thou, O Israel...people saved by the Lord" (Deut. xxxiii. 29). When we are saved by the Lord we cannot help being happy with Him.

4. **Meaning** of Happiness. "Happy shalt thou be, and it shall be well with thee" (Psa. cxxviii. 2). These are twin blessings which come to the one who fears the Lord and walks in His ways.

5. **Feeders** of Happiness. "Happy are ye if ye do them" (John xiii. 17). So our Lord declares to those who do the things of His example.

6. **Helper** of Happiness. When "for righteousness sake" we suffer for Christ, the Lord says "happy are ye" (1 Peter iii. 14).

7. **Condition** to Happiness. "Whoso trusteth in the Lord, happy is he" (Prov. xvi. 20), for he that trusteth in the Lord brings everything to Him in prayer, and thus finds God comes into everything in power.

419. HARD THINGS

HARD things come to hard sinners in their hard ways.

1. **A Hardened Way**. "The way of transgressors is hard" (Prov. xiii. 15). Those who break God's law will surely find hard things in their lives.

2. **A Hardened Heart**. "He that hardeneth his heart shall fall into mischief" (Prov. xxviii. 14). A hardened heart is a heart which will fall in disaster.

3. **A Hardened Neck**. "They hardened their neck" (Neh. ix. 16, 17, 29). Like a horse which will not answer to the driver, so sinners obey not the Lord.

4. **A Hardened Mind**. "His mind hardened in pride" (Dan. v. 20). Pride stiffens to a downfall.

5. **A Hard Bondage**. "Made their lives bitter with hard bondage" (Exod. i. 14). Bondage of Israel is a type of sin's bondage.

6. **Hard Riches**. "How hard it is for them that trust in riches" (Mark x. 24). Riches are hardening if their hardness dominates.

7. **Hard Pricks**. "Hard for thee to kick against the pricks" (Acts xxvi. 14). The goads of sin cut the sinner.

420. HARVEST

HARVEST time is associated with many things.

1. Blessing from the Lord. "Thou crownest the year with Thy goodness" (Psa. lxv. 11, 13). See the "Thou's" of Psalm lxv. God's coronation time is the harvest time.

2. Faithfulness of the Lord. "While the earth remaineth, seedtime and harvest...shall not cease" (Gen. viii. 22). He binds Himself in love to bless us in grace.

3. Communion with the Lord. "One soweth, and another reapeth" (John iv. 37). When we look upon the fields of man's need with the eyes and heart of Christ, we must have fellowship with each other, because we have fellowship with Him.

4. Responsibility to the Lord. In reaping the fields, the poor were to be remembered—Lev. xix. 9; and the firstfruits were to be given to the Lord—Exod. xxiii. 15, 19.

5. Remembered by the Lord. The direction about the forgotten sheaf is very suggestive. What we forget is remembered by the Lord. Our loss is another's benefit, and another's benefit is always a benefit to us—Deut. xxiv. 19.

6. Joy in the Lord. The harvest is a time of joy. God's bounties are inspirations to praise. His givings cause our rejoicings—Isa. ix. 3; Psa. cxxxvi. 6.

7. Gathered Before the Lord. The redeemed who have fallen asleep will be the firstfruits, and the righteous will be gathered in the Lord's garner, but the wicked will be cast out —Matt. xiii. 37-43.

421. HEAD OF CHRIST

1. An **unrested** head in life—Luke ix. 58.
2. An **anointed** head in gratitude—Mark xiv. 3.
3. A **thorn-crowned** head in suffering—John xix. 2.
4. A **bowed** head in atoning love—John xix. 30.
5. An **uncovered** head in resurrection—John xx. 7.
6. A **beautiful** head in revelation—Rev. i. 14.
7. A **crowned** head in victory—Rev. xix. 12.

422. HEALING OF THE BODY

THE Lord gave His disciples power and authority over all demons and to cure diseases. "Power" means ability to do a thing; "authority" speaks of the right to do things; and the fact that the disciples went "healing everywhere" shows that they accomplished what the Lord intended, namely, to "cure" diseases. This raises an interesting question, which is, If the servants of Christ were acting under His authority and power,

would they not have the same ability to heal disease? There
are four reasons why we may expect the Lord to heal.

1. Because of what **He is**—Jehovah Ropheca—Exod. xv. 26.
2. Because of what Christ **has done** on the Cross—Isa. liii. 3, 4.
3. Because of what **He promises**—James v. 15.
4. Because of what the **Holy Spirit can do**—Rom. viii. 11.

423. HEAVY

1. **Heavy Hands.** Brethren hold them up—Exod. xvii. 12.
2. **Heavy Yoke.** Oppression of sin—1 Kings xii. 4, 10, 11, 14.
3. **Heavy Burden.** Consciousness of sin—Psa. xxxviii. 4.
4. **Heavy Ears.** Hardening of unbelief—Isa. vi. 10.
5. **Heavy Eyes.** Drowsiness of slumber—Matt. xxvi. 40, 43.
6. **Heavy Trials.** Opportunities for triumph—1 Peter i. 6.
7. **"Heavy Laden."** Christ the lifter—Matt. xi. 28.

424. HEEDLESS MAN

A HEEDLESS man may be

1. A **Balaam** in good wishes—Num. xxiii. 10.
2. An **Ananias** in profession—Acts v. 3-5.
3. A **Simon Magus** in desire—Acts viii. 19.
4. A **Diotrephes** in prating—3 John 9.
5. An **Esau** in tears—Heb. xii. 17.
6. A **Demas** in friendship—Col. iv. 14; 2 Tim. iv. 10.
7. A **foundationless builder** in folly—Matt. vii. 26.

But these do not suffice, therefore we do well to "take heed"
to God's Word (Luke viii. 18).

425. "HE HATH"

GOD's acts declared in Luke i. 48-54.

1. **Regard.** "He hath regarded...the low estate of His
hand-maiden."
2. **Recognition.** "He that is mighty hath done to me great
things."
3. **Power.** "He hath shewed strength with His arm."
4. **Victory.** "He hath scattered the proud."
5. **Humiliation.** "He hath put down the mighty from their
seats."
6. **Supply.** "He hath filled the hungry with good things."
7. **Refusal.** "The rich He hath sent empty away."
8. **Help.** "He hath holpen His servant Israel."

426. "HE SHALL BE GREAT"

Luke i. 32

SOME of the great things in the great Lord are found in His great love.

1. **Great God in Being.** "Our great God and Saviour" (Titus ii. 13, R.V., margin).

2. **Great Love in Action.** "Great love wherewith He hath loved us" (Eph. ii. 4).

3. **Great Salvation in Blessing.** "So great salvation" (Heb. ii. 3).

4. **Great Mercy in Grace.** "Great is His mercy towards them that fear Him" (Psa. ciii. 11).

5. **Great Power in Operation.** "Great is our Lord and of great power" (Psa. cxlvii. 5).

6. **Great Light in Revelation.** "People that sat in darkness saw great light" (Isa. ix. 2).

7. **Great Rock in Protection.** "Shadow of a great rock in a weary land" (Isa. xxxii. 2).

8. **Great Shepherd in Power.** "Great Shepherd of the sheep" (Heb. xiii. 20).

9. **Great King in Splendour.** "The city of the Great King" (Psa. xlviii. 2).

427. "HE SPAKE"

"Never man spake like this Man" (John vii. 46).

FREQUENTLY in John's Gospel we read, "He spake" and "Jesus spake," which illustrates the head text. Mark the importance of His utterance and the themes to which He refers.

1. Christ's **Resurrection.** "He spake of the temple of His body" (ii. 21).

2. Christ's **Pre-knowledge.** "He spake of Judas Iscariot" (vi. 71).

3. Christ's **Promise.** "This spake He of the Spirit" (vii. 39).

4. Christ's **Revelation.** "He spake again, saying, I am the Light of the World" (viii. 12).

5. Christ's **Attraction.** "As He spake these words many believed on Him" (viii. 19, 20, 27, 30).

6. Christ's **Teaching.** "He spake this parable unto them" (x. 6).

7. Christ's **Death.** "He spake signifying what death He should die" (xviii. 32).

428. "HE WILL...COME"
Heb. x. 37

1. Because **He has said so.** "I will come again and receive you to Myself" (John xiv. 3).

2. Because **He is needed.** "When He shall come to be glorified in His saints" (2 Thess. i. 10).

3. Because **He wants to.** "Behold I come quickly" (Rev. xxii. 12).

4. Because **the Father** hath so **purposed.** "God hath appointed a day in which He will judge the world in righteousness by that Man whom He hath ordained" (Acts xvii. 31).

5. Because **the Scriptures affirm** He will. "The sufferings of Christ and the glory that should follow" (1 Peter i. 10, 11).

6. Because **creation longs** for it. "The earnest expectation of the creature waiteth for the manifestation of the sons of God" (Rom. viii. 19).

7. Because **He alone can adjust** things. "In His days shall the righteous flourish" (Psa. lxxii. 7, see whole Psalm).

429. "HIMSELF"

CHRIST is the embodiment, expression, and example of love.

1. **Love's Satisfaction.** "When He had by Himself purged (atoned for) our sins" (Heb. i. 3).

2. **Love's Substitution.** "Gave Himself for me" (Gal. ii. 20).

3. **Love's Intention.** "Gave Himself for us, that He might redeem us from all iniquity" (Titus ii. 14).

4. **Love's Work.** "Once in the end of the world, He appeared to put away sin by the sacrifice of Himself" (Heb. ix. 26).

5. **Love's Act.** "Christ loved the Church and gave Himself for it" (Eph. v. 25).

6. **Love's Ransom.** "Gave Himself a Ransom for all" (1 Tim. ii. 6).

7. **Love's Deliverance.** "Gave Himself for our sins, that He might deliver us from this present evil world" (Gal. i. 4).

430. HINDRANCES
"What did hinder you?" Gal. v. 7

"THE water is not hot for the bath." So said a servant maid, after the fire in the kitchen grate had been burning for some hours, and in calling attention to what she said was the cause, she held up a piece of coal, and said the coal went to a cinder soon after it was lighted! Attention was drawn by her mistress to the fact, "There is a fire sufficient to roast an ox!" That was an exaggeration, but there was certainly fire enough to roast a joint. The reason why the water did not get hot was not with the coal, but with the maid, for the flue at the back, in front of the boiler was found to be choked with ashes. When the flue was cleared, the fire could get under the boiler, and soon there was hot water enough and to spare. We often blame effects when we should deal with causes. When the causes are adjusted the effects are of benefit. How many hindrances there are which affect the Christian life and hinder its developments!

1. The **lack of adding** the graces of the Spirit will hinder us from seeing "afar off"—2 Peter i. 9.

2. The **want of diligence** will keep us out of God's resting rest—Heb. iv. 1-6, R.V.

3. The **failure to "go on** to perfection" will cause us to be babes in the Christian life—Heb. iii. 12; vi. 1.

4. The **"carnal" state of half-heartedness** will keep us back from the realm of spirituality—1 Cor. iii. 1-3.

5. The **sleepiness of a slothful state** will cause Christ to depart from us, when we might have enjoyed His fellowship—Song of Solomon v. 1-6.

6. The **spirit of legality** will cause us to be left out of the liberty of grace—Gal. v. 1.

7. The **giving heed to the fables** and fancies of men will mar our testimony in the Lord's service—1 Tim. i. 3-19.

431. "HIS"

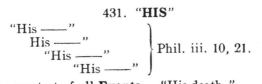

"His ——"
His ——"
"His ——"
"His ——" } Phil. iii. 10, 21.

1. The greatest of all **Events.** "His death."
2. The greatest of all **Sufferings.** "His sufferings."
3. The greatest of all **Power.** "His resurrection."
4. The greatest of all **Blessings.** "His glorious body."

432. "HIS"

ELIHU'S TESTIMONY

THE things that belonged to God are expressively expressed in Job. xxxvi. 22 to xxxvii.

1. "His power" (xxxvi. 22). **Might** of God.
2. "His way" (xxxvi. 23). **Method** of God.

3. "His work" (xxxvi. 24).   **Skill** of God.

4. "His years" (xxxvi. 26).   **Eternity** of God.

5. "His tabernacle" (xxxvi. 29).   **Dwelling** of God.

6. "His light" (xxxvi. 30).   **Essence** of God.

7. "His voice," "His mouth" (xxxvii. 2-6).   **Word** of God.

8. "His lightning" (xxxvii. 3).   **Control** of God.

9. "His strength" (xxxvii. 6).   **Power** of God.

10. "His work" (xxxvii. 7).   **Purpose** of God.

11. "His bright cloud" (xxxvii. 11).   **Glory** of God.

12. "His counsels" (xxxvii. 12).   **Will** of God.

13. "His land" (xxxvii. 13).   **Property** of God.

God has given us two books. The book of nature and the Bible. We cannot understand one without the other. We cannot unlock the lock of nature, without the key of the Bible.

LESSONS.

1. He deals with us to bring us to know ourselves and to know Him—xxxvii. 2, 7, 13. We do well to pray, show me myself, and, show me Thyself.

2. His goodness should cause us to praise Him with life and lips—xxxvi. 31.

3. His power should lead us to trust Him at all times.

4. His wisdom should excite in us the desire to know Him more fully.

433. "HOLD FAST"

1. **An Ideal Believer.**   "Hold fast that which is good" (1 Thess. v. 21).

2. **A Faithful Witness.**   "Holding fast the faithful word" (Titus i. 9).

3. **A Tenacious Evangelist.**   "Hold fast the form of sound words" (2 Tim. i. 13).

4. **A Cleaving Confessor.**   "Hold fast our confession" (Heb. iv. 14, R.V.).

5. **An Expectant Waiter.**   "Hold fast the confession of our hope" (Heb. x. 23, R.V.).

6. **A Resolute Steward.**   "Hold fast till I come" (Rev. ii. 25).

7. **A Jealous Watcher.**   "Hold fast that which thou hast" (Rev. iii. 11).

434. "HOLINESS UNTO THE LORD"

Exod. xxxix. 30

"Holy in all manner of life" (1 Peter i. 15, r.v.).

Murray M'Cheyne prayed, "Lord, make me as holy as it is possible for a child of Thine to be." Such a prayer becomes all who pray. We do well to pray that we may be—

1. Holy in **body**, as expressed in Romans xii. 1, where we are urged to yield our bodies "holy, acceptable unto God."

2. Holy in **prayer**, as directed in 1 Tim. ii. 8, where we are exhorted to "lift up holy hands."

3. Holy in **worship**, as denoted in 1 Peter ii. 5, where believers are called a "holy priesthood."

4. Holy in **citizenship**, as described in 1 Peter ii. 9, where we are named a "holy nation."

5. Holy in **thought**, as suggested by the high priest having on his mitre the words "holiness unto the Lord" (Exod. xxviii. 36).

6. Holy in **business**, as represented by "holiness unto the Lord" being on the "bells" and "pots," as stated in Zechariah xiv. 20, 21.

7. Holy in **heart** as urged in 1 Thess. iii. 13, "hearts unblameable in holiness before God."

435. "HOLY" ("HAGIOS")

"Hagios" denotes that which is sacred, set apart, consecrated. The use of "holy" as applied to the redeemed is far-reaching and suggestive.

1. **Holy Ones**, who are called "saints" (Rom. i. 7). Not called "to be saints," but "called saints."
The words "to be" are not in original. Believers are named "saints" by God, and because of this are to be saintly.

2. **"Holy Scriptures"** (Rom. i. 2). The Holy Spirit is their Author, and holiness is their product.

3. **"Holy Calling"** (2 Tim. i. 9). The vocation of the saint is the opposite to that of the sinner's. The centre of the latter is self, but the attraction of the other is God.

4. **Holy Indwelling.** "The Holy Spirit which dwelleth in us" (2 Tim. 1. 14). To recognise His Holy presence is to experience His sanctifying power.

5. **Holy Identification.** "Chosen in Him...that we should

be holy" (Eph. i. 4). As the altar sanctified the gift under the law, so oneness with Christ makes us holy.

6. Holy Keeping. "Holy Father keep" (John xvii. 11), so Christ prays for His own. The Holy One keeps us holy within and righteous without.

7. "Holy Priesthood" (1 Peter ii. 5). Uncleanness is not tolerated in this priestly service, nor maimed sacrifices in its ministry.

8. "Holy Conversation" (1 Peter i. 15; 2 Peter iii. 11). "Conversation," as R.V., means the whole life. Our behaviour corresponds to our blessings. What we are, tells.

436. HOLY SPIRIT AS THE SPEAKER
IN THE ACTS

AT least seven times we find the Holy Spirit speaking in the Acts of the Apostles, or reference is made to His having spoken, and in each Scripture we are reminded of His personality and authority.

1. He is a **Prophesying** Speaker—i. 16. He draws on one side the veil which hides the future and gives us to see what is to take place in the days to come.

2. He is a **Guarding** Speaker—xv. 28. He points out, as a faithful friend, that which would clog the believer in his walk and hinder him in his usefulness.

3. He is a **Restraining** Speaker—xvi. 6. He is the Lord, the Spirit, hence He does not allow His servants to go where they will. He has the right to command, and the power to forbid.

4. He is a **Warning** Speaker—xx. 23. Danger and persecution lie in the path of every true follower of Christ, but the Holy Spirit is the One who arms us by His forewarning.

5. He is a **Predicting** Speaker—xxi. 11. Peace and persecution, trial and triumph, conflict and conquest go together, but He who tells us of the one assures us of the other.

6. He is a **Reproving** Speaker—xxviii. 25. To be deaf to Christ's entreaties, and blind to His beauty, is to be in a sorry condition.

7. He is a **Separating** Speaker—xiii. 2. Paul and Barnabas did not take upon themselves the task of separating themselves to the Lord's work, neither were they set apart by man, but the Holy Spirit Himself set them apart for the ministry of the Gospel. He called, He equipped, He qualified, and He empowered.

437. HOLY SPIRIT IN GENESIS

1. Power to **Produce.** "God created man" (i. 27).
2. Power to **Act.** "Spirit of God moved" (i. 2).
3. Power to **Declare.** "God said, Let there," etc. (i. 3).
4. Power to **Discern.** "God saw" (i. 4).
5. Power to **Divide.** "God divided" (i. 4).
6. Power to **Designate.** "God called" (i. 5, 8).
7. Power to **Form.** "God made" (i. 7).
8. Power to **Place.** "God set" (i. 17).
9. Power to **Bless.** "God blessed" (i. 22).
10. Power to **Finish.** "God ended" (ii. 2).

438. HOLY SPIRIT "UPON"

1. **Christ.** Power to benefit—Matt. iii. 16; Mark i. 10; Luke iii. 22; John i. 33; Luke iv. 18; Matt. xii. 18.
2. **Mary.** Power to enable—Luke i. 35.
3. **Simeon.** Power to see—Luke ii. 25.
4. **The Disciples.** Power to witness—Luke xxiv. 49; Acts i. 8; ii. 3; ii. 17, 18.
5. **Gentile Believers.** Power to "magnify God"—Acts x. 44-46; xi. 15.
6. **Ephesian Believers.** Power to proclaim—Acts xix. 6.
7. **Suffering Saints.** Power to sustain—1 Peter iv. 14.

439. HOME

"Shew piety at home" 1 Tim. v. 4

"WHAT politics is your husband?" asked a canvasser concerning the absent spouse; and the wife replied: "Well, it's like this— sometimes he goes to a Liberal meeting, and then he's a Liberal; sometimes he goes to a Conservative meeting, and then he's a Conservative." "But," demanded the canvasser, "what is he when he is at home?" "Oh, then," explained the wife, "then he's an old nuisance."

What we are at home is the test of what we are at all.

What should we be at home?

1. **Witnesses,** to tell what the Lord has done for us, as Christ told the saved demoniac—Mark v. 19.

2. **Receivers,** to entertain Christ, as He said to Zaccheus, "To-day I must abide at thy home." (The word "house" in Luke xix. 5, is rendered "home" in 1 Cor. xi. 34.)

3. **Consistent Ones**, for we are "first to shew piety at home" (1 Tim. v. 4).

4. **Faithful Ones**, like Moses, who was "faithful in all his house," or "home" (Heb. iii. 2, 5).

5. **Prayerful Intercessors**, like Cornelius, who prayed in his house or home—Acts x. 30.

440. HOPE

WHEN hope is in the objective, that is, something set before us, it always refers to Christ's Coming for His saints.

1. **"The** Hope" (Col. i. 5). Christ Himself.

2. **"Our** Hope" (1 Tim. i. 1). Common heritage of believers.

3. **"This** Hope" (1 John iii. 3). We shall be "like Him."

4. "Hope of the **Gospel**" (Col. i. 23). Revealed by, and part of, the Gospel.

5. "Hope of **Salvation**" (1 Thess. v. 8). Completion of salvation.

6. "Hope of **Righteousness**" (Gal. v. 5). Vindication of the Lord's own.

7. "Hope of **Eternal Life**" (Titus i. 2; iii. 7). The blessedness of life eternal in the future.

8. "Hope of **Our Calling**" (Eph. iv. 4). What we shall have when Christ comes.

9. "Hope of **His Calling**" (Eph. i. 18). What Christ will have.

10. "Hope of **Glory**" (Col. i. 27). The excellence of His glorious manifestation.

11. **"Living** Hope" (1 Peter i. 3, R.V.). The lastingness of His livingness.

12. **"Blessed** Hope" (Titus ii. 13). Present joy and lasting bliss.

441. HOPE

How Paul plays upon the grace of "hope." "Hope of the promise," "hope to come," "hope's sake." The hope centres in three things—the death, resurrection, and coming of Christ—Acts xxiii. 6; xxvi. 6, 7; xxviii. 20.

1. These are the **objective** realities of the Gospel—1 Thess. iv. 13-18.

2. The **subjective** grace of expectancy is also referred to as the incentive to serve God—1 Thess. i. 9.

3. The objective facts of truth are the power to create the subjective grace within, even as the steam in the engine causes the train to run on the lines.

442. HOUSE

1. The **secure** house of character is built on the Word of the Lord—Luke vi. 48.

2. The **swept** house of reformation, lacking the saving presence of Christ—Luke xi. 25.

3. The **believing** house of faith, a Heaven on earth—John iv. 53.

4. The **perfumed** house of love. What every home should be—John xii. 3.

5. The **earthly** house of the body, and heavenly house of glory—2 Cor. v. 1.

6. The **great house** of Christendom, with its diversified vessels—2 Tim. ii. 20.

7. The **exclusive** house of faithfulness, shutting out the error of evil—2 John 10.

443. HOW TO HELP IN THE LORD'S WORK

1. By the **will of responsiveness** to the Lord, as the workers in the Tabernacle—Exod. xxv. 2.

2. By the **voice of prayer**, as Nehemiah and his helpers—Neh. iv. 9.

3. By the **feet of alacrity**, as Philip the evangelist, when he went to the eunuch—Acts viii. 30.

4. By the **heart of love**, as Paul did the saints at Philippi—Phil. i. 7, R.V.

5. By the **tongue of kindness**, as the apostle did the people on board ship—Acts xxvii. 34-36.

6. By the **ear of deafness**, in not listening to the slander of those who malign us—Matt. xxvii. 14.

7. By the **eye of discernment**, as Peter did Simon the sorcerer—Acts viii. 9.

8. By the **hands of labour**, as the disciples helped each other in fishing—Luke v. 7.

444. HUMILITY

THE QUEEN OF GRACES

HUMILITY is the queen of graces. It does not seek the throne of eminence, but the throne is adorned by it. The excellence of humility is illustrated in the following Scriptures. Humility is—

1. **The Soul of Contentment.** It feels it does not deserve anything, therefore takes with gratitude whatever comes—Phil. iv. 12. It ever sings, "O to grace how great a debtor!"

2. Flower of Grace—Eph. iv. 2. Humility walks consistently, loves generously, serves willingly, acts meekly, forgives heartily, forbears thoughtfully, and responds obediently.

3. Secret of Service—Acts xx. 19. To serve the Lord with all humility of mind is to have the bloom of consecration, the aroma of grace, the unction of love, the warmth of zeal, the ardour of faith, the walk of obedience, and the beauty of holiness.

4. Badge of Obedience. The Lord's command is, "Humble yourselves" (1 Peter v. 6), and it is not without meaning that it is to be "under the mighty hand of God." We only know the mightiness of God's hand when we lie low beneath it.

5. Lesson of Grace. When we are yoked with Christ in God's will we are in the position to learn of Christ, who is "meek" and "lowly in heart" (Matt. xi. 29). To talk about humility is to show we do not possess it, but to keep step with Christ is to have it without knowing it.

6. Mind of Lowliness. "In lowliness of mind let each esteem other better than themselves" (Phil. ii. 3). To see the best in others is to find the worst in ourselves. Self-contemplation leads to self-congratulation, and that always genders pride.

7. Example of Christ. The mind of Christ is illustrated in that He "humbled Himself" (Phil. ii. 8). The three commands of Christ: "Believe in Me," "Abide in Me," and "Follow Me," follow each other. He went down before He was raised up, so we need to pray: "Help us, O Lord, to deeper sink, that we may the higher rise." The downward path is the upward one.

8. Livery of Heaven. "Be clothed with humility" (1 Peter v. 5). This is a suit that is always in fashion; it never wears out, and it is always becoming. Humility is recognised by men, admired by angels, and appreciated by God.

9. Securer of Blessing. "He giveth more grace to the humble" (James iv. 6), or as the margin, "A greater grace." Whether an excelling grace, or "more" of the grace that excels, humility is its own reward, and is rewarded by the Lord's commendation.

10. Harbinger of Reward. "He that humbleth himself shall be exalted" (Matt. xxiii. 12). The heavier the cargo, the more the vessel is sunk into the water, and the greater its worth. When the fruit of humility causes the branch of the soul to bend in lowliness, the Heavenly Gardener plucks the fruit for the garner of His love.

445 "I AM NOT"

It is well to know what we are "not" as well as what we are.

1. **John's Repudiation.** "I am not the Christ" (John i. 20). "I am not worthy" (Matt. iii. 11).

2. **The Pharisee's Pride.** "I am not as other men are" (Luke xviii. 11).

3. **Peter's Denial.** When he was said to be a disciple of Christ's, he replied, "I am not" (Luke xxii. 58; John xviii. 17).

4. **Christ's Avowal.** "I am not of this world" (John viii. 23; xvii. 14, 16).

5. **Centurion's Confession.** "I am not worthy" (Matt. viii. 8).

6. **Christ's Companion.** "I am not alone" (John viii. 16; xvi. 32).

7. **Place in the Body.** "I am not the hand...I am not the eye" (1 Cor. xii. 15, 16). Be what you are, but do not try to be what you are not.

446. "I AM PERSUADED"

1. **Love's Work.** "I am persuaded...this thing was not done in a corner" (Acts xxvi. 26).

2. **Love's Tenacity.** "I am persuaded that neither life nor death," etc. (Rom. viii. 38).

3. **Love's Preservation.** "I am persuaded that He is able to keep that which I have committed unto Him" (2 Tim. i. 12).

447. "I AM WITH YOU"
Haggai i. 13

In the sphere of business, in the temple of worship, and in the home of industry, each is strengthened to do the work of the Lord; and the cause of all is because the Lord says, "I am with you." He is with us—

1. As the **Captain** to lead—Josh. v. 14.
2. As the **Shepherd** to tend—Psa. xxiii. 4.
3. As the **Companion** to cheer—Heb. xiii. 5, 6.
4. As the **Guide** to direct—Isa. xxx. 21.
5. As the **Power** to keep—Isa. xli. 13.
6. As the **Teacher** to instruct—Luke xxiv. 32.
7. As the **Encourager** to stimulate—Isa. xli. 10.

448. "IF ANY MAN"

THE universality of Christ's invitations and claims is comprehensively revealed in the sentence, "If any man," as found in John's Gospel.

1. Eternal Life. "If any man eat of this bread, he shall live for ever" (vi. 51). Eternal life has to do with the Being of God, and is the positive blessing of the Gospel.

2. Secret of Knowledge. "If any man will do His will, he shall know of the doctrine" (vii. 17). The secrets of the Lord are with them who fear Him.

3. Satisfaction. "If any man thirst, let him come unto Me and drink" (vii. 37). He wants everything, who wants Christ, and He is the Meeter of every need.

4. Salvation. "If any man enter in, he shall be saved" (x. 9). Christ is the entrance to every blessing.

5. Walk. "If any man walketh in the day, he stumbleth not" (xi. 9). To walk in the light is the soul of right.

6. Following Christ. "If any man serve Me, let him follow Me" (John xii. 26). The way to serve Him is to follow Him.

7. Honoured. "If any man serve Me, him will My Father honour" (John xii. 26). What is done to Christ is reckoned by the Father as done to Him.

8. Judgment. "If any man hear My words, and believe not...the Word I have spoken, the same shall judge him in the last day" (John xii. 47, 48). How men treat Christ and His Word is the basis of judgment.

449. INDWELLING CHRIST

1. The **Secret of Christ's Life.** "I live, yet not I, but Christ liveth in me" (Gal. ii. 20).

2. The **Power for Progress** in Grace. "I will dwell in them and walk in them" (2 Cor. vi. 16).

3. The **Cause of Fruitfulness.** "I in you" (John xv. 4).

4. The **Illumination to Enlighten.** "The Word of Christ dwell in you" (Col. iii. 16).

5. The **Garrison to Keep** the Mind. "Let the peace of God rule in your hearts" (Col. iii. 15).

6. The **Joy to Gladden** the Heart. "My joy might remain in you" (John xv. 11).

7. The **Hope of Coming Glory.** "Christ in you, the hope of glory" (Col. i. 27).

450. INABILITIES

THE word *"dunamai"* is variously rendered in the following Scriptures. Sometimes "can," but we have given it "not able" in each case.

1. **Inability to Change.** "Not able to make one hair white," etc. (Matt. v. 36).

2. **Inability to Serve** two Masters. "Not able to serve two masters...God and mammon" (Matt. vi. 24).

3. **Inability to Produce.** "A good tree not able to bring forth evil" (Matt. vii. 18).

4. **Inability to Kill.** "Not able to kill the soul" (Matt. x. 28).

5. **Inability to Cure.** "Not able to cure" (Matt. xvii. 16).

6. **Inability to Answer.** "Not able to answer Him" (Matt. xxii. 46).

7. **Inability to Save.** "Himself, not able to save" (Matt. xxvii. 42).

451. "IN CHRIST" AND "IN THE LORD"

THE expression "in Christ" and "in the Lord" in Romans xvi.

1. **Phebe** is to be received "in the Lord."

2. **Priscilla** and **Aquila** are to be greeted as "helpers in Christ Jesus."

3. **Andronicus** and **Junia** are recognised by the apostle as being "in Christ before me."

4. **Amplias** is "beloved in the Lord."

5. **Urbane** is a "helper in Christ."

6. Those of the **household of Narcissus** are saluted as "in the Lord."

7. **Tryphena** and **Tryphosa** are those who "labour in the Lord."

8. **Persis** laboured much "in the Lord."

9. **Rufus** is chosen "in the Lord."

10. **Apelles** is "approved in Christ"—Rom. xvi. 2, 3, 7, 8, 9, 11, 12, 13, 10.

452. "INCLINE THINE EAR"

THE meaning of the Hebrew word for "incline" is "to stretch out," that is, to turn aside and give special attention to the suppliant. *Natah* is rendered "stretched out" in Exodus vi. 6; Isaiah ix. 12, 17, 21; and "turn aside" in Isaiah xxx. 11.

1. **Confidence.** "Thou wilt hear me, O God: incline Thine ear unto me" (Psa. xvii. 6). Confidence in God will secure

communications from Him. The open hand of faith is filled
with the answered request.

2. Salvation. "Incline Thine ear unto me, and save me"
(Psa. lxxi. 2). A consciousness of danger will cause the cry for
deliverance from it.

3. Strength. "Incline Thine ear...for my soul is full of
trouble...I am a man that hath no strength" (Psa. lxxxviii.
2-4). A strengthless condition makes way for the Lord's
strengthful conquests.

4. Trouble. "I am in trouble: incline Thine ear unto me"
(Psa. cii. 2). "Call upon Me in the day of trouble." When we
couple our prayers with God's promises, we command God's
attention and deliverance.

5. Forgiveness. "O my God, incline Thine ear...forgive"
(Dan. ix. 18, 19). We should not only cry for personal forgiveness, but for national forgiveness too. We are united in
the whole, and have a personal responsibility.

6. Victory. "Incline Thine ear, O Lord...save...smote"
(Isa. xxxvii. 15-20, 36). The munitions of prayer are more
effective than the manufacturers of earth.

7. Counterpart. "Incline thine ear" (Psa. xlv. 10). To
incline to the Lord with the heart is to love Him—Josh xxiv. 23;
to His testimonies is to obey Him—Psa. cxix. 36; and to
Himself is to respond to Him—Isa. lv. 3.

453. "IN THE MOUNT"

1. A Substitute Provided. "In the mount it shall be
provided" (Gen. xxii. 14, R.V.).

2. A Pattern Given. "Make...after...pattern showed thee
in the mount" (Exod. xxv. 40; xxvi. 30; xxvii. 8; Heb. viii. 5).

3. A Meeting Place. "Met him in the mount of God"
(Exod iv. 27).

4. A Revelation Communicated. "Moses was in the
mount" (Exod. xxiv. 18).

5. A Rebuked Servant. "Die in the mount...because ye
trespassed," etc. (Deut. xxxii. 50, 51).

6. A Proclaimed Tomb. "Josiah...spied the sepulchres
that were in the mount...which the man of God proclaimed"
(2 Kings xxiii. 16, 17).

7. A Wonderful Fellowship. "We were with Him in the
holy mount" (2 Peter i. 18).

454. INDICATORS

INDICATORS along the track of time of the believer's approach to the eternal city. Some of the indicators are:

1. The **failure** of natural powers—Eccles. xii. 1-7.
2. The **ripening** of Christian character—2 Tim. iv. 7.
3. The believer's inner consciousness that his **work is finished**—2 Tim. iv. 7.
4. Some **special message** from God—Isa. xxxviii. 1.
5. A **longing** to be in the "far better" and be "at home with the Lord" (Phil. i. 23).
6. A **letting go** of the things of earth—1 Kings xix. 19-21.
7. A **contemplation** of the glory land—Isa. xxxiii. 17.

455. INDISPENSABLE THINGS

TALKING with an aged saint, poor in this world's goods, but rich in faith, she remarked, "There are a great many things I can do without." Playfully I said, "Can you do without Jesus?" "No, no," she exclaimed; "ten thousand times no!" Her exclamation reminded me of a Bible reading, which is as follows:

1. **Propitiating Blood.** "Without shedding of blood is no remission" (Heb. ix. 22).
2. **Pleasing Faith.** "Without faith it is impossible to please God" (Heb. xi. 6).
3. **Paternal Chastening.** "Without chastisement,...ye are not sons" (Heb. xii. 8).
4. **Practical Holiness.** "Holiness, without which no man shall see the Lord" (Heb. xii. 14).
5. **Proving Works.** "Faith without works is dead" (Jas ii. 26).
6. **Possessing Love.** Without love, "I am nothing" (1 Cor. xiii. 2).
7. **Providing Power.** "Without Me ye can do nothing" (John xv. 5).

456. "IN HIS SIGHT"

1. **Condemnation.** "No flesh justified in His sight" (Rom. iii. 20).
2. **Comprehension.** "Neither is there any creature that is not manifest in His sight" (Heb. iv. 13).
3. **Consecration.** "Well-pleasing in His sight" (Heb. xiii. 21).
4. **Conduct.** "Do those things that are pleasing in His sight" (1 John iii. 22).

457. "IN THE SIGHT"

1. **Character.** "Great in the sight of the Lord" (Luke i. 15).
2. **Confession.** "Right in the sight of God" (Acts iv. 19).
3. **Confusion.** "Not right in the sight of God" (Acts viii. 21).
4. **Conscience.** "Conscience in the sight of God" (2 Cor. iv. 2).
5. **Care.** "Care for you in the sight of God" (2 Cor. vii. 12).
6. **Charge.** "I give thee charge in the sight of God" (1 Tim. vi. 13; 2 Tim. iv. 1).
7. **Consecration.** "Meek and quiet spirit, which is in the sight of God a great price" (1 Peter iii. 4).

458. INNESS OF THINGS

THE Greek preposition *"en,"* generally translated "in," occurs thirty-five times in Ephesians in relation to Christ and the believer.

1. **"In Christ Jesus"** occurs seven times (i. 1; ii. 6, 7 R.V., 10, 13; iii. 6, R.V., 21). "Christ Jesus" is the anointed and anointing Saviour.

2. **"In Christ"** is found five times (i. 3, 10, 12, 20; iv. 32, R.V.). United to the Anointing One.

3. **"In the Lord"** is stated seven times (ii. 21; iv. 1, R.V., 17; v. 8; vi. 1, 10, 21). We are responsible to obey Him as Lord.

4. **"In Whom"** is declared seven times (i. 7, 11, 13, 13; ii. 21, 22; iii. 12). When we know Him we do not need to name Him.

5. **"In Him"** is given four times (i. 4, 9, R.V., 10; iv. 21, R.V.). To be found "in Him" is to find everything worth finding.

6. **"In Christ Jesus our Lord"** is stated once (iii. 11). We are in the Sanctifier, Saviour, and Sovereign.

7. **"In Himself"** (ii. 15). When believers recognise they are "in Himself" they lose sight of each other.

8. **"In Jesus"** is given once (iv. 21). Truth is found "in Jesus." He must be known to know it.

9. **"In the Name** of the Lord Jesus Christ" is found once (v. 20). When His Name perfumes our praises, how praiseful they are.

10. **"In the Beloved"** is stated once (i. 6). How loved we are when the Beloved loves us! This is tasteful, hence we are graceful.

459. "IN NO WISE"

SOMETIMES "In no wise" is given "In no case" (Matt. v. 20),
"not" (Matt. xxiv. 2), "neither" (Mark xiii. 19), "not in any
wise" (Mark xiii. 31), "by any means" (Luke x. 19), "never"
(John vi. 35), "no" (Heb. viii. 12; x. 17), and "not at all"
(Rev. xxi. 25). In the original in the above Scriptures it is the
double negative (*ov un*), which, as Bullinger points out, means
"a double negative, expressing a strong denial," which gives
an assurance that not anything can make it to be other than it
is said to be. Our words, "by no means," embody its full
significance (Matt. v. 26). Let us see how the full Gospel can
be found in the use of this double negative. We have put in
italics this double negative.

1. **Requirement of Law.** "Thou shalt *by no means* come
out thence till thou hast paid the uttermost farthing"
(Matt. v. 26). Law ever says: "Pay me what thou owest, and
it will not abate its claim, nor compromise its demand." We
owe God perfect obedience to His commandments, and absolute
fidelity to His behests, and because we have broken His laws
we are all "under sin's penalty" (Rom. iii. 9); under sin's
power—Rom. vii. 14; and under law's curse—Gal. iii. 10, 22.

2. **Release by the Lord.** "Blessed is the man to whom the
Lord will *not* ("in no wise") impute sin" (Rom. iv. 8). This
is not merely an act of grace, but it is an act which is based on
the atoning work of the Lord Jesus, for He was "delivered
up for (*dia* rendered "for," with the accusative, means "on
account of") our offences, and was raised for ("on account of")
our justification" (Rom. iv. 25). Because our sins were imputed
to Him, believers have imputed to them His righteousness; as
Luther said, "He is my sin, and I am His righteousness."

3. **Royal Assurance from the Lord.** "Him that cometh
to Me I will *in no wise* cast out" (John vi. 37). What a terrible
fact awaits those who will not come—"Cast out!" What a
gracious invitation the Lord gives in the words, "Him that
cometh;" and what an assurance He gives to those who come,
He will "in no wise cast out." This may also mean that those
whom He takes in shall never be turned out.

4. **Royal Promises in the Lord.** The following "nevers"
may each be read "in no wise." He promises to His own that
they "shall *never* thirst" (John iv. 14), "shall *never* hunger"
(John vi. 35), "shall *never* see death" (John viii. 51), "*never*
taste death" (John viii. 52), "shall *never* perish" (John x. 28),
"shall *never*" be forsaken (Heb. xiii. 5), and that those who are
alive when He returns "shall *never* die" (John xi. 26). Did

you ever find such seven nevers? Can you find such promises outside of Christianity?

5. Rule of the Lord. "I am the Light of the World, he that followeth Me shall *not* ("in no wise") walk in darkness" (John viii. 12). Darkness is the symbol of sin, of ignorance, of unbelief, of uncertainty, of obscurity, of fear, and danger. As long as believers follow the rule, to follow the Lord, sin shall not dominate them, ignorance shall not blind them, unbelief shall not deter them, doubt shall not imprison them, obscurity shall not confuse them, fear shall not daunt them, and danger shall not frighten them.

6. Recompense from the Lord. "Shall *in no wise* lose his reward" (Matt. x. 42). The Lord never loses sight of anything that is done for others out of love to Himself. He takes cognisance of the widow's mite, the work of faith, the labour of love, the patience of hope, the helping hand, the faithful witness, the heart of consecration, and the cup of cold water.

7. Retribution. "They shall *not* ("in no wise") escape" (1 Thess. v. 3), "There shall *in no wise* enter" (Rev. xxi. 27), and "Shall *in no wise* enter the Kingdom" (Luke xviii. 17). These emphatic statements mean something. Laying aside all our theories about everlasting punishment, if we take the opposites of what we read there is undoubtedly eternal loss. Take the double negative as found in other places. *Not* to be hurt of the second death implies being hurt by it—ii. 11. *Not* to have the name blotted out, implies it may be—iii. 11. *Not* to be confounded, implies we may be put to shame—1 Peter ii. 6; not to see death nor taste it, not to hunger and thirst, not to perish, and not to be cast out, implies seeing and tasting death, hunger, and thirst, perishing, and casting out.

460. INTERCESSION

"Intercessions" 1 Tim. ii. 1

THE highest form of prayer is intercession for others, and the most effective ministry is that which we exercise for others' benefit. The following are a few cases of noble intercessors who prayed for blessing upon others.

1. Moses, the self-abnegator, who was willing to be blotted out from the Lord's book so long as Israel was spared—Exod. xxxii. 1-14.

2. Samuel, the faithful prophet, pleaded for Israel and Saul when they were in sore straits because of their sin—1 Sam. vii. 8, 9; xv. 24-31.

3. **Daniel**, the humble statesman, pleaded for the nation of Judah when in captivity by identifying himself with the sin of the nation—Dan. ix. 3-20.

4. **Epaphras**, the loving pleader, interceded for the saints at Colosse that they might stand perfect and complete in all the will of God—Col. iv. 12.

5. **Paul**, the intense suppliant, pleaded for the Church at Ephesus, that they might have God's unparalleled riches—Eph. i. 16-20; iii. 16-21.

6. **John**, the loving disciple, who prayed for his friend Gaius, that he might have soul prosperity—3 John 2, margin.

7. **Christ**, the gracious Lord, who prayed for Peter that his faith might not fail—Luke xxii. 32.

The wonderful intercessory prayer as recorded in John xvii. is a sample of how the Lord is interceding for His people now.

461. IN THE DUMPS, AND OUT OF THEM.

"Why art thou cast down O my soul" Psa. xlii. 5, 6

DR. H. MONTGOMERY, of Belfast, once saw nine boys arm in arm walking along a street. They had recently been brought to Christ, and they were singing this chorus:

> "Down in the dumps I'll never go,
> That's where the Devil keeps me low."

When God's servants get into the dumps, we always find God points the way to deliverance.

1. When Elijah got **under the juniper tree** the angel told him to "arise and eat" (1 Kings xix. 5).

2. When Paul was **threatened with shipwreck**, the Lord told him to be of "good cheer" (Acts xxvii. 25).

3. When John was **banished to the Island** of Patmos, the Lord revealed Himself to him—Rev. i. 11.

4. When Jonah was **in the sea-monster**, the Lord gave him deliverance as soon as he said "salvation is of the Lord" (Jonah ii. 9).

5. When Joshua was **on his face through defeat**, Jehovah said unto him, "Get thee up" (Josh. vii. 10).

6. When Samson was **grinding in the prison**, Jehovah caused his "hair to grow again" (Judges xvi. 22).

7. When Israel was **"groaning"** in Egypt. Jehovah made them glad by bringing them out of it—Exod. vi. 5

462. "IN THE NIGHT"

1. **The Suffering Saviour.** "In the night season" (Psa. xxii. 2); "My sore ran in the night" (Psa. lxxvii. 2).

2. **The Succouring Helper.** "Spake the Lord to Paul in the night" (Acts xviii. 9).

3. **The Gladdening God.** "Who giveth songs in the night" (Job. xxxv. 10).

4. **The Safe Leader.** "Fire to give light in the night" (Psa. cv. 39).

5. **The Encouraging Friend.** "In the night His song shall be with me" (Psa. xlii. 8).

6. **The Directing Redeemer.** "The same night in which He was betrayed," etc. (1 Cor. xi. 23).

7. **The Coming Lord.** "The Lord will come as a thief in the night" (1 Thess. v. 2; 2 Peter iii. 10).

463. "IN VAIN"

1. **"Labour in vain"** (Job. ix. 29; Isa. xlix. 4).   Work without God is always profitless, and brings benefit to none.

2. **"Watch in vain"** (Psa. cxxvii. 1).   Human measures need Divine might.

3. **"Medicines...in vain"** (Jer. xlvi. 11).   Human productions cannot heal sinful maladies.

4. **"Believed in vain"** (1 Cor. xv. 2).   The fact of Christ's resurrection is the basis of our faith.   If He is not risen, there is nothing in which it can rest, it therefore must be in vain.

5. **"Run in vain"** (Gal. ii. 2).   The recognition of those who are in authority is essential to the possession of authority.

6. **"Christ is dead in vain"** (Gal. ii. 21).   Christ having bore the curse of the law in His death for us, we are freed from its curse and consequences.

7. **"Wise...in vain"** (Jer. viii. 8).   To say we are wise when we lack true knowledge is to show we are ignorant of both.

464. "I SEE"

WHAT a number of persons we find exclaiming "I see."

1. The "I see" of **Jeremiah** the prophet—Jer. i. 11, 13.
2. The "I see" of the **King of Babylon**—Dan. iii. 25.
3. Of **the Blind man**—Mark viii. 24.
4. Of **the servant**—John xviii. 26.
5. Of **Stephen**—Acts vii. 56.
6. Of **Paul**—Rom. vii. 23.
7. Of the **other blind man**—John ix. 25.

465. "IN THE PRESENCE"

1. **Standing** "in the presence of God," the secret of worship and work (Luke i. 19).

2. **"Joy** in the presence of the angels over one sinner that repenteth" (Luke xv. 10).

3. **Christ** in His miracles "in the presence of His disciples" (John xx. 30).

4. **Paul** gave "thanks to God in the presence of" his fellow-travellers (Acts xxvii. 35).

5. **Christ** is made everything to us that "no flesh should glory in" the "presence" of God (1 Cor. i. 29).

6. **The Beast Worshippers** will be punished "in the presence of the holy angels and in the presence of the Lamb" (Rev. xiv. 10).

466. "IS ABLE"

WE have ability when our inability is coupled with the Lord's ability.

1. God's ability to **create**. "God is able to raise up" (Matt. iii. 9).

2. Christ's **Keeping**. "None is able to pluck out of My hand" (John x. 29).

3. Lord's **Supply**. "Is able to do" (Eph. iii. 20).

4. The Saviour's **Power**. "He is able to subdue all things" (Phil. iii. 21).

5. Our High Priest's **Succour**. "He is able to succour" (Heb. ii. 18).

6. Living One's **Work**. "He is able to save to the uttermost" (Heb. vii. 25).

7. **Upholder's** Ability. "He is able to keep us from falling" (Jude 24).

467. ISRAEL: GOD'S PECULIAR PEOPLE

1. **Peculiar in Choice**. "Thou shalt be blessed above all people" (Deut. vii. 14). The act of Jehovah was selective and elective.

2. **Peculiar in Place**. "The people shall dwell alone" (Num. xxiii. 9). Separated from the rest of the nations, and to the Land of Palestine.

3. **Peculiar in Title**. "His peculiar people" (Deut. xxvi. 18), and "treasure" (Exod. xix. 5), and "My people" (Exod. viii. 1).

4. **Peculiar in Affection**. "Yea, He loved the people" (Deut. xxxiii. 3), not because they were worthy, but because He would.

5. Peculiar in Purpose. "Thou art a holy people unto the Lord." "Special people unto Himself" (Deut. vii. 6).

6. Peculiar in Relationship. "Treasure unto Me above all people" (Exod. xix. 5). The jewels of the Lord are found in those whom He calls so frequently "My people."

7. Peculiar in Covenant. "His holy covenant" (Luke i. 68-72). See also Exodus ii. 24; vi. 4, 5; Deut. v. 3. He pledges Himself with Abraham, and Isaac, and Jacob to bless His people Israel.

468. ISRAEL'S SINFUL CONDITION
AS DESCRIBED IN ISAIAH I

1. Israel was **Rebellious in soul.** "They have rebelled against Me" (2). Not only had they gone against His word and authority, as the word "rebelled" implies, but they had wounded Him to the heart by their baseless ingratitude. The clenched fist is the outcome of a baseless soul.

2. Israel was **Ignorant in mind.** "Israel doth not know, my people doth not consider" (3). The blight of ignorance had affected the mind of their understanding, and a want of consideration of the Lord and others was the outcome. Ignorance is always inconsiderate.

3. Israel was **Sinful in life.** "Ah! sinful nation" (4). Not only were they full of sin which made them sin to the full, but they were a failure in everything, for the word to sin signifies to miss the mark, to be a failure. They illustrated the Divine saying, "He that sinneth against me, wrongeth his own soul." We miss ourselves, and others, and life's opportunity if we miss God. We are no good if we miss the Supreme Good!

4. Israel was **Weighed in character.** "A people laden with iniquity" (4). The back of their being was heavy with iniquity, and yet for all they had done in burdening themselves, there was nothing of practical value, as the word "iniquity" suggests, for it means faultiness (the word is rendered "fault" in Psa. 59. 4) arising from perverseness. The sin of perverseness is a breaker up of everything. When we have the twist of ill-intent, we shall have the whole being wrongly bent, and have to bend to the load of consequences.

5. Israel was **Evil in conduct.** "A seed of evil-doers" (4). The evil-doing proves the doer is evil. The word "evil-doer" signifies to treat in an evil manner, hence, to break up things, to be one who brings calamity and injury to others. When one is a waster he is always a wrecker. To be a cesspool of iniquity is to be a breeder of disease, and thus to contaminate.

6. Israel was **Corrupt in transaction**. "Children that are
corrupt" or as the R.V. "deal corruptly" (4). The Hebrew
word is stonger than the previous one, it means to mar anything,
and to make it good for nothing. The word is translated
"waster" (Isa. liv. 16), "destroying" (Jer. li. 1), and "battered"
(2 Sam. xx. 15). A destroying wind which kills the sensitive
plant is a fit simile of one who mars another to his destruction.
A waster is always a woe-begetter.

7. Israel was **Apostate in act**. "They have forsaken the
Lord" (4). The word means to leave, and to leave destitute.
It is rendered "leave" in Genesis xliv. 22, and "left destitute"
in Genesis xxiv. 27. To be a traitor and unfaithful is to be
guilty of the blackest sin of Hell. To be untrue to the truth we
know to be true, is to be baseless beyond forgiveness.

8. Israel was **Provocative in speech**. "Provoked the Holy
One of Israel to anger" (4). Wilson says to provoke means
to treat with contempt, joined with hatred and malignity.
Heart-murmurings, slumbering discontent, grumbling speeches,
and a chafing spirit are always displeasing to the Lord. Words
are like thistledown, they cause mischief in the garden of the
soul, and sting others to their hurt.

9. Israel was **Insulting in attitude**. "They are gone away
backward" (4). To turn the back to the Lord was a direct insult
to Him, but to have "gone away," or to be "alienated" (margin),
or estranged from Him is to add injury to insult. The words
might be paraphrased, "Ye have turned your back to Me and
have treated Me as if I were a stranger." To deliberately
cut one without cause is to be guilty of bad manners and an
arrogant temper.

10. Israel was **Sick in head**. "The whole head is sick" (5).
"Head" here means the source of things, as the head of a river,
and "sick" signifies to be worn down in strength, hence, to be in
a condition of weakness and inability. When there is no power
in the source of things, how can the rest of the plant perform
anything? The want of moral fibre is the doom of any nation.

11. Israel was **False in worship**. The sacrifices were not
a "delight" to the Lord; their oblations were "vain," their
incense was an "abomination," their assemblies were "iniquity,"
their keeping of the feasts was hateful, a "trouble," and made
Jehovah "weary" (12-14). Could any charge be more explicit
and pathetic! When rottenness is in the heart, ritual is an
offence and a sin to the Lord.

12. Israel was **Prayerless in Prayer**. "When ye spread
forth your hands I will hide mine eyes from you; yea, when ye
make your prayers I will not hear" (15)

469. "I WILL"

THE late William Sloan, of Glasgow, a well-known Christian merchant in Scotland, once said: "I used to live under the 'Thou shalt's' of the law, but now I live under the 'I will's' of grace." What a difference there is between the two. Under the former there is the effort of self and very often failure, but under the latter there is heart response and rest, with victory. Let the following seven "I will's" of promise speak for themselves.

1. **Rest.** "I will give thee rest" (Matt. xi. 28). Responding to Christ's "Come unto Me," we find rest of conscience about our sins, and rest from fear of death and judgment, and rest of mind and heart.

2. **Service.** "Follow Me, and I will make you fishers of men" (Matt. iv. 19). Follow first, and then fish; even then, He must "make" us fishers, and He promises to do it.

3. **Satisfaction.** "I will pour water upon Him that is thirsty" (Isa. xliv. 3). He alone can slake the thirst and satisfy the soul. The dryness of our need is the opportunity for the supply of His grace.

4. **Upholding.** In Isaiah xlvi. 4, the Lord gives us four gracious I will's: "I will carry," "I will bear," "I will carry," "I will deliver."

5. **Guidance.** "I will even make a way in the wilderness" (Isa. xliii. 19). Where there is no track, He will make one, so that there may be no uncertainty in the path we should tread.

6. **Strength.** "I will strengthen thee; yea, I will help thee; yea, I will uphold thee with the right hand of My righteousness" (Isa. xli. 10). Here is a trinity of promise from the true God.

7. **Victory.** "I will contend with him that contendeth with thee" (Isa. xlix. 25). When the Lord contends with our enemies we may cease to contend with them, for He can do better than we can.

470. "I THANK GOD"

THE Apostle Paul frequently used the expression, "I thank God," as he viewed what God had wrought in the life and labour of others.

1. **A Proclaimed Faith.** "I thank my God...that your faith is proclaimed" (Rom. i. 8, R.V.). Faith in God proclaims itself before men, for faith is not only the instrumental cause which brings us to God, but it is also the incisive grace which brings God into the life.

2. **A Victorious Shout.** "Who shall deliver me out of this body of death? I thank God through Jesus Christ our Lord"

(Rom. vii. 24, 25, R.V.). The realm of spiritual death, which means the rule of sin's authority, is annulled and inoperative because by the Cross of Christ we are lifted out of its dominance and placed in the law of the spirit of life in Christ Jesus, which means victory instead of defeat.

3. **An Enriched People.** "I thank my God always on your behalf, for the grace of God which is given you by Jesus Christ" (1 Cor. i. 4). Only the grace of God could have enriched and borne with such a captious lot of people as the Corinthians were. They were anything but saintly, and yet God in His grace calls them "saints." Paul thanked God for the grace manifested in them, yet he also thanks God he did not baptise only a few of them lest they should make him the head of a factious party—1 Cor. i. 14.

4. **An Evangelistic Church.** "I thank God...for your fellowship in the Gospel" (Phil. i. 3, 5). The saints at Philippi knew the concern of Heaven for the men of earth, and so as men of Heaven on earth they worked in God's working to save men from Hell.

5. **An Enabled Trophy.** "I thank Christ Jesus our Lord who enabled me," etc. (1 Tim. i. 12). The chief of sinners became the choicest of saints through the enabling of the indwelling Christ. The word "enabled" is the same as "strengthened" in Philippians iv. 13 and 2 Timothy iv. 17.

6. **A Clean Servant.** "I thank God, whom I serve in a pure conscience" (2 Tim. i. 3, R.V.). To have a clean conscience through the cleansing Blood and the conquering Christ is no credit to us, but it does call for praise to Him; and certainly whom He cleanses He uses in His work for His glory.

7. **An Appreciating Pastor.** "I thank my God always, making mention of thee in my prayers, hearing of thy love, and of the faith which thou hast toward the Lord Jesus, and toward all the saints" (Philemon 4, 5). There is not anything which rejoices the heart of any true servant of Christ so much as when He sees the Lord's people ardent in their devotion to Christ as expressed in their practical love for each other in obeying Him.

471. "I WILL BRING"

ZECHARIAH

1. **Manifestation.** "I will bring forth my servant the Branch" (iii. 8).

2. **Curse.** "I will bring it forth" (v. 4). The curse to the wrongdoer of verse 3.

3. **Salvation.** "I will bring them (see verse 7), and they shall dwell in Jerusalem" (viii. 8).

4. **Restoration**. "I will bring them again to place them"
(x. 6).

5. **Deliverance**. "I will bring them again out of Egypt
(bondage), and gather them out of Assyria" (x. 10).

6. **Blessing**. "I will bring them into the land of Gilead
and Lebanon" (x. 10).

7. **Purification**. "I will bring the third part through the
fire" (xiii. 9).

472. "I WILL GO"

1. **Faith's Decision**. Ruth said to Naomi, "Whither thou
goest, I will go" (Ruth i. 16).

2. **Love's Decision**. Rebekah said to her parents, when,
asked if she would go with Eliezer to be the wife of Isaac, "I
will go" (Gen. xxiv. 58).

3. **Valour's Decision**. Deborah said to Barak, "I will
surely go with thee" (Judges iv. 9).

4. **Backslider's Decision**. Samson, when shorn of his
strength, said, "I will go out, as at other times," etc. (Judges
xvi. 20).

5. **Fellowship's Decision**. Elisha responded to his young
men, when asked to go with them, "I will go" (2 Kings vi. 3).

6. **Witness's Decision**. David said, "I will go in the
strength of the Lord God, I will make mention of Thy righteousness" (Psa. lxxi. 16).

7. **Prodigal's Decision**. The prodigal, in his repentance,
said, "I will arise, and go to my Father" (Luke xv. 18).

473. "I WILL" OF GOD'S COVENANTING GRACE.

THE Lord covenanted with Himself that He would bless His
people, and He always keeps His word.   See the seven "I wills"
of His pledged word in Exodus vi. 6-8:

1. The I will of **deliverance**. "I will bring you out."

2. The I will of **liberty**. "I will rid you of their bondage."

3. The I will of **power**. "I will redeem you."

4. The I will of **relationship**. "I will take you to Me for a
people."

5. The I will of **friendship**. "I will be to you a God."

6. The I will of **blessing**. "I will bring you into the land."

7. The I will of **inheritance**. "I will give it to you for a
heritage."

474. "I WILL'S" IN ISAIAH LXV

GOD's promises and judgments are always emphatic.

1. "I will" of **action**. "I will not keep silence, but will recompense" (6).

2. "I will" of **retribution**. "I will measure their former work into their bosom" (7).

3. "I will" of **compensation**. "I will bring forth a seed out of Jacob, and out of Judah an inheritor of My mountains, and Mine elect shall inherit it, and My servants shall dwell there" (9).

4. "I will" of **judgment**. "I will number to the sword" (12).

5. "I will" of **joy**. "I will rejoice in Jerusalem, and joy in My people" (19).

6. "I will" of **answer**. "I will answer" (24).

7. "I will" of **promptness**. "While they are yet speaking I will hear" (24).

475. "I WILL SING"

1. Praising His **Name**—Psa. vii. 17.
2. Praising His **Bounty**—Psa. xiii. 6.
3. Praising for **Victory**—Psa. xxvii. 6.
4. Praising His **Mercy**—Psa. lix. 16.
5. Praising His **Strength**—Psa. lix. 17.
6. Praising His **Truth**—Psa. lxxi. 22.
7. Praising for **Deliverance**—Psa. cxliv. 9.
8. Praising the **Lord Himself**—Psa. cxlvi. 2.

476. "JESUS ANSWERED AND SAID"

HE is the answer to every question, and answers all our questions.

1. His reply to **Nathaniel**—John i. 48-51, *re* omniscience.

2. His reply to **the Jews** about destroying the temple and His resurrection—John ii. 18-22.

3. His reply to **Nicodemus** about the new birth—John iii. 2-10.

4. Christ's reply about the **Living Water** He would give, etc.—John iv. 10, 13.

5. His reply to **the people** who followed because of what they received—John vi. 25-27.

6. His reply to the question, "**What shall we do?**"—John vi. 28, 29.

7. His reply about **the doctrine** He taught—John vii. 16, 17.

477. JEHOVAH: A TOWER

"THE Name of Jehovah is a Strong Tower, the righteous runneth into it, and is safe" (Prov. xviii. 10). One of the Names of Jehovah is likened to a Tower—

1. Jehovah is a **High** Tower for refuge—Psa. xviii. 2.
2. Jehovah is a **Strong** Tower from the enemy—Psa. lxi. 3.
3. Jehovah is a **Living** Tower for safety—Prov. xviii. 10.
4. Jehovah is an **Eternal** Refuge for joy—Deut. xxxiii. 27.
5. Jehovah is a **Divine** Refuge for protection—Psa. xlviii. 3
6. Jehovah is a **Present** Refuge in trouble—Psa. xlvi. 1.
7. Jehovah is a **Sure** Refuge for confidences—Heb. vi. 18

478. JEHOVAH PSALM

Psalm xxxiv. A.R.V.

1. Object of **Worship.** "I will bless Jehovah" (1).
2. Object of **Faith.** "Boast in Jehovah" (2).
3. Object of **Glory.** "Magnify Jehovah" (3).
4. Object of **Search.** "I sought Jehovah" (4).
5. Object of **Prayer.** "Jehovah heard" (6).
6. Object of **Fear.** "Jehovah encampeth" (7).
7. Object of **Good.** "Jehovah is good" (8).
8. Object of **Supply.** "Fear Jehovah...no want" (9).
9. Object of **Satisfaction.** "Seek Jehovah" (10).
10. Object of **Instruction.** "Teach you Jehovah" (11).
11. Object of **Regard.** "Eyes of Jehovah" (15).
12. Object of **Judgment.** "Jehovah against evil" (16).
13. Object of **Succour.** "Jehovah heard" (17).
14. Object of **Power.** "Jehovah is nigh" (18).
15. Object of **Comfort.** "Afflictions...Jehovah" (19).
16. Object of **Redemption.** "Jehovah redeemeth" (22).

"Jehovah" is named 16 times in the Psalm, and by implication in the pronouns.

479. J—E—S—U—S

Justifies by the Blood of His atonement—Rom. v. 9.
Endows in His peerless person—Eph. i. 3.
Saves in His vitalising life—Rom. v. 10.
Unites in His baptising Spirit—1 Cor. xii. 13.
Sanctifies by His indwelling presence—Gal. ii. 20.

480. JEHOVAH'S "I WILL'S" IN ISAIAH XLIX

1. Glorified. "I will be glorified" (3). God's glory is always the goal of our good.

2. Identified. "I will also give thee for a light" (6). God's in-fillings make us one with Him and for Him, for His in-fillings are for out-flowings.

3. Preserved. "I will preserve thee" (8). God's preservation is the cause of our perseverance.

4. Blessing. "I will make all My mountains a way" (11). One such mountain is Mount Calvary. It is a way to all blessing.

5. Power—22. "I will lift up Mine hand," etc. The hand of God is a symbol of His power. His liftings up are always leaders to lasting peace.

6. Victory—25. "I will contend with him," etc. Those who stand in the way of the believer's progress are targets for God's prowess.

7. Promise—25. "I will save thy children." The Lord's promise extends to the household of the child of God. Being His children, He promises to bless our children.

8. Judgment—26. "I will feed them that oppress thee with their own flesh." The sinner reaps in kind what he is.

481. JESUS FOUND IN PLACES

OUR Lord is said to be "on" different places.

1. He sat **"on the well"** to meet a needy sinner (John iv. 6).

2. He was placed **"on the pinnacle** of the temple" to be tempted (Matt. iv. 5).

3. He walked **"on the sea"** to succour His disciples (John vi. 19).

4. He wrote **"on the ground"** with His finger to defeat His enemies (John viii. 6).

5. He sat **"on an ass's colt"** to fulfil the Scriptures (John xii. 15).

6. He was **"on the earth"** to glorify God and finish His work (John xvii. 4).

7. He was **"upon the Cross"** in dying for the sins of others (John xix. 31; 1 Peter ii. 24).

8. He is **"on the right hand** of the Father" in approval and blessing (Heb. i. 3, 13; viii. 1; x. 12).

482. "JESUS SAID," or "HE SAITH," and "HE SAID"
IN JOHN I

THE sayings of Christ contain the message of God to us, they are a mould to shape us in life and service, and they are a magnet to attract and keep us.

1. He tells us **what we are.** "He said, Thou art Simon, the son of Jona" (42). Simon was Peter's natural name, as identified with his life in nature and sin.

2. He questions us **when we seek Him.** "Jesus turned...saw. ...saith...What seek ye?" (38). Christ is the answer to all questions.

3. He invites us **to dwell with Him.** "He saitn unto them, Come and see" (39). If we come to Him we shall want to dwell with Him.

4. He bids us **what to do.** "Follow Me" (43). Come, believe, and follow is a triple command from Christ.

5. He appreciates **guilelessness of character.** "Jesus... saith of him" (47). He saw the guilelessness of Nathaniel, and commended it.

6. He answers **our questions.** "Jesus answered and said" (48). The approachableness of Christ creates confidence in Him.

7. He **promises more** than we expected. "Jesus answered and said...Thou shalt see greater things" (50).

8. He **gives us to see** the unseeable. "He saith...Ye shall see" (51). He leads us behind the things that move, and enables us to behold the Power that moves them.

483. "JESUS SAITH," "SAID," "SPAKE," and "CRIED"
IN JOHN XI

1. A Divine **Reason.** "He said...this death...for the glory of God" (4).

2. A Divine **Direction.** "He saith...Let us go" (7).

3. A Divine **Teacher.** "These things said He" (9-11).

4. A Divine **Intention.** "He saith...I go to awake him" (11).

5. A Divine **Explanation.** "Jesus spake of His death" (13).

6. A Divine **Statement.** "Then said Jesus...Lazarus is dead" (14).

7. A Divine **Promise.** "Jesus saith...Thy brother shall rise" (23).

8. A Divine **Revelation.** "Jesus said . I am the Resurrection and the Life" (25).

9. A Divine **Inquiry**. "And said, Where have ye laid Him" (34).

10. A Divine **Direction**. "Jesus said, Take ye away the stone" (39).

11. A Divine **Reminder**. "Jesus saith,...Said I not unto thee" (40).

12. A Divine **Attitude**. "Jesus lifted up His eyes and said" (41).

13. A Divine **Mandate**. "He cried...Come forth" (43).

14. A Divine **Loosing**. "Jesus saith,...Loose him" (44).

484. "JESUS LOOKED ROUND ABOUT"

1. As the Grieved **Saviour**—Mark iii. 5.
2. As the Divine **Kinsman**—Mark iii. 34.
3. As the Compassionate **Healer**—Mark v. 32.
4. As the Searching **Teacher**—Mark x. 23.
5. As the Observing **Lord**—Mark xi. 11.

485. "JESUS TOOK"

CHRIST not only looked upon humanity and saw its need, but He came in contact with it, that its need might be met.

1. **His Incarnation**. "He took not on," or, as American marginal Revised Version: "For verily not of angels doth He take hold, but He taketh hold of the seed of Abraham" (Heb. ii. 16). Christ's incarnation was the door which led to the altar of His sacrifice on Calvary, which secures for us the holy place of His salvation. The word *epilambanomai* means to take on, or upon, and is rendered "caught" in Matthew xiv. 31, "take hold of" in Luke xx. 20, and "lay hold on" in 1 Timothy vi. 12, 19. The thought is, His taking upon Himself human nature in order to benefit the humans with whom He is identified. See how the incident of Peter being "caught" by Christ illustrates.

2. **His Identification**. Christ is the "Lamb of God which taketh away the sin of the world" (John i. 29). The word *airo*, rendered "taketh away," means to take up upon one's self, as when the healed man was commanded to "take up" his bed (Matt. ix. 6); but in Christ's case in being identified with us in our sin, by dying for it, it means also to put away; hence, He was "manifested to take away our sins" (1 John iii. 5). The word is rendered "removed," in Mark xi. 23, "took away" in John xi. 41, and "put away" in Ephesians iv. 31. How

true are the words of Luther: "He is my sin, and I am His righteousness."

3. His Reception. When reference is made to Christ's deliberate action in identifying Himself with the woes and wants of humanity, the words are cited, "Himself took our infirmities" (Matt. viii. 17), as fulfilling them. *Lambano* means to take, or to receive to one's self; hence, it is often rendered "receive." (See its use in John i. 12, 16; vi. 21; xiii. 20; xvi. 24; xvii. 8; xx. 22). The hand of ready help was ever moved by the heart of loving sympathy.

4. His Deliberation. Christ's death was no accident. His star of destiny was His death on Calvary. He knew, too, that death's grip could not hold Him. His own statements are beyond all question as to these acts. He says: "I lay down My life, that I might take (*lambano*, to take to Myself) it again." And He further says: "I have power (or His Father's authority, as the word means, and the context shows) to take it again" (John x. 17, 18).

5. His Commemoration. *Lambano* is used three times in the inception of the Lord's Supper. "Jesus took bread...and said, Take, eat...He took the cup" (Mark xiv. 22, 23). We are not left in any doubt as to the purpose of that death. The Bread represented, as He Himself declares: "This is My body given to you...This cup is the New Testament in My Blood, which is shed for you" (Luke xxii. 19, 20). How terse and telling are the words, "given...shed for you!" We find a sevenfold fact in that giving. Love is its source, Grace is its act, Blood is its price, Men are its object, Salvation is its end, Christ is its Substance, and Glory is its consummation.

6. His Power. "He took the seven loaves" (Matt. xv. 36). When we place what we have in His hands, He makes it meet any emergency. His taking is our making, and others' blessing. There is much in our little when He takes it, for the naught (0) of our insignificance is multiplied by the thousandfold (1000) of His almightiness.

"Little is much, when God is in it."

7. His Example. "Took upon Him the form of a servant" (Phil. ii. 7). What a contrast between "the form of God" and "the form of a slave." Yet His greatness is seen in both. The beauty of a violet, in its lowly bed under the hedge, is as magnificent as the brightness of the sun in the sky. The Babe of Bethlehem in a manger is equal to the Creator of Genesis. He is our Example of Lowliness, hence we are exhorted to have the "same mind" of lowliness as was in Him.

8. **His Object Lesson.** "He took a child and set him in the midst" (Mark ix. 36). Christ was continually referring to things around, and reaching out to things at hand, to illustrate Divine principles and truth. A child is simple in trust, humble in spirit, loving in disposition, and responsive to kindness. Christ not only set the "little child (R.V.) in the midst," but He took it into His arms, and that act He emphasises to point the injunction, that kindness done to a child is a kindness done to Himself; yea, to His Father as well. Here is a law in the Kingdom of grace. He that does a kindness to another does a kindness to Christ.

9. **His Prophetic Act.** "Jesus taketh Peter, James, and John...and was transfigured before them" (Matt. xvii. 1, 2). The word "taketh" has the prefix *para* added to *lambano*, hence it means to take alongside of, which expresses the thought of friendship and fellowship. Christ uses it when He says: "I will come again and receive you to Myself."

486. JEW AND PALESTINE

1. There is **one people** whom Jehovah calls His "peculiar treasure unto Me above all people" (Exod. xix. 5).

2. There is **one land** which is called "holy" (Zech. ii. 12), and promised to Israel for an "everlasting possession" (Gen. xvii. 8).

3. There is **one city** which is called "the beloved city" (literally, "the dearly-beloved"), and which Jehovah will "make a praise in the earth," and that is Jerusalem (Rev. xx. 9; Isa. lxii. 7).

4. There is **one mountain** which has been honoured in the land of Palestine, and that is the Mount of Olives, for Christ's sacred feet last rested upon it ere He ascended to Heaven— Acts i. 12; and it is upon that mountain His holy feet will stand when He returns in manifest glory to the earth, and which mountain will be the object of great and momentous convulsions —Zech. xiv. 4.

5. There is **one temple** which is to be the scene of the greatest sacrilege ever committed in a holy place, and that temple will be the rebuilt one in which the abomination of the Antichrist will be set up—Dan. ix. 27; Matt. xxiv. 15.

6. There is **one throne** upon which Jehovah has said a descendant of David is to sit for ever—2 Sam. vii. 10-17; Luke i. 31-33. and therefore peculiarly honoured and magnified by Him.

7. And there is **one Man** in whom all God's plans centre, and He is a Jew—namely, Christ, for He is distinctly said to be of the Seed of David—2. Tim. ii. 8; of Israel—Rom. ix. 5; and the Son of Abraham and David—Matt. i. 1.

487. JOSHUA, THE LEADER
Josh. xviii. 1-10; xxiv. 1-31

BIBLE characters illustrate some one grace in their lives. In Abraham we see faith, in Joseph purity, in Moses meekness, in David courage, in Jonathan love, in Samuel faithfulness, and in Joshua carefulness as a leader. Joshua was a—

1. **Victorious Leader**—xviii. 1. Under him the children of Israel were able to subdue the land of Canaan and its inhabitants. It may be well for the teacher to recall some of Joshua's victories, and then remind the scholars that Joshua was a type of Christ—Heb. iv. 8-15, R.V. When we are led by our Lord we shall never be defeated. The Conqueror always conquers.

2. **Discriminating Leader**—xviii. 2-10. Several of the tribes had not received their portion of the land, so Joshua sought the Lord's mind as to what they should receive, but omitting Levi, as their inheritance was in the priesthood. In Christ believers are blessed with all spiritual blessing—Eph. i. 3. Every blessing is in Him, and He is every Blessing, so that all we need for advancement in the spiritual life is found in Him (see the seven "in whom's" in Ephesians); but we need to come to our Divine Leader to know what He would have us to do, for the truth of 1 Corinthians xii. and xiii. is, that while all believers are one in Christ, the Holy Spirit gives us the gift for His service as He wills.

3. **Reminding Leader**—xxiv. 1-13. Joshua reminded the tribes and their leading men what God had done for their fathers in the past, and for them. This is strikingly illustrated in the personal pronoun "I" in relation to the Lord God of Israel. We can only indicate and leave the teacher to connect with New Testament truth:

Salvation, "I took...led...multiplied...and gave" (3).

Possession, "I gave" (4).

Commission, "I sent" (5).

Emancipation, "I brought" (6, 7).

Extermination, "I brought," "I gave," "I destroyed," "I delivered" (8-12).

Benediction, "I have given you a land" (13).

In all that was done Joshua saw the hand of God. It was not his prowess, but God's power. Joshua reminded the people of their obligation to Him who had done so much for them— see Psalm lxxviii.

4. **Commanding Leader**—xxiv. 14-25. Joshua's clarion call was to "serve the Lord." From verses 14 to 31 we find the words "serve" and "served" occurring no fewer than fifteen

times, and they cluster round three predominating thoughts, namely, whom we are not to serve, the gods with whom our former life were associated or who may come before us—14, 16, 20; whom we *are* to serve, the Lord—14, 15, 18, 19, 21, 22, 24, 31; and *how* we are to serve Him: in sincerity and in truth—14. Service to the Lord takes in all our life, as the London shoeblack recognised, when he said to the gentleman who commended him for the care he took in shining his boots, "I'm serving the Lord, sir, in serving you." Any drudgery is divinity when it is service for Him.

5. **Faithful Leader**—xxiv. 26-28. Since Israel pledged themselves to serve the Lord—24, Joshua made a covenant with the people, and set up a stone in Shechem to be a witness of their affirmed allegiance to the Lord. Joshua did not take any chances with a fickle people, but set up a monument to remind them of their responsibilities. No service is of any moment unless it is done in heart-faithfulness to the Lord. "I want to please the man who has appointed me to my work," was the reply of an employee, when a man complained of his action when he was carrying out his employer's directions.

6. **Powerful Leader**—xxiv. 31. The influence of Joshua was felt after his death, for we are told, "Israel served the Lord all the days of Joshua, and all the days of the elders that overlived Joshua." Those who truly live for the Lord always find that their works follow them—Rev. xiv. 13. The old American song of "John Brown's soul is still marching on" speaks of the continuance of influence, and so does the hymn which tells us that "kind words can never die." The best memorial that we can leave behind us is the fragrance of a holy life, and the most abiding epitaph is the memory of a helpful influence.

488. JUDGMENT

JEREMIAH XXV

THE language in the chapter is most emphatic in its statements. Sixteen times the word "will" is found in the Revised Reading, as declaring what God will certainly do. In verse 6, by way of promise, "I will do you no hurt"; and fifteen times the words "I will" and "He will," as declaring God's acts of judgment.

1. The **Messenger** of Judgment. "I will send" (9).

2. The **Scope** of Judgment. "I will destroy" (9).

3. The **Misery** of Judgment. "I will take from them the voice of mirth" (10).

4. The **Stroke** of Judgment. "I will punish" (12).

5. The **Desolation** of Judgment. "I will make it desolate" (12).

6. The **Certainty** of Judgment. "I will bring to pass all My words which I have pronounced" (13).

7. The **Righteousness** of Judgment. "I will recompense them according to their deeds" (14, R.V.).

8. The **Effect** of Judgment. "Be mad because of the sword that I will send among them" (16).

9. The **Crushing** of Judgment. "Drink ye, and be drunken, and spue, and fall, and rise no more, because of the sword which I will send" (v. 27).

10. The **Awfulness** of Judgment. "He will mightily roar" (30, R.V.).

11. The **Place** of Judgment. "Jehovah will roar from on high" (30, R.V.).

12. The **Shout** of Judgment. "He will give a shout" (30, R.V.).

13. The **Universality** of Judgment. "He will plead with all flesh" (31).

14. The **Subjects** of Judgment. "As for the wicked, He will give them to the sword" (31).

489. JUBILEE

THE Jubilee is a type of the "acceptable year" of the Gospel (Luke iv. 19). What did the Jubilee mean?

1. **Recognition of the Lord's Claim.** "The land is Mine" (Lev. xxv. 23). "The Lord's release" (Deut. xv. 1-4).

2. Remember the Jubilee was **Based on Atonement**—Lev. xxv. 9. Christ's substitutionary death is the basis of all blessing.

3. **Release from Bondage.** "Proclaim liberty throughout all the land" (Lev. xxv. 10).

4. **Rest.** "A year of rest unto the land." "A Sabbath for the Lord" (Lev. xxv. 4, 5).

5. **Restoration.** "Return every man unto his possession" (Lev. xxv. 10, 13, 28).

6. **Rejoicing.** The meaning of the word "Jubilee" is joy— Psa. lxxxix. 15-18.

7. **Reunion.** "Ye shall return every man unto his family" (Lev. xxv. 10).

490. JUDGMENTS RELATING TO BELIEVERS

1. **God's judgment upon us as sinners** in Christ on the Cross. "By a sacrifice for sin (margin), condemned sin in the flesh" (Rom. viii. 3).

2. **Believers' judgment on himself.** "If we would judge ourselves we shall not be judged" (1 Cor. xi. 31).

3. The **Lord's judgment of His children.** "When we are judged, we are chastened of the Lord" (1 Cor. xi. 32).

4. The **Church's Judgment in Discipline.** "Judged him that hath done this wrong" (1 Cor. v. 3-5).

5. The **Lord's judgment of the "House" of Christendom.** "Judgment must begin at the house of God" (1 Peter. iv. 17).

6. **Believers' judgment of the world and angels.** "The saints shall judge the world...We shall judge angels" (1 Cor. vi. 2, 3).

7. The **Judgment Seat of Christ,** before which believers will be examined—1 Cor. iv. 5; their conduct towards their fellow-believers scrutinised—Rom. xiv; their work tested—1 Cor. iii. 10-15; their motives looked at—2 Cor. v. 9, 10; and rewards given—1 Peter i. 7.

491. JUSTIFICATION

1. **Self-judgment** is its forerunner—Luke vii. 29; xviii. 14.

2. **God** is its Author—Rom. iii. 30; viii. 30, 33.

3. **Grace** is its spring—Rom. iii. 24; Gal. v. 4; Titus iii. 7.

4. **Christ's Blood** is its purchaser—Rom. iii. 24; v. 9.

5. **Christ's obedience** unto death is its basis—Gal. ii. 16; Rom. v. 18.

6. **Christ's resurrection** is its assurance—Rom. iv. 24, 25.

7. **Union** in Christ's death is its freedom—Rom. vi. 7, margin.

8. **Faith** in Christ is its medium—Rom. iii. 26; v. 1; Gal. iii. 24.

9. **The Spirit of God** is its power—1 Cor. vi. 11.

10. **Works** are its outcome—James ii. 21, 24, 25.

492. KING SAUL'S DOWN-GRADE

1. His **impatient act** in sacrifice—1 Sam. xiii. 8-14.

2. His **self-will** *re* Amalek—1 Sam. xv.

3. His **intense jealousy** *re* David—1 Sam. xviii. 8.

4. His **murderous acts** *re* David—1 Sam. xviii. 11, 25;
xix. 10, 15.
5. **Slaying eighty-five priests** and the people of Nob—
1 Sam. xxii. 18, 19.
6. **Hunting for David's life**—1 Sam. xxiv. 2; xxvi, 1, 2, 20.
7. **Resorting to the dead**—1 Sam. xxviii.

493. KNOTTY NOTS

IN HEBREWS III. AND IV.

1. "**Harden not**" of warning (iii. 8, 13, 15; iv. 7).
2. "**Have not**" of ignorance (iii. 10).
3. "**Shall not**" of exclusion (iii. 11).
4. "**Believed not**" of prevention (iii. 18).
5. "**Could not**" of inability (iii. 19).
6. "**Mixed not**" of want (iv. 2).
7. "**Entered not**" of loss (iv. 6).

494. "KNOWLEDGE" *

1. **Conviction.** "Knowledge of sin" (Rom. iii. 20).
2. **Salvation.** "Knowledge of God" (2 Peter i. 2, 3, 8).
3. **Invitation.** "Knowledge of the truth" (1 Tim. ii. 4;
2 Tim. ii. 25; iii. 7; Titus i. 1; Heb. x. 26).
4. **Communion.** "Knowledge of His will" (Col. i. 9).
5. **Growth.** "Increasing in the knowledge of God" (Col.
i. 10; ii. 2; iii. 10).
6. **Every Good.** "Acknowledging of every good thing"
(Philemon 6).
7. **Christ.** "Knowledge of the Son of God" (Eph. i. 17;
iv. 13).

495. LEAN, LOOK, AND LISTEN

A NOTICE at a railway crossing in America reads, "Listen and
Look."
There are three L's in which a heaven of blessing is found,
namely:

1. **Lean hard** upon Christ by faith—Canticles viii. 5.
2. **Look** up to Him by prayer—Psa. v. 3.
3. **Listen to Him** by obedience—John x. 27.

---

* *Epignosis*," rendered "knowledge" and "acknowledge," means an exact knowledge,
which exerts an influence on him who knows.

496. LACK OF VISION

LACK of vision is a—

1. Precursor of **doom**—Prov. xxix. 18.
2. Forerunner of **disaster**—1 Sam. iii. 1.
3. A dungeon of **despair**—Lam. ii. 9.
4. A night of **darkness**—Micah iii. 6.
5. A sign of **spiritual declension**—2 Peter i. 9.
6. An evidence of **lukewarmness** in Divine things—Rev. iii. 18.
7. A state of **unbelief**—Rom. xi. 8, 10.
8. A **want of capacity** to understand things in their true state—Mark viii. 24.

497. "LAMPS"

"Seven lamps" (Exod. xxv. 37).

THE Hebrew word for "lamp" is rendered "candle" (Prov. xxxi. 18), and "light" (2 Sam. xxi. 17).

1. **Man's indestructible spirit** is "the candle of the Lord" (Prov. xx. 27).
2. **God's Word** is a "Lamp to our feet" for guidance (Psa. cxix. 105).
3. Our **Father's** "commandment" is "a lamp" for our obedience (Prov. vi. 23).
4. "**Salvation** as a lamp that burneth" (Isa. lxii. 1).
5. **Supplied** lamps for illumination—Matt. xxv. 4.
6. **Dressed** lamps for clear shining—Exod. xxx. 7.
7. **Useful** lamp for searching—Zeph. i. 12.

498. "LAST"

1. "The **last Adam**" (1 Cor. xv. 45), the Life-giving Spirit.
2. "The **last enemy**" (1 Cor. xv. 26), destroyed by Christ's death.
3. "The **last trumpet**" (1 Cor. xv. 52), in relation to the believer, summoning him to incorruptibility.
4. "The **last time**" (1 John ii. 18; Jude 18), when we may expect the coming of the Antichrist.
5. "The **last days**," which are "perilous" and irreverent (2 Tim. iii. 1; Jas. v. 3).
6. "The seven **last plagues**" (Rev. xv. 1; xxi. 9), which will be fearful in their nature.
7. "The last" and the **Lasting One**. "First and the Last" (Rev. i. 11; xxii. 13).

499. LEADING

1. **Who** leads? "The Lord" (Gen. xxiv. 27; Psa. lxxvii. 20; Deut. xxxii. 12).

2. **Whom** the Lord leads—His redeemed—Exod. xiii. 17; xv. 13.

3. **Where** the Lord leads. "In a plain path" (Psa. xxvii. 11). "In the way everlasting" (Psa. cxxxix. 24); "In the paths of righteousness" (Psa. xxiii. 3); "To the rock that is higher than I" (Psa. lxi. 2); "To the desired haven" (Psa. cvii. 30); "Into the land of uprightness" (Psa. cxliii. 10).

4. **How** the Lord leads. "In mercy" (Exod. xv. 13); "In righteousness" (Psa. v. 8); "By His counsel" (Psa. lxxiii. 24).

500. LEAVING THINGS

"HE left the oxen, and ran after Elijah" 1 Kings xix. 20

SOME things are left behind to our loss, but others to our gain. There are things mentioned in Scripture, that were left behind to the gain of those who left them, and in following the will of God:

1. Abraham **left Ur** of the Chaldees, and its idolatry; and illustrates God's calling in conversion—Gen. xii. 1-4.

2. The Israelites **left the bondage** and bitterness of Egypt; and corresponds to being delivered from sin and the world—Exod. xii. 40-42.

3. Bartimaeus **left his garment** in responding to the call of Christ, and illustrates we should leave anything that hinders us in following our Lord—Mark x. 50.

4. The woman of Samaria **left her water-pot**, in going to her friends to tell them she had found the Saviour, and shows how one may leave legitimate things in the Lord's work—John iv. 28.

5. Joseph **left his coat** in the hands of Potiphar's wife, rather than sin with her. Faithfulness sometimes seems to incriminate us—Gen. xxxix. 1-20.

6. David left behind **the armour of Saul**, for it was an encumbrance to him. What is right to others, may be an encumbrance to us—1 Sam. xvii. 39.

7. Paul left behind his **religiosity**, because it kept him from Christ and the fullness of His blessing—Phil. iii. 4-7.

501. LEANING IN THE WRONG DIRECTION

"Lean not to thine own understanding" PROV. iii. 5

IN a Southern prayer meeting, a coloured brother prayed, "O Lord, support us! Yes, support us, Lord, on every leanin' side!" Should we have any "leanin' side?" If we have any leaning toward anything, we are sure to fall to the thing toward which we lean.

1. Abraham **leaned toward Egypt** in unbelief and soon found himself crippled by it—Gen. xii. 10-20.

2. Lot **leaned toward Sodom** in compromise, and lost all he had gained—Gen xiii. 10; xix. 17.

3. David **leaned toward unholy desire** in laziness, and his name has been smirched ever since—2 Sam. xi. 2-4.

4. Jehoshaphat **leaned toward worldly association** with Ahab, and nearly lost his life—1 Kings xxii. 29-32.

5. King Saul **leaned toward his own inclination** in sparing the Amalekites, and lost his kingdom in consequence—1 Sam. xv. 10-23.

6. Hezekiah **leaned toward pride** when he displayed his riches to the representatives of Babylon, and brought distress to his posterity—Isa. xxxix.

7. Peter **leaned toward self-sufficiency** in his boasted allegiance to Christ, and lost his courage at the taunt of a servant-maid—Luke xxii. 33, 56, 57.

502. "LET DOWN"

NONE of these men were "let down" in the sense of the world, which lets down a person by misrepresentation; but these were letting downs which turned out to be lifting ups. There are certain great principles evidenced in the following men who were said to have been "let down."

1. **Rahab "Let Down" the Spies**—Josh. ii. 15. Fellowship with God's purpose evidenced her faith in Him, and that faith inspired her to help others, and that help brought her blessing and salvation—Heb. xi. 31. The "cord" by which she "let down" the spies was the "scarlet thread" which became a sign of safety to her. Scofield says: "The scarlet* line of Rahab speaks, by its colour, of safety through sacrifice" (Heb. ix. 19, 22). Obedience to God shows our faith in Him, which always secures safety for us.

2. **Michal "Let Down" David**—1 Sam. xix. 12. When no principle is involved, we are warranted to help others to

---

* The Hebrew word for "scarlet" signifies the blood of an insect, the "worm" applied to our Lord in His death, as described in Psa. xxii. 6. His death alone secures our safety.

escape from danger. Michal, by her act, showed she had no fellowship with the cruel hate of Saul; but she had heart-sympathy with the hunted and persecuted David. How full of meaning is Psalm lix. in the light of 1 Samuel xix. 11, for it shows that the persecution of men will drive us in prayer to God, and by this means we find God is our "Defence" and "Refuge" and "Strength" (Psa. lix. 16, 17), and finding Him such, we can sing of His power and mercy.

3. **Jeremiah was "Let Down" into a Dungeon**—Jer. xxxviii. 6. The enemies of God's servants do not care into what mire they may place them. Faithfulness to God will be sure to create opposition from the world. But they were not all enemies in the court of the weak King Zedekiah, for Ebed-Melech not only spoke to the king and got permission to get him, but was also careful to "let down" some clouts and rags, to make it more comfortable to get the prophet out of the dungeon. The opposition of the enemy will often bring the opportune help of our friends; in fact, but for the enemy we should not have known the friends.

4. **The Palsied Man "Let Down" by his Friends to Christ**—Luke v. 19. His letting down in love was the forerunner of his getting up in power. These men knew three things: first, their friend was helpless and needed healing; second, that Christ could heal him, hence their aim to get him to the Saviour; and, third, if the needing man and the Saviour were to meet, they must get him to the Lord. So they lifted up their friend, and brought him along. The difficulties of his dead weight, the impenetrable crowd, the lifting up, and the taking the tiling off the roof, did not deter them. When we are determined to get men to Christ we shall get them there.

5. **The Dead Man "Let Down" into Elisha's Grave**—2 Kings xiii. 21. Contact with the prophet's dead body caused the body to live. Elisha means "God my Saviour." Contact with the Divine brings life to the human. The Lord our Saviour is the only One that can quicken us from the death of sin; but there must be contact with Him by faith, if He is to do it for us, then association with Him in His death is the death of self.

6. **Paul "Let Down" in a Basket**—Acts ix. 24, 25; 2 Cor. xi. 33. An apostle in a basket! In what queer places the saints are found! Jonah in a fish, Elijah under a juniper tree, and now Paul in a basket. Sometimes a letting down is essential to a lifting up, hence we find in the same Epistle, the apostle tells he was "caught up to Paradise" (2 Cor. xii. 2).

7. **Christ Lifted Down from the Cross**—Luke xxiii. 53; Acts xiii. 29. No study or life is complete without Christ.

That lifting down was not an accident, for it was in fulfilment
of what had been written of Him. We gaze with holy wonder
and loving reverence as we see the dead body of our Lord lifted
down from that Cross, for in that death we see Scripture fulfilled,
God satisfied, sin expiated, Hell defeated, Heaven opened,
blessings secured, self annulled, world separated, and death
defeated.

503. LEAVING THINGS

1. **Fleeing from Sin.** "Left his garment in her hand"
(Gen. xxxix. 12, 15). Doing the right thing sometimes brings
us an ill consequence.

2. **Following the Lord.** "Left their nets and followed
Him" (Matt. iv. 20). When the choice is between the nets of a
lawful business and a call to follow the Lord, He must have the
preference.

3. **First be Reconciled.** "Leave thy gift...first be reconciled" (Matt. v. 23, 24). Reconciliation to an offended brother
is pre-requisite to communion with the Lord.

4. **Fascinated by Christ.** "She left her water pot" (John
iv. 28). She forgot what she brought to the well and her quest
in coming, because she found something better.

5. **Following On.** "Leaving the principles of the doctrine
of Christ, go on to perfection" (Heb. vi. 1). Stagnation is the
bane of a consecrated life. We shall go back if we do not "go
on."

6. **Found Wanting.** Elisha "left the oxen," but he wanted
to say "good-bye" to those at home. Elijah would not brook
delay. Earthly ties must not hinder the call to the Lord's
service—1 Kings xix. 20, 21.

504. "LEFT ALL"

1. **Confidence.** "Left all he had in Joseph's hands" (Gen.
xxxix. 6). He had proved himself worthy of confidence, therefore his conduct commanded greater trust.

2. **Apostasy.** "They left all the commandments of the
Lord" (2 Kings xvii. 16). To leave some of the commandments
was bad, but to leave them all was worse.

3. **Devotion.** "We have left all, and have followed Thee"
(Mark x. 28, 29). Renunciation for Christ brings reward from
Him.

4. **Consecration.** "He left all and followed Him" (Luke
v. 28). What a contrast to the rich young ruler who was not
willing to leave all—Luke xviii. 22.

505. "LET GOD"

PONDER the following Scriptures where "Let God" occurs, or its equivalent, and let go all else, that He may be everything.

1. **Salvation.** "Let the God of my salvation be exalted" (Psa. xviii. 46; lxix. 29).

2. **Benediction.** "Let Thy mercy be upon us" (Psa. xxxiii. 22).

3. **Opposition.** "Let the angel of the Lord chase them" (Psa. xxxv. 5).

4. **Adoration.** "Let the Lord be magnified" (Psa. xxxv. 27; lxx. 4).

5. **Preservation.** "Let Thy lovingkindness and truth continually preserve me" (Psa. xl. 11).

6. **Protection.** "Let Thy tender mercies speedily prevent us" (Psa. lxxix. 8).

7. **Beautification.** "Let the beauty of the Lord our God be upon us" (Psa. xc. 17).

506. "LET NOT"

1. Dominion **Over Sin.** "Let not sin reign" (Rom. vi. 12).

2. Dominion **Over Pride.** "Let us not be desirous of vain glory" (Gal. v. 26).

3. Dominion **Over Anger.** "Let not the sun go down upon your wrath" (Eph. iv. 26).

4. Dominion **Over Sloth.** "Let us not sleep" (1 Thess v. 6).

5. Dominion **Over Trouble.** "Let not your heart be troubled" (John xiv. 1).

6. Dominion **Over the Flesh.** "Let it not be named," etc. (Eph. v. 3).

7. Dominion **Over Double-mindedness.** "Let not that man think he shall receive anything from the Lord" (James i. 7).

507. "LIFTED UP"

1. **Eyes** lifted up. "Lifted up their eyes" (Matt. xvii. 8).

2. **Voice** lifted up. "Lifted up her voice" (Luke xi. 27).

3. **Head** lifted up. "Lift up your heads" (Luke xxi. 28).

4. **Hands** lifted up. "Lifting up holy hands" (1 Tim. ii. 8).

5. **Soul** lifted up. "Unto Thee, O Lord, do I lift up my soul" (Psa. xxv. 1).

6. **Heart** lifted up. "Let us lift up our heart unto God" (Lam. iii. 41).

7. **Wings** lifted up. "Lifted up their wings" (Ezek. x. 19).

508. "LETS" WHICH LET IN A BLESSING

1. **Vigilance.** "Let your loins be girded about" (Luke xii. 35).

2. **Diligence.** "Let every man prove his own work" (Gal. vi. 4).

3. **Continuance.** "Let us not be weary in well-doing" (Gal. vi. 9).

4. **Dominance.** "Let the peace of God rule in your hearts" (Col. iii. 15).

5. **Sustenance.** "Let the Word of Christ dwell in you richly" (Col. iii. 16).

6. **Endurance.** "Let us run with patience the race" (Heb. xii. 1).

7. **Supplication.** "Let your requests be made known unto God" (Phil. iv. 6).

8. **Utterance.** "Let your speech be always with grace" (Col. iv. 6).

509. LETTING THE LIGHT SHINE AT HOME

"Go home" (Mark v. 19) "and show how great things God hath done unto thee" (Luke viii. 39). It is in the home we need to have—

1. **Our speech** seasoned with the salt of grace, that we may speak sweetly—Col. iv. 6.

2. **Our manners** tempered with the grace of courteousness, that we may act graciously—1 Peter iii. 8.

3. **Our behaviour** toned with the godliness of chastity, that we may attract powerfully—1 Peter iii. 1, 2.

4. **Our conduct** tuned with the Word of God, that we may act consistently—Titus ii. 1-14.

5. **Our rule** ruled with the authority of Heaven, that we may behave consecratingly—1 Tim. iii. 1-7.

6. **Our office** dominated with the beauty of faithfulness, that we may live blamelessly—1 Tim. iii. 8-13.

7. And **our relations** in life adjusted with the direction of the Spirit, that we may show we have received the Spirit fully —Col. iii. 17; iv. 1; Eph. v. 18; vi. 9.

510. "LET US" IN HEBREWS

1. **A Cautious Believer.** "Let us fear" (iv. 1).

2. **A Diligent Pilgrim.** "Let us labour" (iv. 11).

3. **A Cleaving Saint.** "Let us hold fast" (iv. 14; x. 23).

4. **An Earnest Suppliant.** "Let us come boldly" (iv. 16).

5. **A Progressive Disciple.** "Let us go on" (vi. 1).

6. **A Holy Priest.** "Let us draw near" (x. 22).

7. **A Thoughtful Brother.** "Let us consider one another" (x. 24).

8. **A Wise Athlete.** "Let us lay aside every weight" (xii. 1).

9. **An Enduring Runner.** "Let us run with patience" (xii. 1).

10. **A Possessing Possessor.** "Let us have grace" (xii. 28).

11. **A Separated Son.** "Let us go forth unto Him" (xiii. 13).

12. **A Grateful Chorister.** "Let us offer the sacrifice of praise to God" (xiii. 15).

511. LIFE ETERNAL

1. **Man has not this life** naturally. "Ye have no life in you" (John vi. 53).

2. **Christ** is its **Substance.** "I am the Life" (John xiv. 6).

3. The **knowledge** of God in Christ is its **meaning.** "This is life eternal," etc. (John xvii. 3).

4. **Received by faith** in Christ. "He that believeth on the Son hath eternal life" (John iii. 36).

5. Those who have received Christ have **"passed" from "death into life"** (John v. 24).

6. Christ's indwelling **is its power.** "Springing up into everlasting life" (John iv. 14).

7. This **life reproduces likeness** to itself. "We know we pass from death unto life, because we love the brethren" (1 John iii. 14).

512. LIFTER

ONE of the characters in which our Lord is described is the Lifter.

1. **A Gracious Act.** "Thou hast lifted me up" (Psa. cii. 10).

2. **A Sovereign Lord.** "He bringeth low, He also lifteth up" (1 Sam. ii. 7).

3. **A Victorious Lord.** "Thou hast lifted me up on high above mine enemies" (2 Sam. xxii. 49).

4. **A Living Emancipator.** "Thou that liftest me up from the gates of death" (Psa. ix. 13).

5. **A Great Physician.** "He took her by the hand and lifted her up" (Mark i. 31).

6. **An Exalting Friend.** "The Lifter up (to make high) of mine head" (Psa. iii. 3).

7. **An Almighty Deliverer.** "Lifted him up and arose" (Mark ix. 27).

513. LIFE IN CHRIST

THE positive blessing of the Gospel is life.

1. **God-imparted life** in its bestowment—1 John iv. 9.
2. **Christ-associated life** in its union—John xiv. 6.
3. **Christ-sustained life** in its operation—John vi. 57.
4. **Spirit-inscribed life** in its inscription—2 Cor. iii. 3.
5. **Self-displacing life** in its power—2 Cor. v. 15.
6. **Christ-indwelt life** in its secret—Gal. ii. 20.
7. **Brethren-considered life** in its love—Rom. xiv. 7-9.
8. **Missionary-expressed life** in its sympathy—1 Thess. iii. 8.

514. "LIFE INDEED"

ONE has said: *"Life* is short—only four letters in it. Three quarters of it is a '*lie,*' and half of it is an '*if.*'" We may add, by transposing the letters you can make it into a *"file."* The child of God makes something better of the word *life* by making an acrostic on it in association with Christ, and says—

L **Living in** Christ, I am saved—Rom. viii. 1, 2.

I **Instructed by** Christ, I am rested—Matt. xi. 29.

F **Following after** Christ, I have fellowship with Him—John xii. 24-26.

E **Enduring through** Christ, I am victorious—Phil. iv. 13.

515. LIFE'S BLOOD

"The sacrifice of Himself" Heb. ix. 26

1. **Adam** had an opened side before he got his beautiful bride—Gen. ii. 21.
2. **Isaac** was laid on the altar before he met with Rebekah—Gen. xxii. 2, 9; xxiv. 67.
3. **Jacob** served fourteen years for Rachel before he got her—Gen. xxix. 18-28.
4. **Job** lost his possessions before he got the double portion—Job. xlii. 10.
5. **David's** three mighty men risked their lives before they obtained for the king the desired water from the well at Bethlehem—1 Chron. xi. 17-19.
6. **The apostles** hazarded their lives to propagate the Gospel—Acts xv. 26.
7. **Christ** gave Himself up to death before He could see of the travail of His soul—Matt. xxviii. 20; Isa. liii. 10, 11.

516. LIGHT

THE Bible has a good deal to say about light. The first chapter of Genesis speaks of it—Gen. i. 3, and so does the last chapter of Revelation—Rev. xxii. 5. Light is the symbol of holiness and truth, hence "God is Light" (1 John i. 5). Let us look at light as applied to God's children in the Epistles.

1. Our **Enlightenment**. "God who commanded the light to shine out of darkness, hath shined in our hearts, to give the light of the knowledge of the glory of God in the face of Jesus Christ" (2 Cor. iv. 6). The darkness of sin's condemnation, control and, contamination is taken away by knowing Christ as our Saviour.

2. Our **Environment**. "Called you out of darkness into His marvellous light" (1 Peter ii. 9). The sphere into which we have been brought, and in which we are to move, is the "all things that pertain unto life and godliness" (2 Peter i. 3), and of grace—Rom. v. 2.

3. Our **Enduement**. "Now are ye light in the Lord" (Eph. v. 8). Being in the light, we have all the privileges of the position, and among them is the power of the Holy Spirit.

4. Our **Employment**. "Walk as children of light" (Eph. v. 8). The believer's life, wherever lived, has to be in correspondence to his position.

5. Our **Enjoyment**. "If we walk in the light, as He is in the light, we have fellowship one with another" (1 John i. 7). There is no peace, power, nor joy, so long as we are out of the orbit of the Lord's presence; but remaining there they are all found.

6. Our **Equipment**. "The armour of light" (Rom. xiii. 12). Christ is the Armour of Light. When He stands between us and any foe we are sure of victory.

7. Our **Ennoblement**. "Made us meet to be partakers of the inheritance of the saints in light" (Col. i. 12). The Lord has ennobled us in making us His children, and sufficient for the heavenly inheritance.

517. LITTLE THINGS TO BE AVOIDED

1. The "**little foxes**" of the world's contamination (Cant. ii. 15).

2. The "**little owl**" of fleshly assumption (Lev. xi. 17).

3. The **little service** to the Baal of idolatry—2 Kings x. 18.

4. The **little honey** of self's satisfaction—2 Kings iv. 29, 43.

5. The "**little sleep**" of indolent slumber (Prov. vi. 10).

6. The "**little leaven**" of wickedness (1 Cor. v. 6).

7. The "**little member**" of fiery talk (James iii. 5).

518. "LIFT UP"

1. **Faith's Vision.** "Lift up thine eyes and see" (Gen. xiii. 14; xxxi. 12).

2. **Faith's Prayer.** "Lift up thy prayer" (2 Kings xix. 4).

3. **Faith's Concentration.** "I lift up my soul unto Thee" (Psa. cxliii. 8).

4. **Faith's Worship.** "Lift up your hands in the sanctuary" (Psa. cxxxiv. 2).

5. **Faith's Testimony.** "Thy watchmen shall lift up the voice" (Isa. lii. 8).

6. **Faith's Service.** "Lift up the lad" (Gen. xxi. 18).

7. **Faith's Recognition.** "He lift up his eyes...and he saw" (Gen. xviii. 2).

519. "LIGHT"

THAT WHICH REVEALS

1. **Source** of Light. "God is Light" (1 John i. 5).

2. **Substance** of Light. "I am come a Light into the world" (John xii. 35, 36, 46).

3. **Standing** in Light. "Into His marvellous light" (1 Peter ii. 9).

4. **Walking** in the Light. "Walk in the light" (1 John i. 7).

5. **Gospel** of Light. "Commanded the light to shine out of darkness" (2 Cor. iv. 6).

6. **Protection** of Light. "Armour of light" (Rom. xiii. 12).

7. **Separation** of Light. "What communion hath light with darkness" (2 Cor. vi. 14).

520. "LIGHT"

THINGS OF LIGHT.

1. **Revelation.** "The Light of the world" (John viii. 12).

2. **Reflection.** "Ye are the Light of the world" (Matt. v. 14, 16).

3. **Identification.** "Ye are all the children of the light" (1 Thess. v. 5).

4. **Relationship.** "The Father of Lights" (James i. 17).

5. **Vivification.** "The life was the light of men" (John i. 4).

6. **Possession.** "Have the Light of Life" (John viii. 12).

7. **Satisfaction.** "Full of light" (Luke xi. 34, 36).

521. LIKE

1. Be like a **wise builder**, and build on The Foundation—Luke vi. 47-49.

2. Be like a **faithful watchman**, and be ready for the Lord —Luke xii. 36.

3. Be like a **hind in foothold**, and slip not in life—Psa. xviii. 33.

4. Be like **men in their manliness** and "quit" likewise, and be strong—1 Cor. xvi. 13.

5. Be like **David's mighty men** in valour and courage— 1 Chron. xii. 8.

6. Be like a **"Tree planted beside the rivers of water"** for fruitfulness and freshness—Psa. i. 3.

7. Be like the **"wings of a dove"** for beauty and swiftness— Psa. lv. 6.

522. LIKE PRODUCING LIKE

LIKE producing like is seen—

1. In **creation** producing "after its kind" (Gen. 1. 11).

2. In the **Love** being "kind" (1 Cor. xiii. 4).

3. In the Spirit **producing** "a kind of firstfruits" (James i. 18).

4. In **believers** being "kindly affectioned" (Rom. xii. 10).

5. In **acting** like God—2 Sam. ix. 3.

6. In being **"kind"** like God, and thus show we are His kin —Luke vi. 35.

7. In being **clothed with** "kindness," and thus to prove we are **related to Him** who is Kindness itself—Col. iii. 12; Titus iii. 4.

523. LITTLE SINS

1. Wine—Gen. ix. 21.

2. Calf—Exod. xxxii. 3-8.

3. Wedge—Joshua vii. 20.

4. Stale Bread—Joshua ix. 5.

5. Few Sheep—1 Sam. xv. 21. 23.

6. Lie—2 Kings v. 27.

7. Fear—Mark xiv. 71.

8. Deception—Acts v. 9.

9. Money—Luke xxii. 48.

10. Neglect—Heb. ii. 3.

524. LITTLE THINGS GOD USES

1. A "**little maid**" to cure a great man (2 Kings v. 2).

2. A "**little cloud**" to bring a tremendous shower (1 Kings xviii. 44).

3. A "**little oil**" to supply the need of His servant in a great famine (1 Kings xvii. 12).

4. A "**few little fishes**" to feed a hungry multitude (Matt. xv. 34).

5. A "**little child**" to be an object lesson on humility (Matt. xviii. 2).

6. A "**little flock**" to possess the Kingdom (Luke xii. 32).

7. The "**little children**" in the family of God are victorious (1 John iv. 4).

525. LIVING—HOW?

1. The **prodigal** followed the soul-wasting life by "riotous living" (Luke xv. 13).

2. The **believer** in Christ is declared to "live" because of Christ ("by" means "because of"), hence the Christian life is from the Lord—John vi. 57.

3. The **justified** "live by faith" (Rom. i. 17).

4. As **priests**, we present our bodies a "living sacrifice," and thus live consecratedly (Rom. xii. 1).

5. As the **Lord's own**, we are responsible to "live unto the Lord" (Rom. xiv. 7, 8).

6. As those who are **redeemed**, our motto is, "For me to live is Christ" (Phil. i. 21).

7. To "live **soberly, righteously**, and **godly**" in this world, is to prove we know the grace of God (Titus ii. 12; 1 Peter ii. 24).

8. To "live **in the Spirit**" is to evidence we have life from Him (Gal. v. 25).

526. LONGINGS

Epipotheo is rendered "long," "long after," "desiring greatly," "desire," and "lusteth."

1. A **babe's** longing for food—1 Peter ii. 2.

2. The **Spirit's** longing with love—Jas. iv. 5. See R.V.

3. A **teacher's** longing to instruct—Rom. i. 11.

4. A **believer's** longing to be glorified—2 Cor. v. 2.

5. **Believers'** longing in prayer—2 Cor. ix. 14.

6. An **apostle's** longing for his converts—Phil. i. 8.

7. **Paul's** longing in sympathy with Timothy—2 Tim. i. 4.

527. LOOK AT THE PAST

IT is a good thing for the believer to look at—

1. The **pit** from which he was digged—Isa. li. 1.
2. The **life** from which he has been saved—1 Cor. vi. 11.
3. The **sins** from which he is delivered—Eph. ii. 1-3.
4. The **master** from whom he has been rescued—Rom. vi. 17.
5. The **bondage** which he has left—Gal. v. 1.
6. The **bitterness** he has escaped—Exod. i. 14.
7. The **far country** of the past—Luke xv. 24.

528. "LOOKS"

WE are often, in Holy Writ, exhorted to "Look." In the Old Testament there are over twenty words rendered "Look."

1. **The "Look" In of Sin.** "I see...the law of sin which is in my members" (Rom. vii. 23). Sin is a dominating principle which blights and burns the inner being.

2. **The "Look" To of Salvation.** "Look unto Me, and be ye saved" (Isa. xlv. 22). Salvation is a comprehensive word, and among other things, means deliverance from guilt, forgiveness from sins, peace with God, relationship with God, freedom from sinning, holiness of life, service for God, and eternal glory.

3. **The "Look" Up for Succour.** "In the morning will I direct my prayer unto Thee, and will look up" (Psa. v. 3). Directness of prayer shows itself in patiently looking to the Lord for the answer.

4. **The "Look" Out in Service.** "Look on the fields" (John iv. 35). To look on the needs of others at the Lord's direction means we go forth with Him to meet that need.

5. **The "Look" Around in Contemplation.** "When I consider Thy Heavens...What is man?" (Psa. viii. 3, 4). When we look around and see God's works, we are made conscious of our smallness.

6. **The "Look" Back in Remembrance.** The Lord's Supper bids us look in three directions. We look up and praise the Lord for what He is, we look on and think of Him who is returning, and we look back and remember He died for us— 1 Cor. xi. 23-26.

7. **The "Look" For the Saviour.** "We look for the Saviour" (Phil. iii. 20, 21, R.V.). The truth of the return of the Lord for His own is the goal of salvation, the magnet of love, the meaning of hope, the mould of holiness, the incentive to service, the separator from the world, and the soul of satisfaction.

529. LOOK AT THINGS IN THE RIGHT LIGHT

"The winter of our discontent" is caused by the discontent of our wintry hearts. A well-known writer makes one of his characters reply to an observation associating winter with death: "Winter does not belong to death, although the outside of it looks like death. Beneath the snow the grass is growing. Below the frosts the roots are warm and alive. Winter is only a spring too weak and feeble for us to see that it is living. The cold does for all things what the gardener sometimes has to do for valuable trees. He must half-kill them before they will bear any fruit. Winter is in truth the small beginnings of spring."

It is well we should not judge of things as they seem to be, but look at them from the Divine standpoint.

1. A **Lazarus** with a sore-covered body is nearer Heaven than a richly fed Dives—Luke xvi. 19-24.

2. A seeming self-boasting **Apostle** knows more of the grace of God than a crowd of captious critics—2 Cor. xi. and xii.

3. An unpretentious **Barnabas** is more devoted than a self-consecrated Ananias—Acts iv. 36 to v. 3.

4. A praying **Daniel** is more effective in his work than the Medo-Persian law makers—Dan. vi. 1-24.

5. **Paul**, the chained prisoner, is more royal than the monarch before whom he was charged—Acts xxvi. 28, 29, R.V.

6. **Elijah**, the humble Tishbite, has more power in affairs than the proud and wicked Ahab—1 Kings xvii. 1.

7. The **little maid** of Israel was a greater blessing to Naaman than all the fellow-officers with which he was associated—2 Kings v. 1-3.

530. LOSING THINGS

God's children may suffer loss through failure.

1. Abraham **lost faith** through going down to Egypt—Gen. xii. 10.

2. Samson **lost power** through Delilah—Judges xvi. 19.

3. David **lost joy** through the flesh—Psa. li. 12.

4. Lot **lost possessions** through world-bordering—Gen. xiii. 12; xix. 29.

5. Peter **lost testimony** through cowardice—Luke xxii. 56-60.

6. The Ephesians **lost their first love** through half-heartedness—Rev. ii. 4.

7. Moses **lost place** through discouragement—Num. xi. 25.

531. LOOKS OF THE BELIEVER

1. Look and be **saved**—Isa. xlv. 22.
2. Look and **obey**—Num. xv. 39.
3. Look and **imitate**—Judges vii. 17.
4. Look and **ponder**—James i. 25.
5. Look and **consider**—Phil. ii. 4.
6. Look and **beware**—Heb. xii. 15.
7. Look and **expect**—Titus ii. 13.

532. "LOOK UPON"

1. **Inspection.** "The priest shall look upon it" (Lev. xiii. 43). An illustration of Christ inspecting the sinner to make him conscious of his guilt.

2. **Appreciation.** "Look upon the face of thine anointed" (Psa. lxxxiv. 9). God appreciating Christ, and blessing us for His sake.

3. **Compassion.** "Look upon mine affliction" (Psa. xxv. 18; cxix. 132). The Lord sympathising with His people in their affliction.

4. **Confession.** "What is Thy servant that Thou shouldest look upon a dead dog as I am" (2 Sam. ix. 8). So says every contrite heart.

5. **Qualification.** "The Lord looked upon him, and said, Go in this thy might" (Judges vi. 14). When the Lord sends forth, He fits, furnishes, and encourages.

6. **Recollection.** "Look upon it and remember all the commandments of the Lord" (Num. xv. 39). Observe to practise.

7. **Retribution.** "The Lord look upon it, and require it" (2 Chron. xxiv. 22). Men's sins, in God's judgment, will surely find them out.

533. LORD'S FRIENDSHIP

1. **A Loving Friend.** "A Friend loveth at all times" (Prov. xvii. 17). The times cannot alter His constancy, change His affection, alienate His sympathy, nor check His love.

2. **A Lasting Friend.** "A Friend that sticketh closer than a brother" (Prov. xviii. 24). The word "sticketh" means to adhere to, to cleave closely. He will not let us go, He holds us fast, and always.

3. **A Living Friend.** "As iron sharpeneth iron, so doth the countenance of a man his friend" (Prov. xxvii. 17). "Shar-

peneth" signifies to make sharp, acute, to give an edge. His life will make us live and laugh.

4. **A Lifting Friend.** "A Friend of publicans and sinners" (Matt. xi. 19). He is no friend of sin, but He loves to lift the sinner from the pit of sin, and fit him for the palace of His love.

5. **A Lavish Friend.** "Gavest it to the seed of Abraham, Thy friend for ever?" (2 Chron. xx. 7). Jehovah loves to give the best He has to His own. There is no stint with Him. He gives like God—Isa. xli. 8.

6. **A Listening Friend.** "The Lord spake unto Moses face to face, as a man speaketh unto his friend" (Exod. xxxiii. 11).

7. **A Lovely Friend.** "My Beloved is white and ruddy... this is my Friend" (Song of Songs v. 1-16).

534. LORDSHIP OF CHRIST
2. Thessalonians III

"The Lord" is mentioned six times—1, 3, 4, 5, 16, 16; and "Our Lord Jesus Christ" is mentioned three times—6, 12, 18.

1. "The **Word of the Lord**" associated with prayer and blessing (1).

2. "The **faithfulness of the Lord**" in stablishing and keeping (3).

3. "**Confidence in the Lord**" for the obedience of others (4).

4. **Direction from the Lord** into love and patience—5.

5. **Commanding in the Lord** for faithfulness and discretion—6.

6. **Exhortation by the Lord** for quietness and diligence—12.

7. **Peace from the Lord** in communion and consideration —16.

8. The **Presence of the Lord** for support and comfort—16.

9. "**The Grace of our Lord Jesus Christ**" for graciousness and power (18).

535. LOVE

1. The believer's love has God for its **source**—1 John iv. 7, 8.

2. Christ's love as its **measure**—Eph. v. 2.

3. The Holy Spirit as its **might**—Col. i. 8.

4. Obedience as its **credentials**—1 John v. 2.

5. Labour as its **outcome**—1 Thess. i. 3.

6. Disinterestedness as its **character**—Rom. xii. 9.

7. Believers as its **object**—1 John iii. 11.

536. LOVE

1. In God Himself we see the **Passion of Love**, as expressed in the passion of Christ on the Cross—1 John iv. 10.

2. In Him we behold the **Purity of Love**, as manifest in the holy life of the Saviour—1 John iii. 16.

3. In Him we have evidenced the **Power of Love**, as unfolded in the devotion of consecrated believers—2 Cor. v. 14-16.

4. In Him we discover the **Pre-eminence of Love**, for who but God Himself would and could love a world of sinners?—1 John iv. 16.

5. In Him we find the **Persuasiveness of Love**, as we listen to the telling tones of His tender invitations—Rom. v. 8.

6. In Him we obtain the **Protection of Love**, for He ever shields those who hide in Him—Rom. viii. 35-39.

7. In Him we have the **Perfection of Love**, for there is no flaw nor failure in the glow and gladness of His affection—1 John iv. 18, 19.

537. LOVE

1. Love is the **Oil to lubricate** all our spiritual being, and to cause it to run easily—1 Cor. xiii. 4-8.

2. Love is the **Life to rejuvenate**, so that everything may blossom fruitfully—John xv. 10-16.

3. Love is the **Affection to captivate**, and to cause us to go with others willingly—Ruth i. 16, 17.

4. Love is the **Power to consecrate**, which causes us to sacrifice ardently—1 Sam. xviii. 3, 4.

5. Love is the **Spring to animate**, which will cause us to do something for the benefit of others—1 Chron. xi. 17-19.

6. Love is a **Tonic to stimulate**, to give wings to our feet in service—John xx. 4.

7. Love is the **Grace to elevate**, to lift us above the plain of self—Gal. ii. 20.

538. LOVE FOR THE BOOK

"O how I love Thy law" Psa. cxix. 97

SPURGEON's love for the Bible is happily illustrated in the following, found on the copy he used:

"C. H. Spurgeon, 1856.

"The lamp of my study—

"The light is bright as ever, 1861.

"Oh, that mine eyes were more opened, 1864.

"Being worn to pieces, rebound 1870. The lantern mended and the light as joyous to mine eyes as ever."

Mark the growing appreciation of the Book. In 1856 the Word was the "lamp of my study;" in 1861 his appetite is as keen as ever; in 1864 his prayer is intense for opened eyes, and in 1870 "the light as joyous as ever." May we have a like appreciation. If we love the Word of the Lord, we shall be like the Psalmist in Psalm cxix.

1. **Delight** in God's commandments, "which I have loved" (47).

2. **Lift up** our hands in appeal, for we shall say, "my hands also will I lift up unto Thy commandments which I have loved" (48).

3. **Meditate** in God's law "all the day," and say, "O how I love Thy law" (97).

4. If we love God's law, we shall **turn away** from our own thoughts—113.

5. Gold will have a subordinate place if we **love God's commandments**—127.

6. Because God's Word is "very pure" we shall say, "Thy servant **loveth it**" (140).

7. We shall be **able to say** if we love God's Word, "Consider how I love Thy precepts" (159).

8. We shall turn away from the evil and **keep to the good** —163.

9. We shall **enjoy** "**great peace**" through loving God's law—165.

10. As we go on **keeping** God's testimonies we shall "love them exceedingly" (167).

539. "LOVE" IN JOHN XV

1. **The Source of Love.** "The Father hath loved" (9).

2. **The Correspondence of Love.** "As the Father hath loved Me, so have I loved you" (9).

3. **The Continuance of Love.** "Continue ye in My love" (9).

4. **The Command of Love.** "My commandment, that ye love one another" (12, 17).

5. **The Example of Love.** "As I have loved you" (12).

6. **The Proof of Love.** "If ye keep My commandments, ye shall abide in My love; even as I have kept My Father's commandments, and abide in His love" (10).

7. **The Superlative of Love.** "Greater love hath no man than this, that a man lay down his life for his friends" (13).

540. LOVE OF GOD

1. **Unmerited** in its object—1 John iv. 10.
2. **Unsought** in its action—Rom. v. 8.
3. **Universal** in its offer—John iii. 16.
4. **Unbounded** in its work—Eph. ii. 4.
5. **Unknown** in its fullness—Eph. iii. 19.
6. **Unbroken** in its ministry—Rom. viii. 39.
7. **Unending** in its character—Jer. xxxi. 3.

541. LOVE OF GOD

1. **Inextinguishable** in its flame of affection—Song of Sol. viii. 7.
2. **Inexhaustible** in its flow of supply—Rom. viii. 32-37.
3. **Indefatigable** in its attention of service—John xiii. 12.
4. **Indispensable** in its sustenance of grace—Eph. ii. 4, 5.
5. **Instant** in its readiness of help—2 Cor. v. 14.
6. **Immutable** in its unchangingness of character—1 John iv. 16.
7. **Inseparable** in its strength of holding—Rom. viii. 39.

542. LOVE'S CHARACTERISTICS
In Deuteronomy xxvi

This chapter is the unfolding of what Jehovah was to His people, and the consequent obligation which rested upon them to be to Him. Twelve times the sentence, "The Lord thy God" occurs (1, 2, 2, 3, 4, 5, 10, 10, 11, 13, 16, 19), "Lord" occurs five times (3, 7, 8, 17, 18), "Lord God of our fathers" occurs once (7), "O Lord" occurs once (10), "Lord my God" occurs once (14), "Thy God" occurs once (17). The fitness and fullness of these several uses of the Name of Jehovah and Elohim are full of speaking eloquence.

There are seven things the Lord did for His people.

1. **Love's Giving.** "The land which the Lord thy God giveth" (1, 2). The cause of the Lord's giving is not found in Israel's deserving, but in His grace. The same holds good with us in Christ. Ponder the "when we were" of Romans v. 6, the "while we were" of Romans v. 8, "when we were" of Romans v. 10, and "Even when we were" of Ephesians ii. 5.

2. **Love's Looking.** "The Lord...looked on our affliction, and our labour, and oppression" (7). He saw the "oppression" of their bondage, the "labour" of their toil, and the bitterness of their "affliction." Sin is an exactor, and a hard task-master,

but the Lord sees and succours when we cry out in heart-anguish. See the fourteen things said of what we were before we believed in Christ, in Ephesians ii.

3. **Love's Deliverance.** "The Lord brought us forth out of Egypt" (8). Jehovah not only protected Israel in Egypt, but He brought them out of it. His power and wonders were manifest in doing so, and His skill was displayed. Also the "greatness of His power" was unfolded in Christ's resurrection and our quickening from the death of sin—See Eph. i. 19 to ii. 1.

4. **Love's Placement.** "He hath brought us into this place" (9). The land of Canaan is typical of the fullness of the blessing in Christ. What does that fullness mean? Satisfaction of heart, peace of mind, joy of soul, victory over sin, meekness for service, communion with God, and blessing to others.

5. **Love's Commands.** "The Lord thy God hath commanded thee to do" (13-19). Privileges always bring responsibilities. Obligations rest upon those who have received benefits. Affection commands duties. Love demands obedience. Faith proves itself by devotion, and love by consecration.

6. **Love's Avouchment.** "The Lord hath avouched thee this day to be His peculiar people" (18). The Lord's portion is His people, and also His treasure. He speaks as if He could not do without us, we certainly cannot do without Him; and not only so, but He avouches, that is, solemnly promises, that it is so. His work of grace, His worth of Person, and His word of promise places Him under His own loving obligation.

7. **Love's Making.** "He hath made thee...that thou mayest be an holy people unto the Lord thy God" (19). The fame of holiness is the highest of all fame, providing we remember the Holy One makes us holy. When we are well in soul through the health of holiness, we have the wealth of happiness. His making is the cause of our doing, and the inspiration of our life.

543. LOVE'S SUPERLATIVENESS

1. Love is seen in its **highest form**—1 John iii. 16.

2. Love is revealed in its **lowest stoop**—1 John iv. 9.

3. Love is made known in its **purest grace**—1 John iv. 10.

4. Love is manifest in its **greatest sacrifice**—John iii. 16.

5. Love is unveiled in its **sublimest essence**—1 John iv. 8.

6. Love is bestowed in its **mightiest power**—1 John iv. 16.

7. Love is communicated in its **intensest blessing**— 1 John iv. 17-21.

544. LOVE'S CHARACTER

"The love of God" Rom. v. 5

1. **Divine** in its nature. "God is Love" (1 John iv. 8, 16).

2. **Definite** in its giving. "God so loved...He gave" (John iii. 16).

3. **Decisive** in its assurance. "As My Father hath loved Me, so have I" (John xv. 9).

4. **Deliberate** in its service. "Having loved...He loved to the end" (John xiii. 1).

5. **Dominating** in its power. "The love of Christ constraineth" (2 Cor. v. 14).

6. **Durable** in its affection. "I have loved thee with an everlasting love" (Jer. xxxi. 3).

7. **Dedicating** in its influence. "He that dwelleth in love, dwelleth in God, and God in him" (1 John iv. 16).

545. LOVE'S UNFAILINGNESS

1. Love's unfailing **Promise**—Joshua xxiii. 14.

2. Love's unfailing **Supply**—1 Kings xvii. 14.

3. Love's unfailing **Faithfulness**—Psa. lxxxix. 33.

4. Love's unfailing **Compassions**—Lam. iii. 22.

5. Love's unfailing **Word**—Luke xvi. 17.

6. Love's unfailing **Strength**—Isa. xl. 26.

7. Love's unfailing **Presence**—Deut. xxxi. 6.

546. LUSTS OF THE FLESH

1. **Evil** in their character—Col. iii. 5.

2. **Deceitful** in their appearance—Eph. iv. 22.

3. **Varied** in their manifestation—Rom. vii. 8; 2 Tim. iii. 6; Titus iii. 3.

4. **Fleeting** in their enjoyment—1 John ii. 17.

5. **Hurtful** in their embrace—1 Tim. vi. 9; 1 Peter ii. 11.

6. **Personal** in their origin—2 Tim. iv. 3; 2 Peter iii. 3; Jude 16, 18.

7. **Captivating** in their influence—James i. 14.

547. "MANIFOLD"

1. **An Observing God.** "I know your manifold transgressions" (Amos. v. 12).

2. **A Merciful Lord.** "According to Thy manifold mercies" (Neh. ix. 19, 27).

3. **A Surprising Worker.** "O Lord, how manifold are Thy works" (Psa. civ. 24).

4. **A Wonderful Structure.** "The Church, the manifold wisdom of God" (Eph. iii. 10).

5. **A Weighty Responsibility.** "Stewards of the manifold grace of God" (1 Peter iv. 10).

6. **A Trying Time.** "Divers (same word) temptations" (James i. 2). "Manifold temptations" (1 Peter i. 6).

7. **An Overflowing Reward.** "Who shall not receive manifold more," etc. (Luke xviii. 30).

548. MANNA

THE manna, as we know from Christ's teaching, is a type of Himself as the Bread from Heaven—John vi. 32, 33. The typical teaching of the manna may be gathered from the following.

1. It was **round** in appearance—Exod. xvi. 14; suggestive of Christ, who is the Eternal One, without beginning and without end—Rev. i. 8.

2. It was **small in size**—Exod. xvi. 14; typical of Christ, who became a Babe in Bethlehem, and was a Man among men— Luke ii. 11, 12, 16.

3. It was **white** in colour—Exod. xvi. 31; which indicates Christ as the Righteous One—Heb. vii. 26.

4. It was **sweet** to the taste, it is said to be like wafers made with honey—Exod. xvi. 31; typical of Christ as the precious One, whose Word is often compared to honey—Psa. xix. 10.

5. It is compared to **Coriander seed**, which was used as a condiment—Exod. xvi. 31; and may be taken as typical of Christ, who will season all our life with His presence and grace— Col. iii. 15, 16; iv. 6.

6. It is further described as having the taste of **sweet oil**— Num. xi. 8; and is typical of Christ, who is ever fresh in the livingness of His love and truth—Heb. xiii. 8.

7. It is further identified with the **dew** which fell upon the ground—Num. xi. 9; and may be taken to represent the fact that Christ can only be known and appreciated through the ministry of the Holy Spirit—Eph. iii. 16, 17.

549. "MANY"

1. **"Many infallible proofs"** given by Christ (Acts i. 3).
2. **"Many wonders** and signs" were done by Him (Acts ii. 43).
3. Christ was seen **"many days"** after His resurrection (Acts xiii. 31).
4. **"Many believed** in the Lord" (Acts ix. 42).
5. "Suffer **many things"** (Matt. xvi. 21).
6. **"Many** were **gathered together"** unto Him (Mark ii. 2).
7. **"Many** of His disciples **went with Him"** (Luke vii. 11).

550. MARKS OF A DISCIPLE IN GALATIANS VI
Galatians vi. 17

1. A "spirit of **meekness"** (1).
2. A **bearing** of burdens—2.
3. A **proving** of work—3.
4. A **sowing** to the Spirit—8.
5. A **continuance** in well-doing—9.
6. Doing **good** to others—10.
7. **Glorying** in the Cross—14.

551. MEETING THE LORD

1. The **place** of meeting. The Blood-stained Mercy Seat—Exod. xxv. 22; xxx. 6, 36.
2. The **Person** to meet. God Himself—Exod. xix. 17.
3. Meeting Christ with **praise**—John xii. 13.
4. Going forth to meet the **Bridegroom**—Matt. xxv. 1, 6.
5. Caught up to **meet the Lord** in the air—1 Thess. iv. 17.

552. MEETNESS

1. A **Qualified Believer.** Made meet for the inheritance of the saints in light—Col. i. 12.
2. A **True Penitent.** Bringing forth "fruits meet for repentance" (Matt. iii. 8; Acts xxvi. 20).
3. A **Sanctified Worker.** "Sanctified and meet for the Master's use" (2 Tim. ii. 21).
4. A **Diligent Teacher.** "I think it meet to stir you up" (2 Peter i. 13).
5. A **Humble Apostle.** "I am not meet to be called an apostle" (1 Cor. xv. 9).

553. MEET THINGS

1. **Fruits Meet for Repentance.** "Bring forth fruits meet for repentance" (Matt. iii. 8).
2. **Joy Meet for the Occasion.** "It was meet we should make merry" (Luke xv. 32).
3. **Saints Meet for the Inheritance.** "Made meet for the inheritance of the saints in light" (Col. i. 12).
4. **Vessels made Meet for Service.** "Meet for the Master's use (2 Tim. ii. 21).
5. **Soldiers Meet for the Conflict.** "Pass over all that are meet for the war" (Deut. iii. 18).
6. **Praise Meet for the Subjects.** "We are bound to thank God for you, as it is meet" (2 Thess. i. 3).
7. **Judgment Meet for the Sinner.** "Receiving...that recompense...that was meet" (Rom. i. 27).

554. MERCY

THOSE who cry for mercy obtain the mercy for which they cry.

1. The Lord's mercy is **"great"** in character (Num. xiv. 18, 19).
2. **"Plenteous"** in blessing (Psa. lxxxvi. 15).
3. **"Everlasting"** in extent (Psa. c. 5).
4. **"Good"** in help (Psa. cix. 21).
5. **"Delighting"** in action (Micah vii. 18).
6. **"Tender"** in bestowment (Luke i. 78).
7. **"Rich"** in wealth (Eph. ii. 4).
8. **"Abundant"** in supply (1 Peter i. 3).

555. "ME'S" OF PRAYER

1. The **penitent sinner's** cry is, "Lord, be merciful to me a sinner" (Luke xviii. 13).
2. The **feeble saint's** petition is, "Keep me as the apple of the eye" (Psa. xvii. 8).
3. The **ignorant scholar's** request is, "Teach me Thy paths" (Psa. xxv. 4).
4. The **tempted warrior's** supplication is, "Let not mine enemies triumph over me" (Psa. xxv. 2).
5. The **troubled disciple's** cry is, "Lord save me" (Matt. xiv. 30).
6. The **searched one's** petition is, "Lead me in the way everlasting" (Psa. cxxxix. 24).
7. The **believing suppliant's** prayer is, "Lord, remember me" (Luke xxiii. 42).

556. MESSAGE OF THE GOSPEL

OF Philip's message it is said, "He preached Christ unto them in Samaria, and the things concerning the Kingdom of God;" and when he spoke to the eunuch "he preached unto him Jesus." Christ should be proclaimed in the—

1. **Personality of His Divine Sonship**—Acts ix. 20.
2. **Propitiation of His Glorious Death**—1 John ii. 2.
3. **Power of His Mighty Resurrection**—Acts iv. 33.
4. **Pardoning of His Gracious Love**—Acts xiii. 38, 39.
5. **Peace of His Holy Calm**—Acts x. 36.
6. **Plan of His Outlined Purpose**—Acts xv. 13-18.
7. **Promise of His Practical Blessing**—Acts iii. 19, R.V.

When the Gospel is thus proclaimed, there must be results. The hearers will either be "pricked in their hearts" to their conviction and conversion, as on the day of Pentecost (Acts ii. 37), or they will be "cut to the heart," to their ultimate condemnation and consternation (Acts vii. 54).

557. MILLENNIAL REIGN OF CHRIST
DESCRIBED IN PSALM LXXII

1. **Righteousness** will be the principle of His reign—1, 2.
2. **Peace** will be the character of His reign—3.
3. **Beneficence** will be the blessing of His reign—4, 6, 11-13, 14.
4. **Universality** will be the extent of His reign—8, 11, 17.
5. **Prosperity** will be the consequence of His reign—7, 16.
6. **Victory** over His enemies will be the outcome of His reign—9.
7. The kings of the earth will **acknowledge** His reign—10, 11, 17.
8. **Longevity** will be the time of His reign—17.
9. **Appreciation** will be given in acknowledgment of His reign—15.

558. MILLENNIUM—WHAT IS IT?

"A thousand years" Rev. xx. 2, 3, 4

1. The Millennium will be **inaugurated** by the **Personal Return of Christ**, when He will remove everything that offends, or is a stumbling-block—Matt. xiii. 41.

2. The Millennium will see **the Jews converted** to Christ at its **inception**—Zech. xii. 10, and the lost ten tribes will be united to Judah, and become one nation—Ezek. xxxvi., xxxvii.

3. In the Millennium **Jerusalem** will be the **centre of God's administration**—Jer. iii. 17; Micah iv. 8, and Palestine will be altered in its geographical appearance—Zech. xiv. 4, 10, and extent—Ezek. xlviii.

4. During the Millennium **the land** of Palestine and the earth will become more **fertile** and **fruitful**—Psa. lxvii. 6; Ezek. xxxiv. 27.

5. In the Millennium the **animal creation will be delivered** into the liberty of the glory of the children of God—Rom. viii. 20, 21, R.V.

6. In the Millennium **men will learn war no more,** and will beat their implements of slaughter into implements of agriculture—Hosea ii. 18; Micah iv. 3.

7. In the Millennium **death will be the exception,** and life will be greatly increased in its longevity—Isa. lxv. 20-23.

8. In the Millennium **Satan will be shut up in the abyss,** therefore the tempter will not do his fell work—Rev. xx. 1, 2.

9. The character of the rule in the Millennium will be **an administration of righteousness**—Isa. xxxii. 1; Acts xvii. 31.

10. **The Holy Spirit will be poured out** upon "all flesh" in the Millennium—Joel. ii. 28, 29.

11. Israel will have **great spiritual blessing**—Jer. xxxii. 37-41.

12. In the Millennium **nations will be blest with Israel,** especially Egypt and Assyria—Isa. xix. 23-25.

13. In the Millennium **Jerusalem will be rebuilt** and **a new temple,** and religious worship will be in operation, although not the same as in the past—Ezek. xl. to xlvii.

14. The Lord will be **"King over all the earth,"** and all nations will worship Him—Zech. xiv. 9; Isa. ii. 2, in the Millennium.

559. MILLENNIUM INDICATED

In a Gospel Scene

In Mark vi. 45-56 we have the record of how Christ constrained His disciples to cross the lake while He went up into a mountain, how He saw them toiling in rowing, how He came to them just before daybreak, how He stilled the tempest, and they were safe to land, and then how He went on His way healing the sick.

The whole scene is pictorial of the sequence of events.

1. Christ constrained His disciples to get into a boat and go over to **the other side** of the lake. This is a picture of how He has made us in the boat of existence to voyage on the lake of life,

2. Having "taken leave" of the disciples, He went up into a **mountain to pray,** which may be taken to represent His departure to the right hand of God, where He ever liveth to make intercession for us.

3. While on the mountain He saw the disciples as they were **"distressed in rowing"** (R.V.). Christ sees us in all our toils, sorrows, and difficulties.

4. He came to the disciples in **the fourth watch** of the night, just before daybreak. He also is coming to His own before the daybreak of the Millennium to take us to Himself.

5. When Christ came to the disciples, the **tempest was stilled,** and He brought them safe to land. So when our Lord comes for His own we shall have the stillness of His peace in its fullest sense, and be safe in a glorified Body with Himself.

6. Afterwards He went to the land of Gennesaret, and all who sought Him for healing and health were **made whole.** So when Christ comes in His power to the earth with the Redeemed, He will heal poor broken humanity, and bless the whole earth.

560. MILLENNIUM PICTURED
IN CHRIST'S TRANSFIGURATION
"He made known His power and coming" 2 Peter i. 16, 18

WE are warranted in saying the transfiguration pictures the Millennium, for Christ said before it, "But I tell you of a truth there be some standing here which shall not taste of death till they see the Kingdom of God. And it came to pass about eight days after these sayings," He was transfigured (Luke ix. 27, 28), and this transfiguration Peter states was prophetic, for He "made known" "His power and coming," "when we were with Him in the Holy Mount" (2 Peter i. 16-18).

The whole scene on the Mount and its sequence is full of suggestion.

1. We have the **glorified Christ** as the Object of wonder and praise. "We saw His glory" (John i. 14), and as the glorified One He will be seen.

2. **Moses** was one of the two who "appeared in glory" (Luke ix. 31), and he is a type of those who have fallen asleep, but who will be raised and glorified when Christ comes— Phil. iii. 20, 21.

3. **Elijah** is a type of those who will be alive when Christ returns, and like Elijah will never die, but be caught away to meet Christ in the air—1 Thess. iv. 17.

4. **Peter, James,** and **John** are typical of the Jewish nation, who will see Christ coming with ten thousand of His holy ones,

when He comes to be glorified in His saints—Zech. xiv. 5; 2 Thess. i. 10.

5. Christ coming down from the Mount with His disciples, and meeting the devil-torn child—Luke ix. 37-43, and His emancipating **the child** from the Devil, is a type of Christ delivering poor demon-possessed humanity when He comes to set up His kingdom, and in delivering the oppressed—Psa. lxxii. 4.

6. Christ sending forth, "after these things," **the seventy** to preach the Gospel of "the Kingdom of God" (Luke x. 1-11), is typical of that time when the nation of Israel will be proclaimers that Christ reigns.

7. It was after the seventy had returned and told Christ what they had seen and done, for "in that hour **Jesus rejoiced** in spirit," and said, "All things are delivered to Me of My Father" (Matt. xi. 12-27).

561. "MIND TO WORK"

"The people had a mind to work" (Neh. iv. 6)

IF we have "a mind to work" we shall do our best for the Lord. See how Nehemiah's mind to work worked out.

1. **He prayed** in the face of opposition—iv. 4, 5.

2. **He watched** against the inroads of conspiracy—7-9.

3. **He was the more careful** because of the wiliness of his enemies, and the feebleness of his friends—10-14.

4. **His vigilance** was rewarded with success—15-23.

5. **He got the people to say "Amen"** to the Word of the Lord when differences arose amongst themselves—v. 1-13.

6. **He had confidence** in prayer that God would think of him, since he had thought of God and His people—14-19.

7. **His mind to work** was evidenced in that he minded to work till it was finished—vi. 15, 16.

562. "MINE EYES"

1. **Cause of Confession.** "Mine eyes have seen the King" (Isa. vi. 5).

2. **Cause of Content.** "For mine eyes have seen Thy salvation" (Luke ii. 30).

3. **Cause of Consecration.** "For Thy lovingkindness is before mine eyes" (Psa. xxvi. 3).

4. **Cause of Confession.** "He hath opened mine eyes" (John ix. 30).

5. Cause of Rest. "For Thou hast delivered my soul from death, mines eyes from tears, and my feet from falling" (Psa. cxvi. 8).

6. Cause of Faith. "Mine eyes are ever toward the Lord; for He shall pluck my feet out of the net" (Psa. xxv. 15).

7. Cause of Hope. "Mine eyes shall behold, and not another" (Job. xix. 27).

563. MISTAKES AND MOULDERS OF LIFE

JUDGE RINTOUL, of the City of London Court, gave an extremely interesting address when he spoke to the members of the Bartholomew Club, on "The Fourteen Mistakes of Life." He said pathetically: "I think I have the greatest fitness for speaking on this subject, because I have committed every one of them." And this is the list he gave:

1. To attempt to set up our own standard of right and wrong, and expect everybody to conform to it.

2. To try to measure the enjoyment of others by our own.

3. To expect uniformity of opinion in this world.

4. To look for judgment and experience in youth.

5. To endeavour to mould all dispositions alike.

6. Not to yield in unimportant trifles.

7. To look for perfection in our own actions.

8. To worry ourselves and others about what cannot be remedied.

9. Not to alleviate if we can all that needs alleviation.

10. Not to make allowances for the weakness of others.

11. To consider anything impossible that we cannot ourselves perform.

12. To believe only what our finite minds can grasp.

13. To live as if the moment, the time, the day, were so important that it would live for ever.

14. To estimate people by some outside quality, for it is that within which makes the man.

When we turn to the pages of Holy Writ, we find the opposites to what Judge Rintoul says about mistakes.

1. The Rule of Life is found in the ten commandments—Exod. xx. 1-17.

2. The Example of Life is to be like Christ; that is, to bring enjoyment to others—Acts x. 38.

3. The Word of Life is to think with God, and thus to think with each other—John xvii. 21.

4. The Wisdom of Life is to listen to the voice of experience and wisdom—Prov. i. 8.

5. The Aim of Life is to please the Lord—2 Cor. v. 9, R.V.

6. The Kindness of Life is to yield to others when no principle of right is involved—Rom. xiv. 10-16.

7. The Secret of Life is for Christ to live within us, for He alone can produce perfection in us—Gal. ii. 20.

8. The Joy of Life is to be "anxious for nothing," thankful for anything, and prayerful in everything—Phil. iv. 6, 7.

9. The Work of Life is to alleviate all the misery we can, and thus bring joy to ourselves—Heb. xiii. 16.

10. The Help of Life is to remove the weaknesses we see in others, not forgetting the weakness in ourselves—Gal. vi. 1-3.

11. The Unity of Life is to remember that no man lives to himself, and that we cannot do without each other, any more than one member of the body can do without the other—1 Cor. xii. 14-27.

12. The Fact of Life cannot be explained by the finite, therefore, there are many things which are beyond human comprehension—Job xi. 7.

13. The Future of Life is ever before us; therefore, to live only in the present moment is the greatest folly—Luke xii. 16-40.

14. The Inness of Life is its true character; therefore, to estimate things or people by an outside quality is to miss the guiding principle, that the unseen things are the real, and the seen things are the unreal—2 Cor. iv. 18.

564. "MY FEET"

1. **Set** Feet. "Set my feet in a large room" (Psa. xxxi. 8; xl. 2).

2. **Delivered** Feet. "Delivered my feet from falling" (Psa. cxvi. 8).

3. **Refrained** Feet. "I have refrained my feet" (Psa. cxix. 101).

4. **Illuminated** Feet. "Thy Word a lamp unto my feet" (Psa. cxix. 105).

5. **Sure** Feet. "He maketh my feet like hind's feet" (Psa. xviii. 33).

6. **Pierced** Feet. "They pierced my feet" (Psa. xxii. 16).

7. **Victorious** Feet. "Fallen under my feet" (Psa. xviii. 38).

565. "MOUNTAINS A WAY"

"I will make all My mountains a way" (Isa. xlix. 11).
SOME mountains in Scripture are specially God's mountains,
and they are always a way to something.

1. **Mount Moriah** is the way to see God's gracious provision—Gen. xxii. 14.

2. **Mount Horeb** is the way to God's revelation of His
covenant—Exod. iii. 1; iv. 27.

3. **Mount Sinai** is the way to conviction and commission—
see the mount as mentioned in Exod. xix.; xxiv.; xxv. 40;
xxvi. 30; xxvii. 8; xxxi. 18; Heb. viii. 5; xii. 18.

4. **Mount Hor** is the way to translation—Num. xx. 22-28.

5. **Mount Nebo** is the way to discipline and vision—Deut.
xxxii. 49, 50.

6. **Mount Zion** is the way to victory and joy—Psa. xlviii.
2; Obad. 17; Revelation. xiv. 1.

7. **Mount of Olivet** is the way to Christ—Matt. xxiv. 3;
Mark xiv. 26; Luke xxii. 39; John viii. 1; Acts i. 12; Zech.
xiv. 4.

566. MUSE ON CALVARY

MUSE on Calvary, and let that moving scene move us to act in
soul for Him who acted in love for us, and let us—

1. Believe in Him **trustfully**—Gal. ii. 20.
2. Live to Him **thoroughly**—2 Cor. v. 14-16.
3. Love Him **supremely**—Eph. v. 1, 2.
4. Separate to Him **wholly**—Gal. i. 4.
5. Follow Him **exclusively**—1 Peter ii. 21-24.
6. Praise Him **gratefully**—Rev. i. 5.
7. Expect Him **hopefully**—Titus ii. 13, 14.

567. "MY"

THERE are nine "my's" in 2 Samuel xxii. 2, 3.

1. **Security.**   "Jehovah is my Rock."
2. **Safety.**   "My Fortress."
3. **Deliverer.**   "My Deliverer."
4. **Stability.**   "God is my Rock."
5. **Shield.**   "My Shield."
6. **Strength.**   "Horn of my salvation."
7. **Exaltation.**   "My High Tower."
8. **Refuge.**   "My Refuge."
9. **Saviour.**   "My Saviour."

568. "MOVED" PERSONS

1. **A Compassionate Saviour.** "Moved with compassion"*
(Matt. ix. 36; xiv. 14; xviii. 27; Mark i. 41; vi. 34).

2. **A Jealous Band.** "Moved with indignation concerning
the two" (Matt. xx. 24, R.V.; see Acts vii. 9).

3. **A Stirred City.** "All the city was moved" (R.V.,
"stirred"), "saying, Who is this?" (Matt. xxi. 10).

4. **An Envious Crowd.** "The Jews, which believed not,
moved with envy, took unto them certain lewd fellows...
gathered a crowd" etc. (Acts xvii. 5, R.V.).

5. **A Faithful Worker.** "Noah...moved with fear, prepared
an ark" (Heb. xi. 7).

6. **An Anointed Company.** "Holy men of God spake as
they were moved by the Holy Ghost" (2 Peter i. 21).

7. **A Tender Heart.** "When He saw him, He was moved
with compassion" (Luke x. 33, R.V.).

569. "MY CONFESSION"

1. **Christ for Me.** Salvation—Rom. v. 8.
2. **Christ in Me.** Sanctification—Gal. ii. 20.
3. **Complete in Him.** Supply—Col. ii. 10, R.V.

570. "MY GOD"

"O my God, I trust in Thee" (Psa. xxv. 2)

SEE the words "my God" as to what relationship with Him
means in the following Scriptures:

1. All **need** supplied—Phil. iv. 19.
2. All **enemies** defeated—Psa. vii. 1.
3. All **safety** found—Psa. xviii. 2.
4. All **light** given—Psa. xviii. 28.
5. All **healing** bestowed—Psa. xxx. 2.
6. All **worship** rendered—Psa. xliii. 4.
7. All **thirst** satisfied—Psa. lxiii. 1.

* The Greek word rendered, "*moved with compassion*," also occurs in Matt. xv. 32
xx. 34; Mark viii. 2; ix. 22; Luke vii. 13. x. 33; xv. 20.

571. NAME OF JESUS

BERNARD says: "Jesus is honey in the mouth, melody in the ear, and joy in the heart."

An old coloured woman who had learned the alphabet, said: "Now I want to spell Jesus, for 'pears like the rest will come easier if I learn to spell that blessed Name first."

1. **Music** in His Name—Acts i. 1.
2. **Majesty** of His Name—Acts ii. 36.
3. **Might** of His Name—Acts iv. 2; v. 30, 31.
4. **Message** of His Name—Acts viii. 35.
5. **Magnetism** of His Name—Acts ix. 5, 17, 27.
6. **Melody** of His Name—Acts xvii. 3.
7. **Meaning** of His Name—Matt. i. 21.

572. NAZARITE

"NAZARITE" comes from "Nawzar," to separate. If we ponder Numbers vi. we shall find a sevenfold separation stated and suggested.

1. Separation from the **common run**—2.
2. Separation from **uncleanness**—7.
3. Separation from **strong drink** and all its associations—3, 4.
4. Separation from all that is associated **with death**—6.
5. Separation from the **cuttings of man**—5.
6. Separation from **unclean food**—4.
7. Separation from **self**—2, etc.

573. NEHEMIAH'S PRAYER

"I BESEECH THEE" (i. 4, 5, 6, 8, 11; ii. 4). Couple with "I beseech," "I pray," and "I prayed." Burns says, "They never sought in vain that sought the Lord aright;" and Coleridge declares, "He prayeth best who loveth best." Prayer is—

1. The **empty hand** of need—Jas. v. 15, 16.
2. The **call for aid**—Luke vi. 12.
3. The **expression of faith**—Acts i. 14.
4. The **reliance of trust**—Phil. iv. 6.
5. The **desire of love**—Acts xii. 5.
6. The **work of grace**—Col. iv. 12.
7. The **bloom of holiness**—1 Tim. iv. 5.
8. The **communion of saints**—Eph. vi. 18.

574. NEHEMIAH'S WEEPING
"I sat down and wept" i. 4

THE condition of things so burdened Nehemiah that he "sat down and wept," and more than that, he "mourned and fasted and prayed," and he did all "before the God of Heaven." Christ did the same when He saw the city in its sins and sorrow—Luke xix. 41. Recall—

1. The tears of **Abraham's sorrow**—Gen. xxiii. 2.
2. The tears of **Josiah's repentance**—2 Chron. xxxiv. 27.
3. The tears of the **sinner's love**—Luke vii. 38.
4. Joseph's tears of **sympathy**—Gen. xlv. 2.
5. Israel's tears of **complaint**—Num. xi. 4.
6. Peter's tears of **regret**—Luke xxii. 62.
7. Jesus' tears of **compassion**—John xi. 35.

575. NEW BIRTH

CHRIST repeated the necessity for the new birth twice to Nicodemus—John iii. 3, 7. The Lord Jesus does not argue the matter with Nicodemus, but keeps to this great necessity, if he would see and enter into the presence of God, namely, that he must "be born again."

1. The **necessity** of the new birth is seen, because man is a sinner—Rom. viii. 7, 8.
2. The **Author** of it is the Father—John i. 13.
3. The **procuring cause** of it is the Lord Jesus—1 John v. 1.
4. The **Effective Agent** is the Holy Spirit—John iii. 6.
5. The **instrument** by which the Spirit accomplishes His purpose is the Word of God—1 Peter i. 23.
6. The **evidence** of it is brought out by John in his First Epistle—see ii. 29; iii. 9; iv. 7; v. 1; v. 18.

576. NEW THINGS IN THE NEW CREATION
2 Cor. v. 17, margin

1. A **New Aim.** To please the Lord—9, R.V.
2. A **New Association.** Oneness with the Lord—14.
3. A **New Attitude.** To live "unto Him" who loved us—15.
4. A **New Activity.** To walk by faith—7.
5. A **New Attachment.** To be fused by the love of Christ—14.
6. A **New Ambassage.** To deliver the message of reconciliation—20.
7. A **New Assurance** about the future—1-7.

577. NON-CONSENTERS

1. The **holy ones** not consenting to idolatry—Deut. xiii. 8.

2. The **world** not consenting to the request of God's people—Judges xi. 17.

3. **God's people** not consenting to the world's demand—1 Kings xx. 8.

4. The **saint** not consenting to the sinner's enticement—Proverbs i. 10.

5. The **godly man** not consenting to Christ's death—Luke xxiii. 51.

6. The **servant of Christ** not consenting to remain and minister—Acts xviii. 20.

7. The **professor** not consenting to God's truth—1 Tim. vi. 3.

578. "NO ORDERS, EXCEPT FROM THE KING"
OR, "SEVEN TIMES GO, FROM GOD "

"Things whatsoever I have commanded" (Matt. xxviii. 20).

MAJOR-GENERAL SIR GEORGE YOUNGHUSBAND, the Keeper of the Jewel House of the Tower of London, who has been granted a vacant good service pension, enjoys a curious privilege in that "he hath no superior officer in Court or Kingdom." He receives no orders except from the King himself, or conveyed to him through the Lord Chamberlain. The origin of the rule is clear, for in more turbulent days it would have been easy for some traitor to order the Keeper to hand over the King's jewels to him. In spite of this care, however, the jewels were tampered with and sometimes stolen. The magnificent "aquamarine," which used to be on the top of the King's Crown, was found to be of glass; where the original went none can say.

As the Keeper of the jewels receives no orders but through the King himself, so there are seven commands which the Lord alone gives. These commands are found in seven "Go's."

1. **Adjustment.** "Go and tell him of his fault" (Matt. xviii. 15).

2. **Activity.** "Go and work to-day" (Matt. xxi. 28).

3. **Alertness.** "Go out and meet Him" (Matt. xxv. 6).

4. **Attention.** "Go home to thy friends and tell," etc. (Mark v. 19).

5. **Fruitfulness.** "Go and bring forth fruit" (John xv. 16).

6. **Separation.** "Go and sin no more" (John viii. 11).

7. **Testimony.** "Go and preach the Gospel" (Mark xvi. 15).

When our Lord says "Go," faith recognises His authority, and love is swift to respond to His direction.

579. "NOT I, BUT CHRIST"

"As you grow in your art," said Gounod, to the young poet, "you will judge the great masters of the past as I now judge the great musicians of former times. At your age I used to say 'I,' at twenty-five I said, 'I and Mozart,' at forty, 'Mozart and I;' now I say, 'Mozart'." The same thing is illustrated in the life of the believer who is growing in grace. At first the cry is:

1. "What **must I do** to be saved?" (Acts xvi. 30).
2. Then, "That I may be **found in Christ**" (Phil. iii. 9).
3. Then, "**Christ liveth in me**" (Gal. ii. 20).
4. Lastly, "**Christ is All**" (Col. iii. 11).

580. "NOTS"

THERE are some "not's" which God's children need to ponder, namely:

1. The "**forget not**" of remembered mercies (Psa. ciii. 2).
2. The "**fear not**" of gracious presence (Isa. xli. 10).
3. The "**let not**" of dominating sin (Rom. vi. 12).
4. The "**look not**" of prohibitive command (Prov. xxiii. 31).
5. The "**love not**" of an ensnaring world (1 John ii. 15).
6. The "**sin not**" of entire separation (1 Cor. xv. 34).
7. The "**say not**" of careful speech (Rom. x. 6).

581. NOTS IN ECCLESIASTES V. 1-10

NEGATIVES become positives if we heed them.

1. **Watchfulness.** "Keep thy foot when thou goest to the house of God" (1).
2. **Considerateness.** "Be not rash with thy mouth" (2).
3. **Slowness.** "Let not thine heart be hasty to utter" (2).
4. **Faithfulness.** "Defer not to pay thy vow" (4).
5. **Carefulness.** "Suffer not thy mouth to cause thy flesh to sin" (6).
6. **Look Up.** "Marvel not" (8). There is One above who sees all, therefore keep calm and cool.
7. **Dissatisfaction.** "Shall not be satisfied" (10).

582. "NOT WORTHY"

1. An **Unworthy Forerunner.** "I am not worthy" (John i. 27).
2. An **Unworthy Disciple.** "Taketh not his cross...is not worthy of Me" (Matt. x. 38).

3. **Unworthy Guests**. "They which were bidden were not worthy" (Matt. xxii. 8).

4. An **Unworthy Son**. "I am no more worthy to be called thy son" (Luke xv. 19, 21).

5. **Unworthy Sufferings**. "Sufferings of this present time, not worthy to be compared with the glory" (Rom. viii. 18).

6. An **Unworthy World**. "Of whom the world was not worthy" (Heb. xi. 38).

7. A **Humble Suppliant**. "I am not worthy" (Matt. viii. 8).

583. "NOW"

THE present tense of the Christian life is what faith recognises and enjoys. The word *"nun"* is rendered "present" in Romans xi. 5, and *"at this time"* in 1 Corinthians xvi. 12. The following seven nows in Romans will illustrate.

1. **Mercy Obtained**. *"Now* have obtained mercy" (Rom. xi. 30). We could never attain to the blessings of the Lord, but we can obtain them, for they are all offered to us in Christ.

2. **Righteousness Manifested**. "But *now* the righteousness of God without the law is manifested" (Rom. iii. 21). God can righteously save those who believe in Christ, for He is the righteous One for us in life and death.

3. **Justification Declared**. "Being *now* justified by His blood" (Rom. v. 9). The blood of Christ's atonement is the procuring cause of every blessing, and not least among them is that God accounts us righteous in Him.

4. **Reconciliation Received**. "By whom we have *now* received the reconciliation" (margin, Rom. v. 11). Peace with God is the result of the work of Christ, who has made peace for us by the blood of His Cross.

5. **"Righteousness unto Holiness."** "Even so *now* yield your members servants to righteousness unto holiness" (Rom. vi. 19). Consecration is an act and an attitude. A definite act of yielding to God, and a constant attitude of rightness and separation to Him.

6. **"No Condemnation."** "There is, therefore, *now* no condemnation to them which are in Christ Jesus" (Rom. viii. 1, R.V.). Christ has been judged for our sin and sins, and, there- fore, for our sin and sins, believers will never be judged.

7. **"Salvation Nearer."** *"Now* is our salvation nearer than when we believed" (Rom. xiii. 11). The salvation which is "nearer" is the salvation of the body. This is the consummation of redemption.

584. "NOW" OF THE BELIEVER'S BLESSING

It is a good thing to know our present blessings in Christ. Among the many which the spirit says are ours "now" are the following:

1. **Relationship.** "Now are we the children of God" (1 John iii. 2). The God-given right of children gives the children the right to all the Father possesses.

2. **Reconciliation.** "Now hath He reconciled" (Col. i. 21). Christ did not die to reconcile God to us, for He never went away from us, but He died to reconcile us to God, and to kill in us all that was associated with a state of enmity.

3. **Illumination.** "Now are ye light in the Lord" (Eph. v. 8). As to the past, we were in a condition of "darkness;" as to the present, we are light in the Lord; and as to the future, we are to "walk as children of the light."

4. **Emancipation.** "Now being made free from sin" (Rom. vi. 22). Sin was our master, but when grace mastered us we were freed from the old servitude, that we might know the liberty of Christ's bondage.

5. **Nearness.** "Now in Christ Jesus ye...are made nigh by the Blood of Christ" (Eph. ii. 13). We are nearer than angels, for in the Person of God's Son we are as near as He. Being "made nigh," let us keep near.

6. **Union.** "Now hath God set the members...in the body" (1 Cor. xii. 18). He hath set us in our place, and well placed in Christ. Let us keep our place by holding the Head and the members.

7. **Abiding.** "Now little children, abide in Him" (1 John ii. 28). There is only one way to abide in Him, and that is by obedience. Those who keep His commandments abide in Him, and He also abides in them—1 John iii. 24.

585. NOTABLE COMMANDS

Num. xiii. 1-3, 17-33

There are certain words and expressions which we may take as hubs around which the spokes of thought are found. The—

1. **"Get You Up"** of Commission (17). Moses bids the spies go search the land and see what kind it was, and as to the inhabitants that dwelt in it. It is well to know the strength and character of the enemy we have to conquer. As with Israel, so with us, when the Lord bids us to go in a given direction, it matters not how great the difficulties, or how formidable the foe, we shall have grace to surmount the one and to overcome the other. With every "Go" of command He gives us the "Lo" of His presence—Matt. xxviii. 19, 20.

2. **"Be of Good Courage"** of Fortitude (20). True courage is the outcome of the fear of God. He who fears God need fear no foe. He who has looked into the face of God can look in the face of any man. True courage has consistency as its forerunner—Joshua i. 6, 7.

3. **"Nevertheless"** of Unbelief (28). Unbelief always magnifies difficulties and makes them far larger than they are. "There is always a 'nevertheless' where man is concerned, and when unbelief is at work. The unbelieving spies saw the difficulties—great cities, high walls, tall giants. All these. things they saw; but they did not see Jehovah at all. They looked at the things that were seen, rather than at the things which were unseen. Their eye was not fixed upon Him who is invisible. Doubtless the cities were great; but God was greater; the walls were high, but God was higher; the giants were strong, but God was stronger."

4. **"Well Able"** of Faith (30). The man of faith who looks to God, and remembers what He is able to do, exclaims, "We are well able to overcome." "Faith looks the difficulties straight in the face. It is not ignorant—not indifferent—not reckless; but—what? It brings in the living God. It looks to Him; it leans on Him; it draws from Him. Here lies the grand secret of its power."

5. **"Not Able"** of Despair (31). What a contrast this to the "Well able" of Caleb! "Stronger than we" is the exclamation of despair as the enemy is compared with the self-occupied ones; but surely the foe is not stronger than He! Ah! it makes all the difference whether it be "He" or "We." If the warfare depends upon us there will be defeat, but since it depends upon the Lord there must be victory, if we trust Him. Despair is born of self-occupation and through viewing self's resources. There is only one way to get rid of self, and that is to put Him in front of it; then self reads Himself.

6. **"Evil Report"** of Half-Heartedness (32). Half-heartedness is a worm that will kill any plant of grace. The reason why so many fail is because there is a lack of thoroughness. Half-heartedness is the forerunner of defeat. Half-heartedness magnifies difficulties, hesitates in danger, discourages timid ones, breeds unbelief, lacks backbone, cripples devotion, and thinks much of itself.

7. **"We Saw"** of Short-Sightedness (33). The evil-reporters saw the great ones of the earth, but they did not see the Great One of Heaven. If they had looked at the great ones from God's point of view they would have seen that they were but as "grasshoppers" in His sight—Isa. xl. 22. Instead of this, the

spies say they are "as grasshoppers." If we look at difficulties and dangers through the medium of earth's spectacles we shall be discouraged, and a discouraged man is a defeated one; but if we stand on the mountain-top of fellowship with God, earth's great ones will be pygmies.

586. OBEDIENCE

CONSECRATION is summed up in the voice of the Lord being "obeyed," and the fear of the Lord being recognised.

1. Obedience is the **proof** of being Christ's sheep—John x. 27.
2. The **meaning** of faith—Heb. xi. 8.
3. The **response** of love—1 Peter iii. 6.
4. The **evidence** of union with Christ—Rom. vi. 17.
5. The **soul** of holiness—1 Peter i. 22.
6. The **mark** of abiding in Christ—1 John iii. 24.
7. The **bringer** of the Holy Spirit—Acts v. 32.

587. OBEDIENCE

1. Obedience is essential to **Possession**—Deut. i. 6; iv. 40.
2. Obedience is essential to **Instruction**—v. 1-x. 5.
3. Obedience is essential to **Communion**—x. 10-xii. 32.
4. Obedience is the soul of **Consecration**—xiii. 1-xxvi. 19.
5. Obedience is the secret of **Benediction**—xxvii. 1-xxviii. 68.
6. Obedience is the precursor of **Victory**—xxix. 1-xxx. 20.
7. Obedience is the feeder of **Courage**—xxxi. 1-6.
8. Obedience is the basis of **Confidence**—xxxi. 7, 8.
9. Obedience is the **Harbinger of Help**—xxxi. 9-13.
10. Obedience is the **Soul of Appreciation**—xxxi. 24-xxxii. 43.
11. Obedience is the **Life of the Soul**—xxxii. 44-47.
12. **Blessing** is the result of obedience—xxxiii.

588. "OBEYED NOT"

NOT to obey the Lord is the greatest calamity which can come to anyone. Disobedience to Him is—

1. Cause of **Premature Death**, as seen in the children of Israel being "consumed" in the wilderness—Joshua v. 6.
2. Cause of **Defeat**, and being dominated by our enemies, and the cause of discomfort to ourselves—Judges ii. 2.

3. Cause of **Loss**, impoverishment, and oppression, as is illustrated in Israel when Midian prevailed against them—Judges vi. 10.

4. Cause of **Downfall**, as is seen in King Saul and his disobedience regarding Amalek—1 Sam. xv. 20-23.

5. Cause of **Dishonour**, as is unfolded in the disobedience of the man of God out of Judah—1 Kings xiii. 1-32.

6. Cause of **Bondage**, as is manifest in Israel's being carried away into Assyria—2 Kings xviii. 11, 12; and of Judah into Babylon—Daniel ix. 10-14.

7. Cause of **Shame and Misery**. See right through Jeremiah's prophecy, how many disasters came to those who "obeyed not the voice of the Lord" (Jer. iii. 13, 25; ix. 13; xi. 8; xvii. 23; xl. 3; xlii. 21; xliii. 4, 7; xliv. 23).

589. "OBSERVE "

1. Observe the Lord's Feasts in the light of their spiritual meaning—Exod. xii. 17, 24; xxxiv. 22; Num. xxviii. 2.

2. Observe the **commandments** by obedience to them—see passages in Deut. v. 32; vi. 3, 25; viii. 1; xi. 32; xii. 1, 28, 32; xv. 5; xvi. 12; xvii. 10; xxviii. 1, 15, 58; xxxi. 12.

3. Observe the **Lord's ways** by walking in them—Prov. xxiii. 26.

4. Observe "**all things**" that Christ commanded His servants to teach—Matt. xxviii. 20.

5. Observe the fact that **the Lord observes** us—Hosea xiv. 8.

6. Observe the **Lord's doings**, and thus be wise—Psa. cvii. 43.   See what the Lord is said to do.

7. Observe **to act** in the method the Spirit enjoins, "without prejudice" and "partiality" (1 Tim. v. 21, R.V.).

590. ONLY ONE NAME

In the Name Jesus there is found—

1. **Salvation**—Acts iv. 12.
2. **Forgiveness**—1 John ii. 12.
3. **Strength**—Acts iii. 16.
4. **Eternal Life**—1 John v. 13.
5. **Sonship**—John i. 12.
6. **Answered Prayer**—John xiv. 13, 14.
7. **Leading**—Psa. xxiii. 3.

591. OBTAINING PEOPLE

THE words "taken," "perceived," "attained," "obtain," "comprehend," "apprehend," and "overtake" in the following Scriptures are one and the same in the Greek.

1. **An Obtained Sinner.** "Taken in adultery" (John viii. 3).
2. **An Obtained Knowledge.** "Perceived they were unlearned" (Acts iv. 13).
3. **An Obtained Righteousness.** "Have attained to righteousness" (Rom. ix. 30).
4. **An Obtained Prize.** "So run, that ye may obtain" (1 Cor. ix. 24).
5. **An Obtained Christ.** "May be able to comprehend with all saints," etc. (Eph. iii. 18). Not Christ's love, but Himself.
6. **An Obtained Purpose.** "That I may apprehend that for which I am apprehended" (Phil. iii. 12).
7. **An Obtained Surprise.** "Should overtake you as a thief" (1 Thess. v. 4).

592. "OFF"

THERE are many things the Lord wants to put "off" from us.

1. The offending hand of sin is to be "**cut off**" (Matt. v. 30).
2. The shoes of human irreverence are to be "**put off**" (Acts vii. 33).
3. The works of darkness are to be "**cast off**" (Rom. xiii. 12).
4. The old manner of life is to be "**put off**" by the child of God (Eph. iv. 22; Col. iii. 8, 9).
5. Those who trouble the Church of God are to be "**cut off**" (Gal. v. 12).
6. When the Gospel is deliberately refused, we are to "**shake off**" the dust of the place from our shoes (Matt. x. 14).
7. One thing believers should not do, and that is, to "**cast off**" their "first faith" (1 Tim. v. 12).

593. "OH, THAT I!"

1. The Inquirer's **Lament**—Job. xxiii. 3.
2. The Suppliant's **Prayer**—Job. vi. 8.
3. The Murmurer's **Complaint**—Job. x. 18.
4. The Backslider's **Remorse**—Job. xxix. 2.
5. The Rebel's **Wish**—2 Samuel xv. 4.
6. The Believer's **Desire**—Psa. lv. 6.
7. The Prophet's **Cry**—Jer. ix. 2.

594. "ON"

THERE are many things we are to do in relation to this preposition.

1. **"Believe on** the Name of His Son," in a personal faith in Him (1 John iii. 23).

2. **Build** "**on**" the "most holy faith" of the truth (Jude 20).

3. **"Put on"** the Lord Jesus in the holy habit of life for conquest and power (Rom. xiii. 12, 14; Eph. iv. 24; Col. iii. 10-14).

4. **"Put on"** the armour of God, to be protected in conflict against the evil powers (Eph. vi. 11, 14).

5. **"Go on"** to perfection in the enabling of the Spirit (Heb. vi. 1).

6. **"Meditate on"** the Lord's things, and praise Him, and "muse on" to personal comfort (Psa. cxliii. 5).

7. **"Wait on"** the Lord for power and guidance (Psa. xxv. 3, 5; xxvii. 14; xxxvii. 34).

595. ONENESS

THE Lord prays that all His own may be one. This is seen in John xvii.

1. **One in Life.** "Give eternal life to as many as Thou hast given Him" (2).

2. **One in Love.** "Loved them, as Thou hast loved Me" (23).

3. **One in Preservation.** "Keep those whom Thou hast given Me" (11).

4. **One in Separation.** "They are not of the world" (14).

5. **One in Sanctification.** "Sanctify them in Thy truth" (17).

6. **One in Service.** "As Thou hast sent Me, so have I sent them" (18).

7. **One in Glory.** "Be with Me, that they may behold My glory" (24).

596. "OPENED" THINGS IN LUKE

1. An "opened **Heaven**" in approval—iii. 21.

2. An "opened **Book**" in testimony—iv. 17.

3. An "opened **Door**" to prayer—xi. 9, 10.

4. Opened **Eyes** to faith—xxiv. 31.

5. Opened **Scriptures** in teaching—xxiv. 32.

6. Opened **Understanding** to ignorance—xxiv. 45.

597. OPPORTUNITY
As Made Clear in Acts xiv

A FOURFOLD opportunity came to Paul when he was persecuted at Lystra—Acts xiv.

1. Opportunity to Speak—3. They spoke "boldly" (confidently) "in the Lord." The apostles knew what they knew, and therefore could speak from the certainty of personal experience. When we can say, "He loved me" (Gal. ii. 20), then we have the power to help others.

2. Opportunity to Do Good to Others—8-10. When Paul saw the impotent man he perceived he had faith to be healed, and healed him. When others feel their need of aid it is easy to aid them. We should make it our motto to do all the good we can, to all the people we can, and at all the times we can. A lad the writer knew had hung up in his room a card, upon which were these words:

> "I am only one, but I am one;
> I cannot do everything, but I can do something,
> And by the grace of God I will do what I can."

3. Opportunity to Correct Misapprehension—14-17. The apostles would not receive honour which was due to God, but they seized the occasion to remind their auditors that they owed to their Creator the "good" they received, and the seasons of His favour which they enjoyed. In the magnificent library in Washington, U.S.A., there is inscribed within the words: "He that builds beneath the skies builds too low." The greatest mistake we can make is to live for self, and for the present world alone.

4. Opportunity to Prove the Sufficiency of God's Grace. Paul's being stoned was far from being a pleasant experience, but it was the occasion to prove what God could do for him. He was left for dead—19, and he was not sure whether he was in the body or not—2 Cor. xii. 3, 4, but he was caught up to Paradise and heard "unspeakable words." If he had not been thrown out of the city he would not have been caught up to Paradise. There is good in every ill, a sweet in every bitter, a lifting up in every casting down, and a proving of God's grace in every trial. Remember what Samson said about the lion and the honey—Judges xiv. 14.

598. OUR ATTITUDE TO GOD'S WORD

1. Receive the Word of God with Meekness. "Receive with meekness the engrafted Word, which is able to save your souls" (James i. 21). Receive it as servants, for it is the voice of the Master; receive it as saints, to cleanse from all defilement;

receive it as subjects, for it is the command of the King; receive it as soldiers, to equip for the warfare of evil; receive it as sons, for it is the Father's will; receive it as saved ones, as the direction of grace; and receive it as surrendered ones, as the rule for life.

2. **Let the Word of God Dwell Richly.** "Let the Word of Christ dwell in you richly in all wisdom" (Col. iii. 16). Let it dwell in the heart, as a preservative from evil; let it dwell in the soul, as the propeller in service; let it dwell in the mind, as the plan for direction; and let it dwell in the affection, as the power for conflict.

3. **Keep the Word of God Tenaciously.** "They have kept Thy Word" (John xvii. 6), Christ could say of His disciples. We should keep it as a treasure—securely; as our teacher for instruction, as a tower for protection, and as our trust, we should keep it faithfully and well.

4. **Continue in the Word of God Untiringly.** "If ye continue in My Word, then are ye My disciples indeed" (John viii. 31). Continuance in the Word is the mark of true discipleship, the manifest evidence that we are true followers of Christ.

5. **Live Out the Word of God Faithfully.** "Ye are manifestly declared to be the epistle of Christ" (2 Cor. iii. 3). The Christian is the world's Bible, a living object-lesson. If we are not walking Bibles, then we are walking libels.

6. **Hold Forth the Word of God Boldly.** "Holding forth the Word of Life" (Phil. ii. 16). As the man holds the lighted torch above his head in the dark night, to show himself and others the path in which to tread, so the Christian is to hold up the Word by his life, and its testimony with his lips, that others may be enlightened and benefited.

7. **Muse on the Word of God Prayerfully.** As the well-watered tree by the river's side, grows and is fruitful, so the Christian who muses on, and meditates in, the truth of God, is prosperous in life, and profitable to others—Psa. i. 2.

599. "OUR GOD"
Heb. xii. 29

1. The **"God of Patience"** to console us (Rom. xv. 5).
2. The **"God of Peace"** to calm us (Rom. xv. 33).
3. The **"God of Hope"** to cheer us (Rom. xv. 13).
4. "The **God of all Comfort**" to comfort us (2 Cor. i. 3).
5. "The **God of Love**" to sustain us (2 Cor. xiii. 11).
6. "The **God of all Grace**" (1 Peter v. 10).
7. "**God and Father** of our Lord Jesus Christ" (Eph. i. 3)

600. "OUR GOD" IN THE PSALMS

"He is our God and we are His people" (xcv. 7

1. **Rock** of His Personality. "Who is a Rock save our God?" (xviii. 31; xlviii. 14; cxiii. 5).

2. **Refuge** of His Defence. "In the Name of our God we will set up our banners" (xx. 5).

3. **Remembrancer** for our Thought. "Remember the Name of the Lord our God" (xx. 7).

4. **Returner** to Adjust. "Our God shall come and shall not keep silent" (l. 3; xliv. 21; xcix, 8; cv. 7).

5. **Regarder** to Bless. "Our own God shall bless us" (lxvii. 6; cxxiii. 2).

6. **Object** of Worship. "Exalt ye the Lord our God" (xcix 5, 9; cxlvii. 1, 7).

7. **Embodiment** of Holiness. "The Lord our God is holy" (xcix. 9).

8. **Source** of Salvation. "Save us, O Lord, our God" (cvi. 47; xcviii. 3).

601. "OUR HEARTS"

1. The Gospel **Target**—2 Cor. iv. 6.
2. The Spirit's **Abode**—2 Cor. i. 22.
3. The Lord's **Residence**—Rom. v. 5.
4. God's **Testing House**—1 Thess. ii. 4.
5. Faith's **Concern**—Heb. x. 22.
6. The Believer's **Assurer**—1 John iii. 19.
7. The Spirit's **Tablet**—2 Cor. iii. 2.

602. "OUR SINS"

1. **Confession.** "If we confess our sins" 1 John i. 9

2. **Propitiation.** "He is the Propitiation for our sins" (1 John ii. 2).

3. **Substitution.** "Who His own self bare our sins" (1 Peter ii. 24).

4. **Cancellation.** "He was manifested to take away our sins" (1 John iii. 5).

5. **Emancipation.** "Who gave Himself for our sins, that He might deliver us," etc. (Gal. i. 4).

6. **Supplication.** "Purge away our sins, for Thy Name sake" (Psa. lxxix. 9).

7. **Absolution.** "Washed us from our sins in His own Blood" (Rev. i. 5).

603. "OUR SINS"

THERE are three things to remember about "our sins"

1. **We Have Sinned.** There are sins called "transgressions," which are goings beyond God's law—Num. xiv. 41; there are sins of trespass, which mean unfaithfulness to a trust, and slipping away from God's requirement—Matt. vi. 14; there are sins of iniquity, which denote the perversion of that which is good, and making it bad; hence, being unrighteous—Rom. vi. 13; there are sins of rebellion, which signify the act of self-will and the clenched fists of opposition—Job xxxiv. 37; there are are sins of treachery, which signify an under-current of hypocrisy—Hosea vi. 7, R.V.; there are sins of omission, that is, neglecting to do what we ought to do, and very often through ignorance—Lev. iv. 13; there are sins of debt, failing to do our duty, and paying what we owe—Matt. vi. 12; there are sins of disobedience, failing to respond to God's word of direction, and generally through unbelief—Col. iii. 6; and there are sins of failure, that is, missing the mark of God's Word; hence, "all have sinned, and come short of the glory of God" (Rom. iii. 23).

2. **We Deserve to be Punished Because of our Sins**—Lev. xxvi. 18, 21, 24, 28. Anyone who breaks the law has to bear the consequence. Frequently we are reminded that the one who sins has to "bear his sin" (Lev. xx. 20; xxiv. 15; Num. ix. 13; xviii. 22).

3. **All Sin is Against God.** David's confession—Psa. li. 4; the publican's cry—Luke xviii. 13; the prodigal's lament—Luke xv. 18; and Saul's exclamation, all recognise sin is against God—1 Sam. xv. 24.

There are several passages in the New Testament where the words "our sins" occur.

604. OUTLOOK

DR. MULLINS, of America, in speaking at a meeting in Spurgeon's Tabernacle, referred to the uncertain explanations and definitions which are given of philosophy; and gave a definition of it, as "A blind man in a dark room, looking for a black cat which is not there!"

Some might think the definition over defined, but there is no ambiguousness when we are bidden to think of the future. This is seen if we ponder what we are taught by the Word of God to look for.

1. We are looking for the **"Blessed Hope"** and the glorious appearing of the Lord's return—Titus ii. 13.

2. We are "looking for the **mercy** of our Lord Jesus Christ unto eternal life" (Jude 21).

3. We are "looking for and hasting unto the coming of the **day of God**" (2 Peter iii. 12).

4. We are "looking for **the Saviour**" to give us a glorified body (Phil. iii. 20, 21).

5. We are looking for **Himself** to "appear" (Heb. ix. 28).

6. We are looking for "**new Heavens and a new earth**" (2 Peter iii. 13).

7. Then we are also reminded of this outlook in its **practical power,** when the Spirit says: "Wherefore, beloved, seeing that ye look for such things, be diligent that ye may be found of Him in peace, without spot, and blameless" (2 Peter iii. 14).

605. "OUTERS"

WE read of those who "went out," "came out," and who are told to "get out" and "come out." The greek word, *exerkomai*, in each of the following instances means to get right out.

1. **Separation.** "Get out of thy country" (Acts vii. 3; Heb. xi. 8).

2. **Redemption.** "Came out of Egypt" (Heb. iii. 16).

3. **Consecration.** "Come out" (2 Cor. vi. 17; Rev. xviii. 4).

4. **Persecution.** "Then...Jesus...went out" (John viii. 59).

5. **Intercession.** "He went out into a mountain to pray" (Luke vi. 12; xxi. 37).

6. **Restoration.** "He went out and wept bitterly" (Luke xxii. 62).

7. **Evangelisation.** "They went out and preached" (Mark vi. 12).

606. "OUT OF THE EATER COMETH FORTH MEAT"

1. There is **life** and **honey** in every carcase of death and danger—Judges xiv. 8.

2. There is a **bow of promise** in every dark cloud of providence—Gen. ix. 13.

3. There is a **rose of blessing** in every thorn of adversity—2 Cor. xii. 7-10.

4. There is an **open Heaven** near every pillow of trial—Gen. xxviii. 11-16.

5. There is a **lifting up** in every letting down—2 Cor. xi. 33; xii. 2.

6. There is a **Paradise** found in the Patmos of banishment—Rev. i. 3.

7. A "**good cheer**" in every night of affliction—Acts xxiii. 11.

Out of weakness we are still made strong. He giveth songs in the night, and but for the night we should not have the songs to sing. Refreshment is still found in many a hollow place in life, and but for the hollowness the supply would never have been secured—Judges xv. 19.

607. OUTLOOK IN THE EPISTLE TO THE HEBREWS

THE future things mentioned in the above Epistle are of moment.

1. "A **World** to Come" (i. 6; ii. 5).
2. A **Salvation** to Come—i. 14; ix. 28.
3. A **Coming Subjection**—ii. 9.
4. A **Sabbath Rest**—iv. 9-11.
5. "An **Age** to Come" (vi. 5).
6. A **Covenant** to be Made with Israel and Judah—viii.
7. **Good Things** to Come—ix. 11; x. 1.
8. The **Coming One** Himself—x. 37.
9. A **Shaking of Heaven** and Earth—xii. 25-27.
10. An **Immovable Kingdom**—xii. 28.
11. A **City** that will Abide—xiii. 14.
12. "Them that must **Give Account**" (xiii. 17).

"Jesus Christ, to whom be glory for ever. Amen" (xiii. 21).

608. PATIENCE

1. **A Needed Grace.** "Ye have need of patience" (Heb. x. 36).

2. **A Bestowed Power.** "Strengthened with all might... unto all patience" (Col. i. 11).

3. **A Fruitful Outcome.** "Bring forth fruit with patience" (Luke viii. 15).

4. **A Forming Agent.** "Tribulation worketh patience" (Rom. v. 3).

5. **An Evidencing Witness.** "The ministers of God in much patience" (2 Cor. vi. 4).

6. **A Communicative Blessing.** "Patience, experience" (Rom. v. 4).

7. **A Noble Race.** "Let us run with patience the race set before us, looking unto Jesus" (Heb. xii. 1, 2).

609. "OUTSIDE THE CAMP"

1. **Place of Judgment.** "Without the camp...shall he be burnt" (Lev. iv. 12).

2. **Place of Memorial.** "Burnt offering...ashes without the camp" (Lev. vi. 9-11).

3. **Place of Uncleanness.** Unclean. "Without the camp shall ye put them" (Num. v. 3).

4. **Place of Separation.** "He shall dwell alone: without the camp" (Lev. xiii. 46).

5. **Place of Reproach.** "Shut out from the camp" (Num. xii. 15).

6. **Place of Punishment.** "Brought him without the camp ...stoned...he died" (Num. xv. 36).

7. **Place of Death.** "Without the camp, and one shall slay her" (Num. xix. 3).

8. **Place of Fellowship.** "Suffered without the camp...let us go forth therefore unto Him, without the camp, bearing His reproach" (Heb. xiii. 11-13).

610. PARASITES *

"My familiar friend...which did eat of my bread"
Psa. xli. 9

CAPTAIN CECIL RAWLING, in describing his explorations in New Guinea, among many other things says: "It is quite impossible for anyone who has not visited these parts of New Guinea to realise the density of the forest growth. The vegetation, through which only the scantiest glimpses of the sky can be obtained, appears to form, as it were, two great horizontal strata. The first comprises the giant trees, whose topmost boughs are 150 feet or more above the ground; the other, the bushes, shrubs, and trees of lesser growth, which never attain a greater height than thirty to forty feet. Such is the richness of the soil that not one square foot remains untenanted, and the never-ending struggle to reach upwards towards the longed-for light goes on silently and relentlessly. Creepers and parasites in endless variety cling to every stem, slowly but surely throttling their hosts. From tree to tree their tentacles stretch out, seeming such a close and tangled mass that the dead and dying giants of the forest are prevented from falling to the ground."

There are moral and spiritual parasites which throttle, kill, injure, or retard the growth of the spiritual life.

* A Parasite is one who eats at another's table: hence lives on another, like the ivy, which lives on the tree, and weakens it.

1. The parasite of **sloth** will hinder the grace of watchfulness as it did the virgins—Matt. xxv. 5.

2. The parasite of **worldliness** will kill the grace of devotion, as it did in Demas—2 Tim. iv. 10.

3. The parasite of **pride** will devastate the grace of humility, as it did with the Devil—1 Tim. iii. 6.

4. The parasite of **unbelief** will keep down the grace of faith, as is seen in the children of Israel—Heb. iii. 17-19.

5. The parasite of **self-elation** will kill the grace of self-denial, as is stated of Diotrephes—3 John 9.

6. The parasite of **avarice** will stifle the grace of reality, as is evidenced in Achan—Joshua vii. 21.

7. The parasite of **covetousness** will strangle the grace of generosity, as is manifest in Balaam—2 Peter ii. 15.

611. PATIENCE

1. Patience—Its **Meaning**: Endurance—2 Cor. i. 6.
2. Patience—Its **Need**—Heb. x. 36.
3. Patience—Its **Accompaniment**—Luke viii. 15.
4. Patience—Its **Power**—Col. i. 11.
5. Patience—Its **Attitude**—Heb. xii. 1.
6. Patience—Its **School**—Rom. v. 3.
7. Patience—Its **Bestowment**—Rom. v. 3.

612. PAUL'S CONFIDENCE

2 Tim. i. 12

"I KNOW Him whom I have believed" (R.V.). Christ to Paul was a personal Saviour and Friend. He had more than the knowledge of perception; he had the knowledge of experience. To know by seeing that oranges are oranges is good, but to taste the lusciousness of the orange by eating it is to know it is sweet.

What do we know of Christ?

1. Is He our **Saviour** to save?—Luke i. 47.
2. Our **Power** to keep?—1 Peter i. 5.
3. Our **Victor** to overcome?—Rev. xii. 11.
4. Our **Satisfier** to fill?—Deut. xxxiii. 23.
5. Our **Holiness** to sanctify?—1 Peter i. 16.
6. Our **Lord** to govern?—1 Peter iii. 15, R.V.
7. Our **Hope** to attract?—Titus ii. 13.

613. PAUL'S DEPOSIT
2 Tim. i. 12

"HE is able to keep that which I have committed unto Him."
He says He can keep us, for He is our Keeper—Psa. cxxi. 5-8.
But if He is to keep us we must deposit ourselves with Him, for
the meaning of the word "committed" is "deposited." To
deposit ourselves with the Lord is like placing money in the
bank on deposit for the bank to keep it.

Paul committed to the Lord—

1. The **Reputation** of his character—1 Cor. iv. 13.
2. The **Temple** of His body—2 Cor. iv. 10, 11.
3. The **Life** of his service—Acts xx. 24.
4. The **Work** of his labour—1 Cor. xv. 10.
5. The **Trial** of his infirmity—2 Cor. xii. 9.
6. The **Consecration** of his being—Gal. ii. 20.
7. The **Success** of his service—Eph. iii. 7, 8.

614. PAUL'S EXHORTATIONS AND TESTIMONY
PHILIPPIANS IV

1. The "**I beseech**" of exhortation (2).
2. The "**I entreat**" of affection (3).
3. The "**I say**" of exalting (4).
4. The "**I rejoiced**" of appreciation (10).
5. The "**I speak**," "I have," and "I am," of contentment (11).
6. The "**I know**," the "I know," and the "I am" of initiation (12, R.V.).
7. The "**I can**" of ability (13).
8. The "**I departed**" of itineration (15).
9. The "**I desire**" of fruitfulness (17).
10. The "**I have**" and the "I am" of sufficiency (18).

615. PAUL'S MESSAGE
ACTS XIX. AND XX

PAUL had a message from his Master, and was faithful in giving
it. His message was sixfold in its substance.

1. "**The Kingdom of God**" (xix. 8). The laws of the realm
of grace are "righteousness, peace, and joy in the Holy Ghost"
(Rom. xiv. 17), and this realm is entered by the new birth—
John iii. 5, 8. Life to live is obtained by receiving Christ.
"Righteousness" is doing right because it is the right thing to
do. "Peace" is the calm of God which comes as the result of

obedience, and "joy" is the plant that grows in the soil of holiness.

2. **"That Way"** (xix. 9, 23) indicates God's method of doing things. His way is away from sin, according to His Word, personal faith in Christ, obeying His commands, following Christ, ceasing from self, and consecration to God.

3. **"The Word of the Lord Jesus"** (xix. 10). This is a concrete sentence denoting the sum total of His teaching. Ponder seven of those words: the "come" of invitation (Matt. xi. 28), the "take" of identification (Matt. xi. 29), the "ministered" of substitution (Matt. xx. 28), the "love" of compassion (John xv. 9), the "whatsoever" of prayer (John xiv. 13), the "peace" of bestowment (John xiv. 27), the promise of "power" (Acts i. 8), and the "again" of return (John xiv. 3).

4. **"Repentance towards God"** (xx. 21). Repentance is a change of mind wrought by the Holy Spirit and shown in the action. The Prodigal not only said "I will arise," but he did it. We may be sorry because we suffer the consequence of sin, and not be sorry for the sin which brought the consequences.

5. **"Faith toward our Lord Jesus Christ"** (xx. 21). Faith is the act of the will in receiving Christ—John i. 12, the attitude of the life in resting in Christ—Rom. 1. 5, R.V., and the response of the heart to the commands of the Lord. The trend of the will leads to the track in which we walk.

6. **"The Gospel of the Grace of God"** (xx. 24). A coloured preacher once defined grace as "Receiving everything for nothing when we don't deserve anything." This is good news. See what a beautiful illustration is found in the parable of the prodigal son.

616. PAUL'S MANNER
As Described in Acts xix and xx

His manner was bold or confident in tone, he spoke "boldly."

1. **Persistent in Repetition.** "Three months" and "two years" (8, 10).

2. **Intolerant to Error.** "Disputing" (8).

3. **Persuasive in Utterance.** "Persuading" (xix. 8-10).

4. **Convincing in Argument.** "Turned away" (xix. 26).

5. **Provocative in Declaration**—xix. 26-28.

6. **Consistent in Testimony.** "No cause whereby we may give account of this concourse" (xix. 40).

7. **Humble in Service.** "With all humility" (xx. 19).

8. **Determined in Purpose**—xx. 24. Knowing how to do anything is half the service in doing it.

617. PAUL'S MOLESTATIONS

AS SEEN IN THE ACTS

PAUL was molested in many ways.

1. He was **disturbed** by the "hardened" hearts of unbelief, and the "evil" speaking against "that way" (xix. 9).

2. A "stir" (xix. 23) which developed into a storm of **opposition** which was "full of wrath" (xix. 28), and aimless "confusion" was caused by his witness (xix. 29-32). The town clerk of Ephesus charged the crowd with doing things "rashly" (xix. 37), and were in danger of being called to give an account for the created **"uproar"** (xix. 38-41).

3. Paul had **"tears"** and **"temptations"** because of the "lying in wait of the Jews," who were like cruel beasts waiting for their prey (xx. 19).

4. The outlook was **dark** with further storms of **"bonds and afflictions,"** which caused him to be **"bound in spirit"** (xx. 22, 23); and yet amid it all he was careless of his comfort, and buoyantly declared he was not moved by "these things," or even of life itself (xx. 24). His one ambition was to "finish his course with joy," like the mariner, who knows he must face the storms ere he reaches the port of safety .

There are some things we need to remember. If we do right we are sure to meet with opposition. Difficulties are opportunities for God's deliverances. Temptations prove our metal. Trials sharpen our faith. Seeking the welfare of others will often bring woes to ourselves.

618. PAUL'S PERSONAL EXPERIENCE

EVERY reader of Paul's epistles will be impressed with his personal sense of responsibility. We have only to recall seven of the most familiar sayings to illustrate.

1. The **"I know"** of personal faith in Christ (2 Tim. i. 12).

2. The **"I am"** of personal crucifixion (Gal. ii. 20).

3. The **"I serve"** of personal service (Acts xxvii. 23).

4. The **"I can"** of personal empowerment (Phil. iv. 13).

5. The **"I do"** of personal consecration (Phil. iii. 13).

6. The **"I keep"** of personal mastery (1 Cor. ix. 27).

7. The **"I have"** of personal testimony (2 Tim. iv. 7) demonstrate Paul's sense of personal responsibility.

619. PAUL'S PERSONAL INJUNCTIONS TO
TIMOTHY

1. **A Becoming Behaviour.** "Mayest know how thou oughtest to behave thyself" (1 Tim. iii. 15). A becoming behaviour becomes every one.

2. **An Active Athlete.** "Exercise thyself unto godliness" (1 Tim. iv. 7). The exercise of the soul in godliness is the sure way to avoid gracelessness.

3. **A Meditative Student.** "Give thyself wholly to them" (1 Tim. iv. 15). A concentrated mind is sure to reach a commendable end.

4. **A Careful Custodian.** "Take heed unto thyself, and unto the doctrine" (1 Tim. iv. 16). To apply the Word wholly to oneself, it is necessary to apply oneself wholly to the Word.

5. **A Saved Servant.** "Doing this thou shalt both save thyself and them that hear thee" (1 Tim. iv. 16). To practice the Word fully is the only way to preserve oneself from defeat entirely.

6. **A Clean Man.** "Keep thyself pure" (1 Tim. v. 22). The cleansing from sin's pollution is only possible by the Saviour's presence. We keep as we are kept.

7. **A Separate Saint.** "From such withdraw thyself" (1 Tim. vi. 5). The place of separation is the place of power.

8. **An Approved Worker.** "Study to shew thyself approved unto God" (2 Tim. ii. 15). To please the Lord is the secret of true pleasure.

620. PAUL'S PRAYER

"I HAVE remembrance of thee in my prayers night and day" (2 Tim. i. 3). Prayer was the power that throbbed through the life and labours of Paul.

1. It was the **oil** to lubricate his spiritual nature—Phil. i. 4.

2. The **wind** that moved the vessel of his service—Philemon 4.

3. The **sap** that made him fruitful to his Lord—Col. i. 9.

4. The **outbreathing** of his spirit in petition for others—Acts xvi. 13.

5. The **empty hand** that received that for which he prayed—Phil. i. 9.

6. The **lips of request** that moved in asking for other things—2 Cor. i. 11.

7. The **live wire** that kept him in touch with the supply house of the Spirit's power—1 Thess. v. 23.

621. PAUL'S REGARD FOR HIS BRETHREN

IT is an interesting study to ponder Paul's regard for those with whom he laboured.

1. He was solicitous of **Trophimus**, who was sick—2 Tim. iv. 20.
2. He writes of prayerful **Epaphras**—Col. iv. 12.
3. **The Women** who helped in the Gospel—Phil. iv. 3.
4. The beloved **Timothy**—2 Tim. i. 2.
5. Profitable **Mark**—2 Tim. iv. 11.
6. Refreshing **Onesiphorus**—2 Tim. 1. 16.
7. And **Others**—Rom. xvi.

622. PAUL'S SEVENFOLD CHARACTER
2 Tim. iv. 6, 7, 17

1. The **Ready Servant.** "I am now ready to be offered."
2. The **Commissioned Mariner.** "The time of my departure is at hand."
3. The **Victorious Warrior.** "I have fought a good fight."
4. The **Successful Athlete.** "I have finished my course."
5. The **Faithful Steward.** "I have kept the faith."
6. The **Rewarded Labourer.** "Henceforth there is laid up for me a crown of righteousness."
7. The **Strengthened Sufferer.** "The Lord stood with me and strengthened me."

623. PAUL'S SEVENFOLD BOASTING

THE Apostle frequently uses the word for boasting, and its co-relative, which means to glory in, make a boast of, and to speak loudly about anything or anyone. Sometimes the word is rendered "rejoice," "glory," and "boast."

1. **Boasting in Christ.** "Rejoice ("glory," R.V.) in Christ Jesus" (Phil. iii. 3). When we make our boast in the Lord we have some One who is worthy in whom to glory. If we glory in what we are, in what we can do, or in anything we have, we are missing the mark, and dishonouring the Lord.
2. **Boasting in God.** "But we also joy (boast) in God" (Rom. v. 11). To be reconciled to God, and to be saved in His life is good and better; but the superlative is to joy in Him. "Any salvation short of knowing God Himself is no salvation at all."
3. **Boasting in Tribulation.** "But we glory in tribulations also" (Rom. v. 3). Tribulations are hurtful, and they may be harmful. They may not be toothsome, but they are often

wholesome. The knocks that are meant to bruise, often bless. To glory in them is only possible as we "boast in the Lord."

4. Boasting in the Cross. "God forbid that I should glory (boast), save in the Cross of our Lord Jesus Christ" (Gal. vi. 14). The apostle was not merely boasting in Christ's atonement, but in the sufferings which came to him because of his crucified Lord.

5. Boasting in Infirmities. "Glory in mine infirmities" (2 Cor. xii. 9). The infirmities were bodily weaknesses. He felt them keenly, and prayed about them earnestly, and found in them a strength through the sufficient grace of his Lord.

6. Boasting in Exaltation. "Let the brother of low degree rejoice in that he is exalted" (James i. 9). God's liftings-up are not meant to lift us in pride, but to inspire to thankfulness and humility.

7. Boasting in Hope of the Glory. "Rejoice in the hope of the glory of God" (Rom. v. 2). The outlook of the believer is bright with coming glory.

624. PAUL'S THREEFOLD AMBITION

1. To be **"well-pleasing** to the Lord" (2 Cor. v. 9, R.V.).

2. To **preach Christ,** where He had not been named—Rom. xv. 20.

3. To **mind one's own business**—1 Thess. iv. 11.

625. PAUL'S THREE "I HAVE'S" OF CLIMAX
2 Tim. iv. 6-8

1. A Good Fight. "I have fought a good fight." Paul had not kept on the *defensive* in standing against the forces of evil—Eph. vi. 10-16; but he had been on the *offensive* in waging war against the powers of darkness—2 Cor. x. 4. Christ's victories are ours—Col. ii. 15; so we may be victorious against the world, the flesh, and the Devil. The Spirit is opposed to the internal enemy the flesh, the Father is against the external enemy the world, and Christ is antagonistic to the Devil—Gal. v. 18; 1 John ii. 16; iii. 8.

2. A Course Finished. "I have finished my course." Paul recognised there was a race to run—Heb. xii. 1; a standard of rules to follow—2 Tim. ii. 5; a resolute purpose to fulfil—1 Cor. ix. 25-27; a goal to reach—Phil. iii. 12-14; and a prize to win—2 Tim. iv. 8. The Christian life is no easy thing, but it is a blessed one. The things that cost little are of little worth, while those of value cost much. Like his Lord, Paul "finished" his "course" (John xvii. 4).

3. **A Kept Faith.** "I have kept the faith." "The faith" is the truth of the Gospel. There are seven colours to the bow of the faith, namely, Christ's holy incarnation, His beautiful life, His beneficent ministry, His words of Revelation, His atoning death, His victorious resurrection, and "the blessed hope" of His return. This Paul "kept.". Kept it pure, consistently, prayerfully, carefully, continuously, bravely, and faithfully.

626. PAUL'S WAY IN PRAYER

PAUL as a man of prayer is patent to the most casual reader of Scripture. Mark the characteristics of his praying.

1. **Powerful in Effect**—Acts xvi. 25. The earthquake at Philippi and the soul-quake in the Philippian jailer were the result of the prayers in the inner prison.

2. **Sympathetic in Spirit**—Acts xx. 36. Paul's kindly heart, his human touch, his weeping eyes, his holy concern, all tell out his sympathetic spirit.

3. **Loving in Fellowship**—Acts xxi. 5. He listens to what others have to say, and together they pray about the matter. Matters of difference are best settled on the knees of prayer.

4. **Identifying in Love**—Acts xxviii. 8. Paul's hands laid on the sick man show his whole-souledness in seeking the other's blessing. He identified himself with him.

5. **Continuous in Exercise.** "Without ceasing" Paul prayed (Rom. i. 9). Persistency in prayer proves potentiality in petition. "Praying always for you" (Col. i. 3, 9). "Night and day" (1 Thess. iii. 10; 2 Tim. i. 3).

6. **Intense in Purpose**—Rom. x. 1. The soul of prayer is the prayer of the soul, and without soul it is only a lifeless form.

7. **Definite in Petition.** "I pray to God that ye do no evil" (2 Cor. xiii. 7). There was much evil in the Church at Corinth, and the best way to get it out was to pray it out, for prayer shuts the door on evil.

8. **Pointed in Application.** Mark the three "whats" which point Paul's prayer for the saints in Ephesus—Eph. i. 16-20; and the three "thats" for the Philippians—Phil. i. 9, 10.

9. **Personal in Plea.** Mark the "you's," "your's," and "ye" in 1 Thessalonians i. The saints called forth his thanks, and Paul did not hesitate to mention in detail to the Lord what was worthy of commendation.

627. PEOPLE IN A HURRY

1. **A Compassionate God.** "He *ran*...and kissed him much" (Luke xv. 20, R.V., margin).

2. **A Mistaken Succourer.** "One of them *ran*...and gave Him to drink" (Matt. xxvii. 48; Mark xv. 36).

3. **A Disappointed Woman.** "She *runneth*...and saith... They have taken away the Lord" (John xx. 2).

4. **A Curious Two.** "So they both *ran* together: and the other disciple did outrun Peter" (John xx. 4).

5. **A Speeded Couple.** "They departed quickly...and did *run* to bring His disciples word" (Matt. xxviii. 8).

6. **An Acknowledging Sinner.** "He *ran* and worshipped Him" (Mark v. 6).

7. **A Wondering Disciple.** "Then arose Peter, and *ran* unto the sepulchre: and stooping down, he beheld the linen clothes laid by themselves, and departed, wondering in himself at that which had come to pass" (Luke xxiv. 12)..

628. "PEOPLE OF GOD"
1 Peter ii. 10

THE above is one of the designations by which believers are called.

1. **Their Past History.** "Which were not a people" (1 Peter ii. 10). To remember what we were, is to make us appreciate what we are.

2. **Their Present Position.** "But are now the people of God" (1 Peter ii. 10). Since He owns us, we ought to own ourselves.

3. **Their Practical Conduct.** The result of being separate from things that contaminate us is, God says, "I will be their God, and they shall be My people" (2 Cor. vi. 16).

4. **Their Peculiar Designation.** He calls them "a peculiar people," or, "a people for His own possession" (Titus ii. 14; 1 Peter ii. 9). We are His property, and therefore peculiar in being for Himself.

5. **Their Propitiating Atonement.** Christ has made an atonement for the sins of the people—Heb. ii. 17. That atonement is full, eternal, and God-glorifying.

6. **Their Promised Rest.** "There remaineth a rest for the people of God" (Heb. iv. 9). The outlook for God's people is blessed and bright.

7. **Their Eternal Bliss.** "They shall be His people," is the word of God's promise. Those chosen in time will be well looked after in eternity.

629. "PERFECT HEART"

"PERFECT" is rendered "full" in Ruth ii. 12; "made ready" in 1 Kings vi. 7; "just" in Proverbs xi. 1; and "whole" in Amos i. 6.

1. **A Sad Want.** "Not with a perfect heart" (2 Chron. xxv. 2).

2. **A Holy Requirement.** "Let your heart be perfect" (1 Kings viii. 61).

3. **A Prevailing Plea.** "I have walked before Thee with a perfect heart" (2 Kings xx. 3).

4. **A Necessary Qualification.** "Jehovah shows Himself strong to those who have a perfect heart" (2 Chron. xvi. 9).

5. **A Parent's Admonition.** "Serve Him with a perfect heart" (1 Chron. xxviii. 9).

6. **A Consecrated Band.** "Offered with a perfect heart" (1 Chron. xxix. 9).

7. **A King's Prayer.** "Give unto my son a perfect heart" (1 Chron. xxix. 19).

630. PERFECTION OF CHRIST
IN JOHN X

1. **A Perfect Character.** "The Good Shepherd" (14).

2. **Perfect Knowledge.** "I know My sheep" (14).

3. **A Perfect Sacrifice.** "I lay down My life for the sheep" (15).

4. **Perfect Obedience.** "This commandment have I received," etc. (18).

5. **A Perfect Gift.** "I give unto them eternal life" (28).

6. **Perfect Keeping.** "Neither shall any pluck them out of My hand" (28).

7. **Perfect Unity.** "I and My Father are one" (30).

631. PERISH

1. **A Sad Condition.** "Ready to perish" (Deut. xxvi. 5).

2. **A Startling Cry.** "Master, Master, we perish" (Luke viii. 24).

3. **A Supplying Love.** "Should not perish" (John iii. 15,16).

4. **A Predicted Substitute.** "One die...nation not perish" (John xi. 50).

5. **An Assuring Word.** "Shall not perish" (John x. 28).

6. **A Gracious Waiting.** "Not willing any should perish" (2 Peter iii. 9).

7. **An Ominous Outlook.** "Way of the ungodly shall perish" (Psa. i. 6).

632. PERSONAL POSSESSIONS—"WHOSE"

1. Personal **Sins**. "Whose mouth," etc. (Rom. iii. 14).

2. Personal **Vicariousness**. "By whose stripes ye were healed" (1 Peter ii. 24).

3. Personal **Forgiveness**. "Whose iniquities are forgiven" (Rom. iv. 7).

4. Personal **Faith**. "Whose faith follow" (Heb. xiii. 7).

5. Personal **Record**. "Whose names are in the Book of Life" (Phil. iv. 3).

6. Personal **Property**. "Whose I am" (Acts xxvii. 23).

7. Personal **Retribution**. "Whose end is destruction" (Phil. iii. 19).

633. PERSONAL PLEAS
Psa. cxliii. 1-11

1. **"Answer Me"** of Prayer.

2. **"Hear Me"** of Urgency.

3. **"Cause Me"** of Alertness

4. **"Cause Me"** of Dependence.

5. **"Deliver Me"** of Defence.

6. **"Lead Me"** of Guidance.

7. **"Quicken Me"** of Revival

634. PETER'S BACKSLIDING

CHRIST indicates that Peter was wrong in heart before he was wrong in act, for before he recorded utterances describing his backsliding, He said, "When thou art converted" and "I have prayed for thee that thy faith may not fail" (Luke xxii. 32). Satan sifted Peter in his subtle service, and Peter lost the—

1. Wheat of **confidence**, for he was self-confident in his boasting—Luke xxii. 33.

2. Alertness of **faith** when he was asleep instead of being awake—Luke xxii. 45.

3. Simplicity of **reliance**, when he cut off the servant's ear—Luke xxii. 50; John xviii. 10.

4. Nearness of **fidelity**, when he followed afar off—Luke xxii. 54.

5. Separation of **obedience**, when he sat down among the enemies of Christ—Luke xxii. 55; John xviii. 18.

6. Devotion of **love**, when he denied his Lord—Luke xxii. 57.

7. Reality of **truthfulness**, when he said he was not one of Christ's disciples—Luke xxii. 58.

8. Consecration of **sincerity**, when he declared he knew not what the man said, when he was accused of being "with" Christ—Luke xxii. 60

635. PETER'S EXPERIENCES

As Recorded in Acts x

His experience may be summarised in connection with the uses of his name.

1. **"Peter Went Up"** (9). Peter had a definite object in going to the housetop; it was to pray. Prayer to God preceded his vision from God. All good is ever born of prayer, and no good is enjoyed without it.

2. **"Peter Doubted"** (17). He was not sure what the clean and unclean things meant which he saw in the sheet let down, and, being a Jew, he would not eat anything that was unclean; but he had to learn that what was ceremonially unclean becomes clean when God sanctifies it. Ruskin, in his "Ethics of the Dust," calls our attention to the silent forces of nature, which never appear so grand as when they transmute baser materials into higher forms. We see the pool of slime transformed by the action of light and heat, repose and quiet, so that the clay hardens into blue sapphire, the sand into burning opal, the soot into flashing diamond. And even Jesus never appears so glorious in loveliness as when we see Him transforming the very filth and slime of society into gems fit to burn and shine in an immortal crown.

3. **"Peter Thought"** (19). Thoughtlessness ever breeds a host of evils, while thoughtfulness is like the dawn of the morning, it illuminates and blesses. To think of the consequences of a given action will often prevent us from taking it. To think on the unevenness of our ways is the first step towards mending them.

4. **"Peter Went Down"** (21). Peter's going down showed he obeyed the Divine direction of "get thee down" (20); and happily he went as he was bidden, "doubting nothing." Sir Isaac Newton once said: "It is very difficult to light a candle with the extinguisher on it," and used the simile to denote a man who is blinded by prejudice. Peter had to remove the extinguisher of Jewish prejudice, and we do well to do the same when selfish interests hinder us from doing beneficent actions.

5. **"Peter Went Away with Them"** (23). Being directed by the Lord, he knew he could do some good by going with the three men. When we act under the Lord's direction we are always sure of doing some good to others.

6. **"Peter Took Him Up"** (26). Cornelius was wrong in worshipping Peter, and Peter would have been wrong if he had allowed him to do so. We should not give to those who bring us blessing what belongs to the Lord. We thank God for His servants, but we must not put His servants in the place of Him-

self. A lot of young people once clustered round an evangelist
who had been the means of great blessing to them, and said,
"What shall we do when you go away?" Whereupon he replied,
"If you tie your religion to my coat-tail I shall take it away
with me."

7. **"Peter Opened His Mouth"** (34). The message which
Peter delivered may be summarised under the following points,
all of which centre in Christ:

(1) The word of peace which Christ brought—36, 37.

(2) The work of Christ which He performed through God's
anointing in the power of the Spirit—39.

(3) The walk of Christ in His healing ministry as He went
about doing good, and the cause of it—for God was with
Him—38.

(4) The wonder of Christ's Cross, for while men in their
wickedness slew and hanged Him on a tree, that very tree has
become a beacon light telling of salvation to all—39; Deut.
xxi. 23; Gal. iii. 10.

(5) The witness of God in raising Christ from the dead, and in
showing Him openly to those who were afterwards co-witnesses
of the fact—40, 41.

(6). The ordination of God setting apart Christ to be the
Judge of the living and the dead—42.

(7) And the offer of remission of sins to all who will believe
in Christ—43.

636. PETER'S RESTORATION

1. "Peter **remembered** the word of the Lord," the prelude
to restoration (Luke xxii. 61).

2. "Peter **wept** bitterly," the accompaniment of restoration
(Luke xxii. 62).

3. "Peter **ran**," the urgency to restoration (Luke xxiv. 12;
John xx. 4).

4. "Peter **wondered**," the amazement of restoration
(Luke xxiv. 12).

5. Peter **interviewed** and old "Simon" not omitted, the
searching to restoration—Luke xxiv. 34; Mark xvi. 7.

6. Peter **questioned** by the Lord, the lesson of restoration—
John xxi. 15-17.

7. Peter **commanded** to "follow" Christ, the obedience of
restoration (John xxi. 22).

8. Peter **filled** with the Spirit, and thus restoration consummated—Acts i. 2, 14-18.

637. PHASES OF PRAYER

PRAYER has many phases.

1. Self **cries for help** in distress, like those who are said to have cried unto the Lord—Psa. cvii. 6, 13, 19, 28.

2. The needy cry for **personal aid** when the need of adversity grips them—Neh. i. 6, 11.

3. The abiding one **asks** as Christ would plead—John xv. 7.

4. The servant of God **prays** when he requires the Lord's direction—Exod. xiv. 15.

5. The harassed one **seeks** the Lord's equipment in meeting his enemies—Neh. iv. 9.

6. The communing saint **loves** to pour out his soul in secret—Matt. vi. 6.

7. The unselfish one **gives** himself out in intercession for others—Col. iv. 12.

638. PHILIPPIAN JAILER
Acts xvi

CONVICTED, converted, and consecrated are words which express the experience of the jailer.

1. **Convicted.** The earthquake caused a soul-quake with the jailer. The foundations of his being were shaken, as well as the foundations of the prison—27. His trembling manner, humble demeanour, and earnest cry tell out his anguish of soul—29, 30. Conviction of sin always precedes conversion from sin. The needle of God's law, causing heartache and bitterness of soul, goes before the scarlet thread of the Gospel—Rom. vii. 7-13, 25.

2. **Converted**—31, 34. "He believed in God" sums up the conversion of the jailer. "Believe in the Lord Jesus Christ" is the message that comes to him, like a draught of water to the famished traveller in the arid desert. What does it mean to believe on Christ? At least three things—

To believe on Him as *"Jesus"* is to be *saved* through Him—Matt. i. 21.

To believe on Him as *"Christ"* is to be *sanctified* in Him—1 Cor. i. 2.

To believe on Him as *"Lord"* is to be *swayed* by Him—John xiii. 14.

3. **Consecrated**—33, 34. The jailer evidences his conversion by his kindly treatment to the apostles. He seeks to repair the past and improve the present. It has been well said: "Here is a man converted and he instantly seeks to make up for the past. He tries to rub out yesterday's injury." Christianity always drives men back upon their yesterdays. The Christian says: "I must pay the money that I am owing. I know that the

Statute of Limitations would excuse me, but there is no Statute of Limitations in the regenerated heart." The penitent says: "I must find out the life I once bruised, and if that life is no longer on the earth I must find some descendants, and for David's sake I will love Mephibosheth." The religion that does this proves its own inspiration. It does not need our eloquence, nor ask for our intellectual patronage.

639. PHILIP, THE EVANGELIST

Acts viii

PHILIP was not a man to act on his own authority, nor one who sought to carry a mission in his own power. He was a God-sent servant and a Spirit-controlled worker. When the "angel of the Lord" directed Philip to go to a certain place "he arose and went" (26, 27); when "the Spirit said" to Philip, "Speak to a certain person," he obeyed with alacrity (29, 30); and when the "Spirit of the Lord caught" the evangelist away, he submissively allowed himself to be taken (39). In Philip being controlled by the Lord we have the secret of his success in labour.

Other points in the chapter might be pondered as they relate to Philip—

1. His **Obedience**. "He arose and went" (27).

2. His **Alacrity**. "Philip ran" (30).

3. His **Theme**. "Philip opened his mouth, and preached Jesus" (35).

4. His **Response**. "Philip said" (37).

5. His **Service**. "He baptised him" (38).

6. His **Submissiveness**. "Philip caught away" (39).

7. His **Perseverance**. "He preached in all the cities" (40).

640. PILLARS OF "THE FAITH"

THE live wires of the life-giving faith of truth of Christianity may be summarised under seven pillars of wisdom—Prov. ix. 1.

1. The Pillar of Christ's **Unique Incarnation**. "God manifest in the flesh" (1 Tim. iii. 16).

2. The Pillar of Christ's **Unparalleled Life**. "God was with him" (Acts x. 38).

3. The Pillar of Christ's **Unanswerable Testimony**. "A man approved of God" (Acts ii. 22).

4. The Pillar of Christ's **Unlimited Atonement**. "God set forth" (Rom. iii. 25).

5. The Pillar of Christ's **Unprecedented Resurrection.** "God raised Him from the dead" (Acts x. 40).

6. The Pillar of Christ's **Uniting Spirit.** "God saith, I will pour out My Spirit" (Acts ii. 17).

7. The Pillar of Christ's **Universal Reign.** "God hath appointed," etc. (Acts xvii. 31).

It will be noted we have quoted sentences in each of which we have the statement of what God says about Christ.

641. PLACES WHERE BELIEVERS SHOULD NOT BE FOUND

THERE are some places in which the believer should not live.

1. Not in the **contamination of the world,** like Peter—Luke xxii. 55.

2. Not in the **fog of vexation,** like Lot—2 Peter ii. 7, 8.

3. Not in the **wilderness or desert of pessimism,** like the Psalmist—Psa. cii. 6.

4. Not in the **darkness of fear,** like David—1 Sam. xxvii. 1.

5. Not under the **juniper tree of discouragement,** like Elijah—1 Kings xix. 4.

6. Not in the **ship of backsliding,** like Jonah—Jonah i. 5.

7. Not in the **wilderness of unbelief,** like Israel—Heb. iii. 7-12.

642. "PLEASURE OF JEHOVAH"

"PLEASURE of the Lord shall prosper in His hand." The word "pleasure," in Isaiah liii. 10, speaks of an inward pleasure and delight. It is rendered "purpose" in Ecclesiastes iii. 1, "delight" in Psalm i. 3, "desire" in 1 Kings x. 13, "willingly" in Proverbs xxxi. 13, "pleasant" in Isaiah liv. 12, and "acceptable" in Ecclesiastes xii. 10. Each of these words may be used to express the outlook of God, for—

1. He will fulfil the **"purpose"** of His grace to glorify those whom He has called—Rom. viii. 30.

2. He will **"delight"** to "rejoice" over a redeemed Israel "with joy" (Zeph. iii. 17).

3. His **"desire"** is expressed in the loving words of, "I will betroth thee to Me...in loving kindness and faithfulness, and thou shalt know Me as Jehovah" (Hosea ii. 19, 20).

4. His **willingness** to bless is stated in the loving words, "I will rejoice over them to do them good" (Jer. xxxii. 41).

5. There is a time coming when "Judah and Jerusalem" will "be **pleasant** unto Jehovah," "as in former years" (Mal. iii. 4).

643. "POURED OUT"

1. **A Sorry Statement.** "Thy filthiness was poured out" (Ezek. xvi. 36).

2. **A Suffering Saviour.** "I am poured out like water" (Psa. xxii. 14).

3. **A Supplicating Saint.** "I poured out my soul before the Lord" (1 Sam. i. 15).

4. **A Supplied Suppliant.** "And she poured out" (2 Kings iv. 5).

5. **A Sacrificing Sovereign.** "Poured it out to the Lord" (1 Chron. xi. 18).

6. **The Sent Spirit.** "Poured out the gift of the Holy Ghost" (Acts ii. 17, 18; x. 45).

7. **A Sanctified Servant.** "I am now ready to be poured out as a drink offering" (2 Tim. iv. 6, R.V., margin).

644. POWER

1. **Divine** in its Character. "Divine power" (2 Peter i. 3).

2. **Eternal** in its Blessing. "Save to the uttermost" (Heb. vii. 25).

3. **Saving** in its Operation. "Gospel came...in power" (1 Thess. i. 5).

4. **Healing** in its Touch. "What power?...Jesus" (Acts iv. 7, 10).

5. **Enabling** in its Strength. "Power of Christ may rest upon me" (2 Cor. xii. 9).

6. **Keeping** in its Ministry. "Kept by the power of God" (1 Peter i. 5).

7. **Witnessing** in its Testimony. "Great power gave the apostles witness" (Acts iv. 33).

8. **Moving** in its Service. "Working which worketh in me mightily" (Col. i. 29).

645. POWER

A SEVENFOLD excellence of God's power is seen in the following:

1. "**Exceeding**" in its Greatness (Eph. i. 19).

2. "**Mighty**" in its Essence (Eph. i. 19; vi. 10).

3. "**Effectual**" in its Working (Eph. i. 20).

4. "**Divine**" in its Source (2 Peter i. 3).

5. "**Glorious**" in its Achievement (Col. i. 11).

6. **Eclipsing** in its "Excellence" (2 Cor. iv. 7).

7. "**Spiritual**" in its Nature (Rom. xv. 13, 19).

646. POWER OF CHRIST'S COMING

ARCHIBALD G. BROWN, in speaking of the sustaining power of a personal faith in the personal return of Christ, said: "If the eyes of faith had not brought me to see the Second Coming of Christ as the fulfilment of prophecy, force of circumstances would have driven me into infidelity. When I see iniquity more and more abounding, more heathen than fifty years ago, less godly and converted people, only this hope sustains me, that He will come again—not the weary one, the despised one— but in power and in might, at His Father's right hand. And woe to the despots then! Then shall begin the Millennial age when He shall appear, showing the wounds of the Lamb that was slain, and when righteousness shall cover the earth. The same Christ, He and not another, and we shall know Him by the print of the nails!" Yes, the "Blessed Hope" of Christ's return is—

1. Our **Comfort** in Sorrow—1 Thess. iv. 14.
2. Our **Joy** in Persecution—2 Thess. i. 7.
3. Our **Purifier** in Life—1 John iii. 3.
4. Our **Outlook** of Expectation—Phil. iii. 20, 21.
5. Our **Confidence** in Confession—Heb. x. 23, R.V.
6. Our **Patience** in Trial—James v. 7.
7. Our **Strength** in Endurance—1 Peter i. 13.

647. POWER OF CHRIST'S PRESENCE
Mark iv and v

1. Nature **obeyed** Him—iv. 39.
2. The disciples **"feared"** Him (iv. 41).
3. The demoniac **"worshipped Him"** (v. 6).
4. The demons **acknowledged** His deity—v. 7.
5. The Gadarenes were **"afraid"** of His accomplishments v. 15.
6. The liberated man wanted to be **"with Him"** (v. 18).
7. The **"people gathered** unto Him" (v. 21).

648. POWER OF HIS PRESENCE
"My Presence shall go with thee" Exod. xxxiii. 14

ONE who served in the Great War, in speaking of Sir Douglas Haig, says: "It was just when the Germans had broken our line, and little parties of our men were retreating. At that moment Sir Douglas Haig, then commanding the First Corps, came along the Menin road with an escort of his own 17th Lancers, all as beautifully turned out as in peace time. They approached slowly, and the effect upon our retreating men was instantaneous. As Sir Douglas advanced they gathered and followed him. In the event the Worcesters attacked Gheluvelt, which had been taken by the enemy, drove them out, and restored the line. The Commander-in-Chief's presence was, and is, a talisman of strength to his armies."

1. Power of His presence **to save**. "The angel of His presence saved them" (Isa. lxiii. 9).

2. Power of His presence **for joy**. "In Thy presence is fullness of joy" (Psa. xvi. 11).

3. Power of His presence **to protect**. "Thou shalt hide them in the secret of Thy presence" (Psa. xxxi. 20).

4. Power of His presence **to move**. "Moved at the presence of God" (Psa. lxviii. 8).

5. Power of His presence **to search**. "Whither shall I flee from Thy presence" (Psa. cxxxix. 7).

6. Power of His presence **to break down**. "Broken down at the presence of the Lord" (Jer. iv. 26; v. 22).

7. Power of His presence **to bless**. "Times of refreshing from the presence of the Lord" (Acts iii. 19).

649. POWER OF GOD

1. Power to **Give**—2 Peter i. 3.
2. Power to **Keep**—1 Peter i. 5.
3. Power to **Uphold**—Heb. i. 3.
4. Power to **Calm**—Col. i. 11.
5. Power to **Equip**—Eph. vi. 10.
6. Power to **Prepare**—Eph. iii. 16.
7. Power to **Use**—Acts i. 8.

650. POWER OF THE CROSS

"Christ crucified...the power of God" 1 Cor. i. 18, 23, 24
As we look at the prism of the Cross, we see an eightfold glory of grace. In that Cross there is—

1. The Power to **Reconcile** to God—Eph. ii. 16.
2. The Power to **Separate** from the World—Gal. vi. 14.
3. The Power to **Exalt** to God's Throne—Phil. ii. 8.
4. The Power to **Remove** the Law's Claim—Col. ii. 14.
5. The Power to **Keep** from the Flesh—Gal. v. 24.
6. The Power to **Put Off** the Old Man of Habit—Rom. vi. 6.
7. The Power to **Ignore** the "I" of Self—Gal. ii. 20.
8. The Power to **Inspire** to Obedience—Gal. iii. 1.

651. PRACTICALITY

No devoted Christian can do anything unworthy of the name he bears.

1. As a **Child** of God, he is obedient to his Father—1 Peter i. 14-17.

2. As a **Citizen** of Heaven, he is separated from the evils of earth—1 Peter ii. 11; Heb. xi. 13.

3. As a **Called One**, he is walking worthy of his high and holy calling—1 Thess. ii. 12.

4. As a **Charged Servant**, he is faithful to the trust committed to him—1 Tim. i. 18; v. 21; vi. 13; 2 Tim. iv. 1.

5. As a **Chosen Vessel**, he is selected to be for God's use and service—Acts ix. 15; 2 Tim. ii. 4; 1 Peter ii. 9.

6. As a **Consecrated Believer**, he is wholly devoted to the Lord Himself—Num. vi. 7, 9, 12; 2 Chron. xxix. 31.

7. As a **Covenanted Priest**, he is fearless in his fidelity to his Lord—Mal. ii. 4, 5; Heb. viii. 10.

652. PRAY—HOW TO DO IT

How to do anything is the secret and soul of its accomplishment.

1. Pray **secretly** in the closet of communion—Matt. vi. 6.

2. Pray **watchfully** in the alertness of ' wakefulness—Matt. xxvi. 41.

3. Pray **believingly** in the simplicity of faith—Mark xi. 18.

4. Pray **unceasingly** in the continuance of well-doing—1 Thess. v. 17.

5. Pray **abidingly** in the will of God and in Christ—John xv. 7, 8.

6. Pray **directly** in the pointedness of definite petition—James v. 17, 18.

7. Pray **effectually** in the power of the Spirit—Jude 20.

653. PRAYER

AN ACROSTIC

Pleads the Name of Jesus—John xiv. 13, 14.

Regards the work of Jesus—Heb. x. 19-22.

Abides in the Person of Jesus—John xv. 7.

Yields to the will of Jesus—1 John v. 14, 15.

Expects a fulfilment of the promise of God in Christ—2 Cor. i. 20.

Remembers that there are conditions attached to the fulfilment of the promises in our experience—2 Cor. vii. 1.

654. PRAYER—WHAT IT IS

PRAYER obtained Pentecost, and retained it. Where prayer is lacking in a Church, it will soon die of dry rot.

1. Prayer is the **empty hand** of need, as expressed in the parable of the friend at midnight—Matt. viii. 2, 3.

2. Prayer is the **cry of despair**, bringing deliverance—Psa. cvii. 6, 13, 19, 28.

3. Prayer is the **key to open** the larder of Heaven's supplies—Acts iv. 31.

4. Prayer is the **hedge of protection** keeping back the enemy —Neh. vi. 9.

5. Prayer is the **life's blood** coursing through the spiritual being, keeping all in health—Phil. iv. 6, 7.

6. Prayer is the **sap of fruitfulness** evidencing union with Christ—John xv. 7, 8.

7. Prayer is the **companion of praise**—Acts xvi. 25.

655. PRAYER OF FAITH

James v. 15

1. **Rises** from an uncondemning heart—1 John iii. 20-22.

2. **Recognises** the Will of God—1 John v. 14.

3. **Rests** on the Promise of Christ—John xiv. 14.

4. **Relies** on the Purpose of God—Acts iv. 25-31.

5. **Reckons** on the Power of God—Acts i. 14.

6. **Responds** to the Spirit of God—Eph. vi. 18.

7. **Rejoices** in the Answer from God—Luke i. 13.

656. PRAYER'S ATTITUDE

"He kneeled down and prayed" Luke xxii. 41

1. Kneel **reverently**, as Solomon did at the dedication of the Temple—2 Chron. vi. 13.

2. Kneel **continually**, as Daniel did, three times a day—Dan. vi. 10.

3. Kneel **worshippingly**, as the Psalmist urges, for Jehovah is our Maker—Psa. xcv. 6.

4. Kneel **submissively**, as Christ did in the Garden of Gethsemane—Luke xxii. 41.

5. Kneel **earnestly**, as the leper did when he besought Christ for cleansing—Mark i. 40.

6. Kneel **forgivingly**, as Stephen did when he prayed for his murderers—Acts vii. 60.

7. Kneel **intercedingly**, as Peter did when he prayed for Tabitha—Acts ix. 40.

8. Kneel **faithfully**, like Paul, when he prayed for the Church in Ephesus—Acts xx. 36.

9. Kneel **confidently**, like the apostle, when he recognised God as his Father—Eph. iii. 14.

657. PRAYER'S EFFECTIVENESS

"The supplication of a righteous man availeth much in its working" (James v. 16).

1. Prayer **accomplishes** things, as Elijah demonstrated in obtaining the needed rain—James v. 17.

2. Prayer **concentrates** the mind upon a given object, as Nehemiah illustrates when he repaired the wall in the face of the opposition against him—Neh. iv. 9.

3. Prayer **cleanses** the heart and life, as David experienced, when he prayed: "Create in me a clean heart, O God" (Psa. li. 10).

4. Prayer **enables** the witness to go forward with renewed courage, as is seen in the early Christians, who prayed they might with all boldness preach the Word—Acts iv. 29.

5. Prayer is the **soul of revival**, as the Psalmist recognised, when he pleaded that God would "Quicken" (revive) "me according to Thy Word" (Psa. cxix. 154).

6. Prayer is **one of the weapons** which is a part of the Christian's armour—"all-prayer" (Eph. vi. 18).

Prayer is, as Matthew Henry says: "The **key** of the morning, and the **lock** of the evening."

658. PRAYER AND PERSONS

1. A **Beggar** supplicating a blessing, like the friend at midnight knocking at the door for bread—Luke xi. 5-10.

2. A **Friend** seeking a favour, like Epaphras praying for the Colossians—Col. iv. 12.

3. A **Pastor** pleading for his flock in Ephesus—Acts xx. 36.

4. A **Child** praying to his Father in all things—Matt. vi. 9-15.

5. A **Suppliant** asking for a redress—Luke xviii. 1-8.

6. A **Believer** receiving a benediction—1 John v. 14, 15.

7. A **Priest** interceding for others—1 Tim. ii. 1.

659. PRAYING FOR OTHERS

Two young people, a boy and girl, aged six and eight, were being put to bed by their mother, and she, like a good mother, saw that they prayed before they got into bed, but just before she had taken them to the bedroom, the boy had provoked his mother and she had spoken to him reprovingly.   When the boy was saying his prayers, he said, "O Lord, bless Mamma, and save her from getting cross." When the girlie prayed, she prayed more consistently; she implored the Lord to "Bless Mamma, and save us from making her cross." There is such a thing as balance in prayer, we may pray from our standpoint and reflect upon others.   The better way is to pray that we may be right and be a blessing to others.   When we pray for others, let us endeavour to pray as follows:

1. Pray like **Epaphras**, that others "may stand perfect and complete in the will of God" (Col. iv. 12).

2. Pray like **Paul** did for the Thessalonians, that others may be sanctified wholly—1 Thess. v. 23.

3. Pray like the **Apostles** did for the elected deacons, that others may be qualified by the Holy Spirit for His work—Acts vi. 6.

4. Pray like the **Church** did for Peter, that others may be got out of the prison of difficulties—Acts. xii. 5.

5. Pray as **Peter** and **John** did for the believers at Ephesus, that others may receive the Holy Spirit—Acts viii. 15.

6. Pray as the **Church at Antioch** did for Paul and Barnabas, that others may be led in the Lord's work—Acts xiii. 3.

7. Pray as **The Apostle** did for the elders and church at Ephesus, that others may be kept from error and evil and kept in the grace of God—Acts xx. 36.

660. "PROMISE OF THE FATHER"

Acts i. 4

"The promise of the Father" may be read in three ways.

1. The promise **given** to Christ by the Father as the result of His atoning death—John xiv. 26; xv. 26.   The Paschal Lamb secured the Pentecost of the Spirit.

2. The promise of the Spirit **donates** the gifts of the Spirit. See the association of the gifts of the Spirit in 1 Corinthians xii. in connection with the sevenfold "the same God," "the same Lord," and "the same Spirit" (1 Cor. xii. 4, 5, 6, 8, 9, 11).

3. The promise of Christ **to the believer**—John xvi. 7.

661. PRECEPT AND PROMISE

1. **Acknowledgement and Direction.** Precept: "In all thy ways acknowledge Him." Promise: "He will direct thy paths" (Prov. iii. 6).

2. **Delight and Bestowment.** Precept: "Delight thyself in the Lord." Promise: "He will give thee the desires of thine heart" (Psa. xxxvii. 4).

3. **Obedience and Satisfaction.** Precept: "If ye be willing and obedient." Promise: "Ye shall eat the good of the land" (Isa. i. 19).

4. **Taking and Resting.** Precept: "Take My yoke upon you." Promise: "Ye shall find rest" (Matt. xi. 29).

5. **Bringing and Filled.** Precept: "Bring all the tithes." Promise: "I will open the windows" (Mal. iii. 10).

6. **Seeking and Securing.** Precept: "Seek ye first." Promise: "All these things added" (Matt. vi. 33).

7. **Walking and Peace.** Precept: "Walk in my statutes." Promise: "I will be your God" (Ezek. xi. 20).

662. PRE-MILLENNIAL COMING OF CHRIST

CHRIST unmistakably taught there could be no Millennium until He returned.

There is no more pathetic scene in the life of Christ than when He wept over the city of Jerusalem, and complained that the Jews had not received Him; the consequence was, their house was left unto them "desolate," and He told them that they should not see Him again till they should say, "Blessed is He that cometh in the Name of the Lord." And then Christ, in response to the threefold question which the disciples put to Him, which was, "When shall these things be?" "What shall be the sign of Thy Coming, and of the end of the age?" replies by telling them the conditions that will be found before He returns. If Matthew xxiv. is carefully read, those conditions may be summarised as follows:

1. Spiritual declension, unfaithfulness will abound, hence Christ warns us against false christs, false prophets, and deceivers—Matt. xxiv. 4, 5, 11, 24.

2. Spiritual deception and deceivers and apostasy will precede His Coming, hence iniquity shall abound, the love of the many shall wax cold, the character of the pre-antediluvian days will exist, the evil servant will presume upon the Lord's seeming delay, there will be those who will not be ready as represented in the virgins, the unfaithful servant who did not use his Master's

talent, and also those who did not minister to the Lord's brethren in their need—Matt. xxiv. 12, 37-39, 48-51; xxv. 1-13, 24-30, 41, 46.

3. Instead of finding a condition of peace and tranquillity when He returns, He says there will be wars and rumours of wars, and nation rising against nation, and kingdom against kingdom—Matt. xxiv. 6, 7.

4. Following in the steps of war, there will be famine and pestilence, and so terrible will these things be, that unless the days are shortened no flesh will be saved from their awful consequences—Matt. xxiv. 7, 22.

5. Terrible sufferings will also be characteristic of the time of the end, hence we read of sorrows, affliction, woes, unparalleled tribulation, hatred, killing, and loss—Matt. xxiv. 8, 9, 19, 21.

6. Immediately after the tribulation of those days, there will be wonderful phenomena seen in the heavens and in the earth, in the darkened sun, in the lightless moon, in the falling stars, in the shaking heavens, and in the quaking earth—Matt. xxiv. 7. 29.

7. The budding fig tree of Israel's restoration is yet another sign of the time of the end, and that the summer of blessing for God's covenanted people is near—Matt. xxiv. 32.

8. The time when all these things shall be, is not left in the uncertainty of doubt, for it is when these things shall come to pass that He is nigh even at the doors, and as Christ Himself says, "The Son of Man shall be seen coming with power and great glory" (Matt. xxiv. 30, 33). And following this affirmation of Christ's, He tells us "Heaven and earth shall pass away, but My Word shall not pass away" (Matt. xxiv. 35).

Surely such a state of things goes to prove beyond all question that no Millennium is in existence when the Lord returns, but just the opposite.

663. PRESENCE OF THE LORD

His presence is a—

1. **Searching** presence to convict—Psa. cxxxix. 7.
2. **Saving** presence to convert—Isa. lxiii. 9.
3. **Separating** presence to consecrate—Psa. xxxi. 20.
4. **Settling** presence to calm—Exod. xxxiii. 14.
5. **Satisfying** presence to rejoice—Psa. xvi. 11.
6. **Supplying** presence to refresh—Acts iii. 19.
7. **Sanctifying** presence to humble—1 Cor. i. 26-31.

664. "PRECIOUS BLOOD OF CHRIST"

1. The Blood of **Expiation** to satisfy God's claims—Lev. xvi. 14, 15.
2. The Blood of **Atonement** to cover the sinner's guilt—Lev. xvi. 15; Isa. vi. 7.
3. The Blood of **Cleansing** to remove the sinner's defilement—Lev. xiv. 7.
4. The Blood of **Consecration** to cause the sinner's acceptance—Lev. i. 1-9.
5. The Blood of **Covenant** to secure the sinner's blessing—Exod. xxiv. 6-8.
6. The Blood of **Hallowing** to consecrate to the Lord's service—Exod. xxix. 20, 21.
7. The Blood of **Provision** to restore to fellowship—Num. xix. 1-21.

665. PRESENCE
Psalm xxiii. 4

1. **Redeeming** presence for succour. "Angel of His presence" (Isa. lxiii. 9).
2. **Resting** presence for safety. "My presence shall...give thee rest" (Exod. xxxiii. 14).
3. **Rejoicing** presence for joy. "In Thy presence is fullness of joy" (Psa. xvi. 11).
4. **Regarding** presence for love. "Hide them in the secret of Thy presence" (Psa. xxxi. 20).
5. **Restoring** presence for revival. "Restore us again, cause Thy face" (presence), etc. (Psa. lxxx. 3, 7, 19).
6. **Resuscitating** presence for health. "The health of Thy countenance" (presence), (Psa. xlii. 11; xliii. 5).
7. **Reflecting** presence for beauty. "Cause Thy face (presence) to shine with us" (Psa. lxvii. 1, R.V., margin).

666. PRICE TO BE PAID

BENEFIT to others is always brought by a price that is paid. See how this is brought out in the Sacred Book.

1. The birth of Benjamin was at the **cost of Rachel's life**—Gen. xxxv. 17, 18, margin.
2. The **sufferings of Joseph** were the cost of his after-blessings to his brethren—Gen. xlv. 5-11.
3. **Paul filled up** the sufferings of Christ in allowing His Lord to suffer in him—Col. i. 24.

4. The **three Hebrews were cast into the fiery furnace** that God's Name might be glorified—Dan. iii. 13-23.

5. The **Early Christians suffered** that the truth might be furthered—Acts xvi. 19-24.

6. **John was banished** to Patmos that he might receive the Revelation—Rev. i. 9.

7. **Christ suffered for our sins** that He might bring us to God—1 Peter iv. 1.

667. PRIDE
Study could be Divided into 2, 3, or 4

THE life and death of our Lord Jesus Christ are a standing rebuke to every form of pride to which we are subject.

1. Pride of **Birth and Rank.** "Is not this the carpenter's son?" (Matt. xiii. 55).

2. Pride of **Wealth.** "The Son of Man hath not where to lay His head" (Matt. viii. 20).

3. Pride of **Respectability.** "Can any good thing come out of Nazareth?" "He shall be called a Nazarene" (John i. 46; Matt. ii. 23).

4. Pride of **Personal Appearance.** "He hath no form or comeliness" (Isa. liii. 2).

5. Pride of **Reputation.** "Behold a man gluttonous and a winebibber, a friend of publicans and sinners" (Matt. xi. 19).

6. Pride of **Independence.** "Many others who ministered to Him of their substance" (Luke viii. 3).

7. Pride of **Learning.** "How knoweth this Man letters, having never learned" (John vii. 15).

8. Pride of **Superiority.** "I am among you as He that serveth." "He humbled Himself." "Made a curse for us" (Luke xxii. 27; Phil. ii. 8; Gal. iii. 13).

9. Pride of **Success.** "He came unto His own and His own received Him not." "Neither did His brethren believe on Him." "He was despised and rejected of men" (John i. 11; vii. 5; Isa. liii. 3).

10. Pride of **Self-reliance.** "He went down to Nazareth, and was subject unto them" (Luke ii. 51).

11. Pride of **Ability.** "I can of Mine Own Self do nothing" (John v. 30).

12. Pride of **Self-will.** "I seek not Mine Own will, but the will of Him that sent Me" (John v. 30).

13. Pride of **Intellect.** "As My Father hath taught Me, I speak these things" (John viii. 28).

14. Pride of **Party**. "Forbid him not, for he that is not against us is for us" (Luke ix. 50).

15. Pride of **Resentment**. "Father, forgive them; for they know not what they do" (Luke xxiii. 34).

16. Pride of **Reserve**. "My soul is exceeding sorrowful, even unto death: tarry ye here and watch with Me." "The Son of Man must suffer many things and be rejected" (Matt. xxvi. 38; Luke ix. 22).

17. Pride of **Sanctity**. "This Man receiveth sinners, and eateth with them" (Luke xv. 2).

"Let this mind be in you, which was also in Christ Jesus" (Phil. ii. 5).

668. PROMISE IN JOSHUA I

THERE are many promises given in the chapter:

1. The **Land** of Promise—3, 4.

2. The **Word** of Promise, for He has pledged not to "fail" us nor "forsake" us (5).

3. The **Oath** of Promise—6.

4. The **Prosperity** of Promise—7.

5. The **Success** of Promise—8.

6. The **Joy** of Promise—9.

7. The **Command** of Promise, for when the Lord commands us to "be of good courage," He will give the courage He commands—18.

W. T. Stead, of the *Review of Reviews*, has left on record, as to the influence of this chapter upon his life: "If I had to single out any one chapter which I am conscious of having influenced me most, I should say the first of Joshua, with its oft-repeated exhortation to be strong and to be very courageous."

669. PROMISES

How many promises God gives us as we are journeying along the road of life. The following is a sevenfold bow of promise—

1. He promises **Help** in need—Heb. xiii. 5, 6.

2. **Strength** in weakness—Isa. xli. 10.

3. **Cheer** in despondency—Matt. xiv. 27.

4. **Guidance** in perplexity—Psa. xxxii. 8.

5. **Peace** in trouble—Isa. lxvi. 12.

6. **Joy** in sorrow—Isa. lxi. 3.

7. **Power** in service—Acts i. 4-8.

670. PROMPTNESS OF FAITH

"He went." "He arose" (1 Kings xvii. 5, 10).

1. The **Warrant** of Faith. "The Word of the Lord" (5).

2. The **Reward** of Faith. "Ravens brought him bread" (6).

3. The **Test** of Faith. "No rain" (7).

4. The **Fellowship** of Faith. "Bring unto me...thee... and thy son" (13).

5. The **Promise** of Faith. "Thus saith the Lord" (14).

6. The **Obedience** of Faith. "She went and did" (15).

7. The **Testimony** of Faith. "According to the Word of the Lord" (16).

671. PROOFS

1. **Obedience** proves Sonship. "As many as are led by the Spirit of God, they are the sons of God" (Rom. viii. 14).

2. **Separation** proves Saintship. "As becometh saints" (Eph. v. 3).

3. **Service** proves we are the Lord's. "Serving the Lord" (Rom. xii. 11).

4. **Shining** proves Light. "Ye are the light of the world... Shine" (Matt. v. 14-16).

5. **Walk** proves Life. "Since by the Spirit we live, let us walk in the Spirit" (Gal. v. 25).

6. **Following** proves Discipleship. "If any man will come after Me, let him take up his cross daily, and follow Me" (Luke ix. 23).

7. **Abiding** in Christ proves Union with Him. "Abide in Me, and I in you...the branch cannot bear fruit except it abide in the vine: no more can ye except ye abide in Me" (John xv. 4).

672. PROOFS OF THE NEW BIRTH

THE evidences of being "born of God" are brought out in the First Epistle of John, where we find *gennao* occurring ten times. Let us briefly look at some of these results.

1. **Righteousness of Life**. "Every one that doeth righteousness is begotten of Him" (1 John ii. 29, R.V.). Generally speaking, righteousness is conformity to the standard of right. The standard of right is the ten commandments in the Old Testament, as Arnold says, "Righteousness is the master-word

in the Old Testament;" and the standard of right in the New Testament is Christ, hence, the Christian says, "What would my Lord do?"

2. **Separation from Sin.** "Whosoever is begotten of God doeth no sin, because his seed abideth in him, and he cannot sin, because he is begotten of God" (1 John iii. 9, R.V.). Those who have Divine life do not make it a practice to sin. They are not sinless, nor not liable to fall through temptation, but sinning is no longer a habit of their life.

3. **Love to Others.** "Every one that loveth is begotten of God" (1 John iv. 7, R.V.). Love is not the empty effervescence of animal desire, but the pure flame of an ardent affection, which expresses itself in sacrifice, help, co-operation, sympathy, devotion, thoughtfulness, and service.

4. **Faith in Christ.** "Whosoever believeth that Jesus is the Christ is begotten of God" (1 John v. 1, R.V.). The tense of the verb to believe, is the key to the understanding of these words—"Believeth." Faith is the hand that links us on to Christ, and it is the coupling which keeps us one with Him, even as the couplings of the carriages keep them coupled to the engine. The world wonders we make so much of faith, but the believer knows its worth and power. We know that the "Jesus" of humanity is the Christ of Deity.

5. **Loving the Lord.** "Every one that loveth Him that begat" (1 John v. 1, R.V.). The next verse tells us that we show our love to Him by doing His commandments. The love of God is like the sun to the flowers, it causes them to turn to it; the love of God is like the electric current which moves the needle and sends a message from one operator to another.

6. **Victory.** "Whatsoever is begotten of God overcometh the world" (1 John v. 4, R.V.). God has made no provision for His children to be overcome by the Devil of temptation, the syren of the world, and the whirlpool of the flesh. Victory shows our relationship. Thomas Manton says: "It would be monstrous for the eggs of one creature to bring forth the brood of another kind, for a crow or a kite to come from the egg of a hen. It is as unnatural a production for a new creature to sin." Spurgeon comments on this quotation: "Each creature brings forth after its own kind. Out of a dove's nest we expect only doves to fly. The heavenly life breeds birds of paradise, such as holy thoughts, desires, and acts; and it cannot bring forth such unclean birds as lust, envy, and malice. The life of God infused in the new birth is as pure as the Lord by whom it was begotten, and can never be otherwise."

673. PSALM XLVII

FIVE times in this Psalm we are exhorted to "sing praises" (6, 7), and to sing them "to God," "unto our King," and to "sing with the understanding." Some reasons why we should "sing praises" are—

1. Because of **what the Lord is.** "Jehovah Most High is terrible," "Great King over all the earth," "Our King," and "The God of Abraham" (2, 6, 9).

2. Because of **what He has done.** "God is gone up with a shout," speaking of victory over His enemies (5).

3. Because of what He **is doing, and can do.** He "subdueth," "He chooseth," (R.V.), "God reigneth...sitteth" (3, 4, 8).

4. Because of **what He is to us.** "The God of Abraham" (9).

5. Because of **what He calls us.** "The Excellency of Jacob" (4).

674. PSALM CXLIII

THE personal pronoun "I" in the Psalm reflects the Psalmist in several characters.

1. A **Tracing Pilgrim.** "I remember" (5).
2. A **Thoughtful Saint.** "I meditate" (5).
3. A **Musing Believer.** "I muse" (5).
4. A **Supplicating Beggar.** "I stretch" (6).
5. A **Dependent Child.** "I trust" (8).
6. A **Lifted Soul.** "I lift" (8).
7. A **Pursued Warrior.** "I flee" (9).

675. PURCHASE

1. A **Great Purchaser.** "Denying the Lord that bought them" (2 Peter ii. 1).

2. A **Great Price.** "Bought with a price" (1 Cor. vi. 20; vii. 23).

3. A **Great End.** "Redeemed us to God by Thy Blood" (Rev. v. 9).

4. A **Great Separation.** "Redeemed from among men" (Rev. xiv. 3, 4).

5. A **Great Privilege.** "I counsel thee to buy me gold," etc. (Rev. iii. 18).

The word *agorazo* is rendered "bought," "buy," and "redeemed" in the above Scriptures.

676. QUALIFICATIONS WHICH WORKERS NEED

WE are qualified when we have—

1. The "Go" of Commission, like Isaiah—Isa. vi. 9.
2. The **Glow** of Compassion, like Christ—Matt. xiv. 14.
3. The **Grip** of Conviction, like Paul—1 Cor. ii. 2.
4. The **Godliness** of Consecration, like Barnabas—Acts iv. 36, 37; xi. 24.
5. The **Grace** of Consistency, like Joseph—Gen. xxxix. 10-23.
6. The **Gumption** of Compatibility, like Philip—Acts viii. 30-40.
7. The **Grit** of Continuance, like Moses—Heb. xi. 24-29.

677. QUEEN OF SHEBA
1 Kings x. 1-13

1. A **Listening Ear.** "She heard" (1).
2. A **Ready Foot.** "She came" (2).
3. A **Communing Heart.** "She communed" (2).
4. An **Appreciative Eye.** "When the Queen of Sheba had seen" (4, 5).
5. A **Confessing Tongue.** "She said" (6).
6. A **Giving Hand.** "She gave" (10).
7. A **Prostrated Spirit.** "No more spirit in her" (5).
8. A **Rewarded Suppliant.** "Solomon gave unto the Queen of Sheba all her desire" (13).

678. QUESTIONS ABOUT ABILITY

1. **Christ** to the Blind Men. "Believe ye that I am able?" (Matt. ix. 28).
2. **God** and Forgiveness. "Who can* forgive sins but God only?" (Mark ii. 7).
3. **Satan's Limitation.** "Can* Satan cast out Satan?" (Mark iii. 23).
4. **Salvation.** "Who then can* be saved?" (Mark x. 26).
5. **Christ** the Answer. "How can* we know the way?" (John xiv. 5).
6. **Disciples'** Inability. "Why could* not we cast him out?" (Matt. xvii. 19).
7. The Quandary of **Nicodemus.** "How can* a man be born when he is old?" (John iii. 4).

* The words "can" and "could" are the same as "able."

679. READY

1. **Condition** of the Sinner. "Ready to perish" (Deut. xxvi. 5; Job xxix. 13; Prov. xxxi. 6; Isa. xxvii. 13).

2. **Compassion** of the Lord. "Ready to pardon" (Neh. ix. 17; Psa. lxxxvi. 5; Isa. xxxviii. 20).

3. **Conduct** of the Saint. "Ready to do" (2 Sam. xv. 15).

4. **Commission** of the Servant. "Ready to preach" (Rom. i. 15).

5. **Coming Glory** and Salvation. "Ready to be revealed" (1 Peter i. 5).

6. **Complaint** of the Sorrowful. "Ready to halt" (Psa. xxxviii. 17).

7. **Consequence** of Backsliding. Things "ready to die" (Rev. iii. 2).

680. REDEMPTION—WHAT IS IT?

1. **Subjects of Redemption.** Those who were in bondage to a "vain manner of living" (1 Peter i. 18, R.V.).

2. **Source of Redemption.** Of God it is said that "His grace" operates "through the redemption that is in Christ Jesus," and that the redemption comes to us "according to the riches of His grace" (Rom. iii. 24; Eph. i. 7).

3. **Price of Redemption.** The price is "His Blood" (Eph. i. 7), which Christ gave as "a ransom" (Matt. xx. 28), and is the equivalent for all demands—1 Tim. ii. 6.

4. **Substance of Redemption.** Christ is its Substance and Embodiment, hence, "He is made unto us Redemption" (1 Cor. i. 30).

5. **Receiver of Redemption.** Faith, like Anna, who "looked for redemption" (Luke ii. 38), finds what it looks for in the Redeemer.

6. **Meaning of Redemption** is "deliverance." The Lion of the tribe of Judah breaks every chain—Heb. xi. 35.

7. **Consummation of Redemption** is when our Lord returns. Hence, we are waiting for "the redemption of our body" (Rom. viii. 23).

681. REDEMPTION EXEMPLIFIED

THERE is one chord of truth which the Holy Spirit strikes with repeated emphasis in the Word of God, and that is redemption by blood. In various ways the subject is brought before us.

1. **Israel's deliverance from Egypt** is a picture of redemption's emancipating liberty—Exod. xv. 13.

2. **The Ransom** and **Redemption Money**—Exod. xxx. 12; Num. iii. 49, are types of its protecting and bestowing grace.

3. **The Action of Boaz** in reclaiming the lost inheritance of Naomi, and purchasing Ruth to be his wife, is an illustration of its releasing and claiming power—Ruth iv. 10.

4. **The Year of Jubilee**, with its bestowments of release to the debtor, freedom to the slave, and rest to the captive, depict the blessings of redemption—Lev. xxv.

5. **The Testimony of God's Assuring Word** to the believer is God's guarantee as to his personal benefit of redemption in Christ—Eph. i. 7.

6. **The Song of the Redeemed** in glory has its inspiration in the redemptive work of the Lord—Rev. v. 9.

7. **The Holiness of the Child of God** has its incentive in the redeeming blood of Calvary—1 Peter i. 18, 19; Titus ii. 14.

682. "REJOICE"—THE FOUNDATION

REJOICING in God and in His attributes and blessings as found in the Psalms.

1. **Object** of Rejoicing. "Rejoice in the Lord" (xxxiii.1).

2. **Salvation.** "My heart shall rejoice in thy salvation" (xiii. 5).

3. **Mercy.** "I will be glad and rejoice in Thy mercy" (xxxi. 7).

4. **Protection.** "In the shadow of Thy wings will I rejoice" (lxiii. 7).

5. **Revival.** "Revive us...that Thy people may rejoice in Thee" (lxxxv. 6).

6. **Word** of God. "Statutes of the Lord are right, rejoicing the heart" (xix. 8; cxix. 111).

7. **Israel.** "That I may rejoice in the gladness of Thy nation" (cvi. 5).

683. "REJOICE"*—THE REASONS

1. Because your "names are **written in Heaven**" (Luke x. 20).

2. Because you **see the Lord**"—John xx. 20.

3. Because you can **rejoice in sorrow**—2 Cor. vi. 10.

4. Because the **Gospel is preached**—Phil. i. 18.

5. Because others are **walking in the truth**—2 John 4.

6. Because we are "**counted worthy**" to suffer shame for the sake of Christ (Acts v. 41).

7. Because we are told to "**rejoice evermore**" (1 Thess. v. 16).

* The words "glad" and "rejoice" are the same.

684. REJOICING PEOPLE

THE Greek for "rejoice" is rendered "joyfully," "glad," and "rejoicing" in the following Scriptures.

1. A **Glad Sinner**. "When Herod saw Jesus, he was exceeding glad" (Luke xxiii. 8).

2. A **Glad Shepherd**. "He layeth the sheep on His shoulders rejoicing" (Luke xv. 5).

3. A **Glad Father**. "Be glad" (Luke xv. 32).

4. A **Glad Receiver**. "Received Him joyfully" (Luke xix. 6).

5. A **Glad Anticipator**. "He saw My day and was glad" (John viii. 56).

6. A **Glad Disciple**. "Went on his way rejoicing" (Acts viii. 39).

7. A **Glad Apostle**. "I rejoice" (Phil. i. 18; ii. 17, 18; iv. 10).

685. REJOICING PERSONS

IN THE NEW TESTAMENT

1. **Mary**, the saved. "My spirit hath rejoiced in God my Saviour" (Luke i. 47).

2. **Jesus**, the Lord. "In that hour Jesus rejoiced in spirit" (Luke x. 21).

3. **Eunuch**, the believer. "He went on his way rejoicing" (Acts viii. 39).

4. **Paul**, the minister. "I rejoice;" "I rejoiced" (2 Cor. vi. 10; vii. 7, 9, 16).

5. **John**, the appreciator. "I rejoiced greatly" (2 John 4; 3 John 3).

6. **Jailer**, the grateful. "He set before them and rejoiced" (Acts xvi. 34).

7. **Magi**, the seekers. "Rejoiced when they saw the star" (Matt. ii. 10).

686. RELATIVE POSITIONS

1. **Down in the pit** for misery—Psa. xl. 2.

2. **Through the door** for safety—John x. 9.

3. **Into the Kingdom** for blessing—Col. i. 13.

4. **At the table** for fellowship—Psa. xxiii. 5.

5. **Before the throne** in worship—Isa. vi. 3, 4.

6. **Out in the field** for testimony—Matt. ix. 38.

7. **In the glory** for satisfaction—John xvii. 24.

687. "REJOICE" IN WHAT?

1. **Persecution.** "Rejoice ye in that day" (Luke vi. 23)
2. **Expectation.** "Rejoicing in hope" (Rom. xii. 12).
3. **Communion.** "I therein do rejoice" (Phil. i. 18).
4. **Repetition.** "Rejoice in the Lord alway; and again I say rejoice" (Phil. iv. 4).
5. **Identification.** "Rejoice in my sufferings" (Col. i. 24).
6. **Appreciation.** "But I rejoiced in the Lord greatly" (Phil. iv. 10).
7. **Compensation.** "Rejoice inasmuch as ye are partakers of Christ's sufferings" (1 Peter iv. 13).

688. RELIGION OR CHRIST?

"RELIGION is often put on a pedestal and worshipped instead of Christ," so said a well-known Canon of the Church of England. There are many who are content with an outward show of religion and religious observances who know nothing of heart-faith in Christ and Christly action. The word "religion" only occurs four times in the Bible.

1. **God's Religion.** There is God's description of a true and practical religion, which is to care for the fatherless and widows in their afflictions, and to keep unspotted from the world—James i. 27.

2. **An Empty Religion.** Then there is the Spirit's description of an empty religion, when he describes a person who seems to be religious and who bridleth not his tongue—James i. 26.

3. **Man's Religion.** Paul, in looking upon the empty rites of the idolatrous worship at Athens, said, "I perceive that in all things ye are too religious" (Acts xvii. 22, R.V., margin).

There is often a good deal of religion without Christ, but there is always true religion when there is Christ. In striking contrast to the word religion we find the names and titles of "Christ," "Jesus," and "Lord," which occur 2269 times! The secret of practical religion is the potential Christ.

689. "REMEMBER ME"

1. **A Sinner's Request.** "Remember me when Thou comest into Thy Kingdom" (Luke xxiii. 42).

2. **A Worker's Plea.** "Remember me, O my God, concerning this, and wipe not out my good deeds," etc. (Neh. xiii. 14).

3. **A Suppliant's Argument.** "Remember me...according to the greatness of Thy mercy" (Neh. xiii. 22; Psa. xxv. 7).

4. **A Labourer's Cry**. "Remember me, O my God, for good" (Neh. xiii. 31).

5. **A Covenanter's Petition**. "Remember me, O Lord, with the favour that Thou bearest unto Thy people" (Psa. cvi. 4).

6. **A Needy One's Desire**. "Remember me, and visit me, and revenge me of my persecutors" (Jer. xv. 15).

7. **An Apostolic Appreciation**. "I praise you, brethren, that you remember me in all things" (1 Cor. xi. 2).

690. REMINDERS TO WORKERS
"As" or "According as"

1. The Worker's **Court of Appeal**. "As it is written," or "according as" (Rom. i. 17; ii. 24; iii. 4, 10; iv. 17; viii. 36; ix. 13, 29, 33; x. 15; xi. 8, 26; xv. 3, 9, 21).

2. The Worker's **Administrator**. "The Spirit dividing to every man severally as He will" (1 Cor. xii. 11, 18).

3. The Worker's **Encouragement**. "As we have received mercy, we faint not" (2 Cor. iv. 1).

4. The Worker's **Walk**. "Walk even as He walked" (1 John ii. 6).

5. The Worker's **Instructor**. "Taught by Him, as the truth is in Jesus" (Eph. iv. 21).

6. The Worker's **Becomingness**. "As becometh saints" (Eph. v. 3).

7. The Worker's **Hope**. "Even as ye are called in one hope of your calling" (Eph. iv. 4).

691. RENT THINGS

1. **A Rent Heart—Humiliation**. "Rend your heart" (Joel ii. 13).

2. **A Rent Veil—Propitiation**. "Veil of the temple was rent in twain" (Matt. xxvii. 51).

3. **A Rent Child—Oppression**. "The spirit cried, and rent him sore" (Mark ix. 26).

4. **A Rent Lion—Submission**. "Samson...rent him" (Judges xiv. 6).

5. **A Rent Heaven—Inundation**. "O that Thou wouldest rend the Heavens and come down" (Isa. lxiv. 1).

6. **A Rent Kingdom—Rejection**. "The Lord hath rent the Kingdom from thee" (1 Sam. xv. 28).

7. **A Rent Mantle—Indignation**. "When I heard this thing, I rent my garment," etc. (Ezra ix. 3).

692. "REST"

1. A **sinner's** rest* disturbed—Luke xii. 19.
2. A **restless** one delivered—Matt. xi. 28.
3. A **second** rest found—Matt. xi. 29.
4. A **worker** refreshed*—Philemon 7, 20.
5. The **Spirit** resting upon a saint—1 Peter iv. 14.
6. A **busy group** resting—Mark vi. 31.
7. Tired and **persecuted saints** "rested" (Rev. xiv. 13).

693. REST IN SEVEN ASPECTS

1. **Rest of Conscience** about our sins through faith in the atoning work of Christ—Heb. x. 12.
2. **Rest of Assurance** from judgment through Christ's Word of authority—Luke vii. 50; John v. 24.
3. **Rest of Confidence** from fear of death by entering into Christ's victory—Acts ii. 26.
4. **Rest of Consecration** by being yoked with Christ in the will of God—Matt. xi. 29.
5. **Rest of Heart** by leaving everything in the Lord's hands—Phil. iv. 6, 7.
6. **Rest of Mind** in the Lord's service by fellowship with Christ—Acts ix. 31.
7. **Rest of Glory,** consummated when Christ returns—Heb. iv. 9.

694. RESTORATION OF JEWS TO PALESTINE AND GLORIES

I. **Promise of Restoration to the Land.** "Behold, I will gather them out of all countries whither I have driven them in Mine anger, and in My fury, and in great wrath, and I will bring them again unto this place, and I will cause them to dwell safely." "This place" is specifically stated, namely, "This city" (Jerusalem), and "this land" (Palestine), so there can be no mistake as to locality—Jer. xxxii. 36-41.

II. **Ancient Glories and Sanctity of the Race Regained.** Here are a few of the many promises:

1. "I will build them as at the first" (Jer. xxxiii. 7).
2. "I will no more make you a reproach among the nations" (Joel ii. 19).
3. "I will restore to you the years that the locusts have eaten" (Joel ii. 25).

* The word "rest" in these verses is rendered "ease" and "refreshed."

4. "I will save you from all your uncleanness" (Ezek. xxxvi. 29).

5. "I will bring upon you all the good I have promised them" (Jer. xxxii. 42).

6. "I will make you a name and a praise among the people of the earth" (Zeph. iii. 20).

7. "I will be your God" (Ezek. xxxvi. 28).

Scriptures might be multiplied, but the above emphatic "I will's" of Jehovah are more than sufficient.

695. RESULTS OF COMMUNION

WHEN we have communion with Christ we have—

1. **Joy in sorrow**, as Mary experienced—John xi. 32.

2. **Gladness in persecution**, as Paul and Silas experienced—Acts xvi. 25.

3. **Power in weakness**, as the apostle knew—2 Cor. xii. 8,9.

4. **Success in labour**, as the disciples found out in fishing—John xxi. 6.

5. **Endurance in trial**, as John the apostle was made to know when he was banished to the Isle of Patmos—Rev. i. 9, 12.

6. **Victory in temptation**, as Joseph in Egypt experienced—Gen. xxxix. 9.

7. **Guidance in perplexity**, as the Acts of the Apostles illustrate—Acts viii. 26, 29, 31.

696. REVIVAL

1. **Rule of Revival.** "Revive* Thou me according to Thy Word" (Psa. cxix. 25, 107, 149, 154, 156). Any revival not based on God's Word will be like a sky-rocket, which goes up with a flash, and comes down a stick!

2. **Sphere of Revival.** "Revive* me in Thy way" (Psa. cxix. 37). The way of revival is always the way of holiness of life, lowliness of spirit, and humbleness of mind.

3. **Principle of Revival.** "Revive* me according to Thy righteousness" (Psa. cxix. 40). Righteousness is the principle of doing right because it is the right thing to do.

4. **Attraction of Revival.** "Revive* me after Thy loving-kindness" (Psa. cxix. 88, 159). Love dominates in all true revival, and is ever active in kindness.

5. **Source of Revival.** "Wilt not Thou revive us again?" (Psa. lxxxv. 6). If the Lord revives, He will do it well, and we shall want Him to do it all the time.

* The Hebrew word "*chayah*" is rendered "revive" and "quicken" in these passages.

6. **Subjects of Revival.** "Revive us...Revive me." "Revive Thy work" (Hosea vi. 2; Psa. cxxxviii. 7; Hab. iii. 2). "To revive the humble" (Isa. lvii. 15). When a revival begins in the first person, there are sure to be others joining in it.

7. **Secret of Revival.** Prayer. "Wilt not Thou revive us" (Psa. lxxxv. 6). Prayer is the wire which keeps us in touch with the power house.

8. **Outcome of Revival.** "That Thy people may rejoice" (Psa. lxxxv. 6). "Revive as the corn," etc. (Hosea xiv. 7).

697. RICHES

"Let not the rich man glory in his riches" Jer. ix. 23

A LEADER in a recent newspaper gave the following: "Seventy-nine millionaires and eighty-eight bankers committed suicide in the United States in one year; which proves once more that the mere possession of wealth does not produce happiness or contentment of mind. The eternal struggle for money is based on the false assumption that wealth unlocks the doors to the Elysian fields on earth. Yet no sooner has the goal been reached than the winner of the race finds himself still surrounded by human problems and difficulties in many cases more irksome and exhausting than those from which he has just escaped. The truly rich man is the philosopher who is satisfied, not to be a sluggard or mere drone, but who fills the niche in life for which he is best fitted; who looks on money as a means to an end, and not the end of all, and who cherishes health and the good-will of his fellows above the mere gathering of gold. The contented poor man never commits suicide. He is the one to be envied by millionaires."

When gold is our god how poor we are! When money is our objective, what subjective slaves we are to its rule.

1. Riches are **Unreliable.** "He that trusteth in his riches shall fall" (Prov. xi. 28). Anything short of God will fail us.

2. Riches are **Uncertain.** "Riches certainly make themselves wings and fly away" (Prov. xxiii. 5). When we think we have got them, they are gone.

3. Riches are **Unsatisfying.** "Neither is his eye satisfied with riches" (Eccles. iv. 8). Gold is not bread, and riches cannot feed the heart.

4. Riches are **Unproductive.** "Deceitfulness of riches choke the Word" (Matt. xiii. 22). Riches promise much, but produce nothing.

5. Riches are **Unprofitable.** "How hardly shall they that

have riches enter the Kingdom of God" (Mark x. 23). Riches block the way to higher things.

6. Riches are **Unsettling**. "Trust not in uncertain riches" (1 Tim. vi. 17). If we trust in anything short of the living God, we shall find ourselves unsettled.

7. Riches are **Unfruitful**. "Your riches are corrupted" (James v. 2). A corrupted thing cannot produce anything that is beneficial.

698. RICH FOOL
Luke xii. 16-34

1. **Prosperous** in Business. "Ground...brought forth plentifully" (16).

2. **Self-centred** in Thought. "What shall I do...Layeth up treasure for himself" (17, 21).

3. **Mistaken** in Possessions. "My barns...my fruits... my goods...my soul" (18, 19).

4. **Deceived** in Outlook. "Many years." "This night" (19, 20).

5. **God-forgetful** in Soul. "Thy soul shall be required of thee" (20); "not rich towards God" (21).

6. **Earthly** in Treasure. "Those things which thou hast provided" (20).

7. **Soulish** in Nature. He lived in his soul. "I will say to my soul" (19).

699. ROBBING GOD
"Will a man rob God?" Mal. iii. 8

GOD has to chide His people when they fail to recognise what belongs to Him. Malachi indicates how we may steal in connection with Himself.

1. We rob Him of **obedience** when we depart out of His way—iii. **5**.

2. We rob Him of **reverence** when we profane His holiness—iii. **10**.

3. We rob Him of **allegiance** when we oppress those in need—iii. **5**.

4. We rob Him of **worship** when we neglect His ordinances —iii. **7**.

5. We rob Him of His **rights** when we fail to give Him His tithes—iii. **8**.

6. We rob Him of **glory** when we misrepresent Him, by saying what is not absolutely true—iii. **14, 15**.

700. RIGHT

THE word "right" in other places is rendered "righteous" (Num. xxiii. 10), "straight" (Ezek. i. 7), "upright" (Prov. xv. 8).
1. "Right **Statutes**" to govern us (Psa. xix. 8).
2. Right **Word** to guide us—Psa. xxxiii. 4.
3. Right **Ways** to protect us—Hosea xiv. 9.
4. Right **Work** of the pure is appreciated—Prov. xxi. 8.
5. Right **Life** protects from ill—Exod xv. 26; Deut. vi. 18.
6. Right **Action** brings blessing—Deut. xii. 28.
7. Right **Speech** gives satisfaction—Prov. xvi. 13.

701. "RISE UP"

1. **Saved and Moving.** "Rise up and walk?" (Luke v. 23). Healed from the disease of sin, henceforth we are to walk in the Lord.
2. **Listening and Working.** "Let us rise up and build" (Neh. ii. 18). Listening to the words of Nehemiah led the listeners to activity.
3. **Rebuke and Command.** "Rise up, ye women that are at ease" (Isa. xxxii. 9). Sloth is a curse to the sluggard and an invitation to Satan.
4. **Affection and Concern.** "Rise up, My love, My fair one, and come away" (Canticles ii. 10). The Lover of the Bride wants her at His side.
5. **Christ and Disciples.** "Rise up, let us go" (Mark xiv. 42). The consciousness of danger always calls forth the concern of the Saviour.
6. **Prayer and Deliverance.** "Arise up quickly" (Acts xii. 7). Prayer for Peter brought deliverance to Peter.

702. RULES

THE child of God, as he lives up to his privileges, observes the following rules:
1. He **denies** himself—Luke ix. 23.
2. He **loves** his brother—1 John iii. 14.
3. He **looks** upon the things of others—Phil. ii. 4.
4. He **ministers** to the need of those who are of "the household of faith" (Gal. vi. 10).
5. He **sympathises** with those who are in sorrow—Rom. xii. 15.
6. He **allows** others to be preferred before him—Rom. xii. 10.
7. He **seeks** to please his Lord in all things—Heb. xiii. 21.

703. ROYAL COMMISSIONS

HERE are eight Royal commands of the Lord to His servants. Are there none of them for you?

1. Go and **teach** all nations—Matt. xxviii. 19.
2. Go and **preach** the Gospel—Mark xvi. 15.
3. Go to the **lost sheep**—Matt. x. 6.
4. Go into the **vineyard**—Matt. xx. 4.
5. Go into the **highways**—Matt. xxii. 9.
6. Go into the **streets and lanes**—Luke xiv. 21.
7. Go home to thy **friends**—Mark v. 19.
8. Go and **do likewise**—Luke x. 37.

704. RULES FOR CONDUCT

1. A **personal faith** in Christ to save from sin—Matt. i. 21.

2. An **empowerment** by the Holy Spirit to do the will of God—Acts i. 8; Eph. iii. 16.

3. The blessedness of joy which comes from **heart purity**—Matt. v. 8.

4. **Love**, which shows itself in sympathy and help to others, and that love born of the love of God—1 John iii. 16; 1 Cor. xiii.

5. An **obedience** to Christ which shows itself in keeping His commandments—John xiii. 34, 35; xiv. 15.

6. **Christ** Himself producing His life over again in the **lives** of those who are indwelt by Him—Gal. ii. 20.

7. **Doing the right thing** because it is the right thing to do, or as grace teaches: "To live soberly, righteously, and godly in this present world" (Titus ii. 12).

705. RUNNERS

1. **A Fruitless Task.** "Not of him that runneth" (Rom. ix. 16).

2. **A Heavenly Race.** "Let us run with...the race" (Heb. xii. 1).

3. **A Definite Object.** "So run that ye may obtain" (1 Cor. ix. 24).

4. **A Trained Athlete.** "I therefore so run" (1 Cor. ix. 26).

5. **A Stunted Assembly.** "Ye did run well; who did hinder you?" (Gal. v. 7).

6. **A Hindering People.** "Lest by any means I should run, or had run in vain" (Gal. ii. 2; Phil. ii. 16).

7. **A Successful Word.** "That the Word of the Lord may have free course ("run," R.V., margin) and be glorified" (2 Thess. iii. 1).

706. SABBATH

1. We are **commanded** to keep holy the Sabbath Day— Exod. xx. 8-10. When God commands, it is for us to obey.

2. We are to rest one day in seven, **because God rested** from His creative work on the seventh day—Gen. ii. 2. It is economic and essential that everything that works should have a period of rest.

3. The early Christians **by the practice of gathering together** to worship the Lord, and to remember His death, on the **first day of the week**, proclaim they had the authority of Christ to do so—Acts xx. 7.

4. There is a **special blessing** promised to those who keep God's day of rest—Isa. lvi. 4, 5.

5. **If God's Day is not recognised**, people will drift into the rapids of agnosticism, rationalism, covetousness, self-pleasure, and sin; for if we cut ourselves from one of God's commands, we shall cut ourselves from others—Isa. lvi. 2, 6; lviii. 13.

6. **Disobedience** to remember the Sabbath by self-action always brings punishment, as is evidenced in the man who gathered sticks on the Sabbath—Num. xv. 32-41; and in the case of those who gathered manna—Exod. xvi. 25, 26.

7. And the most important of all, is, the Sabbath is a Holy Day; for **the Lord has sanctified it**—Gen. ii. 3; hence, for man to take what is holy to the Lord for his own use is to commit a trespass in God's holy things; and when any man did this under the law, atonement had to be made for his sin, and reparation—See Lev. v. 14-19. It is a principle we do well to recognise, that in all God's commands He has our best interests at heart, and we study our own interests when we obey His bidding.

707. SAINTS IN WRONG PLACES

1. **A Discouraged Worker.** Elijah under a juniper tree— 1 Kings xix. 4.

2. **A Backsliding Believer.** Abram in Egypt—Gen. xii. 10.

3. **A Disobedient Servant.** Jonah in the sea-monster— Jonah ii.

4. **A Seduced Prophet.** The man of God in the old prophet's house—1 Kings xiii. 19.

5. **A Lazy Saint.** David on the house top—2 Sam. xi. 2.

6. **A Silenced Witness.** Lot in Sodom—Gen. xiv. 12.

7. **A Miserable Disciple.** Peter before the fire—Luke xxii. 55.

708. SAFEGUARDS

1. **On** God's Side. "Who is on the Lord's side?" (Exod. xxxii. 26).

2. **In** God's Hand. "Covered thee in the shadow of Mine hand" (Isa. li. 16; John x. 28, 29).

3. **Doing** God's Work. "My work in the Lord" (1 Cor. ix. 1). "Stablish you in every good work" (2 Thess. ii. 17).

4. **Walking** in God's Way. "I have walked in Thy truth" (Psa. xxvi. 3; Isa. xxxviii. 3).

5. **Energised** by God's Power. "Strong in the Lord and in the power of His might" (Eph. vi. 10).

6. **Enlightened** through God's Word. "Eyes of your understanding be enlightened" (Eph. i. 18).

7. **Aiming** for God's Glory. "Whatsoever ye do, do all to the glory of God" (1 Cor. x. 31).

709. SAINT'S MEDICINE CHEST

ONE pound of the Spirit's Graces in equal portions of one ounce each.

1 oz. Balm of Gilead—Jer. viii. 22.
1 oz. Bark of Calvary—Isa. liii. 4-6.
1 oz. Syrup of Faith—James v. 15.
1 oz. Essence of Love—1 Cor. xiii. 13, R.V.
1 oz. Oil of Confidence—Prov. iii. 26.
1 oz. Honey of the Word—Prov. iv. 20-22; xvi. 24.
1 oz. Spice of Consecration—Song of Songs iv. 12-16.
1 oz. Stalk of Uprightness—Prov. xiv. 2; Rom. xiv. 17.
1 oz. Flower of Discretion—Prov. xxii. 3.
1 oz. Root of Contentment—Heb. xiii. 5, 6.
1 oz. Herb of Joy—Prov. xvii. 22.
1 oz. Milk of Kindness—Prov. xxxi. 20.
1 oz. Frankincense of Worship—Matt. ii. 11.
1 oz. Dew of Humility—Prov. xxii. 4.
1 oz. Crystals of Patience—2 Peter i. 6.
1 oz. Perfume of Praise—Psa. ciii. 1, 2.

Pound these ingredients well in the mortar of believing prayer —1 John v. 14, with the pestle of truth—Eph. iv. 20, 21; add sufficient water of the Spirit's life—Rom. viii. 11, till all are mixed proportionately together, and then put up in the jar of a sanctified memory—2 Peter i. 12. Apply the preparation three times a day, and oftener if required, with the hand of diligence—2 Peter i. 10, and it will be found that this Christ-all compound—Matt. viii. 17, will cure all kinds of ailments— Matt. viii. 16.

710. SALVATION

1. **Establishing** in its Stability. "Rock of His Salvation" (Deut. xxxii. 15).

2. **Exhaustless** in its Supply. "Wells of Salvation" (Isa. xii. 3).

3. **Enabling** in its Strength. "Strength of Salvation" (Isa. xxxiii. 6).

4. **Environing** in its Protection. "Salvation will God appoint for her bulwarks" (Isa. xxvi. 1; 2 Samuel xxiii. 5; Psa. cxlix. 4).

5. **Exhilarating** in its Joy. "The cup of Salvation" (Psa. cxvi. 13).

6. **Enlightening** in its Presence. "Salvation...as a lamp" (Isa. lxii. 1).

7. **Eternal** in its Character. "My Salvation shall be for ever" (Isa. li. 6).

8. **Easy** in its Comfort. "Thy chariots of Salvation" (Hab. iii. 8).

711. SATAN AND JOB

Job. i

1. **Satan Among the Saints.** "Satan came also among them" (6). He is a regular attendant when God's people meet together.

2. **Jehovah's Question.** "Satan, whence comest thou?" (7). Sometimes he has a "seat" and a synagogue—Rev. ii. 9, 24.

3. **Satan's Reply** to Jehovah. "Satan answered, From going to and fro in the earth" (7) (1 Peter v. 8).

4. **Jehovah's Inquiry** about Job. "Hast thou considered My servant Job" (8). The Lord appreciates what He sees in Job.

5. **Satan's Insinuation.** "Satan...said, Doth Job fear God for nought?" (9). Being Job's adversary, he accuses him to God.

6. **Jehovah's Permission.** "The Lord said unto Satan, All that he hath is in thy power" (12). We consider the "end of the Lord" in this permission—James v. 11.

7. **Satan's Going Forth** from the presence of the Lord to afflict Job—12.

Ponder the added afflictions of Job from Satan in Job ii.

712. "SALVATION" *

1. **Power.** "Horn of Salvation" (xviii. 2; xx. 6, margin; xxv. 5).

2. **Protection.** "Shield of Salvation" (xviii. 35).

3. **Person.** "God of my salvation" (xviii. 46; xxvii. 1, 9).

4. **Principle.** "Truth of Thy Salvation" (lxix. 13).

5. **Provision.** "The Salvation of God" (1. 23; lxii. 7).

6. **Pleasure.** "I will joy in the God of my Salvation" (Hab. iii. 18).

7. **Patience.** ' I will wait for the God of my Salvation" (Micah vii. 7).

8. **Prayer.** "Help us, O God of our Salvation" (lxxix. 9).

9. **Presence.** "Surely His Salvation is nigh" (lxxxv. 9).

10. **Prospect.** "Behold thy Salvation cometh" (Isa. lxii. 11).

11. **Platform.** "Rock of our Salvation" (xcv. 1).

12. **Priesthood.** "I will clothe her priests with Salvation" (cxxxii. 16; Isa. lxi. 10).

713. SATAN IN THE BOOK OF THE REVELATION

1. The **Description** of Satan in Revelation xii. Once he is called "the great red dragon" (3), once "the great dragon" (9), six times "the dragon" (4, 7, 7, 13, 16, 17), once "the old serpent" (9), twice "the Devil" (9, 12), once "Satan" (9), and once "the accuser" (10).

2. The **Synagogue** of Satan identifies him with religious circles—ii. 9; iii. 9, in his work among those who profess the Name of Christ.

3. The **"Seat"** of Satan, where he dwells, speaks of his power to oppose the truth and persecute God's faithful ones—ii. 13.

4. The **"Depths** of Satan" (ii. 24), denote his subtle and hidden workings, as he seduces and leads astray by his false ways and doctrines.

5. **Confinement** of Satan in the abyss for a thousand years, where he is kept while Christ reigns—xx. 1-3.

6. **Loosing** of Satan for a short period, and his consignment into the Lake of Fire—xx. 7-9.

* The meaning of "Salvation" is deliverance from danger, to be safe, to be prosperous, and to be in the enjoyment of liberty.

714. SATAN'S ACTIVITIES
No. 1

SATAN has many devices, designs, and doings to accomplish his fell purposes.

1. He **provokes** to wrong action, as seen in David—1 Chron. xxi. 1.

2. He **resists** the grace of God, as illustrated in Joshua—Zech. iii. 1.

3. He **tempts** to gain advantage, as manifest in Christ—Matt. iv. 10.

4. He **takes away** the seed of God's Word, as taught in the parable of the sower—Luke viii. 12.

5. He **desires** to have us, to sift, as stated by Christ to Peter—Luke xxii. 31.

6. He **transforms** himself into an angel of light to lead us astray, as warned by Paul—2 Cor. xi. 14.

7. He **incites to sin**, that he may get us under his power, as unfolded by John—1 John iii. 8.

715. SATAN'S ACTIVITIES
No. 2

1. He **attracts** by the glamour of wonders, as will be evidenced in the coming man of sin—2 Thess. ii. 9.

2. He **seeks** to get "an advantage" over us by misrepresentation, as pointed out by the apostle—2 Cor. ii. 11.

3. He **fills the heart with lies** to keep back what is devoted to the Lord, as practised in Ananias—Acts v. 3.

4. He **hinders** in seeking to thwart God's purposes, as stated by Christ—Matt. xvi. 23.

5. He **seeks to gain possession** of people, that he may carry out his designs, as demonstrated in Judas—John xiii. 27.

6. He **oppresses** that he may harm those whom he dominates, as manifest in Christ's opposing ministry—Matt. ix. 32; xv. 22; Acts x. 38.

7. He **persecutes** the servants of God, who are faithful to Him, as predicted he would—Rev. ii. 10.

716. SATAN'S ACTIVITIES
No. 3

1. He **fights** against the heavenly powers to hinder Christ's rule, as described in Revelation xii. 3-10.

2. He **places** himself upon us when we "give place" to him by inconsistent conduct, as stated in Ephesians iv. 27.

3. He **blinds** the minds of those who are in unbelief, that they may not see Christ, as revealed in 2 Corinthians iv. 4.

4. He **beguiles** by his sophistries to rob us of blessing, as he did Eve—2 Cor. xi. 3.

5. He **works** in the children of disobedience, that he may wreck their career, as we read in Ephesians ii. 2.

6. He **hinders** God's servants in their work, as Paul experienced in his ministry—1 Thess. ii. 18.

7. He **accuses** the brethren to God, and does it night and day, that he may wound God by their inconsistencies, as is revealed in Revelations xii. 10.

717. SATAN'S MANY PARTS

Some years ago, at the Playgoers' Club, a Mr. Osman Edwards delivered an address on "Stage Fiends." In his dramatic career, said Mr. Edwards, as the devil he had played many parts—a Hebrew valet, an Indian sage, a Catholic monster, a Protestant buffoon, an Elizabethan mischief-maker, a Dutch politician, a Spanish professor, a German sceptic, a Shelleian saint, and a Corellian contradiction.

The Bible shows that Satan can play many parts, and among the principal parts he plays are the following seven:

1. He is the **Devil** to deceive—Rev. xx. 10.
2. He is the **adversary** (Satan) to accuse—Luke xxii. 31.
3. He is an **angel of light** to misrepresent—2 Cor. xi. 14.
4. He is an **enemy** to oppose—Matt. xiii. 28, 39.
5. He is the **hinderer** to deter—1 Thess. ii. 18.
6. He is the **god of this age** to blind—2 Cor. iv. 4.
7. He is the **tempter** to allure—Luke iv. 2; 1 Thess. iii. 5.

718. SCRIPTURES

The Scriptures claim to be inspired, and prove the claim they make. They are—

1. **God-breathed** in substance—2 Tim. iii. 16.
2. **Unbreakable** in nature—John x. 35.
3. **Christ-revealing** in contents—John xix. 24, 28, 36, 37; Luke xxiv. 27, 32).
4. **Definite** in message—1 Cor. xv. 3, 4.
5. **Holy** in character—2 Tim. iii. 16.
6. **Profitable** in out-working—2 Tim. iii. 16.
7. **Divine** in authorship—2 Peter i. 19, 20.

719. SATAN'S SUBTLE SERVICE

SATAN means an opponent, the accuser; hence, the adversary. He is God's adversary, and man's, too. He accuses God to us, and accuses us to God.

1. Satan **opposes** the death of Christ, as seen in his use of Peter, when he tried to keep Christ from the Cross, and brought Christ's stern rebuke: "Get thee behind Me, Satan" (Matt. xvi. 23).

2. Satan **catches away** the seed of God's Word, when it falls upon the wayside-bearer, lest it should find a lodgment in the heart—Mark iv. 15.

3. Satan **sifts** the self-sufficient believer, as he did Peter, to get rid of faith in the Lord—Luke xxii. 31.

4. Satan **endeavours** to get people to compromise in their consecration, as he did Ananias, when he and his wife kept back part of the price—Acts v. 3.

5. Satan **tempts** with his devices to get an "advantage" by keeping us from acting after Christ in our actions towards each other—2 Cor. ii. 11.

6. Satan **transforms** himself into an angel of light through his emissaries who come in a false guise to deceive—2 Cor. xi. 11-15.

7. Satan **hinders** the servants of God in their service by putting difficulties in their way—1 Thess. ii. 18.

720. SATAN'S WICKED WAYS

1. Satan's **malignant temptation** of Christ in the wilderness, through the flesh's weakness, the world's glamour, and the pride of life—Mark i. 13.

2. Satan's **cruel work in binding** a woman for eighteen years, so that she could not raise herself—Luke xiii. 16.

3. Satan's **despotic sway** in dominating Judas to betray Christ—Luke xxii. 3; John xiii. 27.

4. Satan's **deceitful working** through the coming man of sin, to get them to believe the lie that his protègè is the Christ—2 Thess. ii. 9.

5. Satan's **purpose in seeking** to turn aside from the right things in the relations of life—1 Tim. v. 15.

6. Satan's **hurtful messenger** in causing the Lord's people to have thorns in their bodies—2 Cor. xii. 7.

7. Satan's **resisting** the angel of the Lord to hinder the blessing of His people—Zech. iii. 1, 2.

721. SATAN'S WILY WILES

SATAN has many wiles and weapons, and by means of them deceives and defeats us.

1. Wiles to **Deceive.** "Wiles of the Devil" (Eph. vi. 11). With cunning and craft he lies in wait, like a wrecker with a false light.

2. Darts to **Hurt.** "Fiery darts of the evil one" (Eph. vi. 16, R.V.). His darts are intended to do us harm, as they did in the case of Job.

3. Snares to **Entrap.** "The snare of the Devil." Pride, riches, and error are some of his snares (1 Tim. iii. 7; vi. 9; 2 Tim. ii. 26).

4. Devices to **Defraud.** "We are not ignorant of his devices" (2 Cor. ii. 11), and those devices are to get advantages over us to rob us.

5. Buffets to **Injure.** "The messenger of Satan to buffet me" (2 Cor. xii. 7). Buffet means to hit one with a clenched fist.

6. Sifts to **Remove.** "Satan hath desired to have you, that he may sift you as wheat" (Luke xxii. 31). He sifts to get rid of faith, love, consecration, prayer, faithfulness, watchfulness, and power.

7. Tares to **Choke.** "Enemy came and sowed tares" (Matt. xiii. 25). The tares resemble the wheat, but they are destructive to it.

722. SAVED "FROM" AND "TO"

1. Saved from the **wrath to come**—Rom. v. 9.
2. From the **curse** of a broken law—Gal. iii. 10.
3. From the **servitude of sin**—Rom. vi. 16.
4. From the **pollution** of sin—1 Cor. vi. 9. 10.
5. From the **corruption of the world**—2 Peter i. 4.
6. From the **selfishness of self**—2 Peter ii. 10.

Saved

1. To **relationship with God**—John i. 12.
2. To **eternal life**—John iii. 36.
3. To **newness of life**—Rom. vi. 4.
4. To **holiness of character**—Rom. vi. 22.
5. To **pureness of heart**—Matt. v. 8.
6. To the **love of Christ**—2 Cor. v. 14.
7. To **righteousness of conduct**—Rom. xiv. 17.
8. To **sweetness of temper**—Eph. iv. 31, 32.
9. To **victory over Satan**—Rev. xii. 11.
10. To **saving** others—Jude 23.

723. "SAVED"

1. **Originator** of our being Saved. The Lord: "Who hath saved us" (2 Tim. i. 9).

2. **Mediator** through whom we are Saved. Christ: "Through Him might be saved" (John iii. 17).

3. **Cause** of our being Saved. Grace: "By grace ye are saved" (Eph. ii. 5-8).

4. **Instrument** of being Saved. Faith: "Thy faith hath saved thee" (Luke vii. 50).

5. **Assurance** to those who desire to be saved and those who are. Word of Christ: "These things I say that ye might be saved" (John v. 34).

6. **Promise** to those who want to be Saved. Prayer: "Whosoever shall call on the Name of the Lord shall be saved" (Acts ii. 21).

7. **Mission** of the Christ and the Gospel. "By which also ye are saved" (1 Cor. xv. 2).

724. "SAVE ME"

1. **A Persecuted Saint.** "Save me from all them that persecute me" (Psa. vii. 1).

2. **A Harassed Sufferer.** "Save me from the lion's mouth" (Psa. xxii. 21).

3. **An Oppressed Suppliant.** "Save me, O God, by Thy Name," etc. (Psa. liv. 1).

4. **A Confident Believer.** "As for me, I will call upon God; and the Lord shall save me" (Psa. lv. 16).

5. **A Happy Worshipper.** "The Lord was ready to save me; therefore we will sing," etc. (Isa. xxxviii. 20).

6. **A Sinking Disciple.** "Lord, save me" (Matt. xiv. 30).

7. **An Agonising Saviour.** "Father, save Me from this hour" (John xii. 27).

725. SAVIOUR

An Acrostic

Saves from sin by His grace—Eph. ii. 5.

Atones for sin by His blood—Rom. iii. 25, 26.

Vivifies from sin by His life—Rom. v. 11.

Inspires to love by His love—2 Cor. v. 14.

Obtains an inheritance by His power—Heb. i. 3, 4.

Unifies to Himself by His Spirit—1 Cor. xii. 13.

Receives to glory at His return—John xiv. 3.

726. SEA OF CRYSTAL

GEORGE FOX, in writing of one of his experiences, said: "I saw a sea of ink and a sea of crystal, and the sea of crystal swept away the sea of ink. " The above quotation suggests what the Gospel of God's grace does in the lives of those who believe in Christ, for, as in the Millennium, there will be an effective living water current which will wash out the Dead Sea, and make it a living stream—Ezek. xlvii.

1. So the Gospel in the cleansing of the precious Blood of Christ **removes** the foulness of sin—1 John i. 7.

2. The water of life **quenches** the fire of unholy passion—John iv. 14.

3. The love of God **supplants** the desire to sin—2 Cor. v. 14-17.

4. The power of Christ **conquers** the dominance of evil—Rom. vi. 14.

5. The holiness of the Lord **electrifies** to whole-hearted devotion to Him—Phil. iv. 12, 13, and thus annuls the failure of self-effort.

6. The presence of Christ **destroys** all fear of man and Devil, for His grace is sufficient—2 Cor. xii. 9.

7. The Coming of Christ **drives** all impurity away, for it is the soul's ambition, when looking for Him, to be ripe and ready, and thus to have His approval—1 John iii. 2, 3.

727. SECOND CHOICE

1. **Abraham** was called at the first to go direct to Canaan, but he chose a second choice in staying at Haran for a time, till the Lord spoke to him again. How significant is the past tense of Genesis xii. 1, "The Lord had said unto Abraham" (Gen. xi. 31; xii. 1-3); also, "when his father was dead" of Acts xii. 1-3, plainly indicating that death had to snap the bond which caused him to tarry in Haran.

2. **Lot** appears to have been only a second-rate believer. He seems to have started wrong. Meanful is the statement that "Lot went with Abram" (Gen. xii. 4), while the latter went with God, in response to His call. Again, Lot "lifted up his eyes, and beheld all the plain of Jordan," etc., while Abraham who did not look, was bidden by the Lord to "look" at Heaven's expanse, as He gave him Heaven's promise—Gen. xiii. 10-14.

3. God wanted **Moses** to go at His bidding and speak to Pharaoh; he hesitated, and complained he could not speak, and passed the honour on to Aaron. Thus Aaron got the best blessing and Moses the second choice—Exod. iv. 14-16; the same thing

is illustrated again when the Spirit was distributed among the seventy elders for administration purposes, instead of resting on Moses alone—Num. xi. 11-17.

4. The **Children of Israel** made the second choice of wandering in the wilderness, instead of entering the Promised Land. They saw many things of the Lord's doings, but they would have had a greater blessing if they had entered into His rest—Heb. iii. 11.

5. **Martha** made the second choice of being cumbered with serving, while Mary had the Lord's rest in sitting at His feet—Luke x. 39-42.

6. **Moses** and **Elijah**, when transfigured on the mount with Christ, had fellowship with Him in conversing about His death; while the disciples were concerned about the place where they were found, and said: "It is good to be *here*." Certainly the better was to be with Him—Luke ix. 33.

728. SECRET OF VICTORY OVER THE WORLD

1. **Keep from it**—James i. 27. The place of separation is the place of power. To "keep unspotted" means not to be stained, therefore we must not be near the world, but keep from the range of its mud-slinging.

2. **Take Christ's victory over it.** His Word is, "I have overcome the world," therefore He bids us "Be of good cheer" (John xvi. 33). See the three references to Christ and "this world" in John's Gospel—John xii. 31; xiv. 30; xvi. 11.

3. **Believe you have got the victory over it.** "This is the victory that overcometh the world, even our faith" (1 John v. 4, 5); and the reasons are, because we have been begotten of God, and because we believe in the Son of God.

4. **Recognise the Lord's indwelling presence.** "Ye... have overcome them, because greater is He that is in you than he that is in the world" (1 John iv. 4). The Lord within keeps the world without.

5. **Remember, the world is an enemy, and the injunction is not to have fellowship with it**—James iv. 4; for if we do, we side with an enemy and make ourselves antagonistic to God.

6. **The uncompromising and specific command of the Lord is,** "Love not the world" (1 John ii. 15). This will be easy if we dwell in the love of God.

7. **Call to mind the prayer of Christ about the world,** and remember you are taken "out of it," sent into it, not of it, and He prays you may be kept from it—John xvii. 6, 7, 14, 15.

729. SEEING CHRIST

1. The shepherds saw Him as the **Incarnate One**—Luke ii. 17.

2. Simeon saw Him as the **Saving One**—Luke ii. 30.

3. His earthly parents saw Him as the **Working One**—Luke ii. 49.

4. Peter saw Him as the **Provider**—Luke v. 8.

5. The leper saw Him as the **Cleanser**—Luke v. 12.

6. The demoniac saw Him as the **Emancipator**—Luke viii. 28.

7. Peter and John saw Him as the **Glorified One**—Luke ix. 32.

8. Zacchaeus saw Him as the **Saviour**—Luke xix. 5.

9. Herod saw Him as the **Silencer**—Luke xxiii. 8.

10. The centurion saw Him as the **Righteous One**—Luke xxiii. 47.

11. The disciples saw Him as the **Risen One**—Luke xxiv. 39.

730. SEEING JESUS
John xii 21

1. To see Him with the **eye of faith** is to be saved by Him—Isaiah xlv. 22.

2. To see Him with the **eye of love** is to be satisfied with Him—Acts vii. 56.

3. To see Him with the **eye of recognition** is to adore Him—John xx. 16.

4. To see Him with the **eye of consecration** is to glory in Him—Cant. v. 16.

5. To see Him with the **eye of spiritual understanding** is to endure like Him—Heb. xii. 1, 2.

6. To see Him with the **eye of reality** is to be glad in Him—John xx. 20.

7. To see Him with the **eye of hope** is to be filled with a holy enthusiasm for Him—Titus ii. 13.

731. SEEING SAVIOUR
Luke xix 5

CHRIST "looked up and saw Zacchaeus." A seeking sinner is never lost sight of by the seeing Saviour. There are seven things the Saviour sees.

1. He sees what we **are** and tells us we have sinned, as He made known to Paul—Rom. iii. 23.

2. He sees what we **have done**, as He made the woman of Samaria to realise—John iv. 29.

3. He sees what we **cannot do**, as He reminded Nicodemus when He told him he needed to be born again or from above—John iii. 5-7.

4. He sees what we **want**, namely, eternal life, as the disciples discovered—John vi. 68.

5. He sees what we **would like to do**, namely, "to do good," and gives us the Spirit to accomplish (Rom. vii. 19, viii. 2).

6. He sees our **difficulties**, as He saw the disciples "toiling in rowing," and gives deliverance (Mark vi. 48).

7. He sees our **trials**, and supplies the sufficient grace, as He did the Apostle—2 Cor. xii. 9.

732. SEEK

1. **Whom** to seek. The Lord. "Seek ye the Lord" (Isa. lv. 6).

2. **When** to seek. "First" (Matt. vi. 33); "Early" (Psa. lxiii. 1); "Continually" (1 Chron. xvi. 11).

3. **What** to seek. "Peace" (Psa. xxxiv. 14); God's "Precepts" (Psa. cxix. 45); "Good" (Amos v. 14); "Righteousness and Meekness" (Zeph. ii. 3); "Things above" (Col. iii. 1).

4. **How** to seek. With a "prepared heart" (2 Chron xix. 3; xxx. 19); with a prayerful spirit—Dan. ix. 3; Matt. vii. 7.

5. **Why** we should seek. Because we "shall not want" (Psa. xxxiv. 10).

733. SEEKING

To have a purpose in life and to fulfil it, is to live to purpose.

1. The Good Shepherd sought the lost **sheep** till He found it—Matt. xviii. 12.

2. The Father seeks **worshippers** to praise Him—John iv. 23.

3. To seek first the **Kingdom of God** is to find the added of His blessing—Matt. vi. 33.

4. To seek **the Lord** by prayer is to find the blessing we desire—Matt. vii. 7, 8.

5. If we seek to **see Jesus** we shall find in Him salvation—Luke xix. 3.

6. To seek **those things** which are above is to find Christ in His risen power—Col. iii. 1.

7. Satan seeks **to devour** the love and faith of the saints that he may find food for his unholy satisfaction—1 Peter v. 8.

734. SEEKING SINNER
Luke xix. 3

ZACCHAEUS "sought to see Jesus who He was;" and he went to some trouble in his quest, for he "climbed" up a tree "to see Him." Who is He? There are many answers to the question. The following seven cover a good deal of ground.

1. Son of God in His Supreme Being. Christ in His personality is the Son of God, God the Son, hence He is said to be "The Express Image of God's Person" (Heb. i. 3). That does not mean the impression of God as the wax bears the impression of the die pressed upon it, but the die that makes the impression.

2. Son of Man in His Spotless Humanity. He became man when He took our nature upon Him, but it does not say He became God. He was perfectly human, and a Perfect Human. He did no sin—1 Peter ii. 22; He knew no sin—2 Cor. v. 21; in Him was no sin—1 John iii. 5; and He was separate from sinners—Heb. vii. 26.

3. Saviour of Men in His Gracious Love. The good Samaritan and loving acts are the unfoldings of His compassion and love—Luke x. 30-35.

4. Suffering Lord in His Sufficient Atonement. The word "atonement" is rendered "satisfaction" in Numbers xxxv. 31, and the New Testament equivalent is the word "propitiation" in Romans iii. 25. God gives what He demands.

5. Successful Combatant Against all Evil, for He has destroyed him who had the power of death, and Christ now holds the keys of Hades and death—Rev. i. 18.

6. Secret of Blessing. All blessing is found in Christ—Eph. i. 3. God has nothing to give us apart from Him, and He has no withholdings with Him—Rom. viii. 32.

7. Sufficient Grace in Meeting our Need. Our need is met "according to His riches, not *out* of them, hence all grace is at our disposal—2 Cor. ix. 8.

735. SERVICE OF THE BELIEVER

THERE are many illustrations we find bringing out the character of those who serve. There is the service of—

1. **The Priest** in the Temple—Heb. ix. 14.
2. **The Slave** in the House—Luke xvii. 8.
3. **The Deacon** in the Church—Luke xxii. 26.
4. **The Elder** in the Flock—Rom. i. 9.
5. **The Son** in the Family—Matt. iv. 10.
6. **The Maid** in the Home—Acts xii. 13.
7. **The Member** in the Body—1 Cor. xii. 21.

736. SELF VOICES
1. **Voice of the World.** "Save thyself" (Luke xxiii. 39).
2. **Voice of the Self-Christian.** "Pity thyself" (Matt. xvi. 22, R.V., margin).
3. **Voice of the Lord.** "Deny thyself" (Matt. xvi. 24).

737. SELF-SEEKING
1. Self-**Pleasing.** "Walk as men" (1 Cor. iii. 3).
2. Self-**Pride.** "I have made" (Daniel iii. 15).
3. Self-**Prayer.** "Prayed with himself" (Luke xviii. 11).
4. Self-**Righteousness.** "I counted loss" (Phil. iii. 4-7).
5. Self-**Opinion.** "I thought" (2 Kings v. 11).
6. Self-**Service.** "I go a fishing" (John xxi. 3).
7. Self-**Eminence.** "Diotrephes, who loveth to have the pre-eminence" (3 John 9).
8. Self-**Placement.** "Reasoning...which should be the greatest" (Luke ix. 46).

738. "SENT FORTH"
THE word *exapostello* is rendered "sent forth," "sent away," "sent," and "send."
1. God "sent forth **His Son**" to the work of redemption (Gal. iv. 4, 5).
2. God "sent forth **the Spirit** of His Son" to assure believers of their sonship (Gal. iv. 6).
3. The Lord "sent **His angel**" to deliver Peter (Acts xii. 11).
4. **Paul** was told by the Lord: "I will send thee far hence to the Gentiles" (Acts xxii. 21).
5. The **rich** in themselves, the Lord hath "sent empty away" (Luke i. 53).

739. "SET FORTH"
1. **The Truth** "set forth" in order (Luke i. 1).
2. **The Death** of Christ "set forth" as a propitiation (Rom. iii. 25).
3. **Christ** "set forth" as the Crucified One in the Gospel message (Gal. iii. 1).
4. **The Apostles** "set forth" as an object lesson (1 Cor. iv. 9).
5. **The Way** of the world, to "set forth" the good first and the bad after (John ii. 10).
6. **The Acceptable Prayer** "set forth" like the evening sacrifice (Psa. cxli. 2).
7. **Sinners** "set forth" as a warning against sin and its consequent judgment (Jude 7).

740. SERMONS IN STONES

1. The **Stone of Hard Circumstances** becoming the blessing of Heaven's manifestation, as demonstrated in Jacob's experience—Gen. xxviii. 11, 12.

2. The **Stones of Gracious Deliverance**, as made known in the memorials of Gilgal, proclaiming Egypt's reproach rolled away from Israel—Joshua iv. 5-9.

3. The **Stone of Ebenezer** testifying to Jehovah's help— 1 Sam. vii. 12.

4. The **Stone of Kidron** heralding the Lord's victory— 1 Sam. xvii. 50.

5. The **Stone of Hindrance** asking for the active labour of Christ's disciples—John xi. 39.

6. The **Stone of Approval** given to the overcomer as his reward—Rev. ii. 17.

7. The **Stone of Death** rolled away announcing Christ's triumphant resurrection—Luke xxiv. 2.

741. SEVEN ACTS

1. An Act of **Faith**. "He, casting away his garment, rose, and came to Jesus" (Mark x. 50).

2. An Act of **Love**. "Perfect love casteth out fear" (1 John iv. 18).

3. An Act of **Confidence**. "Casting all your care upon Him" (1 Peter v. 7).

4. An Act of **Worship**. "Cast their crowns before the throne" (Rev. iv. 10).

5. An Act of **Obedience**. "Cast the net...they cast therefore" (John xxi. 6).

6. An Act of **Consecration**. "Cast that He hath given thee upon the Lord" (Psa. lv. 22, R.V., margin).

7. An Act of **Power**. "Casting down imaginations" (2 Cor. x. 5).

742. SEVEN "GREAT" THINGS IN HEBREWS

1. A "great **salvation**" (ii. 3).
2. A "great **high priest**" (iv. 14).
3. A "great **man**" (vii. 4).
4. A "great **fight**" (x. 32).
5. A "great **recompense**" (x. 35).
6. A "great **crowd of witnesses**" (xii. 1).
7. A "great **Shepherd**" (xiii. 20).

743. SEVENFOLD SANCTIFICATION

1. **"Sanctified in Christ."** Standing of the Saint (1 Cor. i. 2).
2. **"Sanctified by God the Father."** Love separating the believer for Himself (Jude 1).
3. **"Being Sanctified by the Holy Ghost."** Power and Progress (Rom. xv. 16).
4. **"Sanctified in the Truth."** Sphere and Cleansing (John xvii. 19, R.V.).
5. **"Sanctified...by Prayer."** Dependence and Request (1 Tim. iv. 5).
6. **Sanctified by Blood.** Salvation and Dedication—Heb. x. 10, 14; xiii. 12.
7. **"Sanctify Yourselves."** Privilege and Responsibility (Lev. xi. 44; 1 Chron. xv. 12).

744. SEVEN GOLDEN LINKS

ROMANS iv. 25; v. 1-5

1. **Substitution.** "Delivered for."
2. **Justification.** "Justified by."
3. **Introduction.** "Access by faith."
4. **Position.** "This grace wherein we stand."
5. **Exultation.** "Rejoice in hope."
6. **Education.** "Tribulation worketh."
7. **Possession.** "Love of God shed abroad."

745. SEVEN GOLDEN LINKS OF GRACE

TITUS II. 11-14

1. **The Blessing** which Grace brings. "Salvation."
2. **The Instruction** which Grace gives. "Teaching us that denying ungodliness and worldly lusts, we should live soberly, righteously, and godly."
3. **The Hope** which Grace begets. "Looking for that Blessed Hope," etc.
4. **The Price** which Grace paid. "Who gave Himself for us."
5. **The End** which Grace had. "That He might redeem us from all iniquity."
6. **The Acquirement** which Grace claims. "Purify unto Himself a peculiar people."
7. **The Zeal** which Grace inspires. "Zealous of good works."

746. SEVEN GREATEST THINGS

1. The greatest **force** in the world. "The Love of Christ" (2 Cor. v. 14).

2. The greatest **faith** in the world. "The Faith of Christ" (Gal. ii. 16).

3. The greatest **fruit** in the world. "The Gentleness of Christ" (2 Cor. x. 1).

4. The greatest **factor** in the world. "The Power of Christ" (2 Cor. xii. 9).

5. The greatest **fulcrum** in the world. "The Word of Christ" (Col. iii. 16).

6. The greatest **fabricator** in the world. "The Mind of Christ" (Phil. ii. 5).

7. The greatest **fellowship** in the world. "The Afflictions of Christ" (Col. i. 24).

747. SEVEN "I WILLS" OF GRACE

IN HOSEA xiii 14; xiv 4, 5

1. The "I will" of **resurrection**. "I will ransom thee from the power of the grave."

2. The "I will" of **redemption**. "I will redeem thee from death."

3. The "I will" of **retribution**. "O death, I will be thy plagues."

4. The "I will" of **removal**. "O grave, I will be thy destruction."

5. The "I will" of **restoration**. "I will heal their backsliding."

6. The "I will" of **regard**. "I will love them freely."

7. The "I will" of **refreshment**. "I will be as the dew unto Israel."

748. SEVEN SECRETS IN 1 JOHN

1. The Word of God is the **secret of power**—ii. 14.

2. Doing the will of God is the **secret of continuance**—ii. 17.

3. Being born of God is the **secret of holiness**—iii. 9.

4. The love of God is the **secret of service**—iii. 16.

5. The presence of God is the **secret of assurance**—iii. 19.

6. Faith in God is the **secret of victory**—v. 4.

7. The Spirit of God is the **secret of discernment**—iv. 6.

749. SEVEN STARS

1. **Loved** by Christ—Gal. ii. 20.
2. **Loosed** through Christ—Rev. i. 5, R.V.
3. **Lightened** in Christ—Eph. v. 8.
4. **Led** by Christ—John x. 3.
5. **Leaning** on Christ—John xiii. 25.
6. **Living** with Christ—Eph. ii. 6.
7. **Looking** for Christ—Titus ii. 13.

750. SEVEN TRAITS OF FAITH

1. "The word of faith" is **faith's basis** (Rom. x. 8).
2. "The walk of faith" is **faith's life** (2 Cor. v. 7).
3. "The shield of faith" is **faith's protection** (Eph. vi. 16).
4. The service of faith is **faith's business**—Phil. i. 27.
5. The **object of faith** is God Himself—Rom. iv. 5, 20.
6. The **power of faith** is the Holy Spirit—Acts vi. 5, 8.
7. The **prayer of faith** is faith's dependence—Jas. v. 15.

751. "SHALL BE GIVEN"

1. **Provision.** "Bread shall be given him" (Isa. xxxiii. 16).
2. **Promise.** "Ask, and it shall be given you" (Matt. vii. 7).
3. **Power.** "It shall be given you in that same hour" (Matt. x. 19).
4. **Addition.** "Whosoever hath, to him shall be given" (Matt. xiii. 12).
5. **Reward.** "Give, and it shall be given unto you" (Luke vi. 38).
6. **Fellowship.** "Through your prayers I shall be given" (Philemon 22).
7. **Glory.** "The kingdom shall be given to the saints" (Dan. vii. 27).

752. "SHALL COME"

THINGS that "shall come" in the future.

1. "Shall come" of **Separation** (Matt. xiii. 49).
2. "Shall come" of **Glory** (Matt. xvi. 27).
3. "Shall come" of **Fulfilment** (Matt. xxiii. 36).
4. "Shall come" of **Antichrist** (Matt. xxiv. 5; 1 John ii. 18).
5. "Shall come" of **Judgment** (Matt. xxv. 31).

6. "Shall come" of **Return** (Luke xii. 38).

7. "Shall come" of **Gathering** (Luke xiii. 29).

8. "Shall come" of **Ensnarement** (Luke xxi. 35, 36).

9. "Shall come" of **Outpouring** (Acts ii. 17).

10. "Shall come" of **Refreshing** (Acts iii. 19).

11. "Shall come" of **Peril** (2 Tim. iii. 1).

12. "Shall come" of **Assurance** (Heb. x. 37).

13. "Shall come" of **Scoffers** (2 Peter iii. 3).

14. "Shall come" of **Preservation** (Rev. xii. 10).

753. "SHALL COME TO PASS"

THIS sentence in relation to the fulfilment of prophecy occurs in Zechariah many times.

1. **Rebuilding** of the Temple. "Build in the temple of the Lord...this shall come to pass if ye will...obey" (vi. 15).

2. **Restoration**. "It shall come to pass...ye shall be a blessing" (viii. 13).

3. **Identification**. "Shall come to pass...we will go with you" (viii. 20-23).

4. **Judgment**. "Shall come to pass...I will destroy all the nations that come against Jerusalem" (xii. 9; xiii. 2, 3, 4, 8).

5. **Constant Illumination**. "Shall come to pass...at evening time it shall be light" (xiv. 6, 7).

6. **Contention**. "Shall come to pass...his hand shall rise up against his neighbour" (xiv. 13).

7. **Worship**. "Shall come to pass...nations...shall come and worship" (xiv. 16).

754. "SHALL SEE"

1. **Purity of Promise**. "Blessed are the pure in heart for they shall see God" (Matt. v. 8). Purity within is essential to vision without.

2. **Sin and Salvation**. "All flesh shall see the salvation of the Lord" (Luke iii. 6). A consciousness of sin will make us appreciate the call of the Saviour.

3. **Opened Heaven and an Open Way**. "Hereafter (from henceforth) ye shall see Heaven opened" (John i. 51). Christ by His Blood has opened Heaven, and brings Heaven down to us in its supply.

4. **Spirit and Sight**. "Shall see visions" (Acts ii. 17) is one of the outcomes of the Spirit's ministry. We need the vision to fill our vocation.

5. Promise and Prospect. "We shall see Him...and be like Him" (1 John iii. 2). The promise is we "shall see Him," and the prospect is "we shall be like Him."

6. Seed and Satisfaction. "He shall see His seed...He shall see of the travail of His soul and be satisfied" (Isa. liii. 10, 11). He died to have us, and it was for us He died.

7. Person and Partnership. "A little while and ye shall see Me" (John xvi. 16, 17, 19, 22). We shall share what He has gone to prepare, when He comes back.

755. "SHED"

1. Pursuit of the Sinner. "Their feet are swift to shed blood" (Rom. iii. 15).

2. Propitiation of the Saviour. "Blood...which is shed for many" (Matt. xxvi. 28).

3. Power of the Spirit. "He hath shed forth this" (Acts ii. 33).

4. Love of God in the Heart. "The love of God is shed abroad in our hearts," etc. (Rom. v. 5).

5. Supply of the Spirit. "Which He shed on us abundantly" (Titus iii. 6).

6. Faithful Martyr. "The blood of Thy martyr Stephen was shed" (Acts xxii. 20).

7. World's Crime. "Righteous blood shed on the earth" (Matt. xxiii. 35; Luke xi. 50).

756. SHEEP

1. Straying sheep. "All we like sheep have gone astray" (Isa. liii. 6; 1 Peter ii. 25).

2. Sought sheep. "I have found my sheep" (Luke xv. 6).

3. Kept sheep. "A keeper of sheep" (Gen. iv. 2).

4. Called sheep. "He calleth His own sheep by name (John x. 3).

5. Purchased sheep. "Good Shepherd giveth His life for the sheep" (John x. 11).

6. Hearkening sheep. "My sheep hear My voice" (John x. 27).

7. Loved sheep. "Great Shepherd of the sheep" (Heb. xiii. 20).

757. SHOOK OFF

THE Greek word *apotinasso*, rendered "shook off" in Acts
xxviii. 5, is a cognate word to *apotithemi*. In connection with
the latter term there are several things the believer is told to
shake or put off.

1. The **Works of Darkness**—Rom. xiii. 12.
2. **Former Lusts**—Eph. iv. 22.
3. **Lying**, etc.—Eph. iv. 25.
4. **Anger**, etc.—Col. iii. 8.
5. **Every Weight**—Heb. xii. 1.
6. **All Filthiness**—James i. 21.
7. **All Malice**, etc.—1 Peter ii. 1.

758. SHORTNESS

1. **A Self-righteous Man's Rest**. "The bed is shorter
than a man can stretch himself" (Isa. xxviii. 20).
2. **A Wicked Man's Triumph**. "The triumphing of the
wicked is short" (Job xx. 5).
3. **The Sinner's Deficiency**. "Come short of the glory
of God" (Rom. iii. 23).
4. **A Sad Want**. For a saint to "come short" of God's rest
(Heb. iv. 1).
5. **An Incentive to Work**. "The time is short" (1 Cor.
vii. 29).
6. **The Devil's Knowledge**. "Knoweth he hath but a short
time" (Rev. xii. 12).
7. **The Lord's Discipline**. "In those days the Lord began
to cut Israel short" (2 Kings x. 32).

759. SHOULDERS

1. **Redeemed Shoulders**. "Upon their shoulders"
(Exod. xii. 34).
2. **Representative Shoulders**. "Stones upon the shoulders"
etc. (Exod. xxviii. 12).
3. **Upholding Shoulders**. "He shall dwell between His
shoulders" (Deut. xxxiii. 12).
4. **Strong Shoulders**. "He put them upon his shoulders"
(Judges xvi. 3).
5. **Responsible Shoulders**. "They bare it upon their
shoulders" (Num. vii. 9).

6. Saving Shoulders. "He layeth it on His shoulders" (Luke xv. 5).

7. Governing Shoulder. "The government shall be upon His shoulder" (Isa. ix. 6).

The Lord only needs one shoulder for the government of the world, but He needs both shoulders when He brings home a lost sinner. Note the contrast in the last two Scriptures. The shoulder is a symbol of strength.

760. "SHUT IN"

1. Searching. Six times we have the phrase, "shut him up" or "shut him in" (Lev. xiii. 4, 5, 21, 26, 31, 33). If there was no doubt about a person having leprosy he was not shut up—Lev. xiii. 11, but was shut out of the camp—Lev. xiii. 46. Is there not a needs be to be shut in with the Lord our Priest, that He may search us that He may discover to us any leprosy of sin?

2. Salvation. "The Lord shut him in" (Gen. vii. 16). The Lord had first beckoned Noah to "come thou and all thy house into the ark," and when he had obeyed God's "come in," then he knew he was shut in with the Lord, and was as safe and as secure as the Lord Himself. We who are found in Christ are safer than Noah, for we are not in a ship with the Lord, but we are one with the Lord as the member of the body is one with the head.

3. Supplication. "He went in therefore, and shut the door upon them twain, and prayed unto the Lord" (2 Kings iv. 33). The "therefore" tells us why Elisha shut himself in the room, it was because the son of the Shunammite was dead. "He prayed!" How simple and yet expressive are the words. The only way to quicken dead sinners is to get into touch with them, as Elisha did when he stretched himself seven times on the dead body of the lad; and also to get into touch with the Living God by prayer.

4. Supply. "Thou shalt shut the door upon thee and upon thy sons" (2 Kings iv. 4, 5). Being shut in proclaimed two things, she shut out the world and its help, and she was shut up to God to be supplied. No need is truly met, no progress is ever made, no debt of obligation to the Lord is ever paid, only as we get the oil of the Spirit's unction by waiting in soul faith on God.

5. Safety. "Come, My people, enter thou into thy chambers, and shut thy doors about thee; hide thyself as it were for a little moment, until the indignation be overpast" (Isa. xxvi. 20).

In these words the Lord enjoins His people to protect themselves from danger and judgment. Here is a threefold command: "enter," "shut," and "hide." "Enter" means to enter and abide, and speaks of a deliberate act. "Shut" means to be shut up in the entered place, and embodies the thought of giving one self over, hence a deliberate attitude is suggested; and "hide" comes from a word which means to be dark, hence, to hide is not to be seen. It is in "the chambers" we are to be hid; that is, the enclosure or apartment of the Lord's presence. Jehovah is our Dwelling Place, and hidden in Him no enemy can find us nor ill assail us.

6. **Separation.** "Go shut thyself within thy house" (Ezek. iii. 24). Sometimes the Lord puts an embargo upon the lips of His servants, and leaves sinners to their death and doom. He always expects us to be separated from the world of evil, the ways of sin, and the waywardness of the flesh.

7. **Secrecy.** "When thou prayest, enter into thy closet, and when thou hast shut thy door, pray to thy Father in secret" (Matt. vi. 6). The secret life of prayer is the secret of the life of faith, the labour of love, the reality of hope, the soul of communion, the bond of union, the thrill of joy, the calm of peace, and the assurance of victory. The tap-root of prayer finds its feeder in the river bed of God's being.

8. **Service.** "When the doors were shut...came Jesus" (John xx. 19-23). The commissioner in service is Christ. A vision of the Crucified One is essential to service; peace and joy are the outcome of fellowship with Christ in service; and the breath of the Spirit is the power of service.

761. SIGHT OF SIGHTS

1. "We see Jesus" (Heb. ii. 9).

2. "Before whose eyes Jesus Christ hath been set forth crucified" (Gal. iii. 1).

3. "Looking unto Jesus...who endured the Cross" (Heb. xii. 2).

4. "They shall look upon Me, whom they have pierced" (Zech. xii. 10).

762. SILENCE BEFORE THE LORD

THE Hebrew word for silence and stillness is variously rendered in the following Scriptures, and is indicated in the words which are given in inverted commas; and the use of the word may be taken to indicate what silence before the Lord suggests.

1. **Resting** in the Lord. "Rest" in the Lord (Psa. xxxvii. 7).

2. **Waiting** upon the Lord. "Wait" (Psa. lxii. 5).
3. **Silence** before the Lord. "Held...peace" (Lev. x. 3).
4. **Guidance** from the Lord. "Tarry" (1 Sam. xiv. 9).
5. **Arrested** by the Lord. "Stand still" (Joshua x. 12).
6. **Fellowship** with the Lord. "Be still" (Psa. iv. 4).
7. **Made by the Lord.** "A calm" (Psa. cvii. 29).

763. SIN

1. Sin **weakens the body,** as inferred by Christ: "Go and sin no more," to the impotent man (John v. 14).
2. Sin **impairs the mind,** as is illustrated in the King of Babylon—Dan. iv. 28-34.
3. Sin **robs the soul,** for its wages is death—Rom. vi. 23.
4. Sin **mars the spirit,** for it deceives those who are its votaries—Heb. iii. 13.
5. Sin **darkens the understanding,** as Christ told the Pharisees—John ix. 41.
6. Sin **deafens the spiritual sense,** for it causes us to forget the Lord—Deut. viii. 11, 14.
7. Sin **cripples the memory,** for it causes men to turn away from the truth—2 Tim. iv. 3, 4.

764. SIN AND SINS

1. Sin is the **root.** "Sin in me" (Rom. vii. 20).
   Sins are the **fruit.** "Our sins" (1 John iii. 5).
2. Sin is the **cause.** "Sin wrought in me" (Rom. vii. 17, 18).
   Sins are the **effect.** "Your sins" (Col. ii. 13).
3. Sin tells what **we are.** "Sinners" (Rom. v. 19).
   Sins proclaim what **we have done.** "Sins" (1 Tim. v. 24).
4. Sin is **condemned.** "Condemned sin" (Rom. viii. 3).
   Sins are **forgiven.** "Forgiveness of sins" (Acts xxvi. 18).
5. Deliverance **from sin** as a master in Christ—Rom. vi. 10.
   Sins remitted. "Remission of sins" (Matt. xxvi. 28).
6. Sin in the believer, **latent.** "If we say we have no sin" (1 John i. 8).
   Sins, the **habit of life,** forsaken. "Not commit sin" (1 John iii. 9).
7. Sin is not the **believer's master.** "Sin shall not have dominion over you" (Rom. vi. 14).
   Believers are **"dead to sins"** (1 Peter ii. 24).

765. SIN

SIN has a soul as well as a body. We have the contents of sin's inness described in 1 Corinthians v. 9-11.

1. The **"fornications"** of unholy intercourse.
2. The **"idolaters"** of self-adulation.
3. The **"adulterers"** of sinful alliance.
4. The **"effeminate"** of personal abuse.
5. The **"abusers"** of beastly act.
6. The **"thieves"** of sacreligious robbery.
7. The **"covetous"** of grabbing avarice.
8. The **"drunkards"** of sinful excess.
9. The **"revilers"** of ungodly opposition.
10. The **"extortioners"** of pilfering greed.

766. SIN IS A "TRESPASS"

SIN is a deviation, a lapse, a falling aside from God's requirement. The word rendered "trespasses" in Matthew vi. 14 (*paraptoma*) is translated "sins" in Ephesians i. 7; ii. 1, 5; "offence" in Romans v. 15, 16, 17, 18, 20; "fault" in Galatians vi. 1; James v. 16; and "fall" in Romans xi. 11. As a man who slips aside from the path falls into the ditch to his hurt, so the sinner by his deviation from the will of God has lapsed from the truth and trespassed against the God of Truth. Let us take each of the above words in their setting, for they illustrate the meaning of the word "trespass."

1. **Every offence** against God's Word means a fall from God, and damage to us and to others. See the word "offence" in Romans iv. 25; v. 15; 16, 17, 18, 20.

2. **Every departure** from God means a fall from the Divine purpose. See what the Spirit says about the "fall" of Israel in Romans xi. 11, 12.

3. **Every sin** committed is a medium to convey spiritual death and condemnation. See the description of the condition of the Colossian and Ephesian believers before conversion— Col. ii. 13; Eph. ii. 1, 5.

4. **Every slip** from the path of right and duty is damaging to the one who slips. See the word "fault" in Galatians vi. 1 and James v. 16.

5. **Every trespass** is a falling aside from God Himself, and is an affront to Him, which He alone can forgive, but which He does when He acts in grace, for He "forgives our trespasses" through the Blood of Christ's satisfying and vicarious death. See the word "trespass" and "sins" in Matthew vi. 15; 2 Corinthians v. 19; Ephesians i. 7; Colossians ii. 13.

767. SIN IS INIQUITY

INIQUITY is that which is distorted, hence that which is wrong and perverse.

1. "Iniquity in the holy things" (Exod. xxviii. 38) is to do wrong in our service for God.

2. "Iniquities prevail against me" (Psa. lxv. 3). The power of sin over the individual.

3. "Brought low for their iniquity" (Psa. cvi. 43). Sin's humbling and depriving power.

4. "People laden with iniquity" (Isa. i. 4). Aggressiveness of sin's burden.

5. "For your iniquities ye have sold yourself" (Isa. l. 1). Bondage and bitterness of sin.

6. "Your iniquities have separated between Me and you" (Isa. lix. 2). The separating power of sin.

7. "I will punish you for all your iniquities" (Amos iii. 2). Sin brings its own punishment, for the one who breaks God's law is broken by the law he breaks.

768. SIN—ITS FACT

1. Nature proclaims it, for it is under its curse—Gen. iii. 17.

2. Man acknowledges it, like the Prodigal, he says, "I have sinned" (Luke xv. 21).

3. Law discovers it, for by the law is the knowledge of it—Rom. iii. 20.

4. God declares it, for He says, "Because of thy sins" (Micah vi. 13) "I will make thee sick."

5. Christ reveals it, for His holiness makes men like Isaiah say, "I am undone" (Isa. vi. 5).

6. Experience proves the fact of sin, like the Psalmist, it forces from us the confession, "I have sinned against Thee" (Psa. li. 4).

7. The believer knows it, for like Paul, we say, "I know in me dwelleth no good thing" (Rom. vii. 18).

769. SIN—ITS NATURE

THE meaning of the word to sin is, to miss the mark. It is rendered "miss" in Judges xx. 16. The mark in the Old Testament is the Law; and in the New, Christ.

1. Judas missed the mark of love to Christ in betraying Him—Matt. xxvii. 4.

2. The **prodigal** missed the mark of contentment in the Father's will by having his own will—Luke xv. 18, 21.

3. The **impotent man** missed the mark of God's law in sinning against himself—John v. 14.

4. The **adulterous woman** missed the mark of purity by her sin—John viii. 11.

5. The **angels** missed the mark of God's glory by their pride—2 Peter ii. 4.

6. **Israel** missed the mark of God's rest by their unbelief—Heb. iii. 17.

7. The **sinner** misses the mark of God's salvation by refusing Christ in His atonement—Heb. x. 26.

8. The **heretic** misses the mark of God's truth by his error—Titus iii. 11.

770. SIN OF NOT DOING

SOME of the greatest punishments come to people because of what they have not done.

1. Meroz is **cursed** for not helping—Judges v. 23.

2. Those who **love not** the Lord come under His anathema—1 Cor. xvi. 22.

3. The nations that **do not** minister to Christ's brethren go away into eternal punishment—Matt. xxv. 40-46.

4. Those who **know not** God and have not obeyed the Gospel are banished from the Lord's presence—2 Thess. i. 8.

5. **Not to believe** on Christ is the sin of sins—John xvi. 9.

> "It is not the things you do, friend,
> It's the things you leave undone,
> That cause the heartache
> At the setting of the sun."

771. SIN'S INDELIBILITY

"Some men's sins...follow after" 1 Tim. v. 24

WHILE at the World's Fair in St. Louis, I saw the telautograph—an instrument for electrically reproducing at a distance a person's own handwriting or similar matter. I walked over to the booth, took up a pencil having wire attachments, and scribbled my name on a paper pad, when, lo! a miracle occurred. On a perpendicular white surface, about fifteen feet distance, an apparently invisible hand was tracing an exact duplicate of my copy. As I turned to leave the booth I destroyed the page upon which I had written, but there on the wall was that which was beyond my reach and power to destroy.

What a man does stamps itself indelibly on his own personality, and he carries with him the imprint of all his acts. We have many illustrations in the Word of the fact that sin's impress is stamped upon the sinner, hence, in the characters produced we have warning adduced.

1. **Pharaoh's** hardness of heart is a warning against unbelief —Exod. viii. 19.

2. **Cain's self-will** is a beacon against self-action—Jude 11.

3. **Korah's pride** is a danger-signal against self-inflation— Jude 11.

4. The disobedience of **Lot's wife** and God's judgment upon her is a warning against self-will—Luke xvii. 32.

5. **Balaam's** covetousness is a beacon against greed— 2 Peter ii. 15.

6. **Saul's self-action** is a warning against the sin of self-dependence—1 Sam. xv. 22, 23.

7. **Belshazzar's** downfall is a warning against the course of desecration and sin—Dan. v. 22, 30.

772. SINNER COMPARED TO MANY THINGS
1. The uncleanness of the **dog**—Prov. xxvi. 11.
2. The fierceness of the **leopard**—Dan. vii. 6.
3. The subtlety of the **serpent**—Matt. xxiii. 33.
4. The ravening of the **lion**—Psa. xxii. 13.
5. The stupidity of the **sheep**—Isa. liii. 6.
6. The cunning of the **fox**—Luke xiii. 32.
7. The poison of the **viper**—Matt. xxiii. 33.
8. The cruelty of the **bear**—Dan. vii. 5.
9. The wallowing of the **sow**—2 Peter ii. 22.
10. The wasting of the **boar**—Psa. lxxx. 13.
11. The devouring of the **wolf**—John x. 12.
12. The stubbornness of the **ass**—Job xi. 12.

773. SIN—WHAT IS IT?
1. "Sin is **transgression** of the law." (Lawlessness—1 John iii. 4, cf. R.V.)

2. A **grievous malady**, contaminating the whole of man's being—Isa. i. 4, 5; Rom. iii. 10-18.

3. An **obscuring cloud**, which hides the face of God's blessing—Isa. lix. 2.

4. A **binding cord**, which holds man in its power—Prov. v. 22.

5. A **tyrannical owner**, who embitters the lives of his slaves—Neh. ix. 37.

6. A **disturber of rest**, which causes disorder and anxiety—Psa. xxxviii. 3.

7. A **robber of blessing**, which strips and starves the soul—Jer. v. 25.

8. A **terrible devastation**, which brings untold desolation—Micah vi. 13.

9. A **tripper-up**, which continually overthrows the sinner to his hurt—Prov. xiii. 6.

10. A **record writer**, which leaves its indelible mark upon the committer—Jer. xvii. 1.

11. A **betraying presence**, which "will out" no matter what pains are taken to hide it—Ezek. xxi. 24.

12. A **sure detective**, which turns upon the sinner and finds him out—Num. xxxii. 23.

13. An **accusing witness**, which points its condemning finger at the prisoner in the bondage of sin—Isa. lix. 12.

14. A **sum of addition**, which accumulates its weight to the condemnation of the sinner—Isa. xxx. 1.

774. SINS AGAINST THE HOLY SPIRIT

"They rebelled, and vexed His Holy Spirit" Isa. lxiii. 10

A FEW years ago a pioneer in Northern Canada had a pet dove, which he cherished as his own child. He used to spend his evenings reading with the dove gently cooing on his shoulder, and when he woke up in the morning it used to fly and nestle close to his face. In fact, they were inseparable. One day the man came home drunk, and the dove, not knowing his condition, flew as it used to, and lighted on his shoulder, close to his face. With an oath the man shook himself, and, being unaccustomed to such treatment, the dove flew to the window-sill, where it looked around, astonished at its master. After a little while, longing for the usual caress, the dove tried again, and this time perched not so near his face. With another terrible oath the man reeled back, and tried to hit the bird. It seemed as if the bird would fly out this time, but still hoping, as it were, that it was only a sudden fit, and its master would be normal soon, after quite a little while it made another attempt, this time landing on the very extremity of his shoulder, and looked around with a timid and frightened look. The man, as if in a fit of devilish rage, broke forth in terrible curses, and reeling back, he hit the dove with his fist. The poor, wounded bird flew to the window, and, stopping for a moment, it looked around with a look of pain and despair, and then flew out, never to return. How often we treat the Holy Spirit in that very same way; we slam, as it were, the door in His face. No wonder the Scripture likens Him to a dove. Could you have anything more gentle, tender, and faithful, and yet how easily disturbed and frightened away?

1. The Spirit may cease to "strive" through **disobedience**— Gen. vi. 3; 1 Peter iii. 20.

2. The Spirit may be **lied** against by evil promise and untruth—Acts v. 9.

3. The Spirit may be **resisted** by opposition to the truth— Acts vii. 51.

4. We may "**grieve**" the Spirit by inconsistency—Eph. iv. 30.

5. We may "**quench**" the Spirit by discouraging others— 1 Thess. v. 19.

6. We may do "**despite**" to the Spirit by rejecting Christ— Heb. x. 29.

7. We shall be walking after the flesh in **opposition**, if we do not walk after the Spirit—Rom. viii. 4, 5.

775. SINS OF THE BODY

SOMETIMES in thinking of the welfare of the soul, we bring woe to the body.

1. Sins of **unholy passion**. When the flesh has sway, the spirit goes under—Gal. v. 19-21.

2. Sins of **unbridled appetite**. The desire for strong drink is the worst of these—Eph. v. 18.

3. Sins of **expensive adornment**. A small mind is seen in a dressy body—1 Peter iii. 3.

4. Sins of **not yielding** the body to the Lord's keeping— Rom. xii. 1.

5. The sin of **not recognising** that the members of the body are the members of Christ—1 Cor. vi. 15.

6. The sin of **not keeping** the body under the Spirit— 1 Cor. ix. 27.

7. The sin of **not treating** the body as the temple of the Holy Spirit—1 Cor. iii. 16.

8. The sin of **not remembering** the body belongs to Christ— 1 Cor. vi. 20, R.V.

776. SINS OF GOD'S PEOPLE

WHEN we turn to the pages of God's Word we find that the origin of many evils we have to-day, and which have been, would never have arisen if God's people had been true to Him in the past.

1. If **Abram** had not listened to the voice of Sarah in committing fornication with Hagar, there would have been no Arab difficulty to-day—Gen. xvi. 2, 12, 15; xxi. 21.

2. If **Lot** had never gone down to Sodom and been associated with Sodom in marrying a Sodomite, his nameless wife would never have been turned into a pillar of salt—Gen. xix. 26.

3. If **Lot** had not got drunk and committed incest with his daughters, the nations of Moabites and the Ammonites, which became such scourges to Israel, would never have been in existence—Gen. xix. 30-38.

4. If **Jacob** had guarded his daughter Dinah, as he should have done, his sons would not have committed murder in slaying her seducer and the innocent men affiliated with Shechem —Gen. xxxiv.

5. But for the evil of concubinage, **Amalek**, Israel's enemy, would never have been in existence—Gen. xxxvi. 12.

6. But for the evil influence of **Balaam**, the children of Israel would not have committed fornication with the daughters of Moab—Num. xxv.; Rev. ii. 14.

7. But for the sin of **David** in committing adultery with Bath-sheba, the enemies of the Lord would not have had occasion to blaspheme—2 Sam. xii. 14.

8. But for the **sinning brother** in the Church of Corinth, the leaven of wickedness would not have been present, and the evil would not have been allowed to remain if the Church had not been in a carnal state—1 Cor. v. 1-7.

9. The strictures from Christ upon the **Churches in Asia** would not have been made if they had been in a right condition— Rev. ii. and iii.

777. SINS OF THE MIND

THE mind within is the sum total of what we are. "As a man thinketh in his heart, so is he" (Prov. xxiii. 7).

1. The **corrupt mind** of evil thoughts. The sin of the heart within is no less a sin—Matt. v. 27, 28.

2. The **proud mind** of self-esteem. To mind "high things" is to evidence we are puffed up with "conceit" (Rom. xii. 16).

3. The **doubting mind** of unbelief. Not to remember Christ's words is to stifle faith. Doubts will arise if we do not believe—Luke xxiv. 38.

4. The **worrying mind** of anxiety. Worry never helps, it always hinders—Luke xii. 29, margin.

5. The **cumbered mind** of over-carefulness. Burdened with care we shall not reach the better part—Luke x. 40-42.

6. The **selfish mind** of grab. To only think of present things is to miss the essential thing of being rich towards God—Luke xii. 17-21.

7. The **ambitious mind** of self-esteem. To want to be great to the exclusion of others is to be antichrist—Luke ix. 46-48.

778. SKINS

1. **An Atoning Skin.** "The Lord God made coats of skin" (Gen. iii. 21).

2. **A Memorial Skin.** "The priest shall have to himself the skin" (Lev. vii. 8).

3. **A Leprous Skin.** See the expression, "in the skin," in Leviticus xiii., which occurs about thirty times.

4. **A Burned Skin.** "Shall burn in the fire their skins" (Lev. xvi. 27).

5. **A Purified Skin.** "Purify all your raiment and all vessels of skin" (Num. xxxi. 20, margin).

6. **A Broken Skin.** "My skin is broken" (Job. vii. 5).

7. **An Unchangeable Skin.** "Can the Ethiopian change his skin?" (Jer. xiii. 23).

779. SNARES

A SNARE is that which entraps us to our damage, holds us to our loss of liberty, and hinders us from doing good.

1. The snare of **evil companionship**—Joshua xxiii. 3.

2. The snare of a **designing enemy**—Psa. xci. 3.

3. The snare of the **wicked**, who forget God's Word—Psa. cxix. 110.

4. The snare of the **proud** and froward—Psa. cxl. 5; Prov. xxii. 5.

5. The snare of the **fleshly woman**—Prov. vii. 23.

6. The snare of "**an evil time**" (Eccles. ix. 12).

7. The snare of an **ungodly** prophet—Hosea ix. 8.

780. "SO"

WORDS are windows to let the light of thought in. Small words have their mission as well as large ones. "So" frequently occurs in the book of Nehemiah. We give a few instances.

1. **The "So" of Prayer.** "So I prayed" (ii. 4). Nehemiah sandwiched the "request" of the king and his answer with prayer.

2. **The "So" of Purpose.** "So I came" (ii. 11). He did not sit idly at home when the Lord's work called away.

3. **The "So" of Plod.** "So we built" (iv. 6, 10, 18, 21). Difficulties, enemies, rubbish, and discouragements did not hinder.

4. **The "So" of Perseverance.** "So that I cannot come down" (vi. 3). The cure for mischief-makers is to keep on with the Lord's work.

5. **The "So" of Perfection.** "So the wall was finished" (vi. 15). Thus prayer fed purpose, and purpose helped plod, and plod was crowned with perfection.

6. **The "So" of Personality.** "So did I" (v. 15). The man of God does not walk in sin's ways, nor according to his own wishes.

7. **The "So" of Power.** "So the Levites stilled all the people" (viii. 11). According to the law they acted, and so influenced others to be still.

781. SORROWFUL ONES

1. **A Sorrowful Sinner.** "The king was *sorry*" (Matt. xiv. 9).

2. **A Sorrowful Saviour.** "He began to be *sorrowful*" (Matt. xxvi. 37).

3. **A Sorrowful Seeker.** "He went away *sorrowful*" (Matt. xix. 22).

4. **A Sorrowful Servant.** "Peter was *grieved*" (John xxi. 17).

5. **A Sorrowful Spirit.** "*Grieve** not the Holy Spirit" (Eph. iv. 30).

6. **A Sorrowful Saint.** "If thy brother be *grieved*,"* etc. (Rom. xiv. 15).

7. **A Sorrowful Set.** "They were exceeding *sorrowful*" (Matt. xvii. 23; xxvi. 22).

* The Greek word " *lupeo* " occurs in each of the above Scriptures, as indicated by the italics.

782. SONSHIP

1. Constitution of Sonship—**Life**. "Begotten of God" (John i. 13, R.V.).

2. Right of Sonship—**Grace**. "To them gave He the right (margin) to become the sons of God" (John i. 12).

3. Assurance of Sonship—**The Spirit**. "The Spirit Himself beareth witness with our spirit that we are the children of God" (Rom. viii. 16, R.V.).

4. Outcome of Sonship—**Heirship**. "If children, then heirs" (Rom. viii. 17).

5. Trait of Sonship—**Love**. "As dear children, walk in love" (Eph. v. 1, 2).

6. Proof of Sonship—**Holiness**. "Walk as children of light" (Eph. v. 8).

7. Power of Sonship—**Blamelessness**. "Blameless and harmless, the sons of God, without rebuke" (Phil. ii. 15).

8. Evidence of Sonship—**Obedience**. "As obedient children," etc. (1 Peter i. 14).

9. Calling of Sonship—**Assurance**. "Called the sons of God" (1 John iii. 1).

10. Manifestation of Sonship—**Godliness**. "In this the children of God are manifest" (1 John iii. 10).

783. SOULISH LIFE

THE soul is the seat of feeling, and that which is associated with the present order of things and self.

1. **Self** is the **centre** of the soulish life—John xii. 24-27.

2. **Present things** and gain is the occupation of the soulish life"—Luke xii. 47.

3. A soulish life is concerned with the **necessities of this life** and anxious about them—Matt. vi. 25.

4. A soulish life is **dominated by its senses**—Jude 19.

5. A soulish life is **influenced by the flesh**—James iii. 15.

6. A soulish life is dominated by the **mind of envy**. The word "minds" in Acts xiv. 2 is the same as rendered "souls" in other places.

7. A soulish life is a life which is influenced by **its own thought**—Acts xv. 24.

784. SOUND THINGS

1. A Sound Heart. "Let my heart be sound in Thy statutes" (Psa. cxix. 80; Prov. xiv. 30).

2. A Sound Mind. "The spirit of love, and of a sound mind" (2 Tim. i. 7).

3. A Sound Speech. "Sound speech, that cannot be condemned" (Titus ii. 8).

4. A Sound Doctrine. "Things which become sound doctrine" (Titus ii. 1).

5. A Sound Believer. "Sound in faith, in love, in patience" (Titus ii. 2).

6. Sound in the Faith. "That they may be sound in the faith" (Titus i. 13).

7. A Sound Wisdom. Keep sound wisdom and discretion" (Prov. iii. 21).

785. "SPENT"

1. A Sorry Confession. "I have spent my strength for nought" (Isa. xlix. 4).

2. A Useless Quest. "Spent all she had, and was nothing bettered" (Mark v. 26).

3. A Wasted Life. "Spent all" (Luke xv. 14).

4. An Aimless Occupation. "Spent their time in nothing else" (Acts xvii. 21).

5. A Sure Consequence. "Your strength shall be spent in vain" (Lev. xxvi. 20).

6. A Noble Example. "Gladly spend and be spent for you" (2 Cor. xii. 15).

7. An Inspiring Fact. "The night is far spent and the day is at hand" (Rom. xiii. 12).

786. "SPENT ALL"

1. When the **woman** had spent all, she came to Jesus—Mark v. 26, 27.

2. When the **prodigal** had spent all, he came to his father—Luke xv. 14-20.

3. When the **Egyptians** had spent all, they came to Joseph—Gen. xlvii. 18.

4. When the two **debtors** had nothing to pay, the creditor forgave them both—Luke vii. 42.

787. SPECIFIED NEED

WE must name the kind of mercy we need if we would experience the ministry of mercy. Answered prayer is the meeting of specified need, hence—

1. David cried for **pardon**—Psa. li. 9.
2. Peter for **salvation**—Matt. xiv. 30.
3. Leper for **cleansing**—Mark i. 40.
4. Dying thief for **remembrance**—Luke xxiii. 42.
5. Publican for **mercy**—Luke xviii. 13.
6. The Syrophenician woman for **help**—Matt. xv. 25.
7. The blind man for **sight**—Mark x. 51.

We must know what we want if we would know the Lord who can meet it.

788. SPIRITISM

"The doctrine of demons" 1 Tim. iv. 1, R.V.

WE are warned against the doctrine or teaching of having to do with the dead. The departed do not come back, but demons may impersonate them.

1. **Command.** Leviticus xix. 31, where we have a distinct command not to turn to those who have familiar spirits: "Turn ye not unto them which have familiar spirits."

2. **Cut Off.** In Leviticus xx. 6, Jehovah declares that those who resort to the dead can have no fellowship with Him, for He says: "I will even set My face against" them.

3. **Prohibition.** In Deuteronomy xviii. 10-12, the Lord prohibits having to do with those who inquire of the dead, for the meaning of a "necromancer" is one who inquires of the dead.

4. **Separation.** From the experience of King Saul, we know that those who resort to the dead are forsaken by God— 1 Sam. xxviii. 6-13; Isa. xix. 3, R.V.; xxix. 4.

5. **Abomination.** Those who are associated with the dead are said to be "evil," and are an abomination unto the Lord— Deut. xviii. 14; 2 Kings xxi. 6.

6. **Condemnation.** A special judgment from God comes upon those who have to do with the dead—2 Chron. xxxiii. 6; 1 Chron. x. 13, 14.

7. **Darkness.** Those who have to do with the dead are in the darkness of heathenism, and have no light of morning as to the future—Isa. viii. 19, 20, R.V.

8. **Deception.** Those who consort with the dead are deceived by demons who impersonate the departed, for that is what is meant by the "doctrine of demons" (1 Tim. iv. 1, R.V.).

789. SPIRITUAL BLESSINGS
IN EPHESIANS I

1. **Chosen** in His Love—5.
2. **Predestined** in His Purpose—5.
3. **Accepted** in His Beloved—6.
4. **Redeemed** by His Blood—7.
5. **Sealed** by His Spirit—13.
6. **Illuminated** by His Wisdom—17.
7. **Quickened** by His Power—19, 20.

790. SPIRITUAL GRACE FROM GOD
IN EPHESIANS

1. **Supply of Grace**—i. 2.
2. **Standing in Grace**—i. 6.
3. **Salvation by Grace**—ii. 5, 8.
4. **Splendour through Grace**—ii. 7.
5. **Service with Grace**—iii. 2, 7, 8; iv. 7.
6. **Speaking like Grace**—iv. 29.
7. **Supplicating for Grace**—vi. 24.

791. STANDING IN THE WILL OF GOD

"Stand perfect and complete in all the will of God" (Col. iv. 12).
THE wind was blowing the rain across the field, and drenching
everything in its onward rush. A wise old horse in the field
had gone under a sheltering tree, and had turned its back on
the wind, and thus, standing with it, did not feel the blast of
the storm as it would have done had it faced the elements.
The horse's sagacity set the writer pondering, and it said to
him, "Stand with the will of God under the shelter of the Cross,
and you will find things will not be as bad as if you were opposing
it." The will of God is:

1. The **deliverance** from this present evil world—Gal. i. 4.
2. To **serve** the Lord in the daily avocation—Eph. vi. 6.
3. To **work out** our salvation by His willing and working—
Phil. ii. 12, 13.
4. To **thank God** for everything—1 Thess. v. 18.
5. To **be transformed** to prove His will is perfect, good
and acceptable—Rom. xii. 2.
6. To **put to silence by "well doing"** the ignorance of men
—1 Peter ii. 15.
7. To **endure** for ever by **not loving** the world—1 John ii. 17.

792. STANDARD FOR WORKERS
"ACCORDING TO"

1. The Worker's **Authority.** "According to the Scriptures"
2. The Worker's **Message.** Christ died and rose again "according to the Scriptures" (1 Cor. xv. 3, 4).
3. The Worker's **Supply.** "According to the riches of His glory" (Phil. iv. 19).
4. The Worker's **Power.** "According to His glorious power" and "working" (Col. i. 11, 29).
5. The Worker's **Responsibility.** To walk "after" (according to) "the Spirit" (Rom. viii. 4).
6. The Worker's **Prayer.** "According to His will" (1 John v. 14).
7. The Worker's **Reward.** "I will give...according to your works" (Rev. ii. 23).

793. STANDING IN GOD'S PRESENCE

1. **The Place of Confession.** "We are before Thee in our trespasses" (Ezra ix. 15).
2. **The Place of Worship.** "To stand before the Lord to minister unto Him and to bless His Name" (Deut. x. 8; 2 Chron. xxix. 11).
3. **The Place of Service.** "To stand to minister in the Name of Jehovah" (Deut. xviii. 5, 7).
4. **The Place of Judgment.** "The men...shall stand before the Lord" (Deut. xix. 17).
5. **The Place of Fellowship.** "As the Lord God of Israel liveth, before whom I stand" (1 Kings xvii. 1).
6. **The Place of Empowerment.** "As the Lord of Hosts liveth, before Whom I stand" (1 Kings xviii. 15).
7. **The Place of Independence.** "As the Lord liveth before whom I stand, I will receive none" (2 Kings v. 16).

794. STARS
"He made the stars also" Gen. i. 16

THE stars are associated with—

1. The **promise** of His purpose—Gen. xv. 5; xxii. 17.
2. The **omniscience** of His power—Psa. cxlvii. 4.
3. The **reward** of His grace—Dan. xii. 3.
4. The **succour** of His help—Amos v. 8, 9.
5. The **diversity** of His glorified ones—1 Cor. xv. 41.
6. The **coming** of His judgment—Isa. xiii. 10.
7. The **glory** of the Coming Christ—Num. xxiv. 17; Rev. xxii. 16.

795. STEPHEN
A Study in Acts vi and vii

He was a man—

1. **"Full of Faith"** (vi. 5). "Faith is the subtle chain which binds us to the infinite," so writes one. Faith has three main traits: it is the act of the will in receiving Christ—John i. 12; it is accent of the life in obedience to God—Acts v. 29, 32, and it is the consent of the heart in leaving things in His hands—2 Cor. iv. 13, 14. To be "full of faith" means there is no room for doubt, nor fear in the heart, even as there is no room for anything else in a full vessel.

2. **"Full of Grace"** (r.v. vi. 8). Grace means more than favour; it is favour on God's side, and signifies receiving everything for nothing when we do not deserve anything. It shows itself in various ways: it is strength to equip us—2 Cor. xii. 9, salt to preserve us—Col. iv. 6, beauty to beautify us—Acts xi. 23, fragrance to perfume us—Acts iv. 33, life to ennoble us —2 Tim. ii. 1, power to use us—1 Cor. xv. 10, and liberality to bless us—1 Cor. viii. 7-9. When the tree is full of sap, it will be abundant in fruit.

3. **"Full of Power"** (vi. 8). Power is the ability to do things. We have often seen a notice outside a warehouse to let, "To be let with power," so that when a tenant goes into possession he finds there is an electric plant to move things. The Lord never asks us to do anything without giving us the power to do it. With every precept there is a promise. We need to be empty in order that He may fill us, then He will fill us.

4. **Full of Light**—vi. 15. The light within caused Stephen's face to be radiant without, was the Holy Spirit within. His face was like the face of an angel. Sin makes us ugly, but the grace of God makes us beautiful.

5. **Full of Scripture**—vii. If chapter seven is read through or recounted, it will be found that Stephen related the history of God's dealings with the nation of Israel from the call of Abraham to the rejection of Christ.

6. **Full of Courage**—vii. 51. The face and fear of man did not affect Stephen. He did not hesitate to charge those who were opposing the work of the Lord with being "stiff-necked and uncircumcised," also of resisting the Holy Spirit, with not keeping God's law, and with murdering the Lord Jesus—vv. 51-53. His conviction and courage had their after result in the conversion of Paul, for, as Augustine has said, "But for Stephen's prayers and testimony, the Church would not have had the Apostle Paul."

7. Full of Love—vii. 60. The stones which the persecutors hurled at Stephen might break his head, but they could not break his heart of love. His lips might be drenched with the blood of persecution, but they could not stay the pouring forth of his love's intercession. When the grace of God in its love fills the heart and mind, it will enable the servant of Christ to suffer any death.

The great lesson to be gathered from the life and testimony of Stephen is, there is no condition in life, there is no office we are called to fill, there is no testimony we may have to bear, and there is no death we may have to face, but Christ is sufficient to carry us through.

796. STEPHEN'S CHARACTERISTICS

Acts vi. 3, 5, 8, 10

STEPHEN was full of grace (R.V.), faith, power, wisdom, and of the Holy Spirit.

1. "Grace" is the blessing from God, and proves itself in graciousness.

2. "Faith" is reliance on God, and evidences itself in obedience to His Word.

3. "Power" is the ability of God, and reveals itself in accomplishments.

4. "Wisdom" is acting like God, and unfolds itself in knowing how to do things like Him.

5. "Full of the Holy Spirit" is living in **communion with God**. As a sculptor produces the beautiful image from the stone by the mallet and chisel of his ability, so the Holy Spirit reproduces the grace of Christ, and His faith, and His power, and His wisdom.

797. STEPHEN'S SHINING FACE

Acts vi. 15

HE was doubtless unconscious of the shining of his face, but others saw it. Ask the question: "What is the shining face of an angel like?" A shining face will be—

1. **Beautiful** in expression—S. of Sol. ii. 14.
2. **Coloured** with spiritual health—1 Sam. xvi. 12; xvii. 42.
3. **Clear** from the pimples of sin—Dan. i. 4.
4. **Free from** the "crow's feet" of care—1 Peter v. 7.
5. **Indicative of a pure heart** within—Matt. v. 8.
6. **Tender** in its eyes of sympathy—Luke x. 33.
7. **Firm** in its mouth of testimony—Acts x. 43.

798. STEPS IN CONSECRATION

ILLUSTRATED in Elijah's action on Carmel—1 Kings xviii.

1. **Invitation.** "Come near unto Me" (30).
2. **Reparation.** "He repaired the altar" (30).
3. **Construction.** "He built an altar" (32-34).
4. **Supplication.** "Hear me, O Lord," etc. (36, 37).
5. **Expiation.** "Time of the evening sacrifice" (36).
6. **Consecration.** "The fire of the Lord consumed" (38).
7. **Adoration.** "Fell on their faces," etc. (39).
8. **Extermination.** "Let not one escape" (40).

799. STEPS IN THE CHRISTIAN LIFE

1. The Christian life begins by **receiving** Christ—John i. 12.
2. Then follows **confession** of Him—Rom. x. 10.
3. **Abiding** in Him—John xv. 4.
4. **Following** after Him—Luke ix. 23.
5. **Fidelity** to Him—Rev. iii. 10.
6. **Service** for Him—Rom. xii. 11.
7. **Fellowship** with Him—Phil. iii. 10.

800. STEPS INTO THE DEEPER LIFE.

John xii. 21-33

1. Seeing Jesus the **induction to life**—21.
2. Dying with Him the **prelude** to fruitfulness—24.
3. **Hating the self-life** the way to life that is eternal—25.
4. **Serving the Lord** the privilege of the life that lives—26.
5. **Following Christ** the way to "serve"—26.
6. **Serving Christ** the way to honour and position—26.
7. **Victory over the world** and Satan secured by Christ for us—31.

801. STRAIGHT THINGS

"They went every one straight forward" Ezek. i. 12

THE late Sir Henry Campbell-Bannerman, on his deathbed, said to an old friend: "If people should say of me that I tried always to go straight, there is perhaps no credit to me in that. It may have been mere indolence. The straight road always seemed to me the easiest."

To be straight, and go straight, is the soul and essence of a righteous life. We do well to see we have—

1. Straight **feet** in the walk of life, like the Cherubim—Ezek. i. 9, 12, 23.
2. Straight **action** in dealing with others, for this proves that we are taught by grace—Titus ii. 12.
3. Straight **conduct** in life, like Job the perfect—Job i. 8.
4. Straight **dealing** with others when tempted to do wrong like Joseph—Gen. xxxix. 8, 9.
5. Straight **life** in business, like Daniel the faultless—Dan. vi. 2-4.
6. Straight **witness** in testimony, like Elijah, in dealing with Ahab—1 Kings xviii. 18.
7. Straight **work** in the Lord's service, like Nehemiah—Neh. iv. 6.

802. "STRAIGHT"

1. A **Prayer**. "Make Thy way straight before my face" (Psa. v. 8).
2. A **Command**. "Make straight in the desert a highway for our God" (Isa. xl. 4).
3. A **Prophecy**. "The crooked shall be made straight" (Isa. xl. 4).
4. A **Promise**. "I will go before thee, and make the crooked places straight" (Isa. xlv. 2).
5. An **Illustration**. "The kine took the straight way" (1 Sam. vi. 12).
6. A **Direction**. "Let thine eyelids look straight before thee" (Prov. iv. 25).
7. An **Example**. "Straight feet" and "straight wings" (Ezek. i. 7, 23).

803. "STRIPPED"

1. **The Devil's Work**. "Which stripped Him" (Luke x. 30).
2. **The World's Mockery**. "They stripped Him" (Matt. xxvii. 28).
3. **The People's Humiliation**. "Children of Israel stripped themselves" (Exod. xxxiii. 6).
4. **The Friend's Action**. "Jonathan stripped himself of the robe," etc. (1 Sam. xviii. 4).
5. **The Enemy's Defeat**, "And stripped off his armour" (1 Samuel xxxi. 9).
6. **The Saint's Humbling**. "He hath stripped me of my glory" (Job. xix. 9).
7. **The Lord's Warning**. "Lest I strip her," etc. (Hosea ii. 3).

804. "STRONG"

"The Lord is strong and mighty" (Psa. xxiv. 8).

WHAT the Lord is to His people as the Strong One.

1. "A Strong **Rock**" for defence to save (Psa. xxxi. 2, 3).

2. "A Strong **Tower**" to protect from "the enemy" (Psa. lxi. 3).

3. "A Strong **Habitation**" to home for comfort and protection (Psa. lxxi. 3).

4. "A Strong **Refuge**" to preserve from all ills (Psa. lxxi. 7).

5. "A Strong **Lord**" in the might of His ability to shield all about us (Psa. lxxxix. 8).

6. "A Strong **Hand**" to gain the victory over every opposing force (Psa. cxxxvi. 12).

7. "A Strong **Tower**" is found in the Name of Jehovah to meet every emergency (Prov. xviii. 10).

805. "STRONG" THINGS

1. Abraham was "**strong in faith,**" because he believed what Jehovah said (Rom. iv. 20).

2. Christ in the extremity of His need poured out His soul in prayer in "**strong crying** and tears" (Heb. v. 7).

3. The "**strong meat**" of God's Word is not for babes, but for those who are fully grown in grace and faith (Heb. v. 12, 14).

4. "**Strong consolation**" is found by those who rest in God's faithful Word and oath (Heb. vi. 18).

5. Those who are weak in themselves find they are "**strong**" **in God's grace** (2 Cor. xii. 10).

6. Those who are "**strong in the Lord**" have the ability to put on the whole armour of God (Eph. vi. 10).

7. To be "**made strong**" through the ability of the Lord is to find ourselves capable in His power (Acts iii. 16; 2 Tim. ii. 1).

806. "SUCH"

THE distinctiveness of designated ones and things.

1. "**Such a voice**" of appreciation was heard on the Mount of Transfiguration when the Father commended the Son (2 Peter i. 17).

2. "**Such a High Priest**" we have as described as being "holy, harmless, and undefiled" (Heb. vii. 25, 26).

3. "**Such power**" was made manifest in Christ, that the people were bound to acknowledge it (Matt. ix. 8).

4. **"Such things"** as are produced by wicked men are "worthy of death" (Rom. i. 32).

5. **"Such** as have need of **milk"** are those who are undeveloped in the spiritual life (Heb. v. 12).

6. **"Such sacrifices"** as doing good to others are evidences of grace, and bring glory to God (Heb. xiii. 16).

7. **"Such things** as we have,"** when enjoyed with contentment are always a means of grace (Heb. xiii. 5).

807. "SUDDENLY"

GOD is never before time, nor after, but He oftentimes acts suddenly.

1. A Sudden **Revival**. Cleansing and consecration characterised the revival in the time of Hezekiah, and of that revival it is said, "The thing was done suddenly" (2 Chron. xxix. 36).

2. A Sudden **Arrival**. When Christ was born in Bethlehem, and the angel announced the event, "suddenly a multitude of the heavenly host" was seen with the angel "praising God" (Luke ii. 13).

3. A Sudden **Conversion**. When Saul of Tarsus was on his way to Damascus, "suddenly" there "shined round about him, a light from Heaven" (Acts ix. 3, 4).

4. A Sudden **Release**. When Paul and Silas were imprisoned in Philippi, "suddenly there was a great earthquake, and every one's bands were loosed" (Acts xvi. 25, 26).

5. A Sudden **Blessing**. "And suddenly there came a sound from Heaven...and they were all filled with the Holy Spirit" (Acts ii. 2, 4).

6. A Sudden **Return**. Our Lord's command is to watch for His Coming, "lest coming suddenly He find us sleeping" (Mark xiii. 35, 36).

7. A Solemn **Warning**. The sinner who is often "reproved and hardeneth his neck, shall suddenly be destroyed, and that without remedy" (Prov. xxix. 1).

808. SUPPOSITIONS.

"They supposed" Acts xxi. 29

NINE-TENTHS of surmisings about others are born of suppositions, and the other tenth comes from prejudice.

1. The **disciples** supposed Christ was a ghost, but it was Himself—Mark vi. 49.

2. **Christ** was supposed to be the son of Joseph—Luke iii. 23.

3. **Christ's parents** supposed He was with them—Luke ii. 44.

4. **Mary** supposed Christ was the gardener—John xx. 15.

5. **The jailer** supposed the prisoners had fled—Acts xvi. 27.
But they were all wrong.

809. "SURE THINGS"

1. **A Sure Revelation** in God's Word. "The *sure* word of prophecy" (2 Peter i. 19).

2. **A Sure Promise** to Faith. "Therefore it is of faith, that it might be by grace; to the end that the promise might be *sure* to all" (Rom. iv. 16).

3. **A Sure Election** and Calling by adding to faith what the Lord enjoins. "Make your calling and election *sure*" (2 Peter i. 10).

4. **A Sure Confidence.** "Our confidence *stedfast* unto the end" (Heb. iii. 14). The word "stedfast" is the same as "sure" in the above Scriptures.

5. **A Sure Anchor** of Hope. "Which hope we have as an anchor of the soul, both sure and *stedfast*" (Heb. vi. 19).

6. **A Sure Hold.** "Hold fast the confidence and the rejoicing of the hope *firm* unto the end" (Heb. iii. 6).

7. **A Sure Trust.** "Our hope (trust) of you is *stedfast*" (2 Cor. i. 7).

The words in italics are one and the same in the original.

810. SURPRISES
OF CERTAIN PERSONS

1. **Balaam** was surprised to hear the ass speak—Num. xxii. 28.

2. **Jonah** was surprised to find lodgings in the belly of the sea monster—Jonah i. 17.

3. **Nathanael** was surprised to hear that the Lord had seen him under the fig tree—John i. 48.

4. **Zacchaeus** nearly tumbled off his perch when the Lord told him to come down from the sycamore tree—Luke xix. 5.

5. **Ahab** exclaimed, when Elijah confronted him: "Hast thou found me, O mine enemy?" (1 Kings xxi. 20).

6. **Gehazi** was surprised to find Elisha knew the covetousness of his heart—2 Kings v. 20-27.

7. **Hazael** was surprised when the prophet revealed to him the wickedness of his purpose to oust his master as king—2 Kings viii. 7-15.

811. SWALLOWED UP!

THE word *katapino* means to swallow up, rendered "Drowned" and "Devour" under points 5 and 6.

1. **An Over Nice Critic.** "Swallow a camel" (Matt. xxiii. 24).
2. **A Defunct Enemy.** "Death is swallowed up in victory" (1 Cor. xv. 54).
3. **A Discouraged Believer.** "Swallowed up with overmuch sorrow" (2 Cor. ii. 7).
4. **A Mortal Immortalised.** "Swallowed up of life" (2 Cor. v. 4).
5. **A Defeated Foe.** "Assaying to do were drowned" (Heb. xi. 29).
6. **A Purposeful Adversary.** "Seeking whom he may devour" (1 Peter v. 8).
7. **An Inanimate Helper.** "Swallowed up the flood" (Rev. xii. 16).

812. "TAKE HEED TO THE SURE WORD OF PROPHECY"

1. Because of what it **is**. Jehovah says it is "My Word" (Isa. lv. 11). It is His Word because He is its Author, because it reveals Himself through it, and it is His message to us.

2. Because of what it **promises**. "I will hasten My Word to perform it" (Jer. i. 12; xxix. 10). His promises are cheques payable to bearer, cashed by faith, and enjoyed in communion with Himself.

3. Because of what it **does**. "Is not My Word like as a fire?" (Jer. xxiii. 28, 29). As fire burns and warms, so the Lord's Word warms the heart of the saint to his blessing, and scorches the sinner to his undoing.

4. Because of what it **commands**. "Walk in My statutes, execute My judgments, and keep all My commandments" (1 Kings vi. 11, 12). Mark the "If" of command, coupled with the promise, "I will perform My Word." Precepts obeyed secure pledges given.

5. Because of what it **reveals**. "He that heareth My Word" (John v. 24). This great verse reveals God's love in sending Christ; life is given to those who believe on Christ, the believer is passed out of death into life, those who have life "shall not come into condemnation," and are assured by Christ of their personal safety.

6. Because of what it **contains**. Christ again and again speaks of the message He brings as "My Word" (John v. 24; viii. 31, 37, 43; Rev. iii. 8, 10). This specific covers all He said as "The Word."

7. **Because of what His Words impart.** Ponder the following passages where Christ speaks of "My Words," and it will be found by means of *them*, *He* gives reliability—Matt. xxiv. 35; life—John vi. 63; salvation—John xii. 47, 48; revelation—John xiv. 10; His presence—John xiv. 23; and promise of answered prayer—John xv. 7.

> "Believe His words,
> His words are life and beauty,
> His words command thy duty,
> Believe His words."

813. TEARS

1. **The Tears of Faith.** "Said with tears, Lord, I believe" (Mark ix. 24).

2. **The Tears of Humility.** "Began to wash His feet with tears" (Luke vii. 38).

3. **The Tears of Service.** "Serving the Lord with all humility and many tears" (Acts xx. 19).

4. **The Tears of Admonition.** "Cease not to admonish every one night and day with tears" (Acts xx. 31, R.V.).

5. **The Tears of Concern.** "Out of much affliction and anguish of heart I wrote unto you with many tears" (2 Cor. ii. 4).

6. **The Tears of Sympathy.** "Remembering thy tears" (2 Tim. i. 4, R.V.).

7. **The Tears of Earnest Supplication.** "Supplications with strong crying and tears" (Heb. v. 7).

8. **The Tears of Disappointment.** "Though he sought it carefully with tears" (Heb. xii. 17).

814. "TELL ME"

1. **A Commissioner's Request.** "Tell me, I pray thee?" (Gen. xxiv. 23).

2. **A Conquered One's Plea.** "Tell me, I pray thee thy name?" (Gen. xxxii. 29).

3. **A Leader's Demand.** "Tell me what thou hast done?" (Joshua vii. 19).

4. **A Temptress' Question.** "Tell me, I pray thee?" (Judges xvi. 6, 10, 13).

5. **A Prophet's Inquiry.** "Tell me what thou hast in the house" (2 Kings iv. 2).

6. **A Master's Invitation.** "Tell me what thy wages shall be?" (Gen. xxix. 15).

7. **A Lover's Prayer.** "Tell me, O Thou whom my soul lovest, where Thou feedest?" (Cant. i. 7).

815. "TEMPTATION"

1. **Falling through Temptation**—Psa. xcv. 8; Heb. iii. 8; Luke viii. 13. God's testings are for our tempering, and not for our tripping.

2. **Praying against Temptation**—Matt. vi. 13; xxvi. 41. God never leads us to sin in His tryings, but He does test that we may triumph—James i. 13, 14.

3. **Enduring in Temptation**—Luke iv. 13; James i. 12; Luke xxii. 28. To stand the strain and the pain shows there is metal and material in us.

4. **Delivered from Temptation**—Rev. iii. 10. He keeps out of the crucible sometimes, and certainly keeps the temper under control.

5. **Succour in Temptation**—1 Cor. x. 13; Heb. ii. 18; iv. 15. Satan may hedge us in, but he cannot roof us in.

6. **Taken out of Temptation**—2 Peter ii. 9. His eye is watching, His heart is loving, and his hand is ready to rescue.

7. **Christ our Example in Temptation**—Luke iv. 2, etc. Led by the Spirit, and equipped by His Word and armour, we are, trusting in the Lord, victors.

816. TEN LINKS IN GENESIS I

TEN times in Genesis i. the words "God said" occur.

1. **Illumination.** "God said, Let there be light" (3).

2. **Separation.** "God said, Let there be a firmament" (6).

3. **Manifestation.** "God said...Let the dry land appear" (9).

4. **Production.** "God said, Let the earth bring forth grass" (11).

5. **Indication.** "God said, Let there be lights...to divide the day from the night" (14).

6. **Multiplication.** "God said, Let the waters bring forth abundantly" (20).

7. **Reproduction.** "God said, Let the earth bring forth the living creatures after his kind" (24).

8. **Identification.** "God said, Let us make man in our image" (26).

9. **Benediction.** "God blessed them, and God said...Be fruitful and multiply" (28).

10. **Satisfaction.** "God said, Behold, I have given you every herb bearing seed...to you it shall be for meat" (29).

817. TESTS

"He that judgeth (testeth) me is the Lord" 1 Cor. iv. 4

THERE is in the Mint a marvellously delicate machine for assaying the weight of gold. Sovereigns are made to pass through a tube, and when they come to the end, the machine acts so that those which are overweight are thrown to the right, and those under weight are thrown to the left. Only those of exact weight are allowed to pass on.

There are several things which will be tested at the judgment-seat of Christ.

1. The **"hidden things"** of the inner life will be made to stand out in the light (1 Cor. iv. 5).

2. The **"counsels,"** or the purposes of "the heart," will be manifest as they were known (1 Cor. iv. 5).

3. The **"work"** of the Christian worker will be revealed as to its "sort" (1 Cor. iii. 3).

4. The **character** of the material used in the Lord's service will be revealed—1 Cor. xiii. 11-13.

5. Any **work** that will not stand the test of the revealing fire will be "burnt up" (1 Cor. iii. 15).

6. Our **motives** will be examined and scrutinised as to their purity—2 Cor. v. 9, 10.

7. **Reward** will be given to those who have faithfully served their Lord—Luke xix. 16-19.

818. TESTS TO TRY SPIRITS

THERE are seven tests in 1 John iv., that are useful to test any impression, spirit, or doctrine.

1. Does it **confess the true humanity of Jesus Christ**?—2, 3.

2. Does it confess the **true Divinity of Jesus Christ**?—9. 15.

3. Does it confess the **vicarious atonement** of Jesus Christ?—10, 14.

4. Does it tend to **worldliness**, and to a love of the outward?—4, 5.

5. Do the deeply **spiritually-minded agree** with it?—6.

6. Does it **witness** to the **spirit** of Divine love?—7, 8.

7. Does it accord with the **teaching of God's Holy Spirit**?—13. The teaching of the Holy Spirit is found in the hearts of believers and in the Scriptures which He has inspired. The first of these has been mentioned under test five. We ask, secondly: Does it accord with the Holy Scriptures? Not with one text, but with the combined teaching of God's Word?

819. "THAT DAY" IN ZECHARIAH XIV

THE Day of the Millennium.

1. **Arrival.** "The day of the Lord cometh" (1).

2. **Advent.** "His feet shall stand in that day upon the Mount of Olives" (4).

3. **Phenomenon.** "In that day the light shall not be clear nor dark" (6, 7).

4. **Living Waters.** "In that day living waters shall go out from Jerusalem" (8).

5. **Autocracy.** "In that day there shall be one Lord" (9).

6. **Conflict.** "In that day, a great tumult" (13-15).

7. **Holiness.** "In that day there shall be upon the bells of the horses, holiness unto the Lord" (20).

8. **Separation.** "In that day there shall be no more the Canaanite in the house of the Lord" (21).

820. THE CHRIST MIND

1. **A Right Mind** through Christ. "In his right mind" (Mark v. 15).

2. **A Ready Mind** to Believe in Christ. "Received the Word with all readiness of mind" (Acts xvii. 11).

3. **A United Mind** in the Love of Christ. Joined together in the same mind—1 Cor. i. 10.

4. **A Lowly Mind** in the Humble Christ. "Lowliness of mind...This mind" (Phil. ii. 3, 5).

5. **A Steady Mind** in the Word of Christ. "Be not soon shaken in mind" (2 Thess. ii. 2).

6. **A Girded Mind** in the Truth of Christ. "Gird up the loins of your mind" (1 Peter i. 13).

7. **A Sound Mind** in the Spirit of Christ. "Spirit...of a sound mind" (2 Tim. i. 7).

821. "THE CHURCH OF THE FUTURE"

ACCORDING to the teaching of the Holy Spirit, the professing Church (that is, Christendom, not the spiritual body of Christ) will be a degenerate Church.

1. She will mix with the meal of God's Word the **leaven of Rationalism**—Matt. xvi. 6, as described by Christ in the parable of the leaven—Matt. xiii. 33.

2. She will **admit into her community** the bad company of the evil one—Matt. xiii. 4, 19, 32.

3. She will **depart from the faith** and simplicity of the Gospel—1 Tim. iv. 1.

4. She will **scoff at the truth of the Lord's return**—2 Peter iii. 2-4.

5. She will have a **form of godliness**, and know nothing of its power—2 Tim. iii. 5.

6. She will be **nauseous to the Lord**, because of her lukewarm condition—Rev. iii. 15-17.

7. She will be **supported by the world**, as depicted by the woman sitting on the scarlet beast—Rev. xvii. 3; and her end will be the lake of fire—Rev. xviii. 8.

822. "THE EIGHT SPOTS OF GOD'S CHILDREN"

THE spots are:

1. **Faith**—Galatians iii. 14.
2. **Life**—John i. 12, 13.
3. **Assurance**—Romans viii. 16.
4. **Leading**—Romans viii. 14.
5. **Obedience**—2 Corinthians vi. 15-18.
6. **Persecution**—1 John iii. 1.
7. **Love**—Ephesians v. 1, 2.
8. **Victory**—Revelation xxi. 7.

823. THE FAITH

1. **Miracle** of Christ's **Incarnation**—Luke i. 35; 1 Tim. iii. 16; Heb. ii. 9-14.

2. **Majesty** of His **Deity**—Heb. i. 3; Rom. 1. 4; Luke viii. 28; Matt. xxvii. 54.

3. **Music** of His **Life**—Acts x. 38; John xx. 30, 31; Acts ii. 22.

4. **Manifoldness** of His **Atonement**—Matt. xx. 28; xxvi. 28; Rom. iii. 24, 25.

5. **Might** of His **Resurrection**—Eph i. 19, 20; Rom. viii. 11; 1 Cor. xv. 20-25.

6. **Meetness** of His **Priesthood**—Heb. vii; viii. 1-5; Rom. viii. 27, 34.

7. **Manifestation** of His **Glory**—Col. iii. 4; Phil. iii. 20, 21; 1 John iii. 2.

"The Faith" is the truth of the Gospel. It is important to distinguish between "The Faith," and Faith. Faith is the act of believing, "The Faith" is what we believe.

824. "THE FAITH OF OUR FATHERS"

"Contend for the Faith" Jude 3

At a Church Congress in Plymouth, the Mayor stated: "If we want to maintain England and this great Empire in the future, we can only do so as we bring up our children in the faith of our fathers."

"The Faith" is that upon which our fathers lived—namely, the truth of the Word of God, which may be briefly summarised as follows:

1. **God** in the Livingness of His Personality—1 Tim. iv. 10.

2. **Christ** in the Saviourhood of His Deity—Matt. xvi. 16.

3. The **Atonement** of our Lord in His Substitutionary Sacrifice—Matt. xx. 28.

4. The **Holy Spirit** in the Power of His Sanctity—1 Peter i. 2; 2 Thess. ii. 13.

5. The **Example of Christ** in the Steps of His Life—1 Peter ii. 21.

6. The **Devotion of Christ** in the Work of His Ministry—Acts x. 38.

7. The **Love of God** in the Inspiration of His Influence—1 John iv. 16.

8. The **Word of God** in the Principles of its Truth—Psa. cxix. 142, 151.

9. The **Promises of Jehovah** in the Sufficiency of their Grace—2 Cor. i. 20.

10. The **Coming of Christ** in the Magnetism of its Power—2 Peter i. 16.

Many other traits of the Faith of our fathers might be given, but the above will suffice to indicate the magnificence and many-sidedness of its truth. The Faith of the Bible is a mould to shape us, a magnet to attract us, a larder to feed us, a cordial to strengthen us, a power to lift us, a charm to attract us, a sword to protect us, a goad to stimulate us, a harbour to shelter us, and a fortune to enrich us.

825. THE GOOD SAMARITAN

Illustrated in Christ's Friendship—Luke x. 33-35

If the parable of the Good Samaritan is recalled, there will be found in Christ all the traits of real friendship.

1. The **feet** of friendship. "He came where he was."

2. The **eyes** of friendship. "He saw him." He did not look away, He saw his need and met it.

3. The **heart** of friendship. "He had compassion on him." The heart of his love moved the hand of His help.

4. The **service** of friendship. "He bound up his wounds." etc. He binds up the wounds which sin has made, and pours into the heart the wine of His joy and the oil of His grace.

5. The **selflessness of friendship**. "He put him on his own beast." Christ takes our place in death, and gives us His place in glory.

6. The **care** of friendship. "Took care of him."

7. The **spending** of friendship. "I will repay thee." He thinks, and cares, and provides. Cost proves His care.

826. THE GOSPEL

"The power of God unto salvation" Rom. i. 16

BARON UXKILL, of Russia, has put on record that when an infidel, some uneducated evangelists came on his estate, and were the means in God's hands of effecting such a transformation in the lives of his workmen, that although he cared not for Christ, nor the things which belong to Him, he said, "Anything which will make drunken men sober, and dishonest men honest, and immoral men moral, and indolent men industrious, I want to have on my estate."

The Gospel in its onward progress in the power of the Spirit—

1. Turned persecuting Saul into **praying Paul**—Acts ix. 19.

2. Turned the idolatrous Thessalonians into **servants of the Lord**—1 Thess. i. 9, 10.

3. Turned the early Christians into **consecrated believers**—Acts iv. 33-37.

4. Turned the demon-possessed sinners in Samaria into **rejoicing believers**—Acts viii. 5-8.

5. Turned a puzzled courtier into a **devoted** and **rejoicing** chancellor of the **exchequer**—Acts viii. 27-39.

6. Turned a cruel jailer into a **kind minister**—Acts xvi. 24, 34.

7. Turned the witch-craft people of Ephesus into **confessing adherents** of the Lord—Acts xix. 18.

827. THE HEART AND HAND PSALM
PSALM CVII

KEY expression: "His lovingkindness and His wonderful works" (8, 15, 21, 31)—four times. In His heart, "lovingkindness." Once rendered "mercy" (1); four times "lovingkindness" (8, 15, 21, 31, R.V.); and once "lovingkindness" (43, R.V.). The latter is plural, reckoning as two, "lovingkindness" is mentioned seven times.

There are many traits of Jehovah's lovingkindness, but the following are found in the Psalms. Often the Hebrew word is rendered "mercy," as in Psalm cxxxvi., where it occurs twenty-six times, in the well-known sentence, "His mercy (lovingkindness, R.V.) endureth for ever." His lovingkindness is—

1. "Marvellous" in its acts (Psa. xvii. 7; xxxi. 21).
2. Constant in its attendance—Psa. xxiii. 6, R.V.
3. Compassing in its protection—Psa. xxxii. 10.
4. "Excellent" ("precious," R.V.) in its benediction (Psa. xxxvi. 7).
5. "Better than life" (Psa. lxiii. 3).
6. Multitudinous in benefit—Psa. lxix. 13, R.V.
7. "Good" in nature (Psa. lxix. 16, R.V.).
8. "Plenteous" in resource (Psa. lxxxvi. 15, R.V.).
9. "Great" in exercise (Psa. lxxxvi. 13, R.V.).
10. Satisfying in giving—Psa. xc. 14, R.V.
11. "Everlasting" in duration (Psa. c. 5, R.V.).
12. Crowning in bestowment—Psa. ciii. 4.
13. Quickening in its life—Psa. cxix. 88, 124, 149, 159.

The Hebrew word is translated "deal kindly," "kindness," "mercy," "pity," "favour," "goodness," "good deeds," and "lovingkindness;" and in the following cases illustrations will be found of the "exercise" of God's "lovingkindness" (Jer. ix. 24): thus David pleaded with Jonathan to "deal kindly" with him (1 Sam. xx. 8), David showed "kindness" to Mephibosheth (2 Sam. ix. 1, 3, 7), Jehovah had "mercy" on David (1 Kings iii. 6), Job's expressed "pity" to a friend (Job vi. 14), Ahasuerus gave "favour" to Esther (Esther ii. 17), the "goodness" of Hezekiah in his life (2 Chron. xxxii 32), and the "good deeds" of Nehemiah for the house of God (Neh. xiii. 14).

We do well to recall and recount the lovingkindnesses of our God, for they are recorded for our inspiration and our imitation.

The hand of Jehovah in His loving service is expressed in the repeated sentence, "His wonderful works." His "works" are not merely acts, but "wonderful" ones. The Hebrew word is rendered four times "wonderful works," and once "wonders" in Psalm cvii. (8, 15, 21, 24, 31), and it is also translated "marvellous" (Psa. cxviii. 23), "hidden" (Deut. xxx. 11), "accomplish" (Lev. xxii. 21), and in the form of a question, "too hard" (Gen. xviii. 14).

His "wonderful works" in some of their achievements are described in the Psalm before us.

1. **Redemption.** "Redeemed from the hand of the adversary" (2).*

2. **Election.** "Gathered out of the lands" (3).

3. **Emancipation.** "Delivered them out of their distresses" (6).

4. **Direction.** "He led them by a straight way" (7, R.V.).

5. **Satisfaction.** "He satisfieth the longing soul, and the hungry soul He filleth with good" (9).

6. **Salvation.** "He saved them out of their distresses" (13-19).

7. **Pacification.** "He maketh the storm a calm" (23-32).

8. **Transformation.** "He turneth," etc. (33-37).

9. **Benediction.** "He blesseth," etc. (38-43).

828. THE HOLY SPIRIT

1. The Spirit of Truth to **sanctify.** "The Spirit of Truth" (John xiv. 17).

2. The Spirit of Grace to **beautify.** "Full of the Holy Spirit...Grace" (Acts vi. 5, 8, R.V.).

3. The Spirit of Love to **intensify.** "Love in the Spirit" (Col. i. 8).

4. The Spirit of Life to **fructify.** "Fruit of the Spirit is love" (Gal. v. 22).

5. The Spirit of Liberty to **purify.** "Walk in the Spirit" (Gal. v. 16).

6. The Spirit of Wisdom to **qualify.** "Spirit of Wisdom" (Exod. xxviii. 3).

7. The Spirit of Power to **testify.** "Full of power by the Spirit" (Micah iii. 8).

* The Scripture sentences are from the American Revised Version.

829. THE IDEAL CHURCH

THE ideal Church as revealed in the New Testament, like the New Jerusalem, has twelve gates to it.

1. The Christship of Jesus is the **Foundation of the Church.** "Thou art the Christ...Upon this rock will I build My Church" (Matt. xvi. 18).

2. The Blood of Christ is the **Atoning Price of the Church.** "The Church...which He purchased with His own Blood" (Acts xx. 28).

3. The Holy Spirit is the **Administrator of the Church,** hence, He sets "in the Church" His gifts, severally as He will (1 Cor. xii. 28).

4. The ascended Lord is the **Head of the Church,** His mystical body—Eph. i. 23; v. 23.

5. Love is the **Motive and Moving Power of the Church,** hence, the members are to love each other "as Christ loved the Church" (Eph. v. 2, 5, 25).

6. Prayer is the **Life of the Church,** the power that brings release, even as it did to imprisoned Peter, when prayer was "made without ceasing of the Church unto God" (Acts xii. 5).

7. Worship of the Lord is the **Privilege of the Church,** and Christ is ever the One who in the midst of the Church leads her in praise to God—Heb. ii. 12; and the Church is responsible, as well as privileged, to "come together" to remember the Lord's death—1 Cor. xi. 18-26.

8. Edification, or building each other up, is the **Rule of the Church,** hence, the keynote of all ministry in the Church— 1 Cor. xiv. 5, 12, 19.

9. Unity of action is the **Responsibility of the Church,** hence, there are to be no schisms in the body, but each member is to tarry for one another, and hold the Head by recognising the members in mutual helps and assemblage—Eph. ii. 18-22; iv. 16.

10. The truth of God is in the **Custody of the Church,** hence, the Church of God is the pillar and ground of the truth— 1 Tim. iii. 15.

11. God Himself is the **Centre and Circumference of the Church,** hence, the titles by which it is called, and the place where it is found. It is called "the Church of God," "the Church in God the Father, and the Lord Jesus Christ," "the Church of the Firstborn" (1 Cor. i. 2; 1 Thess. i. 1; Heb. xii. 23).

12. The glory of God is the **End of the Church,** hence, it displays His manifest wisdom and is to be to His manifested glory—Eph. iii. 10, 21; v. 27.

830. THE IGNORANCE OF THE UNSAVED

1. **Without Light.** "They know not the light" (Job xxiv. 16).

2. **Without Perception.** "They know not, neither will they understand" (Psa. lxxxii. 5).

3. **Without Peace.** "The way of peace, they know not" (Isa. lix. 8).

4. **Without the Lord.** "They know not Me, saith the Lord" (Jer. ix. 3; Micah iv. 12).

5. **Without Right.** "They know not to do right" (Amos iii. 10).

6. **Without Knowledge** of Christ and His Mission. "They know not Him that sent Me" (John xv. 21). "They know not what they do" (Luke xxiii. 34; xxiv. 16).

7. **Without Guidance.** "Ye...err, because ye know not the Scriptures" (Mark xii. 24).

831. THE LORD BEFORE HIS PEOPLE
Micah ii. 13

1. **Perpetual Protection.** "The Lord went before them," etc. (Exod. xiii. 21). When the Lord stands between us and any foe we are safe.

2. **Perpetual Keeping.** "Behold, I send an angel before thee to keep thee" (Exod. xxiii. 20). The keeping of the Lord is constant in its attention, comforting in its love, and consecrating in its influence.

3. **Perpetual Victory.** "The Lord your God which goeth before you, He shall fight for you" (Deut. i. 30; ix. 3). No enemy can stand before the skill of His might, nor defeat the purpose of His grace.

4. **Perpetual Service.** "Who went in the way before you" (Deut. i. 33). The Lord had to continually adjust the going of Israel, leading them back into the wilderness because of their unbelief, when they might have gone forward if they had trusted Him.

5. **Perpetual Presence.** "The Lord...doth go before thee, He will be with thee" (Deut. xxxi. 8). The Lord's presence means gladness in sorrow, strength in weakness, and progress in holiness.

6. **Perpetual Rectification.** "I will go before thee, and make the crooked places straight" (Isa. xlv. 2). Difficulties become stepping-stones, and dangers helps, when He goes before.

7. **Perpetual Guidance.** "His own sheep, He goeth before them" (John x. 4). The pastures of His promises, and the placid stream of His peace, are not far distant when He leads.

832. THE LIGHT

1. **Walking** in the Light—1 John i. 7.
2. **Worshipping** in the Light—1 Peter ii. 9.
3. **Warring** in the Light—Rom. xiii. 12.
4. **Working** in the Light—John iii. 21.
5. **Watching** in the Light—John xi. 9.
6. **Witnessing** in the Light—Phil. ii. 15.
7. **Waiting** for Christ in the Light—2 Peter i. 19.

833. THE LORD'S WALK

1. **The Almighty Deliverer.** "The Lord thy God walketh in the midst of thy camp" (Deut. xxiii. 14).
2. **The Arresting Reprover.** "They heard the voice of the Lord walking" (Genesis iii. 8).
3. **The Loving Sustainer.** "I see four men loose walking in the fire" (Dan. iii. 25).
4. **The Opportune Succourer.** "Jesus went unto them walking on the sea" (Matt. xiv. 25).
5. **The Minute Searcher.** "Who walketh in the midst of the seven golden candlesticks" (Rev. ii. 1).
6. **The Holy Example.** "He walked" (1 John ii. 6).
7. **The Supreme Exceller.** "Who walketh upon the wings of the wind" (Psa. civ. 3).

834. THE MILLENNIUM

THE Millennium is variously described in the Word.

1. As a **"thousand years"** (Rev. xx. 4-6).
2. As "the **Day of the Lord**" (Zech. xiv. 1; Zeph. i. 7).
3. As **"that Day"** (Isa. ii. 11, 17; xi. 11; xx. 6; xxvi. 1, etc.).
4. As **"the Times of Restitution"** (Acts iii. 21).
5. As **"the Regeneration"** (Matt. xix. 28).
6. As **"the Liberty of the Glory"** (Rom. viii. 21, R.V.).
7. As **"the Age to Come"** (Eph. i. 21, R.V.; Heb. vi. 5. The word "world" in these verses is *"aion,"* which means an age).
8. As **"the World to Come"** (Heb. i. 6; ii. 5). The "world" in these verses is *oikoumene*, and means the inhabited earth, or civilised world.—See Luke ii. 1.
9. As **"His Kingdom"** (Dan. vii. 14; Rev. xi. 15).
10. As typified in the **Feast of Tabernacles**—Lev. xxiii. 33-36.

835. THE MILLENNIUM
IN ISAIAH

WHAT it will mean when the King comes, as stated through Isaiah.

1. A time when **war will be no more**—ii. 4.

2. **The earth will be restored and beautified**—lv. 13.

3. **Human life will be prolonged**, and death will be the exception—lxv. 19-22.

4. When **Israel and Judah will be gathered to Palestine** and Jehovah—xi. 11, 12.

5. **The animal creation will cease to prey upon each other**—lxv. 25.

6. When **all flesh will worship the Lord**—lxvi. 23.

7. When "all the people **will be righteous**" (lx. 21), that is, Jehovah's people ("Thy people.").

836. THE LORD RESTING
IN, ON, AND WITH HIS PEOPLE

1. Resting in them as the **Indweller**—Psa. cxxxii. 8, 14.

2. Resting on them as the **Equipper**—Isa. xi. 2.

3. Resting with them as the **Conqueror**—Isa. xxv. 10.

4. Resting in them as the **Lover**—Zeph. iii. 17.

5. Resting on them as the **Power**—2 Cor. xii. 9.

6. Resting on them as the **Compensator**—1 Peter iv. 14.

7. Resting with them as the **Leader**—Num. x. 12, 36.

837. THE NEW CREATION
2 Cor. v. 17, margin

THERE are several new things named in the "New Testament" of God's grace—Luke xxii. 20.

1. The New Testament brings the **"new teaching"** of the person and work of Christ—Mark i. 27, R.V.; Acts xvii. 19, R.V.

2. Who infuses in the believer the Divine life of a **"new creation"** (2 Cor. v. 17, margin).

3. Which makes all believers to occupy the common position in Christ of the **"one new man"** of the Church—Eph. ii. 15.

4. Which calls all its members to "walk in the **newness of the life**" of the Spirit (Rom. vi. 4).

5. Which again obligates each member to "serve in **newness of spirit**," and not after the letter of the law of Moses—Rom. vii. 6.

6. Which also commands us to keep the eleventh and "**new commandment**" of loving each other as Christ has loved us (John xiii. 34).

7. Which in addition privileges us to put on "the **new man**" of Christly consecration (Eph. iv. 24).

8. While the "**new tongue**" of the Spirit's endowment (Mark xvi. 17).

9. Makes us sing the "**new song**" of redemption (Rev. v. 9).

10. And all these "**new things**" (2 Cor. 5. 17) beget in our hearts the ambition to have the "new stone" of the overcomer's reward (Rev. ii. 17).

11. And make us long for the "**New Jerusalem**" (Rev. xxi. 2), in the "**new Heavens** and the **new earth**" (Rev. xxi. 1).

838. "THEM THAT LOVE HIM"
1 Cor. ii. 9

THOSE who love God have certain traits. They are—

1. **Obedient** to His Word—John xiv. 15.
2. **Fired** with an ambition to please Him—2 Cor. v. 9.
3. **Rely** on His faithfulness—John xiv. 28.
4. **Joyful** in His will—Psa. xl. 8.
5. **Do things** for His love's sake—3 John 7.
6. **Look for** the appearing of Christ—2 Tim. iv. 8.
7. **Love others** by helping them—1 John iii. 16-18.

839. THE PERSONAL ELEMENT
"He gave Himself for me" Gal. ii. 20

1. The **Substitute** for Me. "He loved me" (Gal. ii. 20).

2. The **Shepherd** with Me. "I shall not want" (Psa. xxiii.1).

3. The **Strength** within Me. "I can do all things" (Phil. iv. 13).

4. The **Salvation** Meeting Me. "God is my salvation" (Isa. xii. 2).

5. The **Satisfier** Supplying Me. "My soul shall be satisfied" (Psa. lxiii. 5).

6. The **Shelter** over Me. "I sat down under His shadow" (S. of Sol. ii. 3).

7. The **Spirit** Empowering Me. "I am full of power" (Micah iii. 8).

840. THE PERSONNEL OF PSALM LXIII

1. **Relationship.**   "My God."
2. **Desire.**   "My soul thirsteth for Thee."
3. **Praise.**   "My lips shall praise Thee."
4. **Confidence.**   "I will lift up my hands in Thy Name."
5. **Satisfaction.**   "My soul shall be satisfied."
6. **Joy.**   "My mouth shall praise Thee with joyful lips."
7. **Remembrance.**   "When I remember Thee upon my bed."
8. **Help.**   "Thou hast been my help."
9. **Following.**   "My soul followeth hard after Thee."

Ponder not only the "My's," but the "I's" and the "Me's," and also note the Psalm describes the experiences of David when in the wilderness.

841. THE POWER OF HIS NAME

1. **Promise.**   "Call on the Name of the Lord shall be saved" (Acts ii. 21).
2. **Pardon.**   "Baptised...in the Name of Jesus Christ unto (R.V.) remission of sins" (Acts ii. 38).
3. **Power.**   "In the Name...Rise up and walk" (Acts iii. 6).
4. **Perfection.**   "His Name...perfect soundness" (Acts iii. 16).
5. **Proclamation.**   "Be it known...by the Name of Jesus Christ," etc. (Acts iv. 10).
6. **Provision.**   "Salvation in none other name" (Acts iv. 12).
7. **Prayer.**   "By the Name of Thy Holy Servant" (Acts iv. 30, R.V.).

842. THE PRAYER OF PRAYERS

"Teach me Thy will" (Psa. cxliii. 10)

THERE are other places in the Psalms where this prayer, "Teach me," occurs, but with a different ending—Psa. xxv. 4; xxvii. 11; lxxxvi. 11; cxix. 12, 33, 64, 66, 68, 108, 124, 135.

There are seven things to fulfil in order to fill to the full this prayer of prayers.

"Teach me to do Thy will:"

1. **Instantly**, without question—1 Thess. v. 18-24.
2. **Implicitly**, without doubt—Phil. ii. 12-14.
3. **Continually**, without halting—Col. i. 9-11.
4. **Consecratingly**, without sin—Heb. xiii. 20, 21.
5. **Scripturally**, without self—Heb. x. 7.
6. **Trustfully**, without worry—Col. iv. 12.
7. **Fully**, without reserve—Luke xxii. 42.

843. THE PRAYER OF DANIEL

Daniel vi. 10, 11

THE safety valve of Daniel's persecution was prayer to the Lord. There are five things we note about Daniel's praying.

1. It was **reverent**, for like a humble courtier in the presence of his king, "he kneeled."

2. His prayer was **constant**, for like the regular chiming of a good clock, so he had the regular periods of "three times a day" for prayer.

3. His prayer was **mingled with gratitude**, for as the hen lifts up her head in drinking, so Daniel lifted up his heart in thanksgiving while praying.

4. His prayer was **believing**, for as the child will expect his father to keep to his promise, so Daniel prayed towards the temple of God's atoning love, forgiving grace, and revealed will—1 Kings viii. 29, 30.

5. Daniel's prayer was **known**, for as the scent in the handkerchief will betray itself, so prayer brings the aroma of grace and the fragrance of holiness, and these ever speak out their worth.

844. "THEREFORE"

Phil. iv. 1

THE importance of the "therefore" is seen again and again in the Word. Perhaps not more so than in Philippians iv. 1, for the reason of conduct is founded on the truth of the Lord's Coming. Because He is Coming, we are urged to be alert to keep the following seven commands.

1. The "**so stand fast**" of **fidelity** (iv. 1). Stand fast as a soldier with resolution, as a watchman with alertness, as a steward with faithfulness, as a friend with steadfastness, as a mother with affection, and as a shepherd with concern.

2. The "**same mind**" of **unity** (iv. 2). The mind stands for the soul, the will, and the understanding. The two sisters who were at variance are exhorted to make up their minds to have a fellow feeling, and a clear understanding with each other.

3. The "**help**" of **ability** (iv. 3). To help those who help is to be helped. The help of the heart of love to cheer, the help of the hand of power to lift, the help of the word of comfort to comfort, and the help of the look of solicitude to gladden.

4. The **"rejoice"** of **gladness** (iv. 4). Joy is a flower that blooms in the soil of devotion to the Lord. When the Lord is the aim of our life, His joy is the heart of our gladness.

5. The **"moderation"** of **consideration** (iv. 5). The Revised Version reading is "forbearance," or "gentleness." To forbear with others with the gentleness of love, is to evidence and think of their feelings. When the Lord is "at hand," that is, at our side, that makes us consider Him in thinking of others.

845. THE SEVEN R's OF CHRIST'S RETURN

1. **Revelation** of Christ—John xiv. 3; Acts i. 8; 1 Cor. i. 7; Rev. xxii. 7, 12, 20.

2. **Resurrection** of Sleeping Believers—1 Cor. xv. 23; 1 Thess. iv. 13-18.

3. **Redemption** of the Body—Rom. viii. 23; 1 Cor. xv. 51-54; Phil. iii. 20, 21.

4. **Regeneration** of Israel—Hosea vi. 2; Ezek. xxxvii; Amos ix. 11-15; Acts xv. 16.

5. **Restoration** of Creation—Rom. viii. 19-22, R.V.; Acts iii. 21, R.V.

6. **Renovation** of the Earth—Isa. lv. 13; Psa. lxvii. 6; Isa. lxv. 17-25.

7. **Reign** of Christ—Psa. lxxii.; Luke i. 33; Isa. xxxii. 1; 1 Cor. xv. 25; 2 Tim. iv. 1; Rev. xxii. 5.

846. THE SINNER'S WALK

1. **In Vanity.** "Walketh in a vain show" (Psa. xxxix. 6).

2. **In Pride.** "A wicked man walketh with a froward mouth" (Prov. vi. 12).

3. **In Darkness.** "The fool walketh in darkness" (Eccles. ii. 14).

4. **In Stubbornness.** "Walketh in the stubbornness of his own heart" (Jer. xxiii. 17, R.V.).

5. **In Abomination.** "Walketh after the heart of their detestable things and their abominations" (Ezek. xi. 21).

6. **In Ignorance.** "He that walketh in darkness knoweth not" (John xii. 35).

7. **In Bondage.** "He is cast into a net by his own feet, and he walketh upon the toils" (Job. xviii. 8, R.V.).

847. "THE SPIRIT"
1 CORINTHIANS II

1. The **Effective Power**. "Demonstration of the Spirit and power" (4).

2. The **Effective Revealer**. "But God hath revealed them unto us by His Spirit" (10).

3. The **Effective Searcher**. "The Spirit searcheth all things" (10).

4. The **Effective Knower**. "The things of God knoweth no man, but the Spirit of God" (11).

5. The **Effective Communicator**. "We have the Spirit... that we might know" (12).

6. The **Effective Teacher**. "The Holy Ghost Teacheth" (13).

7. The **Effective Discerner**. "The natural man receiveth not the things of the Spirit of God...they are spiritually discerned (discerned by the Spirit)...We have the mind of Christ" (14-16).

848. THE WORLD

1. **Self** is its Centre. "You...walking according to this world" (Eph. ii. 2).

2. **Pleasure** is its Pursuit. "Having loved this present world" (2 Tim. iv. 10).

3. **Lust** is its Food. "Corruption that is in the world" (2 Pet. i. 4).

4. **Applause** is its Aim. "The world wondered after the beast" (Rev. xiii. 3).

5. **Money** is its God. "Them that are rich in this world" (1 Tim. vi. 17).

6. **Satan** is its God. "The God of this world" (2 Cor. iv. 4).

7. **Reason** is its Authority. "Wisdom of this world" (1 Cor. ii. 6-8).

8. **Present Life** is its Sphere. "This present evil world" (Gal. i. 4).

9. **Seeing** is its Faith. "Shewed Him all the kingdoms of the world" (Matt. iv. 8).

10. **Judgment** is its End "Judge the world in righteousness" (Acts xvii. 31).

849. "THE WORLD, THE FLESH, AND THE DEVIL"

1. **Demas** fell, through the world—2 Tim. iv. 10.

2. **David** fell, through the flesh—2 Sam. xi. 2-4.

3. **Peter** fell, through the Devil—Matt. xvi. 23.

850. "THEY WENT "

1. **Obedience** rewarded—Matt. xxviii. 9.
2. **Testimony** sealed—Mark xvi. 20.
3. **Faith** blessed—Luke xvii. 14.
4. **Diligence** encouraged—Luke xxii. 13.
5. **Service** recognised—3 John 7.
6. **Fellowship** illustrated—2 Kings ii. 2.
7. **Spirit** guided—Ezek. i. 12.

851. THINGS GOD EXPECTS FROM HIS CHILDREN

1. **Exhibition.** "Shew forth His praises" (1 Peter ii. 9).
2. **Fructification.** "Beareth fruit, and bringeth forth" (Matt. xiii. 23).
3. **Separation.** "Let us go forth therefore unto Him" (Heb. xiii. 13).
4. **Determination.** "Reaching forth unto those things before" (Phil. iii. 13).
5. **Illumination.** "Holding forth the Word of Life" (Phil. ii. 16).
6. **Appreciation.** "For His Name's sake they went forth" (3 John 7).
7. **Direction.** "Go thy way forth" (Song of Sol. i. 8).

The word "forth" in each of the above passages represents five different words. No. 1 means to publish, to celebrate; No. 2, 3, and 6, to proceed, to spread abroad; No. 4, to stretch forward, to concentrate one's energies upon a given object; No. 5, to pay attention, to give earnest heed; No. 7, to go, and not to delay.

852. THINGS IN COMMON

1. A common **interest** in Christ—Jude 3.
2. A common **love** to Him—Col. i. 8.
3. A common **place** in His body—1 Cor. xii. 13.
4. A common **desire** to glorify His Name—2 Thess. i. 12.
5. A common **love** for His Word—Acts ii. 42-44.
6. A common **endeavour** in His Work—Phil. i. 27.
7. A common **aim** for His glory—2 Cor. v. 9, R.V.

853. THINGS IN WHICH GOD'S PEOPLE SHOULD DELIGHT

1. The Lord **Himself**. "Then shalt thou delight thyself in the Lord" (Isa. lviii. 14). Note the "then" of the soul's condition in the previous verse, which makes the delighting in the Lord possible.

2. The Lord's **Will**. "I delight to do Thy will, O my God" (Psa. xl. 8). Christ is our Example, for imitation, and our Empowerer for inspiration in doing God's will.

3. The Lord's **Word**. "Thy testimonies also are my delight" (Psa. cxix. 24, 35). To delight in God's Word is a sign of healthy spiritual life—Psa. i. 2.

4. The Lord's **Abundance**. "The meek shall inherit the earth, and shall delight themselves in the abundance of peace" (Psa. xxxvii. 11). The Lord not only favours us with His pardon, but He also feasts us with His promises.

5. The Lord's **Protection**. "I sat down under His shadow with great delight" (Cant. ii. 3). The shadow of Christ's atonement is the protection which shields from God's wrath.

6. The Lord's **Acquaintance**. "Then shalt thou have thy delight in the Almighty." The good of blessing all comes through being acquainted with Him—Job. xxii. 21-30.

854. THINGS OF CHRIST IN EPHESIANS

1. "The **Blood** of Christ" (ii. 13). The Blood is the securer of all blessing, the cause of all victory, and the sanctifier to all devotion.

2. "The **Mystery** of Christ" (iii. 4). "Mystery" means "secret," and the "secret" is that all believers are one in Him.

3. "The **Unsearchable Riches** of Christ" (iii. 8). There is a mine of wealth in Him, which is sufficient to meet all claims and needs.

4. "The **Love** of Christ" (iii. 19). Christ's love is a lake we cannot contain, and it is a fountain which utterly satisfies.

5. "The **Body** of Christ" (iv. 12). The mystical body of Christ is composed of Christ as the Head, and members as a whole and in particular—see 1 Cor. xii.

6. "The **Fulness** of Christ" (iv. 13). All fullness dwells in Him, so we can never lack anything if we abide in Him.

7. "The **Kingdom** of Christ" (v. 5). The Kingdom of His grace—Col. i. 13; and the Kingdom of His administration—Rev. xi. 15.

855. THINGS OF CHRIST

1. A Wonderful **Blessing**. "The love of Christ" (2 Cor. v. 14).

2. A Wonderful **Gift**. "The Blood of Christ" (Heb. ix. 14).

3. A Wonderful **Power**. "The power of Christ" (2 Cor. xii. 9).

4. A Wonderful **Revelation**. "The Word of Christ" (Col. iii. 16).

5. A Wonderful **Faith**. "The faith of the Son of God" (Gal. ii. 20).

6. A Wonderful **Hope**. "The Coming of the Lord" (James v. 7).

7. A Wonderful **Message**. "The Gospel of Christ" (Rom. i. 16).

856. THINGS OF GOD

In 1 Corinthians i

1. **The Will of God**—1. God's will is revealed in God's Word, and we know it experimentally as we walk in His ways.

2. **The Church of God**—2. Some affirm, "It is the Church which makes Christians," but God's truth declares, "It is the Christians (Christ's own) which make the Church."

3. **The Grace of God**—4. Grace stands for favour, strength, and beauty—God's favour towards us, Christ's strength in us, and the Spirit's beauty upon us.

4. **The Power of God**—18. God's power comes in several ways. The Blood has power to cleanse, the Word has power to assure, His love has power to constrain, His peace has power to keep, His joy has power to gladden, His grace has power to enable, and the Spirit is the power of all power.

5. **The Wisdom of God**—21. Wisdom is the right application of knowledge. The Lord knows how to apply His blessings to us. He tempers His blessings to each temperament, and displays His wisdom especially in the Cross of His Son.

6. **The Foolishness of God**—25. God could not be foolish in a positive sense, but comparatively it is so, for what seems foolish in the eyes of foolish men turns out to be the greatest and profoundest wisdom.

7. **The Weakness of God**—25. There is more strength in God's little finger than in all the combined hands of men.

857. THINGS "OF GOD"
2 TIMOTHY I
1. "The **Will** of God" (i. 1).
2. "The **Gift** of God" (i. 6).
3. "The **Power** of God" (i. 8).
4. "The **Word** of God" (ii. 9).
5. "The **Foundation** of God" (ii. 19).
6. "**Lovers** of God" (iii. 4).
7. "**Inspiration** of God" (iii. 16).
8. "The **Man** of God" (iii. 17).

858. THINGS OF GOD
1 CORINTHIANS II
"Deep things of God" 10, 11

1. "The **Testimony** of God" (1). Our testimony is of account and counts when it is what the Lord says.
2. "**Demonstration** of the Spirit" (4). The only effective worker is the Spirit, but if we are usable He will use us.
3. "**Power** of God" (5). When God's power works, things are gripped and governed.
4. "**Wisdom** of God" (7). The wisdom is displayed in the works of His hand, in the heart of His love, and in the grace of His salvation.
5. **Spirit** of God—11, 12, 14, is the source of Truth, its Revealer, and its Communicator.
6. "The **Mind** of the Lord" (16). When we know the Lord we know His mind.
7. "The **Mind** of Christ" (16). "Christ" is the One who thinks of us, thinks in us, and thinks through us.

859. THINGS TO DO
1. **Think** on our ways practically—Psa. cxix. 59.
2. **Trust** in the Lord wholly—Prov. iii. 5.
3. **Tread** the path of life carefully—Eph. v. 15.
4. **Teach** the Word of the Lord helpfully—Deut. xi. 19.
5. **Take** the Lord's supplies gratefully—Psa. cxvi. 13.
6. **Triumph** over sin continually—Rom. vi. 14.
7. **Testify** to the Lord faithfully—Rev. ii. 10, 13.

Then, looking out on the future, we shall rest continually in the Lord's love, and expect the fulfilment of His promise to receive us to Himself.

860. THINGS THAT ARE NEAR

1. The Conscious **Sufferer**. "The Master saith, My time is at hand" (Matt. xxvi. 18).

2. The Approaching **Deliverer**. "Drawing nigh unto the ship" (John vi. 19).

3. The City's **Vicinity**. "The place where Jesus was crucified was nigh to the city" (John xix. 20).

4. A Saving **Gospel**. "The Word is nigh thee," etc. (Rom. x. 8).

5. A Securing **Price**. "Made nigh by the Blood of Christ" (Eph. ii. 13).

6. A Living **Presence**. "The Lord is at hand" (Phil. iv. 5).

7. A Portentous **Time**. "The time is at hand" (Rev. i. 3; xxii. 10).

The words in the above Scriptures rendered "at hand" and "nigh" are one and the same in the Greek.

861. THINGS WHICH ABIDE

1. The Abiding **Christ**. "Christ abideth for ever" (John xii. 34).

2. The Abiding **Spirit**. "Comforter, that He may abide with you" (John xiv. 16).

3. The Abiding **Word**. "The Word of God, which liveth and abideth for ever" (1 Peter i. 23).

4. The Abiding **Fruit**. "Your fruit should abide" (John xv. 16, R.V.).

5. The Abiding **Work**. "If any man's work abide which he hath built upon, he shall receive a reward" (1 Cor. iii. 14).

6. The Abiding **Graces**. "Now abideth faith, hope, and love" (1 Cor. xiii. 13, R.V.).

7. The Abiding **Saints**. "He that doeth the will of God abideth for ever" (1 John ii. 17).

862. "THOU"

1. "To whom **belongest thou**?" (1 Sam. xxx. 13).

2. "What **meanest thou**?" (Jonah i. 6).

3. "What **doest thou**?" (1 Kings xix. 9).

4. "What **wilt thou**?" (Mark x. 51).

5. "Whom **seekest thou**?" (John xx. 15).

6. "Where **dwellest thou**?" (John i. 38).

7. "Whither **goest thou**?" (Zech. ii. 2).

863. THINGS WHICH THE WORLD CANNOT DO *

1. The world could not **touch the life of Christ.** "No man taketh it from Me" (John x. 18).

2. The world cannot **pluck the believer out of the hands of Grace.** "No man is able to pluck them out" (John x. 28, 29).

3. The world cannot **rob the believer of his joy.** "Your joy no man taketh from you" (John xvi. 22).

4. The world **cannot come to God apart from Christ.** "No man cometh unto the Father, but by Me" (John xiv. 6).

5. The world cannot **come to God of itself.** "No man can come to Me, except the Father which hath sent Me draw him" (John vi. 44).

6. The world cannot **understand the things of God.** "The things of God knoweth no man, but the Spirit of God" (1 Cor. ii. 11).

7. The world cannot **serve God and itself.** "No man can serve two masters" (Matt. vi. 24).

864. "THIS."—EXCLAMATIONS

HAVE you noticed the exclamations as recorded in the Gospels about Christ? Let me give but a few in connection with the word "THIS."

1. When the people saw the palsied man healed by Christ, as he was walking away with his bed, they said: "We never saw it on **this fashion**" (Mark ii. 12).

2. When Christ stilled the tempest, the disciples exclaimed, "What manner of **Man is this?**" (Mark iv. 41).

3. When the soldiers were sent to arrest Christ, all they could say to their instructors was, "Never man **spake like this Man**" (John vii. 46).

4. After Pilate had examined Christ, he confessed, "I find **no fault in this Man**" (Luke xxiii. 4).

5. The dying thief confessed that he and his fellow were suffering justly, but as to Christ, he said to his fellow male-factor, "**This Man hath done nothing amiss**" (Luke xxiii. 41).

6. When the centurion saw all the wonders at the Cross, he could not help exclaiming, "Certainly **this was a righteous Man**" (Luke xxiii. 47).

7. When Christ forgave the sins of the woman in the house of Simon the Pharisee, the people present exclaimed, "**Who is this**, that forgiveth sins also?" (Luke vii. 49). Who, indeed, if He is not the Son of God.

* Notice the words "*no man*" in each of the Scriptures.

865. THIRSTING

1. An Unsatisfied Thirst. "Whosoever drinketh of this water shall thirst again" (John iv. 13).

2. An Unfathomable Cry. "Jesus...saith, I thirst" (John xix. 28).

3. An Unspeakable Gift. "Whosoever drinketh of the water that I shall give him shall never thirst" (John iv. 14).

4. An Unlimited Supply. "If any man thirst, let him come unto Me and drink" (John vii. 37; Rev. xxii. 17).

5. An Unchanging Blessing. "He that believeth on Me shall never thirst" (John vi. 35).

6. An Unquestionable Promise. "Blessed are they which do hunger and thirst after righteousness, for they shall be filled" (Matt. v. 6).

7. A Unique Experience. "Hunger no more, neither thirst any more" (Rev. vii. 16).

866. "THIS"—CHRIST'S PERSONALITY

THE Spirit of God points the index finger to Christ, calling attention to Him, in the distinctiveness of His personality.

1. His Peerlessness. "This is My beloved Son" (Matt. iii. 17). The Father knows the Son best, and is the One best able to tell forth His worth.

2. His Powerfulness. When Christ stilled the tempest, it caused the disciples to exclaim, "What manner of Man is this?" (Luke viii. 25).

3. His Persuasiveness. "Never man spake like this Man" (John vii. 46). The charm of His personality, the character of His message, and the persuasiveness of His manner, made Him different to all others.

4. His Philanthropy. "This Man receiveth sinners" (Luke xv. 2). Children and sinners know their Friend, and Christ is the Friend of sinners and children.

5. His Portentousness. "This is the King of the Jews" (Matt. xxvii. 37). His Cross of shame secured for Him the conquest of sovereignty. The shamed Sovereign in His death, the superscription over His head, were portentous of His coming reign.

6. His Proclamation. "This same Jesus...shall come" (Acts i. 11). He who went away will come back to stay. Look out for Him, and watch for His return.

7. His Pre-eminence. "This is the true God and Eternal Life" (1 John v. 20). He stands alone in Deity and humanity. He has what none other hath, because He is unlike any other.

867. "THIS."—DISTINCTIVE MESSAGES

THE distinctive message of the Gospel as found in association with Christ in John's Gospel in connection with the word "this." He is the—

1. **Eternal Son.** "This is the Son of God" (i. 34).
2. **Sent Christ.** "This is the Christ" (iv. 42).
3. **Predicted Prophet.** "This is the Prophet" (vi. 14).
4. **True Bread.** "This is the Bread" (vi. 50).
5. **Exceptional Man.** "This Man" (vii. 46).
6. **Eternal Life.** "This is Life Eternal" (xvii. 3).
7. **Coming King.** "To this End was I Born" (xviii. 37).
8. **Burdened Substitute.** "This Hour" (xii. 27).
9. **Completing Worker.** "After this" (xix. 28).
10. **Equipping Lord.** "When He had said this" (xx. 22).
11. **Risen Saviour.** "On this wise He shewed Himself" (xxi. 1).
12. **Inspired Record.** "Written in this Book" (xx. 30).

868. "THIS" IN ROMANS

1. **"This Cause."** "For this cause God gave them up unto vile affections" (i. 26). Sin the cause of judgment.
2. **"This Time."** "To declare at this time, His righteousness" (iii. 26). Now is the season of grace to those who believe in Christ.
3. **"This Blessedness."** "Cometh this blessedness," etc. (iv. 9). Grace is the ground of justification, and is no respecter of persons.
4. **"This Grace,"** "Access by faith into this grace" (v. 2). The grace which saves, gives the right to stand and commune.
5. **"This Death"** (vii. 24). Spiritual death is the worst of deaths.
6. **"This Mystery"** (xi. 25). God's secrets revealed to God's own.
7. **"This Saying"** (xiii. 9). God's summaries are terse and telling.
8. **"This End"** (xiv. 9). Christ's death was definite in purpose and practical in result.

869. "THIS WISE"

"THIS wise" means, after the manner signified.

1. Incarnation. "The birth of Jesus Christ was on this wise" (Matt. i. 18). He, who was eternally God, became a man in time, that He might accomplish on the earth a redemption that would bless the universe.

2. Resurrection. "On this wise shewed He Himself" (John xxi. 1). In many ways He showed Himself as the Risen One, but in all His manifestations He was the Son of God with power.

3. Revelation. "God spake on this wise" (Acts vii. 6). God's revelation about the seed of Abraham was a forecast of His plan with them.

4. Confirmation. "He said on this wise, I will give you the sure mercies of David" (Acts xiii. 34). God's Word is sure about His "mercies," and they are ensured in Christ's resurrection, for that event ensures things—Acts xvii. 31.

5. Justification. "The righteousness which is of faith speaketh on this wise," etc. (Rom. x. 6). God reckons to faith in Christ, what Christ is.

870. "THIS MAN"

WE often find pivotal expressions in Holy Writ. One such is the phrase, "This Man." Our thought is arrested and our minds interested when such a phrase is pondered in its associations, and at once suggests what manner of Man Christ is.

1. Divine Man. When the centurion saw the phenomenon of the Cross, and listened to His cry, he confessed, "Truly this Man was the Son of God" (Mark xv. 39). When Christ is seen and studied, every honest man must acknowledge His Deity.

2. Faultless Man. Pilate questioned and examined Christ in the light of the accusations against Him, and said, "I find no fault in this Man" (Luke xxiii. 4, 14, 22). Christ's character was like the gold of the Tabernacle—"pure." He did no sin, He knew no sin, and in Him was no sin. He was holy in nature, harmless in action, undefiled in life, and without sin.

3. Powerful Man. When Christ stilled the raging of the sea, His act begat within the disciples the question, "What manner of Man is this?" (Matt. viii. 27). They recognised that nature must obey its Creator, and therefore they were in the presence of the Lord of Nature.

4. Loving Man. "This Man receiveth sinners, and eateth with them" (Luke xv. 2). This statement of scorn embodies the truth of salvation. These words from darkened minds have brought the dawn of hope and faith into many a soul. The word "receiveth" is rendered "waiteth" and "looketh" in other places. He waits in patient grace, and looks out in longing love for sinners, and receives them to Himself when they come, and, further, fellowships with them.

5. **Wonderful Man.** There was a charm and winsomeness about Christ which made everything about Him peculiar and attractive. The soldiers who were sent to arrest Him were so arrested by the matter of His utterances and the manner of His testimony that they exclaimed, "Never man spake like this Man" (John vii. 46).

6. **Completing Man.** "This Man, after He had offered one sacrifice for sins, for ever sat down on the right hand of God" (Heb. x. 12). We have purposely punctuated the words as above. As Newberry gives it, "to perpetuity He has sat down." He will never rise up to open the question of sin, for that has "for ever" been settled by the one Offering for it. A Perfect Offerer has given a perfect offering, which brings in a perfect redemption.

7. **Unchanging Man.** "This Man, because He continueth for ever, hath an unchanging priesthood," and He abideth because He lives in the "power of an indissoluble life" (Heb. vii. 17, 24). His priesthood is not transferable, as Aaron's was; and it is unalterable in character, because He cannot die; and it is unchanging, because He "abideth for ever."

871. "THITHER"

1. The Place of **Refuge.** "That the slayer may flee thither" (Deut. iv. 42).

2. The Place of **Gathering.** "Thither shalt thou come" (Deut. xii. 5).

3. The Place of **Offering.** "Thither ye shall bring your burnt offerings" (Deut. xii. 6).

4. The Place of **Obedience.** "Thither shall ye bring all I command you" (Deut. xii. 11).

5. The Place of **Marshalling.** "Resort ye thither" (Neh. iv. 20).

6. The Place of **Work.** "Thither unto the work" (Neh. v. 16).

7. The Place of **Prayer.** "Resorted thither" (John xviii. 2; Acts xvi. 13).

8. The Place of **Testimony.** "Ran thither to him" (Acts viii. 30).

872. "THIS WOMAN"

ATTENTION is called to certain women in connection with the words, "This woman."

1. A Memorial Act. "That this woman hath done, shall be told for a memorial of her" (Matt. xxvi. 13). Love's offering leaves a perpetual fragrance behind it.

2. A Meritorious Act. "This poor widow hath cast more in" (Mark xii. 43). The worth of a gift is not estimated by amount, but by the heart that moves the hand.

3. A Meanful Act. Christ spoke of "this woman" who washed His feet and wiped them with her hair, and saw beneath her acts her burning heart of love. When love feeds the hearth of the heart, how brightly the fire doth burn—Luke vii. 44-46.

4. A Miserable Act. "This woman was taken in adultery, in the very act" (John viii. 4). If every sinner was discovered in sinning, what revelations there would be!

5. A Memorable Act. "This woman was full of good works" (Acts ix. 36). The summary of her life's ministry is a beautiful testimony to the work of Dorcas.

6. A Musical Act. "She," or "This woman (Phebe) hath been a succourer of many, and of myself also" (Rom. xvi. 2). The music of Phebe's service caused a note of praise to be struck in Paul's commendation.

7. A Ministering Act. "She," or "This woman gave thanks unto God" (Luke ii. 38). Anna was singular in her perception and praise, hence her adoration and worship.

873. THREE BAPTISMS

1. The **Baptism of Suffering**—Luke xii. 40.

The Baptiser,	..	.. The Father.
The Baptised,	..	.. Christ.
The Baptism,	..	.. Christ's Death.

2. The **Baptism of Union**—1 Cor. xii. 12, 13.

The Baptiser,	..	.. The Spirit.
The Baptised,	..	.. All Believers.
The Baptism,	..	.. Union with Christ.

3. The **Baptism of Power**—Acts i. 5, 8.

The Baptiser,	..	.. Christ.
The Baptised,	..	.. Waiting Believers.
The Baptism,	..	.. Power.

874. "THREEFOLD CORDS"

"A threefold cord is not quickly broken" (Eccles. iv. 12).

A FRIEND visiting a Manchester cotton merchant's office says: "I noticed an instrument to test the strength of threads, yarn, etc. I asked my friend the merchant if he would undo a length of three-ply yarn. He did so. He tested the breaking point of the single, and the double, and finally the three-ply, and we found, as I surmised, that the three-ply was far more than three times the strength of a single strand."

God's truths are all threefold.

1. **A Threefold Salvation.** Saved from the penalty of sin by grace—Eph. ii. 8; saved in the life of Christ by power—Rom. v. 10; and saved from the presence of sin by Christ's might—Phil. iii. 20. 21.

2. **A Threefold Life.** Eternal life a gift—Rom. vi. 23; an experience—1 Tim. vi. 19; and a manifestation—Col. iii. 4.

3. **A Threefold Justification.** Justified by God as to cause —Rom. viii. 33; justified by faith as to instrument—Rom. v. 1; and justified by works as to proof—James ii. 21.

4. **A Threefold Choice.** Chosen by God—Eph. i. 4; chosen in Christ—John xv. 16; and proving our election by adding to our faith—2 Peter i. 10.

875. THREE "I KNOWS" OF PAUL

1. **Consciousness of Sin.** "I know that in me (that is, in my flesh) dwelleth no good thing" (Rom. vii. 18). The first step towards being right is to know that we are wrong; not merely that we have done wrong, but that the cause of wrong-doing is in the nature, which is altogether wrong. The fruit of the tree is bad because the tree itself is bad. The stream of the life is polluted because the source of the life—the heart—is defiled— Matt. xv. 19. To know that we are lost is the initiative to seeking that we may be saved. To see that we are under the curse will urge us to crave the blessings of the Gospel of Christ. Do we know, in the Biblical sense of knowing, that we are sinful, that is, do we not merely know it in the head, but is it a thing we have realised in our heart, so that it has made us cry out, "O wretched man that I am?"

2. **Confidence in the Saviour.** "I know Him whom I have believed, and I am persuaded that He is able to guard that which I have committed unto Him against that day" (2 Tim. i. 12, R.V.) There are many who know about Christ, but who do not know Him.

To know Christ as the Saviour, is to trust Him for salvation, and to deposit ourselves in His safe keeping, as the apostle says he had done.   To know Christ as our High Priest is to be continually saved from sinning, as we come to Him in faith and prayer—Heb. vii. 25.   To know Christ as' our Prophet is to be instructed by Him and to sit at His feet, even as Mary did—Luke x. 39.   To know Christ as our Lord is to recognise that we are His property, and to submit ourselves wholly to His rule—John xiii. 13-17.   To know Him as the Christ is to receive Him to live and reign in us—Gal. ii. 20.

3. **Conscience Void of Offence.**   "I know nothing against myself" (1 Cor. iv. 4. R.V.).   The apostle did not mean to say that he had no faults or failings.   As Trapp well says: "Paul a chosen vessel, but yet an earthen vessel, knew well that he had his cracks and his flaws, which God could easily find out."   What the apostle said was that, as far as his conscience went, he knew nothing against himself.   To be able to honestly say this there must be (1) implicit obedience to the Word of God, (2) initiation in the ways of God, (3) instruction in the will of God, and (4) intimate fellowship with God alone.

876. THREE SEPARATED MEN

EVERY believer should have three "S's" in his life—Saved, separated, satisfied—Deut. xxxiii. 29, 16, 23.

1. **Nehemiah.**   Nehemiah found that a magnificent room had been given to Tobiah, but he threw out all the furniture. In the same chapter we find Nehemiah saying, "I chased him from me" (Nehemiah xiii. 8-28).

2. **Caleb.**   He followed the leading of the Holy Ghost fully, and faithfully.   "My servant Caleb, because he had another spirit with him, and hath followed Me fully, him will I bring into the land" (Num. xiv. 24).

3. **Abraham.**   When brought into the land of the separation, he took up the practice of separation, and said, "I have lift up mine hand unto the Lord, the Most High God, that I will not take from a thread even to a shoe-latchet, and that I will not take anything that is thine, lest thou shouldest say, I have made Abram rich" (Gen. xiv. 22, 23).

Nehemiah illustrates separation from known evil by expelling it.   Caleb illustrates separation to the Lord by believing His Word; and Abraham illustrates separation from the world in refusing to have the help of the ungodly.

877. THREE LOOKS

1. **Inward Look** of Examination. "Look to yourselves" (2 John 8).

2. **Upward Look** of Expectancy. "I will direct my prayer unto Thee, and will look up" (Psa. v. 3).

3. **Outward Look** of Exercise. "Look on the fields" (John iv. 35).

878. THREE "SO GREAT" THINGS

1. **Condemnation.** "So great a death" (2 Cor. i. 10).

2. **Consolation.** "So great salvation" (Heb. ii. 3).

3. **Compensation.** "So great faith" (Matt. viii. 10).

879. THREE "WHEREBY'S"

1. **Salvation.** "None other name...whereby we must be saved" (Acts iv. 12).

2. **Possession.** "Ye have received the spirit of adoption, whereby we cry, Abba, Father" (Rom. viii. 15).

3. **Identification.** "The Holy Spirit of God, whereby ye are sealed unto the day of redemption" (Eph. iv. 30).

880. "TIME" AND "TIMES"

Kronos, rendered "time" (Matt. ii. 7), "while" (John xii. 35), "space" (Rev. ii. 21), "seasons" (Acts xx. 18), means a set time, a limited or designated period.

1. "**Times of restitution**" (Acts iii. 21), or restoration, are coming to Israel.

2. "The **time past** of our life," speaks of our sin and folly (1 Peter iv. 3).

3. "When the **fulness of time**" had come, Christ appeared to accomplish His redeeming work—Gal. iv. 4; 1 Peter i. 20.

4. "The **rest of our time**" we should live as becometh believers in Christ (1 Peter i. 17; iv. 2).

5. "In the **last time**" we are warned that "mockers" shall arise (Jude 18).

6. In His grace the Lord gives those who have need to "repent" a **certain** "space" (time) in which to do it—Rev. ii. 21.

7. **There is a** "time" when the Lord will come to reckon with His servants—Matt. xxv. 19.

881. "THYSELF"

PAUL'S weighty injunctions to Timothy are pertinent and powerful in 1 Timothy.

1. **Behaviour.** "How thou oughtest behave thyself" (iii. 15). If we were as careful with our character and our conduct as we are with our clothes and homes, we would be saints indeed.

2. **Exercise.** "Exercise thyself unto godliness" (iv. 7). This is the best kind of exercise. It neither exhausts nor enervates, but strengthens and stimulates.

3. **Diligence.** "Be diligent in these things, give thyself wholly to them" (iv. 15, R.V.). To cultivate the spiritual life with diligence and whole-heartedness is to be fruitful in grace.

4. **Personality.** "Take heed unto thyself" (iv. 16). To look after others and not ourselves is the height of folly, but to develop our own resources is essential and wise and helpful.

5. **Salvation.** "Both save thyself and them that hear thee" (iv. 16). We save ourselves from failure and fruitlessness when we are diligent in duty.

6. **Purity.** "Keep thyself pure" (v. 22). The inner life kept pure, the outward life will be powerful.

7. **Separation.** "From such withdraw thyself" (vi. 5). When brethren are in error or evil we are responsible to withdraw ourselves from them.

882. TIMES OF PROPHECY

1. Christ died at the **appointed time**—Rom. v. 6.

2. The present time is the season for the believer to be **awake** —Rom. xiii. 11.

3. The time when **the Lord will judge** things—1 Cor. iv. 5.

4. Jerusalem will be **"trodden down"** until the "times of the Gentiles be fulfilled" (Luke xxi. 24).

5. The antichrist will be "revealed in **his own time**" (2 Thess. ii. 6).

6. In the **"fulness of times"** God will gather all in Christ (Eph. i. 10).

7. "The **time is at hand**" when Christ will return and prophecy will be fulfilled (Rev. xxii. 10).

883. "TO-DAY"

THE presentness of God's things need to be kept in mind.

1. **Christ.** "Jesus Christ the same yesterday, to-day, and for ever" (Heb. xiii. 8). He is the same without any sameness. In the Cross of His passion, in the communion of His presence, and in the for ever of His glory.

2. **Conversion.** "To-day I must abide at thy house." "This day is salvation come" (Luke xix. 5, 9). Christ's presence is salvation and power.

3. **Consecration.** "Consecrate yourselves to-day to the Lord" (Exod. xxxii. 29). Separation to the Lord and dedication to Him are the soul of consecration.

4. **Concentration.** "To-day if ye will hear His voice" (Psa. xcv. 7; Heb. iii. 7, 13, 15; iv. 7). To hear His voice is to obey His Word.

5. **Command.** "My son, go work to-day in my vineyard" (Matt. xxi. 28). There is work to do, we are commanded to do it, and to do it to-day.

6. **Communication.** "Hearken unto the cry and to the prayer, which Thy servant prayeth before Thee to-day" (1 Kings viii. 28). To communicate to the Lord in prayer we need to keep the communicating way open.

7. **Communion.** "To-day thou shalt be with Me in Paradise" (Luke xxiii. 43). To be with Christ is Heaven.

884. "TOGETHER"

1. **Walk.** "Can two walk together, except they be agreed?" (Amos iii. 3).

2. **Worship.** "Magnify the Lord with me, and let us exalt His Name together" (Psa. xxxiv. 3).

3. **Work.** "Together will build unto the Lord" (Ezra iv. 3).

4. **Joy.** "He calleth together his friends and neighbours," etc. (Luke xv. 6).

5. **Effort.** "Striving together for the faith of the Gospel" (Phil. i. 27).

6. **Love.** "Being knit together in love" (Col. ii. 2).

7. **Example.** "Be followers together of Me" (Phil. iii. 17).

885. "TO HIMSELF"

1. **A Divine Reconciler.** "God was in Christ reconciling the world unto Himself" (2 Cor. v. 19).

2. **A Necessary Mediator.** "Reconciled us to Himself by Jesus Christ" (2 Cor. v. 18).

3. **A Positive End.** "Purify unto Himself a peculiar people" (Titus ii. 14).

4. **A Gracious Choice.** "The Lord hath chosen thee to be a people to Himself" (Deut. vii. 6).

5. **A Separated People.** "Separated you to bring you near to Himself" (Num. xvi. 9).

6. **A Holy Presentation.** "Present it to Himself a glorious Church" (Eph. v. 27).

7. **An Ultimate Goal.** "Reconcile all things* to Himself" (Col. i. 20).

886. TONGUES

1. It was the Devil's **insinuating** tongue that caused our first parents to sin—Gen. iii. 4.

2. It was the **lying** tongues of Joseph's brethren which gave Jacob so much grief—Gen. xxxvii. 32.

3. It was the **deceitful** tongue of Jacob that robbed Esau of his blessing—Gen. xxvii. 18, 23.

4. It was the **obstinate** tongue of Pharaoh that caused the plagues to be sent—Exod. x. 28.

5. It was the **jealous** tongue of Miriam that caused her to be smitten with leprosy—Num. xii. 1, 10.

6. It was the **proud** tongue of Korah and his followers that brought such swift judgment upon them—Num. xvi. 3, 32.

7. It was the **fault-finding** tongues of Job's friends that ministered such trouble to him—Job. xxxii. 10-18.

8. It was the **covetous** tongue of Judas which caused Christ to be betrayed to His death—Matt. xxvi. 15.

9. It was the **boasting** tongue of Peter which made him deny his Lord—Matt. xxvi. 70.

10. It was the **unholy** tongue of Ananias that made him lie to the Holy Spirit—Acts v. 3.

11. It was the **sectarian** tongue of the Corinthians that caused the divisions among them—1 Cor. i. 12.

12. It was the **prating** tongue of Diotrephes which caused so much trouble in the Church—3 John 9, 10.

887. TONGUES
Good Ones

1. A **Choice** Tongue—Prov. x. 20. The "just" (righteous) have such a tongue.

2. A **Wise** Tongue—Prov. xv. 2. He knows what to say and how to say it.

3. A **Wholesome** Tongue—Prov. xv. 4. Such a tongue is a minister of life.

---

* "*Things*" does not mean "*men.*" If it read "men" it would mean universalism; as it is "things", it indicates the universal blessing coming upon creation cursed by man's sin.

4. A **Kind** Tongue—Prov. xxxi. 26. Kindness of tongue comes from heart kindness.

5. A **Confessing** Tongue—Phil. ii. 11; Rom. xiv. 11. To own Christ is to find One worth talking about, for He alone is worthy.

6. A **Scriptural** Tongue. "My tongue shall speak of Thy Word" (Psa. cxix. 172).

7. A **Taught** Tongue—Isa. l. 4, R.V. To be taught by God is to be able to teach others to their profit.

888. TONGUES

BAD ONES

THE tongue if under control can be a blessing, but if it is not it will be a bane.

1. A **Deceitful** Tongue—Rom. iii. 13. A deceitful tongue is a lying one.

2. An **Empty** Tongue—1 John iii. 18. Talk is not help.

3. An **Unbridled** Tongue—James i. 26. Uncontrolled, the tongue is a curse.

4. A **Froward** Tongue—Prov. x. 31. Boasting is the essence of pride.

5. A **Lying** Tongue—Prov. vi. 17; xii. 19; xxi. 6; xxvi. 28. A liar is in league with the Devil, and will be shut out of Heaven.

6. A **Flattering** Tongue—Prov. xxviii. 23. Flattery injects conceit and leads astray.

7. A **Backbiting** Tongue—Prov. xxv. 23. A backbiter not only bites others, but in the end he bites himself.

889. "TOOK"

1. Sin's **Mis-take**. "She took of the fruit of the tree" (Gen. iii. 6).

2. God's **Up-take**. "God took him" (Gen. v. 24).

3. Love's **In-take**. "Isaac...took Rebekah, and she became his wife" (Gen. xxiv. 67).

4. Grace's **Out-take**. "He took him from the sheep-folds" (Psa. lxxviii. 70).

5. Achan's **Wrong-take**. "Took of the accursed (devoted) thing" (Joshua vii. 1).

6. Joshua's **All-take**. "Took all the land" (Joshua xi. 23).

7. Virgins' **No-take**. "Took no oil" (Matt. xxv. 3).

890. "TO," OR "UNTO ME"

1. A **Sad Case**. "Ye will not come to Me" (John v. 40).

2. A **Satisfying Cause**. "He that cometh to Me shall never thirst" (John vi. 35).

3. A **Safe Coming**. "Him that cometh to Me shall in no wise be cast out" (John vi. 37).

4. A **Sanctifying Conclusion**. "Let him come unto Me and drink," etc. (John vii. 37).

5. A **Secret Centre**. His death the power, "to draw all men unto Me" (John xii. 32).

6. A **Saving Call**. "Come unto Me, and I will give you rest" (Matt. xi. 28).

7. A **Separating Condition**. "If any man come to Me, and hate not his father...he cannot be My disciple" (Luke xiv. 26).

891. TRAITS OF A WICKED SINNER

HE has—

1. The **Covetousness** of Balaam—2 Peter ii. 15.

2. The **Double Dealing** of King Saul—1 Sam. xv. 20-23.

3. The **Worldliness** of Demas—2 Tim. iv. 10.

4. The **Cunning** of Absalom—2 Sam. xv. 1-6.

5. The **Keenness** of Gehazi—2 Kings v. 20.

6. The **Greed** of Achan—Joshua vii. 21.

7. The **Grab** of Judas—John xii. 6.

892. TOUCHES

THE following are some of the consequences in touching things.

1. The Touch of **Sin**. Eve not only touched, she took—Gen. iii. 3.

2. The Touch of **Salvation**. The live coal of sacrifice saved—Isa. vi. 7.

3. The Touch of **Sanctification**. Whatever touched the altar became like it, "holy"—Exod. xxix. 37.

4. The Touch of **Strength**. Daniel was touched and set up—Dan. x. 10, 16, 18.

5. The Touch of **Sufficiency**. Jeremiah was qualified for service by the Lord—Jer. i. 9.

6. The Touch of **Submission**. Jacob was subdued by the Lord's touch—Gen. xxxii. 25, 32.

7. The Touch of **Success**. When God touches the heart there is a following—1 Sam. x. 26.

893. TOUCH OF CHRIST

"Jesus put forth His hand and touched him" (Matt. viii. 3).

A MOTHER was deeply anxious to see her child, who was lying very ill in a hospital, but the doctor said the mother's presence might disturb the child. The mother was so persistent to see her child, and at last permission was granted on condition she would dress in the uniform of a nurse, which she did, and sat beside her loved one all the night through. In the night the child was very feverish and restless, and to quieten her the mother placed her cool hand on the forehead of her child. The consequence was the restlessness ceased, and, opening her eyes and seeing the nurse (as she thought), she said, "Your touch is just like mother's." There was a sympathy and love in the mother's touch which nothing could hide.

What a touch there is in the touch of Christ, and how often we read He touched people, and His touches were always benedictions.

Mark the effects of His touches.

1. His **cleansing** touch, when He healed the leper—Mark i. 41.

2. His **cooling** touch, when He restored Peter's wife's mother—Matt. viii. 15.

3. His **compelling** touch, when He banished the blindness from the blind man—Matt. ix. 29; xx. 34.

4. His **comforting** touch, when He told His disciples, "Be not afraid" (Matt. xvii. 7).

5. His **causeful** touch, when He unloosed the dumb man's tongue—Mark vii. 33.

6. His **compassionate** touch, when He raised the widow's son—Luke vii. 14.

7. His **counteracting** touch, when He repaired the damage Peter had done—Luke xxii. 51.

894. "TO WALK"

1. **Command.** "To walk in His ways" (Deut. viii. 6; x. 12; xi. 22; xiii. 5; xix. 9; xxvi. 17; xxx. 16).

2. **Sphere.** "Take heed...to walk before Me" (1 Kings ii. 4).

3. **Covenant.** "Josiah made a covenant to walk after the Lord" (2 Kings xxiii. 3).

4. **Power.** "I will cause them to walk...in a straight way" (Jer. xxxi. 9).

5. **The Good**. "To walk humbly with thy God" (Micah vi. 8).

6. **Faith**. "He will make me to walk upon mine high places" (Hab. iii. 19).

7. **Example**. "Ought...to walk, even as He walked" (1 John ii. 6).

895. TOWERS

1. A **Self-conceived** Tower. The Tower of Babel—Gen. xi. 4. Built by sin.

2. The "**High** Tower" of Safety—2 Sam. xxii. 3. See the six "my's" in the verse as illustrating what the Lord is to His people.

3. The **Exalted** Tower for Security. "He is the tower of salvation" (2 Sam. xxii. 51).

4. The **Strong** Tower for Protection. "A strong tower from the enemy" (Psa. lxi. 3; Prov. xviii. 10).

5. The **Watch** Tower for Observation. "Set me upon my tower" (Hab. ii. 1).

6. A **Judged** Tower. "Every high tower" shall be brought low (Isa. ii. 13-15).

7. The **Intended** Tower in Consideration. "Intending to build a tower" (Luke xiv. 28).

896. TRAITS OF GOD'S WORD

"HE authenticates Himself," says one, in speaking of Christ; so say we of God's Word, it authenticates itself.

1. **Firm and Unalterable**, for it is "settled in Heaven" (Psa. cxix. 89).

2. **True and Reliable**, for it is "true from the beginning" (Psa. cxix. 160).

3. **Enlightening and Guiding**, for it is a "lamp" and a "light" (Psa. cxix. 105).

4. **Expansive and Searching**, for it is "exceeding broad" (Psa. cxix. 96).

5. **Pure and Sanctifying**, for it is "pure" and "tried" (Psa. cxix. 140, margin).

6. **Sweet and Satisfying**, for it is "sweeter than honey" (Psa. cxix. 103).

7. **Divine and Wonderful**, for "Thy testimonies are wonderful" (Psa. cxix. 129).

897. "TRANSGRESSION" *

1. The Cause of **Captivity**. "Carried away...for their transgression" (1 Chron. ix. 1).

2. The Cause of Christ's **Death**. "For the transgression of My people was He stricken" (Isa. liii. 5, 8).

3. The Character of **Sin**. "Sin is the transgression of the law" (1 John iii. 4).

4. The Cause of **Punishment**. "I will visit their transgression with the rod" (Psa. lxxxix. 32).

5. The Cause of **Confession**. "I will confess my transgressions unto the Lord" (Psa. xxxii. 5; xxxix. 8; li. 1, 3).

6. The Charge of **God**. "They have transgressed against Me" (Hosea vii. 13).

7. The Condition of **the Forgiven**. "Blessed is he whose transgression is forgiven" (Psa. xxxii. 1).

898. "TRANSGRESSORS"

1. Transgressors **grieve the godly**. "I beheld the transgressors and was grieved" (Psa. cxix. 158).

2. Transgressors **meet with hardness**. "The way of transgressors is hard" (Prov. xiii. 15).

3. Transgressors **caused Christ to suffer**. "Numbered with transgressors" (Isa. liii. 12; Luke xxii. 37).

4. Transgressors **may be arrested** by a right condition of heart by the Lord's people. "Then shall I teach transgressors Thy ways" (Psa. li. 13).

5. Transgressors were **prayed for by Christ**. "Made intercession for the transgressors" (Isa. liii. 12).

6. Transgressors **found out** by the ways of the Lord. "Transgressors shall fall therein" (Hosea xiv. 9).

7. Transgressors **will meet their doom**. "Transgressors shall be destroyed" (Psa. xxxvii. 38).

899. "TREASURING UP"

1. **Depositing in an Unbreakable Bank**. "Lay up for yourselves treasures in Heaven" (Matt. vi. 20).

2. **Keeping the Lord's Portion for Him**. "Let every one lay by in store" (1 Cor. xvi. 2; literally, "treasure up").

3. **A Parent's Duty**. "Children ought not to lay up for the parents," etc. (2 Cor. xii. 14).

---

* "Transgression" describes the act of those who go beyond the boundary of God's law.

4. The Rich Man's Mistake. "Ye have laid up your treasure in the last days" (James v. 3, R.V.).

5. The Fool's Blunder. "So is he that layeth up treasure for himself" (Luke xii. 21).

6. The Sinner's Legacy. "Treasurest up unto thyself wrath" (Rom. ii. 5).

7. The Heaven's and the Earth's Future. "Have been stored up (treasured up) for fire" (2 Peter iii. 7, R.V.).

900. TREES

1. A Forbidden Tree. "Tree of knowledge of good and evil" (Gen. ii. 17).

2. A Healing Tree. "The Lord shewed him a tree" (Exod. xv. 25).

3. A Juniper Tree. "Sat down under a juniper tree" (1 Kings xix. 4).

4. A Flourishing Tree. "Shall be like a tree...bringeth forth fruit" (Psa. i. 3; xcii. 12).

5. A Corrupt Tree. "A corrupt tree bringeth forth evil fruit "(Matt. vii. 17).

6. A Good Tree. "A good tree bringeth forth good fruit" (Matt. vii. 17).

7. A Christ Honoured Tree. "Cursed is every one that hangeth on a tree" (Gal. iii. 13; 1 Peter ii. 24).

901. TREMBLING PEOPLE

1. A Haunted Patriarch. "Fear came upon me, and trembling, which made all my bones to shake" (Job. iv. 14).

2. An Anxious Sinner. "Jailer came trembling...and said...What must I do to be saved?" (Acts xvi. 29, 30, etc.).

3. A Humble Suppliant. "Saul trembling...said, Lord, what wilt Thou have me to do?" (Acts ix. 6).

4. A Conscious Believer. "The woman fearing and trembling," etc. (Mark v. 33).

5. A Working Saint. "Work out your own salvation with fear and trembling" (Phil. ii. 12).

6. A Weak Servant. "I was with you in...fear, and much trembling" (1 Cor. ii. 3).

7. An Awed Believer. "I will look to him that trembleth at My Word" (Isa. lxvi. 2).

902. "TRESPASS" *

1. **Sin.** "Trespass against the Lord" (Num. v. 6).
2. **Sacrifice.** "Trespass offering" (Lev. v. 6, 15, 16, 18, 19; vi. 6).
3. **Sacrilege.** "Committed a trespass" (Josh. vii. 1; xxii. 20).
4. **Grace.** "Not imputing their trespasses unto them" (2 Cor. v. 19).
5. **Dead.** "Dead in trespasses and sins" (Eph. ii. 1).
6. **Forgiveness.** "Forgiving you all trespasses" (Col. ii. 13).
7. **Example.** "Forgive...that your Father...may forgive you your trespasses" (Mark xi. 25).

903. TRIBULATION: THE GREAT ONE

BEFORE the Lord comes with His saints.

1. The time of **"Jacob's trouble"** must take place (Jer. xxx. 7).
2. The **like of which has never happened** before in the history of the world—Daniel xii. 1; Matt. xxiv. 21.
3. When a **covenant will be made with the Antichrist** —Dan. ix. 26-28.
4. When **two-thirds of the inhabitants** of the land will be "cut off" (Zech. xiii. 8).
5. But it is just at that time the Lord will appear in Person and deliver His earthly people—Zech. xiv.
6. And the Jewish nation will own Jesus of Nazareth, the pierced One of Calvary, to be their Promised Messiah—Zech. xii. 10.

904. "TRIED"

1. A Tried **Testimony.** "The Word of the Lord is tried" (2 Sam. xxii. 31; Psa. xviii. 30).
2. A Tried **Stone.** "A tried stone" (Isa. xxviii. 16).
3. A Tried **Believer.** Abraham. "He was tried" (Heb. xi. 17).
4. A Tried **Servant.** "The Word of the Lord tried him" (Psa. cv. 19).
5. A Tried **Host.** "Many shall be purified, made white, and tried" (Dan. xii. 10).
6. A Tempted **One.** "When he is tried, he shall receive a crown of life" (James i. 12).
7. A Suffering **Saint.** "Tried with fire" (Zech. xiii. 9; 1 Peter i. 7).

* To be unfaithful.

905. TROUBLE

TROUBLE comes from many quarters.

1. **Generally** from sin, as Ahab shows—1 Kings xviii. 18.

2. **Specifically** from self, as Joseph's brethren demonstrate—Gen. xlv. 3.

3. **Testingly** from God, as David confesses—Psa. lxxi. 20.

4. **Circumstantially** from our surroundings, as Eliphaz says—Job v. 6, 7.

5. **Wickedly** from our enemies, as the Psalmist explains —Psa. xxii. 11.

6. **Incidentally** from our testimony, as Paul declares— 2 Cor. i. 8.

7. **Influentially** from our brethren, as Achan illustrates— Joshua vii. 25.

906. TRUE DELIGHT

SEVEN times the Psalmist speaks of delighting in God's Word in Psalm. 119.

1. **Resolution.** "I will delight myself in Thy statutes" (16). When we make up our mind to any given thing, let us mind the thing to which we have consented.

2. **Concentration.** "Thy testimonies also are my delight" (24). Concentration on God's Word in the midst of opposition— see verse 23, ever leads to benediction—Jer. xv. 16.

3. **Compulsion.** "Make me to go in the path of Thy commandments, for therein do I delight" (35). Love easily counsels when the heart is willing to be compelled.

4. **Affection.** "I will delight myself in Thy commandments, which I have loved" (47). The only fuel which will feed the fire of love is God's Word, and when that is fed the sacrifice of pleasure in God's will is ever the outcome.

5. **Opposition.** "Their heart is as fat as grease, but I delight in Thy law" (70). Fatty sinners are ever against flourishing saints. The doings of ungodly men should make us the more determined to do God's Word.

6. **Supplication.** "Let Thy tender mercies come unto me, that I may live, for thy law is my delight" (77). Prayer for "mercies," and faith to believe they are "tender," are sure to come to those whose hearts are right with the Lord by delighting in His Word.

7. **Salvation.** "I have longed for Thy salvation, for Thy law is my delight" (174). The reason why he longed for God's salvation is because he had a heart and a life to obey God's law.

907. TROUBLED ONES

1. **A Striking Simile.** "The wicked are like the troubled sea" (Isa. lvii. 20). Sin is the rest-destroyer and the soul-annoyer.

2. **An Agonised Saviour.** "Now is My soul troubled" (John xii. 27). The hour of His woe was caused by the guilt of our wickedness.

3. **A Defeated Company.** "Why hast thou troubled us?" (Joshua vii. 25). An Achan in the midst will cause defeat in the war.

4. **A Distressed Saint.** "Thou didst hide Thy face, and I was troubled" (Psa. xxx. 7). The Lord's hidings are for the believer's testings.

5. **A Cumbered Servant.** "Martha...thou art careful and troubled about many things" (Luke x. 41). To serve the Lord is good, but to be cumbered with serving is bad.

6. **A Convicted Brotherhood.** "They were troubled at his presence" (Gen. xlv. 3). A bad conscience will prick the heart to its possessor's confusion.

7. **A Routed Foe.** "Troubled the host of the Egyptians" (Exod. xiv. 24). "The troublers of God's people are sure to be troubled by the Lord" (2 Thess. i. 7).

908. TRUTHS ASSOCIATED WITH SINGING

1. **Consecration.** "Offered the burnt offering...with singing" (2 Chron. xxiii. 18).

2. **Dedication.** "Dedication of the wall...with singing" (Neh. xii. 27).

3. **Emancipation.** "Then was our mouth filled with laughter, and our tongue with singing" (Psa. cxxvi. 2).

4. **Satisfaction.** "Rest in His love, shall joy over thee with singing" (Zeph. iii. 17).

5. **Compensation.** "Weeping may endure for a night, but singing (margin) cometh in the morning" (Psa. xxx. 5; cxxvi. 5, margin).

6. **Adoration.** "Come before His presence with singing" (Psa. c. 2; cvii. 22, margin).

7. **Redemption.** "Brought forth His people with joy, and His chosen with singing" (Psa. cv. 43, margin).

909. TWO NATURES

THE two natures—John iii. 6. Naturally we are the children of wrath—Eph. ii. 3; but through faith in Christ we are made partakers of the Divine nature—2 Peter i. 4, R.V., margin, "a Divine nature."

I. The natural man is a **sinner** in a threefold sense.
1. By his connection with Adam—Rom. v. 13.
2. Because he has Adam's nature—Gen. v. 3; Rom. iii. 10.
3. Because he has committed sins—Rom. viii. 5.

II. Those who are believers in Christ are **saints** in a threefold sense.
1. Because we are identified with Christ—1 Cor. i. 2.
2. Because we have the nature of God—John i. 12, 13.
3. Because as saints we live saintly lives—Eph. v. 3.

910. UNBELIEF—ITS POWERS

1. **Destroys** the capacity to see—John iii. 36.
2. **Disturbs** the soul—Acts xiv. 2.
3. **Hardens** the sensibilities—Acts xix. 9.
4. **Questions** the authority of God's Word—Rom. x. 21.
5. **Causes** the feet to stumble—1 Peter ii. 3.
6. **Shuts** up the disobedient in prison—1 Peter iii. 20.
7. **Robs** of blessing—Heb. iii. 18; iv. 2.

911. UNBELIEF—WHAT IT DOES

1. **Hardens** the heart—Acts xix. 9.
2. **Disregards** God's entreaty—Rom. x. 21.
3. **Stumbles** at God's Word—1 Peter ii. 8.
4. **Severs** from the Lord—Rom. xi. 20.
5. The **incentive** to envy and persecution—Acts xiv. 2; xvii. 5.
6. **Synonymous** with disobedience—1 Pet iv. 17.
7. **Forerunner** of destruction—Rom. ii. 8; John iii. 36.

912. UNSEEN

1. The unseen is the **seen to faith**—Heb. xi. 1, 13.
2. For it has **confidence in the Unseen**—2 Cor. iv. 18; v. 1-9.
3. **Love to the Unseen**—Heb. xi. 27.
4. **Joy from the Unseen**—1 Peter i. 8.

913. UNBELIEF

JOHN'S GOSPEL

1. Unbelief **dulls** the faculty of faith—iii. 12.

2. Unbelief **shuts up** in condemnation—iii. 18.

3. Unbelief **keeps out** the blessing of eternal life—iii. 16.

4. Unbelief **sees not** the purpose of Christ's mission—vi. 36.

5. Unbelief **thinks more** of material things than eternal ones—vi. 64.

6. Unbelief **keeps away** from the only One who can deliver from sin—viii. 24.

7. Unbelief **turns a deaf ear** to the Word of Christ—viii. 45, 46.

8. Unbelief **accepts not the testimony of Christ**—x. 25, 26, 37, 38.

9. Unbelief **will not own the working of Christ**—xii. 37. 39.

10. Unbelief is **influenced by the material alone**—xx. 25.

914. "UNTO THE END"

WE are continually exhorted to keep on "unto the end."

1. Those who **"endure unto the end"** shall be saved (Mark xiii. 13).

2. We are to **"hold fast** the confidence and the rejoicing of the hope firm **unto the end"** (Heb. iii. 6).

3. "We are **made partakers** of Christ if we hold the beginning of our confidence stedfast **unto the end"** (Heb. iii. 14).

4. We are to keep the **"full assurance of hope unto the end"** (Heb. vi. 11).

5. We are to **"hope to the end** for the grace" that is yet to come (1 Peter. i. 13).

6. We are to **keep** Christ's **"works unto the end"** (Rev. ii. 26).

7. Then we shall find, as in every case in Scripture, the word of His promise runs parallel with the word of His command, for He promises to **"confirm us unto the end,"** that we "may be blameless in the day of our Lord Jesus Christ" (1 Cor. i. 8).

915. "UNTO THE LORD"

1. **Conversion** is "Turning to God" 1 Thess. i. 9

2. **Christ's substitution** was to "Bring us to God" (1 Peter iii. 18).

3. **Consecration** is to "Live unto the Lord" (Rom. vi. 10, 11, 13, 16, 19, 21; xii. 1).

4. **Communion** with God is to let all service be done "unto Christ" (Eph. vi. 5).

5. **Worship** is "making melody in the heart to the Lord" (Eph. v. 19).

6. **The rule** to regulate our conduct to each other is do everything "unto the Lord" (Rom. xiv. 6-8).

7. **What is the end** God has in view in all things? "To reconcile all things unto Himself" (Col. i. 20).

916. "UNTO YOU"

PREGNANT and personal sentences are full of pertinent blessing. "Unto you" is one of them.

1. **Value.** "Unto you therefore which believe He is precious" (1 Peter ii. 7). Who can value the Value of Christ? Believers have the Value of all values in possessing Christ, and they too are valuable. The Revised Version gives this thought.

2. **Vision.** "It is given unto you to know the mysteries (secrets) of the Kingdom" (Matt. xiii. 11). The initiated are instructed in the Revelation of the Word by the inner illumination of the Spirit.

3. **Life.** "Verily, verily I say unto you," etc. (John v. 24, 25). Eternal life is the positive blessing of the Gospel, and those who are identified with the Living Christ receive the life He is, and are made alive.

4. **Power.** "For the Promise is unto you," etc. (Acts ii. 39). The power of the Spirit has been procured by the propitiation of the Saviour. Passover and Pentecost are the twin blessings of the Gospel.

5. **Knowledge.** "Be it known unto you, therefore, men and brethren, that through this Man is preached unto you the forgiveness of sins" (Acts xiii. 38). To be personally acquainted with Christ is the sum of all knowledge.

6. **Grace and Peace.** "Grace and peace be multiplied unto you" (2 Peter i. 2). Grace here means strength, and peace is quietness. Power to supply and peace to calm.

7. **Healing.** "Unto you that fear My Name shall the Sun of Righteousness arise with healing in His wings" (Mal. iv. 2). To fear Him with holy obedience and humble grace, is to find the healing of His love and the warmth of His power.

917. "UNWORTHY"—"WORTHY"

1. **Confession of the Sinner.** "I am not worthy" (Gen. xxxii. 10).
2. **Character of the Saviour.** "Thou art worthy" (Rev. iv. 11; v. 2, 4, 9, 12).
3. **Calling of the Saint.** "Walk worthy of the vocation" (Eph. iv. 1).

918. UPPER-ROOM MEETING
(John xx. 19-23.)

1. **Presence** of the Risen Christ. "He stood in the midst."
2. **Peace** from the Crucified Lord. "Peace be unto you."
3. **Power** from the Breathing Lord. "He breathed upon them."
4. **Sent Forth** by Christ. "As My Father sent Me, even so send I you."
5. **Revelation** of Christ. "He shewed unto them His hands and side."
6. **Authority** from Christ. "Whose sins ye remit, they are remitted."
7. **Gladness** through Christ. "Then were the disciples glad when they saw the Lord."

919. "UPON A ROCK"

1. The Place of **Revelation.** "Thou shalt stand upon a rock...and...see" (Exod. xxxiii. 21-23).
2. The Place of **Sacrifice.** "Offered it upon a rock" (Judges xiii. 19).
3. The Place of **Safety.** "He shall set me upon a rock" (Psa. xxvii. 5).
4. The Place of **Security.** "Built his house upon a rock" (Matt. vii. 24).
5. The Place of **Vision.** "From the top of the rocks I see" (Num. xxiii. 9).
6. The Place of **Stability.** "Upon this rock I will build" (Matt. xvi. 18).
7. The Place of **Watching.** "Spread it for her upon the rock" (2 Sam. xxi. 10).

920. UPRIGHT

THERE are many blessings which come to the "upright."

1. **Salvation.** "Saveth the upright in heart" (Psa. vii. 10).

2. **Dominion.** "The upright shall have dominion" (Psa. xlix. 14).

3. **Gladness.** "Gladness for the upright in heart" (Psa. xcvii. 11).

4. **Benediction.** "The generation of the upright shall be blessed" (Psa. cxii. 2).

5. **"Light."** "Unto the upright there ariseth light in the darkness" (Psa. cxii. 4).

6. **Privilege.** "The upright shall dwell in Thy presence" (Psa. cxl. 13).

7. **Pleasure.** "The prayer of the upright is His delight" (Prov. xv. 8).

921. UPWARD LIFE

1. Treasure **laid up**—Matt. vi. 20. Christ our Treasure.

2. Faith **looking up**—Psa. v. 3. Christ the Object of Faith.

3. Love **building up**—Jude 20. Christ our Lover.

4. Life **springing up**—John iv. 14. Christ our Indweller.

5. Power **lifting up**—Acts iii. 7-9. Christ the Power.

6. Believer **mounting up**—Isa. xl. 31. Christ our Attraction.

7. **Caught up** to meet Christ—1 Thess. iv. 17. Christ our Hope.

922. VAIN THINGS

1. Vain **"repetitions"** in prayer—Matt. vi. 7.

2. Vain **"imaginations"** in thought—Rom. i. 21; Psa. cxix. 113.

3. Vain **"wisdom"** in carnal reason—1 Cor. iii. 20.

4. Vain **"words"** in speech—Eph. v. 6.

5. Vain **"deceit"** in action—Col. ii. 8.

6. Vain **"jangling"** in discussion—1 Tim. i. 6.

7. Vain **"babblings"** in talk—1 Tim. vi. 20; 2 Tim. ii. 16.

8. Vain **"talkers"** in the Church—Titus i. 10.

9. Vain **"questions"** in debate—Titus iii. 9.

10. Vain **"religion"** in profession—James i. 26.

11. Vain **"help"** in man—Psa. lx. 11; cviii. 12.

12. Vain **"oblations"** in worship—Isa. i. 13.

"Redeemed from." The remedy—1 Peter i. 18.

923. "VERILY, VERILY, I SAY UNTO YOU"

CHRIST was continually using this pregnant sentence. Take seven of the sayings as found in John's Gospel.

1. The **Necessity** of the New Birth. "Verily, verily, I say unto you, Except a man be born from above (margin), he cannot enter the Kingdom of God" (iii. 3, 5).

2. **Eternal Life.** "Verily, verily, I say unto you, He that heareth My Word and believeth on Him that sent Me, hath everlasting life" (v. 24).

3. **Eternal Existence.** "Verily, verily, I say unto you, Before Abraham was I am" (viii. 58).

4. The **Entrance of Blessing.** "Verily, verily, I say unto you, I am the Door of the sheep" (x. 7).

5. **Dying to Live.** "Verily, verily, I say unto you, Except a corn of wheat fall into the ground and die," etc. (xii. 24).

6. **Added Works.** "Verily, verily, I say unto you, He that believeth Me, the works I do shall he do, and greater" (xiv. 12).

7. **Answered Prayer.** "Verily, verily, I say unto you, Whatsoever ye shall ask the Father in My Name, that will I do" (xvi. 23).

924. "VEXED"

1. A **people** vexed by oppression. "The Egyptians vexed us" (Num. xx. 15).

2. A vexed **Holy Spirit** by disobedience. "Vexed His Holy Spirit" (Isa. lxiii. 10).

3. A **daughter** vexed with a devil. "Grievously vexed with a devil" (Matt. xv. 22).

4. A **righteous man** vexed with sin. "Vexed his righteous soul" (2 Peter ii. 7, 8).

5. A vexed **company** healed. "He healed them that were vexed with unclean spirits" (Luke vi. 18).

6. A vexed **one praying.** "My soul is also sore vexed" (Psa. vi. 2, 3).

7. An **afflicted saint.** "The Almighty, who hath vexed my soul" (Job xxvii. 2).

925. VICARIOUSNESS

"Who gave Himself a ransom (*anti-lutron*) for all" (1 Tim. ii. 6). How frequently the Holy Spirit reminds us of the fact, "Christ died."

1. "He died **unto sin once**" (Rom. vi. 10). The sufficiency of His death.

2. "He died for the **ungodly** and **sinners**" (Rom. v. 6, 8). The subjects for whom He died.

3. "Christ died...**risen**" (Rom. viii. 34). The necessary accompaniment.

4. "Christ died for **our sins**" (1 Cor. xv. 3). The thing for which He died.

5. "One died **for all**" (2 Cor. v. 14). Hence, all believers died with Him.

6. "**He** died for all" (2 Cor. v. 15). That believers might live to Him.

7. "**Jesus died and rose again**" (1 Thess. iv. 14). And that is the guarantee that the sleeping and living ones shall be glorified—1 Thess. v. 10.

926. VICTORY

Judges vi and vii

1. Prayer,   ..   The **forerunner** of victory—vi. 7.
2. Presence,   ..   The **secret** of victory—vi. 12, 16.
3. Promise,   ..   The **assurer** of victory—vi. 14; vii. 7, 9.
4. Practice,   ..   The **soul** of victory—vi. 25-27.
5. Power,   ..   The **securer** of victory—vi. 34.
6. Peace,   ..   The **feeder** of victory—vi. 23, 24.
7. Posture,   ..   The **accompaniment** of victory—vii. 5, 7.

927. VICTORY

1. **Crucifixion with Christ** is the secret of victory over self—Gal. ii. 20.

2. **Equipment in the Lord** is the secret of victory over Satan—Eph. vi. 10, 11.

3. **Separation to the Father** is the secret of victory over the world—2 Cor. vi. 14-18; 1 John ii. 14-17.

4. **Walking in the Spirit** is the secret of victory over the flesh—Gal. v. 16-21.

5. **Speech seasoned** with the salt of grace is the secret of victory over the tongue—Col. iv. 6.

6. "**Well doing**" is the secret of victory over the talk of ignorance and foolish men—1 Peter ii. 15.

7. **Christ living in us** is the secret of victory over failure in the Christian life—Eph. iii. 16, 17.

928. VOICES HEARD AROUND THE CROSS

1. **The Voice of Unholy Taunt.** "If Thou be the Son of God, come down from the Cross" (Matt. xxvii. 39, 40).

2. **The Voice of Unconscious Gospel.** "He saved others, Himself He cannot save" (Matt. xxvii. 41-43).

3. **The Voice of Unbelieving Repetition.** "The thieves... cast the same in His teeth" (Matt. xxvii. 44).

4. **The Voice of Mistaken Application.** "This Man calleth for Elias" (Matt. xxvii. 47).

5. **The Voice of Idle Curiosity.** "Let be, let us see whether Elias will come and save Him" (Matt. xxvii. 49).

6. **The Voice of Earnest Appeal.** "Lord, remember me" (Luke xxiii. 42).

7. **The Voice of Compelled Confession.** "Truly this was the Son of God" (Matt. xxvii. 54).

929. WAITING UPON THE LORD

Psa. lxii. 5

THE Hebrew word rendered "wait" in the above verse is translated "rest" in Psalm xxxvii. 7, "cease" in Lamentations ii.18, "forbear" in Ezekiel xxiv. 17, "tarry" in 1 Sam. xiv. 9, "be still" in Isaiah xxiii. 2, "quieted" in Psalm cxxxi. 2. Reading the words into the text, we may say waiting upon the Lord means—

1. **Resting** in the Lord's will.
2. **Ceasing** from self effort.
3. **Forbearing** to answer back.
4. **Tarrying** to be empowered.
5. **To be still** in humble submission.
6. **Quieted** in the peace of God.
7. **Waiting** for the Lord's direction.

930. WAITING ON THE LORD

"Wait on the Lord" Psa. xxvii. 14

"I WILL do what you want me to do," said one friend to another; "but you must wait, while I do it." And the one who was told to wait, replied: "I suppose I shall get what I want, if I wait long enough." In reading through the Psalms, we find continuous reference to waiting upon Him, and then we find how we are to do it, in the attitude expressed in different Scriptures.

1. Wait **Continually**. "On Thee do I wait all the day" (Psa. xxv. 5). Patience will surely be rewarded, therefore wait patiently.

2. Wait **Courageously**. "Wait on the Lord, be of good courage" (Psa. xxvii. 14). Expect to receive from the Lord, and the expectation will surely be met.

3. Wait **Consistently**. "Wait on the Lord, and keep His way" (Psa. xxxvii. 34). We cannot expect to receive from the Lord, unless we are walking in His ways.

4. Wait **Confidently**. "Thou hast done it, and I will wait on Thy Name" (Psa. lii. 9). Past blessings create present confidences.

5. Wait **Calmly**. "Because of His strength, I will wait upon Thee, for God is my defence" (Psa. lix. 9). We need not be disturbed by anything, since God protects us by His presence.

6. Wait **Concentratingly**. "My soul, wait thou upon God" (Psa. lxii. 5). The soul of consecration to the Lord is concentration in Him.

7. Wait **Communicatingly**. "As the eyes of a maiden wait upon the hand of her mistress, so our eyes wait upon the Lord our God" (Psa. cxxiii. 2). The mistress communicates her desire by the indication of her hand to the watching maiden, who thus knows what to do. So we know the mind of the Lord when we look to Him.

931. "WALKETH"

THE present tense of the believer's walk, and the blessedness and power of his walk as he fulfils the Lord's conditions is indicated below.

1. **Dwelling**. "He that walketh uprightly...shall dwell in Thy holy hill" (Psa. xv. 1, 2).

2. **Service**. "He that walketh in a perfect way, he shall serve Me" (Psa. ci. 6).

3. **Blessedness**. "Blessed is every one that walketh in His ways" (Psa. cxxviii. 1).

4. **Answering**. "He that walketh in uprightness feareth the Lord" (Prov. xiv. 2).

5. **Exaltation**. "He that walketh righteously...shall dwell on high" (Isa. xxxiii. 15, 16).

6. **Consolation**. "My words do good to him that walketh uprightly" (Micah ii. 7).

7. **Wisdom**. "He that walketh with wise men shall be wise" (Prov. xiii. 20).

932. "WALK IN"

"WALK" indicates progress in the Christian life as the result of life given; and "in" denotes the sphere "in" which we are to walk.

1. "Walk in **newness of life**" (Rom. vi. 4). The new life shows itself in walking in the new way.

2. "Walk in **the Spirit**" (Gal. v. 16). The sphere in which believers live.

3. "Walk in **love**" (Eph. v. 2) means to live in sympathy, sacrifice, and help.

4. "Walk in **wisdom**" (Col. iv. 5) is to evidence we know how to apply the knowledge we possess.

5. "Walk in the **light**" (1 John i. 7), and thus we are not moving in the realm of sin, unbelief, and ignorance.

6. "Walking in **truth**" (3 John 4) shows we know the truth and are living in it.

7. "Walk in **Him**" (Col. ii. 6) is to demonstrate we have received Christ.

933. WALK IN THE SPIRIT
Gal. v. 25

WHAT does it mean to walk in the Spirit? It means at least the following seven things:

1. "**In the love of God**" (Jude 21) is the sphere of the **believer's affection**.

2. "**In the truth**" is the atmosphere of the **saint's sanctification** (John xvii. 17).

3. "**In the Lord**" is the sphere of the **Christian's joy** (Phil. iv. 4).

4. "**In the Vine**" is the element of the **branch's fruitfulness** (John xv. 5).

5. "**In the light**" is the place of the **child's fellowship** (1 John i. 7).

6. "**In the grace**" of God is the environment of the **servant's fitness** (2 Tim. ii. 1).

7. "**In the Spirit**" is the supply of the **saved one's need** (Eph. v. 18, R.V., margin).

934. WANTING AND NOT WANTING

1. A **Want Supplier**. "Let all thy wants be upon Me" (Judges xix. 20).

2. A **Necessary Condition**. "There is no want to them that fear Him" (Psa. xxxiv. 9).

3. **A Sorry Case.** "He began to be in want" (Luke xv. 14).

4. **An Impossible Sum.** "That which is wanting cannot be numbered" (Eccles. i. 15).

5. **A Happy Quest.** "They that seek the Lord shall not want" (Psa. xxxiv. 10).

6. **A Certain Witness.** "The Lord is my Shepherd, I shall not want" (Psa. xxiii. 1).

7. **A Sad Lack.** "Fools die for want of wisdom" (Prov. x. 21).

935. "WASHED OUT"

"Wash away thy sins" Acts xxii. 16

WALKING down Kingsway, I noticed a pavement artist, who was assiduously applying his art. Against the scene that he was sketching he had chalked, "Five hours' work washed out by the rain." In the earlier part of that afternoon there had been a tremendous downpour of rain, accompanying a terrific storm, and as the poor man indicated, it had completely obliterated all the result of his toil. The words, "Washed out" arrested me, and it made me think of what the Bible says about washing. Both sides are presented to us—what God has done for us for the sake of Christ, and what He would have us do for our own sakes, as well as for His.

1. **A Searching Command.** "Wash you, make you clean" (Isa. i. 16). Till we are willing to be cleansed, and cleanse, the Lord cannot bless us.

2. **A Personal Prayer.** "Wash me and I shall be whiter than snow" (Psa. li. 7). There is no one so clean as the one who has been cleansed in the Blood of Christ.

3. **An Earnest Desire.** "Wash me throughly of mine iniquity" (Psa. li. 2). The Lord's work is always thorough. When He washes, He washes right through.

4. **A Qualified Host.** Those who stand before the throne of God in the glory are those who have "washed their robes and made them white in the Blood of the Lamb" (Rev. vii. 14).

5. **An Assuring Statement.** In reminding the believers at Corinth what they were, and what they are, the Apostle says, "But ye are washed" (1 Cor. vi. 11).

6. **An Essential Qualification.** In drawing near to God in worship, it is necessary to have "our bodies washed with pure water" (Heb. x. 22).

7. **A Grateful Doxology.** "Unto Him that has loved us, and washed us from our sins in His own Blood...be glory and dominion for ever" (Rev. i. 5, 6).

936. WASHING

1. **Separation.** Washed heart. "Wash thine heart from wickedness" (Jer. iv. 14).
2. **Service.** Washed feet. "Wash one another's feet" (John xiii. 14).
3. **Sanctification.** Washed clothes. "Let them wash their clothes" (Exod. xix. 10).
4. **Fasting.** Washed face. "When thou fastest, anoint thine head, and wash thy face" (Matt. vi. 17).
5. **Seeing.** Washed eyes. "I washed and do see" (John ix. 15).
6. **Sympathy.** Washed Stripes. "Washed their stripes" (Acts xvi. 33).
7. **Cleansing.** A washed Church. "Washing of water by the Word" (Eph. v. 26).

937. WATCHING WORKERS

NEHEMIAH IV

MARK the use of the word "work," which occurs seven times.

1. Their **Purpose.** "They had a mind to work" (6).
2. Their **Persecution.** "Cause the work to cease" (11).
3. Their **Personality.** "Every one unto his work" (15).
4. Their **Perseverance.** "Wrought in the work" (16).
5. Their **Protection.** "With one of his hands wrought in the work, and with the other held a weapon" (17).
6. Their **Prospect.** "The work is great and large" (19).
7. Their **Plan.** "So we laboured in the work" (21).

All we do in life's task can be done to and for the Lord. The maid in her service, the scholar in his lessons, the employer in his business, the workman in his task, the mother in the home, the lad in his errand, and the labourer in the field.

938. WEEPING ONES

1. A Weeping **Backslider**—Matt. xxvi. 75.
2. A Weeping **Mother**—Luke vii. 13.
3. A Weeping **Sinner**—Luke vii. 38.
4. A Weeping **Saviour**—Luke xix. 41.
5. A Weeping **Mourner**—John xi. 31-33.
6. A Weeping **Sympathiser**—John xi. 35.
7. A Weeping **Apostle**—Phil. iii. 18.

939. "WE HAVE"

1. **Scripture** as our **Authority**. "We have a more sure word of prophecy" (2 Peter i. 19).

2. **Redemption** as our **Blessing**. "In whom we have redemption" (Eph. i. 7).

3. **Eternal Life** as our **Possession**. "Ye have eternal life" (1 John v. 13).

4. **Peace** as our **Comfort**. "We have peace with God" (Rom. v. 1).

5. **Access** as our **Privilege**. "We have access into this grace" (Rom. v. 2).

6. **Union** with Christ as our **Security**. "We have been planted together" (Rom. vi. 5).

7. Christ's **Advocacy** as our **Care**. "We have an Advocate with the Father" (1 John ii. 1).

940. "WE LIVE"

1. **Sphere** of our life. "In Him we live" (Acts xvii. 28).

2. **Set** of our life. "We live unto the Lord" (Rom. xiv. 8).

3. **Surroundings** of our life. "As dying and behold we live" (2 Cor. vi. 9).

4. **Source** of our life. "By the Spirit we live" (Gal. v. 25, R.V.).

5. **Saviour** of our life. "We might live through (by means of) Him" (1 John iv. 9).

6. **Staple** of our life. "Now we live, if ye stand fast in the Lord" (1 Thess. iii. 8).

7. **Second Coming** of Christ the Hope of our life. "We shall live together with Him" (1 Thess. v. 9, 10).

941. WELLS

A Study in Genesis XXVI

PRIMARILY a well is a pit in the ground into which a water-spring wells up. In a metaphorical sense a well is used in many ways, such as a well of learning, and a well of everlasting life.

I. **Well of Promise**—1-6, 24. When the Lord appeared to Isaac He forbade him, on the one hand, to go down to Egypt, and also told him to sojourn in the land in which he was found. It was a time of famine in the land, and his natural inclination was to go to Egypt for help, as his father Abraham had done —Gen. xii. 10. And then the Lord follows up His prohibition by giving Isaac a series of "I wills" of promise. These promises may be read in the light of the larger blessing of the New Testament.

1. The "I will" of **presence**.   "I will be with thee" (Matt. xxviii. 20).

2. The "I will" of **blessing**.   "And will bless thee" (John xiv. 18).

3. The "I will" of **gift**.   "I will give" (John xiv. 27).

4. The "I will" of **performance**.   "I will perform" (John xiv. 13).

5. The "I will" of **multiplication**.   "I will make thy seed to multiply" (John xv. 5).

6. The "I will" of **continuance**.   "Will give unto thy seed" (Acts ii. 39).

7. The "I will" of **reason**.   "Will bless thee...for My servant Abraham's sake" (John xiv. 14).

All these promises were given to Isaac for Abraham's sake; ours are given to us for Jesus' sake.

II. **Well of Prosperity**—12-16.   The Lord's blessing is seen in that the tilled land of Isaac brought forth a "hundredfold," in that he "waxed great," in that he "went forward," in that he "grew until he became very great," in that he possessed flocks and herds, in that he had a "great store of servants," in that his prosperity was "envied," and in that Abimelech recognised he was "mightier than" the Philistines.   When we serve the Lord by our obedience we always command His blessing.

III. **Wells of Recovery**—17, 18.   The wells that Abraham made were choked by the wanton act of the Philistines; Isaac repaired them.   This action may be taken to illustrate that when it is possible to recover what has been fouled by sinners we should do so.   Sinners will often foul the wells of thought by contaminating literature.   Happy are we if we shall restore our minds by the well-springs of God's Word.

IV. **Well of Contention**—19, 20.   Isaac's servants found a "well of living water" (19, margin).   This provoked opposition from "the herdsmen of Gerar," hence the well was named Esek, which means contention—20, margin.   We shall often find that when by our patient labour we obtain something, others will be jealous of our obtainment.   A strong character will not dispute about his rights, he will give them up rather than contend for them.

V. **Well of Hatred**—21, 22.   Isaac's men "digged another well."   This provoked opposition again, and Isaac called the name of it Sitnah (margin, hatred).   Opposition pursued develops into hatred, but Isaac, in the calm of his surrendered rights, moved on and digged another well. When we are removed from the sphere of those who hate us it is impossible for them to find us.

VI. **Well of Rehoboth**—22. Rehoboth means room (margin). Contention now ceases, and Isaac recognises "the Lord hath made room for us." We shall always find that any thing we give up for the Lord always leads to compensation from Him.

VII. **Well of Communion**—25, 32, 33. Isaac had moved on to Beersheba. Beersheba means the well of the oath—33, margin; and the reason why it is so called is evident from verse 24, where the Lord assures Isaac He will bless him for Abraham's sake. Believers now are assured by God's Word and oath that He will surely bless us in Christ, who is our great High Priest—Heb. vi. 13-20.

An old man, in speaking to his sons on his deathbed, said to them: "I am leaving you a fortune, but you will have to dig for it." Practically, he left his sons no fortune, but the good advice that if they wanted to succeed in life they would have to dig by constant perseverance into the earth of their surroundings and acquire things by diligent labour which would prove a source of sustenance in the after days. The great lesson of the lesson is, press on in the quest of life and do not be discouraged by opposition.

942. WELLS OF SALVATION
Isaiah xii

THE wells of God's supplies are constant in their supply and fullness.

1. His **Life** is perennial in its supply—John iv. 14.

2. His **Love** is expressive of His nature—1 John iv. 8, 16.

3. His **Word** is wonderful in its promises—2 Peter i. 3, 4.

4. His **Joy** is unspeakable in its thrill—1 Peter i. 8.

5. His **Riches** are unsearchable in their wealth—Eph. iii. 8.

6. His **Peace** is beyond human understanding in its quiet—Phil. iv. 7.

7. His **Power** is irresistible in its strength—Isa. xl. 25-31.

8. His **Ways** are undiscoverable in their mystery—Rom. xi. 33.

9. His **Grace** is unlimited in its sufficiency—2 Cor. ix. 8; xii. 9.

10. His **Truth** is holy in its influence—John xvii. 17.

11. His **Holiness** is glorious in its sanctity—Exod. xv. 11.

12. His **Name** is Divine in its contents—Isa. ix. 6.

943. "WELL DOING"
1 PETER

1. **A Commended Citizen.** "Praise of them that do well" (ii. 14).
2. **A Godly Silencer.** "For so is the will of God, that with well doing ye may put to silence, " etc. (ii. 15).
3. **A Patient Sufferer.** "When ye do well, and suffer for it, ye take it patiently, this is acceptable with God" (ii. 20).
4. **A Royal Seed.** "Whose daughters ye are, as long as ye do well" (iii. 6).
5. **An Approved Sufferer.** "Better...ye suffer for well doing than for evil doing" (iii. 17).
6. **A Committed Believer.** "Commit the keeping of their souls in well doing" (iv. 19).

944. "WENT FORTH"
CHRIST is often said to be One who "went forth" and "went out."

1. The "Sower went forth to sow" (Matt. xiii. 3). **Christ's ministry.**
2. "Jesus went forth and saw a great multitude" (Matt. xiv. 14). **His compassion.**
3. "He went forth again...and taught them" (Mark ii. 13). **His teaching.**
4. "He went forth and saw a publican...and said, Follow Me" (Luke v. 27). **His calling.**
5. "He went out, and abode in the Mount of Olives" (Luke xxi. 37). **His isolation.**
6. "He went forth with His disciples" (John xviii. 1). **His sufferings.**
7. "He went forth into...Golgotha" (John xix. 17). **His sacrifice.**

945. "WENT OUT"

1. A **multitude** went out to see—Matt. xi. 7-9.
2. A **householder** went out to hire—Matt. xx. 1-8.
3. A **backslider** went out to repent—Matt. xxvi. 75.
4. A **righteous man** went out to leave—Luke xvii. 29.
5. A **prisoner** went out to liberty—Acts xii. 9, 10.
6. A **believer** went out to blessing—Heb. xi. 8.
7. A **company** went out to pray—Acts xvi. 13.

946. "WENT'S"

1. A Consecrated Saint. Abraham "went out" at the Lord's bidding, and thus found the Lord's blessing—Heb. xi. 8.

2. A Compassionate Saviour. "He went about doing good" (Acts x. 38). The love of His heart moved His hands to labour.

3. A Converted Sinner. "He went on his way rejoicing" (Acts viii. 39). Being saved by the Lord makes us glad in Him.

4. A Concentrated Company. "They went up into an upper room...continued with one accord in prayer" (Acts i. 13, 14). The unity of their fervent prayer brought them the fusing of the Spirit's power.

5. A Conservative Party. "They went to their own company" (Acts iv. 23). Being centralised in Christ, they loved to be with Christ's.

6. A Living Testimony. "Went forth before them all" (Mark ii. 12). Christ's work proves the Christ who works.

7. A Needed Rest. "Went aside privately into a desert place" (Luke ix. 10; compare with Mark vi. 31). The bustle of service must be balanced by communion.

947. WHAT A CHRISTIAN IS SAID TO BE

In 1 Thessalonians i

1. An **Active** Believer. "Your work of faith" (3).

2. A **Diligent** Worker. "Labour of love" (3).

3. An **Enduring** Looker. "Patience of hope" (3).

4. A **Chosen** Beloved. "Beloved your election of God" (4).

5. A **Consistent** Follower. "Followers of us" (6).

6. A **Good** Example. "Ensamples" (7).

7. A **Powerful** Herald. "From you sounded out the Word of the Lord" (8).

8. A **God-honouring** Witness. "Your faith to God-ward is spread abroad" (8).

9. An **Unmistakable** Convert. "Ye turned to God" (9).

10. A **Royal** Servant. "To serve the living God" (9).

11. An **Expectant** Saint. "To wait for His Son from Heaven" (10).

12. A **Saved** Soul. "Jesus, who delivered us from the wrath to come" (10).

948. "WHAT" AND "LIKE MANNER"

1. **Personality.** "What manner of man is this?" (Matt. viii. 27). Who can describe His kind, His worth, His greatness? Ponder the holiness of His nature, the wealth of His worth, the love of His heart, the weight of His words, the beauty of His life, the value of His death, the might of His resurrection, the glory of His ascension, the promises of His Word, and the achievements of His power.

2. **Love.** "Behold what manner of love," etc. (1 John iii. 1). He loves like a Father, providingly; like a mother, tenderly; like a sister, thoughtfully; like a friend, faithfully; like a brother, helpfully; like a king, richly; like Himself, eternally.

3. **Holiness.** "What manner of persons ought ye to be?" (2 Peter iii. 11). Privileges incur responsibilities. Obligations demand returns. God expects more from His children than He does from the world. He has unfolded to us His plans of the future that we might live like Him in the present. Destiny should determine our actions.

4. **Examples.** "Ye know what manner of men we were among you for your sake, and ye became followers of us" (1 Thess. i. 5, 6). Unless preachers are patterns they will become pests. Good samples will command attention.

5. **Reception.** "What manner of entering in we had unto you" (1 Thess. i. 9). It was effective, for they turned to God; it was triumphant in what "sounded out" (i. 8); it was practical in the "ensamples" seen (i. 7); it was demonstrated in the graces evident (i. 4); it was in that it was "not in vain" (ii. 1); and it was unmistakable in their reception of God's Word (ii. 13).

6. **Life.** The Apostle Paul could appeal to the testimony of his life as to its sincerity—Acts xxvi. 4; as to the humility of the manner of his service—Acts xx. 18; and to its manner in the many-sidedness of its reality, as evidenced in his "purpose, faith, endurance, love, and patience."

7. **Advent.** "This same Jesus shall so come in like manner as ye have seen Him go" (Acts i. 11). Who saw Him go? Believers only—Acts x. 41. How did He go? In the act of blessing—Luke xxiv. 50. He will first come *for* His own—1 Thess. iv. 13-18, and then with His own—Zech. xiv. 1-4.

949. WHAT ARE THE WAVES SAYING?

1. **Restlessness.** "The wicked are like the troubled sea" (Isa. lvii. 20).

2. **Vastness.** "The love of God is like, and greater, than all oceans" (Psa. xcvi. 11).

3. **Loss**. The happiest loss that anyone can have is to have his sins lost in the depths of the sea—Micah vii. 19.

4. **Riches**. Who can tell the treasures of the deep?—Deut. xxxiii. 19.

5. **Power**. The power of the sea, who can estimate?—Psa. xciii. 4. Yea, He who holds the believer, holds it in the hollow of His hand—Isa. xl. 12.

6. **Knowledge**. Man can see no path in the sea, but the Lord does—Isa. xliii. 16.

7. **Separation**. The sea is a symbol of separation, but there is a time coming when there shall be "no more sea" (Rev. xxi. 1).

950. WHAT BELIEVERS ARE IN JOHN'S GOSPEL

1. **Sons** as to relationship—i. 12.
2. **Worshippers** as to privilege—iv. 23, 24.
3. **Disciples** as to responsibility—viii. 31; xiii. 15-17.
4. **Servants** as to work—xii. 26.
5. **Friends** as to fellowship—xv. 14.
6. **Brethren** as to love—xx. 17.
7. **Slaves** as to ownership—xiii. 16; xv. 20.

951. WHAT BELIEVERS ARE "MADE"

THE Greek word rendered "made" and "become" means to bring into existence, to become, or for anything to come to pass.

1. **Relationship**. "Power to become the children of God" (John i. 12, R.V.).

2. **Righteousness**. "Made the righteousness of God in Him" (2 Cor. v. 21).

3. **Nearness**. "Made nigh by the Blood of Christ" (Eph. ii. 13).

4. **Service**. "Made a minister" (Eph. iii. 7).

5. **Union**. "Made partakers of Christ" (Heb. iii. 14).

6. **Partnership**. "By these ye might be (made) partakers," etc. (2 Peter i. 4).

7. **Outlook**. "All things are become new" (2 Cor. v. 17).

The same word is rendered "is done" in Revelation xxi. 6. All the above are "done."

952. WHAT CHRIST WAS MADE

1. As to His **humanity**, He was "made of a woman" (Gal. iv. 4).
2. As to His **genealogy**, He was "made of the seed of David" (Rom. i. 3).
3. As to His **identity**, He was "made like unto His brethren" (Heb. ii. 17).
4. As to His **humility**, He "made Himself of no reputation" (Phil. ii. 7).
5. As to His **ignominy**, He was "made a curse" (Gal. iii. 13).
6. As to His **responsibility**, He was "made under the law" (Gal. iv. 4).
7. As to His **substitutionary work**, He was "made...sin for us" (2 Cor. v. 21).

953. WHAT GOD WILL DO IN ANSWER TO PRAYER

As we look to the Lord in prayer—Psa. v. 3, He will give us—

1. **Enlightenment** in perplexity—Psa. xxxiv. 5.
2. **Compensation** in faithfulness—Gen. xv. 5.
3. **Satisfaction** in abandonment—Isa. xvii. 7.
4. **Salvation** in need—Isa. xlv. 22.
5. **Confidence** in desertion—Micah vii. 7.
6. **Peace** in persecution—Acts vii. 55.
7. **Power** in bestowment—Mark vii. 34; Luke ix. 16.

954. "WHAT HAS JESUS DONE?"

"ONCE in the end of the world (ages) hath He appeared to put away sin by the sacrifice of Himself" (Heb. ix. 26).

"Jesus' example is no man's salvation. Rather Jesus' example is every man's condemnation. Christ did not come from Heaven to earth to show men how to live, but to give men life. He gave men life, not by making Himself their Example, but by making Himself their Substitute, taking their sins upon Himself, receiving in Himself the death-penalty of their sins, and dying in their stead. God raised Him from the dead, He returned to Heaven, and now the Holy Spirit through the Word of God and through the testimony of believers is calling upon men everywhere to accept what Christ did for them and be saved. The first and greatest question, therefore, that confronts men to-day is not, 'What would Jesus do?' but 'What has Jesus done?' Only when we accept what He has done can we do what He would do, and what He would have us do."

Christ has "done" in order that we might do. Follow God's order, and we obtain His benefits.

1. Christ has died for our sins, that we should die to them— 1 Peter ii. 24.

2. God has saved us, that we should work our salvation— Phil. ii. 12.

3. God has elected us—Eph. i. 4, that we should make our calling and election sure—2 Peter i. 10.

4. God has made us "**meet**" for the inheritance of the saints in light, that we should be made meet for His use—Col. i. 12; 2 Tim. ii. 21.

5. God has cleansed us in the Blood of Christ—Rev. i. 5, that we should cleanse ourselves from filthiness of the flesh and spirit—2 Cor. vii. 1.

6. God has brought us to Himself—1 Peter iii. 18, that we should be for Himself—Titus ii. 14, R.V.

7. God has loved us, that we may love each other—John iii. 16; 1 John iii. 16.

955. WHAT IS BEFORE US?

THE Lord ever says, "I will go before you" (Mark xiv. 28).

1. He goes before His sheep to provide for them—John x. 4.

2. He sets a hope before us—Heb. vi. 18.

3. He has begotten us to an inheritance ready to be revealed —1 Peter i. 3-5.

4. He assures us we shall be like Him when we see Him— 1 John iii. 2.

5. He pledges Himself to come and receive us to Himself— John xiv. 3.

6. He promises we shall be revealed with Him in His glory— Col. iii. 4.

7. He will present us to Himself faultless, and with exceeding joy—Eph. v. 27; Jude 24.

956. WHAT IS CHRIST TO US?

CHRIST is one of two things to all.

1. He is either the **Stone** on which we are **broken** to penitence and salvation, or He is the Stone to **grind** in pieces to punishment and condemnation—Luke xx. 18.

2. The pillar of cloud was light to Israel and **darkness** to the Egyptians—Exod. xiv. 20.

3. The ways of the Lord are to walk in for our **blessing**, or ways to **stumble** in to our hurt—Hosea xiv. 9.

4. **"God is a Consuming Fire"** to **purify** His people—Mal. iii. 3, and a Burning Fire to **scorch** His enemies—Mal. iv. 1-6.

5. **Christ is life to those** who receive Him—John iii. 36; while He is **wrath** to those who reject Him—Rev. vi. 16.

6. Christ is the **Chief Corner Stone** to those who **rest** on Him in faith for salvation—1 Peter ii. 6; while He is a **Stone of Stumbling** to those who will **not have Him**—1 Pet. ii. 8.

7. Christ is **precious** to those who believe—1 Peter ii. 7, while He is **despised** by those who neglect Him—Isa. liii. 3.

8. When **Christ comes** He brings **eternal rest** for His people, but He gives **eternal destruction** to those who have not obeyed the Gospel—2 Thess. i. 6-8.

957. WHAT IS HEAVEN?

1. **Love** without passion, for we shall be "like Him" (1 John iii. 2).

2. **Service** without weariness, for "His servants shall serve Him" (Rev. xxii. 3).

3. **Holiness** without alloy, for "His Name shall be on our foreheads" (Rev. xxii. 4).

4. **Blessing** without curse, for there shall be "no more curse" (Rev. xxii. 3).

5. **Life** without death, for there shall be "no more death" (Rev. xxi. 4).

6. **Joy** without sorrow, for all tears will be "wiped away" (Rev. xxi. 3).

7. **Light** without darkness, for there shall be "no night there" (Rev. xxii. 5).

8. **Glory** without suffering, for there shall be "no more pain" (Rev. xxi. 4).

9. **Singing** without crying, for there shall be "no more crying" (Rev. xxi. 4).

10. **Satisfaction** without want, for "hunger and thirst" shall cease (Rev. vii. 16).

11. **Rule** without end, for we "shall reign for ever" (Rev. xxii. 5).

12. **Beauty** without infirmity, for we shall be "without wrinkle" (Eph. v. 27).

13. **Living** without sin, for we shall be "faultless" (Jude 24).

14. **Company** without absence, for we shall be "for ever with the Lord" (1 Thess. iv. 17).

958. WHAT IS MAN?

Psalm viii. 4

1. As Created. God's masterpiece—Gen. i. 27.
2. As a Sinner—The Devil's puppet—Eph. ii. 2.
3. As a Saved One. A trophy of grace—1 Tim. i. 16.
4. As a Saint. Christ's reproduction—Gal. ii. 20.
5. As a Temple. God's dwelling—1 Cor. iii. 16.
6. As a Servant. A channel of blessing—John vii. 38.
7. As a Glorified One. Facsimile of the Saviour—1 John iii. 2.

959. WHAT IS SIN?

"SIN" Rom. vi. See references to sin

1. Sin is "transgression," a going beyond the bounds of God's law (1 John iii. 4).
2. Sin is "coming short" of God's requirement, a missing of the mark of the Divine standard (Rom. iii. 23).
3. Sin is a trespass, an offence against God's will—Eph. ii. 1, 5.
4. Sin is iniquity, a falling aside from Divine rectitude—Acts viii. 23.
5. Sin is rebellion against God, an affront to Him—Job xxxiv. 37.
6. Sin is a betrayal, a dealing treacherously with the Lord—Hosea vi. 7, R.V.
7. Sin is a debt, a failure in duty—Matt. vi. 12.

960. WHAT MEN HAVE DONE, AND WILL DO WITH THE SCRIPTURES

WE are told what men have done in the past with the Scriptures, and what they will do in the last days.

1. "Depart from the Faith" (1 Tim. iv. 1; R.V., "fall away"). The word for "depart" is rendered "fall away" (Luke viii. 13), "refrain" (Acts v. 38), "withdraw" (1 Tim. vi. 5). It means a deliberate act, a falling away from a previous position, hence, a departure from the truth of God.

2. Erring is a Straying away from the Scriptures. Christ charged some with being ignorant of the Scriptures; hence, He said, "Ye do err." To "err" signifies to roam from safety, to go astray; hence, to be under a delusion. The word "err" is rendered "be deceived" (Luke xxi. 8), "out of the way" (Heb. v. 2), "wandered" (Heb. xi. 38), "gone astray" (2 Peter ii. 15), and "seduce" (1 John ii. 26).

3. **"Missed the mark,** concerning the faith" (1 Tim. vi. 21, R.V., margin). The word "err" is given "missed the mark," and means to deviate from the truth, by swerving on one side, and thus to miss it. The word is given "swerved" in 1 Timothy i. 6, in calling attention to those who have "missed the mark" (margin R.V.) of holiness of heart and life, as products of the doctrine of grace.

4. **Corrupting the Word of God.** The Apostle speaks of those who "corrupt the Word of God" (2 Cor. ii. 17). To "corrupt" as the margin gives, means, "To deal deceitfully with," or, as the margin of the Revised Version, "To make merchandise of the Word of God." The reference is to retailers of goods, who were notorious for adultering their merchandise, and thus handling their commodities in such a way as to deceive the purchaser.

5. **"Handling the Word of God Deceitfully."** To handle the Word after such a fashion is to falsify it, and make it to be what it is not, as a conjurer, by sleight, deceives an audience, or, as an angler baits the hook by a bait, and thus ensnares— 2 Cor. iv. 2.

6. **Wresting the Scriptures.** Peter speaks of those who "wrest the Scriptures" (2 Peter iii. 16). "Wrest" comes from a word which means to twist, that is, to reverse and turn right round; hence, to torture, to wrench, and by this means to pervert and make the word to mean the opposite to what was intended.

7. Some **"make shipwreck of the faith"** (1 Tim. i. 19, R.V.), that is, allow themselves to run aground on the rocks with "the faith" of God's truth, for the word means, "to suffer shipwreck," and implies it might have been prevented.

961. WHAT THE LORD HATH GIVEN

1. His **Son.** "A Son is given" (Isa. ix. 6).

2. His **Spirit.** "The Holy Spirit which is given unto you" (Rom. v. 5).

3. His **Life.** "Given Himself for us" (Eph. v. 2).

4. His **Bread.** "The bread which the Lord hath given you" (Exod. xvi. 15).

5. His **Testimony.** "The record that God hath given" (1 John v. 11).

6. His **Grace.** "The grace that is given to me of God" (Rom. xv. 15).

7. His **Secrets.** "It is given unto you to know the mysteries" (Matt. xiii. 11).

962. WHAT MAKES A CHRISTIAN?

1. The **Holy Spirit makes** a Christian—John iii. 3, 5.
2. **Faith** in Christ **unites** a Christian to the Father—John i. 12.
3. **Holiness** of life **proves** a Christian—1 Peter iii. 16, R.V.
4. **Trial confirms** a Christian—1 Peter i. 7.
5. **Service** for Christ **helps** a Christian—Eph. iv. 16.
6. **Prayer** to Christ **strengthens** a Christian—John xiv. 13.
7. **Glory** with Christ **crowns** a Christian—Col. iii. 4.

963. WHAT'S OF WEIGHT
IN EPHESIANS

1. "What is the **hope of His calling**" (i. 18). What He is looking for.
2. "What are the **riches of the glory** of His inheritance in the saints" (i. 18). What the Lord has in His people.
3. "What is the **exceeding greatness of His power** to usward who believe" (i. 19). Displayed in Christ's resurrection.
4. "What is the **fellowship of His mystery**" (iii. 9). The oneness of all believers in Christ.
5. "What is the **breadth**" (iii. 18) of **the Christship** of Jesus.
6. "What is the **acceptable will of God**" (v. 10), which we prove by obeying Him.
7. "What the will of **The Lord is**" (v. 17), through the perception of obedience to the Spirit.

964. WHAT THE LORD WILL DO

IF Micah vii. is read it will be seen what the prophet expected the Lord to do, and what He would do for Him. He will give—

1. **Light** in Darkness. "The Lord shall be a light unto me" (8).
2. **Liberty** from Bondage. "He shall bring me forth" (9).
3. **Compassion** for Need. "He will have compassion upon us" (19).
4. **Victory** in Conflict. "He will subdue our enemies" (19).
5. **Mercy** for Sinners. "He delighteth in mercy" (18).
6. **Promise** to Posterity. "Thou wilt perform the truth to Jacob and the mercy to Abraham" (20).
7. **Wonder** for Beholders. "I will shew thee marvellous things" (15).

965. WHAT THE LORD WISHES US TO DO

WE generally see in others what is found in ourselves.

"What paineth thee
In others, in thyself may be."

1. If we **live** consistently—1 Peter i. 22.
2. **Walk** humbly—Micah vi. 8.
3. **Act** individually—Rom xii. 5.
4. **Love** heartily—1 John iii. 23.
5. **Work** personally—Col. iv. 12.
6. **Help** spiritually—Gal. vi. 1, 2.
7. **Forgive** Christly—Eph. iv. 32, we shall fulfil what the Lord wishes us to do towards each other.

966. WHAT THE LORD KNOWETH

1. **The Secrets of the Heart.** "He knoweth the secrets of the heart" (Psa. xliv. 21; Luke xvi. 15; Acts xv. 8).
2. **The Way of the Righteous.** "The Lord knoweth the way of the righteous" (Psa. i. 6; Job xxiii. 10).
3. **Those who Trust in Him.** "The Lord is good...He knoweth them that trust in Him" (Nahum i. 7).
4. **The Frailty of the Body.** "He knoweth our frame" (Psa. ciii. 14).
5. **Those who are His Own.** "The Lord knoweth them that are His" (2 Tim. ii. 19).
6. **How to Deliver the Godly.** "The Lord knoweth how to deliver the godly out of temptation" (2 Peter. ii. 9).
7. **How to Supply the Need.** "Your Father knoweth what things ye have need of" (Matt. vi. 8).

967. "WHAT THINK YE OF CHRIST?"

AN ALPHABET OF BLESSINGS

WHEN a friend was walking with Tennyson in his garden, he challenged the poet: "What do you think of Christ?" After a reverent pause, he said, "Look, here is a flower. What the sun is to this flower, Christ is to me."

What is Christ to the believer?

Advocate to plead .. .. .. 1 John ii. 1.
Beauty to adorn .. .. .. Psa. xc. 17.
Comeliness to perfect .. .. Ezek. xvi. 14.
Deliverer to save .. .. .. Psa. cxvi. 8.
Emancipator to free .. .. John viii. 36.

Fullness to satisfy		Col. ii. 9, 10, R.V.
Grace to strengthen		2 Cor. xii. 9.
Hand to use		Acts xi. 21.
Indweller to sanctify		Gal. 2. 20.
Joy to fill and thrill		John xv. 11.
Kindness to bless		Titus iii. 4.
Lover to inspire		2 Cor. v. 14.
Maker to mould		Isa. xliii. 7; xliv. 2.
Name to charm		Isa. ix. 6.
Overcomer to cheer		John xvi. 33.
Power to keep		1 John v. 18, R.V.
Quietness to calm		1 Chron. xxii. 9.
Redeemer to ransom		Eph. i. 7.
Sovereign to rule		1 Peter iii. 15, R.V.
Truth to sanctify		John xvii. 17.
Upholder to sustain		Isa. xli. 10.
Vine to fructify		John xv. 1-5.
Wall to protect		Zech. ii. 5.
'Xellence to attract		Song of Sol. v. 10-16.
Yoke to unite		Matt. xi. 29.
Zeal to enflame		Psa. lxix. 9.

968. WHAT WILL TAKE PLACE WHEN CHRIST COMES WITH HIS PEOPLE?

THERE are many things that will take place when our Lord returns in manifest splendour to the world with His people.

1. He will **rule the nations** with a rod of iron, and cause them to bow to His Lordly sceptre—Rev. ii. 27.

2. He will **scatter all the workers of unrighteousness**, and make all keep to the principles of right and truth—Isa. ii. 12-21.

3. He will **exercise His power** over the animal world, and cause nature to cease from being "red in tooth and claw" (Rom. viii. 21, 22).

4. He will **lift the curse** from inanimate creation, so that instead of the thorn shall come up the myrtle tree, and the desert shall blossom and bud like the rose—Isa. xxxv. 1, 2; lv. 13.

5. War shall be made to cease, and men then instead of converting implements of argiculture into armaments—Joel

iii. 10, shall beat the instruments of war into implements of husbandry—Micah iv. 3.

6. The **oppressed** and the needy and the downtrodden shall **find deliverance**, emancipation and blessing of every kind when God's King is exercising His authority—Psa. lxxii.

7. **Nations will give to Christ glad homage and service**, and their representatives will go to worship Jehovah in Jerusalem—Micah iv. 2; Zech. xiv. 16.

969. WHAT WILL TAKE PLACE WHEN CHRIST RETURNS

1. The Prophetic Word will be **fulfilled**—2 Peter i. 19.
2. The promise of Christ will be **redeemed**—John xiv. 3.
3. The presence of Christ will be **visible**—Acts i. 11.
4. The "dead in Christ" will be **raised**—1 Thess. iv. 16.
5. The saints will be "**caught up**" to meet Christ—1 Thess: iv. 17.
6. The believer's salvation will be **completed**—Phil. iii. 20, 21.
7. The worker's conduct, motives, and work will be **reviewed** —2 Cor. v. 9, 10.
8. The Jews and Israel will be saved and **restored**—Rom. xi. 26.
9. The antichrist and false prophet will be **destroyed**— 2 Thess. ii. 8.
10. The Devil will be **consigned** to the abyss—Rev. xx. 1-3.
11. The rebuilt City of Babylon will be **consumed**—Rev. xviii. 1, 2.
12. The harlot of a corrupt Christendom will be **overthrown** —Rev. xvii. 14-16.
13. The times of the Gentiles will be **consummated**— Dan. ii. 34, 35; vii. 14; Luke xxi. 24.
14. The details of Zechariah xiv. will **take place**.
15. The nations will be **judged** and **ruled**—Acts xvii. 31.
16. The Millennium will be **inaugurated**—Rev. xx. 6.
17. The world's present conditions will be **rectified**—Isa. ii. 4.
18. Jerusalem will be a **praise** in the earth—Isa. lxii. 7.
19. The Prophetic Vision will be **realised**—Hab. ii. 1-3, 14.
20. The wicked dead will be **judged**—Rev. xx. 11, 15.
21. The golden age will **dawn**—1 Cor. xv. 24-28.

970. "WHEN"

A Point of Time Associated with Christ's Coming.

1. **Signs Appearing.** "When ye see these things coming to pass" (Matt. xxiv. 33).

2. **A Blessed Servant.** "Blessed is that servant...when He cometh, shall find so doing" (Matt. xxiv. 46).

3. **Judgment of the Nations.** "When the Son of Man shall come" (Matt. xxv. 31).

4. **Christ's Appearing.** "When Christ, who is our Life, shall appear" (Col. iii. 4).

5. **Believers Vindicated** and Admired. "When Christ comes to be glorified in His saints" (2 Thess. i. 10).

6. **Sufferers Rewarded and Gladdened.** "When His glory shall be revealed" (1 Peter iv. 13).

7. **Faithful Pastors will Receive** "a **Crown** of Glory." "When the Chief Shepherd shall appear" (1 Peter v. 4).

8. **The Saints will be Glorified** and be "like Christ." "When He shall appear" (1 John iii. 2).

9. **Abiding in Christ.** We who are His will not be ashamed. "When He shall appear" (1 John ii. 28).

971. "WHERE ART THOU?"

Genesis iii. 9

This question has been often applied to the unconverted, hiding behind the trees of iniquity and self-confidence, but let us apply it to the believer in Christ. Many answers may be given to the question: Where Art Thou Positionally? "In Christ" (Eph. i. 1).

Where Art Thou Practically?

1. As to **walk**, we should be in the company of the Lord, like Enoch—Gen. v. 22.

2. As to **worship**, we should be in the holy place of separation, like Moses—Exod. 33. 11.

3. As to **work**, we should be doing it faithfully, like Nehemiah, who worked on amid taunt and opposition—Neh. vi. 3.

4. As to **witnessing**, we should be like Paul, and not shun to declare the whole counsel of God—Acts xx. 27.

5. As to **prayer**, we should be lifting up holy hands—1 Tim. ii. 8, like Daniel, who was ever found at the throne of grace— Dan. vi. 10, 11.

6. As to **consecration**, we should be whole-hearted, like Levi, who feared not to fear God, and therefore feared no one else—Mal. ii. 3-6.

7. As to **power**, we should be in the current of the Spirit's might, like Stephen; then we shall have the shining face, the flashing testimony, and the fearless courage of inwrought conviction—Acts vi. 15.

972. "WHEREFORE'S" AND "THEREFORE'S" OF THE CHRISTIAN LIFE

1. **Injunction.** "Therefore watch," etc. (Acts xx. 31).

2. **Ambition.** "Wherefore we labour" ("make it our aim," R.V.) (2 Cor. v. 9).

3. **Separation.** "Wherefore come out from among them," etc. (2 Cor. vi. 17).

4. **Application.** "Wherefore...make your calling and election sure" (2 Peter i. 10).

5. **Concentration.** "Wherefore we receiving...let us have grace," etc. (Heb. xii. 28).

6. **Attention.** "Wherefore...be diligent," etc. (2 Peter iii. 14).

7. **Expectation.** "Wherefore gird up...and hope," etc. (1 Peter i. 13).

973. "WHEREFORE'S" AND "THEREFORE'S" OF GOSPEL TRUTH

1. **Incarnation.** "Therefore...that holy thing...shall be called the Son of God" (Luke i. 35).

2. **Inspiration.** "Wherefore He saith also in another Psalm," etc. (Acts xiii. 35).

3. **Justification.** "Therefore it was imputed to him for righteousness" (Rom. iv. 22).

4. **Ascension.** "Wherefore He saith, When He ascendeth up on high," etc. (Eph. iv. 8).

5. **Exaltation.** "Wherefore God hath highly exalted Him," etc. (Phil. ii. 9).

6. **Expiation.** "Wherefore when He cometh into the world, He saith,...Lo, I come to do Thy will, O God...by the which will we are sanctified through the offering," etc. (Heb. x. 5-10).

7. **Sanctification.** "Wherefore Jesus also, that He might sanctify the people," etc. (Heb. xiii. 12).

974. WHOLENESS

"Wilt thou be made whole?" (John v. 6).

1. Wholeness means the spirit **made alive**—Eph. ii. 1.
2. The **soul governed**—Col. iii. 1.
3. The **mind illuminated**—Eph. i. 18.
4. The **heart occupied**—Eph. iii. 17.
5. The **life beautified**—Psa. cxlix. 4.
6. The **character moulded**—Rom. viii. 29.
7. The **body benefited**—Rom. xii. 1.

975. WHOLENESS

WHEN the Lord has made us whole, and He keeps us in His risen life, we know, experimentally, that that is the secret of—

1. The **"single eye"** in the Christian life (Matt. vi. 22).
2. The **"pure heart"** for vision (Matt. v. 8).
3. The **"right spirit"** for God (Psa. li. 10).
4. The **"straight paths"** for walk (Heb. xii. 13).
5. The **"willing heart"** for service (Exod. xxxv. 5, 21, 22, 29).
6. The **"true heart"** in worship (Heb. x. 22).
7. The **"faithful" hand** in work (Matt. xxv. 21, 23).

976. "WINGS" OF THE LORD

THE wings of the Lord proclaim the tenderness of His care, the constancy of His service, the strength of His might, and protectiveness of His presence. The wings of the Lord are—

1. **Saving in their Spread.** "I spread My skirt over thee" (Ezek. xvi. 8), said the Lord in saving Israel. (The word "skirt" is same as "wings" in other places.)
2. **Restful in their Repose.** "Under whose wings thou art come to trust" (Ruth ii. 12). (The word "wings" same as "skirt" in Ruth iii. 9).
3. **Supporting in their Strength.** "I bare you on eagle's wings" (Exod. xix. 4; Deut. xxxii. 11, 12).
4. **Safe in their Keeping.** "Hide me under the shadow of Thy wings" (Psa. xvii. 8).
5. **Precious in their Worth.** "How precious (margin) is Thy lovingkindness, O God; therefore the children of men put their trust under the shadow of Thy wings" (Psa. xxxvi. 7).
6. **Protective in their Refuge.** "In the shadow of Thy wings will I make my refuge" (Psa. lvii. 1).

7. Sheltering in their Cover. "I will trust in the covert of Thy wings" (Psa. lxi. 4).

8. Gladdening in their Comfort. "Because Thou hast been my help, therefore in the shadow of Thy wings will I rejoice" (Psa. lxiii. 7).

9. Almighty in their Sufficiency. "He shall cover thee with His feathers (the Almighty, verse 1), and under His wings shalt thou trust" (Psa. xci. 4).

10. Extensive in their Spread. The words "ends" in Job xxxvii. 3, and "uttermost part" in Isaiah xxiv. 16 are the same as rendered "wings" in the other Scriptures.

11. Healing in their Influence. "Healing in His wings" (Mal. iv. 2).

977. WHY DID CHRIST DIE?

1. To **make an atonement** for sin—Heb. i. 3; ii. 17, R.V.; 1 John ii. 2.

2. To **put away** the **hindrance** of sin—Heb. ix. 26.

3. To **take away** the **guilt** of sin—Rom. iv. 25.

4. To **cleanse** from the **pollution** of sin—Rev. i. 5.

5. To **make** us **dead to sins**—1 Peter ii. 24.

6. To **constitute us righteous**—Rom. v. 19, R.V.; 2 Cor. v. 21.

7. To **deliver** us from the **world**—Gal. i. 4.

8. To **separate** us from **self**—2 Cor. v. 14, 15.

9. To **bring us to God**—1 Peter iii. 18.

978. WIDOWS

THERE are five widows mentioned in Luke's Gospel.

1. **Anna, the Prophetess,** who "looked for redemption in Jerusalem" (ii. 36-38).

2. **Widow of Sarepta,** who entertained Elijah in the time of famine—iv. 25, 26; 1 Kings xvii. 9.

3. **Widow of Nain,** who was sorrowed because of the death of her son, and was made glad by his restoration to life—vii. 12.

4. **Widow of the parable,** who was importunate in prayer—xviii. 3-5.

5. **Widow of the two mites,** who was commended by Christ—xxi. 2, 3.

979. "WITH GOD"

1. "With God" all things are possible (Matt. xix. 26). There are no limitations with the Limitless One.

2. "Favour with God" (Luke i. 30). To find favour with God is to have the best of all favours.

3. "With God" there is no respecter of persons. He is impartial in His dealings, and is willing to bless all (Rom. ii. 11).

4. "With God" there is no unrighteousness (Rom. ix. 14). Sovereign rights are His, therefore He is always right and does the right thing.

5. "With God" the absolute wise man's wisdom must be foolishness (1 Cor. iii. 19).

6. "With God" to abide in whatever calling we may be found is to be in the safest place (1 Cor. vii. 24).

7. "With God" to suffer wrongfully when we are right, is to be well-pleasing to Him (1 Peter ii. 20).

980. "WILT THOU?"

1. Question of **Love**—Gen. xxiv. 58.
2. Question of **Sin**—Gen. xxxviii. 17.
3. Question of **Blessing**—Judges i. 14.
4. Question of **Comradeship**—2 Kings iii. 7.
5. Question of **Appreciation**—Exod. iv. 13.
6. Question of **Test**—Matt. xx. 21.
7. Question of **Knowledge**—Acts i. 6.

981. WISE PEOPLE

"Wise in Christ" 1 Cor. iv. 10

WHO are the wise people? The Spirit of God answers the question in His Word.

1. They are wise **who find Christ**, like the Magi of the East—Matt. ii. 1.

2. They are wise who **build on Christ**, like the man who built his house on the rock—Matt. vii. 24.

3. Those who are **faithful to Christ**, like the wise and faithful steward—Matt. xxiv. 45.

4. Those who **build truly for Christ**, like the wise master builder—1 Cor. iii. 10.

5. Those who **administer for Christ**—1 Cor. vi. 5.

6. Those who seize the present opportunity **to labour with Christ**—Eph. v. 15.

7. Those who **live like Christ**—James iii. 13

982. WOMAN OF SAMARIA
1. Her intense **thirst**—John iv. 15.
2. Her intuitive **perception**—John iv. 19.
3. Her argumentive **faculties**—John iv. 20, 24.
4. Her personal **knowledge**—John iv. 25.
5. Her marvellous **spectators**—John iv. 27.
6. Her ardent **purpose**—John iv. 28.
7. Her pertinent **question**—John iv. 26-29.
8. Her attractive **testimony**—John iv. 30.

983. WORD OF GOD
THERE are many things said and implied about the character of Holy Scripture, and among them are the following: It is—
1. **Supernatural** in its origin—2 Tim. iii. 15-17.
2. **Complete** in its structure—Psa. xix. 7-10.
3. **United** in its testimony—Luke xxiv. 27, 44.
4. **Accurate** in its prophecies—1 Peter i. 10-12.
5. **Unique** in its details—John xix. 24, 28, 36, 37.
6. **Distinct** in its claim—1 Thess. ii. 13.
7. **Inerrant** in its contents—Psa. cxix. 89, 140.
8. **Authoritative** in its utterance—Psa. cxix. 11.
9. **Plenary** in its revelation—Heb. i. 1-3.
10. **Divine** in its spirit—2 Peter i. 19, 20.
11. **Peculiar** in its adaptation—Psa. cxix. 133, 154.
12. **Reliable** in its promises—2 Cor. i. 20.
13. **Living** in its nature—1 Peter i. 23, 25.
14. **Faith-begetting** in its ministry—Rom. x. 17.
15. **Beneficent** in its working—Acts xix. 19, 20.
16. **Safeguarding** in its warnings—Psa. xix. 11.
17. **Searching** in its discernment—Heb. iv. 12.
18. **Assuring** in its message—John v. 24; xx. 31.
19. **Reproductive** in its moulding—Rom. vi. 17, margin.
20. **Christ-revealing** in its witness—John v. 39.
21. **God-magnified** in its approbation—Psa. cxxxviii. 2.

984. WORD OF GOD
SEVEN things are said, or implied, of the Word of God in Hebrews iv. 12.
1. **Divine** in its source, hence, it is called "the Word of God."
2. **Living** in its nature, for it is "quick," or living.

3. **Powerful** in its working, hence, it is said to be "powerful."

4. **Keen** in its operation, hence, it is "sharper than any two-edged sword.

5. **Minute** in its dividing, hence, it is said to be able to divide between soul and spirit, etc.

6. **Critical** in its analysis, hence, it is a "discerner of the thoughts and intents of the heart."

7. **Double** in its make, hence, it is called a "two-edged sword."

985. WORD OF GOD: ITS AUTHORITY AND ADAPTABILITY

THE authority and adaptability of the Word of God as the—

1. **Preacher's Message**—Mark xvi. 16-20; 1 Cor. i. 23; Acts v. 20. The true preacher has no fads to air, no fancies to unfold, no fallacies to express, but the facts of the Gospel to proclaim.

2. **Believer's Foundation**—Rom. x. 17; Matt. vii. 24-29; Psa. cxix. 40. Faith has no being nor well-being only as it is founded on, and fashioned by, "as the truth is in Jesus."

3. **Saint's Element**—John xvii. 17, R.V.; Psa. cxix. 133; James i. 25. As we live in the air and the air moves the lungs of the body, so the truth is the saint's environment and equipment for all life's doings and duties.

4. **Christian's Rule**—Phil. ii. 16; 2 Tim. ii. 15; Acts xvii. 11. The Living Word is the Root upon which we grow, and the Written Word is the Rule by which we square. The straight-edge of the Word will always make the walk straightforward in the conduct.

5. **Pilgrim's Guide**—Heb. xi. 10, 13; Psa. lxxiii. 24; John xv. 3. The pilgrim finds the Word a staff to aid him, a cordial to strengthen him, a compass to guide him, a bank to supply him, and a star to cheer him.

6. **Soldier's Weapon**—Matt. iv. 4, 7, 10; 1 Tim. vi. 12, R.V.; Eph. vi. 17. No enemy can defeat us if we obey God's Word fully, believe its promises, and wield it in the power of the Holy Spirit.

7. **Worker's Study**—2 Tim. ii. 15; Psa. cxix. 162; 1 Peter i. 11. We need to study the Word wholly, to be correct; to search it diligently, to be capable; to ponder it prayerfully, to be devout; and to practise it fully, to be assured.

8. **Husbandman's Food**—2 Tim. ii. 6; Jer. xv. 16; John vi. 53, 63. To feed upon the Word is to become like the Word upon which we feed. For brawn and brain we need the right food. Novels and novelties will never make us stalwarts in the Christian life, but the truth will.

986. WORDS

1. Words "against" Christ are forgiven upon repentance—Matt. xii. 32. Words "against" Him hurt Him, as Saul's words did—Acts ix. 4.

2. "Idle" words are accountable to the Lord, and will be judged by Him—Matt. xii. 36.

3. Words are "established" on the evidence of others, and Church discipline carried out on their accuracy—Matt. xviii. 16.

4. Mere words in the worship of the Lord are wearisome to Him—Mal. ii. 17.

5. Words are the witness which will condemn or justify us—Matt. xii. 37.

6. Words of man's wisdom are not enough, we need the Word of the Living God—1 Cor. ii. 4, 13.

7. Words of Eternal Life are found only with Christ—John vi. 68.

987. WORDS

WORDS are variously described as indicating their character.

1. The "Words of Truth" (Acts xxvi. 25).

2. "Unspeakable Words" (2 Cor. xii. 4).

3. "Vain Words" (Eph. v. 6).

4. "Enticing Words" (Col. ii. 4).

5. "Flattering Words" (1 Thess. ii. 5).

6. "Wholesome Words" (1 Tim. vi. 3).

7. "Sound Words" (2 Tim. i. 13).

988. WORDS OF CHRIST

1. Lasting Words, for they "shall not pass away" (Matt. xxiv. 35).

2. Arresting Words, for the disciples were astonished at them" (Mark x. 24).

3. "Gracious Words," for they contained wondrous truths (Luke iv. 22).

4. Living Words, for they contain the Holy Spirit and life —John vi. 63, 68.

5. Inspiring Words, for they lead us to pray aright—John xv. 7.

6. The Father's Words, for He passed them on—John xvii. 8.

7. Repeated Words, for He said of them, "These are the words which I spake" (Luke xxiv. 44).

989. WORK

"Repaired every one over against his house" (Neh. iii. 28).
CHRISTIAN workers will find in Nehemiah iv. how service for
the Lord should be carried out.

1. **The Soul of Work** is the resolute mind of determination
—v. 6.

2. **The Worth of Work** is evidenced when our enemies try
to hinder us in it—v. 11.

3. **The Support of Work** is God Himself, which is illustrated
in the individual sense of responsibility—v. 15.

4. **The Fellowship of Work** is recognised when we work
with others as well as doing our own work—v. 16.

5. **The Proportion of Work** is illustrated in the three things
which characterised the builders under Nehemiah—namely,
the trowel of labour, the sword of defence, and the trumpet of
alarm—vv. 17, 18. See how these are brought out in Ephesians
vi., verses 8, 17, 18.

6. **The Dependence of Work.** The workers being separated
from each other by reason of their several tasks, when danger
was near they gathered together, and knew God would fight for
them—vv. 19, 20.

7. **The Perseverance of Work.** Nehemiah and his labourers
did not consult their own ease, but stolidly and continuously
worked till the task was completed—vv. 21, 23.

990. "WORTHY"

1. An **Acknowledgment.** "The Lord who is worthy to be
praised" (2 Sam. xxii. 4).

2. A **Confession.** "I am no more worthy" (Luke xv. 19, 21).

3. A **Message.** "Worthy of all acceptation" (1 Tim. i. 15).

4. A **Walk.** "Walk worthy of the Lord" (1 Thess. ii. 12;
Col. i. 10).

5. A **Calling.** "Count you worthy of this calling" (2 Thess.
i. 11).

6. A **Reward.** "Labourer is worthy of his reward" (1 Tim. v. 18).

7. A **Kingdom.** "Counted worthy of the Kingdom" (2
Thess. i. 5).

991. WORKERS' EQUIPMENT

IF we keep along God's lines, we shall obtain His power.

1. **One Authority.** The Authority for the worker is the
Word of God. The Spirit's mandate is "Preach the Word"
(2 Tim. iv. 2), then we are sure of the Spirit's application—
Acts x. 44.

2. **One Resource**. The Spirit is our Source and Supply. When we are "endued with power from on high" (Luke xxiv. 49; Acts ii. 4), then we are effective, because He is—1 Peter i. 12.

3. **One Inspiration**. "Love of Christ constraineth" (2 Cor. v. 14). When we are melted and moved by this love, we move and melt others.

4. **One Aim**. To be "well-pleasing unto the Lord" (2 Cor. v. 9, R.V.). When the attitude of our heart is right with the Lord, we shall aim to please Him.

5. **One Principle**. "Serving the Lord" (Rom. xii. 11); and acting "in" Him, then service can never be "in vain" (1 Cor. xv. 58).

6. **One Condition**. "Follow Me and I will make you fishers of men" (Matt. iv. 19). Follow to fish, and be made to catch.

7. **One End**. "The glory of God." "All in Christ, by the Holy Spirit, for the glory of God, all else is nothing."

992. WORTHY THINGS AND MEN

1. A Worthy **Repentance**. "Fruits worthy of repentance" (Luke iii. 8).

2. A Worthy **Saying**. "Worthy of all acceptation" (1 Tim. i. 15; iv. 9).

3. A Worthy **Walk**. "Walk worthy of the vocation"..."of the Lord"..."of God" (Eph. iv. 1; Col. i. 10; 1 Thess. ii. 12).

4. A Worthy **Citizen**. "He was worthy" (Luke vii. 4).

5. A Worthy **Workman**. "Workman is worthy of his hire" (Luke x. 7; 1 Tim. vi. 1).

6. A Worthy **Escape**. "That ye may be accounted worthy to escape" (Luke xxi. 36).

7. A Worthy **Possessor**. "That ye may be accounted worthy of the Kingdom" (2 Thess. i. 5).

993. WRATH OF GOD

1. **Coming** in future—Matt. iii. 7.

2. **Divine** in action—Rom. ix. 22.

3. **Lasting** in effect—John iii. 36.

4. **Revealing** in nature—Rom. i. 18.

5. **Fierce** in separation—Rev. vi. 16, 17; xi. 18; xiv. 10; xvi. 19; xix. 15.

6. **Created** by sin—Rom. i. 18; Eph. v. 6; Col. iii. 6.

7. All **deserve** it—Eph. ii. 3.

994. "YOUR"

PAUL frequently refers to what belongs to the saints. In his second letter to the Church at Corinth he uses the word "your" repeatedly.

1. **Consolation.** "Your consolation and salvation" (i. 6).
2. **Joy.** "Your rejoicing" (i. 14).
3. **Faith.** "Your faith" (i. 24).
4. **Love.** "Your love" (viii. 7).
5. **Zeal.** "Your zeal" (ix. 2).
6. **Generosity.** "Your bounty" (ix. 5).
7. **Righteousness.** "Your righteousness" (ix. 10).
8. **Obedience.** "Your obedience" (x. 6).
9. **Edification.** "Your edifying" (xii. 19).
10. **Perfection.** "Your perfection" (xiii. 9).

995. "YOUR EYES"

1. **Blessed Eyes.** "Blessed are your eyes, for they see" (Matt. xiii. 16).
2. **Seeing Eyes.** "The Lord your God...did for you in Egypt before your eyes" (Deut. i. 30; iv. 3, 34; xi. 7; Joshua xxiv. 7).
3. **Guided Eyes.** "Shall be as frontlets between your eyes" (Deut. xi. 18).
4. **Expectant Eyes.** "Stand and see this great thing which the Lord will do before your eyes" (1 Sam. xii. 16).
5. **Lifted Eyes.** "Lift up your eyes on high" (Isa. xl. 26; Jer. xiii. 20).
6. **Pricked Eyes.** "Pricks in your eyes" (Num. xxxiii. 55; Joshua xxiii. 13).
7. **Closed Eyes.** "The Lord hath closed your eyes" (Isa. xxix. 10).

996. YOUR FAITH

1. **Basis** of Faith. "Faith cometh by hearing, and hearing by the Word of God" (Rom. x. 17).
2. **Object** of Faith. "I believe God" (Acts xxvii. 25).
3. **Secret** of Faith. "I live by the faith of the Son of God" (Gal. ii. 20).
4. **Trial** of Faith. "The trial of your faith" (1 Peter i. 7).
5. **Power** of Faith. "Fruit of the Spirit...faith" (Gal. v. 22).
6. **Prayer** of Faith. "The prayer of faith shall save the sick" (James v. 15).
7. **Victory** of Faith. "This is the victory that overcometh the world, even our faith" (1 John v. 4).

997. "YOUR" versus "OURS"

"Is that your bun, brother?" asked one Christian of another, as they sat at the dinner table. The friend who was questioned took the knife and cut the bun in two, and replied, "Take away the 'y,' brother," as he handed the questioner half of the bun. What a difference it would make if believers would only see that oneness with each other in their oneness with Christ. Let us look at a few of the "our's" in 2 Corinthians i., as illustrating the mutual feeling we should have with each other.

1. **Mutual Relationship.** "Our Father" (2 Cor. i. 2). Believers in Christ have a common ground of relationship to the Lord, and He holds a common relationship to us.

2. **Mutual Responsibility.** "Our Lord Jesus Christ" (2 Cor. i. 3). Purchased by His Blood, we are not our own. He has the right to claim our love and obedience.

3. **Mutual Regard.** "Our tribulation...our consolation" (2 Cor. i. 4, 5). The Lord allows His children to have trial and persecution, that they may know how to comfort others in a like case.

998. "YOURSELVES"

THE Spirit's commands are concise in expression, and consecrating as they are obeyed.

1. **Dead to sin** in the death of Christ. "Reckon yourselves to be dead indeed unto sin," etc. (Rom. vi. 11).

2. **Definite in consecration.** "Yield yourselves unto God" (Rom. vi. 13, 16).

3. **Distinct in discernment.** "Examine yourselves" and prove whether in the faith (2 Cor. xiii. 5).

4. **Desire** to take a second place. "Submitting yourselves one to another" (Eph. v. 21).

5. **Direct** your praise to the Lord, by "speaking to yourselves in psalms and hymns, and spiritual songs," and in all making melody to the Lord (Eph. v. 19).

6. **Divine**, from whence true comfort comes. "Wherefore comfort ye yourselves together" (1 Thess. v. 11).

7. **Disturb** not the Divine word of "Be at peace among yourselves" (1 Thess. v. 13).

999. "YOURSELVES"

WISE and wholesome injunctions are found in the following commands from our Lord.

1. **"Have salt** in yourselves" (Mark ix. 50). The salt of grace will keep us sweet and pungent.

2. **"Take heed** to yourselves" (Mark xiii. 9). Personal application to the Lord's direction will bring untold blessing.

3. **"Come** ye yourselves **apart"** (Mark vi. 31). Separation to the Lord for rest and prayer we constantly need.

4. **"Lay up** for yourselves treasures in Heaven" (Matt. vi. 20). To have riches only on earth is to be bankrupt regarding the lasting treasures.

5. "Ye yourselves like unto men that **wait for their Lord"** (Luke xii. 36). Waiting for Christ is to be rewarded by Him.

6. **"Make to yourselves friends** by means of the mammon of unrighteousness" (Luke xvi. 9, R.V.). Do good by what you have, and you will have good in the days to come.

7. **"Murmur not** among yourselves" (John vi. 43). To murmur is a useless complaint, that benefits no one.

1000. ZEALOUS PEOPLE

THE Greek word for zeal, and kindred ones, are found in the following Scriptures.

1. **A Zealous Saviour.** "The zeal of thine house hath eaten Me up" (John ii. 17).

2. **A Zealous Spirit.** "Fervent in spirit" (Rom. xii. 11).

3. **A Zealous Sinner.** "Concerning zeal, persecuting the Church" (Phil. iii. 6).

4. **A Zealous Service.** "Zealous of good works" (Titus ii. 14).

5. **A Zealous Saint.** "Being fervent in the spirit" (Acts xviii. 25).

6. **A Zealous Servant.** "He hath a great zeal for you" (Col. iv. 12, 13).

7. **A Zealous Shepherd.** "I am jealous over you with godly jealousy" (2 Cor. xi. 2).

Our Worship

"I will worship toward Thy Holy Temple, and praise Thy Name for Thy lovingkindness, and for Thy Truth: for Thou hast magnified Thy Word above all Thy Name" (Psa. cxxxviii. 2).

His Promise

"I will watch over My Word to perform it." (Jer. i. 12, A.R.V.).

Index

The Bible

"Yes, 'tis a mine of precious jewelry,
The Book of God; a well of streams Divine!
But who would wish the riches of that mine
To make his own, his thirst to satisfy
From that pure well; must ear, eye, soul, apply;
On precept precept scan, and line on line;
Search, ponder, sift, compare, divide, combine,
For truths that oft beneath the surface lie."—*Maut.*